Keep this book. You will need it and use it throughout your career.

# AN INTRODUCTION TO HOSPITALITY TODAY

# Educational Institute Courses

## Introductory

**INTRODUCTION TO THE HOSPITALITY INDUSTRY**
Fourth Edition
Gerald W. Lattin

**AN INTRODUCTION TO HOSPITALITY TODAY**
Third Edition
Rocco M. Angelo, Andrew N. Vladimir

**TOURISM AND THE HOSPITALITY INDUSTRY**
Joseph D. Fridgen

## Rooms Division

**FRONT OFFICE PROCEDURES**
Fourth Edition
Michael L. Kasavana, Richard M. Brooks

**HOUSEKEEPING MANAGEMENT**
Second Edition
Margaret M. Kappa, Aleta Nitschke, Patricia B. Schappert

## Human Resources

**HOSPITALITY SUPERVISION**
Second Edition
Raphael R. Kavanaugh, Jack D. Ninemeier

**HOSPITALITY INDUSTRY TRAINING**
Second Edition
Lewis C. Forrest, Jr.

**HUMAN RESOURCES MANAGEMENT**
Second Edition
Robert H. Woods

## Marketing and Sales

**MARKETING OF HOSPITALITY SERVICES**
William Lazer, Roger Layton

**HOSPITALITY SALES AND MARKETING**
Second Edition
James R. Abbey

**CONVENTION MANAGEMENT AND SERVICE**
Fifth Edition
Milton T. Astroff/James R. Abbey

**MARKETING IN THE HOSPITALITY INDUSTRY**
Third Edition
Ronald A. Nykiel

## Accounting

**UNDERSTANDING HOSPITALITY ACCOUNTING I**
Fourth Edition
Raymond Cote

**UNDERSTANDING HOSPITALITY ACCOUNTING II**
Third Edition
Raymond Cote

**BASIC FINANCIAL ACCOUNTING FOR THE HOSPITALITY INDUSTRY**
Raymond S. Schmidgall, James W. Damitio

**MANAGERIAL ACCOUNTING FOR THE HOSPITALITY INDUSTRY**
Fourth Edition
Raymond S. Schmidgall

## Food and Beverage

**FOOD AND BEVERAGE MANAGEMENT**
Second Edition
Jack D. Ninemeier

**QUALITY SANITATION MANAGEMENT**
Ronald F. Cichy

**FOOD PRODUCTION PRINCIPLES**
Jerald W. Chesser

**FOOD AND BEVERAGE SERVICE**
Anthony M. Rey, Ferdinand Wieland

**HOSPITALITY PURCHASING MANAGEMENT**
William P. Virts

**BAR AND BEVERAGE MANAGEMENT**
Lendal H. Kotschevar, Mary L. Tanke

**FOOD AND BEVERAGE CONTROLS**
Fourth Edition
Jack D. Ninemeier

## General Hospitality Management

**HOTEL/MOTEL SECURITY MANAGEMENT**
Raymond C. Ellis, Jr., Security Committee of AH&MA

**HOSPITALITY LAW**
Third Edition
Jack P. Jefferies

**RESORT MANAGEMENT**
Second Edition
Chuck Y. Gee

**INTERNATIONAL HOTEL MANAGEMENT**
Chuck Y. Gee

**HOSPITALITY INDUSTRY COMPUTER SYSTEMS**
Third Edition
Michael L. Kasavana, John J. Cahill

**MANAGING FOR QUALITY IN THE HOSPITALITY INDUSTRY**
Robert H. Woods, Judy Z. King

**CONTEMPORARY CLUB MANAGEMENT**
Edited by Joe Perdue for the Club Managers Association of America

## Engineering and Facilities Management

**FACILITIES MANAGEMENT**
David M. Stipanuk, Harold Roffman

**HOSPITALITY INDUSTRY ENGINEERING SYSTEMS**
Michael H. Redlin, David M. Stipanuk

**HOSPITALITY ENERGY AND WATER MANAGEMENT**
Robert E. Aulbach

# AN INTRODUCTION TO HOSPITALITY TODAY

**Third Edition**

Rocco M. Angelo, CHA
Andrew N. Vladimir, CHE

EDUCATIONAL INSTITUTE
American Hotel & Motel Association

## Disclaimer

This publication is designed to provide accurate and authoritative information in regard to the subject matter covered. It is sold with the understanding that the publisher is not engaged in rendering legal, accounting, or other professional service. If legal advice or other expert assistance is required, the services of a competent professional person should be sought.
—*From the Declaration of Principles jointly adopted by the American Bar Association and a Committee of Publishers and Associations*

The authors, Rocco M. Angelo and Andrew N. Vladimir, are solely responsible for the contents of this publication. All views expressed herein are solely those of the author and do not necessarily reflect the views of the Educational Institute of the American Hotel & Motel Association (the Institute) or the American Hotel & Motel Association (AH&MA).

Nothing contained in this publication shall constitute a standard, an endorsement, or a recommendation of the Institute or AH&MA. The Institute and AH&MA disclaim any liability with respect to the use of any information, procedure, or product, or reliance thereon by any member of the hospitality industry.

©Copyright 1998
By the EDUCATIONAL INSTITUTE of the
AMERICAN HOTEL & MOTEL ASSOCIATION
800 N. Magnolia, Ste. 1800
Orlando, Florida 32803

The Educational Institute of the American Hotel & Motel Association is a nonprofit educational foundation.

All rights reserved. No part of this publication may be reproduced, stored in a retrieval system, or transmitted, in any form or by any means—electronic, mechanical, photocopying, recording, or otherwise—without prior permission of the publisher.

**Printed in the United States of America**
1  2  3  4  5  6  7  8  9  10  03  02  01  00  99  98

**Library of Congress Cataloging-in-Publication Data**
Angelo, Rocco M.
    Hospitality Today : an introduction/Rocco M. Angelo, Andrew N. Vladimir.—3rd ed.
        p. cm.
    Includes bibliographical references and index.
    ISBN 0-86612-171-4 (pbk.).—ISBN 0-86612-172-2 (pbk.)
    1. Hospitality industry—Management. 2. Hospitality industry—Vocational guidance.   I. Vladimir, Andrew.
TX911.3.M27A54 1998
647.94'068—DC21                                                          98–17570
                                                                         CIP

**Editors:**  Robert Bittner
           Jim Purvis

# Contents

Preface .................................................... xi
About the Authors ......................................... xiii
Study Tips ................................................. xv
Prologue: A Brief History of Travel ........................ xvii

## Part I  Introduction

**1  Service Makes the Difference** .......................... 3

What Is Service? ........................................... 5
Problems in Managing and Marketing Service Businesses ...... 7
Achieving Superior Service in a Less–Than–Perfect World ... 11
The Strategic Service Vision .............................. 16
Delivering on the Service Promise ......................... 19
Chapter Summary .......................................... 24

**2  The Travel and Tourism Industry** ...................... 29

The Changing World ....................................... 29
The Nature of the Travel and Tourism Industry ............ 32
Interrelationships within the Travel and Tourism Industry . 35
Why People Travel ........................................ 38
The Social Impact of Travel .............................. 44
Chapter Summary .......................................... 46

**3  Exploring Hospitality Careers** ........................ 53

Hospitality Today ........................................ 53
Careers in the Hospitality Industry ...................... 55
Looking for a Job ........................................ 68
Chapter Summary .......................................... 75
Chapter Appendix A: Key Hotel Management Positions ....... 79
Chapter Appendix B: Key Food Service Management Positions . 81
Chapter Appendix C: Sample Résumé ........................ 83

## Part II  Hospitality Organizations

**4  Understanding the Restaurant Industry** ................ 85

Restaurant Industry Segments ............................. 86
Starting a New Restaurant ............................... 103
Chapter Summary ......................................... 113

## Contents

**5  Restaurant Organization and Management** .............. **119**

    Organizing for Success ........................................ 119
    Financial and Operational Controls ........................ 134
    Chapter Summary ............................................. 150

**6  Understanding the World of Hotels** ..................... **157**

    Hotel Guests .................................................. 157
    Hotel Categories .............................................. 160
    Industry Trends ............................................... 189
    Developing and Planning New Hotels ...................... 191
    Chapter Summary ............................................. 197

**7  Hotel Organization** ...................................... **207**

    How Is a Hotel Organized? ................................... 207
    Revenue Centers .............................................. 209
    Cost Centers .................................................. 233
    Compliance with the ADA ................................... 241
    Control Systems .............................................. 242
    Chapter Summary ............................................. 250

**8  Club Organization and Operation** ....................... **259**

    Background on Clubs ........................................ 259
    Types of Clubs ................................................ 261
    Club Ownership .............................................. 268
    Club Organization ............................................ 269
    Club Operations .............................................. 273
    Chapter Summary ............................................. 277

**9  An Introduction to the Meetings Industry** ............. **283**

    The Size of the Meetings Industry .......................... 283
    The Role of Civic and Government Organizations ........ 289
    Where Meetings Are Held ................................... 289
    The Meeting Planning Process ............................... 290
    Meetings Industry Careers ................................... 293
    Chapter Summary ............................................. 298

**10  Floating Resorts: The Cruise Line Business** ........... **303**

    Early Cruises .................................................. 304
    The Birth of Modern Cruising ............................... 307
    Cruise Ship Organization .................................... 312
    A Case Study in Quality Management ..................... 324
    Chapter Summary ............................................. 334

Contents **vii**

**11 Gaming and Casino Hotels** .......................... **341**

    The Story of Gaming ......................................... 341
    Gaming in America .......................................... 342
    Casino Games ............................................... 344
    Casino Operations .......................................... 346
    Casino Marketing ........................................... 351
    Casino Controls and Regulation ............................. 353
    Career Opportunities in Casino Hotels ....................... 354
    Chapter Summary ........................................... 361

## Part III  Hospitality Management

**12 Managing and Leading Hospitality Enterprises** ............ **367**

    A Manager's Job ............................................ 367
    The Evolution of Management Theories ...................... 373
    Reengineering .............................................. 384
    The Importance of Leadership ............................... 389
    Conclusion ................................................. 392
    Chapter Summary ........................................... 393
    Chapter Appendix: Eight Managerial/Leadership Roles ........ 399

**13 Managing Human Resources** .......................... **403**

    Labor Trends ............................................... 403
    Human Resources Programs ................................ 407
    Chapter Summary ........................................... 429

**14 Marketing and Selling Hospitality** ...................... **435**

    The Marketing Concept ..................................... 435
    Developing a Marketing Plan ................................ 441
    Sales Management and Personal Selling ...................... 446
    Making the Sales Call ....................................... 454
    Selling through Travel Agencies .............................. 457
    Chapter Summary ........................................... 468

**15 Managing Marketing Communications** .................. **475**

    Advertising ................................................ 475
    Choosing Advertising Media ................................ 491
    Public Relations ............................................ 510
    Publicity ................................................... 513
    Sales Promotion ............................................ 514
    Chapter Summary ........................................... 518

**16 How Management Companies Manage Hotels** ............ **527**

    Why Management Companies Exist ......................... 527

The Evolution of Management Companies .................... 528
Management Contracts ...................................... 530
Chapter Summary ............................................ 539

## 17 Franchising Is Big Business ............................ 545

What Is a Franchise? ....................................... 545
The History of Franchising ................................. 547
How Franchising Works ...................................... 551
Owning a Franchise ......................................... 553
Franchising Issues ......................................... 563
Chapter Summary ............................................ 563
Chapter Appendix: Uniform Franchise Offering Circulars ....... 569

## 18 Ethics in Hospitality Management ........................ 573

What Is Ethics? ............................................ 573
Social Responsibility and Business Ethics .................. 574
Ethical Issues in Hospitality .............................. 582
Must There Be a Code of Ethics? ............................ 595
Chapter Summary ............................................ 597

**Appendix: Hospitality Associations and Periodicals** ............... 603

**Index** ................................................................. 617

# Congratulations...

You have a running start on a fast-track career!

Developed through the input of industry and academic experts, this course gives you the know-how hospitality employers demand. Upon course completion, you will earn the respected American Hotel & Motel Association certificate that ensures instant recognition worldwide. It is your link with the global hospitality industry.

You can use your AH&MA certificate to show that your learning experiences have bridged the gap between industry and academia. You will have proof that you have met industry-driven learning objectives and that you know how to apply your knowledge to actual hospitality work situations.

By earning your course certificate, you also take a step toward completing the highly respected learning programs—Certificates of Specialization, the Hospitality Operations Certificate, and the Hospitality Management Diploma—that raise your professional development to a higher level. Certificates from these programs greatly enhance your credentials, and a permanent record of your course and program completion is maintained by the Educational Institute.

We commend you for taking this important step. Turn to the Educational Institute for additional resources that will help you stay ahead of your competition.

# Preface

IN THIS THIRD edition of *Hospitality Today: An Introduction,* we preserve our commitment to build a bridge from the industry to the classroom. This new edition draws on the experiences of many more industry experts than the first and second editions—experts from the United States, Europe, and the Pacific Rim.

We've added three new chapters to this volume. "Service Makes the Difference" is the opening chapter in this text. Ours is a service industry and we emphasize its importance in today's competitive market. There's also a new chapter titled "Floating Resorts—The Cruise Line Business." The fast-growing segment of the industry is recruiting more and more students from hospitality schools, and we're responding to a need of students to know more about it. The same reasoning applies to our new chapter "The Unique Character of Casino Hotels." Gaming is now a $600 billion industry—just in the United States! Many hospitality graduates are involved in it today. Because this book deals with the real world of hospitality, we've profiled six industry innovators who have made a difference in the fundamental structure of the business. Besides this new material, we have extensively revised and updated all the material in the second edition. The purpose of the book has not changed, however: to prepare students for careers in hospitality, and present and describe opportunities in hospitality management. These opportunities include careers in a variety of businesses, including hotels, restaurants, institutions, private clubs, casinos and casino hotels, consulting firms, travel agencies, and cruise ships.

The prologue sets the stage for today's world of hospitality. We expanded the history of hospitality and travel presented in the first edition and added some new anecdotal material.

Chapter 2 presents an overview of the travel and tourism industry. It covers many of the industry's components and shows how businesses within the hospitality industry are interrelated. Travel motivators and emerging travel trends are discussed, along with current concerns about the social impact of tourism.

Chapter 3 deals with hospitality careers. It tells students what the jobs are and where they can be found. A new section can help them get a job. This section introduces the subjects of writing a résumé and preparing for a job interview.

Chapters 4 and 5 describe the food service industry and outline the opportunities in it, not only from a corporate standpoint but from an entrepreneurial point of view as well.

Chapter 6 categorizes hotels and explains the differences between chain hotels and independent hotels. In Chapter 7 we cover developing and planning new hotels, hotel organization, and financial controls. Many hospitality graduates are finding opportunities in private club operations; types of clubs, how they're organized, and their operations are discussed in Chapter 8.

Chapter 9 covers a segment of the market that in recent years has become an identifiable career track: meeting planning. We explain the different kinds of meetings, who holds them, where they are held, and the meeting planning process. The chapter ends with a detailed look at careers in the meetings and conventions field.

Chapters 10 and 11 are brand new, as we previously noted. We believe they will be helpful to students in choosing a career path by explaining to them these new options.

Chapter 12 deals with management theory and practice. We discuss the management theories of Deming, Juran, and Crosby, and there is more material on leadership. We've also recognized and discussed reengineering as a management option. Chapter 13 is about human resource programs—how they are structured and why. Highly motivated and well-trained workers are essential to success today, and this chapter shows how major operators approach the task.

Marketing, advertising, and public relations are the subjects of Chapters 14 and 15. Here we discuss the emerging body of research that separates the marketing of services from the marketing of manufactured goods. There are sections on yield management and direct response advertising (including the use of the Internet as a marketing tool). There are also new examples of successful print, radio, and television advertising campaigns.

Management companies and franchising, which fueled the unprecedented growth of the hotel and restaurant industry, will continue to play a major role in the new millennium. They are analyzed in Chapters 16 and 17, and new trends are identified.

We conclude the text with a chapter about the importance of ethics and values. Although this chapter received the International Institute for Quality and Ethics in Service and Tourism Award for its discussion of hospitality ethics, we revised and expanded it to include new anecdotal material concerning ethical behavior.

At the request of instructors, the key terms sections that follow each chapter were expanded to make them a better resource for students new to the industry.

# Acknowledgments

This book could not possibly be the work of only two authors. A great many people contributed their ideas and time to conceiving and shaping it. We would like to acknowledge the active support and encouragement of Anthony G. Marshall, CHA, Dean of the School of Hospitality Management at Florida International University. Many other friends in the industry and at hospitality schools helped us by reviewing material, suggesting directions for us to pursue, and providing ideas and examples that we use extensively.

Rocco M. Angelo
Key Biscayne, Florida

Andrew N. Vladimir
Coconut Grove, Florida

## About the Authors

ROCCO M. ANGELO (left) is the Associate Dean of the School of Hospitality Management at Florida International University. He is also a full professor and a Certified Hospitality Administrator (CHA). Prior to joining FIU in 1974, Mr. Angelo spent six years as manager of Laventhol & Horwath's Management Advisory Services division in New York City. He was responsible for supervising and conducting economic feasibility studies, operation and control analyses for hotels and restaurants, and tourism studies in the United States, Canada, and the Caribbean. He has also worked in various management positions with the Women's National Republican Club, ARAMARK, Loews Hotels, and Pannell Kerr Forster. He received B.S. degrees from Fordham University and the School of Hotel Administration at Cornell University, and an M.B.A. from the University of Miami. He has taught courses at Cornell University, New York University, and the Centre International dé Glion in Switzerland.

Mr. Angelo has been an advisor to the Club Management Institute of the Club Managers Association of America, and a member of the Corporation of the Culinary Institute of America, the advisory board of Dade County's Academy for Tourism, and of the Certification Commission of the Educational Institute of the American Hotel & Motel Association. He has also served on the Scholarship and Grants Committee of the American Hotel Foundation.

Mr. Angelo is the author of *A Practical Guide to Understanding Feasibility Studies*. He resides in Key Biscayne, Florida.

ANDREW N. VLADIMIR (right) is an internationally recognized marketing consultant with a distinguished track record in the tourism industry. Formerly an Associate Professor at the School of Hospitality Management of Florida International

University, Vladimir taught courses in service management, cruise line management, marketing communications, and promotion strategy.

Before joining FIU's faculty, Mr. Vladimir served as Director of Tourism for the Government of Bermuda, the only non–Bermudian ever to hold that post. Part of his responsibilities as Bermuda's chief tourism regulator was to oversee the government's marketing, advertising, and public relations programs.

Mr. Vladimir has spent most of his career in the advertising business, with a special emphasis on hospitality, travel, and tourism. He has held senior management positions with some of America's best advertising and public relations agencies, including Young & Rubicam, Norman Craig & Kummel, Kenyon & Eckhardt, and Ruder and Finn. In addition, he has headed his own advertising and public relations agencies in San Juan, Puerto Rico; Miami, Florida; and Seattle, Washington; and has owned two travel agencies.

In the course of his career Mr. Vladimir has worked for such hospitality clients as McDonald's, Sonesta Hotels, Loews Hotels, Resorts International, Delta Airlines, Air France, and TravAlaska Tours. He has been a featured speaker at three world congresses of the American Society of Travel Agents.

Mr. Vladimir is the co-author of *Selling the Sea—An Inside Look at the Cruise Industry* (John Wiley & Sons, 1997), *The Complete Travel Marketing Handbook* (NTC Business Books, 1988), and *Fundamentals of Advertising* (Crain Books, 1984). He has written hundreds of newspaper articles on travel for Cox Newspapers and the New York Times Syndicate as well as contributed consumer, trade, and academic magazine articles.

Mr. Vladimir holds a B.A. degree from Yale University and an M.S. degree from FIU's School of Hospitality Management. He is also a graduate of Harvard Business School's Advanced Management Program and a Certified Hospitality Educator (CHE). He is a member of Delta Delta Phi, the hospitality honor society. He has twice received Florida International University's teaching excellence award. He resides in Coconut Grove, Florida.

# Study Tips for Users of Educational Institute Courses

Learning is a skill, like many other activities. Although you may be familiar with many of the following study tips, we want to reinforce their usefulness.

## Your Attitude Makes a Difference

If you want to learn, you will: it's as simple as that. Your attitude will go a long way in determining whether or not you do well in this course. We want to help you succeed.

## Plan and Organize to Learn

- Set up a regular time and place for study. Make sure you won't be disturbed or distracted.
- Decide ahead of time how much you want to accomplish during each study session. Remember to keep your study sessions brief; don't try to do too much at one time.

## Read the Course Text to Learn

- *Before* you read each chapter, read the chapter outline and the learning objectives. Notice that each learning objective has page numbers that indicate where you can find the concepts and issues related to the objective. If there is a summary at the end of the chapter, you also want to read it to get a feel for what the chapter is about.
- Then, go back to the beginning of the chapter and *carefully* read, focusing on the material included in the learning objectives and asking yourself such questions as:

    —Do I understand the material?

    —How can I use this information now or in the future?
- Make notes in margins and highlight or underline important sections to help you as you study. Read a section first, then go back over it to mark important points.
- Keep a dictionary handy. If you come across an unfamiliar word that is not included in the textbook glossary, look it up in the dictionary.
- Read as much as you can. The more you read, the better you read.

## Testing Your Knowledge

- Test questions developed by the Educational Institute for this course are designed to reliably and validly measure a student's ability to meet a standard of knowledge expressed by the industry-driven learning objectives.

- End-of-the-chapter Review Quizzes help you find out how well you have studied the material. They indicate where additional study may be needed. Review Quizzes are also helpful in studying for other tests.
- Prepare for tests by reviewing:
  —learning objectives
  —notes
  —outlines
  —questions at the end of each assignment
- As you begin to take any test, read the test instructions *carefully* and look over the questions.

We hope your experiences in this course will prompt you to undertake other training and educational activities in a planned, career-long program of professional growth and development.

# Prologue
## A Brief History of Travel

SINCE THE WORD "travel" suggests pleasure and adventure to most people, it is not often remembered that "travel" is derived from the French word *travail*, which means "toil and labor." Prehistoric people moved about in search of food and shelter; their travels were by no means pleasant. Travel has been an arduous task for much of recorded history. In fact, only in modern times has travel become relatively comfortable.

Commerce was an important motivator of early travel. By 3000 B.C., caravan routes from Eastern Europe to North Africa and on to India and China were well established. Camels were favored pack animals—a healthy one could carry up to 600 pounds of cargo. By 1200 B.C., Phoenician merchant vessels were plying the Mediterranean, following sea routes stretching from Britain to Africa.

The Romans were the first to travel on land on a large scale. Their desire to expand the Roman Empire resulted in expeditions of discovery and conquest followed by massive road building. The first important Roman highway was the Via Appia, started in 312 B.C. By A.D. 200 the Romans had highways throughout their empire, from Hadrian's Wall in northern Britain to the Sahara Desert—highways that featured wheel-changing stations and rest houses every 15 to 30 miles.

People in ancient times traveled for pleasure as well. Hundreds of years before the birth of Christ, Greeks and barbarians (a "barbarian" was defined by the Greeks as anyone who was not Greek) traveled to the Olympic games. Health, too, provided an impetus for early travel. People believed that waters in certain locations possessed healing qualities, and they would go there to rest and recuperate. The Romans built spas as far away from Rome as Bath, England.

With the growth of organized religion, pilgrimages became common in many parts of the world. Muslims traveled to Mecca; Christians traveled to shrines all over Europe and beyond. A sense of the Christian pilgrimages in the Middle Ages is preserved in *The Canterbury Tales*, which was written in the fourteenth century by Geoffrey Chaucer. The book's narrator is a jovial innkeeper who hosts 29 pilgrims staying at the Tabard Inn in Southwark, England, and subsequently offers to accompany them on their journey to help make the trip an interesting one.

The first European traveler to popularize long-distance trips was Marco Polo. The desire for wealth sent this Venetian in 1275 to trade at the "Hall of the Barbarians" in Kublai Khan's empire. Polo returned from the Far East 20 years later to write a book about his adventures, titled *The Description of the World*, which later became known popularly as *Il milione*—The Millions—because of all the wealth he had allegedly acquired abroad. His adventures captured the imagination of courts all over Europe. Almost certainly, a reader of *Il milione* who eventually set out to find some of the sights Polo catalogued was Christopher Columbus.[1]

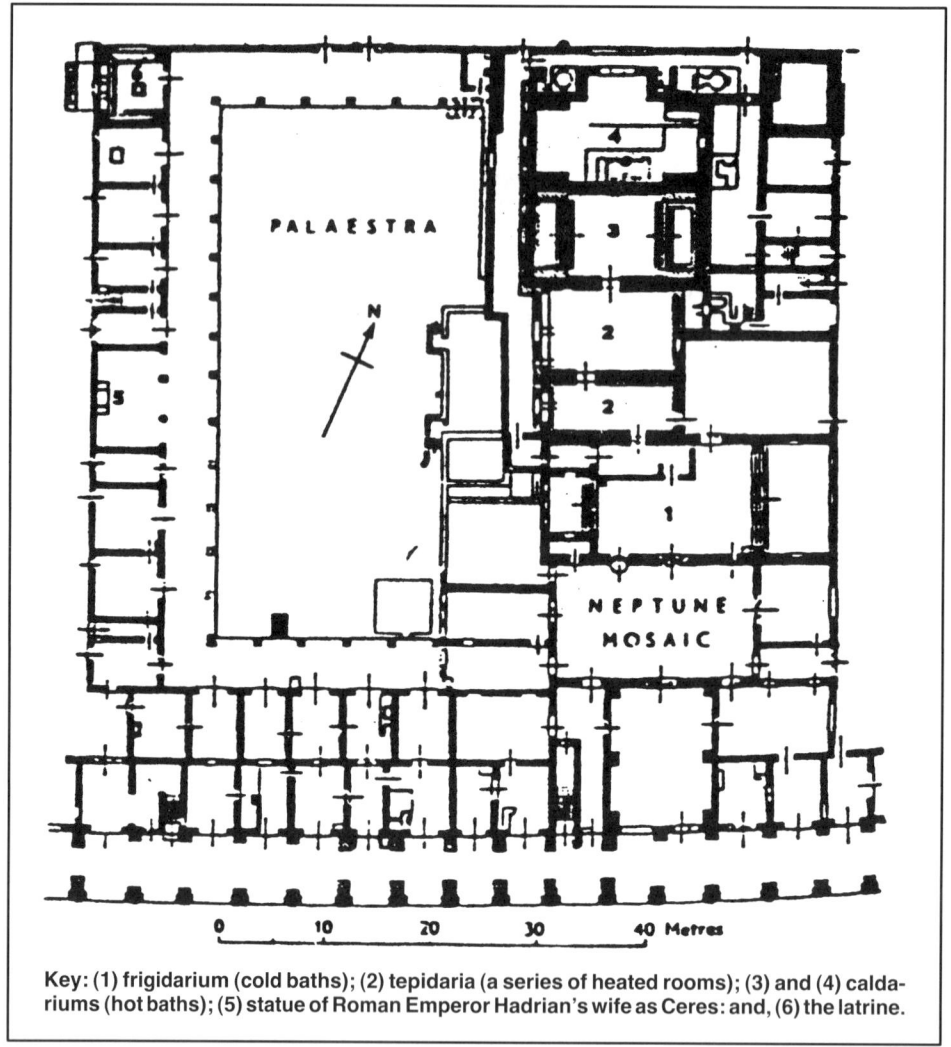

**Key:** (1) frigidarium (cold baths); (2) tepidaria (a series of heated rooms); (3) and (4) caldariums (hot baths); (5) statue of Roman Emperor Hadrian's wife as Ceres: and, (6) the latrine.

**A Roman spa.** Source: Russell Meiggs, *Roman Ostia,* 2d ed. (Oxford: Clarendon Press, 1973).

In the capital city of Hangzhou, home of the "Great Kahn," one of the things that intrigued Marco Polo most was the vast abundance of food. Reay Tannahill, a food historian, points out that

> most countries had their cookshops, but none at this period were as advanced and varied as China's. As well as ordinary eating houses, there were fast food restaurants, hotels, taverns, tea houses, noodle shops and wine shops, all with their own chef's specials—chilled fruits or honey fritters, steamed pork buns, won ton, barbecued meats, fish soups, and so on. Every morning between 1 A.M. and dawn the proprietors hurried off to one of the ten great specialist food markets of Hangzhou for the pork or

silkworms or shrimp from which they made pies to serve with their drinks, or oysters, mussels, or bean curd that nourished the poorer classes.

The fish market, according to Marco, was an extraordinary sight. Every day, "a vast quantity of fish is brought upstream from the ocean, a distance of twenty-five miles. There is also abundance of lake fish, varying in kind according to season, which affords constant occupation for fishermen." So many fish were on sale at the market that "you would imagine they could never be disposed of. But in a few hours the whole lot has been cleared away."[2]

By the thirteenth century trade had emerged as the prime reason for travel. Improved navigation skills and the development of the magnetic compass took much of the uncertainty out of long, hard sea trips. Maps of the continents and two- and three-masted sailing ships helped open the oceans to further exploration in the fourteenth and fifteenth centuries.

During the Renaissance period (beginning in the fourteenth century in Italy and lasting in Europe into the seventeenth century), travel for cultural and artistic reasons became common. Soon it was popular for aristocrats, diplomats, scholars, and other young gentlemen and women to take an extended tour of the Continent, which came to be known as "The Grand Tour." Paris, Rome, Florence, Venice, Munich, Vienna, and other cities of central Europe were fashionable tour stops, and resorts and spas were developed to accommodate the tourists.

An enduring symbol of hospitality surfaced for the first time during this period. Early explorers who traveled to the West Indies were enchanted by pineapple fruit and brought it home to Europe to cultivate in their hothouses. By the seventeenth century it had become a very popular symbol in society and among royalty, and soon the motif appeared carved into their furniture, signifying bountifulness. When the colonists settled North America, they carried with them some of this furniture. Sea captains returning home from long trips would often place pineapples at the doors or on their gate posts to announce their arrival home and invite friends to stop in to celebrate.

Today the pineapple remains a symbol of hospitality and welcome, and you can find it carved into the entrances of hotels, restaurants, and homes.

## The Transportation Revolution

Modern technology became a major force in travel with the development of the steamship, locomotive, automobile, and airplane. These new forms of transportation put long-distance travel within the reach of more people than ever before by decreasing the amount of time and money necessary to take long trips.

### Steamships

Travel to the New World for adventure and profit in the seventeenth and eighteenth centuries opened sea lanes and hastened the development of the great transatlantic ocean liners that were to connect Europe and the Americas in the nineteenth century.

The *R.M.S. Titanic* on a trial run in 1912. It was the most luxurious ocean liner of its day.

The first steamship to cross the Atlantic was the *Sirius* in 1838. In 1840 Samuel Cunard inaugurated regular passenger service across the Atlantic when he formed the British and North American Royal Mail Steam Packet Company, which later took its founder's name and became the Cunard Line. Sea voyages became the most romantic and luxurious form of travel, but only a few could afford them.

Exciting and luxurious as these early steamers may have seemed to landlubbers, the people who actually traveled on them were often uncomfortable during the trip. Harriet Beecher Stowe described a transatlantic voyage she took in 1854:

> At night! the beauties of a night on shipboard!—down in your berth, with the sea hissing and fizzing, gurgling and booming, within an inch of your ear; and then the steward comes along at twelve o'clock and puts out the light, and there you are! Jonah in the whale was not darker or more dismal. There, in profound ignorance and blindness, you lie, and feel yourself rolled upwards, and downwards, and sidewise, and all ways, like a cork in a tub of water; much such a sensation as one might suppose it to be, were one headed up in a barrel and thrown into the sea.[3]

The most famous and tragic sea voyage of all was that of the *Titanic*. The 46,000-ton vessel offered a degree of luxury that was unheard of in the shipping world. One writer called the maiden voyage of the *Titanic* "the millionaires' special." The ship left port on April 12, 1912, and more than two thousand passengers and crew partied their way into the North Atlantic. Only 705 passengers survived the voyage. April 14, 1912—the night the *Titanic* struck an iceberg and sank—is the saddest day in the history of passenger shipping. A woman who survived the tragedy later wrote about that Sunday night in her diary:

> We dined the last night in the Ritz Restaurant. It was the last word in luxury. The tables were gay with pink roses and white daisies, the women in their beautiful shimmering gowns of satin and silk, the men immaculate and well groomed, the stringed orchestra playing music from Puccini and Tchaikovsky. The food was superb—caviar, lobster, quail from Egypt, plover's eggs, and hothouse grapes and fresh peaches. The night was cold and clear, the sea like glass. But in a few short hours every man in that room was dead except J. Bruce Ismay, Gordon Duff, and a Mr. Carter.[4]

Despite this disaster, transatlantic passenger service continued, and the great ocean liners such as the *Queen Mary*, the S.S. *France*, and the *United States* became known throughout the world as the flagships of their nations. Ocean liners were the principal form of luxury travel until the late 1950s, when commercial jets first entered transatlantic service. Soon the great ocean liners became relics of the romantic past. Today the *Queen Mary* is permanently docked and operated as a hotel in Long Beach, California, and the S.S. *France* has taken on a new life as Norwegian Cruise Line's *Norway*. Other older ships still ply the waves, operated by some of the smaller cruise lines.

## Railroads

The first working locomotive was built in England in 1804. In 1830 the railroad age began with the opening of the Liverpool and Manchester Railway in England. One year later America's first public railway, the South Carolina Railroad, began service. It did not take long for entrepreneurs to sense the potential of the railroad to stimulate travel. In 1841 a Baptist preacher named Thomas Cook organized a rail tour from Leicester to Loughborough and back for 570 people to attend a temperance meeting, thus earning himself a place in history as the world's first recognized travel agent.

In the last half of the nineteenth century, railroads grew rapidly in Europe and elsewhere. The Union Pacific and the Central Pacific railroads joined their tracks at Promontory Point near Ogden, Utah, in 1869, making a transcontinental rail trip across America possible for the first time. In 1891 construction started on the Trans-Siberian railroad, which would link Europe to Asia.

After rail travel became popular in Europe, the most desirable place to build a hotel in major European cities was next to the railroad station. In the United States, hotels and restaurants were built beside the railroad tracks as they crisscrossed the country. In many instances, hotels were built well *before* the arrival of the railroad or even before a town had sprung up. The idea was that a proper hotel would attract the railroads and, with them, settlers and commerce. Victorian novelist Anthony Trollope visited North America and makes this point in the book he wrote about his visit:

**In the nineteenth century, railroads put long-distance travel within the reach of ordinary Americans.** (Courtesy of the State of Michigan Archives)

> In the States of America the first sign of an incipient settlement is a hotel five stories high with an office, a bar, a cloak-room, three gentlemen's parlours, a ladies' entrance and two hundred bedrooms. . . . Whence are to come the sleepers in those two hundred bedrooms and who is to pay for the gaudy sofas and numerous lounging chairs of the ladies' parlours? In all other countries the expectation would extend itself simply to travellers; to travellers or to strangers sojourning in the land. But this is by no means the case as to these speculations in America. When the new hotel rises up in the wilderness, it is presumed that people will come there with the express object of inhabiting it. The hotel itself will create a population, as the railways do. With us railways run to the towns; but in the States the towns run to the railways. It is the same thing with the hotels.[5]

Resorts also had their beginnings with the growth of the railroad. The Catskill Mountains were a popular day trip by rail from New York City and eventually became the home of the "borscht circuit," a group of mountain resorts that featured many great entertainers in the 1930s, 1940s, and 1950s. Two of the most famous Catskill resorts were the Concord and Grossinger's. Soon railroad companies started developing resorts of their own. In Florida, Henry Flagler built The Breakers in Palm Beach and other hotels in Miami and Key West to accommodate passengers on his Flagler Line. In West Virginia, the Chesapeake & Ohio Railway company developed the Greenbrier Resort.

**Hotels were sometimes built well before the arrival of the railroad—or even before there was much of a town!** (Courtesy of the State of Michigan Archives)

Trains significantly increased the amount of business travel. With that growth came a demand from business travelers for a uniform standard of hotel quality so that they could go from one city to another and enjoy similar services.

## Automobiles

In the late nineteenth century, horses (for short distances) and trains (for long distances) were the two main modes of land travel in the United States and Europe. This began to change with the invention of bicycles. The bicycle was invented in Paris and first introduced to the European community at the 1867 Paris Exposition. Many people saw it as a faster, safer, more reliable, and less expensive means of transportation than the horse. Bicycles did not require feeding or care and they were not likely to throw off a rider in a fit of temperament. Bicycles did require, however, good, hard-surfaced roads—especially if you wanted to use them to cover long distances fast.

As bicycles grew in popularity, so did the demand for paved roads. It was these hard-surfaced roads that made the motor car a practical device for transportation. Not surprisingly, many of the first cars were made by bicycle manufacturers. Their

**The automobile's potential as a convenient and inexpensive means of travel would not be realized until better roads were built.** (Courtesy of the State of Michigan Archives)

dealers saw the car as an improved bicycle. Companies like Willys in America, Rover in England, Opel in Germany, and Peugeot in France were bicycle manufacturers that realized that many of their customers really wanted fast personal transportation, not bicycles, and that automobiles were the best way to satisfy that need.

As with the first bicycles, the first automobiles were built in France. The early Peugeot cars, built in 1889, were heavy tricycles powered by steam engines. Leon Serpollet, the inventor of the instantaneous steam generator, mounted one of his engines on a tricycle and drove it 295 miles from Paris to Lyon in 1890.[6] At the same time, steam-powered road vehicles of various designs were being built in the United States. In Lansing, Michigan, Ransom E. Olds built one of the earliest models in 1891, which he sold for $400 to a London patent medicine firm for use in its branch in Bombay, India.[7] Soon two American companies were producing steam cars in quantity—the Locomobile and the Stanley Steamer—that could be bought for as little as $600. Steam engines were inefficient, however. There was a brief period of interest in electric cars, but the limited storage capacity of their batteries severely restricted their use.

It was not until the gasoline engine (first invented in 1860 by Etienne Lenoir[8]) was perfected that the modern car became a reality. The first person to improve the engine to the point where it could be attached to a vehicle was Gottlieb Daimler, a German engineer. Daimler, along with his assistant William Maybach, built four experimental motor vehicles between 1885 and 1889. Their engine was the prototype of the modern automobile's power plant.[9] Unfortunately, Daimler crashed one of these vehicles into a wall, giving him another place in history as having the first automobile accident!

The French, who were already enthusiastic cyclists and had a network of good roads, first saw the potential of the gasoline-powered car. By 1901 about 130 automobile manufacturers are estimated to have been in business in the Seine Department of Paris alone, making the Paris metropolitan area the world center of automobile production.[10] At the same time, automobile production was beginning in the United States. Between 1900 and 1908, 485 companies entered the automobile production business in the U.S. Their customers were mostly wealthy professionals who used their vehicles for business travel.

It was Henry Ford who first realized that if an inexpensive car could be built, everyone would want one. In 1908 he introduced the Model T runabout—a 20 horsepower, 1,200 pound car—priced at $825. By 1916, using the assembly line to mass-produce cars, he was able to get the price down to $345. The Model T had none of the sleek lines or sophistication of the European cars being produced in Germany and France during the same period, but it was durable, easy to drive and repair, and its undercarriage was high enough off the road to clear the ruts made by the horse carts and wagons still traveling America's primitive roads. That was enough to make the Model T a huge success.

Cars completely changed the way people lived. It was no longer necessary to buy everything you needed in the town in which you lived. People could live farther away from work. Suburbs began to grow as people moved away from the crowded cities. Small, self-reliant agricultural communities lost many of their businesses and opened some new ones that were dependent on tourists. Touring and sight-seeing became increasingly popular as more Americans acquired cars. There were no places to stay, however. Hotels located in small towns had been built to accommodate traveling salesmen and did not have facilities to serve families with children. Until roadside eating and lodging establishments began to be built in the 1930s, early motorists brought tents with them and camped. It was not until after World War II that the highway hotel and restaurant chains we know today were conceived and built.

According to the Motor Vehicle Manufacturers Association, today there are about 123 million automobiles in operation in the United States.[11] Auto travel accounts for nearly four out of every five miles traveled in the U.S.—more than two trillion miles each year. In fact, about 80 percent of all trips are taken in automobiles. Travel by car remains popular because it is affordable, flexible, and convenient.

## Airplanes

The end of the First World War marked the beginning of commercial aviation on both sides of the Atlantic. The impetus, of course, was the experience gained in flying planes during the war and the number of trained pilots and mechanics available to exploit this new form of transportation. In 1919 the British launched their first trans-channel commercial flights linking the business capitals of London and Paris. The flight took two and a half hours and the first planes used were converted bombers in which the pilot and the passenger sat in open cockpits.

**Many World War I pilots started independent, nonscheduled air transportation services after the war. Passenger comfort was not a consideration.** (Courtesy of the State of Michigan Archives)

In America the first commercial flights were inaugurated in 1918 as joint ventures of the U.S. Signal Corps and the U.S. Postal Service. These flights delivered mail only. However, many pilots who had learned to fly in the war bought surplus planes from the government and started independent nonscheduled service for passengers between various points. Soon, regular flights carried both mail and passengers between major cities.

The air age got a tremendous boost when a young stunt flyer named Charles Lindbergh, whose act of standing on the top wing of a looping plane thrilled crowds all over the country, decided to compete for a prize of $25,000 offered to the first person to fly solo across the Atlantic Ocean. At 7:55 a.m. on May 20, 1927, Lindbergh took off from Roosevelt Field on Long Island, New York, and landed at Le Bourget in Paris 33 hours and 39 minutes later. Lindbergh proved that the airplane was a practical means of traveling over long distances, and, as a result, investors who had been hesitant to put money into this new method of transportation lined up to back commercial aviation.

Also in 1927, a young World War I pilot, Juan Trippe, founded Pan American Airlines with a mail contract from the United States government to fly between Key West, Florida, and Havana, Cuba. The DC3, the first passenger aircraft that met the needs of the flying public, was introduced in 1936. In 1958 the first Boeing 707 went into service. It heralded the start of the jet age and provided a huge stimulus to both the tourist and business traveler markets.

Today, the major airlines operating internationally are owned by corporations or governments from 29 countries. A number of those airlines have multinational ownership.

Almost from the beginning, commercial aviation has had a substantial impact on the hospitality industry. The airplane made affordable mass transportation over long distances possible. Resort areas such as the Caribbean and Hawaii, which had previously been accessible only by boat, could now be visited by a larger number of tourists. The airplane was a boon to the hospitality industry.

## A Closer Look at the Hospitality Industry

Few people realize that there are at least three patron saints for those engaged in providing hospitality to others. The first of these is Saint Julian the Hospitaller. While many acknowledge that he may be mythical, he is listed in the *Oxford Dictionary of Saints* and has seven English churches dedicated to him.[12] In addition, he is depicted in stained glass windows in the cathedrals of Chartres and Rouen. He is the patron saint of innkeepers and travelers. His feast day, for those who wish to celebrate it, is January 29.

The legend goes that while Julian was away from home one day, a traveling couple knocked on the door of his house. His wife answered. She gave the tired travelers food and water and invited them to take a nap in her bed while she went to the market. While she was away, Julian (who was not yet a saint) came home to discover a man and woman asleep in his bedroom. Assuming it was his wife with another man, he killed them both on the spot. As he left the house he met his wife returning from the market. Because of this experience, he decided to spend the rest of his life being hospitable to strangers!

Although not as colorful, Saint Amand, a French monk who lived from 584 to 679, is recognized as the patron saint of innkeepers by the Roman Catholic Church, which holds his feast day on February 26.[13] Saint Amand began his work in Bourges, France, where he was a missionary. His work took him throughout Europe and he founded several monasteries in Belgium. Amand's monasteries were highly regarded as places where weary travelers could find comfortable lodging and good food, and he was supposed to have been a first-class manager.

The third saint, Saint Notburga, has a church dedicated to her in her hometown of Eben/Maurach, Austria. The church literature describes her as a "farm girl who dedicated her life to the welfare of servants," and she is considered the patron saint of food servers.

## History of Lodging

No one knows exactly when the first inns opened. References to them go as far back as recorded history. But certainly the first inns were private homes that offered accommodations to travelers. By 500 B.C., ancient cities such as Corinth, Greece, had a substantial number of establishments that offered food and drink as well as beds to travelers.

The early Roman *hospitia* provided rooms and sometimes food, although whether they were provided hospitably is open to question. The *Cornell Quarterly*, quoting from a 1981 book, *The Laws of Innkeepers*, says, "In ancient Rome, publicans and their houses were held in general contempt, just as they were in Greece. The Romans were a proud race who held that the business of conducting a tavern

**Saint Amand is a patron saint of innkeepers.** (Courtesy of *Lodging Magazine*)

was a low form of occupation, and the running of such establishments was usually entrusted to slaves."

In the Middle Ages, inns built along the highways were of questionable reputation. There is an anonymous English verse written about an inn in Wales that depicts its lack of hospitality this way:

> If you ever go to Dolgelly,
> Don't stay at the Lion's Hotel;
> 'Cause there's nothing to put in your belly,
> And no one to answer the bell!

During this period, landlords were predatory and robberies of travelers were common.[14] Even today the legend of the unscrupulous innkeeper is a part of our cultural heritage. In the popular musical *Les Misérables*, one of the most colorful characters is the innkeeper Thénardier, who sings:

> Welcome, Monsieur,
> Sit yourself down
> And meet the best Innkeeper in town.
> As for the rest,
> All of them crooks
> Rooking the guests
> And cooking the books.

Thénardier himself is not past using a few of these devices, as he tells the audience:

> Charge 'em for the lice,
> Extra for the mice
> Two percent for looking in the mirror twice!
> Here a little slice,
> There a little cut,
> Three percent for sleeping with the window shut![15]

By the middle of the seventeenth century the private inn was well established in England and on the Continent, and its reputation had improved. Samuel Johnson echoed a popular sentiment of the time: "There is nothing which has yet been contrived by man, by which so much happiness is produced as by a good tavern or inn."[16] Inns in those days were important social gathering places, and people congregated at the ones where political and literary figures stayed regularly. One collector of historical anecdotes tells of Thomas Telford, a British engineer who was considered something of a celebrity as well as delightful company: "In London, he stayed at the Ship Inn in Charing Cross, which was always crowded with his friends. A new landlord purchased the inn without knowing that Telford was about to move into a house of his own on Abingdon Street. When he found out he was utterly dismayed. 'Not leaving!' he exclaimed. 'I have just paid seven hundred and fifty pounds for you.'"[17] In France, large buildings that had rooms to let by the day, week, or longer were called *hotel garni*. The word "hotel" was first used in England in about 1760 by the Fifth Duke of Devonshire to name a lodging establishment in London.[18]

In 1794 the first hotel in the United States opened—the 70-room City Hotel on Broadway in New York City. Historian Daniel Boorstin notes that American hotels played a very different role than European hotels:

> Lacking a royal palace as the center of "Society," Americans created their counterpart in the community hotel. Hotels were usually the centers of lavish private entertainment (which, being held there, acquired a public significance) and of the most important public celebrations. The hotel lobby, like the outer rooms of a royal palace, became a loitering place, a headquarters of gossip, a vantage point for a glimpse of the great, the rich, and the powerful.[19]

One of the first hotels to clearly reflect this purpose in its architecture was the 170-room Tremont House, opened in Boston in 1829. Besides having a colonnaded marble portico, it featured formal public rooms with Ionic columns designed to give the hotel a palatial feeling. The Tremont was also the first hotel to have bellpersons, front desk employees, locks on guestroom doors, and free soap for guests. It is considered the first modern American hotel. Its designer, Isaiah Rogers, went on to build many other hotels and became one of the most influential hotel architects of the nineteenth century.

Hotels were often the first places where the public could experience new technology. The Tremont was one of the first large buildings in America to incorporate extensive plumbing facilities. The first public building to be heated by steam was the Eastern Exchange Hotel in Boston. Elevators were first introduced in hotels (New York's Fifth Avenue Hotel installed one in 1859), and less than three years after Thomas Edison announced in 1879 the commercial feasibility of his incandescent lamp, it was tried in hotels. The Hotel Everett on Park Row in New York City was the first hotel lit by electricity.[20]

**Lodging Industry Pioneers.** One of the first prominent hoteliers in the world started his career while still in his teens as an apprentice hotelkeeper in France. César Ritz (1847-1935) subsequently served as manager of the Grand National Hotel in Lucerne, Switzerland, and the Savoy in London, where he introduced live orchestras in the dining room, made evening dress compulsory, and restricted unescorted women.[21] Ritz went back to Paris to found his famous Ritz Hotel, a name that became synonymous with luxury and quality all over the world. Ritz was the first hotelier to give each guestroom a private bath, built-in closets, and telephones. No detail was too small for Ritz's personal attention. He invented the silk lamp shade so that the hotel's electric light bulbs would cast an apricot glow on ladies' faces instead of a harsh glare. On the opening day of the hotel, Ritz thought the dining room tables were two centimeters too high and had them cut down just hours before guests arrived.[22]

One of Ritz's close associates throughout his career was Georgés-Auguste Escoffier. Escoffier became famous in his own right, first as a chef and later for his innovative kitchen management techniques. Escoffier wrote a cookbook called *Le Guide Culinaire* (referred to by most today as *Escoffier*). Many premier hotels still serve dishes prepared from the book's recipes.

The oldest continuously operating hotel in America is the Parker House (now the Omni Parker House) on School Street in Boston. Founded in 1855 by a Massachusetts restaurateur, the Parker House was innovative in several ways. It was one of the first to deviate from the American Plan and embrace the more flexible "European Plan," in which guests paid separately for the cost of a room and whatever meals they ate. It was also the first hotel to offer meals whenever guests wanted them rather than at a fixed time and the first building in Boston with a passenger elevator.[23] Undoubtedly its most famous innovation was the Parker House Roll, a soft, sweet dinner roll "consumed with butter by the tons," according to James Beard.[24]

The need for a uniform hotel standard was first recognized by Ellsworth Statler. He started his hospitality career in 1878 as a bellhop in Wheeling, West Virginia. In 1908 Statler opened the first hotel bearing his name in Buffalo, New York. It featured telephones in every room, modern plumbing, ice water, full-size closets with lights, and other amenities. Soon he had other Statler hotels in Cleveland,

Opening in Boston in 1855, the Parker House gave the world the near-perfect Parker House roll.

Detroit, St. Louis, and Boston. Statler's genius was his ability to increase service and simplify operations on a chain-wide basis. He gave free morning newspapers to guests, provided radios at no extra charge, and even developed "The Statler Service Code," which all employees had to memorize and carry with them.

Another early hotel-chain pioneer was Conrad Hilton, born in 1887 in San Antonio, in the Territory of New Mexico. Young Conrad started his hotel career by renting rooms in his family's home to travelers. In 1919 he bought his first hotel, the Mobley, in Cisco, Texas. Hilton continued to buy hotels throughout his lifetime (he died in 1979), including the Waldorf-Astoria, which his company purchased control of in 1949, and the entire Statler chain, acquired in 1954.

The Sheraton chain—at one time the largest hotel chain in the world—was started in 1941 by Ernest Henderson, a Boston investor. The chain began when Henderson, along with associate Robert Lowell Moore, acquired several New England hotels in the mid-1930s. One of the hotels had an expensive electric sign on the roof bearing the name "Sheraton." Deciding it would be too costly to remove, the owners kept the sign and applied the name to all of their future hotels.[25] Henderson's primary interest was in new forms of financing and other methods for increasing equity. Sheraton was sold to the International Telephone and Telegraph Corporation (ITT) in 1969.

The concept of standardized lodging accommodations built alongside U.S. highways was the brainchild of a former movie theater operator and land developer in Memphis, Tennessee, Kemmons Wilson. Wilson came home very unhappy from a family vacation because he thought he had been overcharged to stay in substandard motel rooms. In 1952 Wilson built his first Holiday Inn in Memphis. Its unique features included a restaurant—most motels did not have one—as well as two double beds in every room. Wilson did not believe in charging parents for lodging their children—he had three children of his own and paying extra for them when he stayed at a motel irked him. Another marketing innovation of Wilson's was a huge property sign (he had learned the value of distinctive signs from his years in the theater business). Wilson also recognized the value of retaining his guests. He instructed his managers to offer to make reservations by telephone for departing guests who wished to stay at another Holiday Inn down the road. Like Statler, Wilson offered free "extras" to his overnight guests—free TV, free ice, and a telephone in every room.

Holiday Inn Worldwide is now one of the largest hotel chains in the world. In 1992 there were 1,630 hotels, with a total of 322,527 rooms, operating under the Holiday Inn name.[26] The company is no longer American-owned, however. In 1989 the Holiday Corporation sold the Holiday Inn chain to Bass PLC, a British company. The original American firm changed its name and continues to operate a gaming division and sell franchises for its Hampton Inn and Embassy Suites products.

Today hotel chains are headquartered all over the globe. Motel 6 and Hilton International are European-owned. The Saison Group of Japan owns Inter-Continental Hotels while the Four Seasons Hotel Company of Canada owns Regent Hotels. Hotel companies based in England, India, Switzerland, Germany, and Hong Kong also own (and in some cases operate) hotels in the United States. U.S. companies such as Sheraton and Marriott continue to expand globally.

## History of Food Service

About the same time that hotels were gaining a strong foothold on both sides of the Atlantic in the seventeenth century, restaurants were also achieving prominence. According to *Food in History*, professionally cooked food was not a new concept:

> It had been known in Mesopotamia in the time of Nebuchadnezzar, and the population of the Near East still, in medieval times, preferred not to cook at home but to buy forcemeat balls, roast mutton, fish fritters, pancakes, and almond paste sweets from the market. It may, indeed, have been from the Arab world, by way of Spain, that the custom of buying ready made food was reintroduced into Europe....[27]

An interest in preparing delicious food on a large scale was stimulated in Europe by Louis XIV of France. He made dining a state occasion. The first restaurant (as distinct from an inn, tavern, or food specialty house) was opened by Boulanger in Paris in 1765. The first London restaurants (which served mainly French food) were not established until about 1830.[28] While he was ambassador to France, Thomas Jefferson learned to appreciate French food and wines and used them in White House functions when he became president. In 1832 America's first continental-style restaurant opened—Delmonico's in New York City.

**Food Service Pioneers.** As well as encouraging the growth of hotels, the railroads were responsible for America's first restaurant chain. In 1875 a 40-year-old English immigrant, Fred Harvey, opened two small restaurants along the Kansas Pacific Railroad.[29] Soon he added more along the Atchison, Topeka, and Santa Fe route. Harvey was a stickler for fine food and quality. His menus featured such delicacies as fresh oysters, sea turtle, and charlotte of peaches with cognac sauce, served on fine linen in scrupulously clean dining rooms. Harvey was also famous for his food servers, who were known as "Harvey Girls." They were chosen to represent impeccable standards of cleanliness, mannerliness, and hospitality—qualities in short supply in the West of those days.

In 1925 Howard Johnson purchased a small drugstore in Wollaston, Massachusetts. He soon started selling a chocolate ice cream product he developed to supplement his drugstore's revenues. The ice cream did so well that Johnson added other flavors until he had developed the "28 Flavors" that became his trademark. Johnson was one of the first franchisors. By 1940 he had 100 roadside restaurants selling Howard Johnson's ice cream and other food.

Like Statler, Johnson was interested in standardization and quality control. The building, decor, and seating arrangements for each restaurant in the Howard Johnson's chain were standardized. Johnson also created a central commissary to make sure his restaurants' food products were consistent and of the proper quality. This commissary prepared frozen entrées for delivery to Howard Johnson's franchises all over the country. Johnson insisted that his franchisees buy everything from him (which was legal at that time) and operate their restaurants exactly as he specified.

Finally, no discussion of food service pioneers would be complete without mentioning Ray Kroc, the man who founded McDonald's. Kroc was a milk-shake-machine salesman who, at the age of 52, called on two brothers who had set up a hamburger stand in San Bernardino, California. They were not interested in expanding their concept, which featured large lighted golden arches, but Kroc was. Within 40 years of making a deal that allowed him to franchise the operation, Kroc had a chain of restaurants stretching first across the nation and then around the world. The success of McDonald's is due largely to its commitment to "QSC&V"—quality, service, cleanliness, and value—combined with a simple standardized concept utilizing many of the same ideas originally pioneered by Howard Johnson.

Today a new McDonald's restaurant opens somewhere in the world approximately every 12 hours. By the end of 1996, McDonald's operated more than 20,000 restaurants in 65 countries, and that figure continues to grow. While the majority of these international operations are in Japan, Canada, England, Germany, and France, there are also McDonald's restaurants in Beijing, Moscow, Copenhagen, and Mexico City. In 1996, 59 percent of McDonald's profits came from overseas units.

# Endnotes

1. *Encyclopedia Britannica,* 15th ed. (Chicago: Encyclopedia Britannica Inc., 1975), p. 757.
2. Reay Tannahill, *Food in History* (New York: Crown Publishers, 1988), p. 138.
3. Cited by Robert Wechsler in *All in the Same Boat: The Humorists' Guide to the Ocean Cruise* (Highland Park, N.J.: Catbird Press, 1988), p. 44.
4. Ellen Williamson, *When We Went First Class* (New York: Doubleday, 1977), p. 112.
5. Daniel J. Boorstin, *The Americans: The National Experience* (New York: Vintage Books, 1965), p. 141.
6. James J. Flink, *The Automobile Age* (Cambridge, Mass.: The MIT Press, 1992), p. 6.
7. Flink, p. 6.
8. Flink, p. 10.
9. Flink, p. 10.
10. Flink, p. 18.
11. The statistics in this paragraph were taken from *Tourism Works for America: A Report of the Travel and Tourism Industry in the United States, 1992 Edition* (Washington, D.C.: National Travel and Tourism Awareness Council, 1992), p. 8.
12. David Hughes Farmer, *Oxford Dictionary of Saints* (Oxford: Oxford University Press, 1987), pp. 243–244.
13. Mark Collins and Robert J. Collins, "In Noble Footsteps," *Lodging,* April 1995, p. 158.
14. "The Evolution of the Hospitality Industry," *Cornell Quarterly,* May 1985, p. 36.
15. *Les Misérables* by Alan Boubil and Claude-Michel Schonberg, based on the novel by Victor Hugo. Lyrics by Herbert Kretzmer. Copyright 1985 Exallshow Ltd.
16. Samuel Johnson, 21 March 1776, in *Boswell's Life of Johnson,* L. F. Powell's revision of G. Hill's edition, vol. 2, p. 452.
17. Clifton Fadiman, *The Little, Brown Book of Anecdotes* (Boston: Little, Brown, 1985), p. 536.
18. Donald A. Lundberg, *The Hotel and Restaurant Business,* 4th ed. (New York: Van Nostrand Reinhold, 1984), p. 21.
19. Boorstin, p. 135.
20. Boorstin, p. 139.
21. Richard A. Wentzel, "Pioneers and Leaders of the Hospitality Industry," reprinted from *Hospitality Management* by Robert A. Brymer (Dubuque, Iowa: Kendall Hunt, 1991), p. 29.
22. "The Cowherd Who Made the Ritz Ritzy," *Lodging,* December 1993, p. 56. This article was adapted from a story by Mary Blume, published in the *International Herald Tribune,* 12 October 1993.
23. "Eating In, All-American Fare," *Lodging,* September 1994, p. 112.
24. "Eating In, All-American Fare," p. 112.
25. Larry Littman, "Despite Its Rocky Start, Hotel Industry Continues to Flourish into the 1990s," *Travel Agent Magazine,* 26 February 1990, p. 62.

26. Richard Turned, ed., *1993 Directory of Hotel and Motel Companies,* 62nd ed. (New York: American Hotel Association Directory Corporation, 1993), p. 343.
27. Tannahill, pp. 173–174.
28. Tannahill, p. 327.
29. Information in this and the following paragraph is cited from John Mariani, "Working on the Railroad," reprinted in *Restaurant Hospitality,* January 1992, p. 71, from Mariani's *America Eats Out* (New York: Morrow, 1991).

# Part I

# Introduction

## Chapter 1 Outline

What Is Service?
Problems in Managing and Marketing
   Service Businesses
      The Nature of the Product
      The Customer's Role in Production
      People Are Part of the Product
      Maintaining Quality Control
      No Inventories
      The Importance of Time
      Different Distribution Channels
Achieving Superior Service in a
   Less-Than-Perfect World
      Strategic Planning, Missions, and
         Objectives
      The Strategic Planning Process
      Planning Challenges in Capacity-
         Constrained Businesses
The Strategic Service Vision
      Targeting a Market Segment
      Focusing on a Service Strategy
Delivering on the Service Promise
      Service Disney-Style
Chapter Summary

## Competencies

1. Define "service," and summarize how service businesses differ from manufacturing businesses.

2. Explain the importance of strategic planning, describe the strategic planning process, and summarize planning challenges in capacity-constrained businesses.

3. Describe a strategic service vision for service companies, summarize key actions companies can take to deliver good service, and describe Disney's four basic service priorities.

# 1

# Service Makes the Difference

IN MANY PARTS of the world, hospitality has become a mature industry. That is to say, it has passed the stage of rapid growth and innovation. There are not many new inventions that affect the way we eat and sleep. In the past, customers were easily able to tell the difference between one hotel or type of restaurant and another. They were easily able to tell the difference between one restaurant type or brand and another, because each was unique within its own market niche. Holiday Inns, Hyatt, McDonald's, and T.G.I. Friday's stood for something special, and different. Within each chain the architecture, decor, amenities, and menus were similar. But there was a clear difference between chains. You could get hamburgers at McDonald's, but if you wanted chicken you headed over to KFC. All Holiday Inns had swimming pools; Days Inn did not.

These distinctions are no longer true. As these chains redefined themselves to appeal to broader markets, their uniqueness began to fade. Chicken is available not only at KFC, but at McDonald's, Burger King, and Wendy's. Tacos are served not only at Taco Bell, but at McDonald's as well. Dunkin' Donuts sells bagels, and if you want a bowl of chili you can find it at Wendy's as well as Chili's.

In the hotel business, atriums were an exclusive feature of Hyatt. Now many hotels have them. They have even become common on many of the new mega cruise ships!

Because obvious physical and product differences have faded, consumers have looked for other ways to differentiate one brand from another. There are many possibilities to choose from. One difference is availability. Some chains have one or more locations in just about every major city; others have just a few. Another difference is price. A steak at Denny's costs much less than one at the Outback Steakhouse. The most compelling difference, however, in the minds of many consumers, is **service**. Why is this so? Much of the answer has to do with lifestyles of today, which have shaped our priorities. The large number of two-income families and the growing number of single-parent families have made *time* a priority in the way we live our lives. Very few consumers today have the luxury of spending a lot of time shopping to find the best value, the highest quality, or the speediest service. The attitude today is that we demand these things...they are a given, and when we don't receive what we expect we become dissatisfied. There is another factor at work here. Many studies show that life has become much more stressful in the last 50 years. The "rat race" is no longer an elusive euphemism, but a reality. One way of escape is to purchase a service so that we don't have to do it ourselves. When we

**The atrium of the Grand Hyatt in Washington, D.C., welcomes guests with its distinctive decor.** (Courtesy of the Grand Hyatt)

do this, we not only relieve some of the pressures of daily life, but we also expect to feel pampered, more important. Someone else is cooking and serving dinner, making the beds, and providing the entertainment. *Expectations* is what service is all about, as we shall see throughout this chapter.

## What Is Service?

Service is generally defined as "work done for others." But this definition falls far short of the real meaning of the word. If a customer sits down at a restaurant, orders a sirloin steak, medium rare, and then after waiting 30 minutes receives a baked chicken breast, we can hardly characterize this as "service." Yet it fits the definition of "work done for others"!

For a better understanding of what service can mean, let's look at a real service experience from one of the most highly praised hotels in the world. According to many travel writers and surveys that have been made among frequent travelers, one of the best hotels in the world is the Mandarin Oriental in Bangkok. Famous writers such as James Michener and Noel Coward have written books while staying there and there are suites named after them. The Oriental's service is considered to be unparalleled anywhere.

How do they achieve this?

Guests who pre-register at the Oriental are asked what flight they will be arriving on and whether they would like limousine service to the hotel. (Traffic in Bangkok is horrendous, taxis are hard to come by, and the hotel's limo costs the same as a taxi.) As soon as guests pass through customs at the Bangkok airport they are greeted by an assistant manager from the hotel. He takes their baggage checks, calls for a Mercedes limousine, and, while they are waiting for the car and the luggage, takes down all of their registration information, including their credit card. When they leave the airport, the assistant manager radios ahead with the guests' names and car number. When they pull up to the hotel entrance, the doorman greets them by name and another assistant manager escorts them immediately to their room. Depending on the level of accommodations, the Mandarin service does not stop there. Every room contains pre-printed personalized stationery. Guests staying in suites are immediately greeted by a butler who offers to unpack for them and press any wrinkled garments. Bowls of fresh fruit in every room are replenished several times a day. All employees greet guests by name. To ensure that the hotel can provide this kind of service there is a staff-to-guest ratio of 3 to 1—an almost impossible level to achieve economically in most countries. Moreover, the hotel runs one of the best hospitality schools in the country. Top graduates are offered a job at the Oriental; others easily find positions at other hotels and restaurants.

Every step of the way, the Mandarin Oriental exceeds guest expectations of what it will be like to stay in that hotel. First-time guests do not expect to be greeted at the airport by an assistant manager, pre-registered while their luggage is being retrieved, greeted by name when they arrive, escorted to their room not by a bellman but by another assistant manager, find personalized stationery, and so on. It is this ability to constantly exceed expectations that has earned the hotel its outstanding international reputation.

Restaurant and hotel customers have certain expectations. Consider the elements that comprise what we would call "good service" at a fine restaurant. The first impression of what kind of service the restaurant offers occurs when guests call for a reservation. How gracious is the person on the other end? Do they sound genuinely interested in taking the reservation or do they act as if the call were an unwanted interruption? The next impression may be the valet parking. Is the car taken quickly? Is the guest welcomed or simply handed a parking ticket? When they walk through the door, who greets them and how? Is the host well groomed, polite, concerned with the customer's needs (for immediate seating or a nonsmoking table, for example)? When seated, how soon before their presence is acknowledged by a server (often simple eye contact is enough) and water and bread are placed on the table? How soon is the order taken? Is the food served on time? Is it what was ordered and prepared the way it was expected? Does the server remember who ordered what? These are just some of the standards that are used in forming a judgment about the restaurant. If all of the parts of this process are performed better than expected, *if reality exceeds expectations*, then customers rate the service received as better than average, or high. This is what we might call a three or four-star restaurant. If reality matches expectations—the guests get what they expected, no more and no less—then service is satisfactory. But if reality is less than what is expected, then service is poor.

One further note. Price may play an important part in how service is evaluated because it influences customers' expectations. When someone buys a hamburger at a fast-food chain unit, what they expect is very different from when they buy a hamburger in the dining room of a fine hotel. They expect more because they are paying more.

It is important to remember that, in all cases, it is the person who is receiving the service (the customer), not the person who is delivering it, whose expectations count. Too often managers assume that if they think they are providing good service that must be so. It is difficult for them to recognize that their perceptions may differ considerably from their customers'.

With this background, we are now in a position to formulate a more compressive definition of service, or, to be more exact, good service. One approach is to look at service as a *performance* directed at satisfying the needs of customers. This is a good analogy and one that is used quite often in books on service management. Those who like this approach compare what a customer experiences in a hotel or restaurant as being similar to a theater. In a theater the audience sees only what happens on stage—the front of the house. Many things happen behind the scenes—the back of the house. The use of these very terms by hotels comes directly from the theater. The employees are compared to actors on a stage. Indeed, at Disney resort hotels and theme parks all employees are "members of the cast" and are "on stage" as soon as they walk into the sight of any of the guests. Through this use of performance terminology, Disney reminds them that they are to "act" at all times the way guests expect them to act, not the way they may feel like acting!

In conclusion, we choose to define good service as *meeting customer needs in the way that they want and expect them to be met*. Superior service, obviously, is exceeding their expectations.

At Walt Disney theme parks, service is a "performance" that seeks to satisfy guest needs. (Courtesy of Walt Disney World, Orlando, Florida)

## Problems in Managing and Marketing Service Businesses

Traditionally, the management and marketing of service businesses (including hospitality) have been described and studied in the same way as manufactured products. The view has been that management is management and marketing is marketing; once you understand the basic principles, it doesn't matter that much whether you're marketing a bowl of soup in a restaurant or a can of soup in a supermarket.

We no longer believe this. There are in fact a number of very important differences that affect the way service enterprises have to be managed. Hotels and restaurants—which deal in such **intangible products** as comfort, security, and positive experiences—have very different management and marketing problems than tangible products such as automobiles or boxes of cereal. Christopher H. Lovelock has identified differences between the two[1]:

- The nature of the product is different.
- Customers are more involved in the production process.
- People are part of the product.
- It's harder to maintain quality control standards.
- There are no inventories.
- The time factor is more important.
- Distribution channels are different.

Let's take a closer look at each of these differences and consider their implications.

## The Nature of the Product

Manufactured goods are tangible products. We can pick them up, carry them around, or in some other way physically handle them. A service, on the other hand, as we have noted, is a performance or process. Marketing a service, like a hotel or restaurant, which of course involves the use of physical objects and goods such as beds and food, is quite a different thing from marketing the goods themselves. For example, when guests choose a hotel, they take into account such factors as the convenience of the location, amenities (spas, business centers, etc.), and the kind of service they expect. When they call for a reservation, we reserve a certain category of room based on price, size, or location, but we seldom reserve the exact room itself (except in the case of a handicapped room), which is assigned at check-in. When guests arrive they use the physical facilities and eat the food, but that's not all they are buying. They are also purchasing the performance of a host of services of people who work in the hotel—room service, concierge service, valet service—all of which are intangible. We have to manage the production of those services as well as of the physical product, and we have to persuade potential guests to buy some things that we cannot show them a picture of or even adequately describe.

## The Customer's Role in Production

Customers have no involvement in the production of manufactured goods. Soup is produced and packaged at the factory and purchased by a consumer at a supermarket or convenience store. The people who make the soup never see the ones who eat

**People are part of the product offered at hotels and restaurants. As a result, their service attitude plays a large part in delivering such "service products" as friendliness and positive experiences.** (Courtesy of The Olive Garden Restaurants)

it, and the ones who eat it don't go to the factory when they want a serving. The two activities, production and consumption, are completely separate. This is not true in a service-based business.

A restaurant or a hotel is, in a very real sense, a factory. It is a factory where service is produced for customers who come inside, see the workers who are putting together the service, and may even participate with them in producing it. A good example is the typical salad bar, where guests assemble their own salads and thus become part of the production process. Another example is the health spa in a hotel where guests use the cycles and Nautilus® equipment as part of the service. Again, they are participating in production. Some kinds of services require more employee interaction than others. But in any case, because it is part of the service (product), that interaction between employees and customers needs to be managed—a task which a manager of manufactured goods never has to face.

## People Are Part of the Product

In a service like a hotel or restaurant, customers not only come in contact with employees but with other customers as well. That makes the other customers a part of the product (which we define as a performance), and often defines the quality of the service. Have you ever been to a movie or play where the people behind you wouldn't keep quiet and spoiled some of your enjoyment? What about a restaurant

**Other guests are an important part of the overall hospitality experience.**

where you went for a quiet, romantic evening and there was a party of 12 loud people at the next table celebrating someone's birthday? Business travelers who pay $200 a night for a room in an elegant city hotel can get very annoyed when their check-in is delayed by a busload of tourists who have just arrived, or when a group of conventioneers insists on being served breakfast before anyone else, so they can be finished in time for their first meeting. Similarly, at an elegant reception, where you have put on your best outfit, the dress of the other guests adds to your own enjoyment.

In short, all of the people whom a guest comes in contact with, both other guests and employees, are an integral part of the product. They often are the main difference in the quality of the experience one hotel provides over another. Surprisingly, not all hospitality managers spend enough time striving to achieve an ideal mix.

## Maintaining Quality Control

When a factory produces a product, it can be inspected for quality before it goes out the door. As long as proper quality control procedures and inspections are in place, defective products are not delivered. But services, like other live performances, take place in real time. That means that mistakes are bound to occur. Professor Christopher Lovelock cites a former package goods marketer who became a Holiday Inn executive and observed:

> We can't control the quality of our product as well as a Procter & Gamble control engineer on a production line can....When you buy a box of Ivory,

you can reasonably be 99 and 44/100ths percent sure that this stuff will work to get your clothes clean. When you buy a Holiday Inn room, you're sure at some lesser percentage that we'll work to give you a good night's sleep without any hassle, or people banging on the walls, and all the bad things that can happen in a hotel.[2]

### No Inventories

Manufacturers can store their inventory in warehouses until needed. But because services are live performances, they cannot be made in advance or stored for future use. That means that there are times when the supply can't be produced on time because the demand is too great. Guests must be turned away from hotels that are completely occupied, or restaurant guests may wait an hour or more for a table. For this reason, service marketing often focuses on controlling demand.

### The Importance of Time

Because most hospitality services are delivered (performed) in the "factory," customers have to be present to receive them (except when they order take-out food from a restaurant, and even then delivery—which is a service—is involved, and time is a crucial factor). When customers are present, they expect the service to be performed "on time," which in their minds means "when they want it." In a restaurant, guests not only expect that their orders will be taken promptly, but that the food will arrive in a reasonable amount of time. Time, then, often plays a more important role in producing services than in producing goods (although "just in time" delivery systems are crucial in certain manufacturing operations). If customers must be kept waiting, hospitality enterprises must devise strategies to keep them from feeling that they are being ignored or are not important.

### Different Distribution Channels

Companies that manufacture goods move their products from the factory by trucks, trains, or airplanes to wholesalers, distributors, or retailers, who then resell them to the ultimate consumer. This is not the case with services where customers come right into the factory or contact it directly. For instance, they may use phones or the Internet to make reservations, or have a secretary or travel agent do it for them. In either case, service industries must train their employees to handle some marketing functions such as dealing with customers. Employees who manufacture goods do not for the most part require those skills. Even when intermediaries are involved (such as travel agents), the relationship requires more "people skills" than the kind where the transfer of physical products is involved, as from a factory to a warehouse.

## Achieving Superior Service in a Less-Than-Perfect World

The most important operational competency of top-level service managers is the ability to plan for the future. While day-to-day operations can be performed by others, someone must be thinking about next year and beyond. This is the job of top managers—to develop the strategy for survival that any business needs to succeed. It is also the key to providing superior service, which must begin at the very top of the organizational ladder.

## Strategic Planning, Missions, and Objectives

Broad, long-range planning is called strategic planning. Companies must formulate general business objectives for themselves, otherwise there is bound to be confusion about where they are going and how they intend to get there. These general business objectives are most commonly called a company's mission and are expressed as a mission statement. Here is the complete mission statement of Chili's Restaurants, named one of America's most admired companies by *Fortune* magazine:

- To be a premier and progressive growth company, with a balanced approach toward people, quality, and profitability.
- To be focused, sensitive, and responsive to our employees, customers, and our environment.
- To empower our team to exceed customers expectations...to become customer obsessed.
- To enhance a high level of excellence, innovation, integrity, and ethics.
- To attract, develop, and retain a superior team.
- To enhance long-term shareholder wealth.[3]

Note the use of the words *quality, empower, team, customer obsessed, innovation, employees,* and *environment*. You will learn to recognize the importance of all of these concepts.

Here is Hilton Hotels' mission statement. It is short and simple:

> To be recognized as the world's best first-class hotel organization, to constantly strive to improve, allowing us to prosper as a business for the benefit of our guests, our employees, and our shareholders.[4]

## The Strategic Planning Process

Once a mission has been clearly established and articulated, there is a series of steps a company must take to make that mission a guiding force.

**Perform a SWOT Analysis. SWOT** stands for *strengths, weaknesses, opportunities,* and *threats*. To do a SWOT analysis, a company examines the internal and external environment in which it is operating. What are the strengths and weaknesses of its operation? What opportunities exist for growth? What threats exist, either from competitors or changing trends? The ultimate goal of this analysis is to determine how well we are serving current markets.

**Formulate Strategies.** Strategies might include appealing to new market segments such as diet-conscious people, adding more units, or developing new products. Marriott did this when it developed three new types of Marriott hotels—Courtyard by Marriott (limited-service), Residence Inns (extended-stay), and Fairfield Inns ("road warriors").

**Implement Strategies.** Once strategies have been developed, they must be implemented. If one of a restaurant chain's strategies is to add salads to its menu, the chain must create a salad that can be made in a uniform manner in all of its units. The chain must also identify suppliers and devise methods of preparation.

Before a company can implement strategies, some fundamental issues must be addressed:

*Leadership.* Managers must explain their strategies to employees. Continuing with the restaurant chain example, the chain's managers must explain why they are introducing salads and persuade them that, even if it involves more work, it will produce benefits for them as well as the organization.

*Organizational structure.* Sometimes the organizational structure must be changed in order to implement a strategy. When Taco Bell decided to concentrate on improving customer service, it freed its unit managers from 15 hours of weekly paperwork so they would have time to coach employees and satisfy customers.

*Corporate culture.* To implement a strategy, you need employees who buy into the corporate culture or way of doing business. They must share the same values and work ethic. Disney spends two days of employee orientation in telling new employees the history of the company. Walt Disney's life story is retold at length. Early Mickey Mouse cartoons are shown. New hires are taught the Disney language—words and concepts unique to the Disney organization. This helps promote a family or "tribal" feeling.

**Monitor and Evaluate Results.** After implementing strategies, managers must monitor them to make sure they are working. Some examples: Marriott reads guest comment cards carefully; Domino's Pizza surveys customers by phone; South Seas Plantation on Captiva Island, Florida, holds customer focus groups.

Tim Firnstahl is the founder and CEO of SGE, Inc., a restaurant management company in Seattle that operates The Kirkland Roaster, Von's, Sharp's, and other popular restaurants. Firnstahl set an objective of making sure that guest satisfaction in all of his restaurants would be guaranteed. Then he developed a plan to reach that objective. He came up with a company slogan: *"Your Enjoyment Guaranteed. Always."* He reduced this to an acronym—YEGA—that all employees could easily remember. After a series of meetings in which Firnstahl explained what he had in mind, all of his 600 employees signed a contract pledging that they would follow through on the YEGA promise. "We created a YEGA logo and put it everywhere," says Firnstahl, "on report forms, on training manuals, on wall signs. We started a *YEGA NEWS* and distributed YEGA pins, shirts, name tags, even underwear. We announced that failure to enforce YEGA would be grounds for dismissal." The final step was empowering employees to make the YEGA objective workable. With this in mind, Firnstahl instituted the idea that employees can and should do anything to keep the customer happy. "In the event of an error or delay, any employee right down to the busboy could provide complimentary wine or dessert, or pick up an entire tab if necessary."[5]

## Planning Challenges in Capacity-Constrained Businesses

One important difference between service organizations and manufacturing firms, as has been previously pointed out, is the inability of service firms to inventory finished products. In the manufacturing of goods, peaks and valleys of supply and demand are managed in part by finishing and storing goods in advance of when they will be needed. Thus it is seldom if ever necessary to produce anything instantly to satisfy demand.

Since service firms cannot finish and store services, their financial success depends on how efficiently they match their productive capacity—their staff, equipment, and resources such as operating inventories—to consumer demand at any given moment. This is very difficult. When demand is low, production capacity will be wasted because there will be an oversupply of workers to serve the customers; when demand is higher than production capacity, there will be more guests than the workers or the building can serve and business will be lost. In other words, hotels and restaurants are **capacity-constrained businesses** and therefore must constantly manage both supply (production capacity) and demand.

**Managing Supply.** Let's first look at strategies for managing supply. In the case of hotels and restaurants, the ability to supply the products manufactured in the service factory is fixed. A hotel has a fixed number of beds; a restaurant has a fixed number of seats. These cannot be altered to increase capacity whenever demand is greater than capacity—that is, when there are more guests than there are hotel beds or restaurant seats. That means that a good part of the time hotels and restaurants must follow a **level-capacity strategy** in which the same amount of capacity is offered no matter how high the demand.

However, some hospitality firms can follow a **chased-demand strategy**, in which capacity can be varied to suit the demand level—in a limited way. For example, there is a measure of flexibility in some parts of a hotel, such as the space set aside for meetings and conventions. Another common tactic in hospitality firms is to have a certain number of part-time employees who work only when the demand is high. Sometimes firms such as caterers can rent extra equipment and thus increase their capacity as needed. Finally, companies can cross-train employees so that they can be shifted temporarily to other jobs as needed. In the long run, of course, a hotel or restaurant organization can increase its capacity by enlarging its property or building a new one.

**Managing Demand.** Because hotel and restaurant capacity is limited, it is important to put most of the strategic planning emphasis on managing demand. One of the goals of managers in a service business is to shift demand from periods when it cannot be accommodated (because the operation is already filled to capacity) to periods when it can be. One way to do this is to encourage business during slow periods. Some restaurants offer early-bird specials to increase demand early in the day, and lounges have happy hours to increase demand early in the evening.

While supply cannot be inventoried, sometimes demand can. This happens when managers or employees encourage customers to stand in line or sit in the restaurant's lounge until the next table becomes available. Reservations systems also are an example of demand inventorying.

**Taking reservations is one way restaurants and hotels can manage demand.**

The most common method used to influence demand in the hotel industry is price. Using pricing strategies to control demand is risky unless the strategies are thoroughly understood. Hotels are faced with pricing decisions every day, such as whether to accept meeting and convention reservations at low group rates, or hold on to those rooms for later sale at higher rates to individual business travelers. One tool managers use to make such decisions is yield management.

Sometimes the product itself can be varied to help balance supply and demand. Restaurants routinely change their menus and level of service between lunch and dinner. Cruise ships reposition themselves to call on ports in the Caribbean in the winter and Alaska in the summer. Sometimes different services can be offered at the same time to accommodate the demand levels of different group as with first-class, business-class, and economy-class airline seats—all on the same plane—or concierge floors in hotels.

Finally, communication strategies can play a large part in balancing demand levels. A carefully thought-out advertising schedule can enable resorts to influence demand by appealing to new market segments with special rates during the off-season; similarly, they can keep demand levels high during the regular season by targeting those guest groups willing to pay full rates.

One of the hard realities that prompt these tactics to manage demand is that hotels and restaurants have a high level of fixed expenses because of their physical plant. These fixed expenses cannot be lowered, so strategies and tactics must be found to utilize a hotel or restaurant to its fullest possible extent. Even a marginal increase in business can produce a significant increase in profit once the break-even point is reached.

**Moments of Truth.** In order to achieve maximum profits, many successful hospitality firms have turned to computers and other modern technology. But this sometimes produces a depersonalized atmosphere, and guests may feel that they are being treated as mere numbers. To combat this guest perception, some companies have identified what they call **moments of truth.** The concept comes from Jan Carlzon, the CEO of Scandinavian Airlines System (SAS) in the early 1980s. Carlzon understood that there was a huge difference in the way SAS defined service levels and the way its customers defined them. "Each of our 10 million customers came in contact with approximately five SAS employees, and this contact lasted an average of 15 seconds each time. Thus SAS is 'created' in the minds of our customers 50 million times a year, 15 seconds at a time. These 50 million 'moments of truth' are the moments that ultimately determine whether SAS will succeed or fail as a company. They are the moments when we must prove to our customers that SAS is their best alternative," Carlzon explained.[6]

Good businesses concentrate their efforts on making sure that moments of truth are handled correctly For hotels, an important moment of truth occurs when guests check in or out and come face-to-face with a hotel employee. Although there are certain check-in/check-out routines that must be followed, guests should be given individual attention so they feel their needs are being addressed in a personal way. One way to do this is to make certain that front desk employees are trained to look up from their computer screens to give guests a warm welcome (by name, if possible), and continue to smile and make eye contact as they perform their duties for the guests. Such seemingly small gestures go a long way toward establishing an overall atmosphere of attentive and pleasing guest service.

## The Strategic Service Vision

James Heskett, professor of business administration at Harvard Business School, notes that all successful service companies share what he calls a "strategic service vision"—a blueprint for service managers. The components of this blueprint are: (1) targeting a market segment and (2) focusing on a service strategy.[7] Let's discuss these elements in more detail, drawing from examples and ideas from the work of Heskett and others.

### Targeting a Market Segment

There is no such thing as a product or service that appeals to everyone. Some people want hotels that have a good restaurant because they enjoy dining while they are traveling. Others don't care that much about food but value a hotel with a fitness club and spa where they can relax and exercise. Some travelers want a comfortable guestroom with a desk where they can work; others plan to spend little time in their room. Similarly, a restaurant can't appeal to everyone. People have different tastes in food and different ideas of what constitutes a pleasant experience when dining out. They differ in how much they are willing to pay for a meal.

Since hotels and restaurants cannot hope to appeal to everyone, they single out groups or market segments and attempt to provide products and services that, in the eyes of these consumers, are superior to those of their competitors. For example, McDonald's primary market has always been families with young children. Wendy's targets adults who want a hamburger cooked to order—historically, it has made little effort to attract children. At the high end of the hamburger-restaurant scale is Fuddruckers, which serves larger and more expensive hamburgers and beer in an atmosphere designed to appeal to adults. The Omni Parker House hotel in Boston focuses on individual business travelers and does not accept business from bus tour groups except on weekends during July and August, which are traditionally slow periods. Mini-vacation weekend packages are offered only when large numbers of business travelers are not in the hotel.

## Focusing on a Service Strategy

The various service concepts that hospitality businesses adopt are not simply amorphous marketing ideas. A hotel or restaurant, including its services, is carefully designed to appeal to a limited segment of the market, *and the way service is delivered is tailored to match the expectations of the segment that it targets.*

Research has shown that most people believe buying an intangible service like a vacation or even a meal in a restaurant is more risky than buying a manufactured product. With a manufactured product, buyers have a better idea of what they're getting for their money, while with intangible products there may be some surprises. It is that element of uncertainty that poses the biggest challenge to service businesses. That is why it is so important for managers and employees to provide consistent services that meet an operation's standards.

**Service Standards.** Successful hospitality companies focus a good deal of management attention on establishing service quality standards, communicating them to employees through training programs, and measuring performance. For example, one service standard that is frequently established and easy to measure is waiting time. Burger King and McDonald's have strict standards for how long customers are expected to wait for their food once it has been ordered. Many airlines and hotels with busy telephone reservation systems have set time limits for how long customers can be kept on hold before their call is handled. Restaurants often manage expectations by telling guests they will have to wait longer for a table than is actually the case. When they are given their table earlier than expected, guests conclude that they have been given special attention—thus their feeling of receiving good service is reinforced.

Another quality control technique restaurants use is to set standards for how quickly a food server should approach a customer after he or she sits down at a table. At some operations the standard is for a server to go to the table immediately and say, "I'll be with you in a minute." Another restaurant may require bread and butter to be served at the same time, to further acknowledge the diners' presence.

Providing consistent services is extremely complex where customer contact is involved, especially when some of the lowest-paid employees make the most contacts.

**Guests may experience more "moments of truth" with a door attendant than with any other employee.**

A former Marriott executive, G. Michael Hostage, described one strategy he used to deal with the problem:

> The *Marriott Bellman* booklet is designed to convince our uniformed doormen that they represent an all-important first and last impression for many of our guests, that they must stand with dignity and good posture, and that they must not lean against the wall or put up their feet when sitting.... Bellmen are often looked at subconsciously by guests as being "Mr. Marriott himself" because many times a guest will speak to and deal with a bellman more often during a visit than with any other employees of the hotel.... They are coached to smile often and to do all they can to make the guest feel welcome and special.[8]

Marriott is known for setting exact standards—including service standards—for all of its jobs and for communicating them clearly in writing as well as in training sessions. The company continually measures how well standards are being met with frequent inspections, and it encourages its employees to provide good service through profit sharing, stock options, and other bonus programs. Pizza Hut rewards its employees with company stock so that everyone feels a personal interest in doing a good job.

**Job Restructuring**. An effective service strategy must also provide a means of achieving levels of productivity that will satisfy the business's economic goals as well as customer expectations. One way managers do this in service companies is by job restructuring—changing the nature of the work or the way it is done. For example, at Benihana of Tokyo, the chef prepares the food at a hibachi in front of the guests, combining the jobs of food server and chef. Professor Heskett observes, "Given the nature of a service concept that combines quality food and entertainment at reasonable prices, as well as the exotic format of a Japanese restaurant, customers of Benihana readily accept a highly economic combination of jobs that is carried out in their full view."[9]

**Payroll Control.** Along with controlling the quality of service goes controlling payroll and other costs involved in providing that service. It would be easy for any hotel or restaurant to have enough employees around to give good service all the time. But they would not be profitable. Every operation must provide good, if not superior, service within its own economic constraints. Companies that do the best job of controlling service quality also excel at controlling labor and other costs, since clearly they are closely connected. Payroll control can be achieved by employee training and careful scheduling, a combination that almost always produces higher productivity and better service.

Remember Seattle restaurateur Tim Firnstahl and YEGA? One of the reasons Firnstahl designed YEGA was to identify systems that were not working and control costs that were out of line. Every time an employee gave a guest a free meal because of bad service, this was reported and considered by Firnstahl to be a "system failure cost." Whenever a meal was given away, Firnstahl asked, "Why is the system failing?" not "Why is the employee failing?" Asking the question proved to be highly productive.

"Our search for the culprit in a string of complaints about slow food service in one restaurant led first to the kitchen and then to one cook. But pushing the search one step further revealed several unrealistically complex dishes that no one could have prepared swiftly."[10] A service strategy helped identify a production problem.

## Delivering on the Service Promise

It is important that students of management understand the reasoning behind all of the theories and ideas that have been mentioned so far in this chapter. The bottom line, however, is doing it—delivering on the promise that a company makes to its owners, employees, and customers. It is easy enough to write a mission statement that says, "We intend to be a premier and progressive lodging company" or, "Our goal is to deliver the best service of any restaurant chain in our class"—but how do you do it? What makes it really happen?

There are hundreds of suggestions that have been made on how to deliver exceptional service. Any good-size bookstore has at least a half-dozen books full of practical ideas that have been tested and work. The Harvard Business School has published dozens of case histories that detail how and why companies succeed and fail. There are many fine training companies that offer seminars on every aspect of service. With all this information available, it is surprising that there is still so much poor service in the hospitality industry.

Everyone understands that customers want superior service and that better service leads to better profits. Understanding it is one thing; doing it is another. This text does not offer a simple recipe for success or a prescription that can turn a one-star restaurant or hotel into a three or four-star one. The authors don't believe that it's that easy. But we do believe that there are a number of tangible things that any organization that cares about good service can do. Here are four of them.

- *Don't forget who you are.* There is a classic story about People's Express, which in the early 1980s was the darling of the airline business. People's started as an airline that promised really low fares to leisure travelers who were willing to accept limited service in return. Their schedules weren't the most convenient, passengers had to buy a ticket on board instead of getting one ahead of time, at the airport people carried their own luggage to the plane, and if they wanted a meal during the flight they paid for it. People's Express employees didn't have a simple job description—they did whatever needed doing. Pilots, for example, also helped out on the ground, which allowed People's Express to save on labor costs. In five short years with this simple strategy the company grew to almost $1 billion.

  As People's Express grew, it acquired more customers and planes. It decided to go after business travelers, and the company added a first-class section. Soon their sheer size meant that they had to change the way they did things. With a small customer base it was acceptable not to take reservations, but when thousands started showing up at the airport, the airline needed some means of forecasting who wanted to go where and when. That meant an expensive computerized reservation system and reservation agents who knew how to use it—just like the big airlines had. It was okay to ask pilots to help out on the ground when they only had a few planes, but when they had more than 100 they needed the pilots in the air. All of this affected their ability to keep their costs down. Even worse, now they were competing with the major airlines for business. They forgot that they had succeeded by being a budget airline that targeted leisure travelers. Five years after the first plane left the ground, People's Express was sold and grounded forever.

  Companies who succeed have a single service strategy for each market segment. They stick to it. They make certain that everyone who works for them understands what they are selling and who they want to sell it to. They don't confuse or anger consumers by offering something they don't deliver.

- *Encourage every employee to act like a manager.* Managers understand the need for repeat business; employees may not. Service-oriented companies motivate, train, and empower their employees to act like it's their business. That means really caring when anyone has a problem, whether it's another employee or a guest. It also means making sure that they can solve problems they run into, which in turn requires that they be given the authority to make the necessary decisions. Authors William Davidow and Bro Uttal talk about Embassy Suites in their book, *Total Customer Service: The Ultimate Weapon*. Embassy Suites uses an upside-down organization chart to dramatize the idea that the frontline employees, the ones who deal with guests, are the most important people

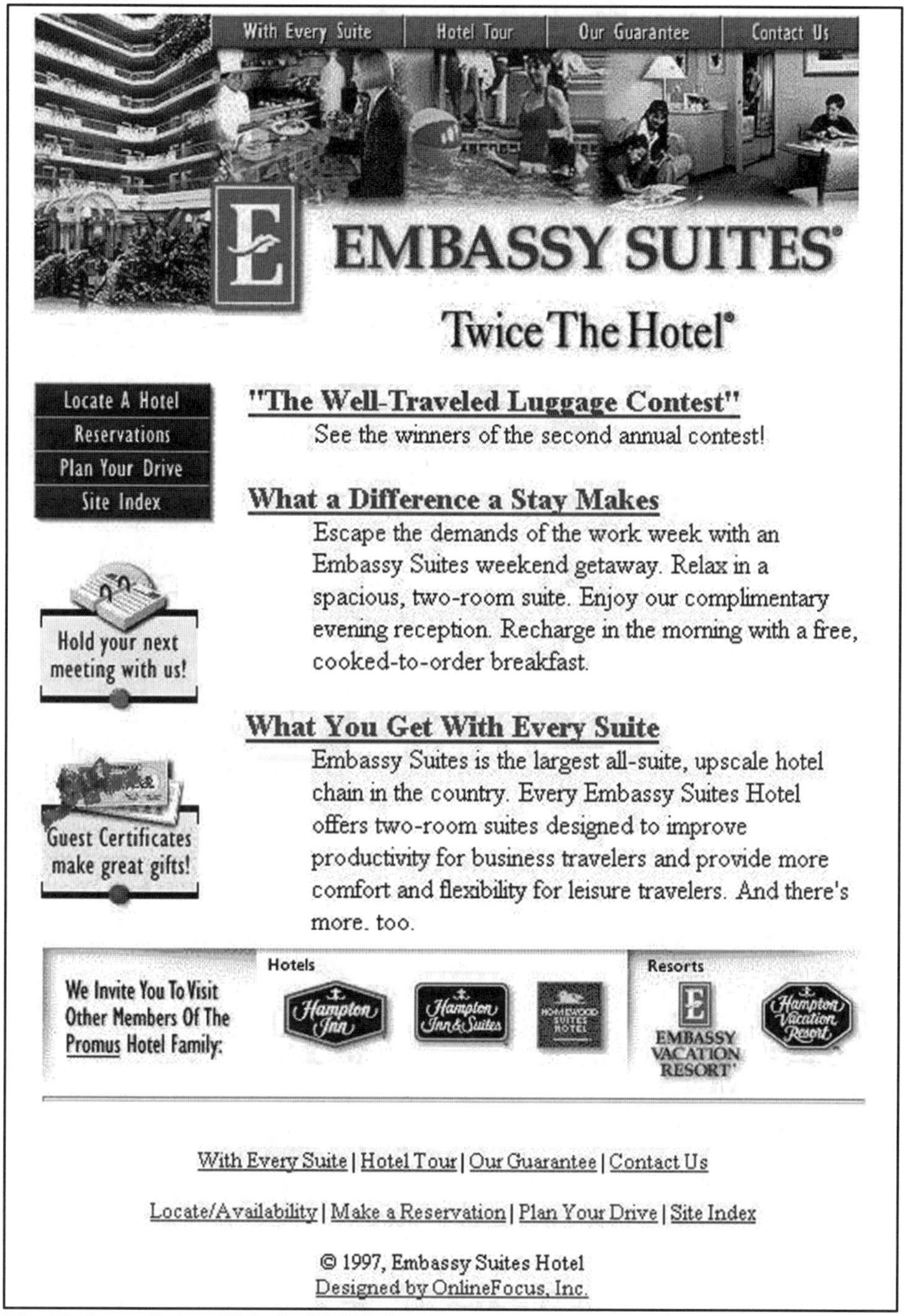

# EMBASSY SUITES
## Twice The Hotel®

**"The Well-Traveled Luggage Contest"**
See the winners of the second annual contest!

**What a Difference a Stay Makes**
Escape the demands of the work week with an Embassy Suites weekend getaway. Relax in a spacious, two-room suite. Enjoy our complimentary evening reception. Recharge in the morning with a free, cooked-to-order breakfast.

**What You Get With Every Suite**
Embassy Suites is the largest all-suite, upscale hotel chain in the country. Every Embassy Suites Hotel offers two-room suites designed to improve productivity for business travelers and provide more comfort and flexibility for leisure travelers. And there's more, too.

- Locate A Hotel
- Reservations
- Plan Your Drive
- Site Index

Hold your next meeting with us!

Guest Certificates make great gifts!

We Invite You To Visit Other Members Of The Promus Hotel Family:

**Hotels**: Hampton Inn | Hampton Inn & Suites | Homewood Suites Hotel
**Resorts**: Embassy Vacation Resort | Hampton Vacation Resort

With Every Suite | Hotel Tour | Our Guarantee | Contact Us

Locate/Availability | Make a Reservation | Plan Your Drive | Site Index

© 1997, Embassy Suites Hotel
Designed by OnlineFocus, Inc.

The Embassy Suites Web site highlights the company's commitment to service. (Courtesy of Embassy Suites)

in the organization. It's not easy to find hotel managers who will accept the idea that when it comes to pleasing the guests, the front desk clerks may be more important than they are. Embassy Suites does that by hiring managers who have the right attitude and then training them to help the people who work for them.[11] Embassy Suites also gives a stake in the company's success by linking everyone's salary to hotel performance. Employees get to see the results of daily guest interviews along with the hotel's occupancy rate and cleanliness. When a hotel meets or exceeds its quarterly targets, employees get a bonus based on their hourly rate and the number of hours they have worked, not their position.[12]

- *Hire good people and keep them happy.* Turnover is the worst enemy superior service has. New people don't know what is expected of them and may have inadequate training or the wrong training. They are often unprepared to give the kind of service that is expected of them. Superior companies make every effort to recruit, hire, and hold onto people who have the right personalities. (Many companies today hire for attitude rather than skill. Skills that are learned on the job are often more easily upgraded than attitudes that employees bring with them.) They regard their people as being as important as their customers. That means training them well, motivating them, and rewarding them. This strategy is inevitably more cost efficient and more successful than constantly finding and training new employees.

- *Responsiveness is crucial.* Guests don't like to wait. It is, for them, a hallmark of poor service. At limited-service establishments even five minutes may seem too long. At family restaurants they expect their food to be on the table in thirty minutes or less. No one likes to hold the phone to make a reservation for an airline ticket, a hotel room, or a rental car. Long check-in and check-out lines spell disaster. None of these is a necessary evil. Excellent companies are constantly monitoring the waiting time of their guests and looking for ways to decrease it, or at least make it less stressful.

Every organization and every situation is unique. Managers need to develop their own lists of key criteria and ways to implement them. It's the difference between wining and losing the battle for satisfied customers.

## Service Disney-Style

A careful look at the way the Walt Disney Company delivers service at its theme parks and resorts provides some insight into how superior service is delivered consistently. It starts with Disney's four basic service priorities: *safety, courtesy, show,* and *efficiency.*

*Safety* is of course a key element, especially in the theme parks, where the potential for accidents is ever-present. For example, cast members (as all employees are called) are trained that if an elderly person with a walker wants to go on the Haunted House ride in the Magic Kingdom, they are empowered to stop the ride while the guest is helped onto the walkway. At the same time, a recorded announcement is played for those on the ride: "Ladies and gentlemen, the ghosts and goblins have taken over for a minute."

**One of the hallmarks of Disney-style service is constant attention to how employees interact with guests.** (Courtesy of Walt Disney World, Orlando, Florida)

*Courtesy* is generated by Disney's attitudes toward its employees and reinforced by specific training techniques in handling guests. A popular Disney saying is "Our front line is our bottom line." As a result, the company is often cited as one of the best employers in the country. Disney also believes that a guest is always a guest, whether they are right or wrong. That means that they are allowed to be wrong with dignity, never reprimanded or put on the defense. If a guest has locked herself out of a car, staff members react in a positive manner even though they know that what has happened is not their fault. They soften it by trying to make the guest feel okay. Body language also is considered a part of courtesy. Cast members are taught to use the "Disney point" when giving directions; the "Disney point" utilizes the entire palm or two fingers—not a single finger, which is considered rude! Another dimension of courtesy is the way the Disney cast interacts with guests. In the morning, when people are full of energy and ready to start off on a day of adventure, the staff too is upbeat and chatty. But at night, when people are tired and returning to their rooms or going home, unnecessary conversation is kept to a minimum.

The other two service priorities, *show* (entertainment) and *efficiency* are obvious throughout the Disney operation. Video monitors and live performances alleviate long waits for attractions. Parades, shows, and fireworks are utilized to draw crowds to specific areas of the park. And Disney World in Florida easily solved a recurring and embarrassing guest problem: remembering where they left their cars in a parking lot that is larger than California's entire Disneyland complex. When guests cannot find their cars, attendants simply ask them what time they arrived. With that information it is easy to tell where to look for a car because specific rows are filled at specific times!

Disney executives estimate that every cast member has 60 moments of truth every day. Clearly, Disney defines quality service as exceeding guest expectations in every one of those encounters, which they achieve by paying attention to the smallest detail. This meticulous approach pays off—and brings customers back for repeat visits, making Walt Disney World the world's largest single tourist attraction.

## Chapter Summary

Because obvious physical and product differences have faded, consumers have looked for other ways to differentiate one brand from another. The most compelling difference in the minds of many consumers is service. Good service is defined as meeting customer needs in the way that they want and expect them to be met. Superior service results from exceeding guest expectations.

Hospitality operations, which often deal in intangible products, have very different management and marketing problems than companies that deal exclusively in tangible products. The nature of the product is different, customers are more involved in the production process, people are part of the product, it's harder to maintain quality control standards, there are no inventories, the time factor is more important, and distribution channels are different.

Broad, long-range planning is called strategic planning. Companies must formulate general business objectives for themselves, otherwise there is bound to be confusion about where they are going and how they intend to get there. These general business objectives are most commonly called a company's mission and are expressed as a mission statement. Once a mission has been clearly established and articulated, there is a series of steps a company must take: Perform a SWOT analysis, formulate strategies, implement strategies, and monitor and evaluate results.

Hotels and restaurants are capacity-constrained businesses and must constantly manage supply and demand. Supply can be managed to some extent by using a level-capacity strategy or a chased-demand strategy. It is more productive to focus on managing demand. Demand can be shifted, inventoried, and controlled by varying price, changing service levels, or using communications strategies such as advertising.

To combat the depersonalized atmosphere generated by modern technology, some companies focus on "moments of truth." These are the times when employees come in contact with guests.

Successful service companies share a "strategic service vision"—a blueprint for service managers. The components of this blueprint are: (1) targeting a market segment and (2) focusing on a service strategy. In addition, successful hospitality companies focus a good deal of management attention on establishing service quality standards, communicating them to employees through training programs, and measuring performance. Job restructuring is another effective strategy.

There are many ways companies have found to make certain they deliver on their promise. Every organization and situation is different. The Walt Disney Company provides some insight into how superior service is delivered consistently.

## Endnotes

1. Christopher H. Lovelock, *Services Marketing*, 2d ed. (Englewood Cliffs, N.J.: Prentice-Hall, 1991), p. 7. The authors gratefully acknowledge the concepts formulated by Dr. Lovelock, upon which much of the following discussion is based.
2. Lovelock, p. 9.
3. Quoted from Chili's Restaurants Employees Recruiting Pamphlet.
4. Quoted from Hilton Hotels Employee Handbook.
5. Timothy W. Firnstahl, "My Employees Are My Service Guarantee," *Harvard Business Review*, July–August 1989, p. 29.
6. Jan Carlzon, *Moments of Truth* (Cambridge, Mass.: Ballinger, 1987), pp. 21–29, cited by William H. Davidow and Bro Uttal in *Total Customer Service* (New York: Harper Perennial, 1989), p. 74.
7. James L. Heskett, *Managing in the Service Economy* (Boston: Harvard Business School Press, 1986), pp. 5–25.
8. Heskett, pp. 96–97.
9. Heskett, p. 93.
10. Firnstahl, p. 30.
11. Davidow and Uttal, p. 115.
12. Davidow and Uttal, p. 117.

## Key Terms

**capacity-constrained businesses**—Businesses that produce "products" or services that cannot be inventoried or stored for future use. Success depends on their ability to efficiently match productive capacity to consumer demand at any given moment.

**chased-demand strategy**—A management strategy in which capacity can, to a limited extent, be varied to suit the level of demand.

**intangible products**—The primary products of hospitality-oriented organizations. Intangible products such as comfort, enjoyment, and pleasant experiences relate to guests' emotional well-being and expectations. They present very different management and marketing problems than tangible products such as automobiles or boxes of cereal.

**level-capacity strategy**—A management strategy in which the same amount of capacity is offered, no matter how high the consumer demand.

**moments of truth**—Critical moments when guests and staff interact, offering opportunities for staff to make a favorable impression, correct mistakes, and win repeat customers.

**service**—Meeting customer needs in the way that they want and expect them to be met.

**SWOT**—An acronym for *strengths, weaknesses, opportunities,* and *threats.* A SWOT analysis helps companies assess how well they are serving their current markets, an important step in the strategic planning process.

## Review Questions

1. How is "good service" defined? What constitutes superior service?
2. What are some of the intangible products that hotels and restaurants provide?
3. What are the different marketing problems between service businesses and manufactured products? Why do these differences exist?
4. Why are employees and other guests considered to be an integral part of the "product" or performance?
5. What are "moments of truth" and how do they affect guests?
6. What is the objective of a company's mission statement? What are some of the important concepts included?
7. What is a SWOT analysis and why is it important?
8. Why is the constant management of supply and demand important?
9. What are the benefits of targeting a market segment?
10. What is meant by YEGA and why is it beneficial?

## Internet Sites

For more information, visit the following Internet sites. Remember that Internet addresses can change without notice. If the site is no longer there, use a search engine to look for additional sites.

*Hotel Companies/Resorts*

Days Inn
www.daysinn.com

Embassy Suites
www.embassy-suites.com

Hilton Hotels
www.hilton.com

Holiday Inns
www.holiday-inn.com

Hyatt Hotels and Resorts
www.hyatt.com

Mandarin Oriental Hotel Group
www.mandarin-oriental.com

Marriott International
www.marriott.com

Service Makes the Difference    **27**

South Seas Plantation
www.southseasplantation.com

### Restaurant Companies

Burger King Restaurants
www.burgerking.com

Chili's Grill and Bar
www.chilis.com

Domino's Pizza
www.dominos.com

KFC
www.kfc.com

McDonald's
www.mcdonalds.com

The Olive Garden
www.olivegarden.com

Walt Disney Corporation
www.disney.com

Outback Steakhouse
www.outbacksteakhouse.com

Pizza Hut
www.pizzahut.com

T.G.I. Friday's
www.tgifridays.com

Taco Bell
www.tacobell.com

Wendy's International
www.wendys.com

# REVIEW QUIZ

When you feel you have covered all of the material in this chapter, answer these questions. Choose the *best* answer.

1. When it comes to judging the quality of service, whose expectations are most important?

    a. the person receiving the service
    b. the staff member providing the service
    c. the staff member's boss
    d. the owner of the company

2. Manufacturing businesses are different from service businesses because in manufacturing businesses:

    a. customers are more involved in the production process.
    b. it's harder to maintain quality control standards.
    c. there are no inventories.
    d. the time factor is less important.

3. What is a SWOT analysis?

    a. It is an analysis of a company's internal and external environments, looking for strengths, weaknesses, opportunities, and threats.
    b. A SWOT analysis helps a manufacturing company determine whether it has the capacity to successfully provide parts to an assembly line or other assembly area "just in time."
    c. It is an analysis of a service company's ability to provide excellent service during "moments of truth"; as such, it focuses on intangibles.
    d. A SWOT analysis looks at a company's ability to meet its financial obligations; it usually takes place at the beginning of each fiscal year.

4. If a restaurant offers the same amount of capacity no matter how high the demand, it is following a _____ strategy.

    a. horizontal-market
    b. chased-capacity
    c. static-market
    d. level-capacity

5. When a lounge has a "happy hour" weekdays from 5:00 p.m. to 7:00 p.m., it is attempting to:

    a. follow a chased-demand strategy.
    b. manage demand.
    c. follow a full-market strategy.
    d. manage supply.

## REVIEW QUIZ *(continued)*

6. A typical hotel or restaurant targets a limited number of market segments because:
   a. it is impossible to appeal to everyone.
   b. for accounting purposes, it is easier to only go after a few groups of customers.
   c. management usually is not aggressive enough to go after all possible segments.
   d. owners do not like to take the risks involved in going after all possible market segments.

7. Disney's four basic service priorities are:
   a. fun, family, food, and fanfare.
   b. opportunity, satisfaction, profits, and vision.
   c. safety, courtesy, show, and efficiency.
   d. enjoyment, recreation, security, and repeat visitors.

**Answer Key:** 1-a-C1, 2-d-C1, 3-a-C2, 4-d-C2, 5-b-C2, 6-a-C3, 7-c-C3

Each question is linked to a competency. Competencies are listed on the first page of the chapter. An answer reading 3-b-C4 translates to:

   3: the question number
   b: the correct answer
   C4: the competency number

## Chapter 2 Outline

The Changing World
The Nature of the Travel and Tourism Industry
Interrelationships within the Travel and Tourism Industry
Why People Travel
    Reasons for Travel
The Social Impact of Travel
    The Planning Process
Chapter Summary

## Competencies

1. List recent world changes that affect the travel and tourism industry, describe in general terms the size of the travel and tourism industry, and explain the importance of the interrelationships within the travel and tourism industry.

2. Summarize reasons people travel and describe travel trends and types of travel research.

3. Describe the social impact travel and tourism can have on a destination, and describe a plan for sound tourism development.

# 2

# The Travel and Tourism Industry

THE HOSPITALITY INDUSTRY is only one of several industries that together make up the travel and tourism industry. In this chapter, we will look at the scope and economic impact of travel and tourism, then examine how businesses within the industry are interrelated. We'll conclude the chapter with a discussion of why people travel, and travel and tourism's effect on society.

## The Changing World

The world has been on an evolutionary path since the beginning of time. But never has the phenomenon of change been as dramatic as in the twentieth century—more specifically, the period following World War II. The pace of change from 1945 to the present has been unprecedented, and there are no signs it will slow down.

More than any other factor, technology is responsible for transforming the way we live. Technological advancement drove much of the world from an agrarian to an industrial society and, beginning in the 1950s, into an information society. Technology has provided us with the means to travel faster and cheaper, manufacture goods more efficiently, and communicate with one another across the globe almost instantaneously. Fax machines, teleconferencing, voice messages, email, the Internet, and cellular telephones enable us to exchange information as fast as thoughts are conceived. Satellites and fiber-optic cables link North America, Europe, and the Far East, carrying voice and electronic communications faster and clearer every day. Even more significantly, new information-transfer technologies can carry a much greater volume of information and calls. "We are moving toward the capability to communicate anything to anyone, anywhere by any form—voice, data, text or image—at the speed of light," write futurists John Naisbett and Patricia Aburdene.[1]

The world's population is growing. In 1980 there were approximately 4.5 billion people on the planet. By 1995 the figure had grown to 5.73 billion. In the year 2000 we can expect a world population of 6.1 billion.

The world's population is not only growing; it is also aging (see Exhibit 1). In many parts of the world, declining birth rates will produce a population with a larger percentage of older people. As we age, we tend to accumulate wealth. Therefore, we can expect that more people will be able to travel and dine out in the years ahead.

**Exhibit 1    The World's Aging Population**

| Countries | % of Population 60 Years or Older 1990 | 2025* |
|---|---|---|
| Ireland | 14% | 18% |
| Poland | 15 | 22 |
| Spain | 18 | 26 |
| France | 19 | 27 |
| Great Britain | 21 | 27 |
| United States | 17 | 27 |
| Netherlands | 17 | 29 |
| Sweden | 23 | 29 |
| Japan | 17 | 30 |
| Italy | 20 | 31 |
| Switzerland | 20 | 31 |
| Germany | 20 | 33 |

*Projected

**The Western world is getting older. In the coming decades, almost all industrialized countries will experience an increase in their older, retired populations. This bodes well for the travel and tourism industry, since older individuals typically have more disposable income, and those that are retired have more time for travel.** Source: *Die Zeit* (a German newspaper), December 24, 1993, p. 24, quoting United Nations' statistics.

Significant political changes have occurred in the international arena in recent years. The Soviet Union dissolved, and, along with most of the former Communist bloc countries, began to move from a socialist system to a market economy. Borders changed in the Balkans and new nations emerged. With the reunification of West and East Germany in 1990, Eastern Europe started a slow but steady transformation toward a more open and traveler-friendly society.

In the Far East, Hong Kong—one of the great financial centers of the world—has become part of the People's Republic of China. China is developing an infrastructure designed to handle more travelers. New hotels are being built, and old ones modernized. Museums and other tourist attractions are being developed.

The balance of economic power between nations is changing as well. Wealth is shifting. The United States, once the world's dominant economic force, now shares that position with Japan and Germany. The European Union (EU) has brought together diverse nations and is shaping them into a unified economic power. Citizens of EU countries carry a common passport that allows them to cross borders with ease. Duty-free allowances have been increased. Currency restrictions have been simplified. The result is that more Europeans are traveling.

Drawing by Ed Fisher; ©1988, The New Yorker Magazine, Inc.

There are many other emerging trends affecting travel. In a number of countries the amount of leisure time is increasing. Of the developed nations, the United States offers fewer legal holidays to its workers than most other countries. While the average American gets 10 legal holidays a year (as does the average Japanese and Canadian), Germans receive 18 days annually, and citizens of Sweden and Denmark receive 30 days.

Many households have two income earners. This means that there are more discretionary funds for travel and a greater need to take a vacation as a relief from stress. But two workers in one family also means shorter vacations. People today tend to take several short vacations rather than one long one.

Seasonality has become less important in travel. Part of this is due to the increased tendency to take vacations when we can, not when we would like to. Also, more and more attractions tend to be "climate controlled." In Japan, for instance, there is an indoor ski resort that is 25 stories high and the length of six American football fields. It holds up to 3,000 skiers, and its temperature is a constant 28°F (−2.2°C).

As a result of an increased awareness of the problems caused by pollution and over-development, ecotourism is growing. In the United States alone, the size of this market is estimated at 60 million people. People all over the world are eager to visit the rain forests of the Amazon, the glaciers of Alaska, and the barrier reefs of Australia. Forty percent of Costa Rica's visitors are eco-tourists.

## The Nature of the Travel and Tourism Industry

When the United States Senate created the National Tourism Policy Act of 1981 to encourage the growth of tourism, it used the following definition of the **travel and tourism industry:**

> An interrelated amalgamation of those businesses and agencies which totally or in part provide the means of transport, goods, services, and other facilities for travel outside of the home community for any purpose not related to day-to-day activity.

Another definition that is somewhat similar but a bit clearer, and therefore the one we will adopt, is provided by Douglas Fretchling, professor of tourism studies at George Washington University. Fretchling defines the travel and tourism industry as "a collection of organizations and establishments that derive all or a significant portion of their income from providing goods and services purchased on a trip to the traveler." Exhibit 2 lists businesses that make up the travel and tourism industry. The businesses under the headings "Accommodations" and "Food and Beverage," along with institutional (generally nonprofit) food service operations, constitute the hospitality industry. As you can see, the hospitality industry is only part of the travel and tourism industry.

One way to define the size of the travel and tourism industry is to add up the amount of money spent on goods and services by travelers. Unfortunately, it is not possible to do this accurately. While just about everyone would agree that airlines and resorts receive almost all of their business from travelers, what about gift shops and gas stations? These businesses on the whole have no way of knowing what percentage of their customers are travelers and what percentage are local residents. Depending on their location, there may be a wide variation in the amount of business they get from each source. Although there is no way of knowing how much of their revenues are from travelers, for statistical purposes the total receipts of these types of businesses are included in projections of the size and scope of the travel and tourism industry.

Statisticians and economists measure the size of the travel and tourism industry by adding together the receipts of the businesses that compose it, but these figures do not tell the whole story. For example, one could argue that the amount of money a hotel takes in is not a true measure of its economic impact on the surrounding community. The real impact is measured by the salaries the hotel pays to its employees, which they in turn spend on housing, clothes, and food for their families; by the taxes the hotel pays to the state and federal governments; by the amount of profits generated by local companies who sell goods and services to the hotel; and by the number of jobs the hotel creates that may keep people off the welfare rolls.

The World Travel and Tourism Council gives these examples of the impact of tourism on other industries:

Exhibit 2    The Travel and Tourism Industry

| Accommodation | Travel Agencies | Luggage |
|---|---|---|
| Hotels/Resorts | Tour Companies | Construction/Real Estate |
| Motels | | |
| Hostels | Hotel/Restaurant Suppliers | Distillers/Brewers/Bottles |
| Caravans | Taxi Services | Auto/Aircraft Manufacturers |
| Camping | | |
| | Cameras and Film | Motor Fuel Producers |
| Transportation | | |
| Airlines | Maps, Travel Books | Clothing Manufacturers |
| Cruise Ships | Shopping Malls | Communication Networks |
| Rail | | |
| Car Rental | Service Stations | Education/Training Institutes |
| Bus Coaches | Sporting Events | Recreation/Sporting Equipment |
| Attractions | Banking Services | Food Producers |
| Man Made | | |
| Natural | Reservation Systems | Advertising Media |
| Food and Beverage | Auto Clubs | Cartographers/Printers |
| Restaurants | Entertainment/Arts Venues | Souvenirs |
| Fast Food | | |
| Wine Merchants | Museums/Historical Sites | |

Source: *Travel and Tourism—Jobs for the Millennium,* World Travel & Tourism Council, 1997.

- When American Airlines did an impact study of employment in the Miami-Dade County community, the company found that it generated 10 percent of the jobs in that area. Of these, 10 percent were directly in aviation and another 10 percent were from companies benefiting from spending by aviation employees. The other 80 percent were jobs in hotels, restaurants, department stores, and other local businesses relying on spending by AA passengers.
- It is estimated that at least 20 percent of the sales in London shops comes from foreign visitors.
- Surveys suggest that 50 percent of all photographs are taken by travelers.[2]

Industry analysts have a name for these indirect or hidden benefits—the **multiplier effect.** The multiplier effect is measured by adding up all the expenditures of travelers in a given geographic area and multiplying that figure by a factor (known as the multiplier) to arrive at the amount of additional income that is generated by these expenditures. While the multiplier effect is highly variable among cities and

**Exhibit 3    Most Tourist Arrivals**

| 1  | France         | 60,640,000 |
|----|----------------|------------|
| 2  | United States  | 45,504,000 |
| 3  | Spain          | 43,232,000 |
| 4  | Italy          | 27,480,000 |
| 5  | Hungary        | 21,425,000 |
| 6  | China          | 21,070,000 |
| 7  | United Kingdom | 20,855,000 |
| 8  | Poland         | 18,800,000 |
| 9  | Austria        | 17,894,000 |
| 10 | Mexico         | 17,113,000 |
| 11 | Czech Republic | 17,000,000 |
| 12 | Canada         | 15,971,000 |
| 13 | Germany        | 14,494,000 |
| 14 | Switzerland    | 12,200,000 |
| 15 | Greece         | 10,072,000 |
| 16 | Hong Kong      | 9,331,000  |
| 17 | Portugal       | 9,132,000  |
| 18 | Malaysia       | 7,197,000  |
| 19 | Singapore      | 6,268,000  |
| 20 | Netherlands    | 6,178,000  |

countries around the world, many industry analysts use a figure of 1.6 as a reasonable multiplier on a general basis.

Although it is difficult to accurately assess the size of the tourism industry, some figures are available that are truly astounding. According to the World Tourism Organization (WTO) there were 592.1 million tourist arrivals worldwide in 1996. The receipts from international travel—excluding airfares—was $423.1 million. The WTO projects that by 2010 arrivals will reach one billion, with receipts of $1.55 billion annually! France, the United States, and Spain had the most tourist arrivals, with Italy, Hungary, China, and the United Kingdom all getting more than 20 million each (see Exhibit 3).

All of these tourists and receipts are creating many, many new jobs—directly and indirectly. Roughly 10.5 percent of the total work force is now employed in jobs that exist because of tourism. The greatest growth in new jobs will be in Asia and the Pacific (see Exhibit 4). That makes tourism one of the most attractive careers for students to consider when surveying the job market.

It is interesting to see where some of these jobs are today. From the standpoint of the percentage of total employment, it is clear that tourism is extremely important for some economies. For example, about 25 percent of all of the jobs in the Caribbean are in tourism. On the other hand, Latin America is way under the world average of 10.5 percent, with only six percent (see Exhibit 5).

**Exhibit 4     The Economic Impact of Travel and Tourism, Part 1**

### Regional Employment Growth between 1997 and 2007
(Percent and Estimated Jobs Increase)

|  | Percent | Millions |
|---|---|---|
| Southeast Asia | 80.1 | 20.94 |
| Northeast Asia | 60.3 | 64.13 |
| South Asia | 43.5 | 17.25 |
| Middle East | 36.6 | 1.35 |
| Eastern Europe | 36.5 | 5.88 |
| Other W. Europe | 30.0 | 0.96 |
| Oceania | 23.2 | 0.55 |
| Sub-Sahara Africa | 22.0 | 2.96 |
| Caribbean | 21.1 | 0.61 |
| North America | 19.3 | 3.40 |
| Latin America | 16.3 | 1.28 |
| North Africa | 11.1 | 0.36 |
| European Union | 9.7 | 1.84 |

Source: *Travel and Tourism—Jobs for the Millennium,* World Travel & Tourism Council, 1997.

# Interrelationships within the Travel and Tourism Industry

An important and unique feature of the travel and tourism industry is the interrelationship of the various parts of the whole. A trip may consist of an airplane flight, a car rental, a stay at a hotel, several restaurant meals, and some gift purchases. Each of these elements must work well in order for travelers to have a pleasant total experience.

For example, suppose the Smiths decide to fly from their home in Minneapolis to vacation at Walt Disney World in Orlando, Florida. The sum total of their experiences determines the quality of their vacation and the likelihood of their becoming repeat guests at Disney World. For instance, the Smiths might have a pleasant flight to Florida, but then their rented car could overheat, leaving them stranded for several hours and cutting short the day they were going to spend at EPCOT. Or their hotel could be undergoing refurbishing so that the pool and the restaurant are closed during their stay and the usually attractive lobby decor is covered with drop cloths and scaffolding. Even worse—suppose they arrive at the Magic Kingdom at a particularly busy time and find that the park has closed its parking lot

**Exhibit 5    The Economic Impact of Travel and Tourism, Part 2**

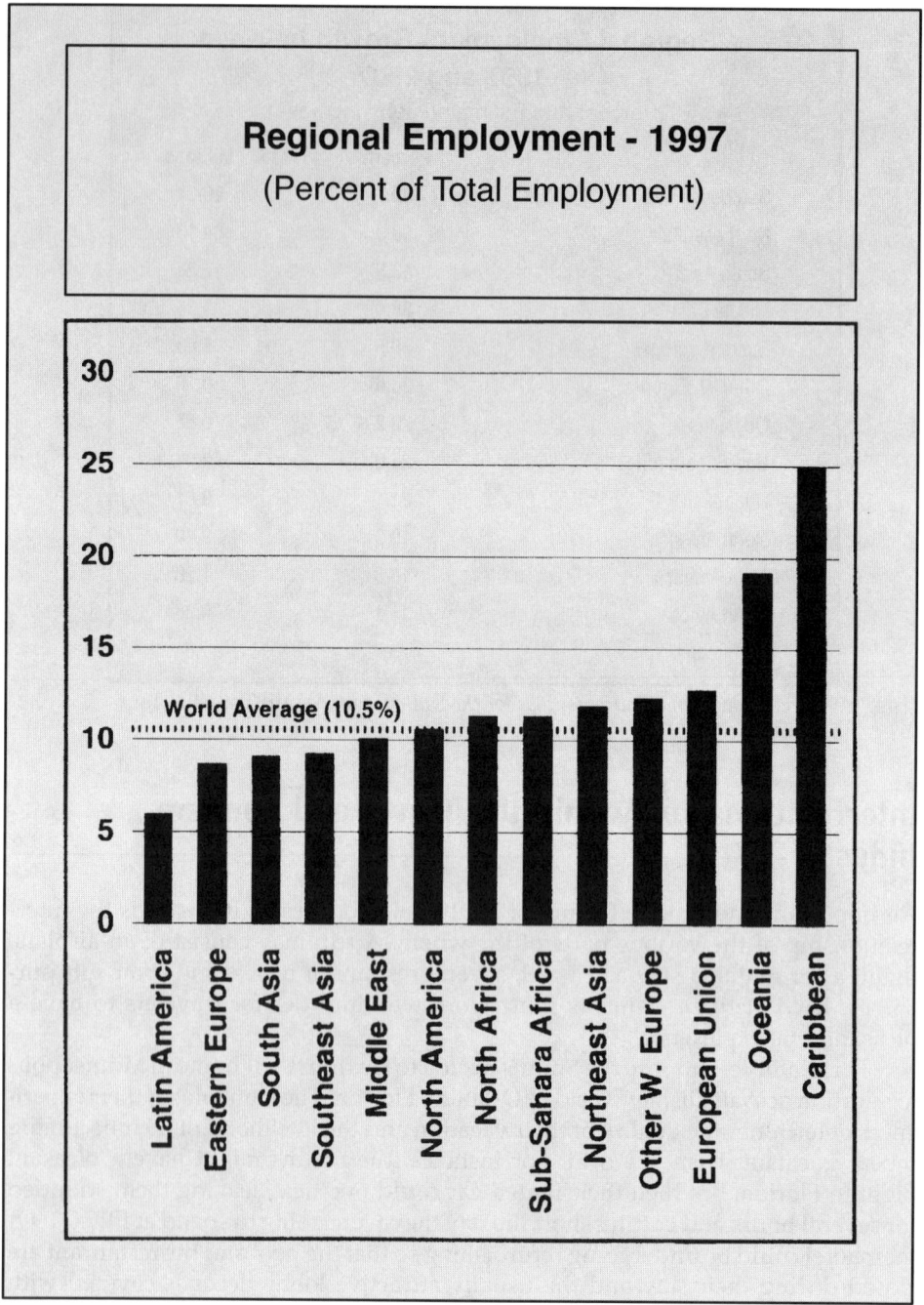

### Regional Employment - 1997
(Percent of Total Employment)

| Region | Percent |
|---|---|
| Latin America | 6 |
| Eastern Europe | 8.5 |
| South Asia | 9 |
| Southeast Asia | 9 |
| Middle East | 10 |
| North America | 10.5 |
| North Africa | 11 |
| Sub-Sahara Africa | 11 |
| Northeast Asia | 12 |
| Other W. Europe | 12 |
| European Union | 12.5 |
| Oceania | 19 |
| Caribbean | 25 |

World Average (10.5%)

Source: *Travel and Tourism—Jobs for the Millennium,* World Travel and Tourism Council, 1997.

**A trip consists of many elements, all of which must work well in order for travelers to have a pleasant total experience.** (Photos courtesy of [clockwise from top left] the San Francisco Convention & Visitors Bureau; Stouffer Cottonwoods Resort, Scottsdale, Arizona; Tacoma Pierce County Visitor & Convention Bureau, Tacoma, Washington; and Red Lobster Restaurants, Orlando, Florida)

and is not admitting any more visitors that day. Any of these incidents could spoil their entire vacation.

Travel-industry businesses have a symbiotic relationship, a mutual dependency. For any one of them to be entirely successful in pleasing the Smiths, all of them must do a good job. If the hotel stay was uncomfortable, the Smiths might enjoy Disney World but still feel on the whole that they had a less-than-perfect vacation. If the hotel did its job but Disney's park was overcrowded, the net sum of their experience could also be negative. Either way, in the long run, all of the travel businesses in the area would suffer because the Smiths may not return to Disney World and might tell their friends in Minneapolis that a trip to Disney World is a disappointing experience.

Some destinations are so aware of this interrelationship that they go to extreme lengths to control all elements of the travel product. Bermuda, for instance, which is only 21 square miles in size, monitors the standards of all hotels, restaurants, and attractions because it believes that if a visitor has a bad hotel room or a bad meal, he or she will go home feeling critical of the whole island. Since more than 40 percent of Bermuda's travel business is repeat, it cannot afford to disappoint its visitors.

Owners and operators of hospitality enterprises often underestimate the importance of the interrelationship of the travel and tourism industry when considering how their enterprise is going to attract consumers. Such vacation spots as Hawaii depend on airlines to deliver almost all of their visitors. If airline fares are too high, business suffers, no matter how strong or how effective marketing efforts are. Atlantic City is a highly successful destination now for motorcoach tours from New York City, but that is entirely a function of the gaming industry that has grown in Atlantic City in the last two decades. Now the casinos depend on the buses, and the buses depend on the casinos. Neither could succeed without the other.

## Why People Travel

Over the centuries, travel has developed for business, health, social, and cultural reasons. But at the most basic level, it can be said that the main reason people travel is to gather information. We want to know how our favorite aunt is doing in Nashville, so we take a trip to visit her. Businesspeople travel to see what is going on in their home office in Chicago or to find out what customers in Madrid think of their products. Some of us travel to France to see how the French vintners grow grapes and produce wine. Others go to Moscow and Beijing to learn more about Russian and Chinese culture.

Travel is an important part of our lives. It helps us understand ourselves and others. It is both an effect and a cause of rapid societal change. Technology has played a huge part in all of this. Commercial jet aircraft have brought foreign places closer, and communications satellites bring news events from around the world into our living rooms and onto our personal computers. These technologies have stimulated interest in traveling abroad.

The three most important factors that determine the amount people spend for travel are employment, disposable income, and household wealth. The more money people who want to travel have, the more likely they are to travel, the more frequently they are likely to travel, and the farther they are likely to travel. While business travel is somewhat less susceptible to economic downturns than leisure travel, it is not immune. Companies invariably tighten their travel budgets during recessions. Research has shown that international travel patterns are very sensitive to shifts in exchange rates. The buying power of a traveler's own currency affects destination choices and the timing of trips.

Conditions at home and in destination countries also affect travel. In 1991 the amount of overseas travel declined significantly as a result of the war in the Persian Gulf and the fear of terrorist incidents. Dubrovnic, a once-popular destination in the former Yugoslavia, has lost most of its tourists.

It is important to note that not everyone is disposed to travel. Some people by their nature are stay-at-homes. Others don't like to fly, or get motion sickness, or simply won't travel no matter what their economic circumstances. Dr. Frank Farley,

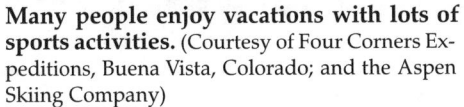

**Many people enjoy vacations with lots of sports activities.** (Courtesy of Four Corners Expeditions, Buena Vista, Colorado; and the Aspen Skiing Company)

a psychologist at the University of Wisconsin, has studied the behavior of travelers versus nontravelers. "People who hesitate to travel may do so because of deep-seated fears," says Farley. "Travelers, though, seem stable enough to expose themselves to uncertainty and adventure. They worry less, feel less inhibited and submissive, and are more self-confident than stay-at-homes."[3] Farley found other differences between people who like to travel and those who enjoy staying at home:

> Most passionate travelers are risk-takers in many areas of life. They're drawn not only to unknown lands but also to taking chances with their investment portfolios. However, their risk taking is rational; it's based on a deep sense that they control their destiny. They enjoy life, love to play, and gravitate towards crowds and parties.[4]

## Reasons for Travel

People travel for many different reasons.

1. *Recreation.* Recreation includes leisure and activities related to sports, entertainment, and rest. Beach vacations, ski vacations, and adventure travel such as white-water rafting all fall into this category. Destinations such as the Caribbean, Disney World, and national parks benefit largely from recreational travel. The Olympic Games in Atlanta, Georgia, drew two million visitors in 1996.

2. *Culture.* People travel for cultural reasons as well—a desire to learn about things and places that interest them. These interests can be historical, ethnic, educational, or they can relate to the arts or religion. Famous battlegrounds such as the beaches of Normandy, France; cathedrals such as St. Peter's in Vatican City; California's Napa Valley; Kenya's national parks; and the Great Wall of China all have educational, religious, historical, or ethnic significance. Destinations often capitalize on these attributes to stage special events and festivals. The Salzburg Music Festival and the Mardi Gras in Rio de Janeiro and New Orleans are examples. The events are marketed very heavily. Many

**Exhibit 6    Web Site Example**

The site for the Utah Shakespearean Festival includes a wealth of information for travelers who want to make the most of their time in the area. (Courtesy of the Utah Shakespearean Festival)

destinations have their own Web sites on which they list all of the events that will take place there (see Exhibit 6).

3. *Business.* Business travel is a significant portion of all travel. This category includes individual travelers and meetings and conventions. The trend now is to combine business and recreational travel—thus business meetings and conventions are held at resort hotels, theme parks, and even on cruise ships, and spouses and even families often come along.

4. *Visiting Friends and Relatives (VFR).* Research has shown that much travel involves visiting friends and relatives. This is difficult to measure, however, and has little economic impact.

**Exhibit 7   Travel Tendencies of Americans**

| Relatively High Tendency To Travel | Relatively Low Tendency To Travel |
|---|---|
| Married | Widowed |
| Male | Female |
| 35 to 44 years of age | 65 years and older |
| Graduate studies | Did not complete high school |
| Professional/managerial | Blue collar |
| Own their home | Rent their home |
| $50,000 to $75,000 family income | Less than $10,000 a year |
| Two wage earners | No wage earners |

Source: U.S. Travel Data Center.

5. *Health.* We believe health is a separate category in classifying travel. Many persons travel to visit diagnostic centers and receive treatment at clinics, hospitals, and spas such as the Mayo Clinic or the Canyon Ranch.

The U.S. Travel Data Center has done a good deal of research to determine what types of Americans travel and how many of them there are. According to the center, 150 million Americans take one or more trips away from home every year. Some groups, as we have pointed out, have a higher propensity to travel. The U.S. Travel Data Center identified them in a survey (see Exhibit 7).

Another kind of research that is helpful in understanding changing travel patterns is psychographic. **Psychographic research** attempts to classify people's behavior not in terms of their age or education or gender, but rather their life-styles and values. Sometimes this information is more useful than **demographic information** in deciding what kind of amenities to offer in a resort or how to advertise a particular destination. For instance, in 1985 the government of Bermuda conducted psychographic research in the United States to determine what kind of people would be most interested in going to Bermuda on vacation. In a sample of persons who were potential vacationers, three different groups emerged:

- The **price and sights group.** These people were interested in seeing the most things for the least amount of money. They wanted tours that covered ten countries in nine days at a bargain price. The best cruises were the cheapest ones that visited the most ports. And a good hotel offered budget-priced accommodations within walking distance of everything they might want to see.

- The **sun and surf group.** These people sought a vacation where they could lie on a beach and get a golden tan. Value was important, but even more important was finding a destination where there was good weather, guaranteed sunshine, and a beautiful beach where they could soak up the sun and swim in clear waters.

- The **quality group.** The quality of the vacation experience was of paramount importance to this group. They felt they had worked hard for a vacation and now it was their turn to relax and be taken care of. This group valued destinations and accommodations that were first class or deluxe. Service was very important—they wanted and expected lots of pampering and were willing to pay a fair price for it. They also wanted gourmet dining and sophisticated entertainment.

The firm of Yankelovich Partners specializes in psychographic research. For many years it has studied how social changes affect American consumer behavior. This information is gathered by surveying a sample base of 4,000 customers, which are representative of the total overall U.S. population. Every year, results are tabulated and provided to subscribers through a service called *Yankelovich MONITOR*™. This study tracks such trends as what kind of vacations people are planning to take, their dining-out habits, and attitudes toward purchasing. *Yankelovich MONITOR* has identified trends that are changing the way people feel and act about traveling.[5]

- The **great-expectations syndrome.** To some extent, the American traveler is a nitpicker. We're more educated than any previous generation, and more of us have traveled to more places more often than at any other time in history. We're not as naive as we once were, willing to settle for bad service because we're away from home. Indeed, the 1996 *MONITOR* survey reported that 53 percent of the population said they would be willing to pay as much as 10 percent more if they were guaranteed better service. We have greater expectations because we have more travel experience and value our leisure time more.

- The **trade-off syndrome.** Because Americans today are so much better traveled than prior generations, they are increasingly inclined to postpone vacations, or trade two weeks in a foreign country for payments on a new car or college tuition. Baby Boomers, who make up a large part of the population today, lead very stressful lives. With both spouses working and two children to care for, they find it difficult to get away for a lengthy period of time. Consumers recognize that they cannot have it all—they have to make trade-offs. The two-week vacation may be well on its way to becoming a dinosaur because of the difficulties of juggling schedules and priorities in today's more complex family structure.

- The **harried traveler.** The *MONITOR* takes a regular look at the type of vacations people say they will take in the future. Here are the leaders:
    - Weekend trip or getaway — 45 percent
    - Visit family, friends or relatives, family reunions or get-togethers (VFR travel) — 45 percent
    - Trip to lake/river/beach — 32 percent
  
  These are relatively short visits and close to home. In fact, 19 percent planned to spend their vacation at home. Only 16 percent reported planning to take some of the more mainstream vacations like cruises; 15 percent planned a resort vacation. Nine percent expected to take a guided tour, and 6 percent were planning an adventure-travel vacation like a safari or white-water rafting expedition. Part of the reason for these choices is that families today don't always have the

luxury of planning far in advance. Last-minute travel has become much more common. Mini-vacations are a way to escape pressures for short periods of time.

- The **strategic traveler.** The *MONITOR* talks about *strategic control*. In the 1980s, people tried to gain total control over every aspect of their lives—their jobs, their family, their health, their appearance. Today's consumers are selectively picking their battles. They set priorities, deciding which decisions are important for them to make personally, which ones they don't have to make at all, and which ones they can delegate. For instance, choosing a brand-name hotel chain is a form of delegation—you decide you can trust them to deliver what you expect. Affluent consumers tend to delegate more financial decisions than others. Rather than searching for the lowest price, today's (and probably tomorrow's) strategic traveler is looking for the best value. Strategic travelers are also information-oriented consumers. They want more information and more access to information. The Internet and World Wide Web are favorite sources for them for travel information.

According to *Yankelovich MONITOR*, consumers today are less interested in traveling as a way of achieving recognition or status. The study asks about various things that people associate with success and accomplishment. At the top of the list are intangible factors such as being satisfied with your life (82%), having people respect you (80%), and having a good marriage (79%). Traveling for pleasure was identified as a symbol of success by only 44 percent, and staying at a luxury hotel by 16 percent.

Yankelovich Monitor Group's Director of Client Services Steve Makadok points out that there has been an increase in the number of people who identify using luxury products and services since 1993. Besides luxury hotels, more people are equating success and accomplishment with owning expensive jewelry, shopping in prestigious stores, and wearing designer clothing. "While intangible things remain very important to people, some of the tangible items are coming back. If you think about the 80s, it was very much a time of ostentatious displays of wealth. People were wearing Rolexes and driving BMWs like they were a badge and were using these things as status symbols to show off a bit. Today we're seeing some of these things bouncing back. We believe it's not necessarily because they're saying to other people, 'Look at me; look what I've accomplished.' It's because they feel they've worked hard and they're rewarding themselves. That's an important reason today for choosing to stay in a luxury hotel or dine in a fine restaurant."

Another reason travel is important, adds Makadok, is fantasy. "We ask their response to a statement like, 'I need to go to places that are so different from my daily experience that they feel like make-believe.' Thirty-two percent of the population agrees with that, and that's higher than it used to be. Consumers are looking for some novelty and excitement in their lives. We also ask whether they agree or disagree with the statement 'I like to imagine myself doing something I wouldn't dare to do,' and 49 percent of the population agrees with that."

The *MONITOR* survey on the whole shows that consumers have a balanced approach to leisure activities, including travel. They are looking forward to doing things that they really enjoy. They don't want to work too hard doing them, however. In the past, if you didn't climb the highest mountain or travel to the most remote corner of the world, you weren't getting enough. But today consumers want their leisure to be fun but easy.

## The Social Impact of Travel

Hotels, restaurants, and attractions can shape and change life in a community and they are almost always at the center of the community's life. For example, Club Med was the first resort to open in Huatulco, Mexico, a community that hardly rated a dot on the map until Club Med decided to build there. Walt Disney World has changed the character of Orlando and Florida forever.

New travelers to any destination bring new money and jobs, but they also bring problems. Whenever you have increased travel to an area you must provide additional public services such as police, fire fighters, water treatment plants, and solid waste disposal facilities. This may increase the cost of living for residents. Crime may increase. New airports bring with them pollution and noise. Hotels and shopping strips change the character of the community. Residents may have limited or no access to beaches and other property that previously had been public.

For these and other reasons, many people feel that their communities have been negatively affected by travelers and are not in favor of development that encourages more tourism. Some areas are ambivalent about the benefits of the travel and tourism industry, and have not gone out of their way to attract tourists or develop facilities for them. Other communities, like Monroe County, Florida (where Key West is located), feel that they may have let development get out of hand and are now trying to put a cap on it.

In developing and Third World countries there are other problems. One is the enormous economic gap that exists between the travelers who stay in luxurious resorts and the employees who witness for the first time new life-styles and behaviors that can change their own expectations and values. Local residents often emulate the dress styles and consumption patterns of visitors. An area's culture and traditional values can be eroded. Racial tensions are not uncommon as a result of these conditions. The seasonality of tourism poses another major problem. When the season is over, often there is a large number of dislocated, jobless workers who have no place to go and few other opportunities to earn a comparable living.

Today's hospitality managers are paying more attention to the social costs of travel and tourism. Modern planning methods make more use of impact studies that consider both social and environmental changes brought about by increased demand. Many countries have mounted impressive marketing campaigns in the off season to attract visitors and keep employment levels high. Countries like Turkey have developed arts and crafts industries so that workers can make products for tourists during the off season.

Pierre L. van den Berghe, a sociology professor at the University of Washington in Seattle, has studied the cultural impact of tourism in depth. He believes that, on the whole, the impact of tourism is positive:

> In complex and unpredictable ways, tourism changes not only the behavior of hosts—their presentation of self—but their very definition of

**Many of today's resorts try to blend in with the surrounding landscape in order to enhance their appeal and minimize environmental damage.** (Courtesy of Club Med, Cancun, Mexico)

self. Far from destroying local cultures, tourism more commonly transforms and revives them. Of all forms of outside contact and modernization that affect isolated local cultures, tourism is probably the least destructive, precisely because it imparts a marketable value to cultural diversity. If the quest for authenticity sometimes initially seems to undermine and corrupt local culture, it can revive and reinvigorate traditions that were languishing under the assault of other modernizing forces such as industrialization, urbanization, Christianization, or Western-style schooling...Locals often have the vitality to recapture their own heritage, the creativity to invent a new, redefined authenticity, and the resilience to resist the encroachments of the global village. To paraphrase Mark Twain, news of the death of Third and Fourth World cultures is greatly exaggerated. And, where cultures die, tourism is seldom to blame.[6]

One answer to solving some of the problems that tourism brings with it is the growth of ecotourism. Ecotourism is defined by the Ecotourism Society as "responsible travel which conserves environments and sustains the well-being of local people."[7] Keep this in mind because the term is frequently misused.

*Condé Nast Traveler* magazine, which frequently publishes articles on ecotourism, believes that ecotourism works best in developing countries where fast-growing human populations threaten wildlife and habitats. "If money brought into such countries by tourism is used to help local economies, and the people see tangible benefits from preserving the environment, that's ecotourism. Ecotourism is effective only when it generates enough jobs or raises enough revenue to create a disincentive for destroying the environment. If locals perceive forests as firewood alone, they'll continue to slash and burn. In Africa, tribespeople will kill elephants that stampede their crops into the soil unless they are given an inducement—from tourism revenues—to desist."[8]

Although this principle is recognized by many governments, it is often ignored because of political pressure fueled by special interests. Costa Rica is cited by critics as an example. With more than half a million visitors annually, tourism has become Cost Rica's leading industry—eclipsing coffee and bananas. The government now blatantly promotes mass tourism, exacerbating the situation.[9]

There are a number of private operators who do business in fragile habitats and are sensitive not only to the environment but to their inhabitants. Some encourage and develop resorts that blend in with the cultural and physical surroundings. Others hire and train local guides and support scientific research in the region. All are careful that their operations will have minimal impact on the environment or the culture. These kinds of steps are the hallmark of real ecotourism.

The bottom line is that travel and tourism is an industry that has its benefits and its costs. Societies and governments must recognize both sides of the coin and plan for the proper balance for their own situation.

## The Planning Process

There is a logical sequence in planning for tourism development that satisfies the requirements of having a policy that is socially, environmentally, and economically sound. It consists of five steps:

1. Define the scope of the project. What is going to be built? Can it be done in a manner that will satisfy the requirements of being socially, environmentally, and economically sound?
2. Analyze the market. What need will this project fulfill? Will the existing infrastructure support it? What about seasonality? What is the demand potential? Who is the competition? Is there an available labor force?
3. Create a master plan. How is the land going to be used? What goes where? Is there a need for new roads, airports, or marine facilities?
4. Determine who is going to develop it. Some projects are built by the government, others by private developers. In the most successful projects, both are involved. Take Cancun, Mexico, where the development of the area as a resort destination was the result of government initiative coupled with the desire of international hotel operators to expand into Mexico.
5. Establish a timetable. Is this a long-term plan or a short-term one? Is everything going to be done simultaneously or in incremental stages?

## Chapter Summary

Technology has provided us with the means to travel faster and cheaper, produce more food with fewer farmers, manufacture goods more efficiently, and communicate with each other globally almost instantaneously. The world's population is changing. There are more of us than ever before and the population continues to grow. Significant political changes have occurred in the international arena in recent years. The balance of economic power among nations is changing.

There are many other emerging trends that affect travel. These include increased leisure time, greater discretionary funds for travel, less seasonality in travel, and growing ecotourism. All of these changes are increasing travel and tourism to an unprecedented degree.

Travel and tourism is now the world's largest industry. We cannot measure its size in receipts alone; expenditures are a truer measure. Moreover, the multiplier effect must be added to get a true picture.

There are many components to the travel and tourism industry, including airlines, hotels, restaurants, and attractions. They are all interrelated and the success or failure of one segment can affect all of them.

People travel for many reasons, but there are four basic travel motivators: physical, cultural, interpersonal, and status and prestige.

There is cause for concern about the cultural impact of tourism. Some believe that the effects of tourism can be detrimental. Others maintain that tourism can stimulate economic growth and preserve rather than destroy native cultures.

## Endnotes

1. John Naisbett and Patricia Aburdene, *Megatrends 2000* (New York: Morrow, 1990), p. 23.
2. These examples are excerpted from "Travel and Tourism—Jobs for the Millennium," published by World Travel & Tourism Council, January 1997. Many of the examples and figures in this chapter are based on material supplied by this organization, for which the authors are grateful.
3. Daniel Goleman, "Head Trips," *American Health,* April 1988, p. 58.
4. Goleman, p. 58.
5. All references to the *Yankelovich MONITOR* are based on an interview with Steve Makadok, director of client services, Yankelovich Monitor Group, March 10, 1997.
6. Pierre L. van den Berghe, "Cultural Impact of Tourism," VNR's *Encyclopedia of Hospitality and Tourism* (New York: Van Nostrand Reinhold, 1993), p. 627.
7. "Can Ecotourism Save the Planet?" *Condé Nast Traveler,* December 1994.
8. "Can Ecotourism Save the Planet?"
9. "Can Ecotourism Save the Planet?"

## Key Terms

**demographic information**—Statistical information (such as age and income) about a population, used especially to identify markets.

**great-expectations syndrome**—The greater travel expectations of the new, more educated, and well-traveled American tourist.

**harried travelers**—New parents and working couples stretched for time. Harried travelers are more likely to make last-minute travel plans and take mini-vacations.

**multiplier effect**—The hidden or indirect benefits of travel and tourism to a community, measured by adding up all the expenditures of travelers in the community and then multiplying that figure by a factor (known as the multiplier) to arrive at the amount of income that stays in the community and is generated by these expenditures.

**price and sights group**—The group of travelers interested in doing the most things for the least amount of money while on vacation.

**psychographic research**—Research that attempts to classify people's behavior in terms of their life-styles and values.

**quality group**—The group of travelers for whom the quality of their vacation is of paramount importance. They want and are willing to pay for first-class accommodations and service.

**strategic travelers**—Travelers who look for the best value, not the lowest price. Strategic travelers are information-oriented consumers.

**sun and surf group**—The group of travelers seeking a vacation spot where there is good weather, guaranteed sunshine, and a beautiful beach.

**trade-off syndrome**—The tendency to postpone vacations in order to purchase some other product or service. Even with the increase in two-earner families, many Americans are finding that they can't have it all.

**travel and tourism industry**—A collection of organizations and establishments that derive all or a significant portion of their income from providing goods and services to travelers.

## Review Questions

1. What were some motivators for early travel?
2. What role has modern technology played in travel?
3. How is the travel and tourism industry defined?
4. What are two ways to estimate the size of the travel and tourism industry?
5. What is the current status of the worldwide travel and tourism industry? the domestic travel and tourism industry?
6. What are some of the changing life-styles and demographics that will affect the growth of the food service industry in the years to come?
7. How are businesses within the travel and tourism industry interrelated?
8. Why do people travel?
9. How are travel patterns changing?
10. What are some of the social impacts that the travel and tourism industry can have on society?

# Internet Sites

For more information, visit the following Internet sites. Remember that Internet addresses can change without notice. If the site is no longer there, use a search engine to look for additional sites.

## Associations

Pacific Asia Travel Association
www.pata.org

Travel & Tourism Research Association
www.ttra.com

Travel Industry Association of America
www.tia.org

## Organizations, Resources

Caribbean Tourism Organization
www.caribtourism.com

Ecotourism Society
www.ecotourism.org

World Tourism Organization
www.world-tourism.org

World Travel & Tourism Council
www.wttc.org

# REVIEW QUIZ

When you feel you have covered all of the material in this chapter, answer these questions. Choose the *best* answer.

1. The world's population is:

    a. slowly declining.
    b. rapidly declining.
    c. staying about the same.
    d. rapidly growing.

2. What are some of the recent world changes that have affected the travel and tourism industry?

    a. The Soviet Union has been dissolved.
    b. China is developing an infrastructure to accommodate travelers.
    c. The European Union has made travel within Europe easier for Europeans.
    d. All of the above.

3. Which of the following statements about travel and economics is *true?*

    a. The amount of business travel is not affected by economic downturns.
    b. International travel patterns remain unchanged even when there are shifts in exchange rates.
    c. The buying power of a traveler's home country's currency affects destination choices and the timing of trips.
    d. a and c.

4. Among potential vacationers, one of the characteristics of members of the price and sights group is their:

    a. willingness to pay for deluxe accommodations and gourmet dining.
    b. desire for good weather and guaranteed sunshine.
    c. interest in seeing the most things for the least amount of money.
    d. desire for personal development, knowledge, and recognition.

5. People who tend to seek a vacation where they can swim and lie on a beach to enjoy the sun belong to the _____ group of travelers.

    a. price and sights
    b. quality
    c. great expectations
    d. none of the above

6. A willingness to postpone vacations because of the difficulties of juggling schedules and priorities is indicative of what trend in traveling?

    a. great expectations syndrome
    b. trade-off syndrome
    c. harried traveler
    d. strategic traveler

## REVIEW QUIZ *(continued)*

7. The travel and tourism industry helps encourage environmental responsibility by:

    a. providing local residents with an economic incentive for preserving habitat and wildlife.
    b. staying out of attractive environmental areas.
    c. giving generously to environmental groups such as Greenpeace.
    d. requiring all management personnel to take "sensitivity training" in environmental issues.

**Answer Key:** 1-d-C1, 2-d-C1, 3-c-C2, 4-c-C2, 5-d-C2, 6-b-C2, 7-a-C3

Each question is linked to a competency. Competencies are listed on the first page of the chapter. An answer reading 3-b-C4 translates to:

   3:   the question number
   b:   the correct answer
  C4:   the competency number

# Part II

## Hospitality Organizations

## Chapter 3 Outline

Hospitality Today
    Lodging
    Food Service
Careers in the Hospitality Industry
    Selecting an Industry Segment
    Career Options
Looking for a Job
    Your First Moves
Chapter Summary

## Competencies

1. Describe in general terms the size and growth pattern of the lodging and food service industries, identify advantages and disadvantages of a career in hospitality, and list the personal characteristics that correspond to each of the three personal skills areas: data, people, and things.

2. Summarize career options in the lodging industry, list the advantages of working in a chain hotel and an independent hotel, and describe typical management positions in lodging operations.

3. Briefly describe segments of the food service industry and the career opportunities available within them, and describe career options in the club and cruise line industries.

4. Summarize the purpose and contents of a résumé, and explain how to prepare and dress for a job interview, strategies for selling yourself during the interview, and effective follow-up techniques after the interview.

# 3

# Exploring Hospitality Careers

THIS CHAPTER FOCUSES on your career in the hospitality industry. The chapter opens with a short discussion of the industry's size. Next we look at the reasons people go into the hospitality field, and how to go about selecting a segment of the industry that interests you. Each segment, from hotels to institutional food service, is described. Finally, there are some ideas and suggestions for getting a job in the industry.

## Hospitality Today

What *is* the **hospitality industry**? This is not an easy question, and books on the subject offer many different answers. Some view the hospitality industry as comprising four sectors: lodging, food, entertainment, and travel. However, usually the hospitality industry is viewed as encompassing mainly lodging and food service businesses. If we define the industry this way we can include such facilities as school dormitories, nursing homes, and other institutions (see Exhibit 1).

The hospitality industry has grown tremendously in recent decades. Some of the reasons for this growth are a generally higher standard of living among Americans, increased leisure time, rapid advances in medicine that have increased life spans, the growth in education, and the greater opportunities available in a rapidly developing society. Services and goods that in the past were only available to the privileged few can now be enjoyed by a much larger percentage of the population. For example, in the past ten years, the number of people who have flown on an airplane or taken a cruise has increased dramatically.

We can get an idea of the hospitality industry's size by examining some of the statistics for the lodging and food service industries.

### Lodging

The World Tourism Organization estimates that there are 11.4 million hotel rooms in the world. More than 3 million of those are in the United States. The number of rooms is increasing as new hotels, resorts, and other lodging facilities open every year.

However, there is no doubt that the lodging industry's growth has slowed in the North American and Western European markets. Notable exceptions in the United States are casino hotels and limited-service hotels. On the other hand, a large number of new hotels are now under construction in Eastern Europe, Asia, and South America.

**Exhibit 1  The Hospitality Industry**

| Lodging Operations | Food Service Operations | Other Operations |
|---|---|---|
| All-suite hotels<br>Casino hotels<br>Conference centers<br>Full-service hotels<br>Limited-service hotels<br>Resorts<br>Retirement communities | Commercial cafeterias<br>Education food service<br>Employee food service<br>Full-service restaurants<br>Health-care<br>Lodging food service<br>Quick-service restaurants<br>Recreational food service<br>Social caterers | Airlines<br>Campgrounds<br>City clubs<br>Country clubs<br>Cruise ships<br>National parks |

Continued expansion of the lodging industry is inevitable. No one knows precisely how many hotels there will be in the next two decades, or where most of the new hotels will be located, or what kind of properties they will be. All that can be said with certainty is that career opportunities in lodging will continue to grow.

## Food Service

The food service industry is experiencing a healthy growth pattern. According to the National Restaurant Association (NRA), food service industry sales are more than four percent of the U.S. Gross Domestic Product. For every dollar spent on food, 43 cents are spent in a food service operation. Over nine million people are employed in the industry. That number is expected to reach 11 million by 2005.[1]

The *Restaurant Industry Pocket Factbook,* published annually by the NRA, highlights some interesting facts and projections about the food service business:

- Most eating and drinking places are small businesses. More than two out of three had annual sales of less than $500,000, and more than four out of 10 are sole proprietorships or partnerships.

- Food service and lodging managers account for the largest number of managerial professions.

- Seven out of 10 supervisors in food preparation and service occupations in 1992 were women. Twelve percent were African American and nine percent were Hispanic.[2]

Most students tend to view the food service business in terms of full-service and "quick-service" (fast-food) restaurants. As can be seen from Exhibit 1, other food service operations deserve serious consideration as well. For example, contract food companies operate cafeterias, dining rooms, snack bars, and catering facilities in office buildings, factories, universities, sports arenas, and retirement homes. The three largest companies in these fields—Marriott, ARAMARK Services, and Canteen—have combined contract sales of more than $6 billion. There are social caterers such as Glorious Foods in New York City. In one typical day Glorious Foods catered seven parties, including a luncheon at the offices of *Redbook* magazine, a cocktail party and buffet at the Metropolitan Museum of Art, and a tribute to actor Clint Eastwood by the Film Society of the Museum of Modern Art. Many hospitals now have the equivalent of a hotel food and beverage manager in charge of their food service. Gourmet meals and wine are available to patients at some hospitals. Hospitals run employee cafeterias, special dining rooms for doctors, and coffee shops for visitors. To maximize kitchen use, some hospitals also market off-premises catering as well.

## Careers in the Hospitality Industry

Why do people go into the hospitality industry? If you were to ask people who have spent their careers in this business what they like most about it, you would get a wide variety of answers. Some of the most popular are:

- *The industry offers more career options than most.* No matter what kind of work you enjoy, and wherever your aptitudes lie, there is a segment of the industry that can use your talents (take another look at Exhibit 1!).

- *The work is varied.* Because hotels and restaurants are complete production, distribution, and service units, managers are involved in a broad array of activities.

- *There are many opportunities to be creative.* Hotel and restaurant managers might design new products to meet the needs of their guests; produce training programs for employees; or implement challenging advertising, sales promotion, and marketing plans.

- *This is a "people" business.* Managers and supervisors spend their workdays satisfying guests, motivating employees, and negotiating with vendors and others.

- *Hospitality jobs are not nine-to-five jobs.* Hours are highly flexible in many positions. (Some see this as a disadvantage, however.)

- *There are opportunities for long-term career growth.* If you are ambitious and energetic, you can start with an entry-level job and move up. The industry is full of stories of people who started as bellpersons or cooks and rose to high management positions or opened their own successful businesses.

- *There are perks associated with many hospitality jobs.* If you become the general manager of a resort, you can dine at its restaurants with your family and friends, and use its recreational facilities. Airline and cruise employees get free or reduced-fare travel.

Despite these advantages, there are some aspects of the business that many people don't like:

- *Long hours.* In most hospitality businesses the hours are long. The 40-hour workweek is not the norm, and 50- to 60-hour workweeks are not unusual.

- *Nontraditional schedules.* Hospitality managers do not work a Monday-through-Friday schedule. In the hospitality field you will probably often find yourself working when your friends are relaxing. As one manager told his employees, "If you can't come to work Saturday or Sunday, don't bother to come in on Monday."
- *Pressure.* There are busy periods when managers and employees are under intense pressure to perform.
- *Low beginning salaries.* Entry-level jobs for management trainees tend to be low-paying compared to some other industries.

## Selecting an Industry Segment

As we have pointed out, one of the attributes that prompts many people to enter the hospitality industry is its diversity. It is difficult to imagine another industry in which there are as many different kinds of work. Before a hotel, restaurant, or club is built, for example, a feasibility study is made by a management consulting firm. Research-oriented hospitality graduates often join consulting firms for the opportunity to combine their interest in collecting and analyzing data with their interest in hotels and restaurants. Others work for hotel owners and investors as asset managers.

Management positions abound in the industry. Although hotels and restaurants may represent the largest sectors, they are by no means the only ones. Hospitality managers are needed in clubs, hospitals, nursing homes, universities and schools, cafeterias, prisons, corporate dining rooms, snack bars, management companies, airlines, cruise ships, and many other organizations. Even the royal palace of the Sultan of Brunei is run by the Hyatt organization!

Within these organizations you can go into marketing and sales, rooms management, housekeeping, cooking, engineering, dining-room management, menu planning, security, accounting, food technology, forecasting and planning, recreation, entertainment, guest relations, and so on. Moreover, you have a wide choice of places to live—you can choose between warm climates and cold; cities, suburbs, and even rural areas; any region of the country or the world. There simply is no other industry that offers more diverse career opportunities.

**Skills Inventory**. One of the best ways to select a career niche you will be happy with is to start by listing your own skills. What are the tasks you do best? Most skills fall into one of three areas: skills dealing with data, skills dealing with people, or skills dealing with things. You will probably find that the majority of your skills will fall into one or two of these areas.

People whose skills fall into the data group are often good in subjects such as math and science and enjoy working with computers. They tend to like such activities as analyzing information, comparing figures, working with graphs, and solving abstract problems. Such individuals might enjoy doing feasibility studies for a hospitality management consulting firm. They might also be happy in corporate planning departments of large hotel and restaurant chains where data is analyzed and demand is forecast. Most auditors and accountants fall into the data-skills group.

## Positions Available in Travel-Related Businesses

Tourist Bureau Manager
Travel Journalist/Writer
Promotion/Public Relations Specialist
Marketing Representative
Group Sales Representative
Tour Operator
Travel Agency Manager
Recreation Specialist
Tour Escort
Retail Store Manager
Incentive Travel Specialist
Consultant
Translator
Planner
Sales Manager
Policy Analyst
Campground Manager
Research/Statistical Specialist
Marina Manager
Economist
In-Transit Attendant
Resident Camp Director
Motor Coach Operator
Concession Operator
Auto-Recreation Vehicle Rental Agency Manager
Destination Development Specialist
Information Officer
Travel Agent
Travel Counselor/Sales Manager
Tour Wholesaler
Reservation Agent
Interpretive Specialist (Museums, Destination Information, Crafts, Art, etc.)
Curriculum Specialist
Business Travel Specialist
Financial Analyst
Teacher/Instructor
Transfer Officer
Market Researcher
Group Sales Manager
Association Manager
Tour Broker
Public Relations Officer
Tour Operator
Receptionist
Tour Leader
Meeting/Conference Planner
Guide
Ski Instructor
Advertising Agency Account Executive
Convention Center/Fair Manager
Sales Representative
Guest House/Hostel Manager
Entertainer
Program Specialist
Recreation Facility/Park Manager
Promoter

Source: The Council on Hotel, Restaurant and Institutional Education, *A Guide to College Programs in Hospitality and Tourism*, 3d edition (New York: Wiley, 1993), p. 21. Reprinted by permission of John Wiley & Sons, Inc.

If you like to deal with people, you probably enjoy helping them and taking care of their needs. You can take and give advice and instructions. You may also enjoy supervising and motivating other people, and may find that they respond to your leadership. Individuals with people skills are often good at negotiating and selling—they like to bargain and are not afraid to make decisions. In the hospitality industry, general managers and marketing and sales managers of hotels often fall into this category. So do independent restaurant owners, catering managers, and club managers.

**There are plenty of opportunities in the hospitality industry for individuals with people skills.**

The third group of skills are those dealing with things. If you excel in this area, you may be good at building or fixing things. You like to work with your hands and use tools and gadgets. You enjoy setting things up—when there is a party in your house you like to put up the decorations, for example. If your skills lie here you may be attracted to food production jobs. Chefs, bakers, and cooks all like working with things. So do the engineers who manage the hotel's physical plant.

Most of us have skills in more than one area. It is important to identify your skills and rank them according to how much you enjoy using them. This exercise will help you find a career niche that suits you.

## Career Options

The type of business you choose for your first hospitality job puts you into a definite career slot. While skills and experience are usually transferable within a particular industry segment (such as resort hotels), generally you cannot easily jump from one kind of industry segment to another. For example, it's unlikely you would progress from managing a Taco Bell to managing food service in a hospital, or from managing a Motel 6 to managing a Ritz-Carlton. However, you might go from being a hotel manager for Hyatt to being a hotel manager of a large cruise ship such as the Grand Princess. Even so, it's important to note that owners and operators of motels and fast-food restaurants often have incomes that are as high as, or higher than, those of managers at some deluxe hotels. With this in mind, let's take a look at the career options open to you.

**Lodging.** There are many types of lodging properties to choose from. There are luxury hotels such as the Mandarin in San Francisco and the Plaza in New York. There are full-service hotels operated by such companies as Hilton, Westin, and Hyatt. Resorts are another type of hotel. Some resorts, like the Boca Raton Hotel and Beach Club in Florida and the Arizona Biltmore, are geared to convention groups. Others, such as the Williamsburg Inn in Virginia and the Trapp Family Lodge in Vermont, cater to individuals and small meetings. Finally, there are casino hotels like the Mirage in Las Vegas and Trump's Taj Mahal in Atlantic City. These specialized operations are organized and managed differently from other hotels.

People who choose the lodging industry as a career often do so because they enjoy traveling and living in different places. Hotel management personnel are in great demand, and since most larger hotels belong to chains, managers are often offered opportunities to move into new positions in different geographic locations. Some people enjoy working in large metropolitan areas and in the course of their careers may live in New York, Chicago, and San Francisco. Others like warm weather resorts and may start in Miami, then move to a better position in Puerto Rico, then on to Hawaii, and so forth. Managers who like to ski or climb mountains often opt for hotels in the Rocky Mountains, the Cascades, or even the Berkshires of New England. Some people enjoy quiet suburban life and move their families to communities where there are independent inns or conference centers. At an independent hotel you are not as likely to be uprooted from your home and community by a transfer.

Would you rather be part of a large chain or work for an independent operation? There are many opportunities in both areas. The arguments for working for a large chain include:

- *Better training.* Companies such as Ritz-Carlton and Hyatt have very sophisticated operating systems. Being trained in these systems provides valuable additional education and experience.

- *More opportunities for advancement.* Marriott has more than 20,000 managers in all of its divisions. Managers who wish to advance are offered opportunities for promotions in the division in which they work or, if none are available there, in different divisions. Hotel managers, for example, might apply for positions in the time share or food service divisions. Since large chains have many units, there are simply more places to climb the ladder of success.

- *Better benefits.* You are more likely to get superior life and health insurance benefits, more generous vacation and sick time, use of a company car, moving expenses, stock purchase options, and so forth from a large chain.

A career with an independent operation also offers some advantages, however:

- *More chances to be creative.* You will have a chance to set standards and initiate changes instead of just adhering to company programs and rules.

- *More control.* You are more likely to be in control of your own destiny. In large chains, decisions that involve your salary, advancement, and place of residence are often made by persons in corporate headquarters thousands of miles away. In an independent operation, however, you deal with the people who will be deciding your fate on a regular basis. And, as mentioned earlier, with an independent you are not likely to be transferred.

- *Better learning environments.* Independent operations offer better learning environments for entrepreneurs. Because all the financial and operating decisions are made on the property, you will have a better opportunity to understand how and why things are done the way they are. If you intend to buy your own lodging operation some day, you will learn more at an independent than at a chain operation where data is forwarded to headquarters for analysis.

**Management positions within lodging operations.** Whether the lodging property is part of a chain or an independent operation, as a hospitality student you have a wide variety of management positions open to you. Many people enjoy aiming for the top administrative job of general manager, but others prefer to specialize in such areas as:

- Catering
- Engineering
- Food and beverage
- Finance and accounting
- Human resources
- Marketing and sales
- Rooms management
- Systems management

Let's take a look at management positions in these areas.

The **general manager** is the chief operating officer of a hotel. He or she is responsible for attracting guests and making sure they are safe and well-served while visiting. The general manager supervises hotel staff and administers policies established by the owners or chain operators. Chains such as Holiday Inn and Marriott have very specific service, operating, and decorating guidelines. The general manager must see that all departments adhere to those standards.

Most general managers hold frequent meetings with their department heads. If a convention is about to arrive, for example, the general manager will want to make sure that the staff is aware of all the details necessary to make the conventioneers' stays pleasant: limousine service, check-in procedures, banquets, meeting rooms, audiovisual facilities, entertainment, and so on.

The general manager's main responsibility is the financial performance of the business. The compensation a general manager receives is often tied to the profitability of the business he or she manages. Hiring and firing when necessary is also part of a general manager's job. The general manager can be involved in union negotiations as well.

*Exploring Hospitality Careers* **61**

| HYATT HOME | @HYATT HOME | PARK HYATT | THE PRESS ROOM | HYATT TRAVEL PARTNERS |
| TRAVEL AGENTS | THE HYATT WORLD OF SERVICES | HYATT VACATION CLUB® | CAREER OPPORTUNITIES ◄ |
| CASINOS | CLASSIC RESIDENCE BY HYATT® |

Reservations
Worldwide Guide
Hot Deals
Gold Passport
Hyatt Resorts
Meeting Planning
@Hyatt

*The Hyatt Management Training Program*

**Hyatt selects only the very best.**

Applicants must meet the following requisites in order to qualify for our Management Training Program:

- Bachelors degree and a G.P.A. of 2.8
- Nine months of relative industry work experience
- Leadership or involvement in campus and/or community activities
- Positive references from two previous work experiences
- Authorization to work in the U.S.

**Initial Placement and Relocation Assistance**

Placement in hotels is determined by geographic preference and availability of trainee positions at participating hotels.

When an individual is selected to begin the Management Training Program, Hyatt will provide relocation assistance. Trainees are reimbursed for mileage driven or cost of air fare, a reasonable cost of lodging, food and beverage, and the transportation of household goods. Hyatt will also provide two weeks lodging in a Hyatt hotel while you arrange for housing.

**Training with Hyatt has its Rewards.**

Hyatt offers a competitive salary for our Management Trainees based on geographic location. Salary is based on a 5-day, 50 hour work week, with additional compensation for any hours worked in excess of 50 hours per week. The first salary review will occur upon successful graduation from the training program.

**Various Destinations, One Great Future**

Completion of the Management Training Program prepares trainees for operational management positions in the following divisions:

*(continued)*

**62**  *Chapter 3*

*(continued)*

> - Rooms
> - Food and Beverage
> - Culinary
> - Accounting
> - Human Resources
> - Catering
> - Sales
> - Engineering
>
> Trainees will receive feedback and evaluations of their performance at the midpoint and the end of the training program.
>
> Because the hotel in which you train has the first opportunity to place you after program completion, you will most likely begin your career in familiar surroundings. If no positions are available at the hotel where you trained, you may be transferred to another Hyatt property.
>
> One of the biggest advantages of a career with Hyatt is the opportunity to live in several different cities over the course of your career. Relocation assistance will be based on position status.
>
> **Explore the Details**
>
> To learn more about the Hyatt Management Training Program, send your resume to:
>
> Hyatt Hotels Corporation
> Dept. HHMTP
> P.O. Box 8440
> Gaithersburg, Maryland 20898
> Fax: 301-519-8418
> E-mail: hyatt@alexus.com
>
> Hyatt Hotels and Resorts is an Equal Opportunity Employer M/F/D/V

Large chains such as Hyatt Hotels frequently offer training programs, placement assistance, good benefits, and numerous opportunities for advancement. (From the Hyatt Hotels Web site at www.hyatt.com)

Good general managers are skilled at getting along with people. They are able to forge positive relationships with employees, guests, and the community at large. They believe in teamwork and know how to get things done through other people. Effective general managers are also technically proficient. They do not subscribe to "seat of the pants" managing; instead, they study problems and carefully formulate short- and long-term solutions.

**Catering managers** promote and sell the hotel's banquet facilities. They plan, organize, and manage the hotel's banquets, which can range from formal dinners to picnic buffets. Knowledge of food costs, preparation techniques, and pricing is essential. Good catering managers are also aware of protocol, social customs, and etiquette. Creativity and imagination are useful qualities as well.

**Chief engineers** are responsible for the hotel's physical operation and maintenance. This includes the electrical, heating, ventilating, air conditioning, refrigeration, and plumbing systems. Chief engineers must have extensive backgrounds in mechanical and electrical equipment and may need numerous licenses.

**Food and beverage managers** direct the production and service of food and beverages. They are responsible for training the dining room and kitchen staffs and ensuring quality control. Food and beverage managers at large properties work with their head chefs to plan menus and with their beverage managers to select wines and brands of liquor. At small properties the food and beverage manager has sole responsibility for these tasks. Menu pricing and cost control are also the province of the food and beverage manager.

Food and beverage managers must have a keen interest in food and wines and an up-to-date knowledge of food trends and guests' tastes. Because food and beverage service is offered from 15 to 24 hours a day, managers in this field must be prepared to work long shifts and endure periods of pressure—dealing with unexpectedly large dinner crowds, serving a banquet, and so on.

The **controller** is in charge of the accounting department and all of its functions, such as the management of credit, payroll, guest accounts, and all cashiering activities. The controller also prepares budgets and daily, weekly, and monthly reports showing revenues, expenses, and other statistics that managers require. Controllers are detail-oriented people and favor an analytical approach to business problems.

**Human resources managers** are responsible for recruiting and training the majority of the hotel's employees. They are also in charge of employee relations within a hotel. This includes counseling employees, developing and administering programs to maintain and improve employee morale, monitoring the work environment, and so on. An important part of the human resources manager's job is to oversee compliance with equal employment opportunity and affirmative action laws and policies. People who choose human resources as a career usually have a good deal of empathy and are excellent negotiators.

The marketing and sales function at a hotel consists of several different activities. Sometimes a large hotel will have two managers overseeing marketing and sales. In that case, the **marketing manager** develops and implements a marketing plan and budget. The marketing plan lays out how the hotel intends to attract business. It includes sections on meeting and convention sales, local sales, advertising, and promotion plans. The marketing and sales manager is also in charge of corporate accounts and may work with an advertising and public relations agency. The **sales manager** conducts sales programs and makes sales calls on prospects for group and individual business. He or she usually reports to the marketing and sales manager. Marketing and sales people tend to be service-oriented and possess good communication skills.

**Resident managers** are often the executives in charge of a hotel's rooms division. Their areas of responsibility include the front office, reservations, and housekeeping, as well as sources of revenue other than the food and beverage department,

**64** Chapter 3

**Exhibit 2   Compensation and Benefits Survey**

| Position | 1st Class | Standard | Suites | Economy |
|---|---|---|---|---|
| Resident manager | $64,400 | $36,400 | $34,300 | $25,300 |
| Front office manager | $32,600 | $27,100 | $26,400 | $20,500 |
| Reservations manager | $56,700 | $40,600 | $25,700 | — |
| Controller | $56,700 | $40,600 | $35,000 | $23,000 |
| Executive housekeeper | $35,100 | $26,200 | $24,200 | $18,700 |
| Chief engineer | $47,300 | $33,500 | $31,000 | $23,900 |
| Sales and marketing director | $63,400 | $43,200 | $44,900 | $28,500 |
| Senior sales manager | $44,300 | $37,200 | — | — |
| Sales manager | $36,300 | $29,100 | $37,300 | $22,400 |
| Catering sales manager | $34,100 | $26,400 | $27,300 | — |
| Security director | $35,800 | $33,000 | — | — |
| Human resources director | $45,400 | $35,600 | $26,900 | — |
| Food and beverage director | $59,000 | $41,500 | $35,000 | — |
| Executive chef | $56,900 | $36,800 | $36,600 | — |
| Sous chef | $34,600 | $24,900 | — | — |
| Banquet chef | $32,000 | $23,500 | — | — |
| Executive steward | $30,200 | $22,900 | — | — |
| Restaurant manager | $31,600 | $27,200 | $25,200 | — |

Source: AH&MA/Coopers & Lybrand

such as gift shops and recreational facilities. In small hotels, resident managers are also in charge of security. They report directly to the general manager and share responsibility for compliance with budgets and forecasts. Resident managers are good leaders and have many of the same qualities that general managers have.

**Systems managers** are the computer experts in a hotel. They are in charge of computerized management information systems—the computers used for reservations, room assignments, telephones, guestroom status reports, accounting functions, and labor and productivity reports. They often know how to write simple computer programs and easy-to-follow instructions for using computers. They have good problem-solving aptitudes and verbal and written communication skills.

The salaries for the hotel management positions just described vary according to the area of the country, the size of the property, and the work experience of the individual. However, Exhibit 2 gives a good indication of average management salaries in various positions. Chapter Appendix A lists hotel management positions, titles, and advancement opportunities.

**Food Service.** There are also a wide variety of job opportunities and geographic locations to choose from within the food service industry. Those who are interested in commercial food service often choose between independent and chain restaurants.

**Independent restaurants.** At the top of the restaurant spectrum are luxury restaurants, which are for the most part owned and operated by independent entrepreneurs. Within the trade, these restaurants are sometimes called "white tablecloth" restaurants. Most of their patrons are on expense accounts. Lutece and the Four Seasons in Manhattan are perennial favorites in this class.

Guests at luxury restaurants usually receive superior service. Some luxury restaurants, for example, feature French service, in which meals are served from a cart or *guéridon* by formally dressed personnel. Tables are waited on by servers, a *chef du rang*, and an apprentice called a *commis du rang*. In the back of the house there is a classic kitchen in the tradition of Escoffier, with an executive chef and a brigade of cooks organized into departments, each headed by a *chef de partie*.

Contrary to popular belief, luxury restaurants are not necessarily high-profit ventures. Often, their rent and labor costs are high, and there is intense competition for a limited number of guests. These restaurants are usually open for both lunch and dinner (some only offer dinner), but the work starts early in the morning, when much of the food is purchased fresh and delivered for cooking that day, and runs until midnight or even later.

Many hospitality students aspire to run and eventually own a luxury restaurant. The top restaurants have a substantial volume and are very sophisticated operations. The Tavern on the Green in New York City sells $27 million in food and beverages annually, for example. Most do considerably less: $5 million to $6 million is a more typical figure for this kind of establishment. The best way to the top is to work in a luxury restaurant and learn the ropes. Many of these restaurants are owned by an individual. They are usually sold to an employee or other entrepreneurs who can get financing when the owner retires. Banks and other lending institutions look to see what experience the prospective owner has before approving loans, so a good track record in management positions at similar restaurants is your best ticket for getting the financing you need to buy your "dream" restaurant.

**Chain restaurants.** Chain restaurants recruit the majority of their managers from hospitality schools. Entry-level jobs for graduates with hospitality degrees are often on the assistant-manager level, with progression to manager, then district manager responsible for a group of restaurants, and then regional manager.

Restaurant chains are the fastest growing part of the restaurant business today. Many of these chains are made up of fast-food restaurants or, as they prefer to be called, quick-service restaurants. Menus rarely change in these restaurants. Their strategy calls for delivering a large number of meals at fairly low prices. The free-standing buildings they occupy are usually specially built food production factories filled with specially designed equipment. Minimum-wage employees turn out a standardized product. Successful fast-food chains depend on a large number of units so that they can engage in regional and national marketing and advertising programs. Expansion is usually accomplished through franchising, although some of the largest fast-food chains own as many as 30 percent of their units. Small fast-food chains such as Subway do as little as $300,000 annually per unit, but large chains like McDonald's average more than $2 million per unit.

Hospitality students often bypass fast-food management opportunities. This is often a mistake. These jobs may pay well and offer security and excellent benefit packages. Many McDonald's managers of single stores earn between $30,000 and $50,000 a year, plus benefits such as stock options and profit sharing. In addition, if you dream of owning your own franchise, the franchise company may help you if you've worked hard and well in one of their units. Domino's Pizza recruits all of its franchisees from its store managers and helps them arrange financing. Burger King and McDonald's have leasing programs that allow successful managers to lease units and pay the rent out of sales until they can afford to buy their unit.

Dinner houses, also known as casual restaurants, are another type of chain restaurant. Such well-known companies as Chili's Grill & Bar, T.G.I. Friday's, and Bennigan's lead the pack. These companies are popular career choices for hospitality graduates because they offer many opportunities for advancement.

**Social caterers.** Social catering is another part of the food service industry that many hospitality graduates become interested in. Catering is another business that is most often started by independent entrepreneurs, as it requires very little start-up capital—facilities can be rented as needed, and equipment can usually be leased on a short-term basis from restaurant supply houses. Food servers can be hired as needed. In some cases, caterers provide only food; in others, they are responsible for tables, chairs, utensils, tents, servers, and decorations.

**Contract food companies.** Contract food companies are generally hired by organizations whose major business purpose is not food service, but they provide it for some reason. The biggest users of contract food services are large manufacturing and industrial concerns in which workers have a short lunch period. Contractors such as ARAMARK and Marriott operate cafeterias and executive dining rooms for these companies. The service is often subsidized by the contracting company, which may supply the space and utilities and, in some cases, underwrite some or all of the food costs. Schools and colleges, hospitals, sports arenas, airlines, cruise ships, and even prisons use contract food companies. In the case of airlines, meals are cooked and prepackaged in central commissaries and then delivered to the airplanes for preparation and service as needed.

Contract food management is somewhat unique because the manager must please two sets of employers—the home office and the client that has contracted for the service. Many contract food programs, such as those at schools and hospitals, have strong nutritional requirements as well. Others, such as airline programs, require a knowledge of advanced food technology.

Careers in contract food service are attractive to many hospitality majors. Contract food managers work more regular hours and are under less pressure than restaurant managers. Why? Because many of the users of contract food service, such as office building tenants, work a regular 40-hour week, Monday through Friday. Also, contract food managers are able to predict with more certainty how many people they are going to feed, what they will feed them, and when the meals will be served.

Because of the large volume of meals involved, contract food managers must be highly skilled in professional management techniques and cost control. For this reason, contract food companies usually hire people with experience within their industry and recruit from hospitality schools.

**Institutional food service.** Although contract food companies can supply food for schools and hospitals, the majority of these institutions handle their own food service programs. Most public schools belong to the National School Lunch Program established by the federal government in 1946. The purpose of this program is twofold: (1) to create a market for agricultural products produced by America's farmers, and (2) to serve a nutritious lunch to schoolchildren at a low cost. Public elementary schools tend to offer only those menu items that qualify for government support, but many high schools add items such as hamburgers, French fries, and even diet sodas. High school food managers work hard to come up with more creative and innovative menu plans to keep students in school cafeterias. Even the look of school cafeterias has changed as managers have developed new methods of merchandising food.

Colleges and universities have also experienced changes in their food service programs. Because more students live off-campus now, there is a trend toward flexible meal plans in which students have a choice of how many meals they wish to purchase from the institution. To compete successfully, many universities have opened special table-service restaurants in addition to their traditional cafeterias. Another move has been to offer a more varied cafeteria menu featuring salad bars and popular items such as croissant sandwiches, bagels, lox and cream cheese, and even Belgian waffles for breakfast. Some have introduced brand names such as Pizza Hut and Taco Bell.

Hospital programs are usually administered by a trained dietitian or a professional food service manager working with one. Menus are generally simple and nourishing. In the past, most hospitals had a central kitchen where all foods were prepared and then sent in insulated carts or trays to the patients' rooms. Some hospitals have decentralized their food service. With a decentralized system, the hospital purchases frozen and portion-packed entrées and salads and keeps them in small pantries in various parts of the hospital. The meals are then plated and heated in microwave ovens as needed. Another trend has been the attempt to turn hospital food service from a cost center into a revenue center. Some hospitals sell take-home food to doctors and employees and even do outside catering.

As you can see, institutions are beginning to compete with commercial food service operations for consumers. This means that there are more opportunities than ever before for hospitality students to enter what is clearly a growing field.

**Management positions within food service.** A restaurant is usually a small business, with average sales somewhere between $400,000 and $500,000.[3] That means that most of the management opportunities in this field, even with large chains, lie in operations or "hands-on" management, as opposed to corporate staff jobs behind a desk. The duties of a food service manager are similar across the spectrum of food service operations, from an independent restaurant to a cruise ship or retirement home.

The Chili's Grill & Bar restaurant chain staffs its units with a general manager and three restaurant managers. The general manager is responsible for overall operations, while each restaurant manager has specific functional duties—managing the dining room, handling beverage service, or supervising the kitchen staff. This simple management structure and division of duties is similar for many other commercial food service operations. Other typical food service management positions include chef, maître d', and banquet manager. Exhibit 3 lists average salaries of unit managers. Chapter Appendix B lists food service management positions, titles, and advancement opportunities.

**Clubs.** Clubs are another career option open to you. Clubs are very different from other types of hospitality businesses because the "guests"—the club members—are also the owners in many cases. There are country clubs, city clubs, luncheon clubs, yacht and sailing clubs, military clubs, tennis clubs, even polo clubs—all with clubhouses and other facilities that must be managed. Some, like the Yale Club in New York City, offer complete hotel services. Large clubs have many of the same positions found in hotels and restaurants: a general manager, a food and beverage director, a catering director (weddings and parties are an important part of club operations), and a controller.

Today there are more than 10,000 recreational and social clubs in the United States that lease or own their facilities and have them run by professional managers. Most clubs are nonprofit organizations owned by and run for the benefit of the members. Some clubs are built by developers as part of housing developments and are proprietary, for-profit enterprises.

Many hospitality managers enjoy working in clubs. First of all, unlike chain food service and hotel operations, there is a chance to exercise one's own imagination and creativity in such matters as menu selection, party planning, and sporting events. Secondly, you interact with the owners (members) in a more direct way. Moreover, clubs with sports facilities often host celebrity tournaments that bring with them media coverage. This can make the job even more stimulating. Since the nature of clubs often requires specialized training and knowledge (such as golf, tennis, and marina operations), club managers often come up through the ranks.

**Cruise Lines.** There are opportunities both on shore and at sea within the cruise industry. Shoreside positions include marketing, accounting, provisioning, itinerary planning, and hotel operations. At sea, there are the same kinds of jobs any fine resort has. Salaries are competitive. Persons who are attracted by travel may enjoy operations jobs at sea but should be prepared to spend a minimum of nine out of every 12 months away from home. Living conditions don't allow for much privacy either, but many like the feeling of having an extended family that occurs on a ship.

## Looking for a Job

Many hospitality students have a preconceived idea of the job they want in the industry. Their parents, someone they admire, or a family friend may have been in the business and advised them to take a particular position. Or they may have had an enjoyable part-time or summer job in a restaurant or hotel. In the view of career

Exhibit 3    Unit Manager Salary Ranges

## Salary Ranges by Location within Region

| Region | State | Location | Median Salary Range |
|---|---|---|---|
| Northeast | Connecticut | Fairfield County | $36,000–37,500 |
|  |  | New Haven | $34,500–36,000 |
|  | Massachusetts | Boston | $30,000–31,000 |
|  | New Jersey | Metro/Northern | $33,000–34,500 |
|  | New York | NYC | $31,500–33,000 |
|  |  | Westchester County | $34,500–36,000 |
|  | Pennsylvania | Philadelphia | $28,500–30,000 |
|  |  | Pittsburgh | $30,000–31,500 |
| North Central | Illinois | Chicago | $30,000–31,500 |
|  | Missouri | St. Louis | $27,000–28,500 |
|  | Nebraska | Omaha | $24,000–25,500 |
|  | Ohio | Cincinnati | $28,500–30,000 |
|  |  | Cleveland | $31,500–33,000 |
|  |  | Columbus | $24,000–25,500 |
|  | Wisconsin | Milwaukee | $33,000–34,500 |
| South |  | Washington, D.C. | $31,500–33,000 |
|  | Delaware | Wilmington | $28,500–30,000 |
|  | Florida | Miami/Ft. Lauderdale | $25,500–27,000 |
|  | Georgia | Atlanta | $28,500–30,000 |
|  | North Carolina | Charlotte | $27,000–28,500 |
|  |  | Winston-Salem/Greensboro | $30,000–31,500 |
|  | Texas | Dallas | $27,000–28,500 |
|  |  | Houston | $28,500–30,000 |
| West | Arizona | Phoenix | $25,500–27,000 |
|  | California | Los Angeles | $33,000–34,500 |
|  |  | San Francisco | $31,500–33,000 |
|  | Utah | Salt Lake City | $25,500–27,000 |

Source: National Restaurant Association, *Compensation for Salaried Personnel in Foodservice—1996.*

counselors, however, it's better to keep an open mind. If you don't explore other career possibilities, you might overlook opportunities that could be more appealing in the long run. A sound understanding of your goals and lifestyle, and a thorough knowledge of the companies that might be interested in what you offer, is an important foundation for your career search.

Every job you take should move you closer to your final goal. If you look at jobs as stepping-stones on a **career path** or **career ladder** (see Exhibit 4), there are several questions you should answer before you decide whether a job is right for you:

- What can I learn from this job that will contribute to my career goals?
- What are the long-term opportunities for growth in this company?
- What is this company's reputation among the people I know? Is it a good place to work? Does it deliver on its promises to employees?
- How good is the training program? Will the company really make an effort to educate me?
- What is the starting salary? What about other benefits? Do they add up to a competitive package?
- How do I feel about the location? Will I be living in a place where I can be happy? What about proximity to friends and relatives?

## Your First Moves

While you are still in school, you probably will want to gain some job experience in the hospitality industry. To do that, you will need some basic knowledge of how to prepare a résumé and handle a job interview. The following sections contain information that may be useful to you.

**Your Résumé.** Whether you mail in a reply to a newspaper ad or apply for a job in person, a basic tool you will need is a well-prepared, typed or printed (not handwritten), and attractive résumé. What follows is a brief introduction to the art and science of writing a good résumé. There are many excellent books in bookstores and libraries on creating résumés; our best advice is to find one and read it!

   **Purpose of a résumé.** Many job seekers do not understand the purpose of a résumé. Put yourself in the shoes of an interviewer. You have just placed an ad in your local newspaper seeking a front desk agent for your hotel. It is not unlikely that you will receive 100 résumés or more for this job. Obviously you can't interview 100 people in person. Their résumés, and the cover letters that usually accompany them, serve as screening guides. They are tools that the interviewer uses to decide whom to see. The purpose of your résumé, therefore, is to make certain that you will be one of the handful of people who will actually be interviewed. Your résumé will not get you a job—no one is hired on the basis of a résumé alone.

   A résumé is an advertisement for yourself. Its purpose is to convince the person doing the hiring that he or she should not fill the job without talking to you first. Résumés have other purposes as well. They introduce you to your prospective employer and provide a brief summary of your educational and employment background. However, their main purpose is to pre-sell you to the company, to persuade the interviewer before the interview starts that you may be the best person for the job.

   **Contents of a résumé.** Once you understand the purpose of a résumé, the information that goes into one and in what order becomes clearer. Start with the

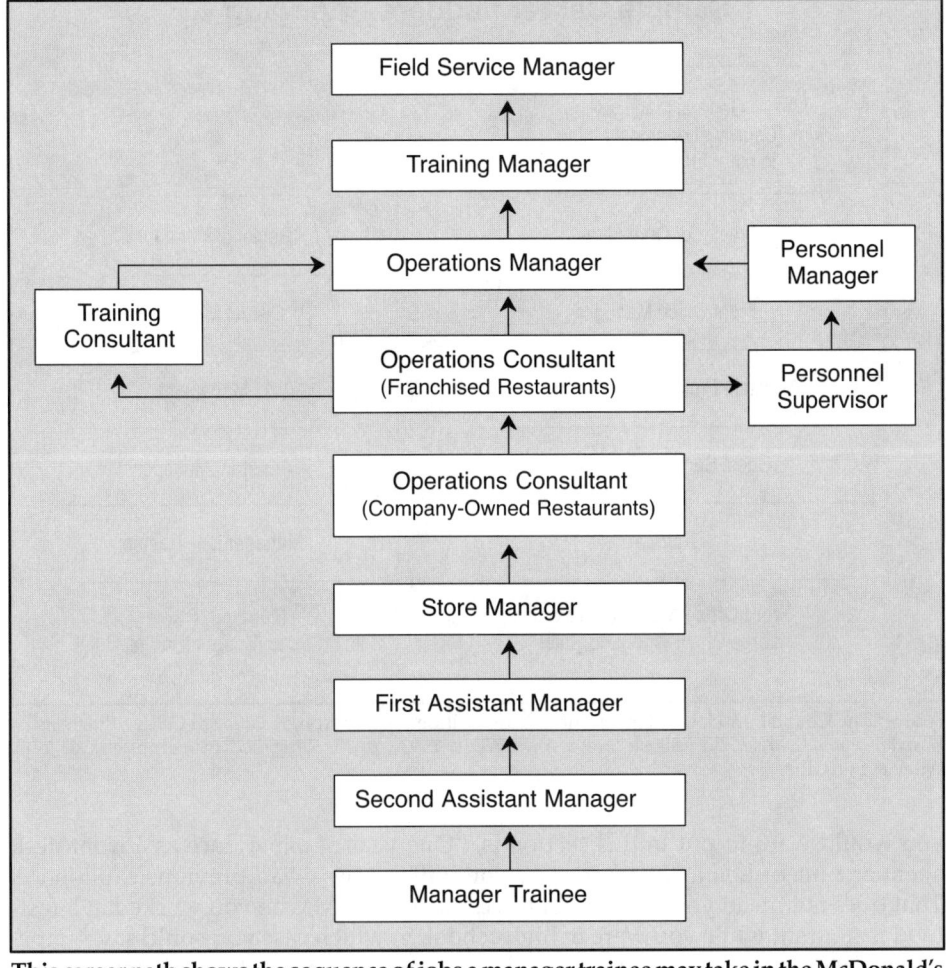

**Exhibit 4   Sample Career Path—McDonald's**

```
                    Field Service Manager
                            ↑
                     Training Manager
                            ↑
  Training  →      Operations Manager      ←    Personnel
  Consultant                                      Manager
                            ↑                        ↑
               Operations Consultant          Personnel
         ↑     (Franchised Restaurants)   →   Supervisor
                            ↑
                Operations Consultant
              (Company-Owned Restaurants)
                            ↑
                     Store Manager
                            ↑
                  First Assistant Manager
                            ↑
                 Second Assistant Manager
                            ↑
                     Manager Trainee
```

**This career path shows the sequence of jobs a manager trainee may take in the McDonald's Corporation as he or she moves up the corporate ladder.** (Courtesy of McDonald's Corporation, Oak Brook, Illinois)

length. Your résumé should not run more than one page. Interviewers don't have time to read more than that, and they don't need to read more in order to decide whether they want to interview you. Remember, your résumé will end up in a file with many others. The interviewer will skim through the file to find the most likely candidates. What should be at the top of the page, after your name, address, and phone number? Whatever you can say that is most likely to make the interviewer want to read more about you.

Many of the best résumés start with a section called "Summary of Qualifications." Continuing with our example, suppose you are applying for the front desk position and you have worked at another hotel before as a front desk agent. What

### Sample Career Ladders—Lodging

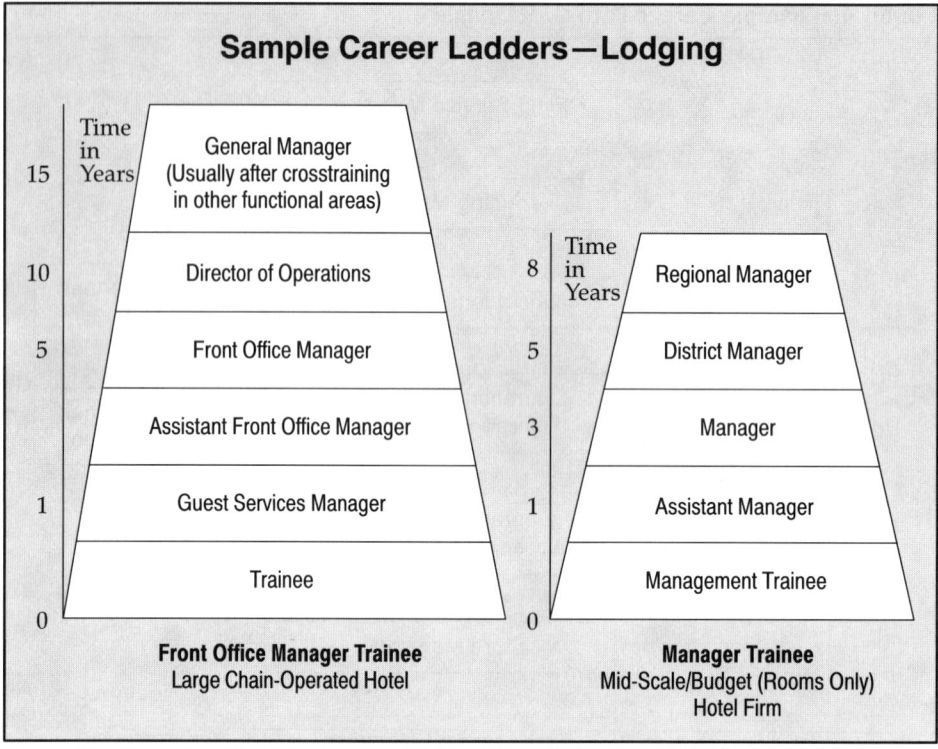

| Time in Years | Front Office Manager Trainee<br>Large Chain-Operated Hotel |
|---|---|
| 15 | General Manager (Usually after crosstraining in other functional areas) |
| 10 | Director of Operations |
| 5 | Front Office Manager |
| | Assistant Front Office Manager |
| 1 | Guest Services Manager |
| 0 | Trainee |

| Time in Years | Manager Trainee<br>Mid-Scale/Budget (Rooms Only) Hotel Firm |
|---|---|
| 8 | Regional Manager |
| 5 | District Manager |
| 3 | Manager |
| 1 | Assistant Manager |
| 0 | Management Trainee |

Source: The Council on Hotel, Restaurant and Institutional Education, *A Guide to College Programs in Hospitality and Tourism,* 3d edition (New York: Wiley, 1993), p. 13. Reprinted by permission of John Wiley & Sons, Inc.

you would want to put in this section is, "One year of experience as a front desk agent at a major hotel." In most cases you will not have had previous experience. That does not mean you are not qualified for the job. Maybe you worked at a fast-food restaurant while you were in high school, in which case you could say, "Experienced at greeting and serving customers." It may well be that you've never held a job before. Your qualifications then might be something like the following: "A personable, enthusiastic worker, quick learner, good team worker." This is the section that you use to market or sell yourself, to show that you have the skills, experience, and basic credentials for the job. If you have received any awards or recognition ("Named 'Employee of the Month'"), this is the place to mention it, to separate you from the crowd.

The next section of a résumé is often a direct presentation of your skills and experience. Here you will be more specific: "One year's experience as a front desk agent at the 100-room Hampton Inn. Duties included taking reservations, checking in and checking out guests, and handling complaints."

What if you've never held a front desk position before? You want to show that the jobs you have held or the work you've done has contributed to your ability to do the job in question. If you said that you were a "personable, enthusiastic

## Sample Career Ladders—Food Service

| Time in Years | Position |
|---|---|
| 15 | General Manager (Usually after crosstraining in other functional areas) |
| 10 | Director of Operations |
| 4 | Assistant Food & Beverage Manager |
|  | Outlet Manager |
| 1 | Assistant Outlet Manager |
| 0 | Trainee |

**Food & Beverage Manager Trainee**
Large Chain-Operated Hotel

| Time in Years | Position |
|---|---|
| 10 | Regional Manager |
| 7 | District Manager |
| 3 | Manager |
| 2 | Assistant Manager |
| 1 | Shift Management: Food Production Manager, Dining Room Manager, or Beverage Manager |
| 0 | Management Trainee |

**Manager Trainee**
Chain Restaurant Firm

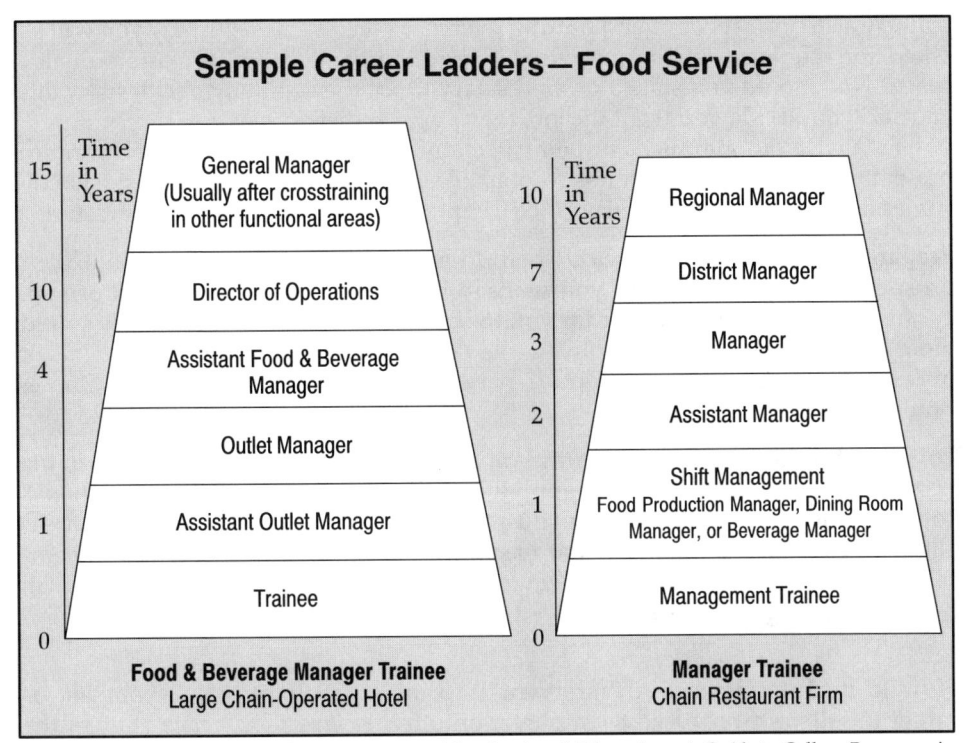

Source: The Council on Hotel, Restaurant and Institutional Education, *A Guide to College Programs in Hospitality and Tourism,* 3d edition (New York: Wiley, 1993), p. 14. Reprinted by permission of John Wiley & Sons, Inc.

worker," you might note that you were a shift leader at McDonald's last summer, or even "Head of the prom committee at Northside High."

List your education at the bottom of your résumé: "Graduate of Northside High. Currently enrolled at Florida International University's School of Hospitality Management." Why not put your education at the top? Simply because most interviewers are not looking for a graduate of Northside High or an FIU student when they start going through résumés. They are looking for someone who can do the job. If they think you can do it, then they'll read your entire résumé carefully and call you in. If they don't, they don't care about your schooling.

Should you list your hobbies? Only if they relate to the job you're trying for. If you're applying for a job as a cook and your hobby is collecting or writing recipes, that would be relevant. But if what you do in your spare time is collect stamps or play the saxophone, leave it out. It not only won't help, it might even hurt (the interviewer might hate the saxophone!).

Other personal information also has no place in a résumé. Your height, weight, age, race, or marital status should not be part of your résumé unless it bears directly on the job qualifications. While some books suggest enclosing a picture, we don't recommend it. Your physical appearance has nothing to do with your ability to do the job, and might unconsciously prejudice the interviewer not to see you. We also don't recommend putting references on résumés. Usually you will be asked for references at the interview if they are wanted—why waste valuable space? Nor should you state a desired salary. Once the company decides it wants you and you decide you want the job, then you can discuss salary.

Finally, avoid gimmicks or being "creative" with your résumé. You want to present yourself as a professional, responsible, and reliable individual. Unusual résumés do not promote that image. (See Chapter Appendix C for a sample résumé.)

**Preparing for the Interview.** You should know as much as possible about your prospective employer before you walk in the door. You want to be informed, because that will make it easier for you to hold a conversation and you will sound more enthusiastic. If you're applying to a hotel or restaurant chain, there's lots of information in the library from trade periodicals, on the Internet, and in Dun & Bradstreet reports.

**Dressing for the Interview.** The way you are dressed makes a big difference in the way you are perceived. If you are applying for a management position, you should consider how you would dress if you were working at the firm, and then dress slightly better. Research shows that reactions to clothing styles, colors, and combinations are fairly predictable. Remember, you want to project a professional, responsible image. The interview is not the time to make a bold or unusual fashion statement.

**How to Be Interviewed.** An interview is your opportunity to sell yourself, or rather to sell your prospective employer on offering you a job. Once you get the offer you can decide whether to take it, but the name of the game is to convince the interviewer to want to hire you.

Going into an interview with this attitude has several implications. First, it gives you a sense of confidence. You are not going to sit back and wait to see what the interviewer asks, because he or she might not ask about the things that make you a superior candidate. You are going to control, to the extent you can, what is talked about. This is not as hard as it sounds. One good way to start off and gain control of the interview is to ask questions. If you have done your homework about the company, some questions will naturally occur to you. Asking questions shows that you are a person who is very interested in working for the company. The answers to your questions may give you clues that will help you sell the interviewer on hiring you.

The more you know about the company (and the interviewer) before you start answering questions, the better job you can do of answering them. Generally, industry recruiters look for people who not only possess specific skills, but also understand the dynamics of our changing business. They want good communicators and leaders who can motivate others, show them what needs to be done, and teach them how to do it. Industry recruiters look for well-rounded individuals who understand financial issues, legislative issues, ethical issues, and, above all, human resources issues.

Often, interviewers have a checklist of topics they want to cover in the interview. Don't be put off; you can still ask your questions in between their questions. Always answer their questions directly and honestly. If you don't know the answer to something, say so. The best thing you can do is sound positive. You want to be remembered after you leave the room as someone who is enthusiastic, confident, energetic, and dependable. Shape every answer to reinforce those images.

Under no circumstances should you say anything bad about a former employer. To do so suggests that you might be disloyal or dishonest.

Finally, encourage the interviewer to make you an offer. Like any good salesperson, ask for the order! Once you have a job offer, you can weigh it along with other possibilities.

After you leave you should always write a follow-up thank-you letter. Thank the interviewer for the time he or she spent with you and for considering you for the position. If you were impressed with the company, say so! Tell the interviewer that you're certain you can make a contribution and you hope you'll be hearing from him or her soon.

If you are offered a job, respond within the time requested. You might have additional questions, so contact the person making the offer to clarify details. If you need more time to make your decision, ask for it. When you have decided, be prompt in letting your prospective employer know. If you call to turn down the offer, follow up with a letter in which you thank the person for his or her interest in you. Remember, you may meet this recruiter again under different circumstances.

## Chapter Summary

The hospitality industry's growth in recent decades has been due in part to the average individual's higher standard of living, higher level of education, increased leisure time, and longer life span. The greater opportunities available in rapidly developing societies have also contributed to industry expansion.

In the past few years, industry growth has slowed in the North American and Western European markets. An exception to this trend in the United States is the casino hotel and limited-service industries. Many new hotels are under construction in Eastern Europe, Asia, and South America.

The hospitality industry offers many career options. The work is varied and there are numerous opportunities for advancement. Some people, however, don't like the occasional pressures and long hours that go along with many hospitality jobs. Management positions in a hotel include general manager, catering manager, chief engineer, food and beverage manager, controller, human resources manager, marketing and sales manager, sales manager, resident manager, and systems manager. Management positions in a restaurant include general manager and restaurant manager.

It's important to select the segment of the industry that will best suit you. To do this you must know whether you work best with data, people, or things. Once you have considered your strengths and weaknesses, you are in a position to evaluate areas of specialization. Your choices include hotels, restaurants, clubs, catering operations, contract food companies, institutional food service, and more.

Three important job-seeking skills are preparing a good résumé, dressing correctly for an interview, and conducting yourself appropriately during an interview. The purpose of your résumé is to gain an interview. It is an advertisement for you;

use it to emphasize your special skills and experience. Research the company you will interview for, dress conservatively for your interview, and "sell yourself."

## Endnotes

1. *1997 National Restaurant Association Restaurant Industry Pocket Factbook* (Washington, D.C.: National Restaurant Association, 1997).
2. *Pocket Factbook.*
3. *Pocket Factbook.*

## Key Terms

**career path/career ladder**—A series of positions an individual may take on the way to his or her ultimate career goal. Some companies lay out sample career paths or ladders for their employees.

**catering manager**—A department within the food and beverage division of a hotel. Responsible for arranging and planning food and beverage functions for (1) conventions and smaller hotel groups, and (2) local banquets booked by the sales department.

**chief engineer**—Responsible for a hotel's physical operation and maintenance.

**controller**—Manages the accounting department and all of its functions, including management of credit, payroll, guest accounts, and cashiering activities.

**food and beverage manager**—Directs the production and service of food and beverages.

**general manager**—The chief operating officer of a hotel or restaurant.

**hospitality industry**—Lodging and food service businesses that provide short-term or transitional lodging and/or food.

**human resources manager**—In charge of employee relations within an organization.

**marketing manager**—Develops and implements a marketing plan and budget.

**resident manager**—In charge of the rooms division in a mid-size to large hotel. Sometimes resident managers are also in charge of security.

**sales manager**—Conducts sales programs and makes sales calls on prospects for group and individual business. Reports to the marketing manager.

**systems manager**—Manages a hotel's computerized management information systems. May write simple computer programs and instruction manuals for employees.

## Review Questions

1. What has the growth pattern for the hotel industry been like in the last few decades? Why?
2. What are some of the advantages and disadvantages of a career in hospitality?

3. How can a skills inventory help you decide on a career path?
4. What are some career options in the hotel industry?
5. What are the advantages of working for a large hotel chain? for an independent hotel?
6. Should a hospitality student bypass fast-food management opportunities? Why or why not?
7. Why are careers in contract food service attractive to many hospitality majors?
8. What are some of the questions you should ask yourself before you decide that a job is right for you?
9. What should appear on a résumé? What should not appear?
10. How should you conduct yourself during a job interview?

## Internet Sites

For more information, visit the following Internet sites. Remember that Internet addresses can change without notice. If the site is no longer there, use a search engine to look for additional sites.

### Associations

American Hotel & Motel Association
www.ahma.com

Asian American Hotel Owners Association
www.aahoa.org

Club Managers Association of America
www.cmaa.org

Culinary Institute of America
www.ciachef.edu

Educational Institute of AH&MA
www.ei-ahma.org

Intl. Assoc. of Hospitality Accountants
www.iaha.org

National Restaurant Association
www.restaurant.org

### Casinos

Ballys Casinos
www.ballys.com

Caesars Palace
www.caesars.com

Circus Circus
www.circuscircus.com

Harrahs Casino
www.harrahs.com

Luxor Casino
www.luxor.com

MGM Grand
www.mgmgrand.com

The Mirage
www.mirage.com

Trump's Taj Mahal
www.trumptaj.com

Windsor Casinos
www.windsornights.com

## Hotel Companies/Resorts

Hilton Hotels
www.hilton.com

Ritz-Carlton Hotels
www.ritzcarlton.com

Hyatt Hotels
www.hyatt.com

Trapp Family Lodge
www.trappfamily.com

Mandarin Oriental Hotel Group
www.mandarin-oriental.com

Westin Hotels
www.westin.com

Marriott International
www.marriott.com

## Organizations, Consultants, Resources

Escoffier Online
www.escoffier.com

Noble & Associates
www.virtuopolis.com/noble

Hospitality Net
www.hospitalitynet.nl

World Tourism Organization
www.world-tourism.org

## Restaurant Companies

ARAMARK Corporation
www.aramark.com

Marriott Management Services
www.marriott.com/mms/

Burger King
www.burgerking.com

McDonald's
www.mcdonalds.com

Canteen
www.canteen.com

Pizza Hut
www.pizzahut.com

Chili's Grill & Bar
www.chilis.com

Taco Bell
www.tacobell.com

Domino's Pizza
www.dominos.com

Tavern on the Green
www.tavernonthegreen.com

## Chapter Appendix A

### Key Hotel Management Positions

| Title | Department | Description | Advancement Opportunity |
|---|---|---|---|
| Food and Beverage Controller | Accounting | Controls food and beverage costs through menu planning and pricing/purchasing decisions, storage, issuing. Works closely with management and provides advice through consultation and reporting. | Assistant Controller |
| Assistant Controller | Accounting | Functions as office manager with responsibility for preparation of financial statements. | Controller |
| Controller | Accounting | Acts as financial advisor to management in achieving profit objectives through detailed planning, controlling costs, and effectively managing assets and liabilities of the hotel. | Area/Regional Controller |
| Director of Operations | Administration | Usually the number two manager in a hotel, responsible for the management of the all operating departments, such as food and beverage, housekeeping, etc. | General Manager |
| General Manager | Administration | Supervises all activities within the hotel. Responsible for the coordination of all departments. | Regional and Corporate Positions |
| Director of Engineering | Engineering | Responsible for the maintenance of the physical and mechanical plant. | Regional Team |
| Steward | Food and Beverage | Purchases and supervises the receipt and storage of food/beverage for the hotel. | Restaurant Manager |
| Director of Food and Beverage | Food and Beverage | Oversees entire food and beverage department. | General Manager |
| Catering Manager | Food and Beverage | Sells banquets and supervises banquet services. | Director of Food and Beverage |
| Convention Services | Food and Beverage | Acts as liaison between meeting planners and the hotel. Responsible for execution of major functions. | Catering, Manager/Director of Food and Beverage |

| Title | Department | Description | Advancement Opportunity |
|---|---|---|---|
| Front Office Manager | Front Office | Acts as a liaison between the guest and the hotel for reservation, registration, and information. | Cross-training in other divisions—Director of Operations |
| Reservations Manager | Front Office or Marketing | Oversees reservations functions, plans for reservations and yield management. | Front Office, Manager/Director of Marketing |
| Housekeeping Manager | Housekeeping | Supervises the work of room attendants and housepersons in assigned areas. | Director of Housekeeping |
| Director of Housekeeping | Housekeeping | Supervises all housekeeping personnel. In charge of all renovation and purchases of housekeeping supplies. | Cross-training in other divisions—Director of Operations |
| Director of Marketing | Marketing | Oversees all marketing and sales functions, develops marketing and sales plans. | Cross-training in other divisions—Director of Operations |
| Director of Sales | Sales | Sells convention facilities for meetings, banquets, and receptions. Sells room to volume purchasers, such as corporate travel directors of large companies. | Director of Marketing |

From *A Guide to College Programs in Hospitality and Tourism,* 3d edition (New York: Wiley, 1993). Reprinted by permission of John Wiley & Sons, Inc.

# Chapter Appendix B

## Key Food Service Management Positions

| Title | Department | Description | Advancement Opportunity |
|---|---|---|---|
| Beverage Manager | Beverages | Orders for and stocks bar, maintains inventories of liquor and glassware, supervise bartending personnel. | Food Production Manager |
| Dining Room Manager | Dining Room | Supervises all dining room staff and activities, including staff training, scheduling, time records, and assigning work stations. | Assistant Manager |
| Pantry Supervisor | Pantry | Supervises salad, sandwich, and beverage assistants. May also supervise cleaning crews and requisition cleaning supplies. | Food Production Manager |
| Cook or Sous Chef | Kitchen | Prepares and portions out all food served. In large restaurants often responsible for specific items such as soups, sauces, or meats. | Executive Chef |
| Pastry Chef or Baker | Kitchen | Bakes cakes, cookies, pies, and desserts, as well as bread, rolls, and quick breads. | Executive Chef |
| Executive Chef | Kitchen | Responsible for all quantity and quality food preparation, supervision of sous chefs and cooks, and menu-recipe development. | Assistant Manager |
| Food Production Manager | Kitchen | Responsible for all food preparation and supervision of kitchen support staff and baker, upholding sanitation standards and cost control. | Assistant Manager |
| Purchasing Agent | Management | Orders, receives, inspects, and stores all goods shipped by suppliers. Oversees distribution to different food preparation departments. Often assists executive chef or assistant manager. | Assistant Manager |

| Title | Department | Description | Advancement Opportunity |
|---|---|---|---|
| Assistant Manager | Management | Performs specified supervisory duties under the manager's direction. | Food Service Manager |
| Food Service Manager | Management | Responsible for profitability, efficiency, quality, and courtesy of the entire food service operation. | Multiunit Regional Manager |
| Personnel Director | Management | Responsible for hiring and training of food service personnel, administration of employee relations, benefits, safety, and communications. | Regional Personnel Manager |
| Merchandising Supervisor (Local) | Management | Plans and carries out advertising and promotional programs to increase sales. May also handle public relations activities. | Regional Merchandising Manager |

From *A Guide to College Programs in Hospitality and Tourism,* 3d edition (New York: Wiley, 1993). Reprinted by permission of John Wiley & Sons, Inc.

# Chapter Appendix C

## Sample Résumé

Chris Jones
911 Maple Avenue
Anytown, USA
(555) 555-1234

Objective: Managerial position in a chain restaurant

## Summary of Qualifications

- Two years experience as successful restaurant entrepreneur
- Innovative problem-solver
- Skilled at customer relations
- Knowledge of computerized point-of-sale equipment

## Relevant Skills and Experience

**Restaurant Management**
Established own take-out pizza restaurant
Achieved sales of $300,000 in first year
Created unique recipes to attract customers
Designed purchasing and cost control procedures
Implemented successful marketing and advertising program

**Customer Relations**
Trained staff to take telephone orders accurately, prepare and deliver pizzas within specified time limits
Called previous customers to encourage repeat business
Effectively resolved complaints and built goodwill
Actively participated in community affairs such as Anytown Runner's Club

## Employment History

| | | |
|---|---|---|
| 1996-1998 | **Partner** | Kiko's Pizza, Anytown, USA |
| 1995-1997 | **Assist. Manager** | Pizza Hut, Anytown, USA |

## Education

State University, School of Hospitality Management B.S., 1998

## REVIEW QUIZ

When you feel you have covered all of the material in this chapter, answer these questions. Choose the *best* answer.

1. The restaurant industry employs more than _____ million people in the United States.

    a. 9
    b. 18
    c. 27
    d. 45

2. Who is the chief operating officer of a hotel?

    a. controller
    b. chief engineer
    c. systems manager
    d. general manager

3. One of the advantages of working in an independent hotel is that you:

    a. receive better training.
    b. have more control over career choices.
    c. have more opportunities for advancement.
    d. are more likely to be transferred.

4. Which of the following statements about chain restaurants is *false*?

    a. Casual chain restaurants such as T.G.I. Friday's and Chili's Grill & Bar typically offer few opportunities for advancement.
    b. Chain restaurants are the fastest growing part of the restaurant business.
    c. Managers of fast-food operations are generally paid well and enjoy other benefits, such as stock options, profit sharing, and opportunities to own their own units.
    d. Menus rarely change in chain restaurants.

5. Which of the following food service operations would probably require the least start-up capital?

    a. quick-service restaurant franchise
    b. social catering business
    c. independent full-service restaurant
    d. casual restaurant franchise

6. Which of the following types of information does *not* belong on a résumé?

    a. Your address and telephone number.
    b. Your educational background.
    c. Your age, height, and weight.
    d. Your qualifications and past job experiences.

## REVIEW QUIZ *(continued)*

7. Which of the following is good advice for handling a job interview?

   a. Never say anything bad about a former employer.
   b. Always ask the interviewer questions about the company.
   c. Always write a thank-you letter after the interview.
   d. All of the above.

**Answer Key:** 1-a-C1, 2-d-C2, 3-b-C2, 4-a-C3, 5-b-C3, 6-c-C4, 7-d-C4

Each question is linked to a competency. Competencies are listed on the first page of the chapter. An answer reading 3-b-C4 translates to:

   3: the question number
   b: the correct answer
   C4: the competency number

## Chapter 4 Outline

Restaurant Industry Segments
    Eating and Drinking Places
    Lodging Operations
    Transportation Market
    Recreational Market
    Business and Industry Market
    Student Market
    Health Care Market
    Retail Market
    Corrections Food Service
    Military Food Service
    Contractors
Starting a New Restaurant
    Why Do Restaurants Fail?
    The Cost of Starting a New Restaurant
    Building a Successful Restaurant
Chapter Summary

## Competencies

1. Describe in general terms the size of the restaurant industry and cite other industry characteristics and statistics, such as the most popular days for eating out, industry employment patterns, and so on; list restaurant industry segments; and describe eating and drinking places.

2. Describe lodging operations; the transportation, recreational, business and industry, student, health care, and retail markets; corrections and military food service; and contractors.

3. Summarize some of the pitfalls of starting a new restaurant, cite reasons restaurants may fail, and outline some of the issues involved in starting a new restaurant, such as working out costs, developing a concept, selecting a site, and having a feasibility study done.

# 4

# Understanding the Restaurant Industry

THIS CHAPTER DESCRIBES the diversity and complexity of the various segments of the restaurant business. We will take a look at eating and drinking establishments; hotel food and beverage operations; food service for airlines, trains, and cruise lines; the recreational market, business and industry, student, health care, retail, corrections, and military markets; and contract food management companies. The chapter also covers starting a new restaurant.

The restaurant industry runs the gamut from gourmet restaurants to hot dog stands. The National Restaurant Association (NRA) projects 1997 food service sales at $320 billion. The industry employs over nine million people in 787,000 establishments and is expected to employ 11 million workers by the year 2005.[1]

Restaurant industry sales equal more than four percent of the U.S. gross domestic product. The percentage of the food dollar spent away from home rose from 42.5 percent in 1990 to 43 percent in 1997. Almost 50 billion meals are eaten in restaurants, schools, and work cafeterias each year. The most popular ethnic cuisines are Italian, Chinese, and Mexican.

In the United States, the most popular day for eating out is Saturday, followed by Friday and Sunday; the least popular day is Monday. NRA statistics show that in Miami, Florida, more dollars are spent per capita on food outside the home than in any other U.S. city. Washington, D.C., ranks second; New York City, third. The typical person consumes an average of 4.1 meals per week outside the home.

The restaurant industry is truly an equal opportunity employer. It employs more minority managers than any other retail industry. Nearly seven out of ten supervisors in food preparation and service occupations are women; 10 percent are African American; and nine percent are Hispanic. Someone entering the food service field might work for a small, independent operator who runs a fine-dining restaurant, pizza parlor, or ice cream stand. Working at an independent operation is good training for future entrepreneurs. Another career track might begin in the management training program of a large corporation like Metromedia, which operates the full-service restaurants Steak & Ale and Bennigan's. There are many opportunities in the fast-food field with McDonald's, KFC, Wendy's, and other companies. The Walt Disney Corporation runs a huge number of diverse food operations and actively recruits hospitality graduates to manage its theme park restaurants and snack bars. Airline meals are supplied by in-flight catering operators such as Dobbs International Services. Many big banks, insurance companies, and advertising agencies have executive dining rooms run by professional food service

**Working at an independent pizzeria can be good training for future entrepreneurs.**
(Courtesy of Bakers Pride Oven Co., Inc., New Rochelle, New York)

managers. Contract food companies such as ARAMARK, Marriott International, and others place future managers in executive or employee dining facilities; schools, colleges, and universities; at tourist attractions such as Ellis Island in New York Harbor; and at fine dining restaurants such as the Carnelian Room in San Francisco's Bank of America building. As you can see, there are many career choices in the restaurant industry.

## Restaurant Industry Segments

The restaurant industry includes many different types of facilities and markets. For reporting and other purposes, the industry can be divided into the following segments:

- Eating and drinking places
- Lodging operations
- Transportation market
- Recreational market
- Business and industry market

- Student market
- Health care market
- Retail market
- Corrections food service
- Military food service
- Contractors

## Eating and Drinking Places

Eating and drinking places constitute the largest segment of the restaurant industry, accounting for 70 percent of total industry sales. This segment includes full-service restaurants, limited-service restaurants, commercial cafeterias, social caterers, ice cream and frozen custard stands, and bars and taverns. Over 90 percent of this segment's sales are made by full-service and limited-service restaurants, which offer the most opportunities for hospitality students. For this reason, most of this section deals with these industry segments.

**Full-Service Restaurants.** There is a wide variety of **full-service restaurants.** According to Mike Hurst, a past president of the National Restaurant Association, full-service restaurants are restaurants that:

- Feature a dozen or more main-course items on the menu, and
- Cook to order.

Full-service restaurants are generally categorized in terms of price, menu, or atmosphere. They can be casual or formal. These categories are not mutually exclusive, however. Many full-service restaurants—as well as other restaurant operations—can fit into more than one of these categories.

*Price.* Restaurants can be categorized as luxury, high-priced, mid-priced, or low-priced establishments. An example of a luxury restaurant is La Côte Basque in New York City, where dinner for two—appetizer, entrée, dessert, coffee, and accompanying bottle of wine—would cost $100 per person. Luxury restaurants are generally small and independently operated. They feature well-trained, creative chefs and employ skilled dining room servers headed by a maître d' hôtel and a cadre of captains. Some luxury restaurants offer table-side cooking. To provide the necessary—and expected—high level of service, luxury restaurants employ more kitchen and dining room employees per guest than do other types of restaurants.

Some luxury restaurants are tourist attractions famous the world over, such as the Eiffel Tower Restaurant in Paris. Others, such as Le Cirque in Manhattan and Masa in San Francisco, cater to "regulars"—members of the jet set, movie stars, corporate executives, and others who lead the lifestyle of the rich and famous. Typically, such establishments are owned or co-owned by a chef who supervises the cooking in the kitchen. While fine dining restaurants have historically featured French cuisine, this is no longer the case. Today's top restaurants often feature regional specialties and fusion cuisine, which blends ingredients and flavors from all over the globe. The industry is led today by innovative young chefs, many of

### Exhibit 1  Top 20 Independent Full-Service Restaurants

| | Restaurant | City | Year Opened | 1996 Sales ($ millions) |
|---|---|---|---|---|
| 1. | The Rainbow Room | New York, NY | 1934 | $32.135# |
| 2. | Tavern on the Green | New York, NY | 1976 | 31.700 |
| 3. | Smith & Wollensky | New York, NY | 1977 | 22.287 |
| 4. | Bob Chinn's Crabhouse | Wheeling, IL | 1982 | 21.014 |
| 5. | Sparks Steakhouse | New York, NY | 1964 | 20.400** |
| 6. | Official All Star Café | New York, NY | 1995 | 19.500** |
| 7. | Joe's Stone Crab | Miami Beach, FL | 1913 | 17.620 |
| 8. | The Manor | West Orange, NJ | 1957 | 14.100 |
| 9. | Scoma's Restaurant | San Francisco, CA | 1965 | 13.605 |
| 10. | Four Seasons | New York, NY | 1959 | 13.600 |
| 11. | The "21" Club | New York, NY | 1923 | 13.518 |
| 12. | Gladstone's 4 Fish | Pacific Palisades, CA | 1976 | 12.741 |
| 13. | Spago Las Vegas | Las Vegas, NV | 1992 | 12.500** |
| 14. | Trattoria Dell' Arte | New York, NY | 1988 | 12.400** |
| 15. | Gibsons | Chicago, IL | 1989 | 11.800 |
| 16. | Del Frisco's Double Eagle Steak House | Dallas, TX | 1985 | 11.600 |
| 17. | Montgomery Inn at the Boathouse | Cincinnati, OH | 1989 | 11.394 |
| 18. | The Lobster House | Cape May, NJ | 1940 | 11.055 |
| 19. | Anthony's Pier 4 | Boston, MA | 1963 | 11.000* |
| 20. | Brennan's | New Orleans, LA | 1946 | 11.000** |

*Restaurant estimate; **R&I estimate; (#) includes entertainment charge

Source: "Top 100 Independents," *Restaurants & Institutions*, April 1, 1997.

whom have been trained in the United States at places like the Culinary Institute of America in Hyde Park, New York.

High-priced restaurants are also usually independently owned and operated, but most have larger seating capacities than luxury restaurants. Menus are extensive, and service can range from formal at New York's Rainbow Room to casual at Joe's Stone Crab in Miami Beach. Every year, *Restaurants & Institutions* ranks the top 100 independent full-service restaurants in America in order of total sales. The Top 20 list for 1997 appears in Exhibit 1.

Menu often defines a restaurant. Steak houses and seafood restaurants are examples of full-service restaurants defined in terms of menu. For example, Outback

**A restaurant with a strong architectural and decorating theme may be visited by many who simply enjoy its atmosphere.** (Courtesy of Rainforest Café, A Wild Place to Shop and Eat®)

Steakhouse specializes in beef; Red Lobster features shrimp, crab, and lobster. **Ethnic restaurants** feature a specific cuisine as their distinctive theme. Brinker International Corporation's Macaroni Grill features Italian food, for example. Other ethnic restaurants serve Chinese, Greek, Japanese, Polynesian, Scandinavian, Korean, or Indian food, to name a few.

Atmosphere can characterize a restaurant's identity. Some restaurants are known primarily for their atmosphere, which can be uniquely identified by architecture, decor, or setting. Show business and sports motifs—currently very fashionable in the industry—provide themes for a growing number of popular restaurants. The Hard Rock Cafe chain, which started in London and now has restaurants in major cities around the world, features Elvis Presley, The Beatles, and other rock star music memorabilia. Planet Hollywood, owned in part by a group of movie stars including Sylvester Stallone and Bruce Willis, uses movie costumes, props, and settings for its decor. Robert Earl, Planet Hollywood's creative developer, launched the first Official All Star Café in Manhattan. Hockey great Wayne Gretzky, tennis star Andre Agassi, and football celebrity Joe Montana are the star investors/spokespersons for this venture.

Old-fashioned, stainless-steel-and-Formica diners—currently enjoying a revival—rely primarily on atmosphere for their appeal. After almost disappearing from the American scene, diners have made a comeback, largely inspired by American architect Richard Gutman, renowned as "The Diner Man." As a result of

**90** *Chapter 4*

Haussner's Restaurant in Baltimore, Maryland, uses a fine-art theme to create a unique atmosphere that keeps guests coming back. (Courtesy of Haussner's Restaurant, Inc.)

Gutman's efforts, other enterprising restaurateurs have opened "old-style" diners. One thriving chain of diners, Chicago-based Ed Debevic's, has a licensed diner in Japan. Debevic's diners—dedicated to traditional diner fare—serve breakfast all

**Exhibit 2  Top 20 Casual Dinner Houses**

| Restaurant | Sales (millions) | Restaurant | Sales (millions) |
| --- | --- | --- | --- |
| 1. Applebee's | $ 1,540.0 | 12. The Black-Eyed Pea | $ 189.6 |
| 2. T.G.I. Friday's | 1,145.2 | 13. Houston's | 177.8 |
| 3. Chili's Grill & Bar | 1,104.0 | 14. O'Charley's | 163.8 |
| 4. Ruby Tuesday | 546.0** | 15. Chart House | 160.6 |
| 5. Bennigan's | 448.0** | 16. Cheesecake Factory | 139.7 |
| 6. Hooters | 325.0 | 17. The Cooker | 110.3 |
| 7. Red Robin | 293.6 | 18. Champe Americana | 103.0* |
| 8. The Ground Round | 285.9 | 19. Grady's American Grill | 100.0 |
| 9. Houlihan's | 251.6 | 20. Claim Jumper | 93.0 |
| 10. Planet Hollywood | 222.5** | *Restaurant estimate; **R&I estimate | |
| 11. Hard Rock Cafe | 216.0** | | |

Source: "Top 400: Dinner Houses," *Restaurants & Institutions*, July 15, 1997, p. 115.

day and feature perennial favorites like meat loaf. Even the food servers are a throwback to the 1950s—they chew bubble gum and pop bubbles in guests' faces!

One of the most famous independent restaurants in America that utilizes atmosphere as a selling point is Haussner's in Baltimore. This 80-year-old restaurant, listed in almost every Baltimore restaurant guide, offers "Masterpieces in Art and Dining." It's the art that draws the crowds. The Haussner family has been collecting original oil paintings since opening their doors. They now have over 700 paintings, 70 percent of which adorn every square foot of the restaurant's walls. Dining at Haussner's is like eating in the main gallery of a fine art museum. The menu lists 75 different entrées as well as specials. It features something for just about everyone, from roast beef and fresh seafood to exotic dishes such as baked rabbit and frogs' legs. Haussner's German specialties include sauerbraten, fresh pig knuckles, and Wiener schnitzel a la Holstein. There's more—every entrée is served with two vegetables, chosen from a list of 35 options. To top it off, Haussner's dessert menu features fresh strawberry pie and 35 other desserts!

**Casual dining houses,** for example, are distinguishable by their combination of decor, informal atmosphere, and eclectic menus that draw from ethnic and traditional offerings. Many consider Steak & Ale and Bennigan's founder Norman Brinker the "father" of this restaurant class. He also founded Chili's, the Macaroni Grill, and others. Almost all casual restaurants are chain-affiliated. Applebee's, T.G.I. Friday's, Red Lobster, and the Outback Steakhouse are all casual dinner houses, one of the largest segments within the full-service category (see Exhibit 2). Applebee's and Chili's are two of the largest chains in this segment. Part of Applebee's success is the attention the chain devotes to the location of each restaurant.

**Exhibit 3    Top 20 Family Dining Restaurants**

| Restaurant | Sales (millions) | Restaurant | Sales (millions) |
|---|---|---|---|
| 1. Denny's | $ 1,933.0 | 12. Steak 'n Shake | $ 283.0** |
| 2. Shoney's | 1,209.8 | 13. Marie Callender's | 263.5 |
| 3. Boston Market | 1,160.0 | 14. Village Inn | 251.7 |
| 4. Big Boy | 970.0** | 15. Country Kitchen | 235.0 |
| 5. IHOP | 796.6 | 16. Carrows | 217.3 |
| 6. Cracker Barrel | 734.2* | 17. Bakers Square | 204.7 |
| 7. Coco's | 710.5 | 18. Eat'n Park | 150.0 |
| 8. Perkins | 677.9 | 19. Lyon's | 130.0* |
| 9. Friendly's | 650.8 | 20. Huddle House | 118.1 |
| 10. Bob Evans | 594.9 | *Restaurant estimate; **R&I estimate | |
| 11. Waffle House | 585.0** | | |

Source: "Top 400: Family Dining," *Restaurants & Institutions*, July 15, 1997, p. 113.

Although there is uniformity in the chain's concept, 40 percent of Applebee's menu items are blocked and tailored to regional food preferences.

**Family restaurants**—another mainstay in the full-service restaurant category—cater to families, with an emphasis on satisfying the needs of children. Family restaurants (see Exhibit 3) serve breakfast, lunch, and dinner, offering traditional menu items. Their pricing falls between casual dinner houses and quick-service restaurants A major source of revenue for some family restaurants—such as Cracker Barrel—is a gift shop.

**Limited-Service Restaurants.** The distinguishing feature of **limited-service restaurants** is that they offer a narrow selection of food, provide limited service, and focus on speed of preparation and delivery.

**Fast-food restaurants** focus on convenience. McDonald's, Wendy's, and Taco Bell fall into this category. Because convenience is such an important element of a fast-food restaurant's appeal, many stay open from early morning until very late at night.

Exhibit 4 lists the 20 leading restaurant chains in 1997. Note that the vast majority are limited-service restaurants. The largest group of limited-service restaurants by far specialize in hamburgers, and the leader of the pack is McDonald's. McDonald's had more than 18,000 units in 91 countries by 1996, with more new units under construction internationally than inside the continental United States. The largest McDonald's in the world is in Vinita, Oklahoma. The busiest, on Pushkin Square in Moscow, serves 40,000 customers per day.

McDonald's is a leader in innovative marketing approaches for new market segments such as the business-lunch segment. In Manhattan, for example, an electronic ticker tape was installed in a McDonald's located three-and-a-half blocks

**Exhibit 4    Top 20 Fast-Food Restaurants**

| 1996 Rank | Restaurant | Segment |
|---|---|---|
| 1 | McDonald's, Oak Brook, IL | QS burgers |
| 2 | Burger King, Miami, FL | QS burgers |
| 3 | Pizza Hut, Dallas, TX | FS pizza |
| 4 | KFC, Louisville, KY | QS chicken |
| 5 | Taco Bell, Irvine, CA | QS Mexican |
| 6 | Wendy's, Dublin, OH | QS burgers |
| 7 | Hardee's, Rocky Mount, NC | QS burgers |
| 8 | 7-Eleven, Dallas, TX | C-stores |
| 9 | Subway Sandwiches & Salads, Milford, CT | QS sandwiches |
| 10 | Domino's Pizza, Ann Arbor, MI | QS pizza |
| 11 | Dairy Queen, Minneapolis, MN | QS sweets/snacks |
| 12 | Little Caesars, Detroit, MI | QS pizza |
| 13 | Arby's, Fort Lauderdale, FL | QS sandwiches |
| 14 | Red Lobster, Orlando, FL | FS seafood |
| 15 | Dunkin' Donuts, Randolph, MA | QS sweets/snacks |
| 16 | ITT Sheraton, Boston, MA | Lodging |
| 17 | Denny's, Spartanburg, SC | Family dining |
| 18 | Holiday Inn Worldwide, Atlanta, GA | Lodging |
| 19 | Hilton Hotels, Beverly Hills, CA | Lodging |
| 20 | Shoney's, Nashville, TN | Family dining |

QS–Quick Service
FS–Full Service

Source: "Top 400 Restaurant Concepts," *Restaurants & Institutions*, July 1, 1996, p. 59.

from Wall Street. The restaurant also has a host and a fax machine that accepts orders for delivery to nearby offices. The McDonald's in the upscale Galleria Mall in Houston, Texas, also has an electronic ticker tape and fax machines as well as telephone jacks at some tables and business publications available for patrons.

Major growth in limited-service restaurants continues to come from hamburger chains as well as chicken, sandwich, and Mexican food chains. Much of the growth is outside the United States (see Exhibit 5). The type or number of menu items alone do not determine the winners. A commitment to good service and providing nutritional menu choices has taken center stage. McDonald's now guarantees "hot food; fast, friendly service; and double-check drive-thru accuracy"—or the next meal is on them. A survey of 27 restaurant chains (including 19 fast-food chains) with 50,000 outlets found that at least three-quarters of them offered menu

**Exhibit 5** Restaurant Units outside the United States

### Selected Chains

| Chain | As of | Total | Canada | Europe | Asia | Latin America | Middle East |
|---|---|---|---|---|---|---|---|
| McDonald's | 3/96 | 7,037 | 763 | 2,671 | 2,780 | 717 | 106 |
| KFC | 12/95 | 4,492 | 883 | 455 | 2,288 | 418 | 448 |
| Pizza Hut | 12/95 | 3,332 | 503 | 1,103 | 1,016 | 512 | 198 |
| Burger King | 3/96 | 1,627 | 223 | 760 | 305 | 288 | 51 |
| Baskin-Robbins | 3/96 | 1,525 | 227 | 268 | 779 | 99 | 152 |
| Subway | 5/96 | 1,439 | 1,075 | 28 | 231 | 83 | 22 |
| Dunkin' Donuts | 4/96 | 1,163 | 244 | 54 | 658 | 202 | 5 |
| Domino's | 5/96 | 1,049 | 184 | 192 | 386 | 232 | 55 |
| Wendy's | 5/96 | 506 | 222 | 32 | 176 | 58 | 18 |
| Churches* | 5/96 | 270 | 105 | 0 | 100 | 65 | 0 |
| Taco Bell | 12/95 | 179 | 112 | 5 | 6 | 47 | 9 |
| Arby's | 2/96 | 162 | 112 | 2 | 10 | 34 | 4 |
| Popeye's | 5/96 | 83 | 4 | 9 | 56 | 8 | 6 |
| Hardee's | 5/96 | 73 | 0 | 0 | 39 | 1 | 33 |
| Sbarro | 5/96 | 59 | 8 | 17 | 4 | 15 | 15 |
| T.G.I. Friday's | 5/96 | 59 | 1 | 26 | 23 | 9 | 0 |

Source: Individual companies. For table purposes, Asia includes Australia, New Zealand, and the South Pacific; Latin America includes the Caribbean, Central America, and South America; Middle East includes Africa. *Operates as Texas Chicken outside the United States and Canada.

Source: *Restaurants & Institutions*, July 1, 1996, p. 92.

choices for health-conscious consumers. Examples included low-fat milk, skinless chicken, and reduced or low-calorie salad dressing. Nine out of ten said they used vegetable fats instead of animal fats for frying.[2]

**Home-meal replacement restaurants** have emerged in recent years. Boston Market—a good example—offers a menu based on roasted chicken, turkey, ham, chicken pot pies, and meat loaf. A plethora of homestyle side dishes are available—soups and salads, mashed potatoes and gravy, string beans, corn, stuffing, creamed spinach, butternut squash—as well as cornbread and desserts. These items are sold separately or as complete meals to be eaten at the restaurant or taken out. Note that this menu is different and more diverse then regular take-out food like fried chicken, hamburgers, and pizza. This market has developed in response to the increase in two-earner and single parent families that are short on time for preparing meals at home. This chain, which has been expanding rapidly since 1993, boasted 1,100 outlets and $1.2 billion in gross revenues by 1997.

### Exhibit 6　Top Eight Hotel Chains in Food Sales per Hotel

| 1995 Rank | Chain | Food Service Sales Per Hotel (By Fiscal Year, in Thousands) |
|---|---|---|
| 1 | Westin International | $6,250 |
| 2 | Hyatt Hotels | 4,100 |
| 3 | Hilton Hotels | 4,000 |
| 4 | Sheraton Hotels | 3,600 |
| 5 | Marriott Hotels & Resorts | 3,500 |
| 6 | Radisson Hotels | 2,200 |
| 7 | Ramada Inn | 630 |
| 8 | Holiday Inn | 380 |

Source: *Nation's Restaurant News*, April 29, 1996, p. 52–53.

Hospitality-school graduates tend to look at careers in limited-service restaurants last, preferring to work for major **fine-dining restaurants.** But fast-food companies offer graduates a chance to assume positions of great responsibility quickly, and the pay is very good due to their liberal bonus and incentive plans.

## Lodging Operations

Food service outlets in lodging operations range from gourmet restaurants to coffee shops and even fast-food outlets. Lodging food service sales are tremendous. In 1995, Marriott Hotels and Resorts alone had food sales of $1.28 billion. Food sales for the top eight hotel chains totaled $5.3 billion.[3] Exhibit 6 breaks this total into food sales per hotel.

In recent years, hotels and motels have marketed their food service outlets more aggressively. According to Atef Mankarios, president of Rosewood Hotels & Resorts, Inc., "Not so long ago, many hotels viewed the hotel restaurant as a necessary evil. This approach resulted in a half-hearted effort with boring and predictable food served with neither flair nor care."[4] Mankarios's Rosewood Hotel Group, which operates the Mansion on Turtle Creek in Dallas as well as other hotels in Hawaii and California, goes out of its way to hire chefs who are recognized as leaders within the industry. Menus are distinctive and feature products indigenous to the hotel's particular region. "A restaurant is not just a service that a hotel must provide," says Mankarios. "It can be a powerful marketing tool. A first-class restaurant helps build a national reputation for a hotel, while at the same time helping to build close ties with the local community by attracting its residents."[5]

## Transportation Market

Travelers eat at highway stops; on airplanes, ships, and trains; at airport terminals and train stations; and at other facilities in the transportation market—a market that will reach $3.7 billion in sales in 1997, according to *Restaurants & Institutions* magazine.[6] United Airlines maintains its own in-flight kitchens. Other airlines buy their meals from Caterair, Ogden Food Service, Sky Chef, or Dobbs International Services. Many airlines today are trying to differentiate themselves by serving more distinctive food in business and first-class sections, using fresh food instead of frozen items when possible. Even the selection of wines available on board has been greatly upgraded in some instances. The trend toward more nutritious meals has become an integral part of many airline food programs. For example, Delta passengers are served oat bran muffins and whole-grain bread. American Airline's Chairman Robert Crandall says, "Our customers now want food that is low in both fat and cholesterol. Chicken, fish, pasta, and fresh vegetables are very much in."[7]

Cruise lines put a great deal of emphasis on their food service. Industry surveys cite the food served shipboard as one of the top reasons for taking a cruise and selecting a specific line. Royal Caribbean International points out that its 72,000-ton *Sovereign of the Seas* was the first cruise ship to receive the Best of the Best Five-Star Diamond Award from the American Academy of Restaurant Sciences for quality, consistency, service, and overall dining experience. Besides an executive chef, the ship carries 95 cooks, 45 cleaners, 12 snack stewards, 200 food servers and buspersons, 12 wine stewards, 37 cocktail servers, and 30 bartenders.

Food service in airports and train terminals is often provided by restaurants—frequently limited-menu restaurants—and contract food companies such as ARAMARK that bid for the opportunity to sell food in the terminals.

## Recreational Market

The recreational market includes food service facilities located at sports arenas, stadiums, race tracks, movie theaters, bowling alleys, amusement parks, municipal convention centers, and other attractions. All together, this amounts to a $9.4 billion market.[8] In many cases, recreational market food service facilities are concessions run by contract food companies. The largest contract food companies in the recreational market include Fine Host, Sportservice, Volume Services, Ogden Corp., and ARAMARK.

The food served at recreational facilities varies greatly. For example, amusement parks tend to sell novelty foods such as elephant ears and cotton candy. Large municipal convention centers may have a variety of food service outlets, ranging from snack bars to full-service restaurants and even private clubs. For example, the Spectrum Sports Arena in Philadelphia has 20 permanent and 10 portable food outlets. It also houses Ovations, a 250-seat members-only upscale restaurant that grosses approximately $2 million a year.[9]

One of the most important companies in the recreational market is Volume Services. It operates concessions for the New York Yankees and the Oakland Athletics as well as other teams. It also operates concessions in national parks such as the Grand Canyon and Everglades National Park.

## Business and Industry Market

The business and industry market was projected to be a $19.95 billion market by 1997.[10] It consists of non-food service businesses that offer onsite food service to

## Exhibit 7  Leading Self-Operated Business and Industry Dining Services

| Company | 1995 F&B purch. ($MM) | Units | Transactions per day | Chain brands |
|---|---|---|---|---|
| **Motorola** Schaumburg, IL | 18.0 | 45 | 45,000 | N |
| **Aetna Life & Casualty** Hartford, CT | 11.0 | 9 | 33,000 | N |
| **Ford Motor Co.** Dearborn, MI | 6.0 | 30[A] | 30,000 | Y |
| **J.P. Morgan & Co.** New York, NY | 5.0 | 4 | 5,500 | N |
| **Procter & Gamble Co.** Cincinnati, OH | 3.5 | 9 | 6,630 | N |
| **3M** St. Paul, MN | 3.1 | 17 | 5,560 | N |
| **Electronic Data Systems Corp.** Plano, TX | 2.6 | 12 | 9,500 | N |
| **Pharmacia & Upjohn** Cincinnati, OH[B] | 1.9 | 13 | 10,000 | N |
| **Pitney Bowes** Stamford, CT | 1.5 | 4 | 3,500 | N |
| **Hallmark Cards** Kansas City, MO | 1.4 | 4 | 4,550[C] | N |

Source: Individual companies, R&H research. (A) 15 main cafeterias with 15 mini food outlets. (B) U.S. operations only. (C) Kansas City and Liberty locations.

Source: *Restaurant & Institutions,* August 1, 1996, p. 80.

their employees. Most businesses that provide employee meals use contract food companies such as Marriott and ARAMARK.

Contract food companies face increasing competition from fast-food and limited-menu restaurants and are responding by entering into agreements with some of these companies to operate franchises.

A number of businesses operate their own employee food programs (see Exhibit 7). Some include very luxurious dining facilities for executives and their clients. Sony Corporation's executive dining facilities cover most of the 35th floor of its New York headquarters and are quite elaborate, according to *The Wall Street Journal:*

Exhibit 8   Top College Contract Food Companies

| Rank | Contractor | # of University Accounts |
|---|---|---|
| 1 | Marriott Management Services | 472 |
| 2 | ARAMARK | 300 |
| 3 | Gardner Merchant Food Services | 150 |
| 4 | Morrison's Hospitality Group | 139 |
| 5 | Seiler's/FDI | 110 |
| 6 | Canteen | 77 |
| 7 | The Wood Co. | 34 |

Source: Adapted from *Restaurant & Institutions,* August 15, 1993, p. 70.

> The main dining room, done in black terrazzo and stainless steel, seats 65 in contemporary elegance, with a reception lounge, a maître d', 12 waiters, and six chefs. Off to one side is the grill room, a casual dining area, with a brick pizza oven. There are four smaller, wood-paneled private dining rooms. And a piano bar.[11]

In the same story, the *Journal* noted that the quality of Eastman Kodak Company's 15 executive and special dining areas helped the company win the "Silver Plate" award, which is considered the "Oscar" of the food service industry.

## Student Market

One of the biggest changes in college food service programs has been the gradual shifting away from mandated meal plans to à la carte operations. Accordingly, college food service operators have been revenue producers instead of revenue consumers. Because more nontraditional students are going to college, dining directors have had to accommodate preferences that are somewhat different from those of the typical 18-year-old.

The Marriott Corporation, which operates hundreds of college food programs, has developed the "Grand Marketplace," a collection of small food boutiques including La Cuisine, which serves steak and lobster, and Greenstuffs, a salad and health food section. ARAMARK's School Nutrition and Dining Services division has also introduced some new concepts to capture the changing student market. These include Deli Corner, Itza Pizza, and Gretel's Bake Shop. At Ohio State, McDonald's runs the food service concession in the student union.

Contract food companies (see Exhibit 8) controlled 42.2 percent of the $7.6 billion college and university food service programs in America in 1992, according to the National Restaurant Association.[12] A contract food company typically guarantees a college or university six to 10 percent of sales in return for a five- to ten-year operating contract.

Many universities still believe they can outdo contract food companies. Some universities that have used contractors in the past, such as Notre Dame and the University of Pennsylvania, are now once again running their own programs. The University of Pennsylvania's program is extensive. It consists of three residence dining halls, the Faculty and Alumni Club, the Penn Tower Hotel, and a full banquet and catering division. The university also does a brisk take-out business with off-campus as well as resident students. "Within four years of self-operation, we went into the black and have been there ever since," says Bill Canney, Penn's dining services director.[13]

## Health Care Market

The health care market consists of three principal segments: hospitals, nursing homes, and retirement communities (including congregate food sites—community-sponsored meal centers for senior citizens). The total 1997 food service sales in this market were projected at $16.7 billion.[14]

Many experts believe that there is enormous development potential for food service management companies in the health care market. This can be attributed to a combination of factors—rapidly changing lifestyles, an aging population, skyrocketing medical costs, restricted federal funds, and a lack of family support systems. Marriott's Management Services Health Care division has more than 1,000 health care accounts, including hospitals, nursing homes, and retirement communities in North America and the United Kingdom. Marriott provides everything from bedside meals for patients to nonpatient food service in hospital cafeterias, some of which feature mall-style food courts with such well-known brands as Pizza Hut, Dunkin' Donuts, and Domino's Pizza. Marriott also provides off-premises catering as permitted by the facility. Some of Marriott's more well-known clients include Johns Hopkins Hospital in Maryland and the Cleveland Clinic in Ohio.

Most health care facilities run their own food service departments. Some of these can be quite extensive. Many hospitals operate vending machines, visitor coffee shops, employee cafeterias, special dining facilities for doctors, day care food programs for employees' children, regular patient food programs, and special patient food programs that can include gourmet meals (with accompanying wines) served in patient rooms. New York Hospital-Cornell Medical Center now includes on its patient menus an item called Bill Blass Meatloaf, created by chefs at Mortimer's, a trendy Eastside establishment. Other menu items include spa cuisine inspired by the Canyon Ranch, a premier U.S. spa hotel located in Tucson, Arizona. The hospital also offers an optional gourmet dining program (at extra cost) that offers fare like Norwegian salmon with yogurt dill sauce.[15] This service uses porcelain dishes and silver flatware.

Hospital food service trends are expected to have a positive impact on the future of this market segment. A few of these trends follow.

- Hospitals are serving more nonpatient meals than ever before. Baptist Hospital in Miami estimates that less than 50 percent of its food is served to patients.

- Hospitals are serving better, more varied food. A sample hospital menu might include an appetizer; freshly grilled filet mignon, lobster, or stuffed shrimp; a dessert; and a beverage served on a tray with fresh flowers—all for $15. Guests can order meals or fruit and gourmet food baskets when visiting patients.

- Many hospitals are adding VIP suites that have carpeting, mini-refrigerators, family sleeping accommodations, and amenity packages that include gourmet meals.
- Off-premises catering is enhancing hospital food service revenues. One franchise company that helps hospitals maximize their kitchen revenue offers a one-week cooking school to teach hospital chefs how to prepare food for catering.
- Hospitals have begun to market their food services off-site.

## Retail Market

Two major trends in food service have surfaced in recent years. The first is the increasing tendency of Americans to eat food prepared outside of the home, as evidenced by the dramatic growth in restaurant food sales. The second trend, which is developing even more rapidly, is the growth in the take-out and delivery segment of the limited-service market. It is clear that Americans are cooking less. It is also clear that there is a growing tendency to buy food prepared outside the home and bring it home to consume it. This last development is in line with marketing trends in other areas such as home electronics and furniture, where research has shown that, at an increasing rate, people use their homes as recreational and entertainment centers.

The major beneficiaries of these trends are home-meal replacement restaurants and retail businesses that sell take-out food—convenience stores and supermarkets, department stores, drug stores, gasoline stations, and specialized retail outlets like gourmet delicatessens. These retail stores have rapidly increased their share of the take-out market, and most industry observers think this trend will continue at an accelerating pace. The food halls found in some department stores, such as Harrod's in London and KaDeWe in Berlin, have traditionally done a large volume of take-out business. Many shoppers visit these stores principally for food purchases. The U.S. retail food service market was expected to reach $5.3 billion in sales in 1997.[16]

A good part of retail business take-out sales are at the expense of traditional restaurants and fast-food outlets. This is due, among other reasons, to increased marketing by convenience stores and supermarkets of their prepared take-out foods. Circle K, for example, spends 85 percent of its marketing dollars on advertising its prepared foods. In some cases, stores have formed alliances rather than compete with each other. For example, in some areas, 7-Eleven stores sell Hardee's hamburgers, and Circle K has a joint agreement to sell Dunkin' Donuts from special display cases that are stocked twice daily with fresh donuts.

Supermarkets are increasing the size and scope of their take-out food operations. Some industry observers expect the average supermarket to increase in size from its present 30,000–50,000 square feet to 200,000 square feet (2,790–4,650 square meters to 18,600 square meters). Much of that space will be devoted to precooked take-out dishes and sit-down food service areas. Many supermarkets already offer take-out salad bars in addition to their traditional deli sections. Using ovens installed in their bakeries, approximately 15 percent of today's supermarkets have small restaurants and cafeterias featuring a complete line of prepared products. Supermarket research shows that supermarket produce is perceived to be fresher than that sold in most restaurants. Some supermarkets are taking advantage of this perception by selling a wide range of freshly prepared salad and vegetable dishes. Some have hired chefs to work in open kitchens so that customers can actually see that dishes are prepared with fresh—not frozen—ingredients.

Another supermarket food service trend is the growth of food courts. Supermarket chains are installing food courts (similar to those found in shopping malls) in hopes of winning back some of the food dollars they have lost to restaurants. According to Nobel & Associates, a food service consulting firm, the percentage of the consumer food dollar spent on groceries to prepare family meals has shrunk to 38 percent.[17]

## Corrections Food Service

Correctional institutions—state and federal prisons and local jails—constitute another segment of the food service industry. Correctional institutions often have a hard time attracting and retaining food service staff because they cannot offer much professional career growth. However, the unique challenge they do offer can be attractive to some people. A prison must offer a **cyclical menu** that is not overly repetitive and has the flexibility to meet special religious and medical dietary needs, while still offering a bit of creativity in both preparation and presentation. Theft is another problem encountered by prison food service systems. Stringent controls must be used. Food costs are a further constraint on operations. Correctional institutions often have limited budgets for food service; economies of scale can thus make a substantial difference in the menus offered to inmates. For this reason, contract food companies are now successfully competing in this area. Their professional expertise and buying power enable them to solve some problems that prison administrators address only occasionally.

ARAMARK operates the food service program at DuPage County Jail in Wheaton, Illinois. The food service director there says, "My job is to keep everyone happy—the client, to keep down chaotic situations, and to get no complaints from inmates. If the meals are fine it keeps riots down."[18] To maintain security, inmates eat in their cells rather than in a cafeteria, so meals are delivered in heated carts. Two security details the food service director must address illustrate the unique challenges that confront prison food service managers: because forks, knives, and bones can be used as or fashioned into weapons, plastic spoons are the only serving utensils allowed, and bones are removed from meat before it is served.

## Military Food Service

Military food service is a very specialized area and it is not within the scope of this chapter. Nevertheless, it deserves mention because of its diversity in terms of geography, type of facility, and size. Military food service sales should reach $4.82 billion in 1997.[19]

Careers in military food service can range from space shuttle food preparation to aircraft carrier or nuclear submarine mess operation to Army, Navy, Air Force,

**Exhibit 9   Contractors and Institutions**

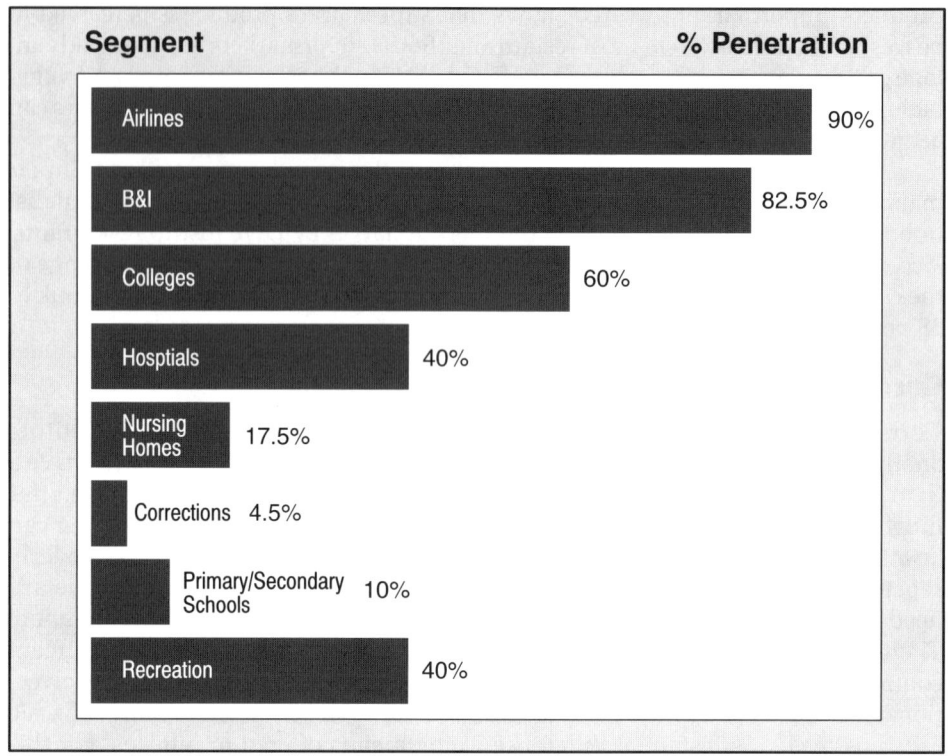

| Segment | % Penetration |
|---|---|
| Airlines | 90% |
| B&I | 82.5% |
| Colleges | 60% |
| Hosptials | 40% |
| Nursing Homes | 17.5% |
| Corrections | 4.5% |
| Primary/Secondary Schools | 10% |
| Recreation | 40% |

Contractors' share of market in all noncommercial segments has been growing steadily since the early 1980s. One estimate of contractors' impact on the noncommercial segment's influence breaks down as indicated in the chart above. Source: *Nation's Restaurant News*, February 24, 1997, p. 56.

Marine, and Coast Guard officers' club management at bases all over the world. Both civilian and military personnel are employed by many of these facilities.

## Contractors

Contract food management companies are the major operators of noncommercial food service. These companies are hired to operate restaurants in convention centers and at tourist attractions, sports arenas, colleges and schools, office buildings, plants, and health care facilities. Exhibit 9 shows the market share within the different food service segments. Many contract companies, such as ARAMARK and Marriott Management Services, recruit on college campuses. These companies offer numerous careers in restaurant management. Unlike free-standing, single concept restaurants, many contract locations implement multiple restaurant concepts. For example, at a corporate headquarters, the food service might consist of an upscale cafeteria, a fast-food outlet, a tableservice restaurant, and banquet facilities.

The two largest contract companies worldwide are the London-based Compass Group and Paris-headquartered Sodexho (see Exhibit 10). Both companies have been acquiring U.S.-based contractors. Compass acquired Canteen and Professional Food-Service Management. However, U.S.-based contractors are also going global—ARAMARK has moved into eleven countries, including Mexico, Korea, Hungary, and the Czech Republic.

Contract management companies have taken advantage of client strategies to outsource noncore businesses. In addition to food service, they provide services such as housekeeping, grounds maintenance, and laundry. This diversification has enhanced management opportunities in the field. For example, a college food service manager may be offered a higher salary to accept the added responsibility of managing building housekeeping.

## Starting a New Restaurant

Many students dream of owning their own restaurant someday. To be sure, huge fortunes have been made in the restaurant business. The entire Marriott empire grew from a single Hot Shoppe Restaurant opened in 1927 in Washington, D.C., by J. Willard Marriott, a 27-year-old sheep herder from Salt Lake City, Utah. (In 1989, the Marriott Corporation decided to abandon its restaurant businesses.) Frank Giuffrida, who owns the Hilltop Steak House in Saugus, Massachusetts, started as a meat manager in a butcher store—which he still owns—next door to his restaurant. America's second largest independent restaurant, the Tavern on the Green in Manhattan, is the creation of Warner LeRoy, whose father, Mervyn LeRoy, produced the movie *The Wizard of Oz*. LeRoy made his fortune by understanding the meaning of showmanship in the restaurant business—his employees often refer to him as a "food impresario." Anthony Athanas, who opened Anthony's Pier 4 in Boston in 1963, is an Albanian immigrant who came to America at age 13 and, despite having had no formal education, became a multi-millionaire.

Another legendary name in the restaurant business is Joseph H. Baum, one of the most important restaurateurs of our time. Among the well-known establishments Baum created and opened are Manhattan's Windows on the World and the Rainbow Room at Rockefeller Center. Many people call him the father of the **theme restaurant**.

Some entrepreneurs never go beyond a single restaurant, nurturing it to perfection. Mike Hurst, past NRA president and creator and owner of Fort Lauderdale's 15th Street Fisheries, is a master of food and beverage merchandising. While managing the kitchen and other back-of-the-house areas is important, his basic philosophy is to emphasize the front of the house and give his guests "recognition, recommendations, and reassurance."

The restaurant business is one of the easiest businesses to enter. Novices recognize few barriers—comparatively little capital and virtually no experience are needed. Used commercial ovens, stoves, and other fixtures are readily available. Almost any location will do—they think—and no special skills or technology are required. Most of the labor (if any is needed beyond the owner's) can be obtained at minimum wage. Anyone can cook—right?

Exhibit 10  The Top 15 Contract Management Companies

| Company | 1995 Worldwide Sales ($MM) | Total Accounts |
|---|---|---|
| **Compass Group**<br>London (in U.S., Charlotte, NC) | 5,000.0 | 8,600 |
| **Sodexho**<br>Paris (in U.S., Waltham, MA) | 3,600.0 | 11,982 |
| **Aramark**<br>Philadelphia, PA | 3,500.0 | 2,400 |
| **Marriott Management Services**<br>Bethesda, MD | 2,800.0 | 3,184 |
| **Service America**<br>Stamford, CT | 715.0 | 7,030 |
| **SHRM Group**<br>Marseille, France (in U.S., Lafayette, LA) | 700.0 | 1,139 |
| **Restaura**<br>Phoenix, AZ | 370.0 | 395 |
| **The Wood Co.**<br>Allentown, PA | 335.5 | 312 |
| **Daka Restaurants**<br>Danvers, MA | 322.5 | 396 |
| **Morriston Health Care**<br>Atlanta, GA | 220.0 | 300 |
| **ServiceMaster**<br>Downers Grove, IL | 200.0 | 1,558 |
| **Universal Ogden**<br>New Orleans, LA | 155.0 | 150 |
| **HDS Services**<br>Farmington Hills, MI | 144.3 | 180 |
| **Guest Services**<br>Fairfax, VA | 126.0 | 118 |
| **Nutrition Management Services**<br>Kimberton, PA | 115.0 | 120 |

Source: "Leading Contract Management Companies," *Restaurants & Institutions,* August 1, 1996, p. 42.

## Industry Innovators

Joe Baum
B.E. Group

Joe Baum has been credited with so many innovations in the restaurant business that is hard to put a label on him. Perhaps the best is "Godfather of Theme Restaurants." There's no question about that.

A graduate of Cornell, Baum joined New York's Restaurant Associates to create and open their first fine-dining restaurant, the Newarker, in the Newark Airport. It was there that Baum first showed his talent for creating a complete dining experience. His knack for exceeding guest expectations quickly attracted notice. Baum added sparklers to desserts. When guests ordered an oyster appetizer, instead of the customary six, they got seven, with the seventh presented on a special plate—to make a point.

With his first success behind him, Baum turned to Manhattan. His first creation there was an extraordinary Italian restaurant, The Forum of the Twelve Caesars, which featured a Roman Empire theme. Wine buckets were shaped like upside-down Roman centurion helmets, and the spigots in the men's room were cast in the likenesses of Roman emperors! The ancient-looking menu offered delicacies such as Quail Cleopatra—truffle-scented, wrapped in grape leaves, and cooked in hot ashes.

Next came La Fonda Del Sol, a high quality Mexican-South American restaurant next to Rockefeller Center. The decor featured bright tiles and handmade glassware and pottery. Baum's next project was the Four Seasons on Park Avenue, a landmark restaurant that took two-and-a-half years and $4.5 million to bring to life. The concept of changing the menu and the decor with each season was an instant success. For the World Trade Center opening in the 1970s, Baum created Windows on the World (WOW), which occupies two acres of the building's 106th and 107th floors. By the late 70s, WOW had become one of the highest grossing independent restaurants in the world. In 1987, Baum took on the renovation of New York's famous Rainbow Room. He brought back the glamour and romance, the cigarette girls, the flaming dishes, and the celebrity clientele. When the city decided to restore Times Square in 1997, Baum teamed up with magician David Copperfield to operate the Magic Underworld.

Almost 200 restaurants in America reflect Joe Baum's touch, including the casual Smithsonian cafeteria in the National Art Gallery. Baum is not a chef, nor does he consider himself a designer. He is a creative genius who is proud to share the credit for his successes. Experts have been involved in all of his projects. For example, James Beard and Jacques Pepin created the menu for Windows on the World.

Baum is a perfectionist with a reputation for getting everything right the first time around.

*(continued)*

> **Industry Innovators** *(continued)*
>
> He has been known to reject restaurant and menu designs, one after another, before finding one he likes. "One detail is as important as the next, no matter how small it is," he says.
>
> Baum's innovations, which have permanently changed American dining, have earned him numerous awards and honors, including induction into the Culinary Institute of America's Hall of Fame. In 1997, at the age of 77, Baum received the James Beard Lifetime Achievement Award.

Staying in business is the real challenge. Being a good cook, a popular host, and a creative promoter are not enough when it comes to running a successful restaurant. Because the business is far more complicated than it appears, those who study the industry at colleges or universities have a much better chance of succeeding. Without business knowledge, prospects can be bleak. Approximately fifty percent of all new restaurants close within a year, and half of the other 50 percent fail in their second year; by their fifth year, 85 percent are no longer in business. Actual figures may be even higher since this data is based on bankruptcy claims and not all restaurant failures result in recorded bankruptcy. Many restaurants simply close their doors when they have exhausted their capital and become unrecorded failures.

## Why Do Restaurants Fail?

There are several reasons why so many restaurants fail every year.

**Lack of Business Knowledge.** The first and most important reason restaurants fail is due to an operator's simple lack of business knowledge. Successful restaurant operators have a working knowledge of marketing, accounting, finance, law, engineering, and human resources. Knowing and loving food is not enough to operate a thriving food service operation.

**Lack of Technical Knowledge.** The second reason for failure is an operator's lack of technical knowledge. Attorneys, accountants, movie stars, and sports figures have all tried the restaurant business. In general, those who have succeeded either invested capital or simply lent their names to the enterprise in return for a share of the profits. They left the planning and operations to professional restaurateurs. Successful restaurant operators must understand site selection, menu planning, recipe development, purchasing, production techniques, and sophisticated service procedures that make it possible to deliver a consistent and reliable experience that meets guest expectations.

**Lack of Sufficient Working Capital.** A third reason for restaurant failure is a lack of sufficient working capital. In the restaurant business, where word-of-mouth recommendations are so important, it takes time to develop a solid guest base. New restaurants usually lose money for a while. Many new operators badly underestimate the amount of capital they will need—to pay for food, labor, and fixed

### Exhibit 11  Restaurant Start-Up Costs

|  | Fine Dining | Café/Bistro |
|---|---|---|
| **Hard Capital Costs** | | |
| Kitchen & other non-public areas | $247,500 | $ 60,750 |
| Dining room & other public areas | 297,000 | 72,900 |
| Plumbing, electrical, decorating, furnishing | | |
| **Soft Capital Costs** | 31,500 | 6,570 |
| Pots, pans, linens, silverware, china & some promotional & marketing costs | | |
| **Professional Fees** | 115,200 | 28,080 |
| Licenses (except liquor), lawyer, accountant, interior designer, etc. | | |
| **Additional Working Capital** | | |
| Beverage & food inventory | 25,000 | 10,000 |
| Three-month payroll | 65,790 | 22,430 |
| **Total*** | **$781,990** | **$200,910** |

*These figures are based on doing a first-class job and buying new equipment. Costs can be reduced considerably by purchasing used equipment.

operating expenses—until they reach the break-even point, which can be six months to a year down the road…or never.

## The Cost of Starting a New Restaurant

Some restaurants fail before they ever get off the ground because their operators underestimate the cost of opening a new restaurant. A few years ago, *Changing Times* magazine asked Stephen Zagon, a food service consulting manager, and Doyle Wayman, president of Index, a Houston restaurant consulting and design firm, to estimate probable start-up costs for two hypothetical restaurants, both in major metropolitan areas. The first column in Exhibit 11 shows costs for a 5,940-square-foot (552.4-square-meter) fine-dining restaurant with 150 seats in the dining room and 30 in the bar. It has a contemporary decor and a new, state-of-the-art kitchen. The second column shows costs for a more modest bistro café with 75 seats—15 in the bar—and a total of 2,430 square feet (226 square meters). The menu choices are more limited and the decor and kitchen less expensive than at the fine-dining establishment. Both lease rather than buy space and have to convert their property for restaurant use. As you can see, even though opening a restaurant is inexpensive compared to starting other businesses, opening costs can still be substantial.

## Building a Successful Restaurant

Let's assume that you have enough business knowledge, technical knowledge, and capital to start a restaurant and keep it going until you reach the break-even point.

What's the first step? How do you decide what kind of restaurant it should be and where it should be located?

Many would-be restaurateurs approach this issue by first deciding what kind of restaurant they would like to have and then picking a location they're comfortable with. You might want to operate an Italian restaurant in the neighborhood where you live, for example. You may then decide to negotiate a lease in a nearby shopping center where some space is available, come up with a name, and hire a contractor to "build out"—do the interior construction needed to add finishing touches to the restaurant, such as Roman columns, trellises from which grapes can be hung, or other details suggesting an Italian setting.

While this approach might succeed, modern management theory suggests that this is putting the proverbial cart before the horse. In the above scenario, you decided on the restaurant's concept and location without any regard to who your guests are likely to be, and without identifying your competition. Fred Turner, former president of McDonald's, was quoted as saying, "We lead the industry because we follow the customers."[20] Part of what makes McDonald's successful is that its product and service concepts are developed in response to customer and potential customer input. For example, breakfast was introduced by McDonald's not to keep stores open longer—although that was a consideration—but because it recognized customer demand for earlier hours and breakfast items.

**The Concept.** Before selecting a concept for your restaurant, you should first ask yourself:

- Who are the people I hope to attract? Are they families, businesspeople, tourists, or other guest groups?
- What guest needs am I trying to satisfy? Do these people want convenient, fast food, or fine dining?
- Where do these people live and work? Are they located near my proposed location?
- When do they buy? Do they eat out at lunch and dinner, or only at dinner? What are their peak days and hours?
- How do they buy? Do they dine in, take out, or want delivery?
- How much competition is there now and is there likely to be in the near future?

If the neighborhood you've chosen for your proposed Italian restaurant already has a half-dozen others, you must make sure there is room for another and that you clearly offer potential guests something the others do not. Smart marketers do a thorough competition analysis that takes into account all the restaurants in the neighborhood and evaluates their menus, prices, and hours of operation.

Once you have addressed all these questions, you are ready to develop a concept. The concept consists not only of the products and services your proposed restaurant will offer, but also the manner in which you will present them. The restaurant's name, atmosphere, location, and menu prices are all elements of the concept. In other words, the concept is the physical embodiment of the answers to

*Understanding the Restaurant Industry* **109**

*"With any entrée, you get unlimited access to the trough."*

Cartoon by Harris;©1995, The New Yorker Magazine, Inc.

the questions you have just asked. It is your idea of a restaurant that will attract the customers you have targeted.

How do you arrive at a concept? A new restaurant's concept can come from an existing concept—as when a restaurant chain expands—or from individuals who create fresh concepts, usually after considering the questions we posed above. In either case, the foundation of the concept is the menu. Will it be ethnic, regional American, eclectic Californian, traditional, or limited? One way to address this question is to study market trends in terms of the popularity of various menu items. Much of this information is available in trade media research (e.g., magazines such as *Restaurant Hospitality* and *Nation's Restaurant News*) as well as from trade associations like the National Restaurant Association.

Once you've decided on the menu, you can put many other aspects of the concept into place—decor, number of seats, type of service, hours of operation, pricing structure, and, finally, the investment required.

You may modify the final investment figure several times in the course of creating your restaurant. To begin with, market research is likely to influence some of the elements of the concept; remember that the focus must be on the potential guests' needs and preferences. Resource limitations may pose another constraint.

Most restaurateurs do not have unlimited funds. Even large restaurant chains are concerned with how long it will take a new restaurant to break even and make a profit. This means that the amount of capital available for investment may be established early on, and that, in turn, may affect many elements of the concept.

**Site Selection.** Another important decision you must make about your proposed restaurant is its location. A restaurant site can be an undeveloped lot where a new building must be constructed or a lot with an existing restaurant or a building that can be converted. Of course, there is no such thing as a universally ideal restaurant site. Some restaurants should be in areas where there is a substantial amount of foot traffic; others should be near a busy highway intersection. Still others rely on neighborhoods with certain predetermined characteristics, such as a minimum number of households within a certain radius or a minimum average household income. In any case, a restaurant's site has a tremendous influence on its success.

Expanding restaurant chains like Chili's Grill & Bar and The Olive Garden provide examples of how site selection works. Most chains start by selecting cities or metropolitan areas with a certain-size population whose average disposable income is within a certain range. For instance, one chain's criterion might be "To locate our new restaurants in cities of more than 250,000 people, where the average annual household income is $20,000 or more." Domino's Pizza units generally serve population bases of 40,000 or more, although Domino's believes it is possible to be profitable in a location with only half that number. Often, rather than thinking in terms of cities or metropolitan areas, sites are selected in specific **areas of dominant influence (ADI).** ADIs describe areas covered by major television station signals, as measured by Arbitron, a national TV rating service. By selecting a site in this manner, a chain knows in advance that it will be able to advertise economically using television.

Restaurant sites often fall into one of four areas:

- *Central city business and shopping districts.* These are near office buildings, downtown department stores, or major commercial hotels.
- *Shopping centers.* Modern shopping centers provide a central focus in suburban communities. City government offices, churches, recreational facilities such as movie theaters and fitness centers, and restaurants usually are in or near shopping centers.
- *Planned communities.* Planned communities can be large suburban developments or urban renewal projects.
- *Highway intersections.*

Usually, large restaurant chains carefully analyze market data in new locations to match potential guest profiles with chain standards. For example, McDonald's depends on families with small children for a large proportion of its business, so it searches for new locations that are surrounded by such families. Red Lobster restaurants appeal to middle-income families who like seafood and eat out regularly. If a proposed restaurant's concept does not match the demographics and lifestyles of those who live or work near the proposed location, a new concept or location is needed.

A good site possesses certain specific characteristics. First, the site must be easily visible. If the proposed site is situated off a highway, it should be near a clearly marked or well-known exit. It should also be possible to put up a sign that can be seen far enough in advance from either direction so that a driver can slow down and exit safely. If the restaurant is in a major shopping complex, the site should not be off in a corner where no one will see it. It should be visible from the parking lot, where shoppers entering the mall or movie theater are bound to notice it.

Second, a good site is easily accessible. Some otherwise favorable sites are rejected because they are hard to find or are on side streets or one-way streets that are inconvenient for customers. Moreover, the restaurant must be accessible to the market it intends to serve. Depending on the type of restaurant, "accessible" can range from a few minutes' walk to a one-hour drive. Restaurants that serve upscale markets or have unique themes may have a large geographic range, while limited-menu or fast-food restaurants tend to serve markets no more than five square miles in size.

The third consideration is availability. Can the property be rented or purchased? When? Are there any zoning restrictions?

A fourth factor to consider is affordability. An undeveloped lot may require extensive and costly site preparation. Are power and other utilities readily available or must they be brought in? What are the terms of the purchase? If you are buying a building on the lot, is the seller willing to help with the financing? Are the taxes reasonable? Can the building be leased? Will the landlord pay for remodeling costs and other improvements, or must you? Since under-capitalization is a major cause of restaurant failure, you must be careful not to commit yourself to higher rent or remodeling costs than you can afford to pay. You should be conservative when deciding what you can afford, because business may not go as well as you expect.

**The feasibility study.** Before deciding on a site, restaurateurs usually have a **feasibility study** done. These studies are similar to the feasibility studies that are done for new hotels. The major difference is that the demand for hotel rooms is usually generated by travelers or others coming from outside a hotel's immediate area, while the demand for restaurants is mostly local. Therefore, local market characteristics are more important for restaurants. Feasibility studies help a restaurateur decide if a particular location is right and if a restaurant has a good chance of success.

In addition to data on local population characteristics, a good deal more information is available from many sources. The National Restaurant Association hires the IRC Survey Research organization to conduct a monthly poll—the Food Service Market Measure—which surveys a national sample of adults using questions such as:

- Which of the following did you do yesterday?

    a. Ate on the premises of a restaurant, fast-food place, cafeteria, or any other place where you purchased a meal or snack.

    b. Purchased take-out food "to go" or had it delivered.

- Was the food you ate on the premises for breakfast, lunch, dinner, or a snack?

- Was the take-out food you had delivered for breakfast, lunch, dinner, or a snack?

Answers to these and other questions are used to determine and forecast seasonal trends by region.

The Bureau of Labor Statistics publishes an annual Consumer Expenditure Survey based on consumer interviews and purchase diaries. This survey is available from the Government Printing Office in Washington, D.C. Using the Consumer Expenditure Survey and data collected from specific zip codes and other sources, several other research services can report exactly how often and which meals people in those zip codes eat out, what they like to eat, and how much they spend.

A computer database called Supersite, available through CompuServe Information Service, provides demographic information for the entire United States, broken down by state, county, zip code, ADIs, and Nielsen TV market areas. Fourteen different demographic reports for any given area are available from Supersite, including income, housing, education, and employment reports. In addition, sales potential reports for restaurants and other services are available.

Information on the buying habits of restaurant patrons is available through ACORN Target Marketing, which can be accessed through the Supersite database. ACORN is the acronym for "A Classification of Residential Neighborhoods," which classifies all households in the United States according to the demographic, socio-economic, and housing characteristics of their neighborhoods. A similar service called PRIZM is available for every zip code in America from the Claritas Corporation.

As you can see, feasibility study writers can draw from many sources to produce qualitative and quantitative analyses of proposed restaurant operations. A feasibility study can identify possible guest markets for a proposed restaurant, evaluate the proposed site, and, finally, analyze the financial prospects of the restaurant.

The financial analysis portion of the study also contains a capital investment budget. The purpose of a capital investment budget is to make certain that enough capital will be available for the following items:

- Land and construction costs (or extended lease costs on an existing building)
- Equipment
- Furniture and fixtures
- Working capital
- Pre-opening expenses for inventory
- Pre-opening staff salaries and training expenses
- Pre-opening advertising and promotion

Finally, the study should contain a proposed operating budget for the restaurant's first three years. Without this information, it's impossible to tell when the proposed restaurant will make money. The budget lets investors and managers know how much cash will be required to meet initial expenses until the restaurant makes a profit. The budget may reveal that the restaurant, as conceived, will never make money, and therefore adjustments must be made.

## Chapter Summary

Food service is a huge industry with over $320 billion in annual sales, 787,000 units, and nine million employees. Career opportunities abound because of the industry's diversity. Some students are attracted by numerous opportunities to climb the corporate ladder at companies ranging from McDonald's to Marriott. Others look forward to hosting movie stars and other celebrities at their own unique restaurants.

Compared to other businesses, the restaurant industry offers unmatched opportunities for entrepreneurship. Restaurant entrepreneurs have followed various paths. Approximately 85 percent of new restaurants that open in a given year will be out of business within five years. Restaurants often fail because their operators lack business or technical knowledge, or because there is insufficient working capital.

Successful restaurateurs start by focusing on the needs and preferences of their potential guests. Then they develop a restaurant concept. Next, they select a site. This step generally involves a feasibility study to analyze the local market and includes a financial analysis and capital investment budget.

## Endnotes

1. Unless otherwise noted, the statistics quoted in this and the following three paragraphs are from *1997 National Restaurant Association Foodservice Industry Pocket Factbook* (Washington, D.C.: National Restaurant Association, 1997).
2. Elizabeth Grudzinski, "In Fast Food, a New Order," *Miami Herald*, 5 January 1992, K1.
3. *Nation's Restaurant News*, 29 April 1996, p. 48.
4. Atef Mankarios, "Great Hotels: Restaurants with Rooms," *Restaurants & Institutions*, 30 October 1989, p. 16.
5. Mankarios, p. 16.
6. "R&I '97 Forecast," *Restaurants & Institutions*, 1 January 1997, p. 64.
7. *American Way*, American Airline's in-flight magazine.
8. *Restaurants USA*, December 1996, p. F19.
9. From a reprint of *Nation's Restaurant News*, Volume 24, No. 50, p. 18.
10. "R&I '97 Forecast," *Restaurants & Institutions*, 1 January 1997, p. 29.
11. Michael J. McCarthy, "In Age of Austerity, Some Still Exalt One Corporate Frill," *Wall Street Journal*, 9 July 1993, p. 1A.
12. "National Restaurant Association's 1997 Foodservice Industry Forecast," *Restaurants USA*, 24 February 1997, p. 56.
13. "Focus—College Feeding," *Nation's Restaurant News*, 20 March 1989, p. F16.
14. *Restaurants USA*, December 1992, p. 31.
15. Karen Benfield, "The Food Is Much More Fanciful, but the Ambience Remains Sterile," *Wall Street Journal*, 9 September 1992, p. B1.
16. "R&I '97 Forecast," p. 42.
17. "A Hankering for Food Courts," *Advertising Age*, 13 December 1993, p. 25.

18. Carolyn Walkup, "Getting a Lock on Jailhouse Food," *Nation's Restaurant News*, Volume 24, No. 50.

19. "*R&I* '97 Forecast," p. 42.

20. Ronald Zemke and Dick Schaat, *The Service Edge* (New York: New American Library, 1989), p. 297.

## Key Terms

**areas of dominant influence (ADI)**—A term used in the television industry to describe areas covered by the signals of major television stations as measured by Arbitron, a national TV rating service.

**casual dining house**—A restaurant distinguishable by a combination of decor, informal atmosphere, and eclectic menu that draws from ethnic and traditional offerings.

**cyclical menu**—A menu that changes every day for a certain number of days, then repeats the cycle. A few cycle menus change regularly but without any set pattern. Also known as cyclic menu.

**ethnic restaurant**—A restaurant featuring a particular cuisine, such as Chinese, Italian, or Mexican.

**family restaurant**—A restaurant that caters to families—with an emphasis on satisfying the needs of children—that serves breakfast, lunch, and dinner, offering traditional menu items.

**fast-food restaurant**—A restaurant that focuses on convenience, offers a narrow selection of food, and provides limited service and speedy preparation.

**feasibility study**—A study commissioned by developers and prepared by consultants that seeks to determine the potential success of a proposed business on a proposed site.

**fine-dining restaurant**—A restaurant that features luxury dining and an exciting menu (not necessarily French or haute cuisine, however), and employs well-trained creative chefs and skilled food servers. Fine-dining restaurants are generally small and independently operated, with more employees per guest than other types of restaurants.

**full-service restaurant**—A restaurant that (1) has more than a dozen or so main-course items on the menu and (2) cooks to order.

**home-meal replacement restaurant**—A restaurant that offers a menu based on homestyle main-course items and a wide variety of side dishes that are sold separately or as complete meals to be eaten at the restaurant or taken out.

**limited-service restaurant**—A restaurant with a small selection of food and limited services. Limited-service restaurants emphasize speed of preparation and delivery, making convenience one of the main reasons for their appeal.

**theme restaurant**—A restaurant distinguishable by its combination of decor, atmosphere, and menu.

## Review Questions

1. What are the two most important food service facilities within the food industry segment called "Eating and Drinking Places"?
2. What characterizes a full-service restaurant? a limited-service restaurant?
3. What two major trends in food service have surfaced in recent years, and how have they benefited certain retail businesses?
4. What changes have been seen in the student food service market?
6. What are some positive trends in hospital food service?
7. Why do restaurants fail?
8. What are some strategies for building a successful restaurant?
9. Most restaurant sites fall into which four classifications?
10. What are some desirable characteristics any restaurant site should have?

## Internet Sites

For more information, visit the following Internet sites. Remember that Internet addresses can change without notice. If the site is no longer there, use a search engine to look for additional sites.

### Associations

National Restaurant Association
www.restaurant.org

### Publications

*Nation's Restaurant News*
www.nrn.com

### Restaurant Companies

Applebee's Neighborhood Grill and Bar
www.applebees.com

ARAMARK Corporation
www.aramark.com

Canyon Ranch Health Resorts
www.canyonranch.com

Chili's Grill and Bar
www.chilis.com

Cracker Barrel Old Country Store, Inc.
www.crackerbarrel.com

Domino's Pizza, Inc.
www.dominos.com

Ed Debevic's Restaurants
www.eddebevics.com

Fine Host Corporation
www.finehost.com

Houston's Restaurants
www.houstons.com

KFC Corporation
www.kfc.com

Marriott International, Inc.
www.marriott.com

McDonald's
www.mcdonalds.com

The Olive Garden
www.olivegarden.com

Outback Steakhouse
www.outbacksteakhouse.com

Pizza Hut
www.pizzahut.com

The Rainbow Room
www.rainbowroom.com

Rainforest Café
www.rainforestcafe.com

Red Lobster Restaurants
www.redlobster.com

Royal Caribbean International
www.rccl.com

Spaghetti Warehouse
www.meatballs.com

Taco Bell Corporation
www.tacobell.com

T.G.I. Friday's, Inc.
www.tgifridays.com

Walt Disney Company
www.disney.com

Wendy's International, Inc.
www.wendys.com

*Understanding the Restaurant Industry* **116-a**

## REVIEW QUIZ

When you feel you have covered all of the material in this chapter, answer these questions. Choose the *best* answer.

1. The National Restaurant Association estimates that the food service industry will employ over _____ million workers by 2005.

   a. 1
   b. 11
   c. 34
   d. 58

2. In the United States, the most popular day for eating out is:

   a. Friday.
   b. Saturday.
   c. Sunday.
   d. Monday.

3. Which of the following is a current trend in the retail market segment of the restaurant industry?

   a. Convenience stores are decreasing the size and scope of their take-out food operations.
   b. The number of food courts located in supermarkets is increasing.
   c. Major cafeteria chains are offering luxury dining options.
   d. a and c.

4. Airport terminals, train stations, cruise ships, and airplanes are part of the _____ market.

   a. contractor
   b. retail
   c. recreational
   d. none of the above

5. Which of the following statements about the health care market is *false*?

   a. Few health care facilities run their own food service departments.
   b. The health care market consists of three principal segments: hospitals, nursing homes, and retirement communities.
   c. Food service experts see opportunities for growth in the health care market.
   d. Hospitals have begun to market their food services off-site.

6. The foundation of a restaurant's concept is its:

   a. menu.
   b. ambiance.
   c. service.
   d. decor.

# REVIEW QUIZ (continued)

7. For a site to be considered a good one for a restaurant, it must be:
   a. easily visible.
   b. affordable.
   c. easily accessible.
   d. all of the above.

**Answer Key:** 1-b-C1, 2-b-C1, 3-b-C2, 4-d-C2, 5-a-C2, 6-a-C3, 7-d-C3

Each question is linked to a competency. Competencies are listed on the first page of the chapter. An answer reading 3-b-C4 translates to:

  3: the question number
  b: the correct answer
 C4: the competency number

## Chapter 5 Outline

Organizing for Success
    Guests
    Ambiance
    Menu
Financial and Operational Controls
    Financial Controls
    Operational Controls
Chapter Summary

## Competencies

1. Describe the importance of guest information and restaurant ambiance to a restaurant's success, summarize rules for creating menus, and give examples of differing guest menu preferences in different parts of the United States and the rest of the world.

2. Describe menu categories, and summarize the importance of menu design and menu pricing.

3. Identify methods of financial and operational control, list the control points of the food cost control cycle, and describe the menu planning, forecasting, purchasing, receiving, storing, and issuing control points of the cycle.

4. Describe the producing, serving, and guest payment control points of the food cost control cycle, outline methods of food cost analysis, and explain how managers can control labor and beverage costs.

# 5

# Restaurant Organization and Management

IN THIS CHAPTER we will focus first on organizing a restaurant for success. We will discuss the importance of guests, ambiance, menu, and menu prices. Then we will describe financial and operational controls for restaurants, including menu planning, purchasing, receiving, storing and issuing, producing, serving, guest payment, and food cost analysis procedures. We will briefly consider labor costs. The chapter ends with a discussion of beverage control.

## Organizing for Success

Restaurant managers must have a broad base of skills to run a restaurant successfully. These include marketing skills (to bring guests in) and quality control and service skills (to satisfy guests so they will want to return). Of course, having guests does not guarantee a profit. Restaurants have gone bankrupt even when running at capacity every night. Often, the difference between successful and unsuccessful food service operations is that the successful ones are organized. Managers of well-organized restaurants are able to budget and control expenses so that they maximize profits. Even the success of managers of nonprofit or subsidized operations, such as school food programs, is measured in financial terms—by their ability to control expenses and operate within their budget limitations.

All types of food service operations have the same mission—to prepare and serve food while staying within financial guidelines. Because their mission is the same, they all operate under similar principles of management and control.

Three elements crucial to the success of any restaurant are a restaurant's guests, ambiance, and menu.

### Guests

Everything starts with the guest or customer. Finding and holding on to this elusive creature is the most important factor in the success of any business. Once you understand where guests will come from and what needs they will have, you can determine the feasibility and optimal location of any food service operation. But a thorough knowledge of guests tells us a good deal more than simply where to put the restaurant. Guests' wants and needs guide new restaurateurs in formulating menus, determining ambiance, setting the level and style of service, and creating advertising and marketing plans.

The marketing research that goes into a feasibility study for a new restaurant is only the beginning. Guest research must be updated continually because we live in a dynamic society where markets change quickly. Continual research makes it possible not only to measure current guest preferences but to discover trends—how those preferences are changing and how fast.

Restaurants with long, successful track records and loyal guests have sometimes lost their guests' allegiance virtually overnight. According to management consultants Albrecht and Zemke, guest loyalty "must be based on a continuously satisfying level of service."[1]

The key word is "continuously." It is not hard to find examples of restaurants that lost touch with their guests and either failed or fell under the control of new companies with new concepts. For example, Sambo's, a limited-menu chain popular for many years, derived its name and decor from the children's story "Little Black Sambo." The civil rights movement focused attention on the racial aspects of Sambo's concept, and the chain died a painful death. The Royal Castle hamburger chain started during the Depression, offering 24-hour service and five-cent hamburgers. Over the years, the units became too small, old-fashioned, and limited in their menu choices. Soon the land on which the 175 restaurants rested was worth more than the company, and the company was liquidated. Then there was the Victoria Station restaurant chain. It had an attractive concept—restaurants in the form of a cluster of railroad cars that served extraordinarily good roast beef and generous drinks at reasonable prices. But beef consumption began to decrease and the restaurant's concept became less popular. The owners tried many new concepts, one after the other, leaving customers guessing about what they might find on their next visit. Eventually, most customers went elsewhere.

Guest attitudes and desires change constantly. In the 1990s, one noticeable trend in the restaurant business was "casualization," also referred to as "downscaling." Many fine-dining restaurants, facing a slowdown in business from the mature baby-boom generation, made their restaurants more casual and revised their menus, offering simpler fare at lower prices. According to *Restaurant Hospitality* magazine, there are hundreds of examples from all over the country of restaurants that have "casualized":

> A Boston bistro, Zuma, adjusted its concept to a more affordable Zuma's Tex-Mex Café; Philadelphia's DiLullo Centro is now the more casual DiLullo Oggi.... Chicago's Metropolis 1800 changed its look and lowered its prices, and San Francisco's Pacific Heights Bar & Grill lowered its dinner menu prices by 20 percent.[2]

One Detroit restaurateur, Jimmy Schmidt, put it this way:

> There's a lot of potential growth in the middle market, which explains why a lot of the independent, upscale guys are moving down, and chains are moving up. It's where the money is.[3]

Meanwhile, the number of casual dinner houses has been increasing, further adding to competition. According to Barbara Caplan, vice president of Yankelovich

**Exhibit 1  Changing Consumer Preferences**

> To: All Employees, Customers, and Suppliers
> From: Taco Management Company
> Subj: A Smoke-Free Workplace
>
> In the interest of providing a safe and healthy environment for employees, customers, and suppliers, Taco Management Company, in accordance with the Michigan Clean Indoor Air Act, has adopted the following policy:
>
> As of January 1, 1994, smoking is prohibited throughout this facility, for the following reasons:
>
> - We want to provide a safe and healthy place for the preparation of our food product.
> - Because of the configuration of our dining rooms, we cannot provide a no-smoking section that is comfortable for everyone.
>
> The success of this policy depends on the thoughtfulness, consideration, and cooperation of smokers and non-smokers. All employees share in the responsibility for adhering to and enforcing this policy.
>
> Thank you.

The managers of some Taco Bell units in Michigan placed leaflets like this one in their lobbies to let customers know about a new no-smoking policy. (Courtesy of Taco Management Company)

Partners (an organization that tracks life-styles with its prestigious *Yankelovich MONITOR* survey), "The main issue now is pleasure as opposed to status and prestige. Status is a victim of the demise of conspicuous consumption. Today status is not a substitute for quality and value."[4] Value now includes not only food but ambiance. Judith Waldrop, the research editor of *American Demographics* magazine, says, "There's a big entertainment component to dining out today—especially among time-pressed families. By eating out, you can kill two birds with one stone. It's getting out of the house; it's atmosphere. It could be a place with nice decor. Or it can be like Chuck E. Cheese, where entertainment is on the menu. There's even a baby-sitting component to a place like that."[5] Consider the Virtual Café, where, in addition to a meal, guests can experience a flight simulator or enter a computer-generated landscape and do battle.

Smoking in restaurants is a good example of how consumer perceptions have changed over the years (see Exhibit 1). Twenty years ago, every restaurant offered ash trays on every table. By the end of the 1980s, surveys showed that more than three-quarters of guests wanted separate smoking and no-smoking restaurants. California has banned all smoking in all restaurants, and other states are considering similar measures. McDonald's has already implemented 100 percent no-smoking policies in all of its company-owned units in the United States and is urging its franchisees to do the same.

Nutrition awareness has dramatically changed the way Americans view menus. Freshness has become an important attribute for menu items, partly because it denotes a healthier and more nutritious product. Restaurant analysts have seen a continuing escalation in the demand for fresh-baked breads and pastries. There has also been an increase in the popularity of fruit and vegetable menu offerings. According to Waldrop:

> Right now, the oldest baby boomers are 46 years old. That's the age when chronic health problems first seem to occur. I'm talking about things that require people to think about what they eat: heart disease, diabetes. It's not just a matter of choice for these people; it's their doctors telling them to exercise and watch their fat intake. A lot of people will be looking for vegetarian meals, low-fat meals. Customers will be requesting preparation methods and restaurants should be prepared for them.[6]

However, whether a trend appears to be taking hold or an old one losing ground is not a reason in itself to make dramatic changes in methods of operation. Few trends are universal. Different regions of the country and different countries have their own values; what is true in California may be less true or not true at all in Vermont. Restaurateurs should use national surveys and studies only as guides. Whether they apply to your city and your restaurant can only be determined by asking your guests.

## Ambiance

In successful food service operations, all types of elements play a role. The decor, lighting, furnishings, tableware, menu, service methods and personalities of the servers, and even the guests all combine to create a feeling about or an identity for a restaurant—that is, they create the restaurant's atmosphere or mood, its **ambiance**. Ambiance often leads guests to choose one restaurant over another. For some patrons, a restaurant's ambiance may be as important as the food, or even more important.

A restaurant's ambiance can even enhance how its food tastes to guests. One reason restaurateurs like to locate seafood restaurants next to the water is that there is a suggestion that the fish they serve are fresh. The restaurants in the Fuddruckers hamburger chain feature a glass-enclosed refrigerated room where fresh sides of beef hang; customers can view the beef while they stand in line for their hamburgers. This reinforces Fuddruckers' claim that its hamburgers are fresh and made on the premises, and may help convince customers that Fuddruckers' hamburgers taste better than those made from frozen hamburger patties.

On Chicago's north side, a restaurant called Ketchup gained a good deal of attention and favorable press when it opened. "Walking into Ketchup is like walking into a cartoon," according to *Restaurant Hospitality* magazine:

> Ketchup-red walls and black-and-white-checked floors frame a kinetic environment where comic book characters from Jughead to Dick Tracy

*Restaurant Organization and Management* **123**

**"One more mackerel and two more calamari."**

Source: Cartoon by Reisinger, appearing in Zagreb, Croatia; Cartoonists & Writers Syndicate, New York, New York.

peer not only *down* from the walls, but *up* from plastic seat covers. Plastic mermaid garnishes join in the upward gazing from the rims of wide martini glasses, even as cartoon videos flicker from a TV screen high on a wall at the far end of the room. And all around customers chatter and laugh.[7]

The average dinner check at Ketchup's is $14. "By and large, people today don't want to go out to *dinner*, they want to go out and get something to eat. Ketchup lets them do just that...and to come as they are," says chef-owner John Terczak.[8]

A legendary industry story about designing a restaurant's ambiance to satisfy the clientele comes from the early days of McDonald's. Founder Ray Kroc decided to concentrate on reaching families with young children. Why? Research showed that this was a large and growing market segment. The research also showed that the children often cast the deciding vote on which restaurant a family visited. With that in mind, Kroc and his associates designed a restaurant that not only served food children would like, but served it in a setting that small children would feel comfortable in. Kroc ordered cameras mounted on three-foot-high tripods to photograph a prototype McDonald's restaurant. Looking at the restaurant through the eyes of a child made the necessity for some changes immediately evident. Counters, for example, were lowered so a child could order without having to strain or stand on tiptoe. Seats and tables were also lowered. The interior was accented with bright yellow and red—the same colors used on many toys at the time.

Benihana of Tokyo is another restaurant chain that owes much of its success to ambiance. Japanese immigrant Rocky Aoiki, the chain's founder, was a stickler for authentic detail. Not only did he train his chefs at a special school in Tokyo before bringing them to the United States, he imported wooden beams from Japan at great expense to create the atmosphere of an authentic Japanese inn. Many of Aoiki's advisors told him that this was an unnecessary expense since the same look could be produced with American materials, but Aoiki refused to compromise.

Restaurant designers today talk about "fusing the decor with the region." Colonial-style furnishings and fabrics are often used in New England inns. Nautical themes are popular at restaurants located in seaports, and Southwest native decor predominates in cities like Santa Fe, New Mexico.

The ambiance of a restaurant's building can dictate the restaurant's concept. For example, some restaurants are housed in old warehouses (the Old Spaghetti Warehouse in Seattle, Washington, to name one) or historic railroad stations. In Europe, castles, country houses, and châteaux are favored locales for restaurants because of their distinctive character.

## Menu

A restaurant's menu is usually the most important element of its success. For that reason, we will discuss menus in some detail. A menu is much more than a list of items for sale. The menu helps define and explain what the restaurant is all about. It should represent what its guests expect and want. There is also a more subtle dimension. The menu should state what the restaurant does best. Unfortunately, what a restaurant does best sometimes changes. This is often the case with independent restaurants that are showcases for famous chefs. Cooking is a creative process; dishes conceived by one chef are not always as deftly executed by assistants and successors. This is one of the main reasons the menus of gourmet independent restaurants should and do change—so that the restaurants they represent can put their best foot forward.

**Basic Rules.** There are some basic rules that good restaurateurs follow when creating menus:

- *Give guests what they want.* Offer your guests what they are looking for at your restaurant. If your restaurant emphasizes convenience and speed of service, then be certain that menu items that take a long time to prepare are not

### Exhibit 2  Sample Standard Recipe

**Fish Fillet Amandine**

| | | Yield: 60<br>Size: 6 oz | IX. MAIN DISHES—FISH 2<br>Baking Temperature: 450°F<br>Baking Time: 14-15 min |
|---|---|---|---|
| Yield: _____ | | | |
| Size: _____ | | | |
| **Amount** | **Ingredients** | **Amount** | **Procedure** |
| _____ | Fish fillets, fresh or frozen 6 oz portion | 22 1/2 lb | 1. Defrost fillets if frozen fish is used.<br>2. Arrange defrosted or fresh fillets in single layers on greased sheet pans. |
| _____ | Almonds, toasted, chopped or slivered | 1 lb | 3. To toast almonds:<br>   a. Spread on sheet pans.<br>   b. Place in 350°F oven until lightly toasted.<br>      *Approximate time:* 15 min |
| _____<br>_____<br>_____<br>_____<br>_____ | Margarine or butter, softened<br>Lemon juice<br>Lemon peel, grated<br>Salt<br>Pepper, white<br>Weight: Margarine-almond mixture | 2 lb 8 oz<br>1/2 cup<br>2 3/4 oz<br>4 tbsp<br>1 tbsp<br>4 lb | 4. Add almonds, lemon juice, lemon peel, salt, and pepper to softened margarine or butter.<br>5. Mix thoroughly.<br>6. Spread margarine mixture on fillets as uniformly as possible.<br>    *Amount per fillet:* #60 scoop<br>7. Bake at 450°F for approx. 15 min or until fish flakes when tested with fork.<br>8. Sprinkle lightly with chopped parsley or sprigs of parsley when served. |

on the menu. If Italian specialties are what you promise, you must offer more than just spaghetti and lasagna.

- *Use standard recipes.* **Standard recipes** are formulas for producing a food or beverage item that specify ingredients, the required quantity of each ingredient, preparation procedures, portion size and portioning equipment, garnish, and any other information necessary to prepare the item (see Exhibit 2). Standard recipes are an essential part of quality control. Guests who come for your Dover sole *à la meunière* expect it to look and taste the same every time they come back for it.

- *Match the menu to the staff's abilities.* Make certain that all of the items on the menu can be correctly prepared and served by your staff. Servers' abilities are especially important when the menu includes items that are prepared tableside.

- *Take equipment into account.* Consider the limitations of your kitchen equipment. Menu items that call for grilling should not be broiled; grilled items do not taste the same as broiled items. Dishes that should have authentic woodsmoke flavors require a hickory or mesquite grill.

## The 800 Club

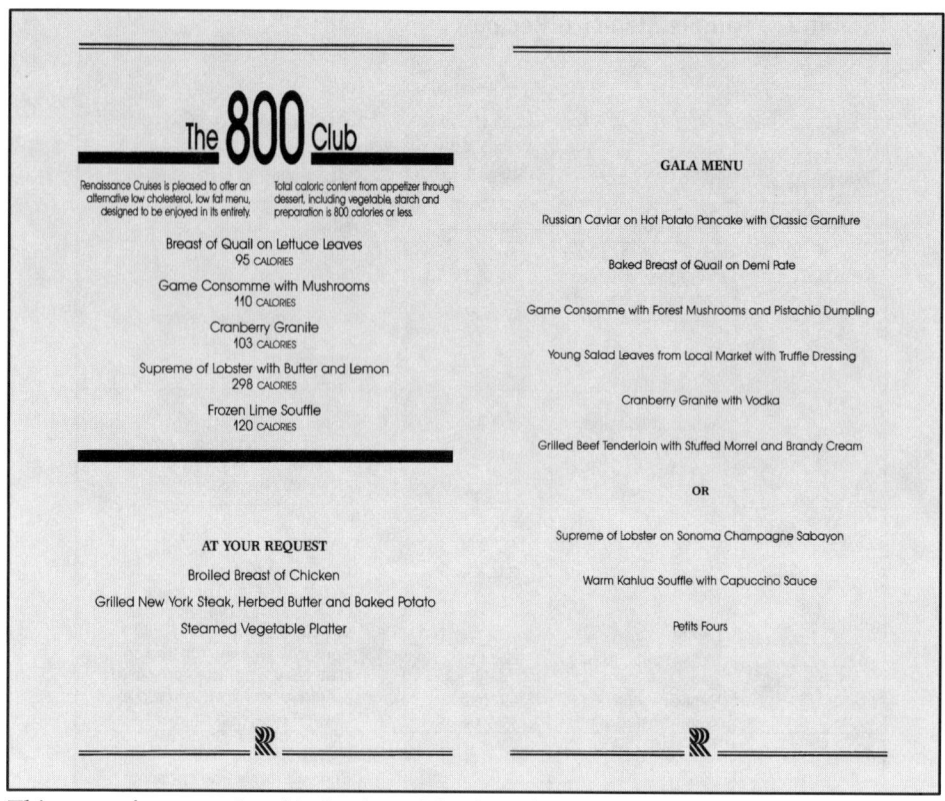

Renaissance Cruises is pleased to offer an alternative low cholesterol, low fat menu, designed to be enjoyed in its entirety. Total caloric content from appetizer through dessert, including vegetable, starch and preparation is 800 calories or less.

Breast of Quail on Lettuce Leaves
95 CALORIES

Game Consomme with Mushrooms
110 CALORIES

Cranberry Granite
103 CALORIES

Supreme of Lobster with Butter and Lemon
298 CALORIES

Frozen Lime Souffle
120 CALORIES

### AT YOUR REQUEST

Broiled Breast of Chicken

Grilled New York Steak, Herbed Butter and Baked Potato

Steamed Vegetable Platter

## GALA MENU

Russian Caviar on Hot Potato Pancake with Classic Garniture

Baked Breast of Quail on Demi Pate

Game Consomme with Forest Mushrooms and Pistachio Dumpling

Young Salad Leaves from Local Market with Truffle Dressing

Cranberry Granite with Vodka

Grilled Beef Tenderloin with Stuffed Morrel and Brandy Cream

OR

Supreme of Lobster on Sonoma Champagne Sabayon

Warm Kahlua Souffle with Capuccino Sauce

Petits Fours

**This menu from a cruise ship begins with a low cholesterol, low fat, low calorie meal as an alternative to the richer fare offered on the facing page. Giving guests a nutritious alternative is especially important on a cruise ship, since the guests are a "captive audience" for the length of the cruise.** (Courtesy of Renaissance Cruises)

- *Provide variety and balance.* Present a variety of items, colors, and textures in your menu. Much of any restaurant's business is repeat, especially at lunchtime. Daily or weekly specials can ensure that there are varying choices for guests. Strive for balance, so that foods complement each other or contrast nicely. Cream soups should not be followed by main courses with cream sauces. Some items should be heavy, others light. Since poultry and meat are white or brown, liven up their presentation with colorful vegetables.
- *Pay attention to the season.* Food costs are higher and quality is lower when you use fresh fruit or vegetables that are out of season. Menu items calling for fresh ingredients that are not readily available should perhaps be dropped from the menu until the ingredients are in season again.
- *Keep nutrition in mind.* Probably a certain number of your guests are committed to eating nutritious meals. Many of today's consumers try to eat a balanced diet. They may also be interested in reducing their intake of salt, fat, or sugar. Don't make that difficult to do in your restaurant.

"If my French is correct, it says 'turkey leftovers'!"

Source: Cartoon by Scott, appearing in London, England; Cartoonists & Writers Syndicate, New York, New York.

- *Use food wisely.* Strive for a menu that will produce profits. Carefully plan how to use perishable items and make full use of leftovers. Throwing away food is like throwing away money. Smart chefs use meat and vegetable scraps for stews and soups. Day-old bread can be used for stuffings and croutons. Good menu planners automatically think of daily specials that chefs can prepare using leftovers from the previous day's production.

**Menu Preferences.** Successful restaurant chains know that menu preferences vary significantly by region. In the United States, people in New England have significantly different tastes than do people in the South or West. Germans from Berlin prefer different dishes than their Bavarian cousins in Munich. Northern Chinese food is much spicier than that of southern China. Darden Restaurants, Inc., which operates such chains as Red Lobster and The Olive Garden, is careful to make sure that, although its restaurants look alike and have many of the same basic items, regional preferences are taken into account. The Olive Garden chain, for example, has 110 different menus for its more than 400 restaurants. By offering seasonal and test menu items and conducting tens of thousands of customer interviews nationwide, The Olive Garden was able to put together a data bank to help in designing new menus. This research showed executives that customers in coastal areas preferred more seafood dishes on the menus, while those in the Midwest preferred more meat options.[9] Before entering a new market, executives sample food at potential competitor restaurants to measure local spice preferences.

**128** Chapter 5

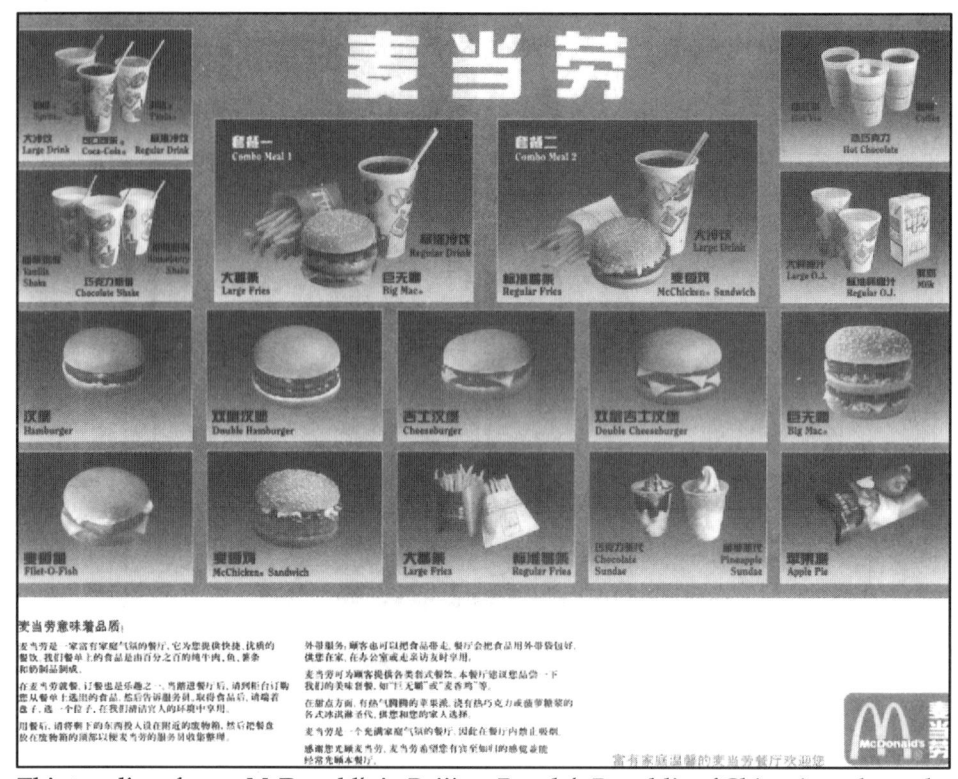

**This tray liner from a McDonald's in Beijing, People's Republic of China, introduces the Chinese to McDonald's products by illustrating the menu items.** (Courtesy of McDonald's Corp., Oak Brook, Illinois)

Global food chains keep their signature items on all menus the world over (McDonald's always offers Big Macs, for example—except in places like India, where the menu is vegetarian), but they also add items that appeal to local tastes. Pizza Huts in Hong Kong offer many more pasta dishes than their counterparts in the United States, since the Chinese have never been large consumers of cheese. McDonald's in Tokyo serves rice balls and miso soup as part of its breakfast menu. McDonald's in Japan has also added fried rice and a Cheese Katsu Burger, which encloses cheese in the traditional Japanese roast pork cutlet, drenched in the traditional katsu sauce and topped with shredded cabbage. KFC in Japan serves a deep-fried chicken cutlet, topped with cabbage and sprinkled with teriyaki sauce.[10]

The National Restaurant Association conducts studies on menu preferences in different parts of the country. In one such study, the most popular menu item in the Northeast was veal and the least popular menu items were Mexican dishes. In the West, Mexican dishes ranked at the top of the most popular items and veal headed the list of the fastest declining items. Enchiladas, which ranked third among the most popular items in the South, were at the top of the least popular items in the Midwest. Midwesterners liked fried fish sandwiches, roast beef sandwiches, and

## Exhibit 3  What's Hot...What's Not

| Rank | Hot Item (Trendy) | Percent of Operators Mentioning | Cool Item (Passé) | Percent of Operators Mentioning | Perennial Favorite | Percent of Operators Mentioning |
|---|---|---|---|---|---|---|
| 1. | Exotic mushrooms | 80% | Organ meats | 73% | Strawberries | 68% |
| 2. | Cappuccino/latte/espresso | 76 | Edible flowers | 67 | Rice | 60 |
| 3. | Hot/chili peppers | 75 | Cold soups | 64 | Cantaloupe | 59 |
| 4. | Meatless/vegetarian dishes | 72 | Blackened dishes | 63 | Potatoes | 57 |
| 5. | Infused oils | 69 | Deep-fried dishes | 62 | Beef | 56 |
| 6. | Alternative red meats | 68 | Cream-based sauces | 59 | Iced tea | 56 |
| 7. | Rotisserie | 68 | Taco salad | 58 | Grapes | 55 |
| 8. | Grilled items | 68 | Chef's salad | 58 | Spinach | 54 |
| 9. | Flatbreads | 67 | Kumquat | 56 | Mozzarella cheese | 53 |
| 10. | Flavored coffees | 66 | Sweet/savory crepes | 55 | Chicken | 53 |
| 11. | Mediterranean cuisine | 65 | Blush wine/rose | 55 | Tossed salad | 53 |
| 12. | Relishes/chutneys | 64 | Kiwi | 54 | French onion soup | 53 |
| 13. | Regional cuisine | 64 | Star fruit | 52 | Broccoli | 51 |
| 14. | Balsamic vinegar | 63 | Rhubarb | 51 | Cheesecake | 51 |
| 15. | Focaccia | 62 | Cobb salad | 51 | Ice cream | 51 |
| 16. | Roasted garlic | 62 | Anchovy | 50 | Fruit pies/tarts | 50 |
| 17. | Hot sauce | 62 | Consomme | 48 | Marinara sauce | 49 |
| 18. | Mango | 62 | Sun-dried tomatoes | 48 | Chowders | 49 |
| 19. | Slow-roasted foods | 62 | Pine nuts | 48 | Pizza | 49 |
| 20. | Ginger | 61 | Persimmons | 47 | Lime | 47 |

Source: Reprinted from *Restaurants USA,* February 1997, with the permission of the National Restaurant Association.

subs. Eggs and omelets were popular in the West but were declining in popularity in the Northeast.[11]

Restaurants are always looking for popular new food items to add to their menus. Exhibit 3 shows a survey of chefs that identifies menu items that are trendy, passé, and perennial favorites. (This kind of information can be useful for more effectively reaching a restaurant's specific market segment.)

**Menu Categories.** There are two menu categories based on how the menu is scheduled: fixed menus and cyclical menus. Menus can be further categorized as breakfast, lunch, dinner, or specialty menus.

**Fixed menus.** A fixed menu, also known as a static menu, is typically used for several months or longer before it is changed. Daily specials may be offered, but a set list of items forms the basic menu.

Fast-food operations are examples of restaurants with fixed menus. Fast-food restaurants can get away with offering the same menu items every day because the items they serve—typically hamburgers, chicken, pizza, or Mexican foods—appeal to a broad market. Many chain-operated full-service restaurants also feature fixed menus.

One of the principal advantages of a fixed menu is its simplicity. Purchasing, staffing, and inventory control are straightforward and uncomplicated. Even the equipment requirements are minimal and less complex. But there are disadvantages. A fixed menu provides no variety and few options for coping with increased costs other than raising menu prices. One solution to the lack of variety is to expand the fixed menu from time to time by adding new menu items on a temporary or permanent basis. Burger King's Bundles of Burgers and McDonald's Shamrock Shakes are both examples of temporary items. Both chains added salads and desserts on a permanent basis to provide more variety and achieve a higher average check per customer.

Some restaurants, such as independent family restaurants, offer daily specials to put a little variety in their fixed menus. The specials are usually printed on a separate sheet and inserted into the regular menu. Adding daily specials to an otherwise fixed menu helps keep regular customers who occasionally want to try something different.

**Cyclical menus.** A **cyclical menu** is a menu that changes every day for a certain number of days before the cycle is repeated. Desktop publishing has made changing menus easy and inexpensive compared to a few years ago, when any major change required a costly reprinting job.

Institutional food service operations and commercial operations that are likely to serve guests for an extended period of time use cyclical menus. A cruise ship where guests typically stay for a week needs a seven-day cyclical menu so that different menus can be offered each day. Menus can be numbered and may run from #1 to #7 before starting with #1 again. Cruise lines that offer longer cruises or whose clientele often take back-to-back cruises may use a much longer cycle menu; Seabourn Cruise Line has a 14-day cycle menu. Hospitals, where patients might be confined for prolonged periods, sometimes use long cycles. Nursing homes may use a very long cycle menu.

**Specialty menus. Specialty menus** differ from typical breakfast, lunch, and dinner menus. They are usually designed for holidays and other special events or for specific guest groups. Most restaurants offer a specialty menu featuring turkey and ham at Thanksgiving and Christmas, for example. Catered events such as birthdays, weddings, bar mitzvahs, and other social occasions may call for specialty menus. In some cases, specialty banquet menus may be created. There are many other kinds of specialty menus used by restaurants, such as children's, early-bird, beverage, senior citizens', dessert, and take-out menus.

Specialty menus are marketing tools—extra incentives to bring patrons in. Their only limit is the menu planner's imagination.

**Menu Design.** Like a brochure for a hotel, a menu is a sales tool and motivational device. A menu's design can affect what guests order and how much they spend. The paper, colors, artwork, and copy all can influence guest decisions and help establish a restaurant's ambiance and image. For example, the breakfast menu from a Bob Evans Restaurant (see Exhibit 4) underscores the chain's reputation for home-style, farm-fresh food. It prominently features their hotcakes with fresh strawberry topping, along with a rich, full-color photograph and descriptive language: "warm syrup," "real butter," and "premium Bob Evans Farms sausage." While menus should not mislead or misidentify the origin and presentation of an item, imaginative embellishment in menu descriptions is often appropriate.

Restaurant Organization and Management **131**

**Exhibit 4  Menu Design**

# Breakfast
*served anytime*

*Hotcakes with fresh Strawberry Topping*

Some places have breakfast specials. At Bob Evans®, every breakfast is special. Our own premium Bob Evans Farms® sausage. Hot buttermilk biscuits baked fresh daily. Warm syrup. Real butter for the asking. Free refills on hot beverages and soft drinks. And more. It's the Bob Evans® way to start the day. So pull up a chair and enjoy. Breakfast at Bob Evans® is served anytime.

## Legendary Breakfasts

**Sausage Gravy & Biscuits** - With home fries _____ $3.99

**Country Skillet** - An open-faced omelette with home fries, Bob Evans Farms® sausage, country gravy and shredded cheese. With your choice of bread _____ $5.29

**Steak & Eggs** - A 5 oz. breakfast steak with two eggs, home fries and your choice of bread _____ $6.59

**Homestead Breakfast** - Two eggs, choice of Bob Evans Farms® sausage patties or links or bacon, sausage gravy, home fries and your choice of bread _____ $6.69

**Fried Mush** - A Bob Evans® Special Recipe. Three slices, fried golden brown with your choice of bacon or sausage patties or links _____ $3.99

*Country Skillet*

*Steak & Eggs*

*Sausage Gravy & Biscuits*

When you start with a good thing, like Bob Evans® sausage, it just gets better and better. Through the years we've created a wide selection of breakfasts and meals the same way we've made our sausage so good: with only the finest ingredients available and extra attention to detail.

I 5/95

Courtesy of Bob Evans Farms

Menu designers stress the importance of tying in the look and language of the menu with the restaurant's concept. Applebee's Neighborhood Grill & Bar includes pictures of its grilled food items and signature drinks on its menu cover, and the time of happy hour on its back cover (see Exhibit 5). Guaymas, a Mexican seafood restaurant in Tiburon, California, uses durable, leather-like synthetic paper for the menu cover and paper the color of tortilla chips for the menu's pages.

When guests sit down at a restaurant table, there is no question about whether they are going to buy something; the question is how much they are going to spend. Blackboards, tent cards, well-trained food servers, and—most important—a well-designed menu can all influence that decision and, ultimately, affect the restaurant's bottom line.

**Menu Prices.** The goal in establishing menu prices is to bring in sufficient revenue to cover operating costs and overhead, and to provide a reasonable return on the investment. In other words, price is related to costs and investment. Clearly, a restaurant with a low investment and low operating costs should be able to charge less than one with high costs and a larger investment. Fast-food restaurants use computer-designed, standardized facilities and specialized equipment to prepare their menu items. The result is a relatively low investment cost plus low operating costs, since the menu and the equipment are designed for use by unskilled labor and with a limited menu in mind. Other operating costs are also kept to a minimum because nothing is added to the system that is not absolutely necessary for the smooth functioning of the unit. Therefore, prices in fast-food restaurants can be kept low.

On the other hand, restaurants such as Charlie Trotter's in Chicago are designed to offer extraordinary dining. These restaurants have lavish appointments, are located on valuable real estate, and provide luxury service with a menu requiring highly skilled chefs, cooks, dining room captains, and servers. Luxury restaurants charge high prices to cover their high food and operating costs and high overhead. They can do this because their guests are willing to pay for a fine-dining experience.

There are a number of mathematical models and other methods that are used to set menu prices. Most of them involve a markup over food and labor costs. Whatever method is used, you should ask some basic questions after pricing menu items:

- Are these prices appropriate for my type of operation? Cafeterias usually charge less than table-service restaurants for the same items, for example.

- Will my guests feel that I am offering a good price/value relationship? In other words, will they feel they're getting a good deal for their money?

- Are my prices competitive? What do similar restaurants in this same locale charge?

- Do these prices deliver a fair profit? Profit, of course, depends on many factors, but, generally, people who invest in restaurants expect their original investment to be paid back in three to five years.

Remember that, for most menu items, the lowest price you can charge a customer is governed by the need for the restaurant to make a profit, but the highest

Restaurant Organization and Management    133

**Exhibit 5    Matching Restaurant Concept with Menu Design**

## DESSERTS

**Fudge Brownie Sundae...$3.25**
A big, thick fudge walnut brownie with a scoop of rich vanilla ice cream topped with hot fudge sauce.

**Apple Honey Cobbler Ala Mode...$2.95**
Apples, cinnamon, raisins & spices baked with a streusel pastry, topped with pecan pieces, vanilla ice cream & honey sauce.

**Chocolate Glacier...$2.65**
White chocolate mousse between slabs of moist Devil's Food cake topped with hot fudge & whipped cream.

**Fudge Nut Fantasy...$3.95**
Indulge yourself with 2 scoops of Macadamia Brittle ice cream smothered in hot fudge & peanut sauce in a crisp cinnamon sparkle tortilla shell, topped with whipped cream, walnuts & a cherry.

**Strawberry Cheesecake...$2.75**
Rich, smooth & creamy on a thin butter cookie crust. Topped with sliced strawberries in sauce.

**Low-Fat & Fabulous Brownie Sundae...$3.25**
Too good to be true! Your favorite dessert in a low-fat version. A brownie wedge with fat-free frozen vanilla yogurt & non-fat hot fudge make it all happen with only 2 grams of fat.

## HAPPY HOUR

3 pm to 7 pm & 10 pm to Close
Everyday
Reduced Drink Prices & 1/2 Priced Appetizers
(Some Restrictions May Apply)
Ask your Server for Details

Ask your Server about our delicious Brunch Menu

**Applebee's**
Neighborhood Grill & Bar

We Will Be Happy To Prepare Most Of Our Menu Items For Takeout.
We Accept American Express, Visa & MasterCard.

Low-Fat & Fabulous

**Applebee's**
Neighborhood Grill & Bar

"Front"    "Back"

Courtesy of Applebee's Neighborhood Grill & Bar

"We use the cheapest ingredients and pass the savings on to you."

Drawing by Weber; ©1988, The New Yorker Magazine, Inc.

price you can charge is governed by the customer's perception of the item's quality and value.

## Financial and Operational Controls

Control is one of management's fundamental responsibilities. Effective control is a result of establishing standards based on the needs of guests and the goals of the business. This principle holds true for all types of food service operations. Whether the establishment is a fine-dining restaurant, a fast-food outlet, or even an institutional food service operation, managers must establish standards for financial performance, operations, and quality control. Without standards, there can be no real management, only organized confusion.

   Clearly, running a successful food service operation requires attention to a lot of details. Managers must know what everything costs, from the salt that's dispensed from shakers on the table to food servers' coffee breaks. Manually collecting that information can be an extremely time-consuming operation. For restaurants with computers, information gathering is much easier.

   A. Dyal Bailey, formerly of Rheinhart's Oysters and Seafood in Augusta, Georgia, is a computer enthusiast. Talking about computerized cash registers in *Restaurants USA,* he says:

Let me tell you in plain words what a computer register does. It counts. It counts how many orders of french fries you sell. It counts the amount of sales you do between 7 P.M. and 8 P.M. on any given night. It counts the total ounces of shrimp used in all your dishes. It counts how much alcohol you sell (as opposed to food sales). Some systems even count how many hours your employees are working—and with those costs it lets you know what your hourly labor cost is. Computers give your management team powerful tools because knowledge is power. After a computer register counts, it compiles the numbers and gives them to you. And with the numbers it gives, you have the knowledge and power to run a more efficient business.[12]

The facts support Bailey's enthusiasm. More than 40 percent of restaurants with annual sales below $500,000 use computers, and more than 75 percent of those with sales exceeding $1 million a year find them a necessary tool. Computers help managers with a wide variety of tasks, from producing financial statements to helping with inventory control and sales analysis.

## Financial Controls

Financial controls are tools managers use to measure the worth of a business and its level of sales, costs, and profitability. They include such documents as balance sheets, statements of income, and statements of cash flow. Managers use an accounting system to gather the financial information that makes control possible.

**Accounting Systems.** An accounting system that provides usable and sufficient information for management decisions is the basis for sound financial control. One such accounting system is the *Uniform System of Accounts for Restaurants.* This system is similar to the *Uniform System of Accounts for Hotels* in that it establishes categories of revenues and expenses, as well as formats for financial statements. The *Uniform System of Accounts for Restaurants* provides a common language for the restaurant industry, so operators can compare the performance of their restaurant with other restaurants in the same chain, with similar establishments in different chains, or with industry performance as a whole.

The following sections discuss two important components of the *Uniform System of Accounts for Restaurants:* the balance sheet and the statement of income.

**The balance sheet.** A restaurant's balance sheet shows the restaurant's financial condition on a given day. It is similar in many ways to a hotel's balance sheet (in fact, to any business's balance sheet), but there are differences. For example, although many restaurants accept credit cards as well as cash, they are, in fact, cash businesses, since the credit card companies rapidly redeem the charges. Therefore, unlike many other kinds of businesses, restaurants do not have high levels of accounts receivable on their balance sheets—that is, money due them from customers.

**The statement of income.** A statement of income shows the results of operations—the sales, expenses, and net income of a business—for a stated period of time. Whereas a hotel has a number of services for sale, a restaurant basically sells only food and, in some cases, alcoholic beverages. (There are exceptions, of course, such as theme restaurants, which may also sell T-shirts, caps, and other souvenirs,

**Exhibit 6  Sample Statement of Income**

---

**St. Julian Restaurant**
**Income Statement**
**Month Ending January 31, 19XX**

| | Amount ($) | Percent* |
|---|---|---|
| Sales | | |
|   Food | $ 577,823 | 77.9 |
|   Beverages | 163,927 | 22.1 |
|     Total Food and Beverage Sales | 741,750 | 100.0 |
| | | |
| Cost of Sales | | |
|   Food | 235,174 | 40.7 |
|   Beverages | 45,736 | 27.9 |
|     Total Cost of Sales | 280,910 | 37.9 |
| | | |
| Gross Profit | | |
|   Food | 342,649 | 59.3 |
|   Beverages | 118,191 | 72.1 |
|     Total Gross Profit | 460,840 | 62.1 |
| | | |
| Other Income | 8,250 | 1.1 |
| Total Income | 469,090 | 63.2 |
| | | |
| Controllable Expenses | | |
|   Payroll | 196,563 | 26.5 |
|   Employee Benefits | 35,604 | 4.8 |
|   Direct Operating Expenses | 51,923 | 7.0 |
|   Music and Entertainment | 6,676 | .9 |
|   Advertising and Promotion | 17,802 | 2.4 |
|   Utilities | 18,544 | 2.5 |
|   Administrative and General | 40,055 | 5.4 |
|   Repairs and Maintenance | 12,610 | 1.7 |
|     Total Controllable Expenses | 379,777 | 51.2 |
| | | |
| Profit Before Occupation Costs | 89,313 | 12.0 |
| | | |
| Occupation Costs | 59,340 | 8.0 |
| | | |
| Net Income Before Taxes | 29,973 | 4.0 |

*All ratios are to total sales except cost of sales and gross profit, which are ratios to their respective sales.

---

and restaurants with gift shops.) Hence, the statement of income generally is uncomplicated and relatively easy to understand.

Exhibit 6 shows an income statement for the fictional St. Julian Restaurant. Note the division of sales into "food" and "beverage" sales. (Food sales include sales of nonalcoholic beverages; beverage sales are sales of alcoholic beverages.) The cost of sales is also divided into "food" and "beverage" categories, representing the cost of the food and beverages sold to guests. "Other income" includes income derived from service charges, cover and minimum charges, banquet room rentals, and gift shop sales. Although this other income can be profitable, it is not very significant in food service operations. "Controllable expenses" relate to the entire operation, with "payroll" the largest single controllable expense.

"Occupation costs" relate to the financial structure of the restaurant. The levels of these expenses do not vary with sales as operating expenses do—with the exception of rent on the land or building(s), which may contain a percentage clause related to sales. (For example, the rent may be $20,000 a year plus 2 percent of gross sales.)

## Operational Controls

**Budgeting.** Budgeting—the forecasting of revenues, expenses, and profits—is another tool managers must use to track a restaurant's performance and make necessary adjustments. The headquarters of many chain restaurants collect the sales figures from each restaurant in the chain on a daily basis, using telephone/computer hookups. This process is called "polling." Managers at headquarters then compare actual sales with forecasted sales and take appropriate action. If sales are down, management can increase advertising, lower prices, add promotional items to the menu, or take other steps. Without standards and budgeting procedures, restaurant managers can and do allow difficult situations to develop past the point where anything can be done about them and financial disaster becomes almost a certainty.

Many management experts feel that budgeting for the first year of operation for any food service enterprise is as much an art as a science. The reason, of course, is that the venture is new—there are no sales history records on which to base forecasts. That means that estimates of the number of guests to expect and the expenses that are likely to be incurred ought to be made by persons with experience or with at least a solid understanding of what goals are reasonable in terms of revenues and costs. Once the business has been running for a year or more and has a track record, the forecaster's work becomes easier.

Since food is the primary tangible item for sale in a restaurant, the procedures related to menu planning, the acquisition of food products, and the processing of food through storage, production, and service are important elements of a restaurant's control system. Equally important is control over labor costs. The cost of food sold plus payroll costs and employee benefits (such as paid vacation, sick leave, employee meals, and bonuses) constitute the largest costs of operation. Together they are known as **prime costs,** representing approximately 60 percent of sales. While all expenses must be controlled, prime costs are management's major concern.

The following sections will discuss strategies for controlling food, labor, and beverage costs.

**Controlling Food Costs. Food cost** is defined as the cost of food used in the production of a menu item. To control food costs, most restaurants use a system of control points that are linked in a cycle similar to the one shown in Exhibit 7. A problem anywhere in the food cost control cycle can weaken the operation's control over food costs. Let's take a closer look at each of the cycle's control points.

**Exhibit 7  Food Cost Control Cycle**

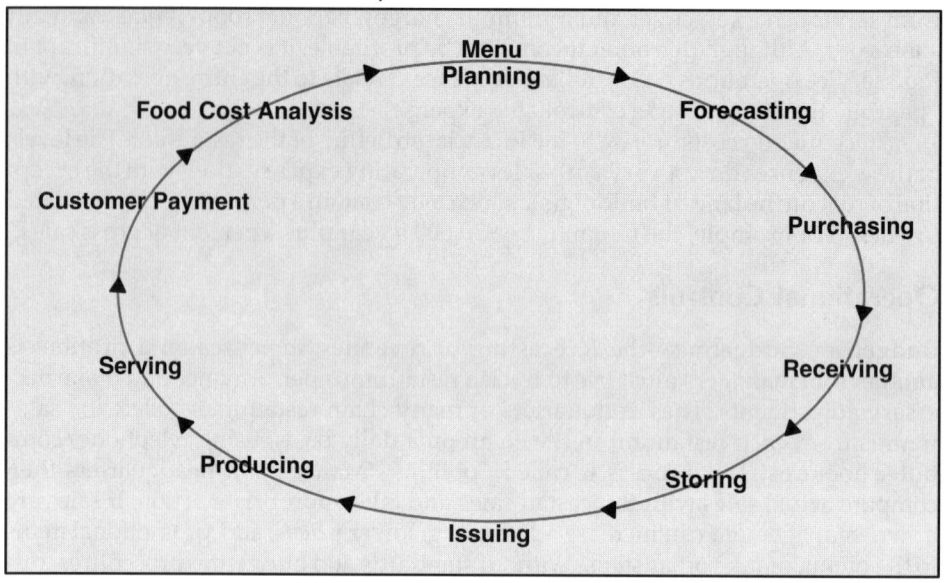

*Cycle diagram showing the following stages in clockwise order: Menu Planning → Forecasting → Purchasing → Receiving → Storing → Issuing → Producing → Serving → Customer Payment → Food Cost Analysis → (back to Menu Planning)*

**Menu planning.** Once a restaurant is in operation, ongoing market research is needed to update the existing menu or develop a new one. Such research includes periodic analyses of menu items sold. Computerized point-of-sale (POS) systems make this analysis easier. Sales of menu items can be tracked by meal period or, if necessary, by the hour. This information can help menu planners develop a menu guests will like. (Their choice of menu items is not unlimited, however; they must keep in mind their operation's concept, equipment, staff, and budget.) With such an analysis in hand, the planner can remove menu items that are not selling and replace them with items that may prove more popular. To achieve an optimal mix of popular and profitable menu items, managers perform a menu analysis. The following discussion is not intended to give you a detailed understanding of menu analysis; its purpose is to introduce you to the subject and acquaint you with some of the methods used in the industry.

There are a number of ways to analyze a menu. The earliest was proposed by Jack Miller, who used a "cost percentage" scheme that suggested that the best menu items ("winners") were those that achieved the lowest food cost percentage and the highest popularity.[13] A second method, proposed by Michael Kasavana and Donald Smith of the Boston Consulting Group, placed all menu items into a chart consisting of four sections labeled **stars, plowhorses, puzzles,** and **dogs.** Under this system, the best items (stars) were those that produced the highest **contribution margin** (the menu item's selling price minus the cost of the food that went into preparing the item) and the largest sales volume. A third method was suggested by David Pavesic. Pavesic said that the best items, the **primes**, were those with a low food cost and a high contribution margin, which he weighted by

## Exhibit 8  Levels of Profitability Analysis

|  | | | | | |
|---|---|---|---|---|---|
| Level 1 The Operation | | The Restaurant | | | |
| Level 2 Meal Segments | Breakfast | Lunch | Dinner | Catering | |
| Level 3 Menu Categories | Appetizers | Entrées | Desserts | Beverages | Beer & Wine |
| Level 4 Menu Items | Prime Rib / Top Sirloin / Veal | Fried Chicken / Pasta / Salmon / Lamb Shank | | | |

Source: Mohamed E. Bayou and Lee B. Bennett, "Profitability Analysis for Table-Service Restaurants," *Cornell Quarterly*, April 1992, p.53.

sales volume.[14] All of these methods rely on averages to separate the winners from the losers.

David Hayes and Lynn Huffman suggested a fourth method that created an individual profit and loss (P&L) statement for each item. Their system calculates the P&L for each item by allocating all variable and fixed costs incurred in the restaurant among the items on the menu. Variable costs are those that change when business volume changes (for example, food servers or table linens). A fixed cost is an item such as insurance, which does not vary according to volume. The best items, according to Hayes and Huffman, are those that contribute the greatest profit.

Finally, Mohamed E. Bayou, assistant professor of accounting at the University of Michigan, and Lee B. Bennett, an experienced restaurant-chain controller, have proposed a method that begins by analyzing the profitability of the restaurant as a whole, and then the profitability of each of its meal segments (breakfast, lunch, dinner, and catering). Once this is done, a margin for each menu category, such as appetizers, entrées, and desserts, is calculated and from there a margin for each item within the category is established (see Exhibit 8). On the surface, this procedure sounds complicated, but when Bayou and Bennett surveyed the managers of 103 table-service restaurants in southeastern Michigan, they found that 55 percent used an approach that was similar to their "segment-contribution analysis" method.[15]

Professor Stephen Miller of Boston University suggests that "the proliferation of personal computers and low-cost, easy-to-use software means virtually any organization can quickly and easily perform menu analyses anytime at little or no additional expense."[16] Miller calls his system "The Simplified Menu-Cost Spreadsheet."

**140** *Chapter 5*

**Exhibit 9  Sample Menu-Cost Spreadsheet**

| E | F | G | H | I | J | K |
|---|---|---|---|---|---|---|
| Menu Item | Cost per Entrée | Cost of Side Dishes | Total Cost | Selling Price | Food-Cost % | Gross Profit |
| Beef Kebob | $2.82 | $1.25 | $4.07 | $8.75 | 46.51% | $4.68 |
| Chicken Kiev | $2.07 | $1.25 | $3.32 | $8.50 | 39.06% | $5.18 |
| Chopped Beef Stk | $0.93 | $1.25 | $2.18 | $7.95 | 27.42% | $5.77 |
| Delmonico Stk | $5.46 | $1.25 | $6.71 | $9.95 | 67.44% | $3.24 |
| Filet Mignon | $4.43 | $1.25 | $5.68 | $15.95 | 34.61% | $10.27 |
| Fried Shrimp | $3.62 | $1.25 | $4.87 | $9.95 | 48.94% | $5.08 |
| Lamb Chops | $3.15 | $1.25 | $4.40 | $12.95 | 33.98% | $8.55 |
| Liver & Bacon | $1.49 | $1.25 | $2.74 | $7.50 | 36.53% | $4.76 |
| London Broil | $1.80 | $1.25 | $3.05 | $8.95 | 34.08% | $5.90 |
| Perch | $1.84 | $1.25 | $3.09 | $8.95 | 34.53% | $5.86 |
| Pork Chops | $1.49 | $1.25 | $2.74 | $8.50 | 32.24% | $5.76 |
| Prime Rib | $6.50 | $1.25 | $7.75 | $14.95 | 51.84% | $7.20 |
| Scallops | $4.22 | $1.25 | $5.47 | $11.95 | 45.77% | $6.48 |
| Scrod | $2.11 | $1.25 | $3.36 | $8.95 | 37.54% | $5.59 |
| Seafood Kebob | $3.27 | $1.25 | $4.52 | $9.95 | 45.43% | $5.43 |
| Seafood Platter | $3.99 | $1.25 | $5.24 | $15.50 | 33.81% | $10.26 |
| Sole/Crabmeat | $4.20 | $1.25 | $5.45 | $10.95 | 49.77% | $5.50 |
| Strip Steak | $4.99 | $1.25 | $6.24 | $14.95 | 41.74% | $8.71 |
| Swordfish | $4.94 | $1.25 | $6.19 | $12.95 | 47.80% | $6.76 |
| Turkey | $1.59 | $1.25 | $2.84 | $8.25 | 34.42% | $5.41 |
| Whitefish | $2.73 | $1.25 | $3.98 | $12.95 | 30.73% | $8.97 |

Source: Stephen G. Miller, "The Simplified Menu-Cost Spreadsheet," *Cornell Quarterly,* June 1992, p. 87.

Under Miller's system, a spreadsheet listing all ingredients and their costs is first set up, then the cost of menu items and side dishes is calculated along with selling price and **gross profit.** A portion of Miller's spreadsheet is reproduced in Exhibit 9.

**Forecasting.** Once the menu is created and a restaurant has been open long enough for a sales pattern to be established, management should forecast total expected business by meal period, as well as by menu item, in order to determine purchasing needs and plan production. Accurate forecasting keeps food costs down because food is not purchased to be left sitting in a storeroom, perhaps to spoil before it is needed.

## Exhibit 10  Sample Purchase Specification Format

_____
(name of food and beverage operation)

1. Product name: _____

2. Product used for:

> Clearly indicate product use (such as olive garnish for beverage, hamburger patty or grill-fry for sandwich, etc.).

3. Product general description:

> Provide general quality information about desired product. For example, "Iceberg lettuce; heads to be green and firm without spoilage, excessive dirt or damage. No more than 10 outer leaves. Packed 24 heads per case."

4. Detailed description:

> Purchaser should state other factors that help to clearly identify desired product. Examples of specific factors, which vary by product being described, may include:
>
> - Geographic origin
> - Variety
> - Type
> - Style
> - Grade
> - Product size
> - Portion size
> - Brand name
> - Density
> - Specific gravity
> - Container size
> - Edible yield, trim

5. Product test procedures:

> Test procedures can occur at the time the product is received and/or after product is prepared/used. For example, products that should be at a refrigerated temperature upon delivery can be tested with a thermometer. Portion-cut meat patties can be randomly weighed. Lettuce packed 24 heads per case can be counted.

6. Special instructions and requirements:

> Any additional information needed to clearly indicate quality expectations can be included here. Examples include bidding procedures, if applicable, labeling and/or packaging requirements, and special delivery and service requirements.

**Purchasing.** In any food service operation, the goal in purchasing is to keep food costs down by obtaining the right product for the best price. To accomplish this, **purchase specifications** must be developed for all food items used in the restaurant, so that bids based on those specifications can be obtained from suppliers. A purchase specification is a detailed description of a food item for ordering purposes (see Exhibit 10). The description might include size by weight ("3 lb. chicken") or by volume ("#2 can"); grade ("Rib of Beef—USDA Prime" or "Peaches—Fancy"); and packaging ("Iceberg Lettuce—24 count" or "Eggs—30 dozen").

According to Lendal H. Kotschevar, author of *Management by Menu* and other food service industry texts, most food specifications should include the following:

- Name of the item
- Grade of the item, brand, or other quality information
- Packaging method, package size, and special requirements
- Basis for price—by the pound, case, piece, or dozen
- Miscellaneous factors required to get the right item, such as the number of days beef should be aged, the region in which the item is produced, and the requirement that all items be inspected for wholesomeness[17]

Purchase specifications enable the restaurant's purchaser to communicate to suppliers an exact description of what is needed to meet the restaurant's standards. Veteran operators are able to establish these specifications based on need and personal experience. Beginners and others who would like assistance can turn to sources such as the National Association of Meat Purveyors in Chicago, which publishes the "Meat Buyers Guide to Portion Control Meat Cuts" and the "Meat Buyers Guide to Standardized Meat Cuts." The U.S. Department of Agriculture offers a variety of helpful publications covering the purchase of produce, milk, and fresh and processed food products.

Once you have developed purchase specifications, the next task is to determine how much of each item to purchase. As explained earlier, the best way to accomplish this is to forecast the number of guests you expect and identify the menu items they are most likely to order. Delivery schedules also play a part in determining how much to order. Delivery schedules depend in part on the restaurant's location in relation to its suppliers—the greater the distance, the costlier the deliveries. Many restaurants order large quantities of the items they can stock up on (such as nonperishable items) so fewer deliveries are needed. Restaurants typically like to receive fresh fish and produce daily; meats twice weekly; canned and frozen items weekly or biweekly; and nonperishable items, such as napkins or sugar packets, quarterly or even semi-annually. The level of inventory already on hand is another obvious factor in determining how much to order. Computers make it easier to track inventory levels closely and make rate-of-consumption information on individual items readily available.

Recent years have seen an important development in food purchasing—not unlike the change that overtook household shopping when supermarkets replaced traditional grocery stores. The concept is known as **one-stop purchasing.** Some food distributors have expanded their product lines so that it is now possible to find one supplier who sells everything from produce and dairy products to fresh meat and poultry or even kitchen equipment. One-stop purchasing helps food service operations streamline their ordering, receiving, and accounting procedures.

**Receiving.** Acceptable receiving procedures mandate that the employees receiving the food items clearly understand the food specifications adopted by the restaurant. Receiving clerks help keep food costs down by verifying that:

- The items delivered are those ordered and correspond to the quantity on the supplier's invoice
- The quoted price and the invoice price are the same
- The quality and size of the items delivered match the restaurant's specifications

In addition, receiving clerks handle the initial processing of invoices and deliver the food to the kitchen or to storage areas. Some operators favor a "**blind receiving**" system. With this system, suppliers give the receiving clerk a list of items being delivered but not the quantities or weights. This forces the clerk to count or weigh the incoming products and record his or her findings on the invoice. Later these figures are compared with (1) the supplier's invoice received by the accounting office, and (2) the restaurant's purchase order.

Receiving clerks must check large shipments on a random basis for quality and count. Items that do not meet the restaurant's standards are generally returned and a credit is recorded on the invoice. Those items that are acceptable are placed in storage, ready to be used as needed.

Controlling the receiving process is an important part of keeping food costs down, because receiving is an area in which dishonest employees or suppliers can take advantage of employers. For example, suppliers may deliver a lower-grade product than ordered, with the hope that it will pass unnoticed, or use extra packing material to increase the weight of goods delivered.

**Storing.** Food storage facilities consist of dry storerooms, refrigerators, and freezers. Ideally, food storage areas should:

- Have adequate capacity
- Be close to receiving and food preparation areas
- Have suitable temperature and humidity levels
- Be secure from unauthorized personnel
- Be protected from vermin and insects

In addition, careful consideration should be given to storage shelves and the arrangement of items within the storage facility. Obviously, the items used most frequently should be stored near the entrance. Sometimes goods are stored on shelves by groups ("vegetables" might be one group, for example) and then alphabetically within those groups (asparagus, broccoli, cauliflower, corn, and so on).

A standard inventory system of **first-in, first-out (FIFO)** is almost always adopted. With this system, older products (those received first) are stored in front so that they will be used first, and newer shipments are stored behind them for use later. Proper storage reduces spoilage and waste.

**Issuing.** Formal procedures for transferring food from storage to production or service areas are an essential part of any control system. The purpose of such procedures is to keep track of inventory usage, and make sure only authorized employees take food from storage.

In some instances, a small amount of food goes directly from the receiving area to the kitchen or dining room, bypassing the issuing system used to requisition food from storage areas. This is known as a **direct purchase.** Most direct purchases consist of items that will be used that day, such as fresh-baked goods and fresh fish. Food service operations can calculate their daily food costs by adding together direct purchases and storeroom issues.

The bulk of the inventory received in each shipment goes to various storage areas. Items from storage are issued using a requisition system. A **requisition form** identifies the person who ordered the items and the type, amount, and price of each item. Sometimes the area the items are going to—for example, the pantry or kitchen range area—is identified. Although many operations manually calculate the cost of requisitioned food, the trend is to use computerized systems to calculate this cost. Some operators track food by categories such as meat, fish, fresh produce, or staples. This enhances control by showing how the restaurant uses specific food categories and, within each category, specific food items.

Modern food service operations with relatively uncomplicated menus have been the first to adopt computerized issuing. For computerized issuing to work, standard recipes must be used. When food is requisitioned for a specific menu item, the computer determines the quantity to be issued based on the standard recipe. Computerized issuing systems work best in hospitals, schools, and other institutional food service operations that prepare large numbers of the same types of meals. Few hotels have adopted the system, due to their many different restaurant concepts and menus. But as new software becomes available, this technology is expected to spread.

**Producing.** Standard recipes are essential in controlling food costs. With a standard recipe, managers can calculate exactly how much it should cost to produce each menu item. As a result, managers have something to compare actual costs with, and can take into consideration the cost of producing menu items when setting menu prices. Standard recipes are also important in controlling labor costs, since employees using such recipes require less training and supervision.

Standard recipes play a major role in customer satisfaction. By using standard recipes, operators are able to provide consistency in quality and quantity no matter who is in the kitchen. Standard recipes enable restaurants to ensure that every time a repeat customer orders a particular item, the same product and portion will be served.

**Serving.** If service is not friendly and efficient, all other efforts in the control cycle are in vain because most guests will stop going to a restaurant where they receive poor service. Well-trained food servers who know the menu and have good people skills can help overcome production problems. However, if servers are not attentive to the needs of guests, the best efforts of the chef and others in the kitchen will not be enough to produce a satisfactory experience. It is a mistake to assume that operations that do not offer table service need not be concerned with their level of service. Even the food servers in a cafeteria serving line help set the mood for guests.

**Customer payment.** Obviously, a restaurant can't recoup its food costs if customer payments are not collected. There is no one universal payment system—systems vary from operation to operation. Here are some of the ways payment can be settled:

- The customer pays a cashier who tabulates the food order (as in a cafeteria).

Servers have a tremendous impact on the guests' experience—and the bottom line.

- The customer pays an order-taker/cashier who rings up the order on a cash register before the food is delivered (as in fast-food operations).
- The server writes the order and prices on a check, or the order is machine-printed and priced on a check. The check is then settled in one of the following ways: (1) the customer pays the cashier; (2) the customer pays the server, who pays the cashier; or (3) the customer pays the server, who maintains a bank.

The goal of any cash control system is to ensure that what comes out of the kitchen is in fact served, recorded as a sale, and paid for. In those establishments where the server takes the order, the server writes the order on a check. The original is kept for presentation to the customer for payment at the end of the meal, and will eventually be placed in the cash register. A duplicate is carried to the kitchen so that production personnel know what to prepare. Computerized point-of-sale systems can help servers perform this process faster and with less legwork. Servers input the order into a hand-held or stationary point-of-sale terminal in the dining room. The order is electronically transmitted to the kitchen, where it is shown on a kitchen video display monitor or printed by a small work station printer. Whether checks are recorded manually or by computer, control records (that is, the machine data, the check, and the duplicate check) are created that can be reconciled at the end of the meal.

**Food cost analysis.** A common statistic used throughout the food service industry is the **food cost percentage**. This number represents the cost of food sold to

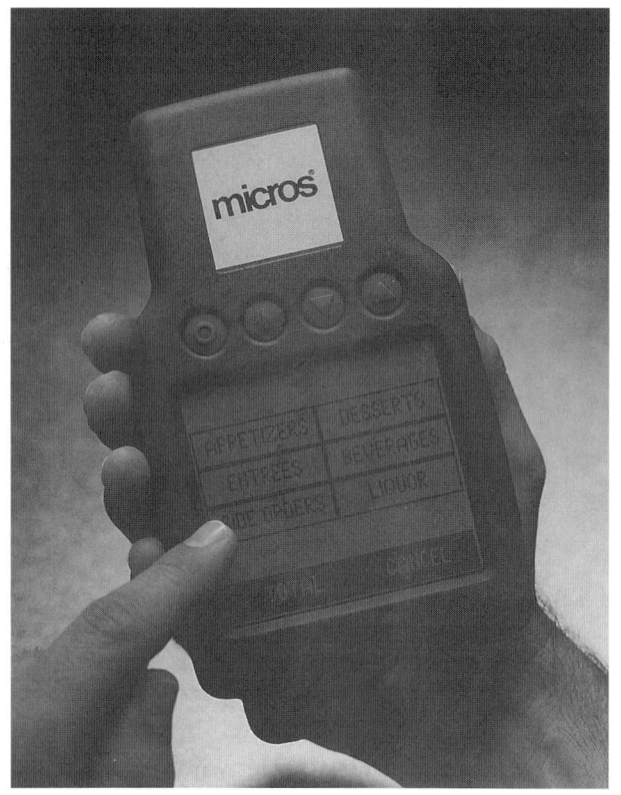

**Hand-held server terminals speed ordering and help with control.** (Courtesy of Micros Systems, Inc.)

customers in a given period (the month of June, for example), divided by food sales for the same period.

To reach the **cost of food sold,** one must deduct meals that are consumed but not sold, such as complimentary meals. The cost of food sold is based on beginning and closing inventories and food purchases for the period between the two inventories, minus complimentary meals. The following figures illustrate how this works:

| | |
|---|---|
| Beginning Inventory | $ 20,000 |
| Add Food Purchases | + 15,000 |
| Total | $ 35,000 |
| Deduct Closing Inventory | −  4,000 |
| Cost of Food Consumed | $ 31,000 |
| Deduct Employee Meals ($1,500) and Complimentary Meals ($500) | −  2,000 |
| COST OF FOOD SOLD | $ 29,000 |

Assume food sales for this period (the month of June, for example) were $100,000. To compute the food cost percentage, the formula is:

$$\frac{\$29{,}000 \text{ (cost of food sold)}}{\$100{,}000 \text{ (food sales)}} = .29 \times 100\times = \times 29\%$$

In this example, 29 percent reflects the actual cost of food sold (expressed as a percentage of food sales) during June. This percentage has little value unless it can be compared to a goal or an acceptable food cost percentage range established by management.

How do managers come up with a food cost goal or an acceptable range within which food costs should fall? They often use a standard cost system based on standard recipes. Since each standard recipe is an exact formula for making $X$ number of menu items, the exact or standard cost of preparing a menu item can be computed. Managers can total the standard costs for all the menu items sold during June, divide this figure by the total menu item sales for June, multiply by 100, and come up with the **standard food cost percentage**, which would match the actual food cost percentage for June if everything worked exactly as it should have. Assuming the manager assessed standard food costs in June at $27,000, the standard food cost percentage would be calculated as follows:

$$\frac{\$27{,}000 \text{ (standard food costs)}}{\$100{,}000 \text{ (food sales)}} = .27 \times 100 = 27\%$$

In this case, the standard food cost percentage for June is 27 percent. The actual food cost percentage for June was 29 percent—2 percentage points higher than the standard. Since a standard food cost represents the ideal cost that management can expect if everything goes exactly as planned, the actual food cost percentage is almost always higher than the standard food cost percentage. Management at each restaurant must determine an acceptable limit for actual food costs. For example, one operation may set a limit of 2 percentage points over standard food costs. This means that if the standard food cost percentage for a period of time is 22 percent, an actual food cost percentage of 24 percent or below for that time period is acceptable.

Each individual menu item has a standard food cost percentage and, of course, some menu items have a higher food cost percentage than others. However, it is unwise to decide to keep an item on the menu or add a new one by looking at the item's food cost percentage alone. The following comparison between two menu items shows why.

|  | **Lamb Chops** | **Deluxe Omelet** |
|---|---|---|
| Menu Price | $18.00 | $8.00 |
| Standard Food Cost % | 52.8% | 25% |
| Gross Profit | $8.50 | $6.00 |

The deluxe omelet has a lower food cost percentage, which is desirable, but the lamb chops provide a higher gross profit. Obviously, it's preferable to sell the lamb chops, despite the higher costs associated with them, because their gross profit gives the operation $2.50 more ($8.50 - $6.00) to cover other costs and add to profits.

**Controlling Labor Costs.** The cost of payroll and employee benefits averages about 30 percent of sales for most full-service restaurants. This is a high figure when you consider that restaurants have more entry-level and minimum-wage employees than most other businesses. Food service is highly labor-intensive, and quality service on any level demands that employees be well-trained, efficient, and productive. Quick-service restaurants and cafeterias have lower payroll costs primarily because of their methods of service and, in the case of quick-service restaurants, their limited menu and production-line system of food preparation.

Commercial food service establishments have a unique problem in controlling payroll. The amount of money an operation must allocate to payroll depends on two factors: (1) the rates of pay for employees, and (2) the time required to do a given job—that is, productivity. While payroll costs escalate every year, productivity does not. Indeed, many full-service restaurants prepare and serve food today with the same type of equipment and in the same way as did restaurateurs many years ago. (Even quick-service restaurants with new technology will always need a base staff.) As a result, the industry, for the most part, has responded to higher payroll costs by raising menu prices rather than increasing employee productivity, adhering to the conventional wisdom that you cannot raise productivity when you are dealing with low-paid, inexperienced personnel.

However, you can't raise productivity if there aren't enough customers in the restaurant. Even the hardest-working employees can't be productive if there is no one to serve. And the best managers can only trim payroll costs to a certain point, because a minimum number of employees must be on hand when a restaurant opens, even when business is projected to be terrible. Therefore, keeping payroll costs in line depends in part on having a concept and menu that appeal to the target market and having a marketing program strong enough to keep guest demand high.

**Controlling Beverage Costs.** In recent years, the dangers of excessive alcohol use have gained greater recognition in the United States and elsewhere, and consumption of all kinds of alcoholic beverages has dropped dramatically. Nevertheless, wine, malt beverages (beer, ale, stout), and distilled spirits—the major categories of alcoholic beverages—are still an important part of restaurant revenue. Alcoholic beverages account for approximately 22 percent of sales in medium-priced full-service restaurants. These sales are highly profitable because of the high markup on beverages. In fine restaurants, a markup of 100 percent for a bottle of wine is not unusual. Most drinks are easy to pour or mix, and the labor and beverage costs combined represent a small part of the sales price.

Purchasing alcoholic beverages is relatively uncomplicated compared to purchasing food. Purchase specifications are limited to brand (Dewars White Label scotch, Budweiser beer, Robert Mondavi wine); size (liters, quarts, fifths, kegs); and, in the case of wine, vintages. Competitive bidding is usually not necessary. Some states, known as monopoly or control states, set beverage prices and allow

"And what is your preference in wine -- single or double figures?"

Source: Cartoon by Levin, appearing in the United States; Cartoonists & Writers Syndicate, New York, New York.

beverage purchases to be made only from state-owned stores. Most states, however, are license states. In these, operators can buy from private wholesalers licensed by the state. Even in these states, state laws are typically designed to limit price wars, and prices do not vary a great deal among wholesalers. Most license states publish a monthly master list of wholesalers in the state, the beverages they carry, and the prices they charge.

Receiving is also straightforward. For example, weighing or checking for wholesomeness is not necessary. The receiving clerk simply verifies that what was ordered—brand, size, amount, and vintage—is what was delivered and billed on the invoice.

Secure storage is of prime importance. Access to beverage storage areas should be limited to authorized personnel. All items should be grouped by brand. Wine bottles should be stored on their side or bottom-up to keep the cork moist. Temperature control during storage is crucial. The ideal storage temperature for red wines is 65°F (18.3°C) and for white wines 45°F to 50°F (7.2°C to 10°C).

Issuing is generally done by requisition. If there is more than one bar, separate requisitions are written by personnel at each bar. Some operations stamp their liquor bottles with their name or logo to prevent unscrupulous bartenders from bringing in their own bottles, pouring drinks from them, and pocketing the money.

In most operations, a perpetual inventory of beverage items is maintained either manually or by computer. A **perpetual inventory** is a record that shows what should be on hand in the storeroom at any one time. It is compiled from daily invoices and requisitions by adding each day's purchases and subtracting each day's issues. Of course, inventory levels should be checked by a physical count on a regular basis, usually monthly. The perpetual inventory system is particularly helpful for purchasing managers, since it tracks inventory usage on a daily, weekly, and monthly basis.

Control over individual drink sales may take one or more forms. Many operators have employed automated systems with electronic or mechanical devices attached to each bottle that record every drink poured. The advantages are obvious. The manager or owner can easily determine how many drinks have been sold and thus what the receipts should be. The system reduces loss from spillage and overpouring and prevents a bartender from underpouring or offering complimentary drinks to friends. The disadvantage of an automated system is that it impedes those bartenders who make pouring drinks a theatrical presentation.

Managers can control the amount of beverages on hand at a bar by establishing a "par." A **bar's par** is the amount of each type of beverage that managers want to be available behind the bar. It is based largely on expected consumption. Levels are set high enough so that the bar will not run out of an item during a bartender's shift, but not so high that theft is encouraged. At the end of each shift, empty bottles are replaced so that the bar's beverage stock is at par for the next shift.

Beverage control is crucial to running any establishment that sells beverages to customers. Product consistency and the threat of theft are the primary areas of concern. Only through proper controls can these concerns be addressed and customer satisfaction and profitability be ensured.

## Chapter Summary

Food service operations that are organized for success focus on their customers. Since preferences and tastes constantly change, a restaurant's management team should keep track of national trends and conduct ongoing research of its own customers to make sure that the restaurant's concept and menu reflect current preferences.

A restaurant's ambiance is also important. Decor, lighting, furnishings, and other features should all be a natural extension of a restaurant's concept.

A third important element of a successful restaurant is its menu. A good menu offers customers what they want, is based on standard recipes that can be prepared and served by the staff of the establishment, takes into account equipment limitations, and lists a variety of items. Menus can be categorized as either fixed menus or cyclical menus. Menus can be further categorized as breakfast, lunch, dinner, or specialty menus. It should be remembered that the menu is primarily a sales tool that should be constructed and presented with marketing in mind.

Pricing menu items correctly is also a key element of organizing for success. Menu prices are related to costs and investment. Basic considerations when setting menu prices include the type of operation, the customers' perception of the price/value relationship, the competition, and the desired level of profit.

Sound financial management is achieved through efficient budgeting, using a system such as the *Uniform System of Accounts for Restaurants*. Components of this system include a balance sheet and a statement of income.

A successful operation keeps its costs within budgeted levels. Prime costs are the most important costs for management to control. Prime costs consist of the cost of food and the cost of payroll and related employee benefits.

There are many control points in the food cost control cycle that help restaurant managers keep food costs down. The first is menu planning. A correctly planned menu has few, if any, unpopular menu items. This helps control food costs by reducing or eliminating the need to purchase food for unpopular menu items. Such food may spoil and have to be thrown away before it is used. Accurate forecasting also helps to reduce food costs because unnecessary food is not ordered. A restaurant's purchaser can minimize food costs by obtaining the right products for the best price. Purchase specifications play an important role in this. If suppliers have a restaurant's purchase specifications in hand as they're formulating a bid, their bids are more likely to be truly comparable, since they are all basing their bids on the same criteria. One development in purchasing that keeps food costs down is one-stop purchasing.

Receiving procedures can also affect food cost. What is received must be verified and compared with what was ordered.

Storage and issuing also require attention if food cost is to be adequately controlled. Storage must protect the operation's inventory from deterioration or theft. Issuing procedures allow managers to keep track of inventory and calculate a daily food cost figure. Daily food cost is calculated by adding together direct purchases and storeroom issues.

Standard recipes that yield standard portions reduce food waste. Standard recipes also reduce food and labor costs. The cost of preparing menu items can only be calculated accurately when standard recipes are used.

Service and cash control concerns include the manner in which customer payments are handled. This varies by type of establishment, but the goal of all cash control systems is to ensure that what comes out of the kitchen is in fact served, recorded, and paid for.

Food cost calculation is essential for the operation of a successful and profitable establishment. A restaurant's overall food cost percentage for a given period is calculated by dividing the cost of food sold during the period by total food sales during the same period. Each menu item has its own food cost percentage and contribution margin. Although, as a rule, a low food cost percentage is desirable because a high contribution margin results, some menu items with high food cost percentages also have high contribution margins. Therefore, operators should keep contribution margins as well as food cost percentages in mind when making decisions about whether to drop or add menu items.

Payroll expenses, including employee benefits, represent about 30 percent of sales in the food service industry, but payroll costs vary considerably by type of establishment.

Alcoholic beverages account for approximately 22 percent of medium-priced full-service restaurant sales—sales that have a high profit margin. Purchasing beverages is fairly uncomplicated since purchase specifications are largely limited to brands and sizes, and competitive bidding is not necessary. Receiving is also straightforward. Issuing is usually tracked by a perpetual inventory system that shows what ought to be on hand in the beverage storeroom. These records should be checked by taking a physical inventory on a regular basis, usually monthly. Finally, a bar par, based mostly on expected consumption, is established at each bar.

## Endnotes

1. Karl Albrecht and Ron Zemke, *Service America* (Homewood, Ill.: Dow Jones-Irwin, 1985), p. 49.
2. Michael Sanson, "The Casual '90s," *Restaurant Hospitality*, January 1992, pp. 95–96.
3. Sanson, p. 96.
4. "What Does Today's Customer Want?" *Restaurants USA*, December 1992, p. 37.
5. "What Does Today's Customer Want?" p. 37.
6. "What Does Today's Customer Want?" p. 37.
7. Terry Breen, "Cartoon Caper," *Restaurant Hospitality*, January 1992, p. 125.
8. Breen, p. 126.
9. "The Marketing 100," *Advertising Age*, 5 July 1993, p. S-24.
10. Yumiko Ono, "Japan's Fast Food Companies Cook Up Local Platters to Tempt Local Palates," *Wall Street Journal*, 28 May 1992, p. B1.
11. "The Hungry Host Restaurant," *Lodging*, December 1991, pp. 20–21.
12. A. Dyal Bailey, "How Computer Registers Saved My Family Life," *Restaurants USA*, October 1992, pp. 12–13.
13. Mohamed E. Bayou and Lee B. Bennett, "Profitability Analysis for Table-Service Restaurants," *Cornell Quarterly*, April 1992, p. 50.
14. Bayou and Bennett, p. 50.
15. Bayou and Bennett, p. 55.
16. Stephen G. Miller, "The Simplified Menu-Cost Spreadsheet," *Cornell Quarterly*, June 1992, p. 85.
17. Lendal H. Kotschevar, *Management by Menu*, 2d ed. (Chicago: National Institute for the Foodservice Industry/William C. Brown, 1987), p. 261.

## Key Terms

**ambiance**—The decor, lighting, furnishings, and other factors that create a feeling about or an identity for an establishment.

**bar par**—The amount of each type of beverage established for behind-the-bar storage, based on expected consumption.

**blind receiving**—A receiving system in which the supplier gives the receiving clerk a list of items being delivered but not the quantities or weights, thereby forcing the clerk to count or weigh the incoming products and record the results. These results are later compared with the supplier's invoice.

**contribution margin**—A food or beverage item's selling price minus the cost of the ingredients used to prepare the item.

**cost of food sold**—The expense of the food that is sold to a customer.

**cyclical menu**—A menu that changes every day for a certain number of days, then repeats the cycle. A few cyclical menus change regularly, but without any set pattern. Also known as a cycle menu.

**direct purchase**—Food sent directly from the receiving area to the kitchen or dining room rather than to a storage area.

**dogs**—Unpopular menu items with a low contribution margin.

**first-in, first-out (FIFO)**—An inventory method for rotating and issuing stored food that requires items that have been in storage the longest to be used first.

**fixed menu**—A menu with a set list of items that is used for several months or longer before it is changed. Also known as a static menu.

**food cost**—The cost of food used in the production of a menu item.

**food cost percentage**—A ratio comparing the cost of food sold to food sales, calculated by dividing the cost of food sold during a given period by food sales during the same period.

**gross profit**—Price minus the cost of food.

**menu analysis**—A system whereby the cost of each menu item is calculated and deducted from the sales price of the item to reveal its gross profit. A menu item's gross profit is the amount of money it generates that can be used to cover all other operating costs.

**one-stop purchasing**—A convenience offered to food service operations by food distributors with broad, expanded product lines, enabling a purchase to buy everything from produce to kitchen equipment from one supplier.

**perpetual inventory system**—A system for tracking inventory by keeping a running balance of inventory quantities—that is, recording all additions to and subtractions from stock.

**plowhorses**—Popular menu items with a low contribution margin.

**prime costs**—The cost of food sold plus payroll cost (including employee benefits). These are a restaurant's highest costs.

**primes**—Menu items with a low food cost and a high margin.

**purchase specifications**—A detailed description—for ordering purposes—of the quality, size, weight, and other characteristics desired for a particular item.

**puzzles**—Unpopular menu items with a high contribution margin.

**requisition form**—A written order used by employees that identifies the type, amount, and value of items needed from storage.

**specialty menu**—A menu that differs from the typical breakfast, lunch, or dinner menu. Specialty menus are usually designed for holidays and other special events or for specific guest groups. Examples include children's, beverage, dessert, and banquet menus.

**standard food cost percentage**—The ideal food cost percentage that managers should expect when a menu item is prepared according to its standard recipe. It is calculated by dividing the standard food cost of the menu item by its sale price and multiplying by 100.

**standard recipe**—A formula for producing a food or beverage item specifying ingredients, the required quantity of each ingredient, preparation procedures, portion size and portioning equipment, garnish, and any other information necessary to prepare the item.

**stars**—Popular menu items with high contribution margins.

## Review Questions

1. What are the most important success factors for a restaurant?
2. Why is keeping up with customer preferences so important?
3. What elements contribute to a restaurant's success?
4. What are some basic rules to keep in mind when creating menus?
5. How do fixed menus differ from cycle menus?
6. What is a balance sheet? a statement of income?
7. What control points make up the food cost control cycle?
8. A purchase specification should include what kinds of information?
9. What is a food cost percentage and how is it calculated?
10. In what ways does beverage cost control differ from food cost control? In what ways is it similar?

## Internet Sites

For more information, visit the following Internet sites. Remember that Internet addresses can change without notice. If the site is no longer there, use a search engine to look for additional sites.

*Restaurant Companies*

Applebee's Grill & Bar
www.applebees.com

Burger King
www.burgerking.com

Fuddrucker's
www.fuddruckers.com

McDonald's
www.mcdonalds.com

The Olive Garden
www.olivegarden.com

Pizza Hut
www.pizzahut.com

Planet Hollywood
www.planethollywd.com

Red Lobster
www.redlobster.com

## Point-of-Sale (POS) Systems

Javelin Systems
www.jvln.com

MICROS Systems, Inc
www.micros.com

Remanco International
www.remanco.com

## REVIEW QUIZ

When you feel you have covered all of the material in this chapter, answer these questions. Choose the *best* answer.

1. Offering menu items that use fresh fruits and vegetables that are out of season is likely to:

   a. make menu planning easier.
   b. lower food quality.
   c. increase food costs.
   d. b and c.

2. The most important element of a restaurant's success is usually its:

   a. management.
   b. decor.
   c. menu.
   d. employees.

3. The primary goal in establishing menu prices is to:

   a. bring in enough revenue to cover costs while providing the owners with a reasonable return on investment.
   b. attract as many customers as possible.
   c. keep prices lower than the competition without letting the operation lose money.
   d. keep income control procedures as simple as possible while maintaining a steady revenue stream.

4. Forecasting a restaurant's revenues, expenses, and profits is known as:

   a. food cost analysis.
   b. budgeting.
   c. inventorying.
   d. requisitioning.

5. You are the manager of the Laredo Restaurant. You want to make sure that Ted, your receiving clerk, is careful about checking in suppliers, so you set up a food receiving system in which suppliers give Ted a list of items being delivered but not the quantities or weights. This receiving system is called a _____ system.

   a. masked invoicing
   b. blind receiving
   c. controlled receiving
   d. purchase specification

## REVIEW QUIZ *(continued)*

6. The following restaurant food figures refer to a single time period:

   | | |
   |---|---|
   | Beginning Inventory | $20,000 |
   | Food Purchases | $15,000 |
   | Closing Inventory | $ 4,000 |
   | Cost of employee and complimentary meals consumed | $ 2,000 |

   What is the restaurant's cost of food sold for this time period?

   a. $15,000
   b. $29,000
   c. $41,000
   d. $43,200

7. Which of the following statements about restaurant customer payment systems is *true?*

   a. Hand-held server terminals allow guests to pay their checks by electronically accessing their checking or savings account.
   b. Guest checks should not be duplicated.
   c. Guest payment systems vary from restaurant to restaurant.
   d. Because of computerization, all restaurants use the same guest payment system.

**Answer Key:** 1-d-C1, 2-c-C1, 3-a-C2, 4-b-C3, 5-b-C3, 6-b-C4, 7-c-C4

Each question is linked to a competency. Competencies are listed on the first page of the chapter. An answer reading 3-b-C4 translates to:

- 3: the question number
- b: the correct answer
- C4: the competency number

## Chapter 6 Outline

Hotel Guests
    Corporate Individuals
    Corporate Groups
    Convention and Association Groups
    Leisure Travelers
    Long-Term Stay/Relocation Guests
    Airline-Related Guests
    Government and Military Travelers
    Regional Getaway Guests
    Guest Mix
Hotel Categories
    Location
    Ownership
    Price
    Other Hotel Categories
Industry Trends
    Global Performance
    The United States
Developing and Planning New Hotels
    Site Selection
    The Feasibility Study
    Financing
Chapter Summary

## Competencies

1. List and briefly describe important hotel guest segments.

2. Describe center city, resort, suburban, highway, and airport hotels, including their services and facilities, and summarize their historical development.

3. Explain various ways hotels can be owned and operated; define "independent hotel," "management company," "hotel chain," "franchise," "franchisor," "franchisee," and "referral system"; and explain how hotels can be categorized by price.

4. Identify and describe the following hotel categories: conference centers, interval ownership/timeshare, condominium hotels, and continuing-care retirement communities.

5. Identify industry trends, and outline the following steps in developing and planning new hotels: site selection, the feasibility study, and financing.

# 6

# Understanding the World of Hotels

IN THIS CHAPTER we will discuss types of hotel guests and the various types of hotels they patronize. You will learn about hotel branding concepts and some of the differences between chain and independent hotels. Major players will be identified so you can become familiar with the business philosophies of the most successful hotel companies. Finally, there is a section on developing and planning new hotels. Included in this section is information on the use and structure of feasibility studies.

## Hotel Guests

In his book *Hospitality in Transition,* Albert J. Gomes describes the most important guest segments that constitute the market for the hotel industry today.[1] They are:

- Corporate individuals
- Corporate groups
- Convention and association groups
- Leisure travelers
- Long-term stay/relocation guests
- Airline-related guests
- Government and military travelers
- Regional getaway guests

### Corporate Individuals

**Corporate individuals**—not part of any group—are guests who travel for business purposes. They usually stay one or two nights. The most frequent users of lodging services, corporate guests typically stay in hotels 15 to 20 times per year. U.S. companies spent $33 million on lodging in 1997. Sixty percent of the hotel industry's business comes from the business traveler. A study by *Lodging Hospitality* lists the top five reasons—in order of preference—that a business traveler chooses a hotel:[2]

1. Location
2. Room rate
3. Reputation

4. Employer preference
5. On-site amenities

Forty percent of these travelers make their reservations through a travel agency, 29 percent call a hotel company's toll-free phone number, and 28 percent call a hotel directly. Use of the Internet to make hotel reservations is steadily increasing. On-site amenities that business travelers use most often include restaurants, lounges, and room service. They also take advantage of exercise facilities, concierge floors, and business centers. Business travelers have very definite ideas about what they need to facilitate their work on the road. A working desk is their highest priority, followed by access to a fax machine, proper lighting, a phone at the desk, access to a copy machine, and a comfortable desk chair. Travelers who use laptop computers also need data ports.[3]

Business travelers care about recognition and special treatment. Frequent-stay programs such as Hilton Honors and Hyatt's Golden Passport have proven particularly effective with part of this market segment. Individual corporate travelers are often members of airline frequent-flyer programs, and they may choose hotels and rental car companies tied in with such programs when they have a choice.

## Corporate Groups

**Corporate groups** travel purely for business purposes but, unlike individual corporate travelers, are usually attending a small conference or meeting at the hotel or at another facility in the area, and their rooms are booked in blocks by their company or a travel agency. These travelers usually stay from two to four days. While top managers are typically assigned single rooms, middle- and lower-level managers often share rooms.

Corporate group travelers favor hotels that offer intimate meeting rooms and private dining facilities. Several conference centers with these features have been constructed in suburban locations conveniently located near major cities and airports. The idea is to do away with big-city distractions and give participants a chance to interact not only during meetings but between them as well.

## Convention and Association Groups

Generally, what distinguishes **convention and association groups** from other corporate groups is their size. The number of people in a convention or association group can run well into the thousands. For example, a world congress of the American Society of Travel Agents typically attracts 5,000 to 7,000 delegates, and every year the National Restaurant Show in Chicago attracts approximately 90,000 visitors. Delegates tend to stay in large hotels where a negotiated package price covers rooms, meals, functions, and often athletic events. Hotels that have fewer rooms and limited function space often compete for group business in slow periods by offering extremely competitive rates. Convention delegates usually share rooms and stay three to four days. Large convention groups choose their venues several years in advance, so a hotel's selling efforts are often prolonged and may involve cooperation from airlines and local convention and visitors bureaus.

## Leisure Travelers

**Leisure travelers** often travel with their families on sightseeing trips, or on trips to visit friends or relatives (VFR travel). Except at resorts, they typically spend only one night at the same hotel, and a room may be occupied by a couple as well as one or more children. Because they travel during peak season, they usually pay full rack rates unless they are members of such organizations as the American Automobile Association or the American Association of Retired Persons, which have been able to negotiate discounts with many hotels.

## Long-Term Stay/Relocation Guests

**Long-term stay/relocation guests** are primarily individuals or families relocating to an area and requiring lodging until permanent housing can be found. Often they are corporate, government, or military personnel. Their needs include limited cooking facilities and more living space than is available in a typical hotel room. All-suite and extended stay hotels such as Embassy Suites and Residence Inns by Marriott are examples of products designed specifically for the needs of long-term guests. A Residence Inn unit is about twice the size of an average hotel room and typically contains a living area, a bedroom, extra closet space, and a small kitchen.

## Airline-Related Guests

Airlines negotiate rates with hotels for airplane crew members and for passengers who need emergency accommodations because they are stranded by some unforeseen event such as a winter storm. Rooms for **airline-related guests** are usually booked in blocks at rock-bottom prices.

## Government and Military Travelers

**Government and military travelers** are reimbursed on fixed per diem allowances, which means they only receive a certain amount for lodging expenses no matter what they have to pay for a room. Therefore, as a general rule these guests stay only in places that have negotiated acceptable rates with their organizations or offer very low rates.

## Regional Getaway Guests

**Regional getaway guests** are important to hotels that normally cater to commercial and convention groups on weekdays. They promote special weekend packages designed to entice nearby residents to leave the kids at home, check into a hotel for Friday and Saturday nights, and enjoy a night or two "on the town." Family packages are also available. Rates are discounted substantially and often include some meals and entertainment.

## Guest Mix

"**Guest mix**" refers to the variety or mixture of guests who stay at a hotel. A hotel's guest mix might consist of 60 percent individual business travelers, 20 percent conventioneers, and 20 percent leisure travelers, for example. Guest mix is carefully managed in successful hotels.

With few exceptions, hotels—no matter where they are located or what their price structure is—strive to capture multiple market segments. A hotel's guest mix depends on its location, size, facilities, and operating philosophy. To fill up rooms not booked by convention groups, hotels geared to convention sales seek individual business travelers and vacationers willing to pay nondiscounted rates. At any one time, a hotel such as the 2,000-room New York Hilton in Manhattan will lodge several groups, some individual business travelers, families on vacation, airline crews, and government employees. By diversifying their guest base, hotels hope to minimize the effect of seasonality, economic recessions, and changing market dynamics.

Students should recognize that there are dangers inherent in this strategy. Sometimes different kinds of guests do not mix well together. For example, business executives paying a top rate for a room may be annoyed to find a noisy tour group blocking their way to the coffee shop in the morning. Some luxury hotels control their mix very carefully, only allowing groups on weekends and, even then, setting up special facilities for group registration and dining so the groups will not interfere with regular guests.

## Hotel Categories

It's important to understand the ways in which hotels are categorized. Hotels can be categorized by location, ownership, price, and other factors.

### Location

Many hospitality publications and consulting firms categorize hotels by location. Some of the most generally recognized hotel location categories are:

- Center city
- Resort
- Suburban
- Highway
- Airport

**Center City.** After the Great Depression of the 1930s, there was a considerable amount of rebuilding and construction in the United States as part of President Franklin Roosevelt's New Deal. One result of that program was that by 1941, when America entered World War II, most cities had at least one downtown hotel built to create jobs and stimulate the economy. Major cities like New York, Chicago, and Los Angeles had many downtown hotels, some of which were internationally famous. These hotels were usually built near railroad stations, for at that time railroad stations were located at or near the center of a city's business district. This followed the pattern that had been established in other major cities of the world as early as the late nineteenth century. London's famous Savoy Hotel, built in 1889, and Frankfurt's Parkhotel are early examples of this trend. In New York City, the Commodore (the Grand Hyatt Hotel now occupies the site) was built right over

The Plaza Hotel, overlooking Central Park in New York City.

Grand Central Station. In St. Louis, the Head House (now the Hyatt Regency) was part of Union Station. Other popular downtown locations for hotels were near centers of government such as city halls and courts, and in financial districts such as merchandise marts or stock exchanges. In those days virtually all of the nation's important business took place near these downtown areas.

After World War II the face of the world began to change. In the United States, automobiles and airplanes replaced trains as the favored means of transportation. Automobiles and good road systems made suburbs possible. Soon the suburbs began attracting office parks, shopping centers, airports, and other businesses. Downtown areas in many parts of the country began to decline. This was not the case in Europe, where trains remained a viable means of transportation. As a consequence the downtown centers of major European capitals continued to flourish.

But most Americans were not ready to let their downtown metropolitan areas die. In the mid-1960s a trend began (which is still continuing today) to restore and rebuild downtown areas. This included building new hotels and refurbishing many of the old ones. In 1969 the Parker House in Boston was bought by the Dunfey hotel chain and a total renovation took place. In Seattle, the Four Seasons purchased the historic Olympic Hotel from Westin. In 1986 Washington D.C.'s Willard Hotel—the hotel of choice for foreign dignitaries, several presidents-elect, and other notables in the nineteenth century—was reopened as an Inter-Continental Hotel after $113 million was invested in its restoration. And in Chicago, the 3,000-room Conrad Hilton Hotel, built in 1927, was closed in 1984 and reopened in 1988 as the Chicago Hilton and Towers after a $180 million renovation. The Roosevelt Hotel in New York City near Grand Central Station was acquired by InterState Hotels in 1997 and refurbished.

The majority of downtown or **center city hotels** today are properties built within the last 25 to 30 years. Along with these hotels, skyscrapers such as the John Hancock Building in Chicago, Columbia Center in Seattle, and the World Trade Center in Manhattan have sprung up. These buildings have kept corporate headquarters in town and attracted new businesses as well. As you would expect, the hotels that surround them attract mostly business travelers. The profile of guests for center city hotels is primarily commercial and convention guests. In general, center city hotels achieve the highest average room rate of all the nonresort hotel categories. These hotels cost more to develop and operate than other categories because of the high cost of real estate, construction, and urban wages.

The majority of center city hotels today are chain operated or managed full-service facilities (see Exhibit 1). In addition to rooms, center city hotels may have a coffee shop as well as other restaurants, at least one bar or cocktail lounge, room service, laundry and valet services, a newsstand and gift shop, and a health club.

Because of the unpredictable arrival and departure times of the business clientele who patronize these properties, extended room service hours are considered essential. The room service menu for the Oriental Hotel in Bangkok states that if guests do not see anything on the menu that they like, the kitchen will be pleased to prepare a requested dish for them at any hour!

Many older center city hotels have no parking facilities on the premises and must offer valet services to park guest automobiles off-site. Consequently, parking fees can be high. Some of these hotels contract at special rates with nearby independent garages, thus lowering their costs somewhat.

**Resort. Resort hotels** are generally found in destinations that are desirable vacation spots because of their climate, scenery, recreational attractions, or historic interest (see Exhibit 2). Mountains and seashores are favorite locales. It is not unusual for resorts to have elaborately landscaped grounds with hiking trails and gardens, as well as extensive sports facilities such as golf courses and tennis courts.

The Romans were the first to build hotels for recreational purposes—usually around hot springs. Famous spas dating back to the Roman Empire still exist, though in modern form, in Baden-Baden, Germany; Bath, England; and other countries. In the United States, early resorts were linked to the transportation system—the highways, rivers, and railroads. Reputedly, the first American resort advertisement appeared in 1789 for Gray's Ferry, Pennsylvania. Guests were offered fishing tackle and free weekly concerts. Transportation to and from nearby cities

## Exhibit 1  Top 20 Center City Hotels

| Rank | Sales Per Room | Property/Location | Rooms and Suites | Total Sales ($000) | Average Occupancy |
|---|---|---|---|---|---|
| 1 | $ 213,753 | The Lowell Hotel<br>New York, NY | 65 | $ 13,894 | 76% |
| 2 | 163,265 | Four Seasons Hotel<br>Washington, DC | 196 | 32,000 | 78 |
| 3 | 148,883 | The Plaza Hotel<br>New York, NY | 806 | 120,000 | 81 |
| 4 | 144,214 | The Rittenhouse Hotel<br>Philadelphia, PA | 98 | 14,133 | 74 |
| 5 | 128,571 | Stanhope Hotel<br>New York, NY | 140 | 18,000 | 72 |
| 6 | 122,685 | Hotel Crescent Court<br>Dallas, TX | 216 | 26,500 | 70 |
| 7 | 117,694 | The Mark<br>New York, NY | 180 | 21,185 | 74 |
| 8 | 106,976 | Ritz-Carlton/Four Seasons<br>Chicago, IL | 430 | 46,000 | 77 |
| 9 | 101,869 | Ritz-Carlton<br>New York, NY | 214 | 21,800 | 80 |
| 10 | 101,388 | Hotel Du Pont<br>Wilmington, DE | 216 | 21,900 | 74 |
| 11 | 99,233 | Rihga Royal Hotel<br>New York, NY | 496 | 49,220 | 83 |
| 12 | 98,666 | Chateau Marmont<br>Hollywood, CA | 63 | 6,216 | 85 |
| 13 | 94,444 | Grand Bay Hotel<br>Coconut Grove, FL | 180 | 17,000 | 70 |
| 14 | 91,628 | Charles Hotel in Harvard Square<br>Cambridge, MA | 296 | 27,122 | 81 |
| 15 | 89,442 | Willard Inter-Continental Hotel<br>Washington, DC | 341 | 30,500 | 66 |
| 16 | 88,790 | The New York Palace<br>New York, NY | 901 | 80,000 | 75 |
| 17 | 85,282 | The Bellevue Hotel<br>Philadelphia, PA | 170 | 14,498 | 65 |
| 18 | 83,934 | Hotel Westbury<br>New York, NY | 229 | 19,221 | 66 |
| 19 | 83,766 | Fitger's Inn<br>Duluth, MN | 60 | 5,026 | 84 |
| 20 | 83,113 | Brown Palace Hotel<br>Denver, CO | 230 | 19,116 | 75 |

Source: "400 Top Performers, "*Lodging Hospitality,* August 1996, p. 31.

## Exhibit 2  Top Five U.S. Resort Destinations—ADR and Occupancy

| | **Average Daily Rate** | | **Occupancy** | |
|---|---|---|---|---|
| 1) | Phoenix/Scottsdale: | $125.16 | Las Vegas: | 81.3% |
| 2) | Hawaii: | $122.04 | Reno, NV: | 78.3% |
| 3) | San Francisco: | $115.95 | Hawaii: | 76.0% |
| 4) | New Orleans: | $115.32 | Phoenix/Scottsdale: | 75.1% |
| 5) | Western Ski Areas: | $115.25 | San Francisco: | 75.0% |

Source: Smith Travel Research, E&Y Kenneth Leventhal Real Estate Group, 1996.

was provided by "a handsome State Waggon mounted on steel springs, with two good horses."[4]

Early American resorts were also built around hot or mineral springs. The Greenbriar in White Sulphur Springs, West Virginia; the nearby Homestead in Hot Springs, Virginia (which owns 15,000 acres of Allegheny mountain forests); and the many facilities in Saratoga Springs, New York—all survive today as popular vacation destinations.

Major growth in U.S. resorts came in the nineteenth century. The Mountain View House in Whitefield, New Hampshire, opened in 1865. The Del Coronado (still in operation today) opened its doors in 1888. That was the same year Henry Flagler opened the Ponce de Leon in St. Augustine, Florida, followed by the Royal Poinciana in Palm Beach in 1893 and the Royal Palm Hotel in Miami in 1896. Another great resort, the Grand Hotel on Mackinac Island in northern Michigan, opened in 1879 and has preserved its original turn-of-the-century atmosphere to this day—helped greatly by the island's ban on all automobiles.

The first American resorts were summer retreats only. In the winter, fashionable people stayed in the cities to work and attend the opera, theater, and other cultural events. One went to the mountains and seashore in the hot summer months to escape the heat of the city. California resorts were the first to solicit winter vacation business, followed by Florida hoteliers who recognized the potential profit in offering those in northern cities a way to get out of the cold.

European resorts were also first built as summer retreats, only later becoming popular in the winter as well. The Palace, a famous Swiss resort in St. Moritz, was founded in 1856 by Johannes Badrutt. His clientele came only in the summer until one year Badrutt made a bet with some of his wealthy British guests. He told them that if they would visit him in the winter, he would charge them nothing if they did not agree that wintering in St. Moritz was more pleasant and not as cold as staying home in London. They came and Badrutt won his bet. Today the Palace dominates St. Moritz and remains one of Europe's most luxurious resorts, attracting royalty and celebrities from all over the globe.

The trend today is for resorts to stay open year-round. Even resorts that used to stay open only part of the year have concluded, for the most part, that this policy is no longer economically feasible in today's business climate. Moreover, it is often

> ## How the U.S. Government Categorizes Lodging Properties
>
> The U.S. government has its own way of categorizing hotels and other lodging properties. The basis of government classification of all businesses in the United States is the **Standard Industrial Classification code (SIC)**. This code is based on the U.S. census reports. Businesses covered by the census were assigned kind-of-business classifications. Most hotels, rooming houses, camps, and other lodging places are listed together in this classification system's SIC Major Group 70. Tourist homes and hotels that provide accommodations for permanent residents are classified in Major Group 65, which covers real estate.
>
> Within these two major groups, there are smaller classifications for census purposes. For instance, all hotels, motor hotels, and motels within Major Group 70 are classified together under Industry Group 701. In some government reports the data within this group is broken down even further into subdivisions such as:
>
> - Hotels, 25 guestrooms or more
> - Hotels, less than 25 guestrooms
> - Motels and tourist courts
> - Motor hotels
>
> Rooming and boarding houses (including bed and breakfast establishments) are in Industry Group 702. Establishments renting rooms, with or without board, on a fee basis to permanent or transient guests are covered by this classification. However, nursing homes and homes for the aged and disabled have different code numbers entirely.
>
> Sporting and recreational camps that provide lodging and meals or lodging only are in Industry Group 702. Dude ranches, fishing camps, hunting camps, and children's camps also fall into this classification. Trailer parks and camp sites that provide overnight or short-term sites for trailers, campers, and tents have a different classification number—Industry Group 703.
>
> Finally, Industry Group 704 covers hotels and lodging houses that are operated by membership organizations for the benefit of their members and guests and are not open to the public. Some of these groups operate commercial hotels, which are classified as hotels, motels, and motor hotels (Group 701).
>
> Knowing these government classifications can help you should you need to look at government data when conducting research. Developers or hoteliers contemplating building a new hotel can consult government data to find out the number and type of hotels that are located near the site of the proposed hotel.

more practical to stay open all year because if you close your property and lay off employees it may be difficult to get them back when you wish to reopen. In a service industry—and especially at resorts, where service is expected to be at a high level—a trained staff is essential and is difficult to achieve without full-time employees who have job security on a 12-month basis. Nevertheless, many year-round resorts let part of their staff go, curtail some services in the off-season (such as 24-hour room service), and train the permanent personnel to do double duty.

A resort's guest base may vary greatly according to the season. For example, in Palm Springs, California, the winter months are the peak season. That is when

**The Mena House Oberoi in Cairo, Egypt, is a luxury resort featuring 40 acres of ornamental gardens; seven deluxe restaurants (including a night club and a discotheque); 24-hour room service; and recreational attractions that include a casino, a golf course, lighted tennis courts, and horse or camel riding.** (Courtesy of Oberoi Hotels International, Delhi, India)

movie stars and other celebrities are in town and rates are at their highest. In the summer, when temperatures often approach 100 degrees in the shade, the same resorts offer bargain prices to tour operators, conventioneers, and individual guests who could never afford to come during the cooler months.

Early resorts did not have extensive entertainment or recreational facilities. The principal activities consisted of dining, walking, climbing, horseback riding, swimming, and lawn games. These resorts all featured large verandas with comfortable chairs for sitting, reading, and enjoying the scenery. Dinner was served early, and many guests retired to their rooms by 10 P.M. On weekends there might be a dinner dance. Contemporary resorts offer much more to their guests. In Las Vegas resorts, for example, there are nightly shows featuring star entertainment, all-night casinos, discos, elaborate health spas, two or even three golf courses, tennis courts, boating, arts and crafts classes, and children's programs. Fine dining is an important part of all resort operations. Guests expect it and are not willing to pay high room prices unless the resort has a superior restaurant.

Compared to other segments of the industry, resorts still remain largely independent from chains, but there is a trend toward chain affiliation. For example, in an analysis made by Kenneth Leventhal & Company of 16 major worldwide resort market areas, large chains such as Hilton, Sheraton, and Marriott commanded aggregate market shares of 70 percent of total available rooms.

**Most resorts are expensive to build because of the high cost of desirable land and the expenses involved in constructing golf courses, swimming pools, and tennis courts.**
(Courtesy of Rancho Las Palmas, near Palm Springs, California, and the Marriott Corporation)

Today it is estimated that there are 450,000 resort hotel rooms in the United States; over 90,000 of these are considered luxury rooms. Few new resorts are being built because construction costs per room do not make it economically feasible. Most resorts require a good deal of capital to develop—desirable land in scenic locations or on the waterfront has appreciated greatly in recent years, and the necessary amenities are costly to build and maintain. An 18-hole golf course, for example, can easily cost $11 million or more to build, not including the cost of the land. In California the 393-room Ritz-Carlton Laguna Niguel cost $100 million to build in 1984—a cost of approximately $250,000 per room. In 1996, the Westin Rio Mar Beach Resort in Puerto Rico cost almost $300,000 per room.

Successful resorts achieve higher occupancy and higher sales per room than other categories of hotels (see Exhibit 3). However, resorts are the most expensive hotels to operate. They average a higher number of employees per room, and thus their payrolls are much higher than for other kinds of hotels.

Resorts are attracting more business guests than ever before. Business travelers make up nearly half of the resort lodging market for large resort hotels that have conference and convention facilities. In smaller resorts the guest mix may be skewed toward leisure visitors, but groups and meetings nevertheless remain important target markets. Because of the increase in business guests, many resorts are adding or increasing amenities that are important to this market segment, such as fax machines, computer centers, secretarial services, and on-site travel agencies.

**Suburban.** With the rebirth of American cities in the two decades after World War II, the U.S. economy expanded rapidly, and construction of major office buildings in

**Exhibit 3  Top 25 Resort Properties**

| Rank | Sales Per Room | Property/Location | Rooms and Suites | Total Sales ($000) | Average Occupancy |
|---|---|---|---|---|---|
| 1 | $ 248,000 | Auberge Du Soleil<br>Rutherford, CA | 50 | $ 12,400 | 81% |
| 2 | 180,901 | Timberline Lodge<br>Timberline, OR | 71 | 12,844 | 78 |
| 3 | 156,462 | Barton Creek Resort<br>Austin, TX | 147 | 23,000 | 80 |
| 4 | 153,465 | Ponte Vedra Inn & Club<br>Ponte Vedra Beach, FL | 202 | 31,000 | 81 |
| 5 | 152,336 | Resort at Longboat Key Club<br>Longboat Key, FL | 223 | 33,971 | 75 |
| 6 | 147,661 | Ventana Country Inn Resort<br>Big Sur, CA | 59 | 8,712 | 82 |
| 7 | 145,100 | Turnberry Isle Resort<br>Aventura, FL | 340 | 49,334 | 76 |
| 8 | 127,883 | The Lodge at Vail<br>Vail, CO | 60 | 7,673 | 78 |
| 9 | 123,463 | The Mirage<br>Las Vegas, NV | 3,044 | 375,822 | 97 |
| 10 | 119,565 | Pinehurst Resort<br>Pinehurst, NC | 460 | 55,000 | 49 |
| 11 | 119,418 | Boca Raton Resort & Club<br>Boca Raton, FL | 963 | 115,000 | 71 |
| 12 | 117,320 | Kona Village Resort<br>Kailua-Kona, HI | 125 | 14,665 | 55 |
| 13 | 116,868 | Salish Lodge & Spa<br>Snoqualmie, WA | 91 | 10,635 | 72 |
| 14 | 115,808 | Doral Arrowwood<br>Rye Brook, NY | 272 | 31,500 | 76 |
| 15 | 113,920 | Claremont Resort & Spa<br>Berkeley, CA | 239 | 27,227 | 84 |
| 16 | 109,090 | Best Western Yacht Harbor<br>Dunedin, FL | 55 | 6,000 | 75 |
| 17 | 108,771 | Rancho Bernardo Inn<br>San Diego, CA | 285 | 31,000 | 71 |
| 18 | 108,333 | Shephard's Lagoon Resort<br>Clearwater Beach, FL | 60 | 6,500 | 83 |
| 19 | 104,778 | Stein Eriksen Lodge<br>Park City, UT | 131 | 13,726 | 64 |

**Exhibit 3**  *(continued)*

| Rank | Sales Per Room | Property/Location | Rooms and Suites | Total Sales ($000) | Average Occupancy |
|---|---|---|---|---|---|
| 20 | 101,593 | Pacific Islands Club<br>Tamuning, GU | 502 | 51,000 | 94% |
| 21 | 98,970 | Don Cesar Beach Resort<br>St. Petersburg Beach, FL | 275 | 27,217 | 82 |
| 22 | 97,665 | Sam's Town Hotel<br>Las Vegas, NV | 648 | 63,287 | 96 |
| 23 | 97,087 | Apple Farm Inn<br>San Luis Obispo, CA | 103 | 10,000 | 90 |
| 24 | 96,000 | Trump Taj Mahal<br>Atlantic City, NJ | 1,250 | 120,000 | 93 |
| 25 | 94,720 | Hotel Jerome<br>Aspen, CO | 93 | 8,809 | 57 |

Source: "100 Top Performers," *Lodging Hospitality,* August 1997, p. 31.

downtown areas reached a new peak of activity. Landowners soon realized that new buildings commanded a much higher rent than older ones, and real estate prices in many downtown areas doubled and tripled.

Many corporations that did not want to pay the higher downtown rents moved to the suburbs. Land there was available at a more reasonable price and, with improved highway systems, proliferating suburban housing developments, and gigantic shopping centers, it made sense to relocate. IBM, for example, moved its world headquarters from Manhattan to Armonk, New York. Many of the other large business tenants in Manhattan moved to Connecticut, New Jersey, and upstate New York.

Inevitably, a strong demand arose for building new hotels near these suburban businesses. Land developers recognized this need and found meeting it particularly attractive. Unlike suburban townhouses and rental apartments, a hotel seemed to be a more profitable investment. After all, when you rented out a new apartment you were tied into a lease at a set price for a year or more. Inflation could easily erode your profits because you couldn't raise the rent whenever you wanted to cover increased costs. A hotel was different. You were not locked into fixed rates at all. If your costs went up, you could raise rates in less than 24 hours. While many land developers didn't know the first thing about running a hotel, a solution was readily available. Large hotel chains were selling franchises, and management companies were available to completely take over the new hotels from those developers who were not really interested in hotelkeeping.

In addition to the new businesses, there were other reasons for locating hotels in the suburbs. Newer and larger hotels offering parking space and other amenities could be built much more economically in suburban locations than downtown. Moreover, the growth of motels (which were on their way to being called motor hotels), combined with the need for suburban accommodations, further eroded the desirability of building hotels downtown.

Today it is difficult to distinguish between a **suburban hotel** and any other kind of hotel. It is the location that makes the difference. Nevertheless, there are some characteristics that suburban hotels have in common:

- As a group, they tend to be somewhat smaller than downtown hotels. Many suburban properties have 250 to 500 rooms and limited banquet facilities.

- They are primarily chain affiliated; just about every major chain operates suburban properties.

- Their major source of revenue is from business meeting and convention attendees and from individual business travelers.

- They often have the same kinds of facilities that center city hotels offer. Because they depend heavily on local patronage, restaurants in suburban hotels frequently offer superior dining experiences. Hotel services such as laundry, valet, and room service are on a par with center city standards.

- Many of these properties have sports and health facilities as well as swimming pools.

- Suburban hotels are often cornerstones of their communities. They frequently host weddings and bar mitzvahs as well as weekly meetings of such major service clubs as Rotary and Kiwanis.

**Highway.** As soon as America began to develop its highway system in the 1920s and 1930s, small **tourist courts** began to spring up along major roads such as the Boston Post Road (U.S. Highway 1) from Maine to Florida. At first these tourist courts were a row of simple cabins with direct access to the outside. Many of them did not even have private baths. These early motels averaged 20 rooms and were usually owned by a couple who lived on the premises and did all the work. No effort was made to provide food or other services. Because rooms were sometimes rented for just a few hours with no questions asked, early highway motels in some communities developed an unsavory reputation.

It was not until after World War II, when the pent-up demand for automobiles and travel was finally released, that the highway motel business really grew. With the new interstate highways came a need for families and business people to have a safe and comfortable place to stay en route to their destination. One of the first to recognize this need was Kemmons Wilson, whose Holiday Inn chain was launched in 1952 in Memphis, Tennessee. One of Wilson's major innovations was to put a restaurant in his motel so that travelers could eat a meal without leaving the property. This upgraded the status of these properties considerably, making them more like hotels. Soon the evolution from tourist court to motel to motor hotel was complete. Today's **highway hotels** offer the same facilities found in downtown and suburban hotels, but with a distinct identity of their own.

Most highway hotels feature a large sign that can be seen from the highway and an entrance where travelers can leave their automobiles while they check in. Parking space is plentiful and the atmosphere is informal. Beyond that, the

### Highest Sales Per Room by Location

| Location | Hotel | Sales Per Room |
|---|---|---|
| Center City | Lowell Hotel<br>New York, NY | $213,753 |
| Resort | The Lodge at Ventana Canyon<br>Tucson, AZ | $238,061 |
| Suburban | The Lodge & Beach Club<br>Ponte Vedra Beach, FL | $121,212 |
| Highway/Airport | The Russell Inn<br>Russell, MB | $ 78,871 |

Survey of more than 29,000 hotels, motels, and resorts in the United States, its possessions, and Canada. (Source: "400 Top Performers," *Lodging Hospitality*, August 1996).

distinction blurs—a highway hotel can be just like any other hotel except that it is on the highway.

Most highway hotels are franchised. The nature of highway hotels—often located away from urban centers—presents management and quality control problems that can best be solved by independent entrepreneurs operating a franchise.

Highway hotels have a lower number of employees per room than suburban or center city hotels. This is because highway hotels generally provide fewer services. Guests spend less time at this kind of hotel than in other kinds of hotels; consequently, total sales per room are generally lower. Like most other types of hotels, highway properties depend mainly on commercial traffic.

Many highway hotels are older properties. This is causing an interesting phenomenon in the business—an increasing number of franchise conversions. Rather than upgrading and modernizing their properties to keep up with new standards, many franchise owners have elected to convert their hotels to franchises that offer fewer services and a lower-price product. For instance, many older full-service Holiday Inns have been converted to Holiday Inn Express properties.

**Airport.** It did not take long for hotel chains to identify another growing need for hotel space in the United States—guestrooms near airports. Eighty-five percent of **airport hotels** today are affiliated with chains. Even though airport hotels tend to have difficulty attracting weekend guests because most airline travel occurs on weekdays, airport hotels enjoy some of the highest occupancy rates in the lodging industry. In fact, demand can be too high at times. A problem that airport hotels face is the need to respond to a high demand almost immediately. A severe snow storm or an airline strike can fill up an airport hotel instantly and put a severe strain on the rooms division and food service facilities.

Airport hotels in the United States and Europe have begun changing from facilities designed just for overnight guests to hotels that can accommodate the needs of business travelers who may plan to stay more than one night and might require meeting space. Why are they changing? Because fewer guests are airline passengers. Busy industrial parks have sprung up in areas surrounding major airports. *Business Traveler* magazine reports that hotels near the airports serving London, Brussels, and Frankfurt draw much of their business from executives visiting nearby firms, and many of these executives arrive by auto.[5] "European airport hotels derive at least half of their business from the commercial infrastructure that has grown up around the airport," says Alan Parker, senior vice president and managing director for Holiday Inn.[6]

Another trend, according to *Business Traveler,* is "to incorporate at least one hotel into the design of a new terminal or airport. For instance, the Munich airport has a single five-star Kempinski next to the terminal, while the Eurohub terminal at Birmingham (England) boasts a Novotel on site."[7] The magazine points out that there are fewer airport hotels in the Far East and Asia. For example, Singapore's award-winning Changi airport has no hotel on-site.

## Ownership

Hotels can also be categorized by ownership. There are six different ways hotels can be owned and operated. Hotels can be:

- Independently owned and operated.
- Independently owned but leased to an operator.
- Owned by a single entity or group that has hired a hotel management company to operate the property.
- Owned and operated by a chain.
- Owned by an independent investor or group and operated by a chain.
- Owned by an individual or group and operated as a franchise of a chain. The franchise holder may be an individual or a management company.

An **independent hotel** is not connected with any established hotel company and is owned by an individual or group of investors. A **management company** contracts with hotel owners to operate their hotel. The management company may or may not have any of its own funds invested. It is usually paid by a combination of fees plus a share of revenues and profits. A **hotel chain** is a group of affiliated hotels.

A **franchise** is the authorization granted by a hotel chain to an individual hotel to use the chain's trademark, operating systems, and reservation system in return for a percentage of the hotel's revenues plus certain other fees, such as advertising fees. A **franchisor** is the party granting the franchise. Holiday Inn Worldwide is an example of a franchisor. A **franchisee** is the party granted the franchise. A franchisee can be a hotel management company—Richfield Hotel Management Inc., for example—or an individual who has applied and been granted a license to do business under the franchisor's name.

There are also **referral systems.** Referral systems tend to be made up of independent properties or small chains that have grouped together for common marketing purposes. Best Western is the largest of these. Its properties have no

**Exhibit 4   Top 25 Hotel Chains**

| Rank | Corporate Chain | Rooms | Hotels | Rank | Corporate Chain | Rooms | Hotels |
|---|---|---|---|---|---|---|---|
| 1 | HFS Inc. Parsippany, NJ USA | 490,000 | 5,300 | 14 | Grupo Sol Meliá Palma de Mallorca, Spain | 47,371 | 203 |
| 2 | Holiday Inn Worldwide Atlanta, GA USA | 386,323 | 2,260 | 15 | Forte Hotels London, England | 46,847 | 259 |
| 3 | Best Western Int'l Phoenix, AZ USA | 295,305 | 3,654 | 16 | Doubletree Hotels Phoenix, AZ USA | 43,555 | 166 |
| 4 | Accor Evry, France | 279,145 | 2,465 | 17 | Westin Hotels & Resorts Seattle, WA USA | 42,897 | 97 |
| 5 | Choice Hotels Int'l Silver Spring, MD USA | 271,812 | 3,197 | 18 | Club Méditerranée SA Paris, France | 37,906 | 133 |
| 6 | Marriott Int'l Washington, D.C. USA | 251,425 | 1,268 | 19 | Société du Louvre Paris, France | 36,059 | 567 |
| 7 | ITT Sheraton Corp. Boston, MA USA | 130,528 | 413 | 20 | La Quinta Inns San Antonio, TX USA | 32,096 | 249 |
| 8 | Promus Cos. Memphis, TN USA | 105,930 | 809 | 21 | Red Roof Inns Hilliard, OH USA | 28,000 | 248 |
| 9 | Hilton Hotels Corp. Beverly Hills, CA USA | 101,000 | 245 | 22 | Prince Hotels Inc. Tokyo, Japan | 26,643 | 86 |
| 10 | Carlson Hospitality Worldwide Minneapolis, MN USA | 91,177 | 437 | 23 | Tokyu Hotel Group Tokyo, Japan | 23,130 | 109 |
| 11 | Hyatt Hotels/Hyatt Int'l Chicago, IL USA | 80,598 | 176 | 24 | Circus Circus Las Vegas, NV USA | 19,585 | 16 |
| 12 | Inter-Continental Hotels London, England | 69,632 | 193 | 25 | Walt Disney Co. Burbank, CA USA | 19,415 | 18 |
| 13 | Hilton International Watford, England | 51,305 | 160 | | | | |

Source: *Hotels*, July 1997, p. 48.

common designs or standard amenities, but a room at a Best Western can be reserved anywhere in the United States through a central reservations number.

**Chain Hotels.** Hotel chains account for a large percentage of the world's hotel room inventory. The largest of these chains is Hospitality Franchise Systems in Parsippany, New Jersey (see Exhibit 4). This company is a franchise system with such brand names as Ramada, Howard Johnson, HoJo Inns, Days Inns, and Super 8. Holiday Inn Worldwide in Atlanta, Georgia, is the second largest. The French-based Accor chain ranks fourth internationally, but it is the largest chain in Europe and is represented in most countries of the world.

In the past, the world's most deluxe hotels were independent. There was a perception that a chain could not possibly achieve the level of service of an independent hotel owned and operated by hoteliers who were there every day. This is no longer true. Most travel writers consider the Oriental Hotel in Bangkok to be the world's single best hotel. The Oriental is part of the Mandarin chain, with nine hotels (including the Mandarin in Hong Kong and San Francisco). The Ritz-Carlton Hotel Company, headquartered in Atlanta, Georgia, manages 23 hotels in the United States and two in Australia. In 1992 it was awarded the Malcolm Baldrige National Quality Award, created by the U.S. Congress to recognize quality achievements. It was the first hotel company ever to win this prestigious award. Four Seasons Hotels and Resorts of Toronto, Ontario, Canada, operates 33 hotels worldwide, including London's famous Inn on the Park and Hong Kong's luxurious Regent Hotel.

It should be noted that the figures in Exhibit 4 can be somewhat misleading without a more complete understanding of these organizations. For example, the "Hotels" column is misleading, since it does not indicate how many of the properties are company-owned, franchised, under management contract, or simply independent hotels that have banded together solely to advertise and set up a common reservation system. Hospitality Franchise Systems (ranked first on the list) does not own or manage a single property, but merely sells franchises to other companies that use Hospitality Franchise Systems' brand names and operating systems. Best Western International (ranked third) does not own, franchise, or manage any of its properties. The only affiliation between Best Western hotels is that all of them are part of a common reservation and marketing system. On the other hand, Hilton Hotels Corporation (ranked eighth) owns, partially owns, and manages or franchises hotels.

**Independent Hotels.** Most hotels that are classified as independent are independently owned and managed but are allied with a referral or marketing association. Three such associations are Preferred Hotels, The Leading Hotels of the World, and Relais & Chateaux. The Breakers Hotel in Palm Beach, Florida, and the Hotel DuPont in Wilmington, Delaware, are Preferred Hotels. The famous Hotel Bristol in Paris is a member of both Preferred Hotels and The Leading Hotels of the World. Relais & Chateaux properties include Horizons and Waterloo House in Bermuda, Little Palm Island in Florida, Ashford Castle in Ireland, and Las Mananitas in Mexico. It is sometimes difficult to differentiate hotels that are independent from those that are actually managed or owned by chains. For example, the Pierre Hotel in New York City, which many consider to be a fine independent hotel, is actually managed by the Four Seasons chain.

## Price

Another way of categorizing hotels—or **segmenting**—is by the prices they charge. In order to accomplish this, a hotel chain creates several different brands or names

> **How Hotel Chains Got Their Names**
>
> **Accor**
> **Evry, France**
> The name was taken from the French word *accord*, which means "agreement" or "bringing together."
>
> **Hampton Inns**
> **Memphis, Tennessee**
> The name was found in a colonial-style home furnishings magazine by an executive's wife.
>
> **Holiday Inn**
> **Atlanta, Georgia**
> Named for the Hollywood movie *Holiday Inn*, starring Bing Crosby.
>
> **Howard Johnson**
> **Parsippany, New Jersey**
> Named for founder Howard Dearing Johnson.
>
> **Hyatt Hotels**
> **Chicago, Illinois**
> Named for the first hotel the chain bought, a property owned by a man named Hyatt Von Dahn.
>
> **Radisson**
> **Minneapolis, Minnesota**
> Named for Pierre Esprit Radisson, an explorer of the upper midwestern United States. The name was suggested by a student who won $50 in an essay contest sponsored by the manager of the first Radisson hotel. (Radisson's computer reservation system is named Pierre.)
>
> **ITT Sheraton**
> **Boston, Massachusetts**
> After the chain's founders bought one of their first hotels, they discovered that removing an electric rooftop sign from it would cost more than the hotel's purchase price. So the sign remained. The name of the hotel was Sheraton.

Source: Adapted from Sally Wolchuk, "How Chains Got Their Names," *Hotels*, June 1993, p. 19.

that offer different benefits and charge different prices. While this is a fairly recent development in service businesses such as hotels, consumer products have been "branded" for a long while. For example, General Motors manufactures economy automobiles like Chevrolets, mid-price automobiles like Oldsmobiles, and luxury cars such as Cadillacs. The idea is that different segments of the consumer market are attracted to different brands at different price levels, and if you want to sell a car to everyone you must have different kinds of cars with different prices. When Henry Ford started his automobile business, his intention was to offer only one kind of car—a basic black Model T that he could sell for the lowest-possible price of $500. It was not until General Motors demonstrated that it could sell more cars

## Industry Innovators

J.W. Marriott, Jr.
Chairman of the Board and Chief Executive Officer
Marriott International Inc.

J.W. "Bill" Marriott did not start the Marriott empire—he inherited it from his father, who opened his first Hot Shoppe restaurant in 1927 in Washington, D.C. In one sense, the company that Bill Marriott runs today is very much the same as it was in 1985, the year his father died and Bill was named chairman of the board. The same core values and corporate culture that the senior Marriott instilled continue, but Bill Marriott has transformed the company. The once-thriving enterprise that concentrated its efforts on a few brands of hotels and restaurants is now the world's leading lodging and contract services company. That's only part of the story. When Marriott split his operations into Marriott International and Host Marriott Companies, a third company, Host Marriott Services Corporation, was created.

Marriott International runs Marriott Lodging, which manages or franchises Marriott Hotels, Resorts, and Suites; Courtyard by Marriott; Residence Inns; Fairfield Inns; and Renaissance, New World, Ramada, and Ritz Carlton Hotels worldwide. Another part of Marriott International—Marriott Service Group—has three divisions: Management Services, Senior Living Services, and Distribution Services. These divisions service institutional and corporate food service facilities, manage senior living communities, and provide food and related products for Marriott's own operations and clients.

Host Marriott is one of the largest lodging real estate companies in the world—its assets exceeded $5 billion in 1996. In addition to the properties it owns outright, Host Marriott also owns interests in many real estate partnerships that own other properties. Marriott Services Corporation manages restaurant and retail operations at airports, stadiums, turnpikes, and tourist attractions.

A devout Mormon, Bill Marriott has always been known for his ethics, values, and integrity. He believes that if he takes good care of his employees, they'll take good care of his guests. He spends about one-quarter of his time on the road, practicing what he calls "Management by walking around." For Bill Marriott, this means talking with employees on the job, eating with them in company cafeterias, having photos taken with them—a tradition that dates back to his father's time—and paying attention to details. It is not unusual, on these visits, for Bill to suggest changes in the food, to order new pillows for guestrooms, or to pick up trash. Perhaps this is Marriott's most unique characteristic as CEO. Raised in the business, he understands the importance of guest satisfaction to his huge empire, and that is where he concentrates his efforts. "I come up with some of our ideas but, really, I'm not so much a deal-cutter as an operations man," he says. "I leave that part to the people I hire."[8] Marriott offers these other rules for success:

- Continually challenge your team to do better.

*(continued)*

> **Industry Innovators** (continued)
>
> - Celebrate your people's success—not your own.
> - Do it now. Err on the side of taking action.
> - It's more important to hire people with the right qualities than people with specific experience.
> - Eliminate the cause of a mistake—don't just clear it up.[9]

by having a range of brands at different price levels that Ford decided to change his strategy of offering only one product at a rock-bottom price.

Similarly, in the lodging industry the major hotel chains started by offering one kind of brand only. Initially these were mid-price products introduced by Sheraton, Hilton, and Marriott. They were priced to appeal to the largest segment of the traveling public—mid-level business executives. Top executives in those days wouldn't dream of staying at a chain hotel—they stayed at independent properties or properties that may have been part of a group but were perceived to be unique or independent, such as the Plaza Hotel in New York City or the Drake in Chicago (now a Swissôtel property).

As the market for full-service hotels became saturated, some of the leading hotel chains developed new concepts to appeal to a growing economy-minded market. Also, there was increasing demand from families and business people for more spacious, reasonably priced hotel accommodations. The industry responded by developing several full-service and limited-service brands at different prices.

Today, chains have properties in one or more full-service or limited-service segments. Through development and acquisition, the Marriott Corporation, for example, has chosen to enter every price category to maximize its market share. Marriott adheres to the philosophy that, if it is no longer possible to appeal to everyone with one kind of hotel, they will build/acquire as many kinds of hotels as necessary to ensure that as many people as possible who stay in hotels will stay in one of theirs. On the other hand, Four Seasons identifies its expertise not in the management of hotels in general, but in the management of a particular kind of hotel. To maintain this specialized identity, Four Seasons offers only hotels that appeal to its current guest base. Exhibit 5 shows how the market looks for the Marriott Corporation, which has decided to follow a segmentation strategy and offer different products at different prices for different markets.

**Limited Service: Economy and Budget.** There are many **limited-service hotels** in the marketplace today (see Exhibit 6). The first hotel chain to go after a low-price consumer market was Holiday Inn. Holiday Inns were not budget properties, however. Their construction costs were relatively high because they included restaurants and other amenities and services, and their aim was to provide a better product than previously available on the highway.

**Exhibit 5   Marriott Market Segmentation, 1997**

| Market Segment | Marriott Products | | |
|---|---|---|---|
| Economy/Budget | Fairfield Inn | Fairfield Suites | |
| Mid-Price | Courtyard | Towne Place Suites | Residence Inn |
| First Class | Marriott Hotels | Marriott Suites | |
| Luxury | Ritz-Carlton | | |

It was not until the 1960s that the first budget motels were introduced—Motel 6 in California, Days Inn in Georgia, and La Quinta in Texas. Sam Barshop, founder of La Quinta, explained his idea this way: "We have a very simple concept. What we're doing is selling beds. Not operating restaurants, not running conventions—just selling beds." By eliminating the restaurants and the lobby and meeting space that Holiday Inns offered, La Quinta and other budget properties were able to offer Holiday Inn-type rooms at 25 percent less. Some chains, like Motel 6, sold rooms for as low as $6. They were able to offer such low prices by using modular and prefabricated construction materials and choosing less-than-ideal locations where land costs were lower. These chains offered hardly any amenities at all. In the early days, some had a coin slot in their guestroom television sets for pay-as-you-view TV!

The early budget motel segment has evolved into two price levels, **economy hotels** and **budget hotels.** Both of these hotel segments have a low per-room construction cost. Depending on the geographic location, currently the per-room cost could range from $25,000 (for an economy hotel) to $45,000 (for a budget hotel). Because they provide limited services and facilities, labor and other operating costs are well below those for full-service hotels. The average daily rate for these hotels is under $60. However, pricing varies by market area and changes with inflation. Generally, rates are offered at 20 to 50 percent below prevailing mid-market rates. Of course, hotel rates are constantly changing. Holiday Inn, once at the low end of the price scale, is now considered a mid-price hotel. That company's Holiday Inn Express now competes at the low end of the market. Choice Hotels, the fifth largest hotel company worldwide, developed Comfort Inns and Comfort Inn Suites as part of its low price strategy.

The market for limited-service hotels is 51.4 percent tourist and 45.8 percent business.[10] In a 1996 Smith Travel Research study, limited-service hotels showed strong profitability with pretax income of 23 percent of total revenue. Chain-affiliated hotels were more profitable than independent hotels. In 1995, economy hotels achieved 71.9 percent occupancy,[11] whereas the budget had an occupancy of 69.1 percent.[12]

**Mid-Price (Full-Service and Limited-Service).** In the 1960s, Sheraton, Hilton, Ramada, Quality Inns, and Holiday Inn used the term "inn" to designate their mid-price products. At that time the mid-price hotel segment was the fastest-growing segment of the industry. Fueled by a growing economy and the development of automobile and commercial air traffic, a strong need existed for mid-price lodging

**Exhibit 6  Top 25 U.S. Economy/Limited Service Chains**

| Rank | Chain Name | No. of Properties |
|---|---|---|
| 1 | Days Inns of America | 1,630 |
| 2 | Comfort Inns | 1,292 |
| 3 | Super 8 Motels | 1,271 |
| 4 | Motel 6 | 768 |
| 5 | Econo Lodge | 658 |
| 6 | Travelodge | 485 |
| 7 | Hampton Inns | 454 |
| 8 | Holiday Inn Express | 275 |
| 9 | Courtyard by Marriott | 237 |
| 10 | La Quinta Inns | 229 |
| 11 | Red Roof Inns | 220 |
| 12 | Knights Lodging | 185 |
| 13 | Fairfield Inn by Marriott | 184 |
| 14 | Budget Host Inns | 176 |
| 15 | National 9 Inns | 171 |
| 16 | Scottish Inns | 161 |
| 17 | Ramada Limited | 153 |
| 18 | Red Carpet Inns | 148 |
| 19 | Hojo Inns | 145 |
| 20 | Friendship Inns | 114 |
| 21 | Rodeway Inns | 110 |
| 22 | Budgetel Inns | 109 |
| 23 | Shoney's Inns | 74 |
| 24 | Allstar Inns | 72 |
| 25 | Drury Inns | 67 |

Source: *Hotel & Motel Management*, July 24, 1995.

facilities with restaurants and some other amenities previously found only in higher-price establishments. Today, however, the term "inn" no longer identifies a specific category. For example, Hampton Inns and Days Inns are both economy products.

Although many consider **mid-price hotels** to be those with average prices from $65 to $90, there is considerable variance by market. In Manhattan a mid-price hotel could easily average $150 a night. In Sacramento, California, a room in a similar hotel might cost as little as $60.

The mid-price segment is attractive to many consumers who want to trade up from the economy/budget segment. However, when the rate difference between first class and mid-price hotels is not significant, travelers are drawn to the higher class hotel. As the rate difference grew, the mid-price hotels became more attractive. Many mid-price hotels offer facilities and services similar to those at higher priced hotels. They have restaurants and bars, and many have meeting space. The challenge for mid-price hotels is to maintain a clear difference from both increasingly upscale hotels in the economy/budget segment and first class hotels with high room rates.

ITT Sheraton has introduced Four Points Hotels, a mid-price concept that is, in some cases, a re-branding of the Sheraton Inns. Although the facilities have not necessarily changed, the name has changed because the term "inn" was considered to represent a limited facility. Holiday Inn Select, Candlewood Hotels by Doubletree, and Hilton Garden Inns are other brands that compete in the mid-price segment.

Smith Travel Research has reported that properties in this segment have an average of 226 rooms. In 1995, mid-price hotels achieved an average 70.6 percent occupancy rate—slightly higher than the economy/budget class—with an average room rate of $64.97.[13]

**Full-Service/Luxury.** At the top of the price scale there is a range of **full-service/luxury hotels**, from the full-service hotels of Hyatt, Hilton, Stouffer, and Marriott to the luxury properties of Four Seasons, Ritz-Carlton, and Inter-Continental. Before these chains offered successful luxury hotels, "luxury chain hotel" was considered a contradiction in terms. By definition, a luxury hotel used to be an independent property in which the owner/manager was present to greet guests and see that their every need was satisfied. A perfect example of this kind of property was the Ritz Hotel in Paris on the Place Vendôme. Its founder, the legendary César Ritz, set unusually high standards for facilities and services. But Ritz also recognized the marketing advantages that could accrue from having more than one Ritz Hotel and so, with his partner Georges-Auguste Escoffier, he acquired an equity interest in the Carlton Hotel in London and then formed the Ritz-Carlton chain. Other luxury chains followed. One highly successful example is the Canada-based Four Seasons hotel company. The company's strategy is to operate only mid-size hotels of exceptional quality and have the finest hotel or resort in each destination where it locates.

There was considerable development of first class and luxury hotels in the 1980s, although occupancy was declining. This downward trend reversed in 1991. Occupancies and profits began a record climb, but few first class or luxury hotels were constructed. Most of the activity in this segment was in mergers and acquisitions and in the changing of one brand for another, known as re-flagging. According to Smith Travel Research, luxury and upscale (their term for full-service, first class hotels) hotels were the most profitable segments in the United States in 1995. Their pretax income was 9.6 percent of total sales. Chain-affiliated hotels recorded a higher occupancy but lower average rate than did independent hotels. The chain hotels were more profitable, however. Their pretax income was 12.5 percent of total sales, whereas the independents experienced a 2.6 percent pretax income.[14] This higher profitability could be attributed to the ability of chains to benefit from economies of scale.

The Westin Hotel, Singapore.

**All-Suite Hotels.** There are a number of all-suite hotel chains, including Embassy Suites, Residence Inn by Marriott, and Guest Quarters Suite Hotels. Although all-suite chains can be viewed as a different kind of hotel chain, they also provide a way for traditional hotel chains to expand their product.

When **all-suite hotels** were first introduced, the concept was simple—two connected hotel rooms for approximately the price of one, at a price much lower than that for a traditional hotel suite. One room was furnished as a typical hotel

**The Radisson Suite Hotel Tucson.** (Courtesy of the Radisson Suite Hotel Tucson, Tucson, Arizona)

guestroom with a bed, the other with a fold-out sofa (or a table and chairs) in place of the bed. The first all-suite hotel was built in 1961—the Lexington Apartments and Motor Inn in Grand Prairie, Texas. It took 11 years for one of the major chains to embrace the idea; Guest Quarters Suite Hotels opened its first property in Atlanta in 1972. Residence Inns developed an all-suite concept in the early 1980s and had more than 100 hotels when it was acquired by the Marriott Corporation in 1987.

All-suite hotels were originally positioned to attract extended-stay travelers, but they proved popular to other kinds of travelers as well. An all-suite hotel gave guests more private space, but the trade-off was that much of the hotel's public space—the lobby, meeting rooms, health club, and (most importantly) restaurant and kitchen—was eliminated.

All-suites continue to develop and be embellished; today there are all-suite hotels that are upscale, mid-price, extended-stay, and resort. Some of these hotels still embrace the original concept, but others have added back the lobbies, restaurants, health clubs, and more.

All-suite hotels appeal to several kinds of travelers. Business travelers are still the primary target and account for two-thirds of the guests. Executives find all-suites attractive because they can hold private meetings outside of a bedroom setting. Families also like all-suites. The children can sleep on the convertible sofa in the living room, leaving the parents with the master bedroom. And the ranges and microwave ovens are great for preparing meals or popping popcorn while watching the news or the movie of the week.

## Other Hotel Categories

Other hotel categories include:

- Conference centers
- Condominium hotels
- Interval ownership/timeshare
- Continuing-care retirement communities

**Conference Centers.** Although all hotels with meeting facilities compete for conferences, there are specialized hotels called **conference centers** that almost exclusively book conferences, executive meetings, and training seminars. While they provide most of the facilities found at conventional hotels, conference centers are built to provide living and conference facilities without any of the outside distractions that might cloud or detract from meetings held in ordinary hotels.

According to the International Association of Conference Centers, for a facility to be classified as a conference center, a minimum of 60 percent of its total sales must come from conferences and, of the facility's total meeting space, 60 percent must be devoted exclusively to meetings.[15]

Conference centers almost always have more audiovisual equipment on-site than is available at other hotels. Theaters, videotaping facilities, closed-circuit television, secretarial services, and translation facilities are common amenities. Conference centers are usually accessible to major market areas but are in less busy locations. They generate some $3.5 billion in annual revenues and range in size from 32 guestrooms (The Beaver Hollow Lodge and Conference Center in Java Center, New York) to 400 guestrooms and four suites (the Dallas/Fort Worth Hilton Executive Conference Center in Grapevine, Texas).[16] Exhibit 7 charts the growth of the conference center segment.

As with other kinds of hotels and resorts, conference centers can be classified according to usage. There are four general classifications:

- *Executive conference centers,* which cater to high-level meetings and seminars.
- *Corporate-owned conference centers,* used primarily for in-house training.
- *Resort conference centers,* which provide extensive recreation and social facilities in addition to conference facilities.
- *College and university conference centers,* which tend to be used mostly by academic groups. These facilities range from dormitory accommodations to modern hotels.

Conference centers operated by American Express, IBM, and the Chase Manhattan Bank are used expressly for private conferences. Private and public universities such as Columbia, Duke, Babson, and the Universities of Virginia and Pennsylvania have entered the conference center business with great success, attracting overseas visitors and weekend meetings.

One company that specializes in conference center management is Benchmark of Woodlands, Texas. Benchmark manages more than 15 conference resorts,

**Exhibit 7    U.S. Conference Centers Growth 1991–95**

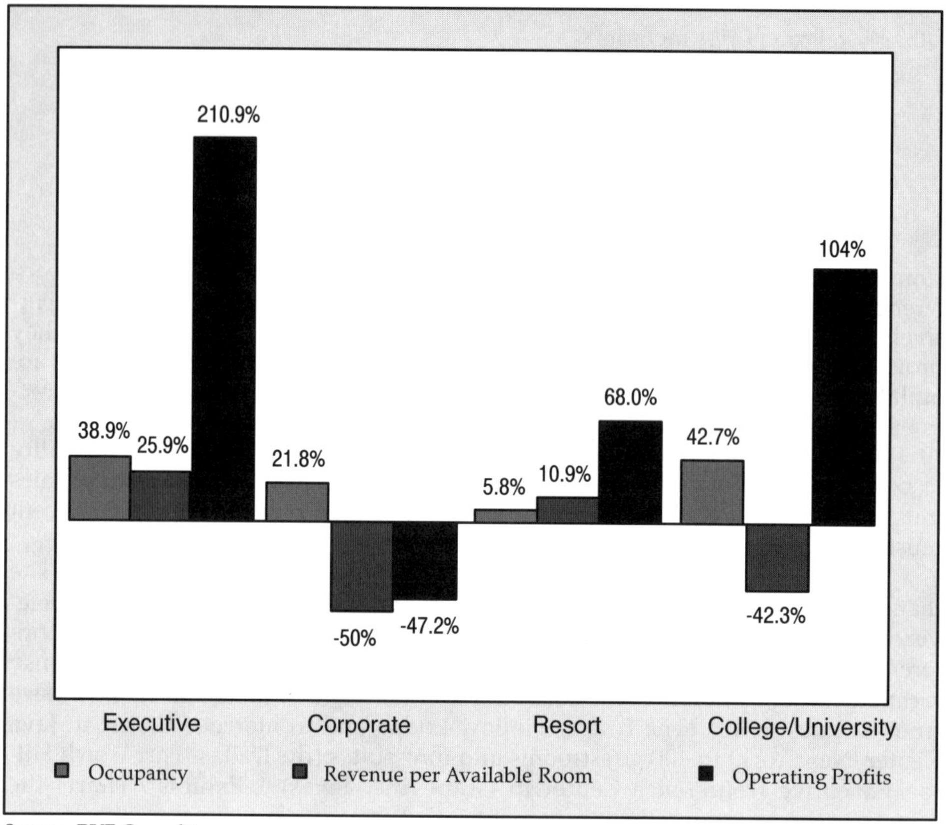

| Category | Occupancy | Revenue per Available Room | Operating Profits |
|---|---|---|---|
| Executive | 38.9% | 25.9% | 210.9% |
| Corporate | 21.8% | -50% | -47.2% |
| Resort | 5.8% | 10.9% | 68.0% |
| College/University | 42.7% | -42.3% | 104% |

Source: PKF Consulting

corporate, and executive conference centers in nine states. Their first international project was in Thailand. Another company that specializes in this segment is Dolce International, which operates 10 properties in the United States, Canada, and Europe.

According to a study conducted by PKF Consulting and the International Association of Conference Centers, U.S. conference centers have been making impressive gains in occupancy and profitability. Between 1991 and 1995, occupancy increased 27.2 percent, revenue per occupied room was up 18.9 percent (at resort and executive conference centers only), and operating profit before fixed charges increased 174 percent. Corporate and college and university conference centers are primarily limited to servicing their own in-house constituencies, and therefore have less opportunity to benefit from the increasing demand for these specialized facilities.[17]

**Interval Ownership/Timeshare.** In an age of inflation, time sharing—which first started in the French Alps in the 1960s—seemed like an idea whose time had come. Many people enjoyed taking their vacation every year at the same time and at the

**Exhibit 8  Location of Timeshare Projects Worldwide**

| | |
|---|---|
| United States | 37.3% |
| Europe | 29.7% |
| Mexico | 7.0% |
| South America | 5.6% |
| Caribbean | 4.9% |
| S.E. Asia/Japan | 3.9% |
| South Africa | 3.4% |
| Australasia | 2.8% |
| Canada | 2.2% |
| Elsewhere | 3.2% |

Source: Ragatz Associates

same place. Many Californians, for example, went to Hawaii every winter for a week or two, rented a hotel room at the same property, played the same golf course, and had a group of friends who would go at the same time. The more affluent Californians bought condominiums, but for most people it didn't make sense to buy a $50,000 to $100,000 condominium that they might use for only a few weeks a year.

The **timeshare condominium** concept seemed the perfect answer. Instead of selling an individual an entire condominium, developers reasoned, why not sell them only one-twelfth of one, which would give them the use of it for 30 days—or even one-fiftieth of one, which would allow buyers to use the condo for one week every year? You could pick your own month or week and actually own the condo for that period of time. If you couldn't go on your designated week, you could trade with another owner. By buying a block of time in a timeshare condominium you would not only be assured of getting the accommodations you wanted when you wanted them, but over the years your rate would stay the same even if hotel room rates doubled or tripled. Moreover, if you got bored with going to the same place every year, you could join an association such as Interval International or RCI and trade the use of your timeshare unit for another timeshare unit somewhere else in the world (see Exhibit 8).

Timeshare arrived in the United States in the 1970s. Problems with the first timeshare developments occurred when too many unscrupulous developers tried to unload bankrupt or aging hotels and condominiums by luring purchasers with high-pressure sales tactics. In a number of cases, management of such facilities was left to unsuspecting buyers who lacked the technical expertise needed to operate a

**Exhibit 9   Hotels' Share of the Vacation Ownership Pie**

| Company | Type of Business | No. of Properties | No. of Owners | Cost/Week |
|---|---|---|---|---|
| HFS Inc. | HFS recently acquired Resorts Condominiums International (RCI), the world's largest exchange organization. | N/A | 2 million in total exchange system | N/A |
| Ramada | Timeshare developer Preferred Equities has a deal with Ramada Franchise Systems to license and operate properties under the Ramada Vacation Suites banner. | 7—in Hawaii, Nevada, Florida, and Colorado | About 60,000 | Approx. $10,000 |
| Marriott | Marriott Vacation Club International is the largest timeshare operator. | 30 in 15 locations | 80,000 and another 20,000 expected in 1997 | N/A |
| Walt Disney Corp. | Operates Disney Vacation Club timeshare resorts. | 2 in Orlando, 1 in Vero Beach, FL, and 1 in Hilton Head, SC | More than 21,000 | Approx. $15,000 |
| Hilton Hotels Corp. | Operates Hilton Vacation Club resorts. | 18 | 11,500 at 2 properties in Las Vegas and Orlando. Total: 43,000 | $11,000 to $18,000 |

Source: *Lodging,* February 1997, p. 44.

transient hotel. Consequently, many properties were poorly maintained and a number went bankrupt. The federal government and most of the states enacted consumer protection laws and policies including a grace period for buyers to reconsider their decision to purchase a timeshare. However, it was not until the 1980s, when respected management companies such as Marriott International, Hilton, and Disney entered the timeshare arena that the concept became a serious contender for the vacation market. Other well-regarded companies followed: Promus, Hyatt, Westin, Inter-Continental, and Four Seasons.

Successful entry into the timeshare market for these hotel companies has been accomplished through joint ventures, separate subsidiaries, or franchises (see Exhibit 9). For example, the Promus Hotel Corporation has a licensing agreement with Signature Resorts—the fastest growing timeshare developer in North America—to develop Embassy Vacation Resorts. Promus has other agreements, like a joint venture with Visitana Development Ltd., another leading developer of vacation ownership resorts, to acquire, develop, and market both Embassy Vacation

Resorts and Hampton Vacation Resorts. Marriott International, the leading established hotel company in the timeshare market, has created Marriott Vacation Club International to continue its aggressive growth. Marriott entered the timeshare business in 1984 with the acquisition of American Resorts, operators of three timeshare properties at Hilton Head, South Carolina. As of mid-1997, Marriott had 30 timeshare properties in 15 locations and about 100,000 owners.

**Exchange Programs.** Another important development that promoted public acceptance of timeshare is the flexibility of trading slots and units for other locations and other times. Companies like Marriott and Disney can offer such exchange programs among their company-operated timeshare hotels. However, about 90 percent of timeshare facilities are owned by independent companies. How do they administer exchange programs? Enter RCI and Interval International, the first and second largest exchange companies. RCI has 3,000 participating resorts in 84 countries and two million member timeshare owners. Interval's worldwide membership is about 1,300 resorts in 60 countries with 700,000 timeshare owners. The flexibility provided by exchange programs—vacationing practically anywhere in the world—is a major attraction that has boosted timeshare sales. "Anywhere in the world" includes urban locations, but not too many. The Manhattan Club in New York City, located in midtown Manhattan across from Carnegie Hall, is the city's first timeshare. Boston and San Francisco have timeshares, and other large cities have timeshares in the planning stages.

Initially, the majority of timeshare units sold were deeded one-week intervals. While that type is still popular, many timeshare resorts now offer a flexible time system. Other programs have emerged as well. Vacation point systems enable vacation owners to purchase a minimum number of points—rather than property—that can be used like currency to select the preferred time of year, number of days, and type of unit. Points can be used all at once, or can be spread throughout the year for shorter vacations.

**An Appealing Investment.** Hotel companies are entering the timeshare business for a number of reasons. First, of course, is the potential for profit. The average price of a timeshare unit is $15,000 for one week. If that is sold for 50 weeks—typical to allow for maintenance—the total revenue on that unit is $750,000. After a deduction of approximately 45 percent for sales and administrative costs, $375,000 remains to cover the cost of the unit and profit. According to the developer of the New York City Manhattan Club, the renovation cost of combining two rooms into a suite, including furnishings and other related costs, was $320,000 per unit for his project. That leaves a profit of $93,000 per room.[18] In addition, there is potential for a management fee and a contribution for advertising, as well as a profit from providing financing for purchasers.

The timeshare business has other advantages for hotel companies, especially in mixed-use projects that include a resort hotel where operating expenses can be shared. For example, timeshare residents increase hotel food and beverage revenue and can balance the demand for staff such as housekeeping personnel.

From the management company's standpoint, there are significant differences in managing traditional hotels and timeshare facilities. Timeshare properties—where there is deeded interest—are considered harder to manage because owners are always present and concerned about their investments. Managers must deal with numerous owners, all of whom have their own ideas about improvements. Many timeshare developers only sell rooms for 50 weeks of the year, allowing only two weeks for cleaning and refurbishing.

Selling must be handled more aggressively and sales costs are considerably higher for timeshare properties than for traditional hotels. After all, when a deeded interest is involved, you are selling a piece of property, not simply an overnight stay. Salespersons with strong closing techniques are required for the initial sell-out period.

Timeshare is big business—a $5 billion industry that grew 900 percent between 1980 and 1996.[19] In 1996, Marriott's timeshare sales were estimated at $300 million—a 40 percent increase over 1995. Disney's sales for the same period were $90 million. Hilton sold $78 million—an increase of 60 percent over the previous year.[20] There are more than 4,000 timeshare resorts in 81 countries with over three million unit owners representing 174 countries. The United States currently dominates the industry, with more that 37 percent of all timeshare resorts, but its share of the market is waning as timeshare properties expand in Europe, South America, and South Africa.[21]

**Condominium hotels,** also known as condo hotels or even condotels, first surfaced in the 1960s and weathered some difficult early years as a result of dishonest practices by some developers. A condo hotel is one in which investors take title to specific hotel rooms. Investors stay in their rooms whenever they wish, and inform management of the times during the year when they will not be using their rooms. When an investor does not occupy his or her hotel room, it is placed in the pool of hotel rooms available for renting to vacationers and other travelers. The investor expects to receive a gain from the increase in value of the condominium hotel over time, as well as ongoing income from the rental of his or her room.

**Continuing-Care Retirement Communities. Continuing-care retirement communities** (CCRCs) are facilities for seniors that offer independent senior apartments, assisted living units, and skilled nursing facilities. CCRCs are much like residential hotels in campus-like settings that offer different specialized personal services in each segment. For example, independent senior apartments provide residents the freedom to live as they wish along with options such as housekeeping, group activities, and meal service. Assisted living operations provide similar services plus personal assistance with daily living needs like bathing, dressing, and taking medication. Skilled nursing facilities provide full-time assistance with daily living activities and medical oversight.

CCRCs are getting the attention of hotel corporations and major real-estate developers with hotel interests. The reason for the growing interest is the "graying of America," which so many marketing people have commented on and written about. Although in 1980 only 11.3 percent of the U.S. population was over 60 years old, that figure is projected to reach 12.2 percent by the turn of the century, and 18.3 percent by 2030. In sheer numbers, the size of America's elderly population will more than double—from 25.5 million to 55 million—in just 50 years.[22]

In the past, many elderly Americans moved in with their children; retired to states like Florida, Arizona, or California; or entered nursing homes. However, today's senior citizens are a different breed. For example, the very term "senior" is rejected by some older citizens. They think of themselves as active, mature people with distinct needs. They are, on the whole, more educated and affluent than their parents. And many of them prefer the new CCRCs to other options.

There is no doubt that CCRCs, or "life-care" centers (as they are sometimes called to distinguish them from "health-care" facilities like nursing homes), are targeted at the affluent. Residents can buy apartments or rent them, but many cost over $100,000 to buy, and rents of $1,500 or more per month are common. Buyers or renters typically get small studios or one- or two-bedroom apartments with small kitchens where they can prepare their own meals, although usually at least two meals a day are included in the rent or maintenance plans. Often there are activities every day, including daily trips to shopping malls and grocery stores, movies, and fitness centers. Market studies show that CCRCs appeal mostly to women (approximately 75 percent of residents), especially widows. Married couples account for most of the other residents.[23]

The Marriott Corporation was one of the first hotel companies to enter this market when it established its Senior Living Service division in 1984. Marriott's first two developments were the Fairfax in Ft. Belvoir, Virginia, and the Quadrangle, in Haverford, Pennsylvania. Each had more than 80 percent of its units spoken for on opening day. Marriott has since acquired the Forum Group, which increased its senior complexes from nine to 69. The Hyatt Corporation started Classic Residence by Hyatt in 1987 to develop and manage high-end independent, assisted living, and skilled nursing facilities. Manor Care, the parent of Hotels, is also aggressively developing senior communities.

# Industry Trends

## Global Performance

The hotel business is, indeed, a global business. Inter-Continental Hotels, headquartered in London, England, but owned by the Seison Group of Japan, operates hotels in over 65 countries. The French company Accor has hotels in 68 countries. London-based Ladbroke's Hilton International chain has hotels in 49 countries. United States-based ITT Sheraton has hotels in 60 countries. The world's top 200 chains, headquartered in 40 countries, operate 28,000 hotels with more than 3,800,000 rooms.[24]

The hotel industry is dynamic, subject to frequent change. Companies and hotels change ownership and new companies and brands enter the marketplace; currently popular brand names may not be around in the next decade. Hotel demand is affected as the economic fortunes of countries, regions, and cities rise and fall. For example, Renaissance Hotels of Hong Kong acquired Stouffer Hotels (formerly a U.S.-based company) from the Nestle Corporation of Switzerland and converted them into Renaissance Hotels, which were then acquired by Marriott International. The Stouffer hotel name no longer exists and, thus far, Marriott has no plans to replace the Renaissance name, either.

According to Smith Travel Research, Hong Kong, the Dominican Republic, and Australia have the highest occupancies worldwide. However, the highest average room rates are recorded in Japan, Switzerland, and France. Hotels in Asia report the highest operating profit of any region.[25] Strong economies in Asia are fueling rapid hotel growth with an increasing demand for trained staff to maintain the high level of service that is the trademark of the region. To meet regional training needs, both Shangri-La Hotels and Resorts of Hong Kong and Atlanta-based Holiday Inn Worldwide operate training centers in Beijing, China.

International chains have not significantly penetrated the Latin American market. International brands are represented by only 12 percent of the hotel supply. U.S.-based companies are the major presence in Latin America, with 45 percent of the supply; 30 percent is associated with European brands.[26] According to Smith Travel Research, Latin American hotels report the lowest occupancies and the lowest average room rates.

## The United States

In the 1960s, the development of new hotel locations fueled the expansion of the industry. Prior to that time, hotels were built primarily in city centers and resort areas. As commerce and industry spread from urban centers to rural, suburban, and airport locations, hotel companies like Hilton, Sheraton, and Marriott recognized opportunities to develop their brands in these new locations.

In the 1970s, intense competition among established and emerging hotel chains created a need for chains to better differentiate their product. Some did this with architecture and decor—for example, the atrium lobby became Hyatt's signature for its Regency brand. Hotel companies adopted distinctive motifs—Ritz-Carlton's decor was traditional, Hyatt's was contemporary.

Pampering the hotel guest was the strategy of the 1980s. Room and bathroom amenities—specialty soaps, sewing kits, mouthwash, shampoo, and a variety of other personal care items—could be found in most hotels, whatever the rate category. Of course, the higher-rate hotels provided more elaborate amenity packages. Some first class and luxury hotels set aside one or more guest floors as "club" areas. For a higher rate, club guests could enjoy a number of special services including an exclusive club desk for check-in and check-out, and complimentary breakfast, afternoon tea, evening cocktails, and before-bed snacks served in the club's private lounge. Even the room amenities were enhanced. Exercise rooms or complete spa facilities were added to many hotels to satisfy travelers' growing interest in physical fitness. Hotels with predominant business traveler markets added business centers to provide secretarial and translating services as well as computer and fax capabilities.

In the early 1990s, the concept of quality service as a differentiating factor came to the fore. Hotel companies implemented quality assurance programs and referred to the quality of their service in their advertising. For the first time, a hotel company, the Ritz-Carlton, won the prestigious Baldrige Award, presented to an organization for outstanding quality.

As the 1990s progressed, the industry emphasized innovation and new business strategies. Segmentation strategy was one of the most important tactics implemented by many of the chains to increase their market share. Actually, the concept was not new. Hilton and Sheraton each had established hotel and inn divisions 30 years before. The hotels were in cities, and the inns were in suburbs, at airports, and off highways. Now, segmentation was based not on location, but on market. Between 1992 and 1996, there were 25 new brand announcements. Some of these brands were divisions of established chains, such as Wingate Inns by HFS and Marriott International's Towner Place Suites. Other brands, namely Extended Stay America by Huizenga Holdings and U.S. Franchise Systems' Microtel Inns, were new companies.

Other significant trends have marked the last decade of the twentieth century. Mergers, acquisitions, joint ventures, and strategic alliances have changed the competitive environment in the U.S. and globally. Some notable transactions follow:

- Forte Plc was acquired by the Granada Group, which created the Forte Hotels division. Both companies are based in England.
- U.S.-based HFS purchased Travelodge from Forte Hotels.
- Doubletree Hotels acquired Red Lion Hotels and Inns. Both are based in the United States.
- Wharf Holdings Ltd. of Hong Kong sold Omni Hotels to TRT Holdings of the United States.
- ITT Sheraton was acquired by the Starwood Capital Group.
- Patriot American Hospitality acquired Carnival Hotels and Resorts.

Acquisitions were not the only vehicle for growth. Companies expanded through partnerships and alliances. For example, Carlson Hospitality Worldwide, owners of Radisson Hotels, partnered with Four Seasons-Regent Hotels and Resorts of Canada. The agreement gave Carlson rights to the Four Seasons-Regent name and to the development of new hotels, while Four Seasons continues to manage existing and new properties. Inter-Continental Hotels established Global Partners, an alliance with other hotels of their class for whom they provide marketing and reservation services. Seattle-based Westin Hotels and Resorts partnered with Paris-based Demeure Hotels, and Scandic Hotels of Stockhom allied with Holiday Inn Worldwide.

## Developing and Planning New Hotels

Before a new hotel is built, (1) a site is selected, (2) a feasibility study is conducted to determine the potential success of the planned hotel, and (3) financing is arranged.

### Site Selection

Choosing the site for a hotel is usually first in a series of critical decisions affecting the eventual success of the hotel. The site must be accessible to the market it hopes to attract. If the location is downtown, for example, it should be convenient to the central business district, the financial district, the entertainment district, or a major convention hall. It also should be accessible by public transportation. If it is a highway location, whether the highway is a major route and will continue to be one should be established. Many of the old "ma and pa" tourist courts and motels were put out of business when new freeways and turnpikes bypassed their locations.

The site must be adaptable to the type and size of the proposed hotel. A 400-room commercial hotel with meeting space can't be built on a site where zoning laws prohibit a building of that size. Zoning ordinances could also limit the type and size of ancillary facilities that would make the property more attractive and marketable, such as restaurants and lounges. Parking requirements are another consideration. Many cities have ordinances that dictate the number of spaces that must be available to employees and guests. That requirement must be satisfied before a hotel can be constructed.

## The Feasibility Study

After the site is selected, a market study and financial analysis, called a **feasibility study,** is conducted to determine the economic viability of the hotel project. Among other things, a feasibility study determines the size and scope of the potential guest market for the new hotel. It would be unwise to construct a hotel without first making sure that a market for it exists and learning about the market's size and characteristics. The kinds of questions the study should address include: What kind of hotel is most likely to succeed in this location? What types of guests is it likely to attract? How much will these guests be willing to pay? What occupancy rate can be expected? How many competitors are there and where are they located?

A feasibility study helps prospective owners in a number of ways. They can use the study to help them obtain financing and negotiate contracts for a franchise, lease, or management contract. A feasibility study can guide planners and architects of the facility. A study also helps the new hotel's management team formulate operating and marketing plans and prepare the initial capital and operating budget.[27]

Feasibility studies are conducted at the request of lenders, investors, franchisors, or management companies. Usually the person or persons conducting the study are independent consultants, although it is not uncommon for developers, management companies, or institutional investors to conduct their own study as well.

The person or consulting firm commissioned to conduct a feasibility study should have expertise and prior experience in the areas of hotel marketing, operations, and finance. There are a number of domestic and international companies that are considered experts in these disciplines. Most are firms of certified public accountants that have developed special consulting divisions for the hospitality industry. These include Arthur Andersen, and Coopers and Lybrand. Personnel in the consulting divisions of these and other accounting firms are often graduates of hospitality management schools rather than accounting schools.

Most feasibility studies are performed to determine the suitability of a location for a hotel-chain property. Hotel chains already have brand-name recognition, tested hotel concepts, and established markets. Consumers have definite expectations of these hotels. Therefore, an important purpose of a feasibility study is to find out whether the proposed site and hotel can meet these consumer expectations.

**The Report.** The final product of a feasibility study is a written report that typically includes the following sections.

**Market area characteristics.** This section contains a review of demographic and relevant economic data for the area surrounding the site. The purpose is not to provide an in-depth economic evaluation, but to obtain a sampling of those factors that support or reject the need for the proposed hotel. For example, a profile of the commercial and industrial sectors of the area can indicate the degree of economic stability and strength of the market. Population statistics, along with growth trends and income levels, are valuable for determining the potential demand for food, beverage, and catering facilities. Employment statistics are helpful as well. Not only are they another indicator of economic strength, but they also may be useful in forecasting potential employment problems or opportunities in operating the hotel. Highway traffic counts, air arrivals and departures, and tourism statistics often are analyzed in relation to their potential impact on the proposed project.

**Site and area evaluation.** The father of the modern American hotel, Ellsworth Statler, was reputed to have said that there were three reasons for a hotel's success: location, location, and location. That maxim may be as true today as it ever was. As pointed out earlier, convenience and accessibility are key components to a new hotel's success. There may be a real demand, but if the proposed hotel is not easily accessible to the source of that demand, it cannot succeed. Moreover, ideally the proposed hotel should be *more* accessible than existing or proposed competing hotels.

Accessibility is a relative concept, of course, which varies according to the kind of facility proposed. Club Med has built one of the largest hospitality organizations of its kind by going into areas that are by definition inaccessible—except to its own guests. To make sure that guests can get to its hotels, Club Med often charters aircraft and buses, and it has even developed airports in partnership with governments (as was necessary in Mexico). Resort hotels may not need to be accessible by automobile as long as they are convenient by air, train, bus, or even ferry (as is Nantucket Island in Massachusetts). On the other hand, highways are the lifelines of motels.

Finally, the reputation of the area may well be an important factor in determining the feasibility of the proposed hotel. Travelers avoid areas with high crime rates, blatant poverty, or political unrest. Unless there is an overriding reason for building a hotel in these areas, they are best avoided.

**Competition analysis.** A good feasibility study carefully describes all of the competition in the area in order to reveal the size and nature of the market as it currently exists. Facilities, services, and price levels of competitors are noted. This section of the report is a good place to look for opportunities that may have been overlooked or simply not taken advantage of by competitors. There may not be a fine-dining restaurant in the area, for example, or there may be a need for a health club—both of which a hotel could include in its concept. Hyatt often puts revolving restaurants on top of its properties because both the height and the concept are unique.

**Demand analysis.** The feasibility study must answer a number of questions about potential guests. Who are they and where are they going to come from? How many are there? Is this number likely to grow or decline in the future? Which hotels are they going to now? How are we going to take these guests away from

The pristine beaches and tropical foliage surrounding The Naples Beach Hotel and Gulf Club have made the property a popular destination since 1946. (Courtesy of the Naples Beach Hotel and Gulf Club, Naples Beach, Florida)

those hotels? A detailed approach to demand analysis is a vital part of any sound marketing plan.

If demand is expected to be generated from local industry and commercial activity, then surveys of potential guests in the area are one of the best ways to confirm that demand. On the other hand, if the potential market is anticipated to come from incoming travelers such as conventioneers and sightseers, then the market survey should be extended to cover those groups. The market as a whole must be quantified, then the potential for the proposed property to gain a fair share of that market must be appraised. Generally, through a series of interviews with potential guests, a profile of the needed facilities and services can be formulated.

**Proposed facilities and services.** After analyzing market area characteristics, evaluating the site, reviewing the competition, and preparing a demand analysis, the next step in a feasibility study is the proposal of facilities and services. At this stage the analysts conducting the study are expected to recommend the size and type of facilities the proposed hotel should have, as well as the services that should be provided. Their goal is to establish a market difference that gives the hotel a competitive advantage. Recommendations may cover architectural and design considerations as well as overall concept and ambiance.

**Financial estimates.** The last section of the study contains estimates of revenues and expenses, based on (1) the proposed hotel's type and the services it will offer, and (2) the size of the projected guest demand.

Feasibility studies vary at this point. Some will present estimates of operating results only, while others, at the request of those commissioning the study, provide additional information, such as (1) the fixed charges that can be anticipated—for example, property taxes, insurance on building and contents, and interest on borrowed capital and depreciation; and (2) an analysis of the expected return on investment (ROI). A study that includes ROI is a true feasibility study. Most studies end at the point of forecasting income before fixed charges—that is, they estimate only operating revenues and expenses. Those studies are known as market studies with estimates of operating revenues and expenses.

## Financing

Investors who are asked to participate in the financing of a new hotel look carefully at several components:

- *The land on which the hotel will be built.* How large is the site? What condition is it in? What is its appraised value? What is its market value? What has comparable land sold for in the last year?

- *The building.* What construction costs are involved? How long will it take to construct the hotel?

- *Furniture and fixtures.* What is needed to decorate rooms and public areas? How much will it cost?

In addition to these **hard costs,** there are some **soft costs** that should be factored into any financing package:

- *Architectural fees.* These include site elevations, final blueprints from which contractors will work, and models.

- *Pre-opening expenses.* Certain members of the management team will be on board months before opening day. New managers and employees must be trained. Security guards will be needed to protect the property. An advertising campaign should begin several months before opening day. Working capital will also be needed until the hotel is open and generating its own.

There are two general types of hotel financing—permanent financing loans and construction financing loans.

**Permanent financing loans** are long-term mortgage loans—traditionally no longer than 25 years. Long-term mortgage loans are obtained from institutions such as insurance companies, pension funds, and banks. These lending institutions provide the financing and charge interest at what the going rate is when the loan is made. In addition, they sometimes take an equity position in the property—that is, they become part-owners of the hotel. Typically these institutions put up as much as 65 to 75 percent of the cost of the entire project. The developer, either alone or with partners, is expected to provide the remainder, as lenders do not wish to loan

**Exhibit 10  Hotel Construction and Occupancy Rates**

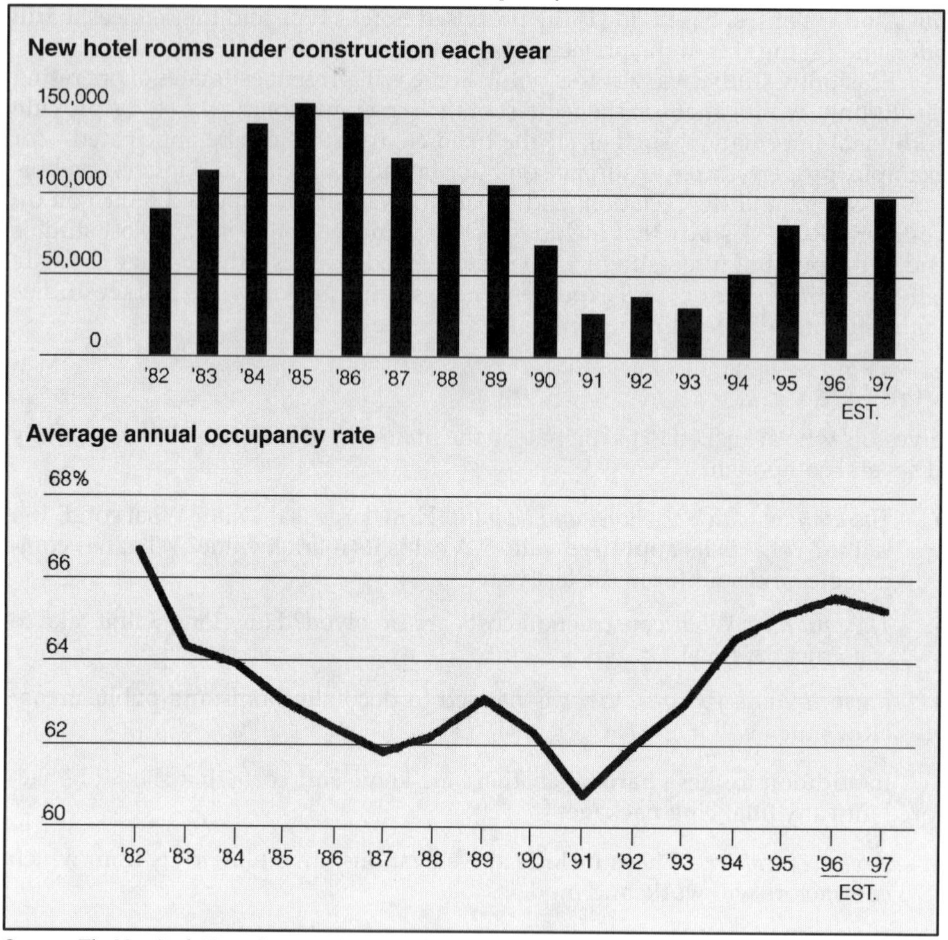

**New hotel rooms under construction each year**

[Bar chart showing new hotel rooms under construction from '82 to '97 EST., with values ranging from approximately 80,000 in '82, peaking around 150,000 in '85-'86, declining to a low near '91-'93, and rising back to near 100,000 by '96-'97.]

**Average annual occupancy rate**

[Line chart showing occupancy rate from '82 to '97 EST., starting near 66.5% in '82, declining to around 61.5% in '87, rising slightly to '89, dropping to a low of about 60% in '91, then rising steadily to about 65% by '96-'97.]

Source: *The New York Times,* January 2, 1997, C6.

money to projects if the developer is unwilling or unable to risk any of his or her own funds.

**Construction financing loans** are obtained from a bank or a group of banks. This is a short-term loan to be used while the hotel is being built, with repayment to be made in three years or less. In most cases the construction financing loan is approved only after permanent financing, known as "**take-out**," has already been granted, since once the hotel opens and the permanent financing is in place, part of the permanent financing will be used to pay off the construction financing loan.

Exhibit 10 shows U.S. hotel construction and occupancy from 1982 to 1997 (estimated). Construction—of mostly first class and luxury hotels—continued through the 1980s, although occupancy was on the decline. In 1991—the lowest occupancy year—the hotel industry lost $5.7 billion. When construction resumed after 1991, primarily economy and budget-class hotels were developed. With a few exceptions,

Las Vegas was the only location where full-service upscale hotels were built during the 1990s. As of 1997, it was cheaper to buy first class and luxury hotels than to build them, and many hotels changed owners as the major chains reversed their strategy to manage rather than to own. Other buyers were foreign interests, pension funds, and real estate investment trusts.

A real estate investment trust (REIT) is an investment vehicle, similar to a mutual fund, that provides the general public the opportunity to invest in real estate. As defined by the U.S. Internal Revenue Service, if 95 percent of the trust's net taxable income is distributed to stockholders as dividends—and other requirements are met—REITs are not subject to income tax like a regular corporation. REITs are traded on the stock exchange, providing a high level of liquidity for the investor. Generally, REITs are prohibited from actively managing the real estate they own; however, there are four REITs, known as paired-share REITs, that can own property and manage non-real estate businesses. Both Patriot American Hospitality, Inc. and Starwood Lodging Trust, two of the largest hotel REITs, are paired-share REITs. In 1997 and 1998, Patriot American acquired Wyndham Hotels, Carnival Hotels and Resorts, and Interstate Hotels. During the same period, Starwood acquired Westin Hotels and ITT Sheraton.

Exhibit 11 highlights lending institutions that finance new construction, acquisitions, and hotel refinancing. Some major franchisors—most notably HFS, Choice, and U.S. Franchising Systems—have also developed loan programs for their franchisees.

## Chapter Summary

Hotel guests can be classified by market segment. The major market segments are corporate—individuals, corporate groups, convention and association groups, leisure travelers, long-term stay/relocation guests, airline-related guests, government and military travelers, and regional getaway guests.

Hotels can be categorized by location: center city, resort, suburban, highway, and airport are common categories. Center city hotels have experienced growth in recent years with the rebirth of downtown areas. More than half of downtown hotels today are less than 12 years old. The majority serve business guests and are operated or managed by chains.

Resorts are built in destinations that are desirable because of climate, scenery, recreational facilities, or historic interest. Many resorts are patronized for health reasons. While early resorts were usually open only in the summer, today most resorts are open year-round. Most resort business comes from leisure travelers, but resort use by businesses for meetings and incentive programs is increasing. Most resorts are still independent operations. They are expensive to build and operate.

Suburban hotels followed corporations and factories that relocated from downtown to the suburbs because of land costs. Suburban hotels tend to be somewhat smaller than downtown properties and are primarily chain affiliated. Individual business travelers represent their single largest market, although their food and beverage operations are often patronized by the local community.

**Exhibit 11    Sourcing Financing**

| Market Segment | Acquisition and Refinancing | New Construction |
| --- | --- | --- |
| Budget | Community and regional banks<br>SBA loan providers | Community and regional banks<br>SBA loan providers |
| Economy | Community and regional banks<br>SBA loan providers<br>Mortgage conduit programs | Community and regional banks<br>SBA loan providers<br>Mortgage conduit programs |
| Midmarket | Regional banks<br>Mortgage conduit programs<br>Credit companies<br>Life insurance companies | Regional banks<br>Mortgage conduit programs<br>Credit companies |
| First Class* | Money center banks<br>Mortgage conduit programs<br>Credit companies | Money center banks<br>Mortgage conduit programs<br>Credit companies |
| Luxury* | Money center banks<br>Life insurance companies<br>Pension funds | Money center banks<br>Life insurance companies |

*The availability of new construction financing in these categories, although growing, is only poor to fair at best. Additionally, in these categories, the number of financing sources is much narrower than in all other categories.

Source: *Lodging Hospitality,* May 1997, p. 30. Survey conducted by HMBA: America's Hotel Broker.

Highway hotels have evolved from early tourist courts. Large signs, easy access, and ample parking facilities are distinguishing characteristics. Many are franchised by companies like Holiday Inn and are relatively new structures. Business travelers are their main source of revenue.

Airport hotels are for the most part affiliated with chains and enjoy some of the highest occupancy rates in the lodging industry. Their biggest operating problem is the need to respond to high demand instantly when weather or other conditions delay flight arrivals and departures.

Hotels can also be categorized by ownership. Most hotels today are owned, leased, managed, or franchised by a chain. Nevertheless, many independent hotels have overcome the chains' advantage of economies of scale with other business strategies that allow them to compete effectively.

Business philosophies vary from chain to chain. Some hotel chains prefer to own, others to franchise, and others to manage. Many have a mix of the three. In addition, there are some successful management companies that operate and manage chain properties.

Hotels can also be categorized by price. The most important classifications are: economy and budget, mid-price, first class, and luxury.

A fairly recent development in the lodging industry has been the growth of segmentation strategies. In order to capture more guest markets, companies like Choice Hotels International and Marriott now offer a complete line of properties that range from economy to luxury.

Other hotel classifications include conference centers, timeshare and condominium hotels, and continuing-care retirement communities (CCRCs).

Feasibility studies are conducted when new hotels are developed and planned. They help prospective owners obtain financing and help managers prepare marketing plans. Location is a key consideration in all new hotel projects.

Financing covers the land, building(s), furniture and fixtures, and equipment, as well as architectural fees and pre-opening expenses. Financing for new hotels is usually provided in two types of loans—long-term permanent financing loans (mortgage loans) and short-term construction financing loans.

## Endnotes

1. Albert J. Gomes, *Hospitality in Transition* (Houston, Tex.: Pannell Kerr Forster, 1985), pp. 32–34. Although the hotel industry has been through many changes since Gomes' book was published, the industry's guest market can still be categorized as described in the following sections.
2. Megan Rowe, "The Smart Business Hotel," *Lodging Hospitality,* October 1996, p. 21.
3. Rowe, p. 21.
4. Donald E. Lundberg, *The Hotel and Restaurant Business,* 5th ed. (New York: Van Nostrand Reinhold, 1989), p. 185.
5. *Business Traveler,* April 1992, p. 12.
6. *Business Traveler,* p. 12.
7. *Business Traveler,* p. 12.
8. Anthony Falola, "The Bill Marriott Way," *The Washington Post,* 19 August 1996, p. 12.
9. Falola, p. 13.
10. *Trends in the Hotel Industry USA Edition - 1996,* PKF Consulting, p. 74.
11. *Hotel Operating Statistics, 1996,* Smith Travel Research, p. 25.
12. *Hotel Operating Statistics, 1996,* p. 27.
13. *Hotel Operating Statistics, 1996,* p. 17.
14. *Hotel Operating Statistics, 1996,* pp. 14–15.
15. "Conference Centers," *The Convention Liaison Council Manual,* 6th Edition (Washington, D.C.: Convention Liaison Council, 1994), p. 17.
16. Edwin McDowell, "Shorter Meetings on Short Notice Are the Rule," *New York Times,* 9 February 1992, p. F10.
17. David Arnold, "Conference Centers Coming of Age," *Lodging,* February 1997, p. 17.
18. Mike Sheridan, "Warming Up to Vacation Ownership," *Hotels,* March 1997, p. 70.
19. Robyn Taylor Parets, "Vacation Ownership," *Lodging,* February 1997, p. 42.

**200** *Chapter 6*

20. Sheridan, p. 67.
21. M. Chase Burritt and Mark A. Lunt, "Its Fair Share," *Lodging*, June 1996, p. 75.
22. Robert Meyer, "The Hospitality Industry Entering the Life Care Market: Implications for Hotel Restaurant and Institutional Management Curricula," *Hospitality Education and Restaurant Journal*, 1988, p. 242.
23. Robert L. Roher and Robert Bibb, "Contemporary TLC," *CCRC*, May 1986, p. 51.
24. "200 Corporate Chains," *Hotels*, July 1997, pp. 58, 60.
25. Mark V. Lomano, "Worldwide Performance," *Hotel & Motel Management*, 16 December 1996, p. 17.
26. "200 Corporate Chains," pp. 58, 60.
27. Rocco M. Angelo, *A Practical Guide to Understanding Feasibility Studies* (East Lansing, Mich.: Educational Institute of the American Hotel & Motel Association, 1985), p. 25.

## Key Terms

**airline-related guests**—Airplane crew members; sometimes includes passengers needing emergency accommodations.

**airport hotels**—Hotels built near airports. These full-service hotels are more likely to have in-room movies, computerized property management systems, and call accounting systems.

**all-suite hotel**—A hotel that features units including two connected hotel rooms for approximately the price of one at lower prices than traditional hotel suites. One room is furnished as a typical hotel guestroom with a bed, the other with a fold-out sofa and/or table and chairs.

**budget hotels**—A type of limited-service hotel. They have low construction and operating costs, allowing them to charge between $45 and $60 per night.

**center city hotels**—Full-service hotels located in downtown areas.

**condominium hotels**—Hotels in which an investor takes title to a specific hotel room that remains in the pool to be rented to transient guests. The investor expects to receive a gain from the increase in value of the hotel over time as well as ongoing income from rental of the room.

**conference centers**—Specialized hotels, usually accessible to major market areas but in less busy locations, that almost exclusively book conferences, executive meetings, and training seminars. A conference center may provide extensive leisure facilities.

**construction financing loan**—A short-term loan to be used while a hotel is being built, with repayment to be made in three years or less.

**continuing-care retirement communities (CCRCs)**—Facilities for seniors that offer independent senior apartments, assisted living units, and skilled nursing facilities. CCRCs are much like residential hotels in campus-like settings that offer different specialized personal services in each segment. Independent senior apartments provide residents the freedom to live as they wish along with options such as housekeeping, group activities, and meal service. Assisted living operations provide similar services plus personal assistance with daily living needs like bathing, dressing, and taking medication. Skilled nursing facilities provide full-time assistance with daily living activities and medical oversight.

**convention and association groups**—Groups of businesspeople attending a convention or association meeting. The number of people attending can run into the thousands.

**corporate groups**—Groups of people traveling for business purposes, usually to attend conferences or meetings.

**corporate individuals**—Individuals traveling for business purposes.

**economy hotels**—A type of limited-service hotel. They have the lowest construction and operating costs, allowing them to charge 25 percent less than budget hotels.

**feasibility study**—A study commissioned by developers and prepared by consultants to determine the potential success of a proposed hotel on a proposed site.

**franchise**—Refers to (1) the authorization given by one company to another to sell its unique product and service, or (2) the name of the business format or product that is being franchised.

**franchisee**—The individual or company granted the franchise.

**franchisor**—The franchise company that owns the trademark, products, and/or business format that is being franchised.

**full-service/luxury hotels**—Hotels with high room rates and exceptional service and amenities.

**government and military travelers**—Travelers in government or the military on a fixed per diem allowance who typically are reimbursed for hotel and other travel expenses. That is, they receive a certain amount of money to pay for their hotel room, no matter what the hotel rate is.

**guest mix**—The variety or mixture of guests who stay at a hotel or patronize a restaurant.

**hard costs**—The land, building, furniture, fixtures, and equipment (FFE) costs that are basic to hotel and restaurant development.

**highway hotels**—Hotels built next to a highway. These hotels typically feature large property signs, an entrance where travelers can leave their cars as they check in, and a swimming pool. Parking space is plentiful and the atmosphere is informal.

**hotel chain**—A group of affiliated hotels.

**independent hotel**—A hotel owned by an individual or group of investors not connected with any hotel company.

**leisure travelers**—Travelers—often entire families—who typically spend only one night at a hotel unless the hotel is their destination.

**limited-service hotels**—Hotels that do not offer the full range of services customarily associated with hotels. For example, they do not have restaurants or bars. Types of limited-service hotels include budget and economy hotels.

**long-term stay/relocation guests**—Individuals or families relocating to an area who require lodging until permanent housing is found.

**management company**—A company that manages hotels for owners, typically in return for a combination of fees and a share of revenues. A management company may or may not have any of its own funds invested in a hotel that it manages.

**mid-price hotels**—Hotels that offer facilities and services similar to those at full-service/luxury hotels, but at average rates. They have restaurants and bars, and many have meeting space. Average prices vary by market.

**permanent financing loan**—A long-term mortgage loan for a hotel, usually up to 25 years. Long-term mortgage loans are obtained from institutions such as insurance companies, pension funds, and banks.

**referral systems**—Independent properties or small chains that do not share common operating systems, decor, purchasing systems, etc., but are linked by (1) a common reservation system, and (2) a common marketing strategy. The reservation system and marketing campaigns are funded by the hotels in the referral system.

**regional getaway guests**—Guests who check into a hotel close to home—with or without children—in order to enjoy a weekend away from daily responsibilities.

**resort hotels**—Usually located in desirable vacation spots, resort hotels offer fine dining, exceptional service, and many amenities.

**segmenting**—A method of categorizing hotels by the prices they charge.

**soft costs**—Development costs other than the land, building, furniture, fixtures, and equipment (FFE) for a hotel or restaurant project. Soft costs include architectural fees and fees for pre-opening activities such as advertising.

**standard industrial classificiation code (SIC)**—The basis of government classificiation of all businesses in the United States. Most hotels and lodging places are in Major Group 70.

**suburban hotels**—Hotels located in suburban areas that typically have 250 to 500 rooms, restaurants, bars, and other amenities found at most downtown hotels. Suburban hotels usually belong to major hotel chains.

**take-out**—The permanent financing secured for a new hotel.

**timeshare condominiums**—Condominiums for which an owner can purchase a portion of time at the condominium—typically one week to one month—for one-twelfth or one-fiftieth of the condominium's price, and share the condominium with other owners. Owners have the right to stay at the condominium during their assigned time or to trade their slot with another owner.

**tourist courts**—The forerunners of motels, built along highways in the 1920s and 1930s. Tourist courts usually included a simple row of small cabins that often had no private baths.

## Review Questions

1. What are some of the differences between a center city hotel and a resort hotel?
2. What are some characteristics of suburban hotels? highway hotels?
3. Airport hotels possess what unique characteristics?
4. What are some hotel price categories?
5. How can economy and budget hotels offer such low rates?
6. What are some important guest categories?
7. What are the differences between chain and independent hotels?
8. What is a feasibility study and what does it cover?

## Internet Sites

For more information, visit the following Internet sites. Remember that Internet addresses can change without notice. If the site is no longer there, use a search engine to look for additional sites.

### Hotel Companies/Resorts

Accor
www.accor.com

Benchmark Hospitality
www.benchmark-hospitality.com

Choice Hotels International
www.hotelchoice.com

Club Med
www.clubmed.com

Days Inn
www.daysinn.com

Dolce International
www.dolce.com

Doubletree Hotels
www.doubletreehotels.com

Embassy Suites
www.embassy-suites.com

Four Seasons Hotels and Resorts
www.fshr.com

Hilton Hotels
www.hilton.com

Holiday Inn Worldwide
www.holiday-inn.com

Inter-Continental Hotels
www.interconti.com

La Quinta Hotels
www.laquinta.com

The Leading Hotels of the World
www.lhw.com

Mandarin Oriental Hotel Group
www.mandarin-oriental.com

Marriott International
www.marriott.com

Motel 6
www.motel6.com

Preferred Hotels
www.preferredhotels.com

Relais & Chateaux
www.britain.co.uk/relais.html

Sheraton Hotels
www.sheraton.com

Signature Resorts
www.sigr.com

Starwood Lodging
www.starwood.com

Swissôtel
www.swissotel.com

Westin Hotels
www.westin.com

## *Organizations, Consultants, Resources*

American Society of
Association Executives
www.asaenet.org

Arthur Andersen Consulting
www.arthurandersen.com

Coopers and Lybrand
www.colybrand.com

International Association of
Conference Centers
www.iacconline.com

PKF Consulting
www.delve.com/pkf/pkf.html

Smith Travel Research
www.str-online.com

## *Publications*

*Meetings & Conventions*
www.meetings-conventions.com

# REVIEW QUIZ

When you feel you have covered all of the material in this chapter, answer these questions. Choose the *best* answer.

1. Rooms for _____ are usually booked in blocks at rock-bottom prices.

   a. regional getaway travelers
   b. leisure travelers
   c. corporate groups
   d. airline-related guests

2. Guests in the _____ segment are typically reimbursed for hotel stays on a fixed per diem basis.

   a. convention and association group
   b. leisure traveler
   c. government and military traveler
   d. a and c

3. Guests at center city hotels tend to be primarily:

   a. corporate and leisure travelers.
   b. corporate travelers and conventioneers.
   c. convention groups and regional getaway guests.
   d. individual corporate and governmental travelers.

4. Which of the following statements about resorts is *false*?

   a. A large number of resorts are being built today.
   b. Many of the first resorts were built around hot or mineral springs.
   c. Compared to other segments of the hotel industry, resorts still remain largely independent from chains.
   d. Resorts are the most expensive hotels to operate.

5. Which of the following statements about franchising is *true*?

   a. A "franchisor" is the party granted the franchise.
   b. A "franchise" is the authorization granted by a hotel chain to an individual hotel to use the chain's trademark, operating systems, and reservation system in return for a percentage of the hotel's revenues plus certain other fees.
   c. A "franchisee" is the party granting the franchise.
   d. All of the above.

6. Which of the following statements about conference centers is *true*?

   a. According to the International Association of Conference Centers, for a facility to be classified as a conference center, a minimum of 90 percent of its total sales must come from conferences.
   b. Colleges and universities do not operate conference centers.
   c. Executive conference centers tend to be used mostly by academic groups.
   d. The demand for conference centers is increasing.

## REVIEW QUIZ (continued)

7. Which of the following is *not* a soft cost?
    a. furniture and fixtures
    b. architectural fees
    c. pre-opening expenses
    d. a and c

**Answer Key:** 1-d-C1, 2-c-C1, 3-b-C2, 4-a-C2, 5-b-C3, 6-d-C4, 7-a-C5

Each question is linked to a competency. Competencies are listed on the first page of the chapter. An answer reading 3-b-C4 translates to:

  3: the question number
  b: the correct answer
C4: the competency number

## Chapter 7 Outline

How Is a Hotel Organized?
    Revenue Centers versus Cost Centers
Revenue Centers
    Rooms Division
    Food and Beverage Division
    Other Revenue Centers
Cost Centers
    Marketing Division
    Engineering Division
    Accounting Division
    Human Resources Division
    Security Division
Compliance with the ADA
Control Systems
    Financial Controls
    Quality Controls
Chapter Summary

## Competencies

1. Explain how a hotel is organized, distinguish revenue centers from cost centers, and describe the rooms division.

2. Describe a hotel's food and beverage division, and describe the following hotel revenue centers: telephone department; concessions, rentals, and commissions; and fitness and recreation facilities.

3. List hotel cost centers, describe the marketing, engineering, accounting, human resources, and security divisions; and give examples of what a hotel must do to comply with the Americans with Disabilities Act.

4. Describe hotel control systems, give examples of financial controls used in hotels, and summarize the need for (and give examples of) quality controls used in hotels.

# 7

# Hotel Organization

IN ORDER TO GAIN a perspective on how hotels are organized, a few hotel characteristics should be noted at the outset:

- All hotels are in the business of renting rooms.
- Hotels vary in size from under 100 rooms to over 5,000.
- Hotels vary in type. As pointed out in the previous chapter, hotels can be suburban, airport, all-suite, and so on.
- Hotels vary in the nature and extent of their facilities. Some hotels offer only rooms, while others have coffee shops, gourmet restaurants, swimming pools, golf courses, and other facilities.
- Hotels vary in the level of service they offer. For example, some offer 24-hour room service, others offer room service from 7 A.M. to 10 P.M. only, and some do not offer room service at all.

Clearly, hotels are not all alike. No matter what category a hotel falls into, however, it must be organized in order to: (1) coordinate the many specialized tasks and activities necessary to attract and serve guests, and (2) produce a reasonable profit consistent with the amount of money and time invested in the enterprise. Organizing is one of the principal jobs of management.

## How Is a Hotel Organized?

In order to attract and serve guests and make a reasonable profit, hotels are organized into functional areas or divisions[1] based on the services the hotel provides. For instance, all hotels have a rooms division to manage guestrooms. If the hotel operates a restaurant or lounge, it is likely to have a food and beverage division as well. Within each division there are specialized functions. The rooms division handles reservations, check-in and check-out activities, housekeeping, uniformed service, and telephone service. At a small hotel, these functions are performed by personnel who report to and take their instructions from the general manager. At a large hotel, rooms personnel report to a rooms division manager. The tasks each employee is responsible for also vary with the size of the hotel. For example, in a small hotel, one person behind the front desk may act as receptionist, cashier, and hotel operator. In a large hotel, different individuals handle these jobs.

**Exhibit 1    Sample Organization Chart—Small Hotel**

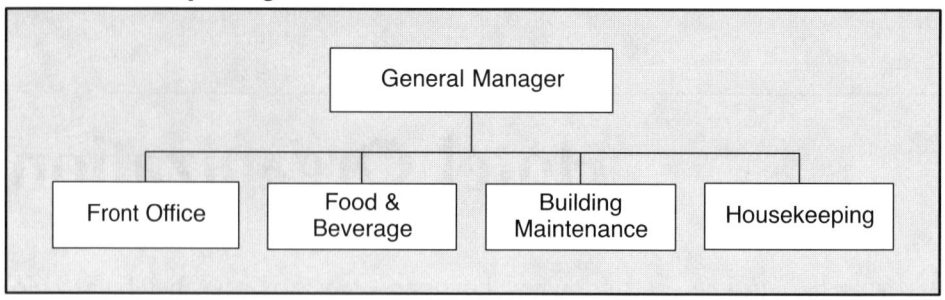

```
                    General Manager
        ┌───────────────┼───────────────┬───────────────┐
   Front Office    Food &         Building        Housekeeping
                   Beverage       Maintenance
```

## Revenue Centers versus Cost Centers

The divisions in a hotel can be categorized as revenue centers or cost centers. **Revenue centers** generate income for the hotel through the sale of services or products to guests. **Cost centers,** also known as support centers, do not generate revenue directly. Instead, they support the proper functioning of revenue centers.

Probably the easiest way to understand revenue and cost centers is to take a look at hotel organization charts. Exhibit 1 shows a typical organization chart for a small hotel. As you can see, this hotel has four divisions. The general manager supervises four people, each of whom has the responsibility and the authority to take care of one of the four principal areas in this hotel. Each of these individuals may or may not supervise other employees, depending on the size of the property.

Let's examine a much larger hotel that has a more complex organization (see Exhibit 2). The divisions and departments shown in Exhibit 2 can be thus categorized:

| Revenue Centers | Cost Centers |
| --- | --- |
| Rooms | Marketing |
| Food and Beverage | Engineering |
| Telephone | Accounting |
| Concessions, Commissions, Rentals | Human Resources |
| Fitness and Recreation Facilities | Security |

In order to make hotels more efficient and profitable, there is a trend to combine some departments and eliminate certain middle-management positions. At some hotels, rooms and food and beverage operations have been combined under one operating division, for example. Those areas responsible for generating revenue, such as sales, guestroom reservations, and catering, might be combined into a revenue division. Finally, there is an administrative division that includes human resources and accounting.

In some chains, regional management clusters have been formed. Under this system, a single manager—i.e., general manager, comptroller, or human resources director—is in charge of more than one hotel in the region.

At other hotels a different kind of reorganization is taking place. Based on management concepts that put the customer first, front-line employees are being given more authority to solve guest problems and make other decisions—by themselves or in teams formed to solve work problems. Authority is pushed down to the lowest level in the organization. Thus, as we move into the twenty-first century, hotel organization is in a state of flux. For some hotels, the sample organization charts shown in this chapter may be more representative of the functions that occur in a hotel rather than the individuals who do the job.

Now let's take a closer look at each revenue and cost center.

## Revenue Centers

### Rooms Division

In most hotels, the **rooms division** is the major division and the central reason for the business entity. Casino hotels are an exception to this rule, since their rooms are occupied by guests whose primary reason for being at the hotel is to gamble, not spend the night. However, most of any hotel's square footage is devoted to guestrooms and areas that support the operation of those rooms. Therefore, the major segment of the building investment and, in most cases, the land cost is related to the rooms division.

For all hotels except casino hotels, guestroom rentals are the single largest source of revenue (see Exhibit 3). Not only do rooms occupy the most space in a hotel and produce the most revenue; they generate the most profit. In a study of U.S. hotels done by PKF Consulting, rooms division income (defined as room revenues or sales less room operating expenses) amounted to 73.2 percent of rooms revenue. In other words, for every dollar spent on guestrooms, 73.2 cents were available for general overhead after deducting the direct rooms division expenses.[2]

**Organization of the Rooms Division.** No matter what the size or category of hotel, rooms divisions are organized and function in a similar manner. Large hotels have more departments and personnel within the division, but this does not change the basic tasks that must be performed.

In a small hotel, the general manager or owner directly oversees the rooms division because of its paramount importance. In a mid-size to large hotel (300 rooms or more), there is likely to be a rooms manager or an executive assistant manager in charge of rooms. In either case, the rooms division is usually organized like the sample division shown in Exhibit 4. As you can see, the rooms division has four departments or functions:

- Front office
- Reservations
- Housekeeping
- Uniformed service

**Front office.** The **front office** is the command post for processing reservations, registering guests, settling guest accounts (cashiering), and checking out guests.

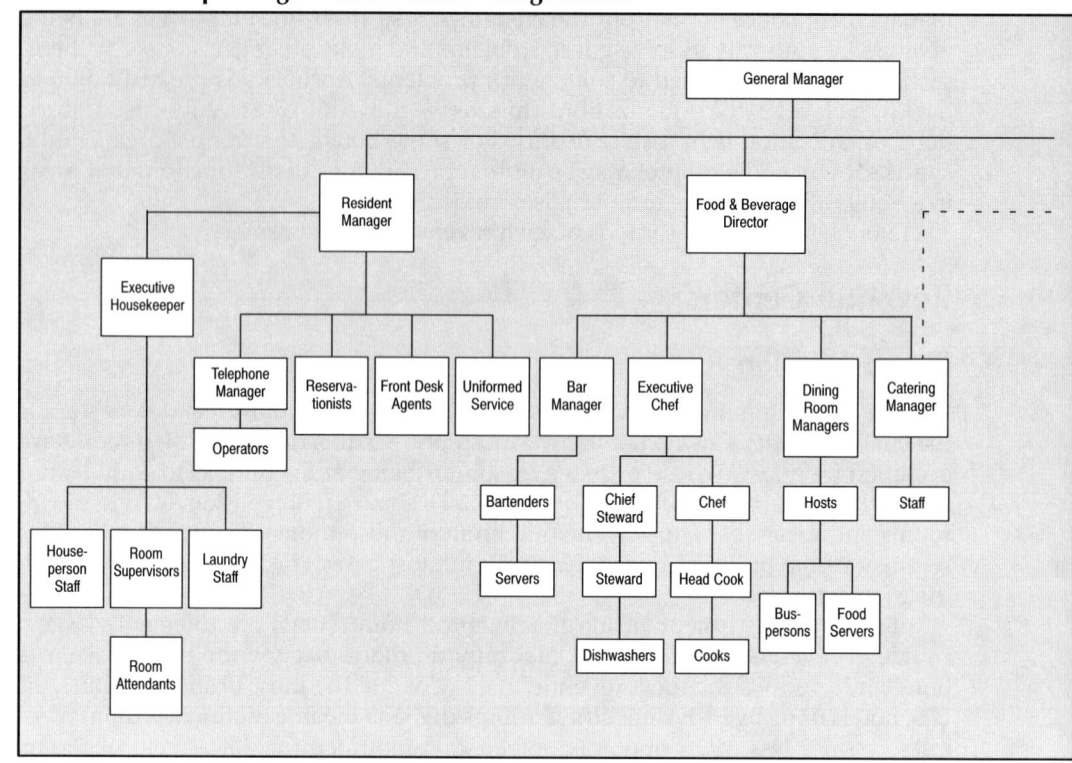

**Exhibit 2 Sample Organization Chart—Large Hotel**

```
                                General Manager
                         ┌───────────┴───────────┬──────────────┐
                    Resident                Food & Beverage
                    Manager                     Director
        ┌──────────────┼──────────────────┐        │
   Executive      (front office)              (F&B sections)
   Housekeeper
```

- General Manager
  - Resident Manager
    - Executive Housekeeper
      - Houseperson Staff
      - Room Supervisors
        - Room Attendants
      - Laundry Staff
    - Telephone Manager
      - Operators
    - Reservationists
    - Front Desk Agents
    - Uniformed Service
  - Food & Beverage Director
    - Bar Manager
      - Bartenders
    - Executive Chef
      - Chief Steward
        - Steward
        - Dishwashers
      - Chef
        - Head Cook
        - Cooks
    - Dining Room Managers
      - Hosts
        - Buspersons
        - Food Servers
    - Catering Manager
      - Staff

Front desk agents[3] also handle the distribution of guestroom keys and mail, messages, or other information for guests.

The most visible part of the front office area is of course the front desk. The front desk can be a counter or, in some luxury hotels, an actual desk where a guest can sit down and register. Traditionally, the front desk was placed so that the person behind it had a view of both the front door and the elevator. This was so front desk agents could discourage unwelcome individuals from entering and keep non-paying guests from departing. Because of modern credit and security procedures, such front desk placement is no longer necessary.

The duties of front desk agents include:

- Greeting guests
- Registering guests
- Establishing a method of payment for the guestroom—credit card, cash, or direct billing
- Assigning guestrooms that are unoccupied and have been cleaned
- Assigning guestroom keys to guests

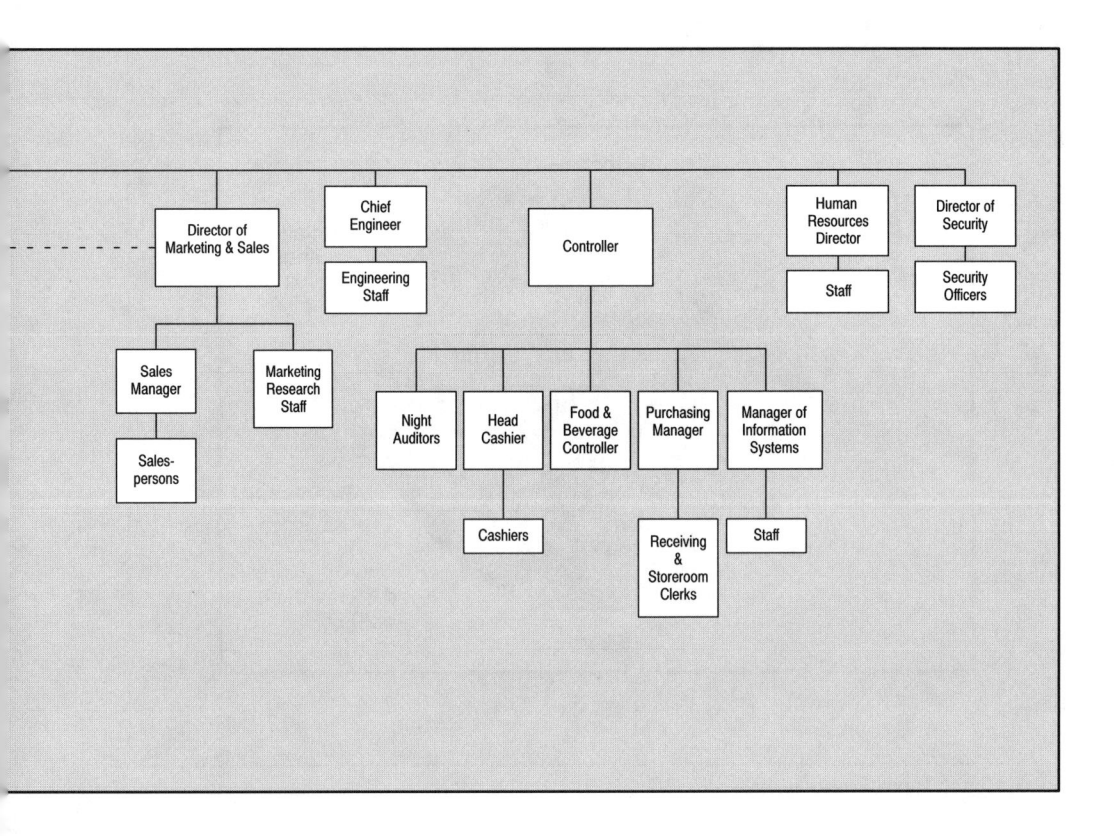

```
                                  Chief                                    Human          Director of
            Director of          Engineer                                Resources         Security
        Marketing & Sales                          Controller             Director
- - - - -                       Engineering                                                 Security
                                   Staff                                    Staff          Officers

          Sales       Marketing
         Manager      Research
                        Staff          Night      Head      Food &     Purchasing   Manager of
                                      Auditors   Cashier   Beverage     Manager    Information
           Sales-                                          Controller                Systems
          persons
                                                 Cashiers             Receiving      Staff
                                                                          &
                                                                      Storeroom
                                                                       Clerks
```

- Informing guests about their room location and special hotel facilities, and answering questions about the property and the surrounding community
- Calling a bellperson to assist guests with their luggage if such service is normally provided

In small and mid-size hotels the front desk agent is also the cashier. Although the front desk station and cashier's station are usually separated in large hotels, employees are often cross-trained to handle both jobs. One important duty of a cashier (or a front desk agent performing cashier duties) is to post charges to the guest's account. This means that the cashier must make sure that any expenses the guest incurs, such as restaurant bills and telephone calls that were charged to the room, are added to the bill before it is presented. This task is not necessary in hotels that have a computerized **property management system (PMS)**, where electronic cash registers at points of sale (dining rooms, bars, and gift shops, for example) automatically post charges to guest accounts. Once the posting has been accomplished (either manually or electronically), guests can settle their account when they check out. Checking out guests requires tact and diplomacy. Guests often have questions about their charges and, in some cases, may not even be aware that they incurred a charge when using a particular service (such as making telephone calls).

**Exhibit 3    U.S. Lodging Industry Sources of Revenue**

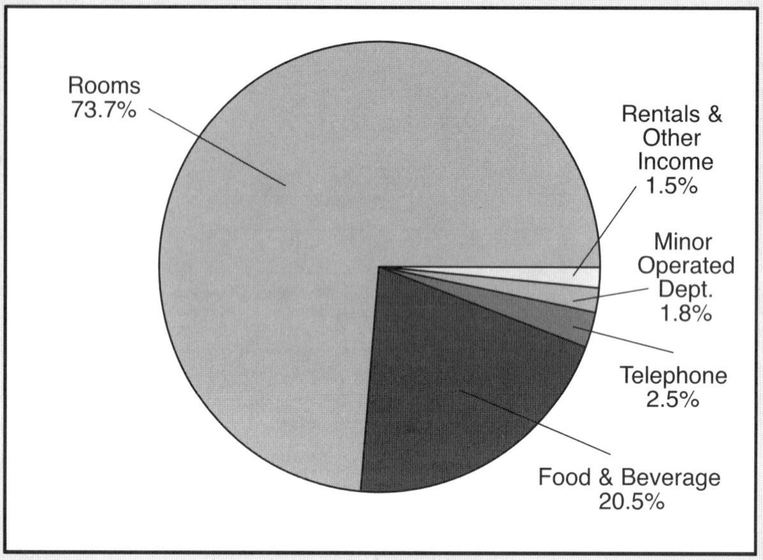

- Rooms 73.7%
- Rentals & Other Income 1.5%
- Minor Operated Dept. 1.8%
- Telephone 2.5%
- Food & Beverage 20.5%

Source: Smith Travel Research, 1996.

Computerized property management systems have simplified check-in. Marriott's "First 10" program refers to the first ten minutes of a guest's stay in one of their hotels. Upon arrival, guests with reservations are greeted personally at the door by an employee, who then escorts them to a special rack. In the rack is a packet for each pre-registered guest. The packet contains a room key and a registration card already filled out. The employee checks with the guest to see if the information is correct. If it is, the employee offers to escort the guest to the guestroom or simply gives directions. Hilton has introduced a similar program called "Zip-In Check-In," in which guests go directly to a "Zip-In" station, have an imprint of their credit card taken, and are given an arrival packet that includes a room key. At Hyatt Hotels, guests can even check in by phone before they arrive at the hotel.

Other hotels are trying different check-in approaches. The O'Hare Airport Hilton in Chicago, the Opryland Hotel in Nashville, and the Oriental Hotel in Bangkok check guests in at the airport. The Mandarin Oriental Hotel in Hong Kong has employees meet guests at the airport, transport them to the hotel in a limousine, and take them directly to their room—only then are they checked in, in the privacy and comfort of their guestroom. Most of these programs are designed for frequent business travelers, since leisure guests often prefer to check in at a front desk where they have an opportunity to ask questions.

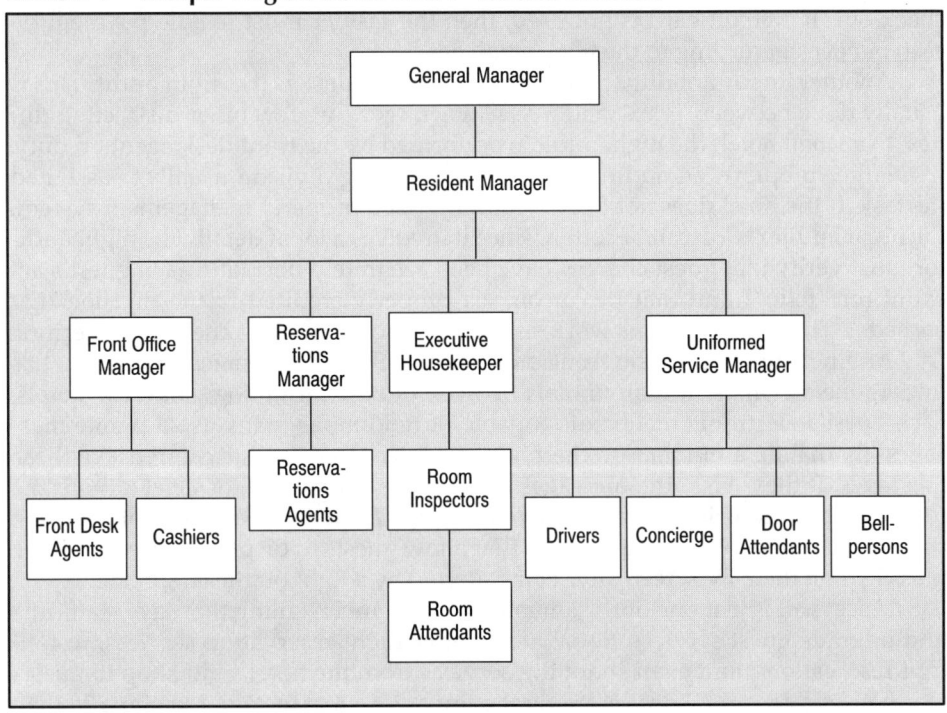

**Exhibit 4    Sample Organization Chart—Rooms Division**

```
                        General Manager
                              |
                        Resident Manager
    _____|_____
    |             |              |                |
Front Office  Reserva-      Executive         Uniformed
 Manager      tions         Housekeeper       Service Manager
              Manager
    |             |              |          _____|_____
    |             |              |          |         |         |        |
Front Desk   Reserva-        Room         Drivers  Concierge  Door    Bell-
Agents |     tions           Inspectors                      Attendants persons
Cashiers     Agents             |
                             Room
                             Attendants
```

Checking out has benefited from computer technology also. For example, the Milford Plaza Hotel in New York City has installed check-out stations in their lobby that are similar to the cash-dispensing automatic teller machines that banks use. Guests can use the machine to check out and get a copy of their bills. Many hotels allow guests to review their bills on the television screen in their guestroom and then send a signal through the channel selector to acknowledge that their account is in order and authorize payment. The bill is then charged to their credit card. A copy of the bill can be mailed directly to them at home or picked up in the lobby upon departure. In guestrooms with fax machines, the bill is faxed to the guest before he or she leaves the room.

Since many hotels do not yet have "high-tech" check-out systems, another common procedure is to slip a copy of the final bill under the door of the guestroom during the night, while the guest is sleeping. This system saves time because the guest doesn't need to request the bill, and it allows the guest to study the bill before check-out. If guests have no questions, they can simply phone the front desk and tell the cashier that they agree with the charges as posted. Any charges incurred between the time the bill is okayed and the time check-out actually occurs are added to the guest's final account. The total amount of guest charges will appear on the guest's personal or corporate credit card statement.

This system presumes that the guest has used a credit card and that an imprint of that card was taken at registration. Usually, approval of the card and the guestroom charges is obtained from the credit card company at check-in, not check-out. If a credit card is not used, then the cashier must handle payment by cash or check according to the hotel's policies.

Another important duty performed at the front desk is the **night audit**. This is usually done between 11 P.M. and 6 A.M., when there are few other distracting duties. In a small hotel, the night audit is performed by the front desk agent on duty. In a larger property, an auditor from the accounting division usually is assigned the task. If the hotel does not have a computerized property management system, the night auditor's job can be tough, since it involves a lot of detail. The night auditor must verify that guest charges have been accurately posted to each guest's account (or "folio") and that the income is properly credited to the division that earned it. This can be tedious work, especially since it involves checking for errors.

Another function of the front desk staff—relaying messages to guests—has undergone a change in many hotels because of new technology. In these hotels, each guest's electronic mailbox is capable of holding as many as 25 phone messages. By dialing a number on the phone in their room, guests can retrieve these messages. If they wish, the messages can be repeated, saved, or deleted with the touch of a button. This automated system relieves front desk personnel of handling this chore. Other hotels have systems that allow guests to display incoming phone messages on their TV screen after being alerted by a light on the telephone.

Voice mail is just one of the amenities hotels are installing that save staff time and upgrade guest services. Some hotels offer flight-reservation services, restaurant reservations, and even shopping services from the hotel's gift shop to guests via their guestroom television. Several companies have installed keyboards that, when attached to a TV set, turn the television into a computer terminal that is capable of these new functions.

Even the typical metal guestroom keys and locks have been replaced in most instances by electronic locking systems that operate with disposable plastic **card keys**—and sometimes with a guest's own credit card. An electronic connection between guestroom door locks and a console at the front desk makes it possible to code a card key with each check-in, matching the card key's code with a code programmed into the console for the guest's room. When the guest inserts the card key into a slot in the guestroom doorknob assembly, the door is unlocked. The door will stay locked if someone tries to use a card key with a code that does not match the electronic code for the lock. These new card keys usually do not have the name of the hotel or the room number on them, so if they are lost they are of no use to whoever finds them. Some new card key systems connect guestroom locks to a central computer so that the hotel has a record of everyone who has entered the room (each housekeeping and maintenance employee's key registers its owner's code), along with the time of entry.

In addition to all of their other duties, front desk employees represent the first and last (and often the only) contact the guest has with hotel personnel. The front desk agents' ability to make the guest feel welcome and special has a tremendous impact on the quality of a guest's experience. It's essential, therefore, that the front desk staff be well trained and that morale be kept high so that interactions with guests and among staff members are always positive.

**Friendly, attentive front desk agents help set the right tone for a guest's lodging experience.** (Courtesy of The Dusit Thani, Bangkok, Thailand)

In order to improve guest relations, more and more hotels are encouraging employees to take the initiative in resolving disputes themselves rather than referring them to a supervisor. For example, the Ritz-Carlton hotel chain permits front desk agents to take off up to $2,000 from a guest's bill. "When a guest complains, we call that an opportunity to make things better for them," says Sima Hawn, a front desk agent at The Ritz-Carlton in McLean, Virginia. She waived a two-night bill of $405.25 when a guest complained that the housekeeping wasn't up to par and that the fitness center attendant was rude.[4]

**Reservations.** Another part of the rooms division is the **reservations department** or office. A reservations department should be staffed by skilled telemarketing personnel who are able to accept reservations over the phone, answer questions about the facilities, and quote guestroom rates and available dates. Since some callers are shopping around, reservationists should be trained to sell the property as well as simply accept reservations. Reservationists also process reservations that may arrive through central computer reservation systems or through third parties such as travel agents and hotel representatives.

When travel agents and hotel representatives call in a reservation, their calls must be handled with skill and efficiency if they are to be served properly. They require immediate and correct information on current room status. These travel professionals are compensated by commissions that the hotel sends to them after guest stays are completed. Naturally, a major concern of theirs is that the hotel will keep accurate records so that they will be paid promptly.

The largest percentage of advance reservations comes into hotels through direct inquiry. The remainder are received through the following sources:

- Own reservation system
- Travel agents
- Hotel representatives
- Tour operators
- Independent reservation system
- Airlines, cruise lines, and other transportation companies

Some hotels use **yield management** techniques in the reservations department. For many years, airlines have used sophisticated yield management pricing systems. These are automated marketing programs that allow the airlines to control the inventory and pricing of airplane seats by forecasting the demand for seats on a given flight or route and then adjusting prices to maximize revenue. Warren H. Lieberman of Arthur D. Little, a consulting firm, defines yield management for hotels as "using information, historical and current, in combination with policy supports, procedural supports, and statistical models, to enhance a hotel's ability to carry out a number of common business practices, and thereby increase both its revenues and its customer service capabilities."[5] Lieberman says these practices include:

- Setting the most effective pricing structure
- Limiting the number of reservations accepted for any given night or room type, based on the expected profitability of a reservation
- Reviewing reservation activity to determine whether any inventory control actions should be taken (for example, discounting rates)
- Negotiating volume discounts with wholesalers and groups
- Providing customers with the right product (the right guestroom type, rate, etc.)
- Obtaining more revenue from current and potential business
- Enabling reservations agents to be effective sales agents rather than merely order takers

Eric Orkin, an industry consultant and president of a company that provides yield management computer software, says:

> Performance benchmarks in the hotel industry are commonly keyed to room-night or dollar volume. Volume criteria like these make perfect sense when selling a product with a sustained value, but the value of a hotel room varies from day to day and over time. For example, a room on a Saturday during New England fall foliage season is a lot more valuable than the same room on a "mud season" night in the spring. Less obvious, the value of that fall foliage night was high until two days before the date, when bad weather caused a major tour to cancel. Because the hotel was now faced with the prospect of empty rooms, the value of the hotel's rooms dropped.[6]

Yield management requires the use of complex computer programs to (1) forecast the number of reservations an operator can expect on a given day (as well as

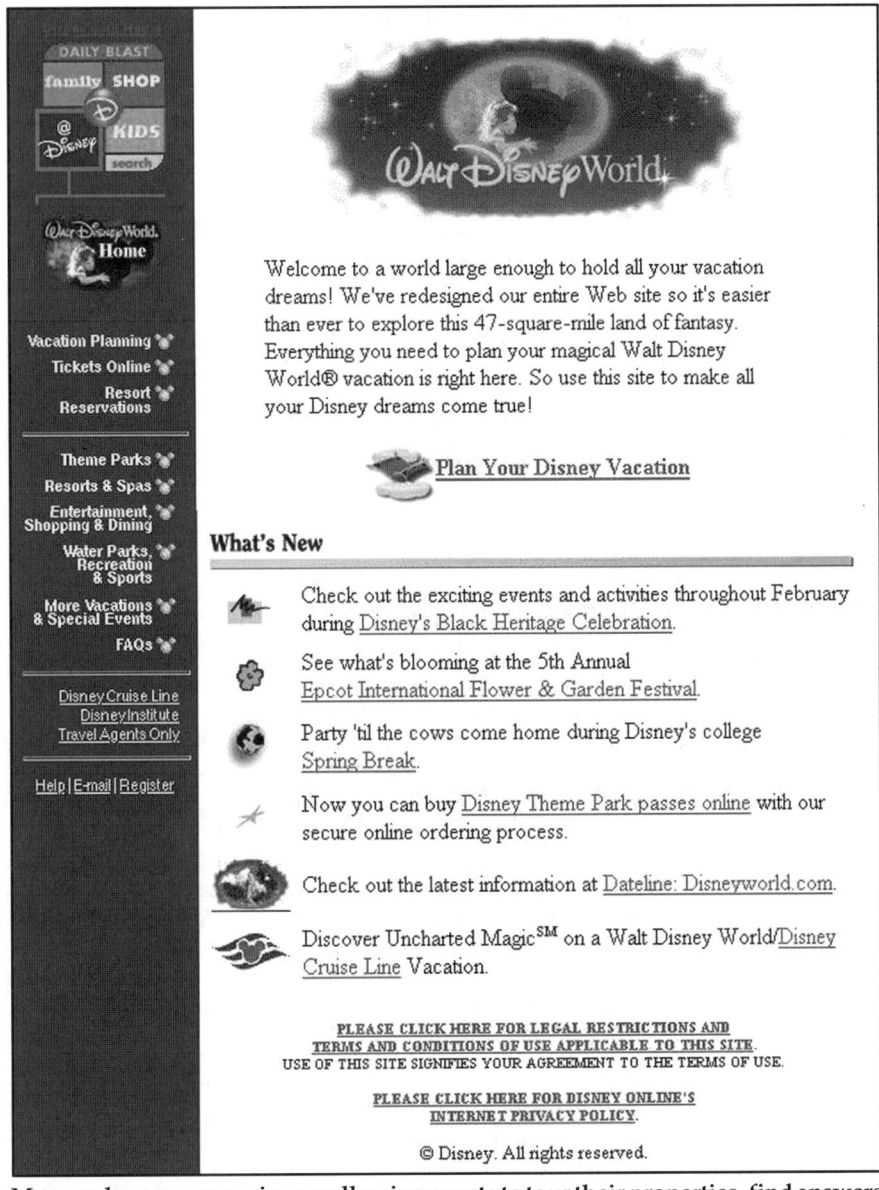

More and more companies are allowing guests to tour their properties, find answers to common questions, plan their vacations, and make reservations on the Internet.
(Courtesy of Walt Disney World, Orlando, Florida)

cancellations and no-shows), (2) track the availability of rooms, and (3) compute the maximum rates that those rooms can be sold for. Holiday Inn, for example, uses a program designed by American Airlines Decision Technologies called HIRO, an acronym for Holiday Inn Revenue Optimization.

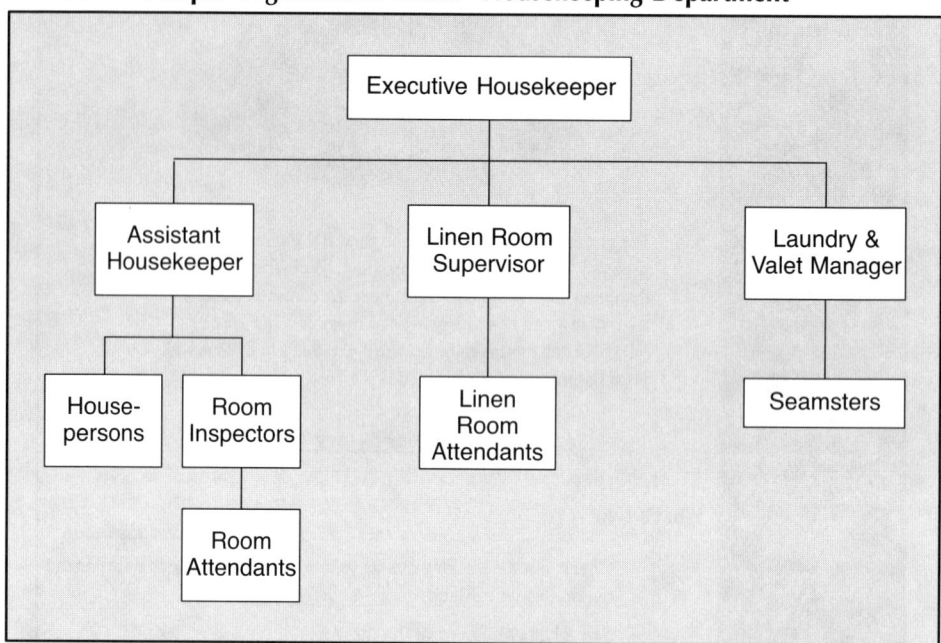

**Exhibit 5  Sample Organization Chart—Housekeeping Department**

```
                    Executive Housekeeper
                             |
         ------------------------------------------
         |                   |                    |
    Assistant          Linen Room          Laundry &
    Housekeeper        Supervisor          Valet Manager
         |                   |                    |
   ------------           Linen Room          Seamsters
   |          |           Attendants
House-     Room
persons    Inspectors
              |
           Room
           Attendants
```

Some hoteliers feel that yield management systems sometimes encourage discounting. Others see yield management as incompatible with good customer service because it confuses guests and requires them to accept the most expensive rooms. This may be an ethical consideration as well. But, properly used, there is no doubt that yield management can be an effective reservations tool.

The issue of perceived fairness in hotel pricing has received a lot of attention. Many customers have an idea of what a hotel room in a specific situation is worth. If a hotel increases the price of a room without a good reason, guests may consider this unfair. Hotels have used various strategies to overcome this perception. For instance, hotels selling packages that include food make it more difficult for guests easily calculate the real price of a room. Since most travelers get some kind of discount off the rack rate, by increasing the rack rate a hotel can raise its price without being perceived as unfair. Sometimes additional amenities—such as a discounted or free breakfast or dinner—are added. There is an inherent danger in using yield management systems, and that danger must be addressed in order to make yield management systems an effective and profitable reservations tool.

**Housekeeping.** The **housekeeping department** is another department of the rooms division. Housekeeping is responsible for cleaning the hotel's guestrooms and public areas. In many hotels, this department has the largest staff, consisting of an assistant housekeeper, room inspectors, room attendants, a houseperson crew (which cleans the public areas and handles the logistics of moving housekeeping supplies throughout the hotel), linen room attendants, and personnel in charge of employee uniforms (see Exhibit 5). Many hotels also have their own laundry and valet service. Hotels with laundry and valet equipment may use it only for hotel linens and uniforms and send guest clothing to an outside service where it can be handled with specialized equipment.

The housekeeping department is directed by an executive housekeeper. The executive housekeeper has an enormous amount of responsibility—not only for cleaning and maintenance, but also for training staff and controlling large inventories of linens, supplies, and equipment.[7] Room inspectors supervise room attendants. Room attendants are responsible for cleaning guestrooms according to specified procedures and for maintaining a predetermined level of supplies in the linen closets located on each floor. They are usually assigned a quota of rooms to clean in a given number of hours. Fifteen guestrooms per shift is average, although this figure may vary considerably because of such conditions as geographic location, union contracts, the size of the property, and the wage scale. In most hotels, room attendants are paid relatively low wages.

When guests check out, it is the room attendants' responsibility to clean the guestrooms so that they are available again for rental. This includes such duties as:

- Removing soiled linen and towels and replacing them with fresh ones
- Checking the bed and blankets for damage
- Making the beds
- Emptying trash
- Checking the guestroom for broken appliances, damaged shades or blinds, and leaky faucets
- Checking closets and drawers for items forgotten by guests
- Cleaning the guestroom and bathroom
- Replacing bathroom towels and amenities

Some hotels contract with outside cleaning services to clean the hotel's lobbies, restaurants, restrooms, and windows. With the exception of windows, much of this cleaning must be done late at night, and hotels often find it difficult to find supervisors and employees willing to work at those hours. Contract cleaning firms, many of whom handle offices and airline terminals as well, are geared to handle these cleaning tasks and unusual hours efficiently.

**Uniformed service.** The **uniformed service department** is sometimes referred to as the guest service department. Employees in this department include bellstaff (so called because originally they were summoned by a bell), a concierge, and transportation or valet-parking employees. Some large hotels have door attendants who move luggage from cars or taxicabs into the hotel.

Bellstaff move guest luggage to and from guestrooms. They also escort guests to their rooms, inspect guestrooms while rooming the guest, and explain the features of the room and the hotel to guests. Good bellstaff possess a detailed knowledge of the hotel, including the hours of operation of the hotel's restaurants, lounges, and other facilities. They also know the local community.

Some hotels have adopted the European system of concierge service. The concierge performs many of the functions that a host might perform for guests in his or her home. The goal is to give guests personal and attentive service. The concierge is the main source of information about the hotel. He or she is not only familiar with the hotel's facilities and services but also has a thorough knowledge of the local area. A good concierge knows what's going on in town. He or she can recommend a romantic candlelit bistro within walking distance or the best steak house in the city. The concierge can make reservations and get theater tickets—or suggest someone who can. He or she can also recommend secretarial services and copying centers, order limousines, and perform many other services that give guests the feeling that they are important and well cared for.

Transportation services include valet parking, either in the hotel's own garage or a nearby facility. If other transportation services are provided, such as airport vans, these are normally handled by the same department. In most large hotels, garages and limousines are handled by outside contractors.

**Measuring the Performance of the Rooms Division.** The three most commonly used room department statistics for measuring department performance are the **average daily rate (ADR),** the **occupancy percentage,** and **revenue per available room (REVPAR).** These statistics can be calculated daily or for any other time period.

The average daily rate is simply the amount of rooms revenue divided by the number of rooms occupied for the same period of time. Here is an example of how this is calculated for a single day and a three-day period:

| Day | Rooms Revenue | ÷ | Rooms Occupied | = | Average Daily Rate (ADR) |
|---|---|---|---|---|---|
| Monday | $11,900 | | 170 | | $70.00 |
| Tuesday | $15,000 | | 185 | | $81.08 |
| Wednesday | $14,500 | | 178 | | $81.46 |
| **Three-day Figures** | $41,400 | | 533 | | $77.67 |

In this example, $77.67 indicates the average amount of revenue for each of the 533 occupied rooms for the three-day period. Most hotels have a number of rate classes targeted at different market segments. There may be rates for government employees, corporate travelers, and senior citizens, among others. The rates also vary according to room size, location, furnishings, and service. For example, a large corner room on a high floor overlooking a park is more expensive than a smaller room on a lower floor that faces an alley. The price the room is finally sold for will depend on who it is sold to, the location, the day of the week, and possibly the season of the year. Management's goal is to sell the most expensive rooms first. However, guests usually request the lowest-priced rooms. Therefore, the average daily rate is an indicator of the sales ability of those taking reservations, as well as the demand for the various types of guestrooms.

An equally important marketing statistic is the occupancy percentage. It is computed by dividing the number of rooms occupied by the number of rooms available for sale for the same period and multiplying by 100. The number of rooms available for sale may be different from the number of rooms in the hotel.

This discrepancy occurs when rooms are being used to house managers and other personnel on a permanent basis, or when rooms are being remodeled. Like the average rate, the occupancy percentage can be calculated for any period of time:

| Day | Rooms Occupied | ÷ | Rooms Available | × 100 | = | Occupancy Percentage |
|---|---|---|---|---|---|---|
| Monday | 170 | | 200 | | | 85.0% |
| Tuesday | 185 | | 200 | | | 92.5% |
| Wednesday | 178 | | 200 | | | 89.0% |
| **Three-day Figures** | 533 | | 600 | | | 88.8% |

Revenue per available room (REVPAR) is the third statistic operators use in evaluating the performance of the rooms department. It is computed by dividing room revenue by the number of available rooms for the same period. Alternatively, it can be determined by multiplying the occupancy percentage by the average daily rate for the same period:

| Day | Occupancy Percentage | × | Average Daily Rate | = | REVPAR |
|---|---|---|---|---|---|
| Monday | 85.0% | | $70.00 | | $59.50 |
| Tuesday | 92.5% | | $81.08 | | $75.00 |
| Wednesday | 89.0% | | $81.46 | | $72.50 |
| **Three-day Figures** | 88.8% | | $77.67 | | $68.97 |

These three statistics are used by managers to assess how the hotel is doing in relation to the budget and forecast of performance. Also, from these forecasts the marketing department can easily see what weeks and months ahead need extra sales effort. It should be noted that these figures cannot be used by themselves to measure a hotel's financial performance. A hotel might have a 99 percent occupancy percentage and still be failing if the average daily rate or revenue per available room is not high enough to cover all costs and provide a reasonable return on investment.

## Food and Beverage Division

Although in most hotels the rooms division generates the greatest amount of revenue, this is not always the case. In a few hotels (most often resorts and convention properties with extensive banquet sales), the **food and beverage division** may produce the same or more revenue than does the rooms division. This is because guests in resorts tend to stay on the premises and may be less price-sensitive because they are on vacation. In convention hotels, the added food sales come from the multitude of restaurants, banquet rooms, and bars.

Whether the food and beverage operation is large or small, most hotel managers have found that their food and beverage facilities are of paramount importance to the reputation and profitability of the hotel. There is no doubt that in

**The Caxton Grill in London's Stakis Ermins Hotel.** (Courtesy of Stakis Hotels, Glasgow, Scotland)

many cases the quality of a hotel's food and beverages powerfully affects a guest's opinion of a particular property and influences his or her willingness to return. In fact, some hotels are as famous for their restaurants as for their guestrooms. For example, Les Celebrites, in Nikko Hotel's Essex House in New York City, has been called one of the fifty best restaurants in the United States. Truffles Restaurant, located in the Four Seasons Hotel in Toronto, has for years enjoyed a reputation as Toronto's best restaurant. According to many reviewers, the best Chinese restaurant in Hong Kong is located on top of the Mandarin Oriental Hotel overlooking Victoria Harbour.

Successful hotel operators no longer consider dining facilities merely a convenience for guests. A hotel's food and beverage outlet(s) must attract members of the local community, convince hotel guests to dine on the premises, and return a fair profit. The **capture rate**—that is, the percentage of guests who eat meals at the hotel—is measured regularly by some chains.

Except for limited-service hotels and motels (which achieve that status partially by staying out of the restaurant business), virtually all lodging facilities offer some level of food and beverage service. Large hotels usually have a wide array of facilities, while small properties may have just one dining room that serves breakfast,

**Exhibit 6  Types of Hotel Food and Beverage Outlets**

| Food Service | Beverage Service |
|---|---|
| Dining Room | Cocktail Lounge |
| Specialty Restaurant | Public Bar (for guests) |
| Coffee Shop (mid-price restaurant) | Service Bar (for servers) |
| Supper Club | Banquets |
| Snack Bar | Discotheques |
| Take-Out | Mini-Bars (in guestrooms) |
| Cafeteria | |
| Room Service | |
| Banquets | |
| Employee Food Service | |

lunch, and dinner. Exhibit 6 lists the types of food and beverage outlets that may be found in a hotel.[8]

**Selecting Food and Beverage Outlets.** There are several criteria managers use to decide what type of food and beverage service should be offered in any given hotel. It is worthwhile to think about these carefully, both in the initial planning stages of a new hotel and as a hotel matures and the market it appeals to changes.

The first criterion is the type of hotel. Does this property primarily serve transient businesspeople or conventioneers? Is the property a resort? Business clientele are more interested in private dining, while convention hotels need ballrooms for large gatherings. Resorts often do well with specialty restaurants.

Next is the class of hotel. Five-star hotels need five-star restaurants. Moderate-price hotels could not sustain this kind of restaurant quality, nor would their guests expect it.

Competition is another consideration. What kinds of restaurants are already available in the area? If you are surrounded by Italian restaurants, putting one in your hotel would probably not be a good idea. It might be wiser to try something completely different.

Product availability also counts. A fresh-fish restaurant might have a difficult time making it unless it limited itself to the kind of fish that is readily available. The cost of flying in Maine lobster and Dover sole could easily price it out of the market.

Availability of labor is another important consideration. A menu that requires a lot of employees—for example, one that features tableside cooking with dishes like Steak Diane and desserts such as crêpes Suzette—might not be practical in a tight labor market.

Finally, there is the question of demand. Certain kinds of food are more popular in some areas of the country than others. Mexican restaurants are more in demand in the Southwest than the Northeast, for example. Is the type of restaurant in the hotel one that the hotel's guests will want to patronize?

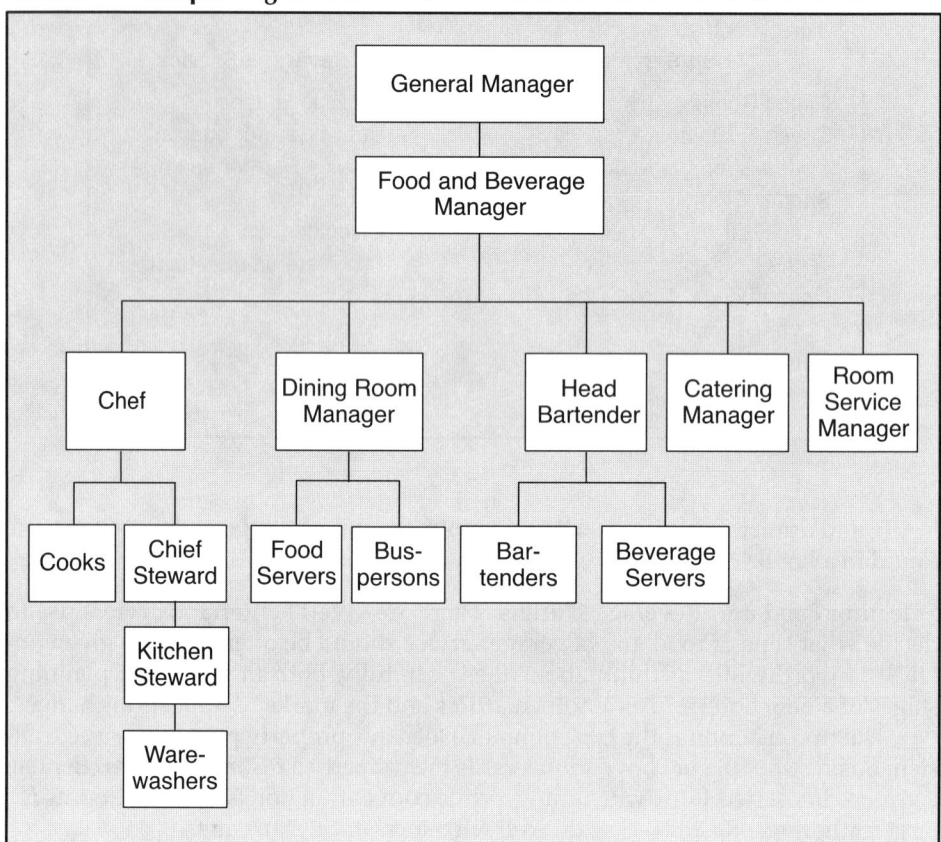

**Exhibit 7    Sample Organization Chart—F&B Division in a Mid-Size Hotel**

```
                        General Manager
                              |
                    Food and Beverage
                         Manager
     _____|_____
     |            |            |            |            |
   Chef      Dining Room      Head       Catering      Room
             Manager      Bartender     Manager      Service
                                                     Manager
   __|__      ___|___      ___|___
   |   |      |     |      |     |
Cooks Chief  Food  Bus-  Bar-   Beverage
      Steward Servers persons tenders Servers
        |
      Kitchen
      Steward
        |
      Ware-
      washers
```

**Organization of the Food and Beverage Division.** The food and beverage division of a major hotel can be complex, offering a variety of different kinds of restaurants and bars, each with its own unique decor, menu, and style of service. Such a division requires well-trained employees and highly skilled and versatile managers in the kitchen, bar, and service areas.

We can examine an organization chart of a typical food and beverage operation in a mid-size hotel to get an idea of how a food and beverage division works (see Exhibit 7). As can be seen from the exhibit, the person who is in charge of the food and beverage division reports to the general manager and is known as the food and beverage manager. (Some hotels assign this function to an executive assistant manager.) Since this job entails responsibility for a major business entity of the hotel staffed by persons with specialized technical skills, the food and beverage manager should have a thorough knowledge of general business and management practices. He or she should also be well versed in the technical aspects of food and beverage preparation and service.

## Meal Plans

There are several meal plans that hotel food and beverage divisions offer. They include the Full American Plan, the Modified American Plan, the Continental Plan, and the European Plan.

The Full American Plan and the Modified American Plan are usually seen in resort hotels. Under the Full American Plan, the room rate quoted includes all major meals—breakfast, lunch, and dinner. In effect, guests are offered a package price that includes their room and all three meals for as long as they stay. This has great appeal to guests who are concerned with the total cost of their resort vacation and like to budget for it ahead of time. The Modified American Plan provides two meals only—usually breakfast and dinner.

The Continental Plan includes a continental breakfast with the room rate. This plan is also called a Breakfast Plan, and in Bermuda it's known as the Bermuda Plan. With the European Plan, no meals are included in the room rate.

Isolated resorts with few or no restaurants in the surrounding area and no centers of population nearby are more likely to offer an American Plan. These were especially popular in the early 1900s, when travelers stayed at resorts for two weeks or more. Most guests today don't want to be locked into a meal plan—they prefer the freedom to try other restaurants in the area. As a result, offering a meal plan is not a growing hotel service since demand for it, on the whole, is decreasing. Hotel managers can be sympathized with for wishing this were not so. From the hotels' standpoint, there is much better control over purchasing, preparing, and staffing when the number of meals that will be served is known in advance. Moreover, both American plans guarantee food revenue and, to a great degree, beverage revenue as well, since guests often order cocktails before dinner, wine with dinner, or after-dinner drinks.

Reporting to the food and beverage manager is the chef, sometimes called the executive chef or head chef, who is in charge of the kitchen staff. An important member of the chef's team is the chief steward, who directs the kitchen steward and warewashers and makes sure all dining rooms, bars, and banquet rooms have sufficient inventories of clean china, glassware, and silverware.

The dining room manager must see that guest service goes smoothly, that there is a sufficient number of food servers and buspersons on duty, and that all dining room employees are well trained and are meeting the property's service standards. The job may also include training new employees.

In mid-size hotels with a lounge, a head bartender oversees the lounge's operation. He or she supervises bartenders and beverage servers.

**Catering.** The food and beverage divisions of some hotels contain catering departments. **A catering department's** importance is twofold. Not only is it an image-maker for the hotel, but it also can be the most profitable segment of the food and beverage division. Catering arranges and plans food and beverage functions for (1) conventions and smaller hotel groups, and (2) local banquets booked by the sales department. Catering sales, in some instances, represent as much as 50 percent of a hotel's total food and beverage sales.

Catering is a highly competitive business in most market areas. To succeed, a catering department must have employees with a broad range of abilities and knowledge. Good catering departments excel in sales, menu planning, food and beverage service (including wines), food production, product knowledge, cost control, artistic talent, and a sense of theater. All of this requires sound technical knowledge as well as skillful use of the hotel's facilities and equipment.

Superior marketing tools are also needed. St. Michaels Harbour Inn on Chesapeake Bay in Maryland is a relatively small resort property, but they have learned how to successfully sell catered events. From their dinner catering menu, customers can choose between table service or a buffet. There are 16 table service menu items and four suggested buffets. Everything is clearly described and priced so that clients who are not sure what they want or what the hotel offers can make an easy choice. The beverage service menu also offers three different grades of open bar—per person, per hour, or per drink. This kind of flexibility is important if a catering operation hopes to serve a wide variety of customers.

The catering manager generally reports to the food and beverage manager. There are exceptions to this rule, however. In some instances, the catering manager reports to the director of sales or directly to the hotel's general manager. When hotels are organized in this manner, the banquet manager usually reports to the food and beverage manager. Such a division of labor separates the selling function from the production and service function. To help cut costs, some hotels combine the positions of food and beverage manager and catering manager.

**Room service.** Most hotels with a food and beverage division provide some type of food service to guests in their rooms. **Room service**—or "private dining," as the highly marketing-oriented Walt Disney Corporation refers to it—is one of the most difficult areas of hotel food service to manage and has the greatest potential for losing money.

There are two main difficulties with room service. First, food and beverages are served at great distances from production areas. In resorts where there are cabins for guests, electric carts are often used to transport food. Because of frequent stops along the way, there is a real likelihood of hot items arriving cold and cold items becoming tepid. Second—and, again, because of distance—the productivity of food servers is low; they can take care of fewer guests in a given amount of time. The revenue generated, therefore, is often not sufficient to cover costs. These problems are made worse by the fact that the greatest demand for room service is at breakfast and the most popular type of morning meal is the continental breakfast (juice or fruit, roll with butter and jam, and a beverage). This meal has a low check average compared to room service items served the rest of the day.

To deal with room service costs, many hotels charge higher prices for room service food, as well as an additional charge per order (or per person) for the service. The cost problem can be further alleviated by limiting (1) the number of items on the room service menu, and (2) the hours of service. This does not solve the problem of potentially inferior food quality, however.

To retain food quality, the food must be delivered to the room as quickly as possible and at the appropriate temperature. This requires proper equipment and a highly efficient organization in the room service area. Many hotels use a doorknob

# Industry Innovators

Stephen F. Bollenbach
President and Chief Executive Officer
Hilton Hotels Corporation

Steve Bollenbach is "one of the sharpest pencils in corporate America," according to *Time* magazine. In the last decade, he has changed the face of five of the largest hospitality organizations in the world, and he shows little sign of slowing down.

Bollenbach has a simple philosophy that has appealed to shareholders of every company he has ever been associated with: increase the value of the organization's shares. He does this fervently with a series of innovative techniques that include splitting companies, selling assets, taking on large amounts of debt, swapping debt for equity, paying special dividends, and restructuring loans.

In 1989 Bollenbach joined Holiday Corporation as chief financial officer and a member of the board of directors. The recapitalization and operational restructuring he spearheaded resulted in a healthier company whose stock value rose 250 percent.

Part of Bollenbach's job at Holiday involved successfully repelling hostile suitors, including Donald Trump. Impressed by his business acumen, Trump offered Bollenbach a job as chief executive officer of the Trump Organization, which Bollenbach accepted in 1990. His primary responsibilities involved refinancing a variety of assets and companies owned by Donald Trump—including a personal loan guarantee of $650 million.

Bollenbach's success with Trump's organization led to an offer to join Marriott Corporation as chief financial officer. In 1993 he led the company through an innovative restructuring that resulted in two separate companies: Host Marriott and Marriott International. Bollenbach was named Host Marriott's president and CEO. During his two-year tenure, stockholders saw their shares appreciate by 158 percent.

In 1995, Bollenbach became senior executive vice president and CFO of Walt Disney Company. He persuaded Disney Chairman Michael Eisner, who had turned down media acquisitions for years because of their likely drain on Disney resources, to purchase ABC/Capital Cities—the giant media conglomerate—for $19 billion. It was the second-largest business acquisition in U.S. business history, and it resulted in a steady rise in Disney's profits.

After just one year, however, Bollenbach was again on the move. In 1996, Barron Hilton named him president and chief executive officer of Hilton Hotels Corporation. He now oversees Hilton's hotel and casino operations, as well as all of the company's financial affairs.

Today, Stephen Bollenbach is recognized as one of the world's leading authorities on the hospitality and entertainment industries and financial affairs and transactions. He is one of hospitality's most notable innovators.

menu that invites guests to order their breakfast the night before, indicating the items they want and the time they would like to be served. The menus are then placed on the outside doorknobs of the room, for collection during the night. This allows the hotel to do a better job, because the hotel can plan the number of breakfasts to be served in each time period and organize delivery to the rooms. Another innovative approach to room service has been used at the Palmer House Hilton in Chicago. They have a special large elevator equipped with a telephone, food service equipment, and limited selection of breakfast food items. A guest's room service call is routed directly to the elevator, so service is provided within minutes of the call. Since most hotels do not have this luxury, they must tightly manage their service elevators—which means room service personnel get top priority during peak serving hours.

Because of the problems associated with delivering a satisfactory room service experience, some hotels have been cutting back on room service, curtailing the number of hours it is available or doing away with it altogether. On the other hand, some first class and luxury hotels view room service as an opportunity. Hoteliers at these properties see it as part of the overall guest experience. To help guarantee its success, they have redesigned their menus to focus on foods that travel well and to include a wider variety of selections. For example, Ritz-Carlton includes pizza, hamburgers, and salads; The Four Seasons serves homestyle dishes such as chicken pot pie and meat loaf.

**Support and control services.** Support and control services related to the food and beverage division include the purchasing department and the accounting division. Large hotels have a purchasing manager who is responsible for buying all of the products used in the hotel, including food and beverage items. Usually, orders are given to the **purchasing department** by the chef, by the bar manager (or head bartender), and often by the food and beverage manager directly. The purchasing department then receives competitive bids on the basis of precise specifications for each of the food and beverage items.

The control aspect of food and beverage is generally under the supervision of the hotel's controller. Reporting to the controller are:

- Receiving clerks, who verify the number and quality of food and beverage items received

- Storeroom clerks, who are responsible for properly storing and issuing items from the food and beverage storeroom

- Cashiers in restaurants, coffee shops, and other food and beverage outlets, who handle the settlement of guest checks

Some properties also have a food and beverage controller who reports to the hotel's controller. This individual is the food and beverage expert in the controller's office and is responsible for ensuring that optimum value is attained in the food and beverage division. A food and beverage controller's duties include:

- Tracking food and beverage costs

- Monitoring ordering and receiving procedures, including adherence to purchasing specifications

- Costing and pricing menu items
- Conducting monthly storeroom inventories
- Keeping management informed of costs and, when necessary, recommending actions to lower costs
- Creating monthly and daily reports on food and beverage costs

In some hotels, the food and beverage controller reports to the food and beverage manager. From a control standpoint, this arrangement is not desirable, because the food and beverage controller, in effect, is the watchdog over the food and beverage division, with his or her reports serving as an evaluation of the division. However, the food and beverage controller is sometimes positioned that way because the job is often an early step in the career path toward food and beverage manager.

**Problems in Food and Beverage Operations.** Although the food and beverage divisions of many hotels show a substantial profit in all of their food and beverage operations, not all food and beverage divisions are profitable. Some lose money in all areas, while others lose money in their food operations but make a profit with their beverage operations. Sometimes losses are attributed to bad management alone, but there are a number of other reasons that have been identified and can often be corrected:

- *Long hours of operation.* Hotel restaurants must maintain an adequate level of service even during slow periods in order to satisfy the needs of hotel guests. But the low volume of business during slow times is not always sufficient to cover the cost of operation. Tightly managed employee scheduling can help alleviate this problem.
- *Low check averages.* Low-priced breakfasts and inexpensive snacks served at odd hours are frequently cited as reasons for unprofitability. Clever marketing of more profitable items can help overcome this problem.
- *Too many facilities.* Trying to satisfy a wide variety of hotel guests by having several different types of food and beverage facilities tends to be inefficient from a cost standpoint. However, proper planning, central kitchens, and coordinated menus (so that different recipes use many of the same ingredients) can help solve this problem.
- *High turnover.* Because of the increasing complexity of the food and beverage division, there is a greater need for highly paid personnel. This labor cost cannot be avoided. What can be avoided is a high turnover rate among this group, which increases recruiting and training costs. Good human resources management can make a real difference here.
- *Costly entertainment.* Some hotels with several restaurants and bars hire entertainers to entice guests into a night out. Although entertainment is a specialized business, prices charged by entertainers are negotiable. Hotels that use experienced booking agents often have lower entertainment costs and get better entertainers.

- *Insufficient marketing.* In the past, few hotels marketed their food and beverage outlets. Some are still guilty of that omission today. But one of the most significant changes in most hotels in recent years is that they are aggressively marketing their restaurants and lounges. Now many hotels compete successfully with free-standing restaurants by employing some of the same techniques that these independents have used so effectively: exciting themes and decor, interesting and dramatic menus, and quality entertainment.

## Other Revenue Centers

**Telephone Department.** Hotel managers know that good telephone service adds to a guest's positive impression of the hotel, while poor service causes frustration and a negative perception of the hotel. This can result in lost repeat business.

The use of modern telephone systems and equipment has lessened the guest's dependence on the hotel's telephone operators. Many hotel services can be accessed directly by dialing a given extension. Guests can retrieve their own phone messages, if they are taken (or recorded) correctly, by dialing a digital code. Wake-up calls can be automated, although clock radios in guestrooms often eliminate the need for these calls completely. Local and long-distance calls no longer require the assistance of the hotel's operator. As a result of these advances, the **telephone department** in a modern hotel not only provides better service than ever before but has a greater potential for profit than previously realized.

There is no doubt that good phone service is appreciated, and guests may be willing to pay extra for it. Writing in the *Miami Herald,* travel columnist Peter Greenberg praised hotels that featured phones with two lines and a "hold" button, such as the Four Seasons Hotel in Beverly Hills, whose telephones also include a special port for personal computers. Greenberg also singled out the Hilton Hotel in Lake Buena Vista, Florida, where telephones in each room have buttons to turn on heat and air conditioning and to regulate fan speed. Other buttons serve as a remote control for the TV set. In the Drake Swissotel in New York, touch-tone phones are placed on the desk as well as on the bedside table of guestrooms, and every phone has a call-waiting feature to let you know that someone else is trying to reach you.

Many first-class hotels now offer guests a voice-mail service that allows guests to send and receive recorded messages. Beeper service and cellular phones are also offered, so that guests can contact business clients quickly, whether the guests are in the hotel or out at a meeting. Other innovations in hotel telephone services are coming. One system developed by Spectradyne, Inc., a telecommunications firm located in Dallas, Texas, uses a 900 number to connect guests directly to stock market and weather information, and allows guests to reserve airline and theater tickets. AT&T has an over-the-phone translation service. A non-English-speaking guest simply calls a front desk agent, who can contact an AT&T operator to act as a translator for the guest and the front desk agent. Westin Hotels offers this system in all of its U.S. hotels.

**Concessions, Rentals, and Commissions.** If there is enough guest demand, a hotel has the potential to sell more than rooms, food, and beverages. Gift shops,

## Telephone Deregulation—What It Has Meant to Hotels

In the United States, as in most countries, major forms of mass communication, including telephone service, are regulated by the government. The Federal Communications Commission regulates interstate communications, while public service commissions in individual states regulate communications within the state's borders.

Prior to 1968, all hotels were required to lease their telephone equipment from the American Telephone and Telegraph Company (AT&T), which had been given its authority by the federal government. As a result of the *Carterfone* decision in a Texas court, private companies other than AT&T were allowed to manufacture and sell telephone equipment to hotels and other businesses. This meant that hotels could avoid paying an often expensive monthly rental fee to AT&T by buying their own equipment. However, governmental authorities continued to define how a hotel could be compensated for providing telephone service to guests. The Federal Communications Commission prohibited hotels from charging guests for interstate calls (long-distance calls between states), but hotels could receive commissions from AT&T. For intrastate calls (calls within the same state), the procedures established by the public service commissions of the different states varied. In some states, the telephone company was permitted to pay commissions to hotels for each call placed by guests (the amount of the commission was regulated by law). Other states instituted a guest fee system, and still others used a combination of guest fees and commissions. Some states, however, simply avoided the problem by not giving any clear direction.

In 1981, as a result of far-reaching telephone deregulation, other telephone companies were allowed to compete with AT&T. Companies such as Sprint and MCI installed their own long-distance lines or rented AT&T's lines and resold them. They solicited hotels and other businesses to provide long-distance service to their guests.

Deregulation also meant that hotels were no longer required to use costly operator-assisted long-distance service. Hotels could purchase long-distance service at low direct-dial rates and charge their guests the operator-assisted rates they were used to paying. The equipment that enabled them to accomplish this is known as a call accounting system. Call accounting systems gave hotels the ability to keep track of their guests' long-distance time and charges, rather than rely on phone company operators to do so.

Another piece of equipment that hotels were able to purchase was a least-cost router. This equipment allowed hotels to connect with telephone systems other than AT&T so that they could route calls the least expensive way. This provided greater flexibility and profitability for hotels.

It should be noted, however, that there have been some abuses of the system. The Federal Communications Commission has warned alternative operator systems that they are responsible for identifying themselves to callers, supplying callers with rate information, and—should the callers desire—providing access to other carriers. Some hotels that initially imposed surcharge fees on certain types of calls, such as credit card calls and collect calls, have decided to drop these as a result of consumer resistance.

*(continued)*

> Today there exists a considerable divergence in the way hotels charge and are charged for calls. Not every hotel has purchased a call accounting system or a least-cost router, and some still have their long-distance calls handled by AT&T, Sprint, MCI, or other operators. Some hotels levy surcharges on local calls; others do not. What hotels charge for long-distance calls depends on the telephone company and equipment the hotel uses and on what policy it has adopted in charging for telephone service.

newsstands, flower shops, laundry and dry cleaning services, beauty salons, jewelry stores, secretarial services, and even office space are just a few of the types of services that can be made available within the hotel and accessible through the lobby or a separate street entrance. Hotel management has the choice of either operating these services themselves or bringing in others to do it for them.

A **concession** is a facility that might well be operated by the hotel directly, such as a beauty salon or fitness club, but instead is turned over to an independent operator who is responsible for the concession's equipment, personnel, and marketing. The hotel's income from concessions is determined in several ways. It can be a flat fee, a minimum fee plus a percentage of the gross receipts over a specific amount, or simply a percentage of total gross sales.

**Rentals** are common in many properties. With a rental, the hotel simply rents space to an enterprise such as an office or a store. The rent charged is typically spelled out in a lease, usually on a long-term basis with options to renew and annual rent adjustments specified.

**Commissions** are fees paid to the hotel by suppliers that are located outside the hotel but provide services for hotel guests. Some examples are car rental agencies, photographers, and dry-cleaning services. They pay a commission to the hotel based on a percentage of their gross sales to guests.

One important aspect of these kinds of arrangements is that unless the company or individual providing the service within the hotel is recognized in its own right (such as Bally's Scandinavian Fitness Centers), as far as most guests are concerned, their relationship is not with the vendor but with the hotel. Therefore, the quality and service standards of vendors must conform to the rest of the hotel's operation, or they can affect the guest's perception of the hotel itself. For example, if a gift shop sells tasteless novelties, guests are likely to conclude that the hotel itself has those same tastes and standards. An agreement with a vendor should explicitly spell out standards of cleanliness, personnel dress codes, and other "image" issues, as well as more practical matters such as hours of operation.

**Fitness and Recreation Facilities.** Today's businessperson may well travel with a pair of running shoes and feel that a daily run or workout of some kind is important. Hotels that have recognized this and provided workout facilities and indoor swimming pools have been able to capitalize on this new demand and increase their guest base. Other hotels have not kept up with the times and have lost guests who insist on some provision for exercising while they are away from home.

Often guests are not charged for the use of basic exercise facilities, although there may be a fee for extras like massages, rental bicycles, or the use of a luxury

**Fitness centers are increasingly popular amenitites at properties catering to business travelers.**

spa. Some hotels have recognized the potential to sell access to their health club to office workers and residents near the hotel and have sold health club memberships, thus turning what started out as a cost center into a revenue producer.

Another growing trend in travel is to combine business with pleasure. It is not uncommon to see businesspeople traveling with their spouses and children. As a result, some properties have installed video game rooms, which have turned out to be exceedingly popular. Such rooms can gross more than $500 per week, with approximately half of that ending up on the bottom line as profit to the hotel.

A major source of recreation revenue comes from pay TV in guestrooms. There are many systems for delivering television programming to hotel guestrooms and lounges. In addition to regular broadcast channels, there are cable channels such as HBO, Showtime, ESPN, and MTV. First-run movies are also available on a pay-per-view basis. This is one service that a deluxe or even middle-market hotel can hardly afford not to offer. Many guests expect to be able to watch movies in their room—often with pizza or popcorn delivered by room service.

## Cost Centers

As mentioned earlier, cost or support centers are hotel divisions that do not directly generate revenues. These divisions include:

- Marketing
- Engineering
- Accounting
- Human resources
- Security

## Marketing Division

The mission of a hotel's **marketing division** is to (1) identify prospective guests for the hotel, (2) shape the products and services of the hotel as much as possible to meet the needs of those prospects, and (3) persuade prospects to become guests. This task begins before the first brick is laid.

One way to understand marketing is to look at what it is not. Marketing is not selling. It has been said that the difference between marketing and selling is that selling is getting rid of what you have, while marketing is having what people want. If you have what people want and you tell them about it, sales will come easily—assuming that not too many others have it at the same place for the same price at the same time! If you don't have what people want and you are forced to get rid of what you have, you may have to discount it or promote it heavily, and even then it might not sell.

Marketing a hotel is not an activity confined to the marketing division; every employee is involved in providing what guests want. It is part of the job of the marketing division to understand the needs and wants of the hotel's guests and advise management of them, so that managers can train employees in how to meet those needs and wants.

The marketing division is charged with the responsibility of keeping the rooms in the hotel occupied at the right price and with the right mix of guests. It accomplishes this through many activities, including:

- Contacting groups and individuals
- Advertising in print and on radio and television
- Creating direct mail and public relations campaigns
- Participating in trade shows
- Visiting travel agents
- Arranging **familiarization tours** (free or reduced-rate travel programs designed to acquaint travel agents and others with the hotel and stimulate sales)
- Participating in community activities that raise the community's awareness of the hotel

On average, hotels spend approximately five percent of sales on such efforts. This figure is misleading, however, and should be considered cautiously. For example, marketing a new hotel is much more expensive than marketing an established one. The marketing expenses involved in opening a new hotel, such as parties for community leaders and familiarization tours for travel agents, are often

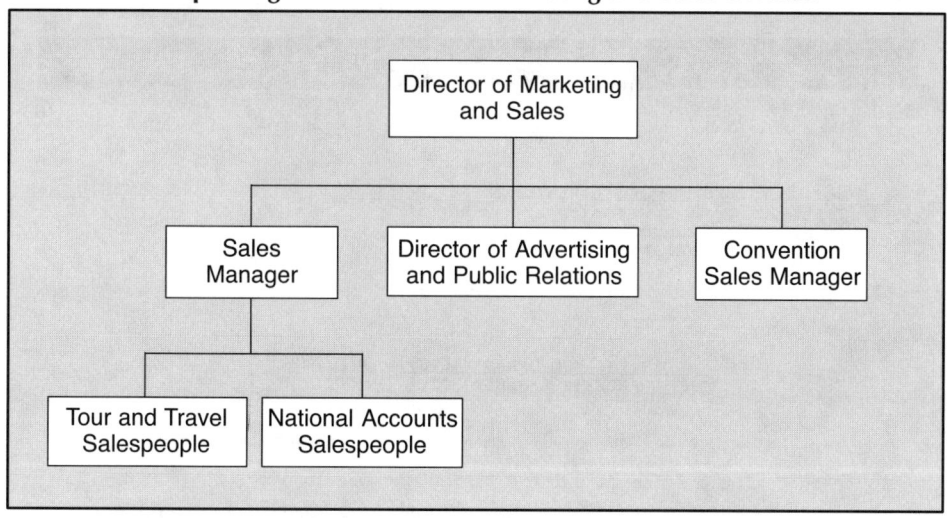

**Exhibit 8  Sample Organization Chart—Marketing and Sales Division**

```
                    Director of Marketing
                         and Sales
                              |
        ┌─────────────────────┼─────────────────────┐
        |                     |                     |
    Sales            Director of Advertising    Convention
    Manager          and Public Relations       Sales Manager
        |
   ┌────┴────┐
Tour and Travel   National Accounts
Salespeople       Salespeople
```

capitalized and charged off over a period of time. The cost of reservation systems is often charged to the rooms division, although it could be argued that such a system is a marketing tool and ought to be treated as a marketing expense.

In most large hotels, the marketing division is headed by a director of marketing and sales (see Exhibit 8). Reporting to the director is a sales manager, an advertising and public relations director, and a convention sales manager. Each of these individuals heads a department that is responsible for a distinct and separate activity within the overall marketing mission.

The sales department is responsible for prospecting for business and making sales calls on individuals and companies. The advertising and public relations department attempts to attract guests through advertising and create a positive image of the hotel. Commonly used public relations techniques are news releases about the hotel and its employees or guests, and involvement by managers and employees in community service (see Exhibit 9). The convention sales manager specializes in finding and booking group and convention business.

In many ways, the marketing and sales function of a hotel can be considered the very essence of the operation. A frequently quoted remark by management consultant Peter Drucker puts it this way: "There is only one valid definition of business purpose: to create a customer."[9]

## Engineering Division

Taking care of the hotel's physical plant and controlling energy costs are the responsibilities of the **engineering division**.[10] The physical upkeep of the building, furniture, fixtures, and equipment is essential to:

- Slow a hotel's physical deterioration
- Preserve the original hotel image established by management

**236** Chapter 7

**Exhibit 9    Sample News Release**

---

### GRAND NEWS

For more information, contact:
Eric Hiss or Joanna Massey
at Fleishman Hillard
Tom Bruny at MGM Grand

### JUST THE MGM GRAND FACTS -- BUILDING THE GRANDEST, LARGEST HOTEL IN THE WORLD

LAS VEGAS -- "The sky is the limit" is the phrase that best describes the sense of purpose behind the development of the MGM Grand Hotel, Casino & Theme Park, scheduled to open Dec. 18, 1993. When finished, the project will have the distinction of being the largest hotel and casino in the world, complementing Nevada's only theme park -- MGM Grand Adventures -- and the 15,200-seat MGM Grand Garden special events arena.

The MGM Grand represents a remarkable combination of technical ingenuity, modern eco-sensitive engineering, and a true sense of fantasy with lavish attention to detail. What follows are construction highlights that illustrate the scope of this landmark development:

<u>Monty Hall's Nightmare -- 18,000 doors!</u>
"Door number one, door number two, or door number three ... " Hardly. This mammoth hotel has enough doors to fit more than 1,600

- (More) -

**WORLD'S LARGEST HOTEL, CASINO & THEME PARK**
**MGM GRAND**
3799 LAS VEGAS BOULEVARD SOUTH
LAS VEGAS, NEVADA 89109

---

**This is the first page of a news release containing interesting facts about the MGM Grand Hotel, Casino & Theme Park.** (Courtesy of MGM Grand, World's Largest Hotel, Casino & Theme Park, Las Vegas, Nevada)

## Exhibit 10  Sample Organization Chart—Engineering Division

```
                        Chief Engineer
                              |————————— Secretary
                        Assistant
                        Chief Engineer
    ┌──────────┬──────────┬──────────┬──────────┬──────────┐
  Head       Head       Head       Head       Head       Head
  Plumber    Electrician Sound     HVAC/      Carpenter  Painter
                        Technician Refrigeration
    │          │          │          │          │          │
  Plumbers  Electricians Sound    Refrigeration Carpenters Painters
                        Department Technicians
                        Staff
                                              Locksmith
```

Courtesy of Professor Fritz Hagenmeyer, Florida International University

- Keep revenue-producing areas operational
- Keep the property comfortable for guests and employees
- Preserve the safety of the property for guests and employees
- Create savings by keeping repairs and equipment replacements to a minimum

The engineering division is also responsible for heating and air-conditioning systems and the systems that distribute electricity, steam, and water throughout the property.

In order to accomplish the many tasks of the engineering division, several types of technicians may be employed: electricians, plumbers, carpenters, painters, refrigeration and air-conditioning engineers, and others. The division is headed by a chief engineer. In small hotels one all-purpose engineer may perform all these functions or subcontract work as needed. In a large hotel, the chief engineer may be called a plant manager. When the size of the hotel warrants, there is also a secretary or administrative assistant to deal with the logistics of handling repair requests and scheduling service. Exhibit 10 shows a sample organization chart for the engineering division of a 700-room convention/resort hotel.

The maintenance and repair work performed by the engineering staff is one of two kinds: preventive or as needed. Preventive maintenance is a planned program of ongoing servicing of the building and equipment in order to maintain operations and prolong the life of the facility. Outside contractors may be hired for some jobs either on an as-needed basis or through a service contract. An important aspect of maintenance work is that in all areas there should be documentation to track labor and material costs. A master checklist groups the preventive maintenance work to be done on a daily, weekly, and monthly schedule. Detailed equipment checklists outlining tasks to be performed and how long it should take to perform them assist managers in scheduling employees.

In addition to preventive maintenance, the engineering staff performs routine repairs. Repair logs should be used to keep track of the start and finish of each repair assignment. Major projects that require the purchase of building materials may also be undertaken by the engineering division. Management usually determines whether extensive repairs or replacement of equipment not covered by service contracts is to be done by the hotel's own staff or given to an outside contractor.

In a study of full-service U.S. hotels, PKF Consulting reports that its sample spent 5.2 percent of total sales on maintenance. Energy cost was 4.3 percent.[11]

**Controlling Energy Costs.** Controlling energy and utility costs while maintaining guest comfort and operational efficiency is one of the functions of the engineering division. A sound cost-control program begins with an understanding of how energy is used. This requires a careful analysis of energy-consuming equipment and electricity, water, and fuel bills.

**Water.** According to Robert E. Aulbach, president of RoBach Inc. and an energy consultant to major hotel chains and independent hotels, over a period of three months a single dripping faucet can waste about 2,000 gallons (7,560 liters) of water.[12] When you think of the potential for costly water loss in a hotel, with all its toilets, sinks, and bath tubs, it is clear that diligence is important if costs are to be managed at all. Moreover, environmental concerns are causing more and more hotels to conserve water because of its scarcity in some areas.

It should be noted that some water conservation measures might affect guest perceptions of the hotel. Although visitors are not likely to be concerned about whether the boiler is metered or the rinse cycles in the laundry are reduced, serving water in the dining room only on request or lowering the water pressure in the hotel and restricting the flow of shower heads may be noticed and disapproved of by some guests. These measures, therefore, should be tempered with a firm understanding of the business strategy of the hotel and the needs and expectations of the guests it is trying to attract.

**Electricity and fuel.** Heating and air-conditioning systems are major users of energy in a hotel. The cost of energy varies depending on both consumption and time of day. Utility companies commonly charge premium rates for peak periods, when demand is greatest.

Many hotels have adopted energy control systems that allow front desk personnel to turn off or turn down heat or air-conditioning in a guestroom when it is vacated. An even more efficient system is one in which each guestroom is equipped with a motion detector. If no motion is detected, the room's air-conditioning and heating systems are shut down; when motion is detected, the guestroom's systems are turned on to predetermined levels set by management.

Computerized property management systems can control peak demand by leveling off consumption. This is accomplished by automatically reducing non-essential

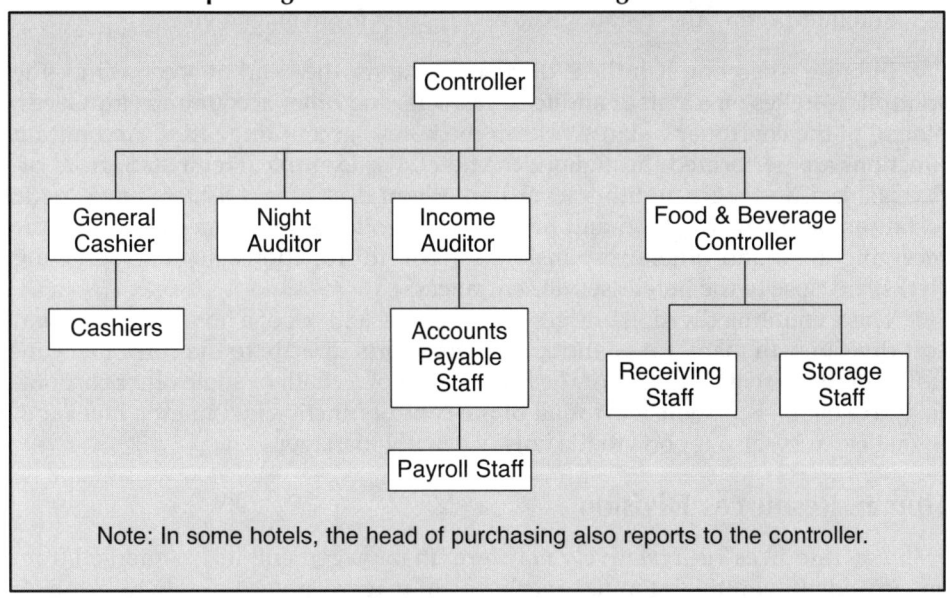

**Exhibit 11    Sample Organization Chart—Accounting Division**

```
                            Controller
        ┌───────────────┬──────────────┬──────────────────┐
   General         Night          Income          Food & Beverage
   Cashier        Auditor         Auditor            Controller
      │                              │                   │
   Cashiers                      Accounts          ┌─────┴─────┐
                                 Payable        Receiving   Storage
                                  Staff           Staff      Staff
                                    │
                               Payroll Staff
```

Note: In some hotels, the head of purchasing also reports to the controller.

energy requirements at times of greatest energy demand. Many hotels without sufficient budgets for computerized property management systems rely on well-trained and energy-conscious employees who manually monitor heating and air-conditioning systems and make periodic adjustments as needed.

Hotels committed to energy conservation have a wide range of options. As more energy-efficient heating, air-conditioning, and lighting systems become available, opportunities for even greater savings will increase.

## Accounting Division

A hotel's **accounting division** is responsible for keeping track of the many business transactions that occur in the hotel. The accounting division does more than simply keep the books—financial management is perhaps a more appropriate description of what the accounting division does. An organization chart of an accounting division might look like the one shown in Exhibit 11.

The responsibilities of the accounting division include:

- Forecasting and budgeting
- Managing what the hotel owns and what money is due from guests
- Controlling cash
- Controlling costs in all areas of the hotel—revenue centers as well as cost centers and payroll
- Purchasing, receiving, and issuing operating and capital inventory such as food and beverages, housekeeping supplies, and furniture

- Keeping records, preparing financial statements and daily operating reports, and interpreting these statements and reports for management

In order to accomplish these diverse functions, the head of accounting—the controller—relies on a staff of auditors, cashiers, and other accounting employees. Not all of the controller's staff works in the hotel's accounting office. Accounting functions are performed throughout the hotel. For example, credit staff, front office cashiers, and night auditors work in the front desk area. Cashiers work in the restaurant and bar. The food and beverage controller is sometimes located in the receiving area, and others responsible for control functions, such as receiving clerks, are close to the hotel's service entrances.

The accounting division bridges and interacts with all of a hotel's revenue and cost divisions. In many cases, the controller reports directly to the corporate controller of the parent company (if the hotel is part of a chain or some other corporation). He or she is responsible for all of the control functions within the hotel and, in that capacity, also reports to the hotel's general manager.

## Human Resources Division

"Human resources" is a relatively new term in management. It has emerged from an expanded definition of a manager's job. Managers are not simply directors of people, but are also facilitators. Today's managers see themselves as developers of people and as guardians of their company's most important asset—its employees. Thus, the traditional personnel division is slowly going the way of the dinosaur. In the old days the personnel manager of a company was little more than a clerk. His or her job was to accept applications, check references, and keep records of who was hired, fired, and promoted.

Today's **human resources division** does much more. Modern human resources managers are concerned with the whole equation of people and productivity—as well as salaries, wages, and benefits. Their job description includes recruiting, orienting, training, evaluating, motivating, rewarding, disciplining, developing, promoting, and communicating with all of the employees of the hotel.

## Security Division

The security of guests, employees, personal property, and the hotel itself is an overriding concern for today's hotel managers. In the past, most security precautions concentrated on the prevention of theft from guests and the hotel. However, today such violent crimes as murder and rape have become a problem for some hotels. Hotel owners and operators are concerned about their ethical and legal responsibility to protect guests and their property. Not giving security the attention it deserves can be costly. Courts have awarded plaintiffs thousands (in some cases, millions) of dollars as a result of judgments against hotels for not exercising reasonable care in protecting guests.[13]

A hotel security program should be preventive. While ultimate responsibility for security remains with the general manager, most hotels have one or more security officers on staff who are professionally trained in crime prevention and detection.

Traditionally, security has been the responsibility of the front office. The trend today is to give security the status of an independent division or department reporting directly to the general manager or resident manager. In large hotels, the head of the **security division** may be called the chief of security. This person usually has an extensive background in law enforcement.

Those involved in security should have specialized training in civil and criminal law. They must work closely with local police and fire departments to ensure that all regulations pertaining to hotels are enforced. Applicants for security positions should be trained in self-defense.

A comprehensive security program includes all of the following elements:

- *Security officers.* Security officers make regular rounds of the hotel premises, including guest floors, corridors, public and private function rooms, parking areas, and offices. Their duties involve observing suspicious behavior and taking appropriate action, investigating incidents, and cooperating with local law enforcement officials.

- *Equipment.* Security equipment includes two-way radios; closed-circuit television (CCT) to monitor entrances, elevators, and corridors; smoke detectors and fire-alarm systems; fire-fighting equipment, including extinguishers, hoses, and fire axes; and adequate interior and exterior lighting.

- *Master keys.* Security officers should be able to gain access to guestrooms, storerooms, and offices at all times.

- *Safety procedures.* A well-designed security program includes evacuation plans in case of fire, bomb threats, terrorism, or some other emergency. All employees should be familiar with these plans. Employee training and procedure manuals should include sections on safety.

- *Identification procedures.* Identification cards with photographs should be issued to all employees. Name tags for employees who are likely to have contact with guests not only project a friendly image for the property but are also useful for security reasons.

## Compliance with the ADA

As a result of the Americans with Disabilities Act (ADA), all of the divisions of a U.S. hotel must modify existing facilities to some extent and incorporate design features into new construction that make hotel facilities accessible to disabled persons.[14] Disabled persons, as defined by the act, include persons in wheelchairs, other persons with mobility impairments who may suffer from neuromuscular conditions such as multiple sclerosis and muscular dystrophy, and persons with sensory impairments such as blindness and deafness. The act affects employees as well as guests.

All hotels are expected to have at least 4 percent of their parking spaces designated as "handicapped" (the figure drops to 2 percent if the parking lot has more than 100 spaces). Parking spaces for persons with disabilities must be wide enough for wheelchairs to be unloaded from a van and for users to easily enter the hotel by means of accessible ramps and doors. Entrances to hotels must have accessible pick-up and drop-off points without curbs or any other obstructions for a person using a wheelchair or crutches.

Many areas within hotels are affected by the ADA. One section of the registration desk should be low enough for a person in a wheelchair to comfortably see over it. Ramps should be equipped with handrails; stairs require handrails and beveled risers. Restrooms must have accessible stalls that are wide enough for a disabled person to receive assistance from another individual if needed, or to allow a blind individual to enter with a guide dog. Meeting rooms must be equipped with accessible ramps to platforms and special listening systems for persons who are hearing impaired. Restaurants must have "accessible paths" at least 36 inches (91.4 centimeters) wide between tables or counters and bars. Merchandise racks in hotel retail shops must be spaced far enough apart for persons in wheelchairs to move around and between them.

Guestrooms must be fitted with equipment that can be manipulated by persons with severe arthritis, an amputation, or poor control of their hands. Visual fire alarms are required in designated rooms for hearing-impaired guests. Numbers on doors must be tactile so they can be read by touch.

Many of these changes involve new construction or modifications of existing facilities that are "readily achievable." In time, hopefully, all public facilities in the United States, including hotels, restaurants, museums, theaters, shops, and even parks, will have made the changes necessary to be accessible to disabled persons. Other countries, notably the United Kingdom and Germany, are making great strides in improving their handicapped facilities.

## Control Systems

An important part of managing is to measure performance levels and take corrective action if they do not meet the goals of the enterprise. In order to maintain control over all aspects of an organization, managers and owners must first establish goals against which results can be measured. For example, an organization may establish a payroll goal of 30 percent of revenues—that is, the operating plan is to spend 30 percent or less of sales on salaries and other payroll expenses. The plan may also provide that a variance of 2 percent is acceptable, but that anything above that is not. If payroll expenses exceed 32 percent, management must take action.

The ideal control system allows managers to quickly recognize and correct deviations from the operating budget (or some other management standard) before they become major problems. One way hotel managers accomplish this is to have accurate forecasting systems. To continue with our payroll example: By being able to forecast with a high degree of accuracy what sales are likely to be in a given period, managers can adjust staffing levels accordingly to meet the payroll goal. For instance, if the dining room manager knows from sales history records that on Monday evenings in February the dining room is likely to serve only 100 meals, then the number of food servers and cooks that will be required is no longer a matter of guesswork but can be carefully planned. Of course, current occupancy and other circumstances must also be taken into account.

In too many cases, corrections are made long after the problem starts. The longer the period between the variation from property goals and the correction, the weaker the control system and the greater the potential for lost revenue and increased costs.

Training plays a key role in control systems. A certain number of errors by front desk personnel and food servers is inevitable. No human system is perfect. But careful training can minimize errors and bring performance levels up to standard.

Many of management's goals can be quantified. The more specific the goal and the easier it is to quantify, the more likely it is that the goal will be met. Guestroom occupancy levels, guest counts in restaurants, and revenue and expense targets are examples of quantifiable goals. Not all goals are easy to measure. For example, an operating plan might have a goal of increasing guest satisfaction or employee morale. However, even there it is possible to be more specific and measure the results accordingly.

Two of the most important types of controls for managers are financial controls and quality controls.

## Financial Controls

One of the most useful **financial control** tools is financial statements. Investors use them to monitor profitability. Lenders read them as a measure of financial stability. Managers base their planning on them and monitor the success of their planning with them.

In order to understand a hotel financial statement, it is necessary to be familiar with the hotel industry's financial terminology and to understand the manner in which revenues and expenses are grouped by division.

**Uniform System of Accounts.** In March 1926 the American Hotel & Motel Association (at that time it was called the American Hotel Association of the United States and Canada) adopted a manual called the *Uniform System of Accounts for Hotels.* The system was formulated by a committee of accountants and hoteliers in New York City. The ninth edition, published in 1996, bore a new title to better encompass all segments of the industry: *The Uniform System of Accounts for the Lodging Industry.*

The *Uniform System of Accounts for the Lodging Industry* classifies the different types of hotel revenues and expenses and groups them in the statement of income by division or department. The **statement of income** is one of management's major control tools. It shows the total sales by product or service category (rooms, food, beverage, and so on) for a stated period of time, the expenses incurred in generating those sales, and the profit earned or the loss incurred as a result of those activities (see Exhibit 12).

There are three types of hotel expenses: divisional expenses, overhead expenses, and fixed charges or capital costs. Divisional expenses include a wide range of items, such as rooms division payroll expenses, restaurant laundry, and telephone supplies like message pads and pencils. Overhead expenses are costs such as marketing and energy—costs that relate to the entire hotel and not to one specific department. Fixed charges or capital costs are expenses related to the

**Exhibit 12   Sample Hotel Statement of Income**

### XYZ Hotel
### Statement of Income
### For the year ended December 31, 19XX

| | | |
|---|---:|---:|
| **Net Revenue** | | |
| Rooms | $ 897,500 | 56.3% |
| Food | 393,320 | 24.6 |
| Beverage | 131,250 | 8.2 |
| Telecommunications | 51,140 | 3.2 |
| Other Operated Departments | 63,000 | 3.9 |
| Rentals and Other Income | 61,283 | 3.8 |
| Total Departmental Revenue | 1,597,493 | 100.0 |
| **Costs and Expenses** | | |
| Rooms | 205,239 | 12.8 |
| Food | 360,652 | 22.6 |
| Beverage | 76,541 | 4.8 |
| Telecommunications | 75,763 | 4.7 |
| Other Operated Departments | 50,354 | 3.2 |
| Administrative and General | 164,181 | 10.3 |
| Marketing | 67,868 | 4.2 |
| Property Operation and Maintenance | 61,554 | 3.9 |
| Utility Costs | 47,312 | 3.0 |
| Rent, Property Taxes, and Insurance | 80,738 | 5.1 |
| Interest Expense | 192,153 | 12.0 |
| Depreciation and Amortization | 146,000 | 9.1 |
| Total Costs and Expenses | 1,528,355 | 95.7 |
| **Income Before Income Taxes** | 69,138 | 4.3 |
| Income Taxes | 16,094 | 1.0 |
| **Net Income** | $ 53,044 | 3.3% |

investment, such as insurance on the building and contents, and interest on the mortgage loan.

The uniform system also classifies **assets** (something of value that is owned) and **liabilities** (what is owed to creditors). Examples of assets might be the hotel building itself, furniture and equipment, and courtesy vans to transport guests to and from airports. Liabilities include items such as the mortgage loan and food purchases for which payment is due. All of these items are grouped together in the financial statement known as the **balance sheet** (see Exhibit 13). A balance sheet reports the financial position of a business by presenting its assets, liabilities, and owner's or shareholders' equity on a given date.

## Quality Controls

It is a relatively simple task to standardize the quality and cost of a manufactured product. This is because products, whether they be toasters or skis, are produced in

**Exhibit 13  Sample Hotel Balance Sheet**

### XYZ Hotel
### Balance Sheet
### December 31, 19XX

#### ASSETS

**Current Assets**
| | | |
|---|---|---|
| Cash | $ 58,500 | 1.9 % |
| Short-Term Investments | 25,000 | .8 |
| Accounts Receivable (net) | 40,196 | 1.2 |
| Inventories | 11,000 | .3 |
| Prepaid Expenses | 13,192 | .4 |
| Total Current Assets | 147,888 | 4.6 |

**Property and Equipment**
| | | |
|---|---|---|
| Land | 850,000 | 26.2 |
| Building | 2,500,000 | 77.0 |
| Furniture and Equipment | 475,000 | 14.6 |
| Total | 3,825,000 | 117.8 |
| Less Accumulated Depreciation | 775,000 | 23.9 |
| Total | 3,050,000 | 93.9 |
| Leasehold Improvements | 9,000 | .3 |
| China, Glassware, and Silver (net) | 36,524 | 1.1 |
| Total Property and Equipment | 3,095,524 | 95.3 |

**Other Noncurrent Assets**
| | | |
|---|---|---|
| Security Deposits | 1,000 | — |
| Deferred Charges | 3,000 | .1 |
| Total Other Assets | 4,000 | .1 |
| **Total Assets** | **$3,247,412** | **100.0%** |

#### LIABILITIES AND SHAREHOLDERS' EQUITY

**Current Liabilities**
| | | |
|---|---|---|
| Accounts Payable | $ 13,861 | .4 % |
| Federal and State Income Taxes Payable | 16,545 | .5 |
| Accrued Payroll | 11,617 | .4 |
| Other Accrued Items | 7,963 | .2 |
| Unearned Revenue | 3,764 | .1 |
| Current Portion of Long-Term Debt | 70,000 | 2.2 |
| Total Current Liabilities | 123,750 | 3.8 |

**Long-Term Debt**
| | | |
|---|---|---|
| Mortgage Payable, less current portion | 2,055,000 | 63.3 |
| **Total Liabilities** | 2,178,750 | 67.1 |

#### SHAREHOLDERS' EQUITY

| | | |
|---|---|---|
| Common Stock, par value $1, authorized and issued 50,000 shares | 50,000 | 1.5 |
| Additional Paid-In Capital | 700,000 | 21.6 |
| Retained Earnings | 318,662 | 9.8 |
| Total Shareholders' Equity | 1,068,662 | 32.9 |
| **Total Liabilities and Shareholders' Equity** | **$3,247,412** | **100.0%** |

a factory under strictly controlled conditions. Some assembly lines are computerized, and many use robots to perform some functions. Moreover, quality control inspectors not only monitor all operations but can inspect each finished item before it leaves the plant and a consumer purchases it.

Service businesses such as hotels operate under an entirely different set of circumstances. The "product" that a hotel produces—the experience of staying there—is manufactured in the hotel "factory" right in front of the consumer. For example, a guest enters a hotel, goes into the lounge, sits down at a table, and orders a strawberry daiquiri. The product in this case is not simply the daiquiri—it also includes the lounge, the server, and the bartender who mixes the drink. It is this total experience that the guest pays for. If the guest had just wanted a strawberry daiquiri, he or she could have made one at home or bought a bottled one at the corner liquor store.

Because of the nature of a service business, it is extremely difficult to standardize or even control the service that guests receive. There are too many variables that can interfere with the process—including the guests, who, for example, may be rude and insensitive and receive similar service in return.

Opportunities for dissatisfaction abound. Take our guest who ordered the strawberry daiquiri. Possibly the guest had to wait for a table because none was available or the host was out of the room temporarily. Maybe the seating was prompt, but the guest had to wait longer than expected for the order because the ice machine or the drink mixer was broken. Perhaps the bartender was preoccupied with a personal problem instead of concentrating on fixing a perfect strawberry daiquiri. Even if everything else goes well, it can all be spoiled if the guest has to wait too long for the check or if there is a mistake on it. All of these possibilities exist whenever a guest enters the lounge. Any of them can affect the quality of the experience (the product) and thus the guest's perception of the lounge and the hotel. This one transaction is a single example of the many kinds of things that can go wrong in a hotel that is open 24 hours a day, where guests interact regularly with, and receive service from, front desk agents, food servers, room attendants, bellpersons, concierges, valets, maintenance people, and gift shop employees.

Product and service consistency is of primary importance and can only be achieved through **quality controls** such as:

- Setting standards that answer the needs and expectations of guests
- Selecting employees who are capable of achieving those standards and who are motivated to do so
- Conducting continual training and certification programs for all employees at every level
- Involving employees in structuring job descriptions, setting performance standards, and solving problems
- Evaluating the program so that all managers and employees know they are achieving what they have set out to do—satisfy the guest
- Rewarding managers and employees for achieving goals

Quality programs at hotels go by various names: "quality assurance" (QA) and "total quality management" (TQM) are two examples. Although their names vary, the goal of all such programs is to provide quality service to guests.

**Setting Standards.** Quality is an overriding concern in the hotel industry, but what does "quality" mean? There is no universal industry agreement on what quality is, nor should there be. Quality has to do with expectations versus reality. When guests check into a $35-a-night budget hotel, they expect a certain standard of service and no more. If they get what they expect (or a little more), they have enjoyed a quality experience from their point of view. If they get less than what they expected or thought they were paying for, then they will think they received poor-quality service. The formula is the same for a hotel room that costs $200 a night. A guest who pays that amount has certain expectations. His or her perception of quality depends to a large degree on whether those expectations are met or exceeded.

Most hotels strive for quality for their type of product and target market. Quality, then, means that the guest experience—in terms of the cleanliness of the rooms, the taste and presentation of the food, and the physical condition of the hotel—is consistent with what the management has promised and is trying to deliver.

Some lodging chains that emphasize food and offer the same menu at all of their units go to great lengths to ensure that food quality will be the same at every unit, because that is what their repeat visitors expect. Club Med, for example, which operates more than 100 resorts in 34 countries, relies on lavish buffets that are more or less identical all over the world:

> The buffets at each and every Club Med are a veritable catalog of traditional French cuisine: pungent cheeses, freshly baked baguettes and croissants, pâtés and terrines, crudités, ratatouille, côte d'agneau, quiche, coulibiac, even frogs legs....To add a touch of the indigenously exotic, local specialties account for at least five percent of each club's menu.[15]

To achieve consistency, Club Med resorts in the western hemisphere fly the majority of the required items from Miami, although some items, such as wine, are imported from France. The amounts are staggering: 7 million eggs, 95 tons (86.5 metric tons) of cheese, 300 tons (273 metric tons) of meat, and 235 tons (213.9 metric tons) of fish each year. In a single day, guests at any one resort eat 500 croissants and 120 baguettes.[16]

Ritz-Carlton also sets very high standards. According to the management of the Ritz-Carlton chain, "Customer satisfaction is a deeply held belief at the Ritz-Carlton and begins with an absolute understanding of the needs and expectations of our customer." The chain achieves this understanding by forming focus groups of Ritz-Carlton current and prospective guests and by recording guest preferences that are detected and reported by all front-line employees. This information is used to set guest-service standards.

To achieve quality standards, hotel managers—with the help of individual employees and "quality teams" formed from hotel personnel—must create procedures for hotel staff to follow. For example, when a room attendant has finished cleaning a guestroom, the position of the furniture, the number of towels and other guest amenities, and—most important—the overall cleanliness of the room must be exactly the same every day for every room. How many towels to leave in the bathroom or what constitutes "clean" should not be left to the discretion of the person doing the cleaning. Procedures must be established for each task to be performed. At the same time, a standard of what is acceptable and what is not must be spelled out for each procedure. It is not reasonable to set standards without specifically detailing the procedures that must be followed in order to achieve those standards.

The following example of a food service procedure and standard concerns the task of greeting guests at a table:

*Procedure:* After table is seated, greet the guest(s): "Good morning. May I offer you some coffee?" Be pleasant, unhurried. Pour coffee with cup on table, and to right of guest. If tea is served, the tea pot is served on a butter plate with a doily, lemon on top of tea pot.

*Standard:* Make the guest feel comfortable. Strike a positive note in your "beginning" with the guest.

**Selecting Employees.** Ritz-Carlton emphasizes the importance of employee selection in its quality management program. Jim Vail, general manager of The Ritz-Carlton Buckhead in Atlanta, Georgia, tells all new employees, "You are not hired; you are selected."[17] Ritz-Carlton has devised a highly sophisticated predictive instrument, using superior employees as a benchmark, that allows them to determine whether the candidates for a specific position are capable of living up to the chain's service standards.

**Training Employees.** It is not enough for a hotel to establish standards and procedures and select employees to carry them out. Employees must be shown how to perform the procedures. Employees who have never cleaned a guestroom or waited on a table can't be expected to know what to do simply because they've been given a manual.

To succeed, training must be ongoing and have the full commitment of management. At Ritz-Carlton, all hotels have a director of human resources on staff who is assisted by the hotel's quality leader, who acts as an advisor. Each work area has a departmental trainer who is charged with the training and certification of new employees at their unit. According to Horst Schulze, president and chief operating officer of Ritz-Carlton, "At the Ritz-Carlton, it is everybody's job, daily, to make our people more valuable."[18]

**Involving Employees.** All successful quality programs use a participative style of management. Judy King, owner and president of Quality Management Services, lists basic beliefs in employee involvement in problem solving:

1. The person doing the job knows how the job can be done better.
2. Problem solving and decision making should be done at the lowest capable level in the organization.
3. People are the greatest untapped resource in the organization.

4. People will meet expectations if they have been enabled to do so and, with encouragement, will exceed them.[19]

Ritz-Carlton employees are expected and empowered to solve problems. On the Ritz-Carlton "Gold Standards" card that every employee carries, it says, "Any employee who receives a customer complaint 'owns' the complaint." Employees are encouraged to break out of their regular routine and solve guest problems immediately and ensure that they do not recur. Teams of workers from different divisions are often put together to resolve conflicts between internal operation problems and external guest expectations.[20]

**Evaluating Quality Programs.** Management must verify the consistency of product and service quality in order to evaluate the success of its quality efforts. Ritz-Carlton, for example, depends heavily on real-time reports, called "guest incident action forms," that are generated daily by employees. These reports are analyzed and quickly acted on so that incidents of guest dissatisfaction will not be repeated.

One of the simplest ways to evaluate the quality of an operation is called "management by walking around." Successful hotel managers have found that periodic tours of the hotel, and alertness to what is going on around them, is one of the best ways of ensuring that the quality program is working. There is a saying in the United States Navy that also applies to the hotel business: "You get what you inspect, not what you expect."

Guest comment cards are another important evaluation tool (see Exhibit 14). Although many managers feel these cards encourage negative comments, they are nevertheless a valuable tool. Cards typically are placed in guestrooms on the dresser or desk. Some hotels require front desk agents to ask departing guests if they have completed a card. Experience has shown that open-ended questions that ask guests to write a description of their experiences do not work as well as simple rating scales, where guests can indicate their level of satisfaction with various components of the hotel's service and facilities. There should be room on the card, however, for guests to add comments if they choose and to identify employees whom they wish to single out either positively or negatively.

Another evaluation method involves hiring outside inspectors, usually referred to as "mystery shoppers." These inspectors, who are not known to hotel employees, make reservations, stay in a guestroom, eat in the dining room, check out, and then prepare elaborate reports on the level of service they received. Some hotels announce inspections in advance and the inspectors are known. While employees often favor this system, the level of management confidence in the results of such inspections tends to be much lower.

**Rewarding for Achievement.** Today, hotel management executive compensation almost always includes both a salary and a bonus. The bonus can be quite substantial and is a result of hotel owners' desire to motivate their executives to a higher level of performance. Very often bonuses are tied to achieving and/or surpassing specific outcomes—for example, financial performance or guest satisfaction as reported by comment cards.

Employee recognition programs are also common. These may involve posting photographs of the "employee of the month" in a special frame in the lobby, giving

### Exhibit 14  Sample Guest Comment Card

| | Rating scale: sehr gut/excellent – gut – befriedigend/satisfactory – unterdurchschnittlich/poor – mangelhaft/very poor |
|---|---|
| **1.** Wie beurteilen Sie dieses Holiday Inn Hotel? / How do you rate this Holiday Inn hotel? | ☐☐☐☐☐ |
| **2.** Wie beurteilen Sie den Service in diesem Hotel? / How do you rate this hotel's service? | |
| Freundlichkeit / Friendliness | ☐☐☐☐☐ |
| Hilfsbereitschaft / Helpfulness | ☐☐☐☐☐ |
| Aufmerksamkeit / Attentiveness | ☐☐☐☐☐ |
| Leistungsfähigkeit / Efficiency | ☐☐☐☐☐ |
| Unaufdringlichkeit / Discretion | ☐☐☐☐☐ |
| **3.** Bitte beurteilen Sie wie folgt: / Please rate the following: | |
| **a)** Ihr Gästezimmer – Your Room | |
| Preis/Leistungsverhältnis / Value for money | ☐☐☐☐☐ |
| Erster Eindruck / Appearance | ☐☐☐☐☐ |
| Einrichtung / Furnishing | ☐☐☐☐☐ |
| Sauberkeit / Cleanliness | ☐☐☐☐☐ |
| Funktionsfähigkeit / Functioning of facilities | ☐☐☐☐☐ |
| Badezimmer / Bathroom | ☐☐☐☐☐ |
| Zimmerservice / Room service | ☐☐☐☐☐ |
| Allgemeiner Eindruck / Overall impression | ☐☐☐☐☐ |
| **b)** Die Restaurants – The Restaurants | |
| Qualität der Speisen / Food quality | ☐☐☐☐☐ |
| Preis/Leistungsverhältnis / Value for money | ☐☐☐☐☐ |
| Bedienung / Service | ☐☐☐☐☐ |
| Allgemeiner Eindruck / Overall impression | ☐☐☐☐☐ |
| Welche Mahlzeit(en) haben Sie eingenommen? / Which meal(s) taken? | Frühstück/Breakfast ☐  Mittagessen/Lunch ☐  Abendessen/Dinner ☐ |
| **c)** Die Bars – The Bars | |
| Allgemeiner Eindruck / Overall impression | ☐☐☐☐☐ |
| Qualität der Getränke / Beverage quality | ☐☐☐☐☐ |
| Preis/Leistungsverhältnis / Value for money | ☐☐☐☐☐ |
| Bedienung / Service | ☐☐☐☐☐ |
| Welche Bar(s) haben Sie benutzt / Which bar(s) used | _____ |
| **d)** Die Rezeption/der Empfang / The Reception/Front Desk | |
| Handhabung Ihrer Ankunft/Abreise / Handling of check-in/check-out | ☐☐☐☐☐ |
| Leistungsfähigkeit / Efficiency | ☐☐☐☐☐ |
| Freundlichkeit / Friendliness | ☐☐☐☐☐ |
| **e)** Konferenz-Einrichtungen / Conference Facilities | |
| Bequemlichkeit / Comfort | ☐☐☐☐☐ |
| Beleuchtung / Lighting | ☐☐☐☐☐ |
| Klimatisierung / Temperature | ☐☐☐☐☐ |
| Bedienung / Service | ☐☐☐☐☐ |
| **f)** Eindruck des Hotels / Hotel Appearance | |
| Außenansicht des Gebäudes / Building exterior | ☐☐☐☐☐ |
| Eingangshalle/öffentliche Bereiche / Lobby/public areas | ☐☐☐☐☐ |
| **4.** Haben Sie von unseren Freizeiteinrichtungen Gebrauch gemacht? / Did you use our leisure facilities? | Ja/Yes ☐  Nein/No ☐ |
| **5.** Haben Sie in den letzten 12 Monaten in irgendeinem Holiday Inn Hotel gewohnt? / Have you stayed at any Holiday Inn hotel in the last 12 months? | Ja/Yes ☐  Nein/No ☐ |
| **6.** Würden Sie sich bei Ihrem nächsten Aufenthalt in dieser Gegend wieder für dieses Hotel entscheiden? / If you return to this area, will you stay at this hotel again? | Ja/Yes ☐  Nein/No ☐ |

Guest comment cards are an important evaluation tool for managers. These are two panels of a six-panel comment card from a Holiday Inn Crowne Plaza in Germany. Note the simple rating scale ("*sehr gut*/excellent" to "*mangelhaft*/very poor"). Another panel (not shown) provides room for guests to add comments if they wish. (Courtesy of Holiday Inn Worldwide, Brussels, Belgium)

gift certificates and other monetary rewards, or providing special parking spaces for recognized employees.

## Chapter Summary

Managers manage by organizing hotels into various functional areas and then delegating responsibility and authority. The functional areas are divided into revenue and cost (or support) centers. Divisions such as rooms and food and beverage are revenue centers; others, like engineering and accounting, are cost centers. The number of such centers (or divisions) depends on the size of the hotel.

In most hotels, the rooms division is the largest and generates the most revenue and profit. It generally consists of four departments: front office, reservations, housekeeping, and uniformed service. Front office duties include checking guests in and out, posting charges to their accounts, and collecting payments. In small hotels, front desk agents may also accept reservations, relay messages to guests, and handle the telephone switchboard.

The housekeeping department is responsible for cleaning guestrooms and public areas. Often it has the most employees. Besides cleaning, the housekeeping department also takes care of laundry and valet services.

Uniformed service employees deal with guest luggage and transportation, and provide concierge services.

The food and beverage division is of paramount importance to a hotel's profitability and reputation. There may be many different types of food and beverage outlets in a hotel. Factors that influence the level of food and beverage service that is offered include the type of hotel, the class of hotel, the competition, product availability, availability of labor, and guest demand. The food and beverage manager typically has restaurant managers, beverage managers, and a catering director reporting to him or her. Support and control personnel for the food and beverage division include purchasing managers, receiving clerks, storeroom clerks, cashiers, and a food and beverage controller.

The overall profitability of food and beverage operations depends on several factors, including hours of operation, guest check averages, the number and kind of facilities, employee turnover, entertainment costs, and marketing.

A well-managed telephone department can also contribute to a hotel's profits. Modern telephone systems have made a big difference in the way hotel telephone departments function and have helped increase guest satisfaction with telephone service.

Concessions, rentals, and commissions are other sources of hotel revenue. However, managers should make sure that the standards of concessionaires are compatible with the hotel's.

Guests' changing lifestyles have made hotel health spas, cable movies, and video game rooms popular and important.

The marketing division is charged with identifying prospective guests, seeing that management understands and responds to their needs and wants, and persuading prospective guests to stay at the hotel. To accomplish these tasks, the marketing division usually has a director of marketing and sales, a sales manager, a director of advertising and public relations, a convention sales manager, salespeople, and support staff.

The engineering division takes care of the hotel's physical plant and utility systems. The division is headed by a chief engineer, assisted by his or her own staff and outside contractors. Preventive maintenance duties and repairs are performed. One important aspect of the engineering division's mission is the conservation of energy and water.

The accounting division is charged with the hotel's financial management. Accounting is headed by a controller who oversees the general cashier, the night auditor, the income auditor, and the food and beverage controller.

The human resources division is responsible for recruiting, orienting, training, evaluating, motivating, rewarding, disciplining, developing, promoting, and communicating with hotel employees.

Security of hotel employees and guests is of overriding importance. Hotel security programs are preventive and should be under the direction of a person with law enforcement experience.

As a result of the Americans with Disabilities Act (ADA) enacted by the U.S. Congress, all of the divisions of a U.S. hotel must modify existing facilities to some extent and incorporate design features into new construction that make hotel facilities accessible to disabled persons. Disabled persons, as defined by the act, include persons in wheelchairs, other persons with mobility impairments who may suffer from neuromuscular conditions such as multiple sclerosis and muscular dystrophy, and persons with sensory impairments such as blindness and deafness. The act affects employees as well as guests.

Hotel managers have two major kinds of controls: financial controls and quality controls. Important financial controls are the hotel's financial statements. These statements are based on those found in the *Uniform System of Accounts for the Lodging Industry*. In this accounting system, hotel expenses are classified as divisional, overhead, and fixed. Assets and liabilities are also classified.

Quality controls are essential in order to ensure that standards established by management are adhered to. Hotels must establish standards appropriate for their type of hotel, create procedures, and select employees carefully if quality guest service is to be achieved. All quality programs require employee involvement. Employees are encouraged to solve problems that interfere with good guest service. Quality programs must be evaluated to make sure they are truly effective, and both management and employees must be rewarded for achievement.

## Endnotes

1. The use of the terms *division* and *department* is not standardized in the industry. Some properties call their main functional areas (rooms, food and beverage, etc.) departments; the smaller functional areas within departments (room service, for example) may be called sub-departments. Large properties often call their main functional areas divisions and units within divisions, departments. Neither option is better than the other. For consistency, however, throughout this chapter we will call the main functional areas "divisions" and the smaller areas "departments."

2. PKF Consulting, "Trends in the Hotel Industry—1996."

3. The titles for front desk employees vary within the industry. Hotels may refer to their front desk employees as front desk agents, front desk clerks, guest service representatives, front office agents, or something similar. However, for the sake of consistency we will refer to front desk employees as front desk agents throughout this text.

4. Front office operations are covered in detail in Michael L. Kasavana and Richard M. Brooks, *Managing Front Office Operations,* 4th ed. (East Lansing, Mich.: Educational Institute of the American Hotel & Motel Association, 1995).

5. Warren H. Lieberman, "Debunking the Myths of Yield Management," *Cornell Quarterly*, February 1993, p. 36.

6. Eric B. Orkin, Yield Management Conference, March 26–27, 1992, Dallas, Texas.

7. The housekeeping department, from an executive housekeeper's perspective, is the subject of Margaret M. Kappa, Aleta Nitschke, and Patricia B. Schappert, *Managing Housekeeping Operations,* 2d ed. (East Lansing, Mich.: Educational Institute of the American Hotel & Motel Association, 1997).

8. For students desiring a good introductory text to food and beverage operations, see Jack D. Ninemeier, *Management of Food and Beverage Operations,* 2d ed. (East Lansing, Mich.: Educational Institute of the American Hotel & Motel Association, 1990).

9. Peter E. Drucker, *Management: Tasks, Responsibilities, Practices* (New York: Harper & Row, 1974), p. 61.

10. For more information on the responsibilities of a hotel's engineering division, see David M. Stipanuk and Harold Roffmann, *Hospitality Facilities Management and Design* (East Lansing, Mich.: Educational Institute of the American Hotel & Motel Association, 1992); and Michael H. Redlin and David M. Stipanuk, *Managing Hospitality Engineering Systems* (East Lansing, Mich.: Educational Institute of the American Hotel & Motel Association, 1987).

11. PKF Consulting, "Trends in the Hotel Industry—1996."

12. Robert E. Aulbach, "Water and Energy: Limited Commodities," *Lodging,* December 1988, p. 43.

13. Legal ramifications of hotel security are covered in Part Three of Jack P. Jefferies, *Understanding Hospitality Law,* 3d ed. (East Lansing, Mich.: Educational Institute of the American Hotel & Motel Association, 1995). The security responsibilities of hotel managers and hotel security programs are the subjects of Raymond C. Ellis, Jr., and the Security Committee of AH&MA, *Security and Loss Prevention Management* (East Lansing, Mich.: Educational Institute of the American Hotel & Motel Association, 1986).

14. Much of the following information appeared in John P. S. Salmen, "The ADA and You," *Lodging Magazine,* November 1991, pp. 97–107.

15. Beverly Stephen, "Fed by Med," *Food Arts,* January/February 1993, p. 77.

16. Stephen, p. 77.

17. *Miami Herald,* Weekly Business, April 12, 1993, from the *New York Times.*

18. Horst Schulze, speaking at the "Quest for Excellence" conference, February 1993.

19. Judy Z. King, Sixth Annual AH&MA National Conference for Quality, San Francisco, July 7–9, 1993.

20. Cheri Henderson, "Putting on the Ritz," *TQM Magazine,* November/December 1992.

## Key Terms

**accounting division**—Responsible for keeping track of the many business transactions that occur in a hotel and managing the hotel's finances.

**assets**—Resources available for use by the business, i.e., anything owned by the business that has monetary value.

**average daily rate (ADR)**—A key rooms department operating ratio: rooms revenue divided by number of rooms sold. Also called average room rate.

**balance sheet**—A financial statement that provides information on the financial position of a business by showing its assets, liabilities, and equity on a given date.

**capture rate**—The percentage of hotel guests who eat meals at the hotel.

**card keys**—Plastic cards, resembling credit cards, that are used in place of metal guestroom keys. Card keys require electronic locks.

**catering department**—A department within the food and beverage division of a hotel. Responsible for arranging and planning food and beverage functions for (1) conventions and smaller hotel groups, and (2) local banquets booked by the sales department.

**commissions**—Retailers located off the hotel site (such as gift shops, car rental agencies, and photographers) that pay a commission to the hotel based on a percentage of their gross sales to guests.

**concessions**—Facilities that might well be operated by the hotel directly, such as a beauty salon or fitness club, but are turned over to independent operators. The hotel in turn receives a flat fee, a minimum fee plus a percentage of the gross receipts over a specific amount, or a percentage of total gross sales.

**cost centers**—Divisions or departments within a hotel that do not directly generate income. They provide support for the revenue centers. Also known as support centers.

**engineering division**—Responsible for taking care of the hotel's physical plant and controlling energy costs.

**familiarization (fam) tours**—Free or reduced-rate travel programs designed by hotel personnel to acquaint travel agents and others with the hotel and stimulate sales.

**financial controls**—Financial statements, operating ratios, and other financial statistics that managers can use to keep track of operations and make sure financial goals are being attained.

**food and beverage division**—Responsible for preparing and serving food and beverages within a hotel. Also includes catering and room service.

**front office**—A hotel's command post for processing reservations, registering guests, settling guest accounts, and checking guests in and out.

**housekeeping department**—A department of the rooms division responsible for cleaning the hotel's guestrooms and public areas.

**human resources division**—Responsible for recruiting, orienting, training, evaluating, motivating, rewarding, disciplining, developing, promoting, and communicating with hotel employees.

**liabilities**—Obligations of a business—largely indebtedness related to the expenses incurred in the process of generating income.

**marketing division**—Responsible for identifying prospective guests for the hotel, conforming the products and services of the hotel as much as possible to meet the needs of those prospects, and persuading prospects to become guests.

**night audit**—An accounting task usually performed between 11:00 P.M. and 6:00 A.M. A night audit verifies that guest charges have been accurately posted to each guest

**occupancy percentage**—A ratio indicating management's success in selling its "product." For hotels or motels, it is referred to as the occupancy rate and is calculated by dividing the number of rooms sold by the number of rooms available. For food service operations, it is referred to as seat turnover and is calculated by dividing the number of people served by the number of seats available.

**property management system (PMS)**—A computerized system that helps managers and other personnel carry out a number of front-of-the-house and back-of-the-house functions. A PMS can support a variety of applications software that helps managers in their data gathering and reporting responsibilities.

**purchasing department**—Responsible for buying, receiving, storing, and issuing all the products used in a hotel.

**quality controls**—Standards of operation, quality assurance programs, and other controls that seek to establish and maintain products and services at quality levels established by management.

**rentals**—Enterprises such as offices or stores that pay rent to a hotel.

**reservations department**—A department within a hotel's rooms division staffed by skilled telemarketing personnel who take reservations over the phone, answer questions about facilities, quote prices and available dates, and sell to callers who are shopping around.

**revenue centers**—Divisions or departments within a hotel that directly generate income through the sale of products or services to guests.

**revenue per available room (REVPAR)**—A statistic used by operators to evaluate the performance of the rooms department. It is computed by dividing room revenue by the number of available rooms for the same period. It also can be determined by multiplying the occupancy percentage by the average daily rate for the same period.

**rooms division**—The largest, and usually most profitable, division in a hotel. It typically consists of four departments: front office, reservations, housekeeping, and uniformed service.

**room service**—The department within a food and beverage division that is responsible for delivering food or beverages to guests in their guestrooms. May also be responsible for preparing the food and beverages.

**security division**—Responsible for the protection of guests and their property, employees and their property, and the hotel itself.

**statement of income**—A financial statement of the results of operations that presents the sales, expenses, and net income of a business for a stated period of time.

**telephone department**—Responsible for providing telephone and other services (such as wake-up calls) to hotel guests.

**uniformed service department**—A hotel department within the rooms division that deals with guests' luggage and transportation and provides concierge services. Also referred to as the guest service department.

**yield management**—A hotel pricing system adapted from the airlines that uses a hotel's computer reservation system to track advance bookings and then lower or raise prices accordingly—on a day-to-day basis—to yield the maximum revenue. Before selling a room in advance, the hotel forecasts the probability of being able to sell the room to other market segments that are willing to pay higher rates.

## Review Questions

1. What is the difference between a revenue center and a cost center?
2. Which division provides the largest source of revenue for most hotels?
3. What are some of the duties of a front desk agent?
4. How is a typical housekeeping department organized?
5. Why do some food and beverage divisions lose money?
6. What changes have occurred in hotel telephone departments?
7. What are the marketing division's challenges and responsibilities? the engineering division's?
8. How have the new human resources divisions changed from the old personnel divisions?
9. What are the elements of a good security program?
10. What are two of the most important types of controls for managers and how are they used?

## Internet Sites

For more information, visit the following Internet sites. Remember that Internet addresses can change without notice. If the site is no longer there, use a search engine to look for additional sites.

*Hotel Companies/Resorts*

Club Med
www.clubmed.com

Four Seasons Hotels
www.fourseasons.com

Hilton Hotels
www.hilton.com

Holiday Inns
www.holiday-inn.com.

Mandarin Oriental Hotel Group
www.mandarin-oriental.com

Marriott International
www.marriott.com

Opryland Hotel
www.opryhotel.com

Ritz-Carlton Hotels
www.ritzcarlton.com

St. Michaels Harbour Inn
www.friend.ly.net/harbour

Swissôtel
www.swissotel.com

Walt Disney Corporation
www.disney.com

Westin Hotels
www.westin.com

*Organizations, Consultants, Resources*

Americans with Disabilities Act
www.jan.wvu.edu/links/adalinks.htm

Arthur D. Little Consultants
www.arthurdlittle.com

AT&T
www.att.com

PKF Consulting
www.delve.com/pkf/

*Publications*

LODGING
www.lodgingmagazine.com

TQM
www.mcb.co.uk/tqm.htm

*Software/Hardware Companies*

CLS Software (yield management)
www.maisystems.com

CSS Hotel Systems (PMS)
www.csshotelsystems.com

RBS Computer Systems (PMS)
www.rbscc.com

Yield Management TriCorp, Inc.
www.ymwerks.com

## REVIEW QUIZ

When you feel you have covered all of the material in this chapter, answer these questions. Choose the *best* answer.

1. Which of the following is a responsibility of the executive housekeeper of a large hotel?

    a. controlling linen inventories
    b. scheduling maintenance employees
    c. re-coding card keys
    d. training bellpersons

2. What is the formula for calculating the average daily rate?

    a. rooms occupied divided by rooms revenue
    b. rooms occupied divided by rooms available
    c. rooms revenue divided by rooms available, multiplied by 100
    d. rooms revenue divided by rooms occupied

3. A business operated inside a hotel by an independent operator, from which the hotel receives income, is called a:

    a. commission.
    b. rental.
    c. concession.
    d. vendor.

4. Which of the following statements about a hotel's catering department is *false?*

    a. Depending on the hotel, the catering manager may report to the food and beverage manager, the director of sales, or the hotel's general manager.
    b. Catering sales can represent as much as 75 percent of a hotel's total food and beverage sales.
    c. The catering department is an image-maker for a hotel.
    d. The catering department plans and puts on food and beverage functions for local banquets booked by the hotel's sales department.

5. Which of the following is a typical activity of a hotel marketing division?

    a. taking reservations
    b. designing banquet formats
    c. participating in trade shows
    d. training front desk agents

## REVIEW QUIZ *(continued)*

6. As a result of the Americans with Disabilities Act:
    a. all hotels are expected to have at least 10 percent of their parking spaces designated as "handicapped" parking.
    b. hotel restaurants must have accessible paths at least 36 inches (91.4 centimeters) wide between tables.
    c. visual fire alarms are required in all guestrooms.
    d. a and c.

7. Guests' perception of quality depends to a large degree on:
    a. their expectations.
    b. how far they have traveled that day.
    c. how much money they make.
    d. their level of education.

**Answer Key:** 1-a-C1, 2-d-C1, 3-c-C2, 4-b-C2, 5-c-C3, 6-b-C3, 7-a-C4

Each question is linked to a competency. Competencies are listed on the first page of the chapter. An answer reading 3-b-C4 translates to:

- 3: the question number
- b: the correct answer
- C4: the competency number

## Chapter 8 Outline

Background on Clubs
Types of Clubs
    City Clubs
    Country Clubs
    Other Clubs
Club Ownership
    Equity Clubs
    Corporate or Developer Clubs
Club Organization
    The Club Manager
Club Operations
    Revenue
    Expenses
    Control
Chapter Summary

## Competencies

1. Summarize background information about clubs; list and describe types of city clubs; and describe country, yacht, fraternal, and military clubs.

2. Compare equity clubs with corporate or developer clubs; outline club organization and the duties, personal attributes, and advancement opportunities of a club manager; list and describe typical revenue sources for clubs; and give examples of club expenses and controls.

# 8

# Club Organization and Operation

IN THIS CHAPTER we will discuss the organization and management of private clubs. The chapter explains the different kinds of clubs and their membership composition. It also describes how clubs are owned, organized, and managed. We then examine the unique aspects of clubs, including their sources of revenue, and profile several prominent clubs and their memberships.

## Background on Clubs

Private clubs are gathering places for club members only. They bring together people of like interests. Those interests could be recreational, social, fraternal, or professional.

Private clubs are not an invention of modern society. Wealthy citizens of ancient Greece and Rome formed clubs. Clubs have been an integral part of the social fabric of upper-class English society for centuries. As the English colonized the world, they established clubs. English social clubs and the golf club of St. Andrews in Scotland are the forerunners of city clubs and country clubs in the United States. Some U.S. city clubs, such as the Somerset Club in Boston, the San Francisco Commercial Club, and the Wilmington Club in Delaware, date back to the mid-nineteenth century. Perhaps the oldest country club—founded in 1882—is located in Brookline, Massachusetts.

In many parts of the world the club you belong to is an indication of your position in society. Comedian Groucho Marx sent a telegram to the Friar's Club in Manhattan, to which he belonged: "Please accept my resignation. I don't want to belong to any club that will accept me as a member." Marx was commenting on the fact that many people join clubs to enhance their own social status. While some clubs continue to be vestiges of the class system, by and large the exclusionary aspect of private clubs in the United States has changed due to equal rights legislation and society's increased social consciousness.

Today there are about 14,000 private clubs in America, providing diverse opportunities in management. Private club management is closely related to hotel and food service management. Many of a club manager's responsibilities in the areas of guest relations, human resource management, marketing, control, and maintenance are similar to those of a hotel manager's. Most clubs have dining facilities. In fact, some have multiple dining rooms and lounges as well as extensive private meeting rooms for catering. In addition to these facilities, many city

**Some clubs are like resort hotels. In fact, some clubs become resort hotels. The Jekyll Island Clubhouse on Jekyll Island, Georgia, was built in 1887 and was the nucleus for many of the private club's activities. A large clubhouse annex was built around the turn of the century. Following a $17 million restoration, the clubhouse opened in December 1986 as a world-class hotel—The Jekyll Island Club.** (Courtesy of the Jekyll Island Authority, Jekyll Island, Georgia)

clubs have gymnasiums, racquetball courts, and guestrooms for overnight guests. Country clubs may have dining rooms, meeting rooms, one or more golf courses, a tennis club, a beach club, and even a skeet-and trap-shooting club. Such country clubs are like resort hotels, except that they are not open to the public.

Clubs managed by the same company, as well as independent city and country clubs, have various types of reciprocal agreements so that their members can use the facilities of similar clubs when traveling. The Downtown Athletic Club in New York City has reciprocal agreements with clubs all over the United States, including the Petroleum Club of Los Angeles, the Bankers Club in Miami, and the Boston Athletic Club, as well as with clubs in Hawaii, Australia, the Bahamas, Canada, England, Hong Kong, Japan, Germany, and even Hungary! Typically, members secure an introductory guest card or letter of introduction to the club they wish to visit before leaving on their trip, although simply presenting their current membership card in their own club will often get them into an affiliated club.

There are some similarities in the organization of clubs and hotels. A basic difference between clubs and hotels is that the club's "guest" is a dues-paying member with a financial and emotional attachment to the club, whereas hotels are open to the public and the relationship between the guest and the hotel is less personal.

# Types of Clubs

There are two basic types of private clubs: city clubs and country clubs. There are also some private clubs that do not easily fit into either of these classifications, which we will discuss under a third classification called "other private clubs."

## City Clubs

**City clubs** vary in size, type, facilities, and membership. Some clubs own their own real estate; others lease space in office buildings or hotels. What they have in common is that food service is generally offered and a manager is hired to oversee the entire operation. The basic types of city clubs are:

- Athletic
- Dining
- Professional
- Social
- University

**Athletic.** Athletic clubs are as varied as the club industry itself. The Downtown Athletic Club, known for its annual award of the Heisman Trophy, occupies an entire building in downtown Manhattan in New York City. Its 35 stories—plus a sun deck—contain 136 guestrooms; dining rooms with a total capacity of 1,000; conference rooms; and extensive health club facilities, including squash and handball courts and an indoor swimming pool. It also sponsors many social programs. The Dayton Racquet Club in Dayton, Ohio, is a more modest facility located on the top floor of a 29-story office building. Squash is the main athletic activity, but a running track and fitness equipment are available. The club also has dining facilities.

**Dining.** The number of dining clubs located in office buildings proliferated in the 1960s. Building owners offered them mainly to induce companies to lease office space. Many dining clubs are only open for lunch—these clubs are usually referred to as luncheon clubs. In some instances, facilities that are used exclusively as private luncheon clubs during the day are open to the public for dinner in the evening. Some dining clubs located in downtown office buildings remain open for cocktails after work, and a few even serve dinner, but most shut down quite early unless they have some lodging facilities.

The Marco Polo Club, located in the Waldorf-Astoria in New York City, is a dining club that leases space from the hotel. Although the club is operated as a separate entity open only to club members and their guests, the food served in the club is made in the Waldorf-Astoria's kitchens, with production supervised by the club's manager.

**Professional.** Professional clubs are dining and social clubs for people in the same profession. Clubs of this nature include the Press Club in Washington, D.C., for journalists, the Lawyers' Club in New York City for attorneys, and the Friars Club (also in New York City) for actors and other theater people.

**The Downtown Athletic Club.** (Courtesy of the Downtown Athletic Club, New York, New York)

One famous professional club located on Gramercy Park in New York City is the National Arts Club, founded in 1898 by Charles de Kay, at that time the literary and art critic for the *New York Times*. De Kay's aim was to unite all the arts—painting, sculpture, music, and literature—and allow serious patrons to mingle with the men and women whose works they admired and collected.[1] Mark Twain was one of the early members of this club, as was the American painter George Bellows.

**Social.** Members of a social club may have no affiliation except that they enjoy being in each other's company. These clubs were modeled originally after men's social clubs in London such as Boodle's, St. James, and White's, where persons from similar backgrounds could meet with each other at the end of the day for cocktails and general companionship or entertainment unrelated to business. Indeed, in some social clubs it was considered bad manners to talk about business.

**Some city clubs offer facilities such as lounges and swimming pools to their members.** (Courtesy of the Downtown Athletic Club, New York, New York)

The oldest social club in America is said to be the Fish House in Philadelphia, founded in 1832. To ensure that the Fish House would always be socially oriented rather than business oriented, it was formed as a men's cooking club, with each member taking turns preparing meals for the membership.[2] Social clubs in Manhattan include the Union League Club, founded in 1863; the Knickerbocker Club, started by author Washington Irving for gentlemen with New York roots; and the Links Club, which was originally established "to promote and conserve throughout the United States the best interests and true spirit of the game of golf." Links Club members include business leaders and politicians from all over the country. In New Orleans there's the Louisiana Club, and on the West Coast the most famous social club is San Francisco's Bohemian Club, founded in 1847. This club, which occupies a handsome red-brick Georgian clubhouse on the side of Nob Hill, has a 750-seat theater where members perform amateur theatricals. The club also owns a 280-acre estate in the Sierra Nevada, where members gather every summer for a two-week "encampment," during which there are poetry readings, musical productions, and concerts presented by the club's own 70-piece orchestra.[3]

In recent years social clubs have been founded for other purposes besides leisure, recreation, and camaraderie. One such club is the Commerce Club in Atlanta, Georgia, whose stated purpose is "to provide, for the political, business, and civic leadership of metropolitan Atlanta, club facilities and programs designed to stimulate and maintain vigorous and healthy communication and discourse on issues of common interest affecting metropolitan Atlanta, in an environment offering comfortable surroundings, modern meeting facilities, and the finest food and service."

**University.** University clubs are private clubs for university graduates or individuals otherwise affiliated with a university (university employees, for example). Some clubs of this nature are quite open. For instance, the University Club in Seattle is not affiliated with any university, and to be eligible to join you only have to be a university graduate. Other university clubs are for graduates of specific schools and exist in cities where there may be a large concentration of alumni who either live there or visit often. In New York City, for example, Harvard, Princeton, Yale, and Cornell have their own clubs with restaurants, health clubs, guestrooms, and regular activities such as lectures and concerts. The largest of these clubs is the Yale Club. Guestrooms, dining facilities, meeting and banquet rooms, an indoor swimming pool, and a gymnasium are provided for Yale (and Dartmouth) alumni. The club stands on the exact spot where one of Yale's most celebrated sons, Nathan Hale, uttered the famous phrase, "I regret that I have but one life to give for my country," before being hanged by the British during the Revolutionary War for spying.

## Country Clubs

The largest single type of private club is the country club. **Country clubs** are primarily recreational and social facilities for individuals and families who live nearby. These clubs often have separate children's facilities and do a large catering business, since it is common for members to hold bar and bat mitzvahs, weddings, and other social events at them.

In one study of 30,000 club members, dining and golf were cited as the most important reasons for joining a club. In fact, dining was mentioned by more than 50 percent as the most important activity. Frank Vain, president of the McMahon Group (which did the study), tells club managers, "The food at your club must compete with, and surpass, the wide choices of dining that are available in the community if you expect to have consistent member usage."[4]

Since country clubs need a great deal of land (one 18-hole golf course typically requires a minimum of 110 acres), they are usually located in suburban or rural locales. Exceptions sometimes occur when a nearby city develops to the extent that the urban sprawl comes up to or surrounds the club. The Hillcrest Country Club in Los Angeles is a case in point. When it opened in 1920, the locale was suburban Los Angeles. Now it is surrounded by Beverly Hills and Century City. Other once-suburban country clubs include the Chevy Chase Country Club in metropolitan Washington, D.C., and the Everglades Country Club on fashionable Worth Avenue in Palm Beach, Florida.

In some cases, new clubs are financed by prospective members, who are asked to invest in the club by buying shares of stock. A new club can cost $50 million to build. It is not unusual for members who wish to join to be asked to buy as much as $150,000 worth of stock, as well as pay membership dues of at least $1,000 a month.

In addition to a clubhouse with one or more dining rooms and function rooms, most country clubs have at least one golf course and one swimming pool. In

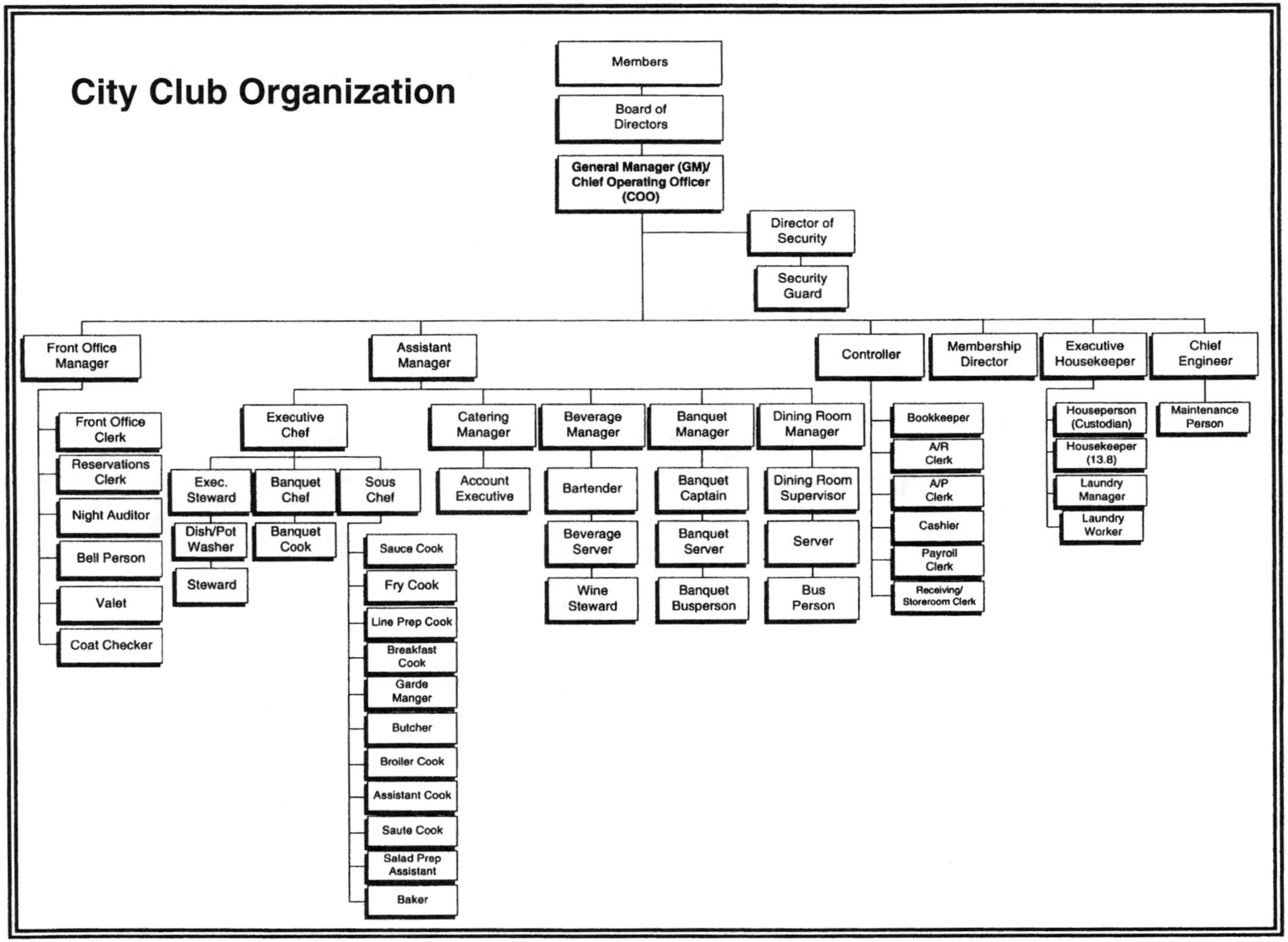

# City Club Organization

Source: CMAA.

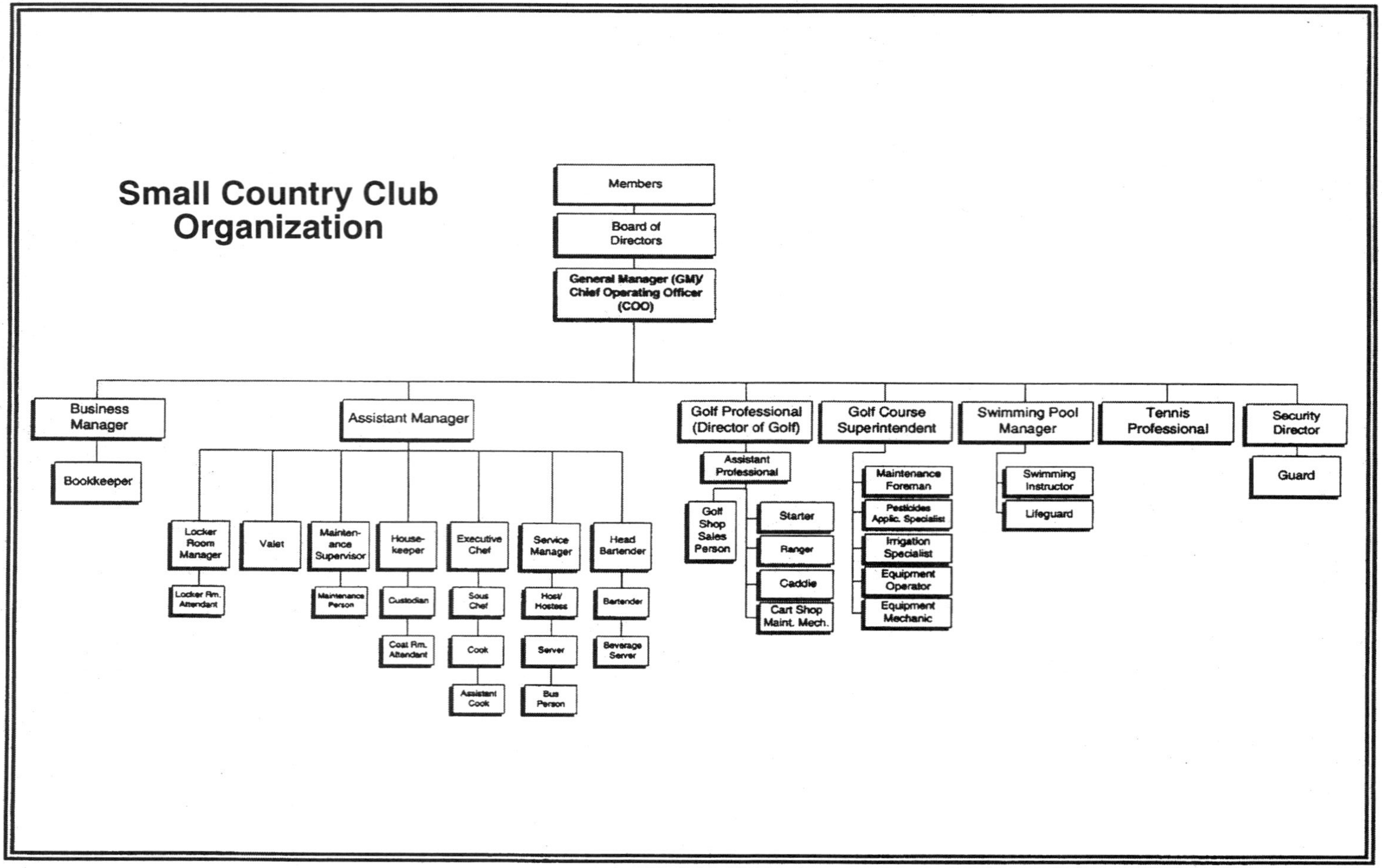

# Small Country Club Organization

- Members
- Board of Directors
- General Manager (GM)/Chief Operating Officer (COO)

## Business Manager
- Bookkeeper

## Assistant Manager
- Locker Room Manager
  - Locker Rm. Attendant
- Valet
- Maintenance Supervisor
  - Maintenance Person
- Housekeeper
  - Custodian
  - Coat Rm. Attendant
- Executive Chef
  - Sous Chef
  - Cook
  - Assistant Cook
- Service Manager
  - Host/Hostess
  - Server
  - Bus Person
- Head Bartender
  - Bartender
  - Beverage Server

## Golf Professional (Director of Golf)
- Assistant Professional
  - Golf Shop Sales Person
- Starter
- Ranger
- Caddie
- Cart Shop Maint. Mech.

## Golf Course Superintendent
- Maintenance Foreman
- Pesticides Applic. Specialist
- Irrigation Specialist
- Equipment Operator
- Equipment Mechanic

## Swimming Pool Manager
- Swimming Instructor
- Lifeguard

## Tennis Professional

## Security Director
- Guard

Source: CMAA.

the 1970s, the popularity of tennis grew so much that tennis courts became almost a mandatory part of the recreational facilities for a country club. In a study conducted by the Club Managers Association of America (CMAA), 80 percent of the country clubs reporting had outdoor tennis courts and 10 percent had indoor courts. Other facilities indicated in the study were steam rooms, fitness and exercise rooms, paddle tennis, and racquetball.

There are a number of country clubs known for their beautiful facilities and exclusivity. One such is the Owentsia Club in Lake Forest, Illinois, its name derived from the Iroquois word meaning "a meeting place in the country for sporting braves and squaws." The golf course of the Mid-Ocean Club in Bermuda (founded in 1921) was played by Sir Winston Churchill, Presidents Eisenhower and Bush, and baseball legend Babe Ruth; the *World Atlas of Golf* calls its par-4 fifth hole "one of the world's unforgettable holes."[5] Other clubs are famous for their outstanding golf courses and the tournaments held there. Examples include the Pebble Beach Country Club in Pebble Beach, California, and the Royal St. George's Golf Club in Sandwich, England.

## Other Clubs

There are other types of private clubs that engage professional managers to operate their facilities and manage their social and recreational programs.

**Yacht.** Yacht clubs are located near large bodies of water. Their main purpose is to provide marinas and other facilities for boat owners. While many of these clubs have tennis courts, swimming pools, and elaborate clubhouses with dining rooms and lounges, others provide only the bare necessities of dock space, fuel, and boating supplies.

One famous club is the Grosse Pointe Yacht Club in Grosse Pointe Shores, Michigan, founded in 1923 by a group that included automaker Edsel Ford. The club's facilities include an enormous ballroom, a domed main dining room overlooking the harbor, and slips for 300 boats. The club is managed by John "Jack" R. Sullivan, a past president of CMAA. Sullivan made family entertainment an important part of club activities. For example, he introduced a family evening the night before the annual regatta dinner—as many as 600 club members and guests attend. Some families have three or four generations in attendance.[6]

**Fraternal.** The Elks and the Veterans of Foreign Wars are examples of fraternal clubs. Fraternal organizations sometimes own or rent entire buildings or floors within a building. Some offer food and beverage service, overnight accommodations, and rooms for meetings and recreation. Fraternal clubs also require professional managers.

**Military.** The armed services operate officers clubs and noncommissioned officers clubs. Most have clubhouses with dining and function facilities. Some have lodging facilities, recreational facilities, and social programs similar to civilian private clubs and resorts. One such facility is the Hale Koa Hotel at the Armed Forces Recreation Center in Fort DeRussy, Hawaii, which is on one of the nicest parts of Waikiki Beach. In Europe, the armed forces operate hotels and recreation centers in

Garmisch, Berchtesgaden, and Chiemsee—all in Bavaria. In recent years the Department of Defense has hired civilians to manage military clubs instead of using military personnel. Some commissioned and noncommissioned clubs have been combined as part of the U.S. military's downsizing.

## Club Ownership

Private clubs are usually owned in one of two ways. A club can be owned by some of its members; such clubs are called equity clubs. Those members who fund the purchase or development of an equity club are known as founder-members. Or a club can be owned by a company that sells memberships in the club. These for-profit clubs are also known as corporate or developer clubs or, less frequently, as proprietary clubs.

### Equity Clubs

**Equity clubs** are generally nonprofit, since they are typically formed not for money-making purposes but simply for the enjoyment of their members. Members are either (1) founder-members, or (2) other members who pay a one-time initiation fee and annual dues. If an equity club has an excess of revenues over expenses, the profits are not given back to the founder-members but are invested in improving the club's facilities and services. Because equity clubs are not formed to make a profit, the nonprofit statute of the tax law exempts the club from federal and state income taxes, although clubs may be required to pay taxes on unrelated income (such as nonmember functions) as well as federal and state payroll taxes.

Nontransfer of profits to members is only one part of what gives an equity club its nonprofit status. To receive a tax exemption, an equity club must be formed solely for pleasure and recreation, and must not discriminate on the basis of sex, race, or religion against anyone who wishes to become a member. Discrimination is often practiced on other grounds, however. Sometimes clubs charge high initiation fees or require members to buy expensive bonds or membership shares. And it is perfectly within the rights of a club to turn down applicants because they are not qualified by reason of accomplishment, professional occupation, or—as in the case of the Bohemian Club—artistic talent.

### Corporate or Developer Clubs

As mentioned earlier, **corporate clubs** or developer clubs operate for profit and are owned by individuals or corporations. Persons who wish to become members purchase a membership, not a share in the club. Members may or may not be involved in running the club.

Corporate or developer clubs proliferated with the real estate boom in office buildings, condominiums, and single housing developments. Just as having a dining club in office buildings helped developers rent office space, a country club at the center of a condominium or housing development was a good marketing tactic that not only helped to sell or lease properties but raised their prices by offering an added value to buyers.

The major company in the business of club management is the ClubCorp Company. This Dallas-based company operates 250 country and city clubs nationwide. In 1984, with the purchase of the Pinehurst Resort and Country Club, CCC broadened its business by going into resort hotel management. Later, they added daily-fee golf courses to their management portfolio. This was not surprising in view of the similarity between country clubs and resorts.

Some corporate or developer clubs are built exclusively for the use of employees of particular companies and are owned and operated by those companies. The DuPont Country Club in Wilmington, Delaware, is one of those clubs. Only employees of the DuPont company, members of their immediate families, and retired employees may join this club. The 10,300-member club is one of the largest private clubs in the world. Its facilities include 29 tennis courts, a lawn-bowling green, and four 18-hole golf courses. There are three dining rooms and 13 banquet and meeting rooms. The club has annual sales of more than $10 million, with food and beverage accounting for half that volume.[7]

# Club Organization

How a club is organized depends to a large extent on whether the club is nonprofit or for-profit. In a nonprofit equity club, the members elect a board of directors (sometimes called a board of governors) to oversee the budget and set policy affecting membership and club use. Here the board is the governing body, and the club manager reports to the board and implements its policies and decisions (see Exhibit 1). In a for-profit corporate or developer club, the club manager reports to and receives instructions as to club policies, procedures, and standards from the club's owners (see Exhibit 2). A corporate or developer club may have a board of directors made up of club members, if the owners wish to give the members some sense of authority, but generally this board merely advises the owners and does not make policy.

The number of members on an equity club's board usually ranges from 12 to 25, although sometimes it is even higher. Board officers typically include a chairperson (usually last year's president), president, vice president, and treasurer.

Committees are extremely important to club morale and operation because they allow more members to participate in managing the club. In addition to special committees that are appointed for specific social or sporting events, clubs generally have five standing committees: a house committee, a membership committee, a finance and budget committee, an entertainment committee, and an athletic committee.[8]

## The Club Manager

Club managers were not considered to be necessary until the early 1920s. Up to that time, most private clubs were managed by the members through the standing committees and the board of governors. Generally, the clubhouse was run by a steward, and the sports facilities were overseen by a sports professional. Today, we recognize that club management is a profession requiring special training and expertise.

The duties of a **club manager** can vary considerably, depending on the kind of club he or she works for and the way it is organized. Some clubs have a general

**Exhibit 1    Sample Organization Chart for an Equity Club**

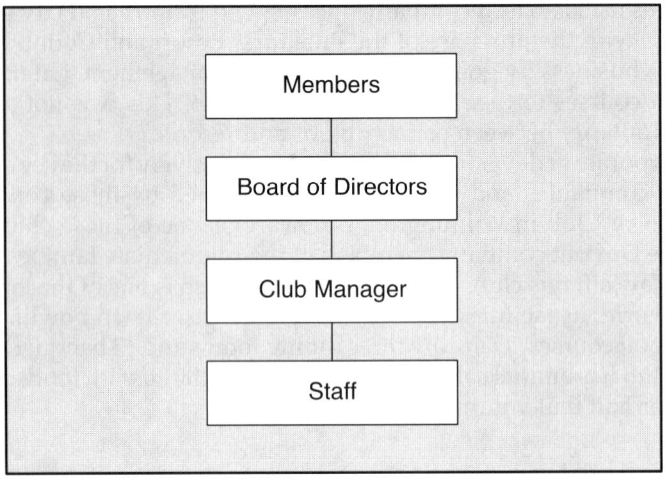

```
        Members
           |
   Board of Directors
           |
      Club Manager
           |
         Staff
```

In an equity club, the members own the club and elect a board of directors (who are also members of the club) to oversee the budget and set club policies. The club manager reports to the board or a member of the board.

**Exhibit 2    Sample Organization Chart for a Corporate or Developer Club**

```
    Owners  - - - - -  Board of Directors
       |
   Club Manager
       |
     Staff
       |
    Members

- - - - - - -  Advisory only
```

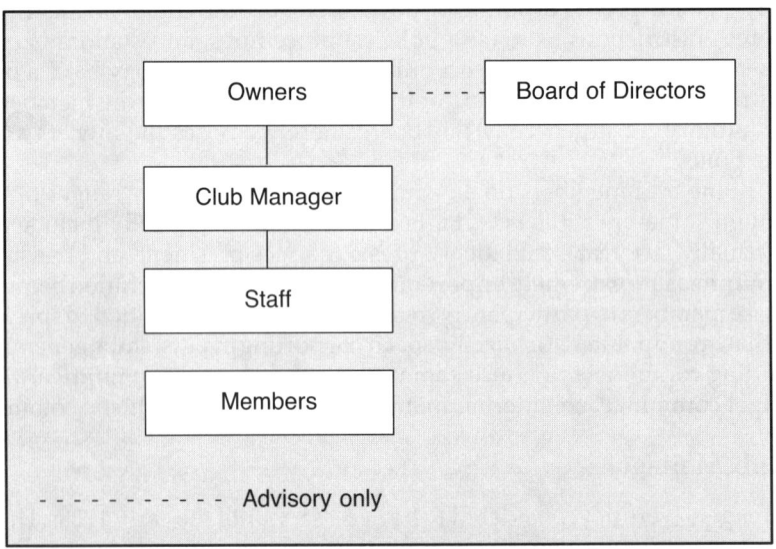

In a corporate or developer club, the club is owned by a corporation or developer, not the club's members. Members may or may not be involved in running the club. For example, the club's owners may form a board of directors, made up of club members, to advise them on club matters. The club manager reports to the corporation or developer, not the club's members.

manager; others have a clubhouse manager. The difference is that a general manager has responsibility for all the employees of the club, while a clubhouse manager may only be responsible for employees working in the clubhouse. For example, a country club may have a clubhouse manager in charge of clubhouse operations and personnel, while the club's sports facilities are operated by athletic professionals. A list of the areas of competency needed by general managers is shown in Exhibit 3. In corporate or developer clubs the trend is to have one general manager in charge of everything, because members are too busy to take an interest in all of the details involved in running a club.

According to CMAA, club managers who excel have certain personal qualities and abilities in common:

1. Effectiveness in interpersonal relations
2. Dedication—commitment to the welfare of the club
3. Integrity
4. A strong sense of organization and an ability to administer
5. Creativity and vision
6. Intelligence
7. Professionalism
8. Ability to communicate well
9. Strong leadership capability
10. Industry experience[9]

A career in club management can be very rewarding, but a club manager's job is extraordinarily complex. The Thornblade Club in Greenville, South Carolina, finally had to resort to an "executive headhunter" to find a qualified professional. The Thornblade Club's manager "has to know golf, tennis, pools, maintenance—not to mention 190 wines on the club's wine list," bemoaned Howard Covington, Jr., the club's president. "He's responsible for all the budget numbers, the pro formas, and responding to membership."[10] Wages for club managers vary according to the size and type of club (see Exhibit 4).

In one respect a club manager's job is more complex than that of a hotel or restaurant manager's. The jobs are similar to the extent that each manager must manage physical facilities, employees, and services in order to meet economic objectives. In addition, each must hire, train, fire, and set standards of service. Where the jobs differ—and what makes a club manager's job more complex—is that club managers must share planning and budgeting responsibilities with an on-site board of directors, and club members have a more direct say in whether a manager keeps his or her job than hotel or restaurant guests do. In an equity club, a club manager must find a way to keep two groups relatively happy: (1) a board whose members may have diverse points of view because they were elected by different factions within the membership who do not agree, and (2) a variety of members with differing wants and needs. To do this, a club manager must be a master politician.

**Exhibit 3    Club Management Competency Areas for the GM/COO**

I. **Private Club Management**
- History of private clubs
- Types of private clubs
- Membership types
- Bylaws
- Policy formulation
- Board relations
- Chief Operating Officer concept
- Committees
- Career development
- Golf operations management
- Golf course management
- Tennis operations
- Swimming pool management
- Yacht facilities management
- Fitness center management
- Locker room management
- Club job descriptions

II. **Food and Beverage**
- Sanitation
- Menu Development
- Nutrition
- Pricing concepts
- Ordering/receiving/controls/inventory
- Food and beverage trends
- Quality Service
- Creativity in theme functions
- Design and equipment
- Food and beverage personnel
- Wine list development

III. **Accounting and Finance in the Private Club**
- Accounting and finance principles
- Uniform system of accounts
- Financial analysis
- Budgeting
- Cash flow forecasting
- Compensation and benefit administration
- Financing capital projects
- Audits
- Internal Revenue Service
- Computers
- Business office organization
- Long range financial planning

IV. **Human and Professional Resources**
- Employee relations
- Management styles
- Organizational development
- Balancing job and family responsibilities
- Time management
- Stress management
- Labor issues
- Leadership vs. management

V. **Building and Facilities Management**
- Preventive maintenance
- Insurance and risk management
- Clubhouse remodeling and renovation
- Contractors
- Energy and water resource management
- Housekeeping
- Security
- Laundry
- Lodging operations

VI. **External and Governmental Influences**
- Legislative influences
- Regulatory agencies
- Economic theory
- Labor law
- Privacy
- Club law
- Liquor liability
- Internal Revenue Service

VII. **Management and Marketing**
- Communication skills
- Marketing through in-house publications
- Professional image and dress
- Effective negotiation
- Member contact skills
- Working with the media
- Marketing strategies in a private club environment

Source: CMAA.

Exhibit 4   Club Manager Salaries

|  | Base Salary | Bonus | Fringe Benefits | Total |
|---|---|---|---|---|
| All Managers | $101,923.66 | $11,190.89 | $9,809.21 | $122,582.68 |
| Country Club | $101,095.45 | $10,472.75 | $9,951.72 | $121,566.75 |
| City Club | $111,522.35 | $16,373.06 | $10,024.95 | $136,654.75 |

Note: Figures reflect the average from the top 25 percent of the study. Source: Compensation and Benefits Summary Report 1995, Table IV, CMAA.

Exhibit 5   Sources of Club Revenue

|  | Country Clubs | City Clubs |
|---|---|---|
| Dues | 44.8% | 39.3% |
| Food | 24.9 | 36.0 |
| Beverages | 8.2 | 9.3 |
| Rooms | — | 2.8 |
| Sports Activities | 18.0 | — |
| All Other | 4.1 | 12.6 |
|  | 100.0% | 100.0% |

Source: *Clubs in Town & Country 1996* (New York: Pannell Kerr Forster Worldwide, 1996), pp. 9, 20.

Advancement in the club management field may require more mobility than in the hotel field. According to surveys done by CMAA, fewer than 20 percent of all CMAA-member club managers were employed as an assistant manager or department head at the same club they now manage.[11] An assistant manager or department head who wishes to advance usually must move to a different club. Club managers who wish to advance to a larger and more prestigious club obviously have to change jobs, which usually requires moving. But many club managers develop such a satisfying relationship with club members and officers that they never consider moving on.

## Club Operations

Clubs are similar to other hospitality businesses in that they generate revenue and incur expenses. Differences between clubs and other hospitality businesses can be found in the clubs' sources of revenue.

### Revenue

Since a club is a private enterprise used primarily by members, the bulk of its revenue is derived from its members (see Exhibit 5). Typical sources of club revenue are:

- Membership dues
- Initiation fees
- Assessments
- Sports activities fees
- Food and beverage sales
- Other sources of revenue

Membership dues, initiation fees, assessments, and sports activities fees help set clubs apart from hotels and restaurants, since hotels and restaurants do not earn revenue from these sources.

**Membership Dues. Membership dues** are the cost to a member for the exclusivity of the club. Unlike an operation open to the public, a private club has a limited number of patrons and hence a limited source of revenue. Membership dues subsidize all of the club's operating costs and fixed charges. Dues vary based on the type of club (city or country), the number of members, and the extent of the club's facilities and services. Because country clubs are generally more expensive to operate than city clubs, they usually have higher dues. According to a study by Pannell Kerr Forster, in 1995 the income per member derived from dues alone averaged $2,360 for country clubs, compared to only $1,032 for city clubs.[12]

It is common for a club to have several different membership dues based on different types of membership. This makes it possible for more persons to join and thus increases the membership base, which decreases costs for each member.

A good example of how a city club offers different types of memberships is the Cornell Club of New York. The Cornell Club occupies a 15-floor building with guestrooms, dining rooms, a lounge, and private meeting rooms. Here are the different memberships (each with a different dues structure) that are available:

- Resident—a member who resides within New York City
- Suburban—a member who resides within 50 miles of New York City but not within the city itself
- Nonresident—a member who resides more than 50 miles from New York City

Each of these memberships has six different levels of dues based on the number of years the member has been out of college. It is presumed, of course, that the ones who have been graduates for the greatest number of years can afford the highest dues.

In addition to these memberships, the Cornell Club offers special memberships for persons who are not Cornell graduates but are associated with the university (such as full-time faculty and staff). These special memberships are also categorized as resident, suburban, or nonresident. There is even a Cornell couple membership and a spouse membership.

Country clubs usually have a larger number of membership categories than city clubs. Some people are just interested in a social membership at a country club—they wish to eat there and socialize with friends at the swimming pool but are not interested in playing golf or tennis. Other members want to make full use of the club's recreational facilities and purchase a regular or active membership. Some clubs offer single or family memberships. A few country clubs have a nonresident category. Many have a lifetime membership option for those willing to make a large one-time payment for lifetime privileges.

An example of a club that offers its members a wide variety of memberships is the Grosse Pointe Yacht Club mentioned earlier. This club offers a choice of an active membership, an intermediate I membership for members aged 21-27, an intermediate II membership for members aged 28-34, two types of social memberships for those aged 21-34 and two for those 35-plus, two types of junior memberships, a nonresident membership, and even a special membership for clergy.

**Initiation Fees.** Most clubs charge new members an **initiation fee,** which in most cases is nonrefundable. Clubs vary in how they handle initiation fees. Some consider them contributions to capital and show them as additions to founder-members' equity (for equity clubs) or owners' equity (for corporate or developer clubs). Others add them to reserve funds for specific capital improvement projects such as refurbishing the clubhouse. Initiation fees typically range from $500 to $10,000, although a few clubs charge $100,000 or more.

**Assessments.** One-time or periodic **assessments** are sometimes imposed on members instead of increasing dues. Some assessments cover operational shortfalls. Others are used to raise capital for improvements to the club. Assessments are unpopular with members since they are unanticipated expenses. Therefore, instead of assessments, many clubs prefer to impose minimum spending requirements, usually on food and beverages. If a member does not spend a specified amount on food and beverages either on a monthly, quarterly, or annual basis, a bill is sent for the difference.

**Sports Activities Fees.** City clubs do not record revenue from sports activities because they typically do not charge members extra for using the club's recreational facilities. On the other hand, **sports activities fees** account for 18 percent of total country club revenues.[13] In country clubs where golf and tennis are significant activities, a golf professional and a tennis professional are responsible for programs in these sports. Fees are charged for playing tennis or golf and, in the case of golf, rental fees are charged for golf carts.

A golf course is an expensive facility, each year costing more than $54,800 per hole to maintain.[14] As Exhibit 6 shows, revenue derived directly from golf operations covers only a little more than half of golf costs. Membership dues or profits from other departments are necessary to make up the difference.

Sometimes other recreational facilities exist, such as a swimming pool, a health spa, and volleyball or squash courts. Members at most country clubs pay fees to use these facilities, with the exception of the swimming pools; swimming is usually free. If a club offers a lot of sports options, an athletic director might well be added to the staff to supervise all of the club's recreational facilities and programs.

Clubs with athletic facilities have committees for specific sports. Country clubs with a golf course have a **golf committee** that reports to the club's board and advises it on golf course policies such as appropriate course use and the course's

### Exhibit 6  Golf Course Expenses

| Average Cost per Hole, 1995 | Overall Averages |
|---|---|
| Payroll | $19,432 |
| Payroll Taxes and Employee Benefits | 4,144 |
| Course Supplies and Contracts | 6,766 |
| Repairs to Equipment, Course Buildings, Water and Drainage System, Etc. | 3,006 |
| All Other Expenses | 5,099 |
| Total Golf Course Expenses | $38,447 |
| Add: Golf Shop, Caddy, and Committee Expenses | 16,354 |
| Total Golf Expenses | $54,801 |
| Less: Income from Golf Fees, Golf Carts, Etc. | 31,876 |
| Net Golf Expenses | $22,925 |

Source: *Clubs in Town & Country 1996* (New York: Pannell Kerr Forster Worldwide, 1996), p. 11.

hours of operation. The committee works with the club's management in planning tournaments and preparing the golf course budget.

**Food and Beverage Sales.** After dues income, sales of food and beverages are the major source of revenue in both city clubs and country clubs. Like hotels and resorts, clubs often have more than one dining facility. City clubs with a single dining room tend to keep it formal and add a more informal tap room or grill. Country clubs usually operate snack bars at the pool or golf course, an informal dining room for lunch, and a formal dining room.

A club's dining facility must compete with independent restaurants in the surrounding area in terms of food quality and value. The Lake Mead Golf and Country Club near San Francisco conducts wine tastings and frequently puts on special dinners prepared by renowned European chefs to draw members away from competing restaurants. Club chefs are often promoted heavily and in some instances have become celebrities. Former executive chef Thomas Catherill of the Cherokee Town and Country Club in Atlanta is a gold medalist from the Culinary Olympics in Frankfurt, Germany. In Dallas, the Club at San Simeon lured a sizable share of banquet business away from prominent hotels by offering the locally renowned cuisine of their club chef.

In general, club members hold their club to higher standards of food quality and service than public restaurants. For this reason, in many cases food service becomes the main focus of the club, requiring the greatest part of the club manager's efforts.

**Other Sources of Revenue.** In addition to membership dues, initiation fees, assessments, sports activities fees, and food and beverage sales, there are other sources of revenue at some clubs. Most clubs charge **visitors' fees** for nonmembers who are guests of members and use rooms, buy food and beverages, or use recreational facilities. Often there are service charges on food and beverage sales, which may be

Exhibit 7  Sources of Club Expense

|  | Country Clubs | City Clubs |
|---|---|---|
| Operating Supplies and Expenses | 35.1% | 26.3% |
| Payroll and Related Costs | 46.2 | 50.3 |
| Cost of Food and Beverages Sold | 11.7 | 14.5 |
| Real Estate Taxes and Insurance | 5.0 | 5.2 |
| Balance Available for Debt Service, Capital Improvements, Etc. | 2.0 | 3.7 |
|  | 100.0% | 100.0% |

Source: *Clubs in Town & Country 1996* (New York: Pannell Kerr Forster Worldwide, 1996), pp. 9, 19.

distributed to employees or, as in most cases, are used to offset the club's labor costs. City clubs with overnight accommodations generate revenue from guestroom sales and may offer laundry and valet services for a fee. Country clubs have pro shops, operated by the club or by a concessionaire, that sell sports equipment, apparel, and (in some cases) a broad range of gift items.

## Expenses

Payroll is the single largest expense in operating a club, representing more than 46 percent of club expenses in country clubs and about 50 percent in city clubs (see Exhibit 7). The largest segment of payroll expenditure is in the food and beverage operation. Administrative payroll, which includes management and accounting staff, makes up about 12 percent of a country club's payroll and 16 percent of a city club's payroll.

In Exhibit 7, "Balance Available for Debt Service, Capital Improvements, Etc." shows how much income remains after all of the club's operating expenses have been paid. This income is used to pay fixed charges such as real-estate taxes, insurance on the club's buildings and their contents, and interest on borrowed money.

## Control

Like hotels and restaurants, clubs have a uniform accounting system. The *Uniform System of Financial Reporting for Clubs* is a manual published by CMAA.[15] In addition to a classification of accounts, the system provides for a reporting method that separates revenues and expenses into departments. This allows a club's managers, board of directors, members, and—if it is a corporate or developer club—owners to easily review operating results by department.

## Chapter Summary

Private clubs date back to ancient Greece and Rome, but the true forerunners of American private clubs (which now number more than 14,000) are the social and golf clubs of England and Scotland. While there are many similarities to managing clubs and hotels, there are some differences as well.

There are two basic types of clubs—city clubs and country clubs. City clubs can be categorized as athletic, dining, professional, social, or university.

Athletic clubs are often quite large, sometimes occupying entire downtown buildings, and may include lodging and dining facilities as well as gymnasiums, swimming pools, and courts for squash, handball, and racquetball.

Dining clubs are generally found in office buildings. Many of these clubs are open only for lunch.

A professional club is a dining or social club for people in a particular profession. There are clubs for lawyers, actors, artists, journalists, and other professionals.

Social clubs were originally modeled after men's social clubs in England. Although most social clubs do not discriminate on the basis of sex, race, or religion, some try to limit their membership to persons of the same social and economic background.

University clubs are private clubs for university graduates. Some university clubs have dining and meeting rooms, guestrooms, and extensive libraries and recreational facilities.

Other kinds of clubs include yacht clubs, fraternal clubs, and military clubs.

Most private clubs are equity clubs or corporate or developer clubs. Equity clubs are owned by a group of founder-members and are generally nonprofit, since they are formed not for money-making purposes but only for the enjoyment of their members. Corporate or developer clubs are for-profit clubs owned by companies that sell memberships in the clubs.

A club's organization depends on whether it is an equity or a corporate or developer club. The club manager is the hired professional responsible for guiding all of the elements of a club's operation.

The bulk of club revenues is derived from club members. These revenues fall into the following classifications: membership dues, initiation fees, assessments, sports activities fees, food and beverage sales, and other sources of revenue.

Membership dues are the cost to a member for the exclusivity of the club. It is common for city and country clubs to have several different types of memberships. A city club might have different membership dues for resident, suburban, and nonresident members, reflecting the location of the member's residence in relation to the location of the club. Country clubs tend to use a different type of dues structure, based on use of recreational facilities, a member's age, and other factors. In addition to dues, clubs generally charge initiation fees and, in some cases, special assessments.

Next to dues, food and beverage sales are the major source of club revenue. In recent years clubs have upgraded their food service in order to more successfully compete with public dining facilities.

Other sources of revenue include guestroom sales (for city clubs), visitors' fees, and service charges on food and beverage sales.

A club's payroll is its largest expense. Payroll represents approximately half the costs for operating city clubs and slightly less for country clubs.

Like hotels and restaurants, clubs have their own uniform system of financial reporting that helps club managers control and manage operations.

## Endnotes

1. Carole Klein, *Gramercy Park: An American Bloomsbury* (Boston: Houghton Mifflin, 1987), p. 159.
2. Stephen Birmingham, *America's Secret Aristocracy* (New York: Berkley Books, 1990), p. 209.
3. Birmingham, p. 213.
4. Frank Vain, "You've Heard of 'Everyman,' Now Meet 'Everyclub,'" *Club Management*, May–June 1993, p. 37.
5. Bermuda Department of Tourism.
6. Tom Finan, "Right on Pointe," *Club Management*, May–June 1993.
7. William Sullivan and Mary Lynn Duffy, "The DuPont Country Club: A Study in Automation," reprinted in *The Bottomline*, the Journal of the International Association of Hospitality Accountants, from Glenn R. Collins, *Hospitality Information Technology*. (Dubuque, Iowa: Kendall-Hunt, 1992).
8. Ted E. White and Larry C. Gerstner, *Club Operations and Management*, 2d ed. (New York: Van Nostrand Reinhold, 1991).
9. Club Managers Association of America, *Club Management Operations*, 4th ed. (Dubuque, Iowa: Kendall-Hunt, 1989), p. 27.
10. Amanda Bennett, "Grass Looks Greener for Golf-Club Managers," *Wall Street Journal*, 25 January 1990, p. B1.
11. *Club Management Operations*, p. 32.
12. *Clubs in Town & Country 1996* (New York: Pannell Kerr Forster Worldwide, 1996), pp. 4, 13.
13. *Clubs in Town & Country 1996*, p. 9.
14. *Clubs in Town & Country 1996*, p. 12.
15. Club Managers Association of America, 1733 King Street, Alexandria, Virginia 22314.

## Key Terms

**assessment**—A one-time or periodic charge imposed on private club members to cover operational shortfalls or raise capital for improvements to the club.

**city club**—An urban recreational and social facility that can be categorized as athletic, dining, professional, social, or university.

**club manager**—The hired professional responsible for guiding all of the elements of a private club's operation.

**corporate club**—A for-profit private club owned by a company that sells memberships in the club. Also called a developer or proprietary club.

**country club**—A private recreational and social facility for individuals and families who live in the surrounding area.

**equity club**—A nonprofit private club whose members buy shares in the club and, after expenses have been paid, invest any revenues left over into improving the club's facilities and services.

**golf committee**—A private country club committee composed of club members who establish golf course policy, review golf course budgets and operations, and oversee the care of the golf course(s).

**initiation fee**—A typically nonrefundable charge that new members must pay to join a private club.

**membership dues**—The cost to a private club member for the exclusivity provided by the club's limited membership. Membership dues subsidize all of the club's operating costs and fixed charges.

**sports activities fees**—Fees that country clubs charge members and visitors for using the club's recreational facilities.

**visitors' fees**—Charges to nonmembers of a private club who are guests of members and use rooms, buy food or beverages, or use recreational facilities.

## Review Questions

1. What is a basic difference between clubs and hotels?
2. What are the similarities and differences among the various types of city clubs?
3. What are the similarities and differences between city clubs and country clubs?
4. What are two basic ways private clubs can be owned?
5. What are some criteria an equity club must meet to maintain its nonprofit status?
6. How is an equity club organized? How is a corporate or developer club organized?
7. What are some problems and opportunities associated with a career in club management?
8. What are typical sources of club revenue?
9. What are some common types of club memberships?
10. What are typical sources of club expenses?

## Internet Sites

For more information, visit the following Internet sites. Remember that Internet addresses can change without notice.

*Associations*

Club Managers Association of America
www.cmaa.org

Educational Institute of AH&MA
www.ei-ahma.org

International Health, Racquet and
Sports Club Association
www.ihrsa.org

***Organizations/Resources***

Club Services
www.clubservices.com

National Restaurant Association
www.restaurant.org

The Virtual Clubhouse
www.club-mgmt.com

## REVIEW QUIZ

When you feel you have covered all of the material in this chapter, answer these questions. Choose the *best* answer.

1. Which of the following types of clubs is considered a city club?

    a. university
    b. fraternal
    c. equity
    d. yacht

2. Members of a social club usually have what type of affiliation?

    a. They are in the same profession.
    b. They enjoy being in one another's company.
    c. They have mutual business interests.
    d. They have similar political backgrounds and goals.

3. The main purpose of a yacht club is to:

    a. gain social prestige for its membership.
    b. provide dining and social facilities for people interested in boating.
    c. provide marinas and other facilities for boat owners.
    d. sponsor races and other boating competitions.

4. A member of a corporate club owns:

    a. shares in the club.
    b. a membership in the club.
    c. part of the real estate development surrounding the club.
    d. shares in the corporate sponsor of the club.

5. Which of the following usually does *not* have a direct effect on club membership dues?

    a. type of club
    b. extent of the club's facilities and services
    c. number of members
    d. age of the club

6. Which of the following statements about equity clubs is *false?*

    a. If an equity club has an excess of revenues over expenses, the profits are given back to the founder-members.
    b. Equity clubs are exempt from federal and state income taxes as long as they meet certain conditions.
    c. Equity clubs are usually nonprofit.
    d. An equity club can legally discriminate against applicants on other grounds besides sex, race, or religion.

## REVIEW QUIZ *(continued)*

7. In an equity club, the club manager reports to the club's:
   a. owner (usually a corporation or developer).
   b. controller.
   c. board of directors.
   d. house committee.

**Answer Key:** 1-a-C1, 2-b-C1, 3-c-C1, 4-b-C2, 5-d-C2, 6-a-C2, 7-c-C2

Each question is linked to a competency. Competencies are listed on the first page of the chapter. An answer reading 3-b-C4 translates to:

- 3: the question number
- b: the correct answer
- C4: the competency number

## Chapter 9 Outline

The Size of the Meetings Industry
    Types of Meetings
The Role of Civic and Government Organizations
Where Meetings Are Held
The Meeting Planning Process
    Planning the Meeting Itself
    Choosing a Location
    Choosing a Facility
Meetings Industry Careers
    Travel and Tourism Careers Associated with Meeting Planning
Chapter Summary

## Competencies

1. Describe the size of the meetings industry, list and describe types of meetings typically held in lodging facilities, explain the role of civic and government organizations in the meetings industry, and describe where most meetings are held.

2. Outline the meeting planning process, and summarize career opportunities in the meetings industry.

# 9

# An Introduction to the Meetings Industry

**A**NY DISCUSSION OF the meetings industry should begin with a definition of what we mean by a meeting. For the purposes of this text, we define a **meeting** as a planned event in which a group of people gather together to accomplish something. The gathering can take place in a hotel, on a cruise ship, in a convention center, or at airports or colleges. It can also take place at several locations simultaneously through teleconferencing.

A meeting can consist of a few people in a conference room or 100,000 delegates at a major convention center utilizing a dozen or more hotels in a large city. In some cases, especially where a convention is involved, a meeting may include a trade show. For example, the International Hotel and Restaurant Exposition, held annually in New York City, consists of: a general industry association meeting, at which industry issues and trends are discussed; committee meetings; educational programs; and a trade show. At the trade show, vendors of products and services such as furniture, property management systems, and design services demonstrate and explain what they have to offer. There are also numerous receptions, meals, and other social events held all over the city in conjunction with the exposition. The American Society of Travel Agents holds annual world congresses in cities such as Glasgow, Bangkok, and Miami, typically attracting 6,000 or more delegates.

In order to stage such complicated events, many specialized services, facilities, and technologies are used. For example, transporting a huge body of people to a single location at the same time involves the use of airlines, motorcoaches, limousines, and rental cars. Meeting planners must arrange for this transportation. They must also book hotels to house and feed the delegates, and reserve convention centers to hold the meetings and trade shows. Vendors must contract with exhibit designers to build booths where the vendors will show their products. Meeting planners may contract with audiovisual and satellite services to record and film the guest speakers or produce and broadcast the presentations.

## The Size of the Meetings Industry

The **meetings industry**, also referred to as the conventions, expositions, meetings, and incentive travel industry (CEMI), generated $82.8 billion in direct spending in 1994, according to a study done by the international accounting and consulting firm of Deloitte & Touche. The industry is ranked 22nd among all U.S. private-sector businesses (in contribution to the U.S. Gross Domestic Product). Conventions

**Exhibit 1   The Meeting Industry's Impact on Hotels**

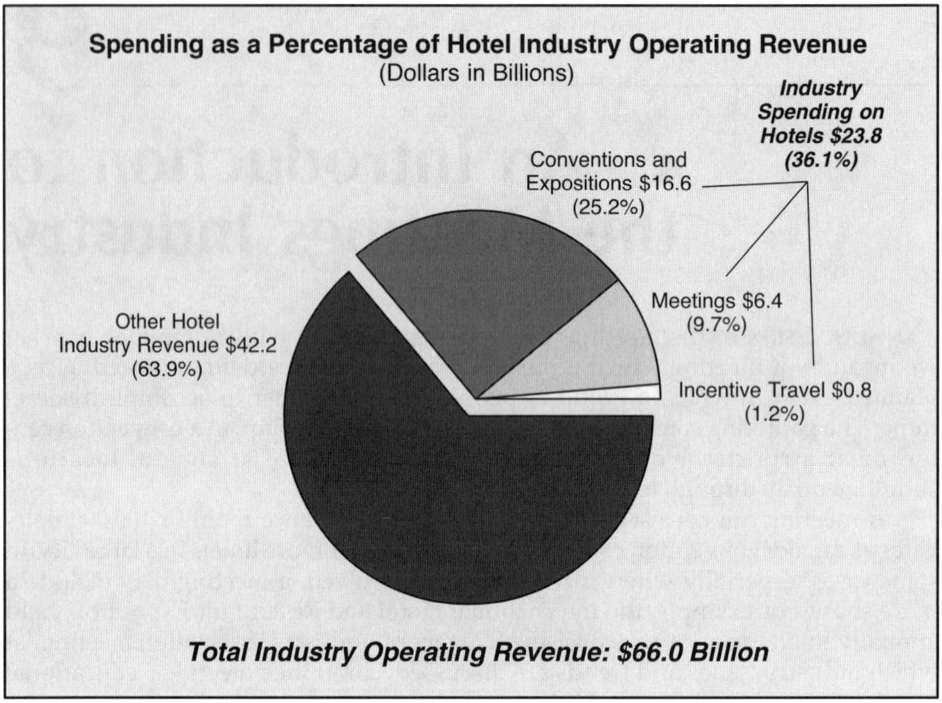

**Spending as a Percentage of Hotel Industry Operating Revenue**
(Dollars in Billions)

- Industry Spending on Hotels $23.8 *(36.1%)*
- Conventions and Expositions $16.6 (25.2%)
- Meetings $6.4 (9.7%)
- Incentive Travel $0.8 (1.2%)
- Other Hotel Industry Revenue $42.2 (63.9%)

**Total Industry Operating Revenue: $66.0 Billion**

Source: American Hotel & Motel Association.

and expositions accounted for $52.2 billion, or 63 percent, of the $82.8 billion in direct spending. Association, corporate, and government meetings constituted $27 billion (32.6 percent) of the total; incentive travel represented $3.5 billion (4.2 percent) of the total. Total direct spending generated 1.6 million full-time equivalent jobs and $12.3 billion in federal, state, and local tax revenues.[1]

The meetings industry has an enormous impact on hotel business, generating 36 percent of all hotel operating revenue (see Exhibit 1). Nearly a quarter of the airlines' annual operating revenues come from the meetings industry, accounting for $19.3 billion in spending.[2]

## Types of Meetings

**Association Meetings.** Many people belong to an association of some kind. Association events generated almost $56.1 billion (67.8%) of the $82.2 billion in direct spending for meetings. Associations range from trade groups, such as the American Medical Association, to social groups, such as the American Association of Retired Persons (AARP). Labor unions, like the Teamsters or the American Federation of Labor—Congress of Industrial Organizations (AFL-CIO), are also associations. Service associations include the Junior Chamber of Commerce (Jaycees) and the Rotarians.

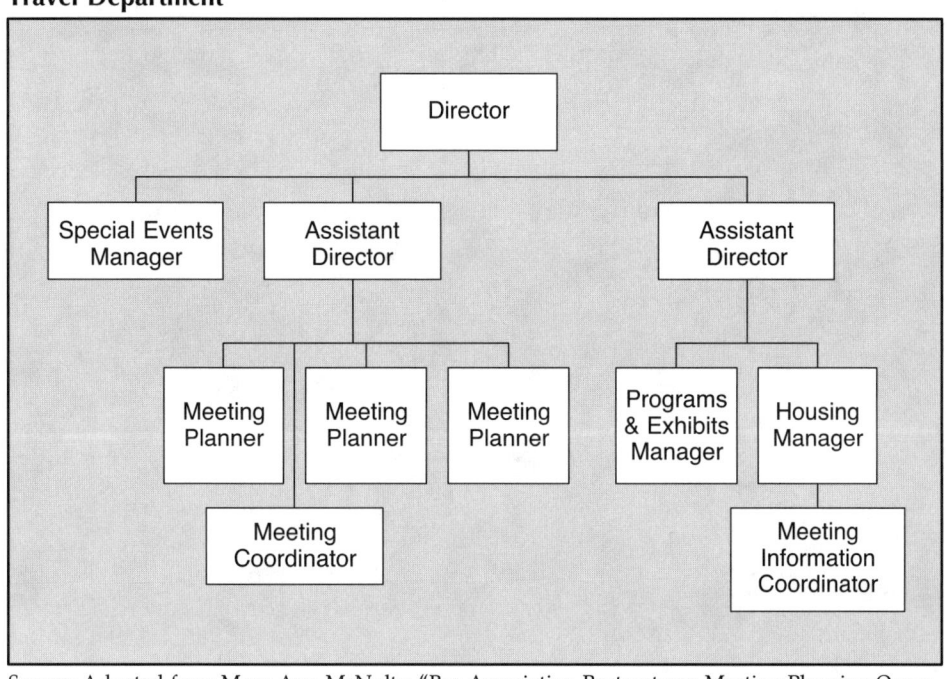

**Exhibit 2   Sample Organization Chart for a Large Association's Meetings and Travel Department**

```
                          Director
           ┌────────────────┼────────────────┐
    Special Events    Assistant         Assistant
       Manager        Director          Director
                   ┌────┬────┐        ┌────┬────┐
                Meeting Meeting Meeting  Programs  Housing
                Planner Planner Planner & Exhibits Manager
                                        Manager
                     │                              │
                  Meeting                        Meeting
                 Coordinator                   Information
                                               Coordinator
```

Source: Adapted from Mary Ann McNulty, "Bar Association Restructures Meeting Planning Operations," *Meeting News,* April 1993, p. 8.

Some associations are large enough to employ a full-time meetings and travel department. Exhibit 2 shows a sample organization chart for such a department.

Virtually all associations hold at least one annual meeting when the entire association gets together to elect officers, set budgets, and plan activities. Association members take this opportunity to learn about the issues that may affect their future, such as government regulation. In between these annual meetings, members network with each other and hold local chapter meetings.

Some associations meet frequently. Besides annual national or international conventions, some associations hold regional meetings, board meetings, and educational seminars. These meetings typically range in length from one day to one week. For example, in a typical year the American Bar Association might hold an annual meeting (attended by 12,000 delegates), a mid-year meeting (attended by 3,200 delegates), and 350 local meetings throughout the year.

An important characteristic of association meetings is their timing cycle. National or international meetings or conventions are usually held annually. Often the site is selected two to five years before the event, especially when large numbers of persons are involved. (Smaller meetings are scheduled as needed, with a typical lead time of five to eight months.) These large conventions usually last from three to five days. From a large association's point of view, the number of cities that can accommodate 50,000 delegates or more is limited. Sites must be selected years

**Incentive trips are a way for corporations to reward employees. Such trips are usually to destinations with a warm climate, and spouses are often invited.** (Courtesy of Bonaventure Resort & Spa, Ft. Lauderdale, Florida)

in advance to be sure that hotel rooms and airline seats are available. A hotel or convention center's goal is to maximize the use of its facilities, and this long lead time allows them to plan sales and marketing efforts.

The need for adequate exhibit space is another important characteristic of association meetings. More than 40 percent of all conventions feature exhibitions that require at least 20,000 feet of exhibit space.

Attendance at association meetings is voluntary, so association meeting planners must pay special attention to site selection and social programs.

**Corporate Meetings.** According to the Professional Convention Management Association, the types of corporate meetings held off company premises include:[3]

- *Management meetings.* Management meetings include everything from financial reviews to strategic planning sessions. Management meetings make up the largest category in the corporate meetings market. Average attendance: 45.
- *Training seminars.* Training seminars rank second in number of meetings held. They provide training for employees at all levels.

- *Sales meetings (both national and regional).* Sales meetings are essential for teaching sales techniques, introducing new products, building morale, and motivating sales personnel. National sales meetings average 3.6 days with 104 attendees. Regional sales meetings average 42 attendees and last an average of 2.5 days.

- *New product introductions.* New products are showcased to employees at new product introductions. These meetings are also used to motivate dealers or distributors who are not employees (for example, introducing new car models to dealers). New product introductions last 2 days on average; average attendance is 60 people.

- *Professional and technical meetings.* Professional and technical meetings are used to provide information or teach new techniques to employees who work in technical and professional fields. Accountants need to learn about new tax laws and rulings every year, for example. The average length of these meetings is 2.3 days; average attendance, 62 people.

- *Incentive trips.* Often a combination of meetings and recreation, incentive trips are rewards to customers, retailers, distributors, or employees. Spouses are often invited to attend.

- *Stockholders meetings.* Stockholders meetings are annual events usually lasting a day, with an average attendance of 95 owners of company stock.

- *Other corporate meetings.* Other corporate meetings include press conferences, public forums, and any other meetings a corporation might sponsor.

Corporate meetings require much less lead time than association meetings, since for the most part they are smaller and don't last as long. Because corporate meetings are often mandatory, corporate meeting planners do not need to take as much care to promote the meeting or plan special social programs as do association meeting planners.

**Trade Shows and Expositions. Trade shows,** also known as **expositions,** usually take place at convention centers, at exhibit halls, or in exhibit space in hotels. Sometimes public arenas are used. Trade shows are sponsored by trade associations, private companies who are in the business of organizing trade shows, or by governments. Trade shows can be part of a convention or association meeting. When they are, they can represent a significant amount of revenue for the sponsoring association.

According to professor Denney G. Rutherford of Washington State University, there are four different kinds of trade shows:

- Industrial shows
- Wholesale and retail trade shows
- Professional or scientific exhibitions
- Public or consumer shows[4]

Industrial shows, says Rutherford:

**288** *Chapter 9*

**This award-winning ad from Opryland Hotel is aimed at groups that put on trade shows.** (Courtesy of Opryland Hotel and Ericson Marketing Communications, Nashville, Tennessee)

are events used by manufacturers of equipment and products to exhibit their products to other manufacturers. At an industrial show, buyers are typically purchasing materials and inventory that they will re-manufacture into a processed product or resell either direct or in some adapted form.[5]

Wholesale and retail trade shows are "a collection of exhibits that are specific to one or more closely allied or associated trade. In most instances the buyers represent businesses that are shopping for services and products to use in the conduct of their business."[6] The World Trade Show, held annually in London, is an example of a wholesale and retail trade show. At this show, several hundred hotels, airlines, cruise lines, tour operators, and tourism boards from major countries staff booths and attempt to persuade travel agents to recommend their offerings. One of the largest wholesale and retail trade shows in the United States is held every May in Chicago by the National Restaurant Association. This show attracts almost 2,000 exhibitors and is attended by more than 100,000 delegates from all over the world.

Professional or scientific exhibitions are "usually associated with meetings of professional groups, educators, scientists, and other people who could be considered end users."[7] Public or consumer shows are the only wholesale and retail trade shows open to the public. Many newspapers and other media sponsor travel shows for their advertisers. At these shows, the public can: browse among exhibits prepared by destinations, hotels, tour operators, and cruise lines; view videos; and listen to presentations about various vacation options. Popular consumer shows include antique shows, art shows, and other shows that appeal to collectors.

## The Role of Civic and Government Organizations

Almost every city has a **convention and visitors bureau (CVB)** or a chamber of commerce. These are nonprofit organizations whose job it is to market their destinations. Counties often have their own tourism department. Virtually every country in the world has a Department or Ministry of Tourism that often includes a division whose function is to attract meetings and conventions. These entities field salespeople to call on meeting planners. They also run advertisements in meeting publications suggesting that their locations are ideal for a meeting or convention. They help groups find meeting sites and accommodations, and organize activities for delegates. They will frequently offer personnel to assist with greeting and registering delegates as well.

## Where Meetings Are Held

Almost any kind of facility can be used to hold a meeting. Meetings have been held in amusement parks, football stadiums, and castles. All modern cruise ships have conference centers and meeting rooms. Meetings have even been held on luxury trains such as the Orient Express. However, most meetings are held in hotels or motels. More than 50 percent of the business in hotels with 1,000 or more rooms comes from meeting groups.

Almost all of the business of conference centers, which are specifically designed to house small meetings, comes from the meetings market segment. Conference centers range in size from 32 guestrooms to 400. Some are owned by corporations, which use them primarily for their own purposes and occasionally rent them out to other corporations and, in some cases, even open them to the public on weekends. Corporations that own their own conference centers include American Express, Xerox, IBM, and Chase Manhattan Bank. Many universities have also built conference centers. For example, Columbia University operates Arden House on its Harriman, New York, campus.

## The Meeting Planning Process

The meeting planning process comprises three parts: planning the meeting itself, choosing a location, and choosing a facility.

### Planning the Meeting Itself

To do a good job, a meeting planner must know the objective(s) of the meeting. This will give him or her a better idea of how much time to schedule for the meeting, what time of year to schedule it, and what type of format or agenda is best. The following sections will cover each of these meeting planning components: objectives, scheduling, and format.

**Objectives.** One of the first questions a meeting planner must deal with is the objective(s) of the meeting. There are three general meeting objectives: business, educational, or social (or any combination of the three). The appropriateness of a meeting site depends on the meeting's objectives. For example, a two-day meeting of fast-food franchisees from all over the United States might best be held in a centrally located large hotel in (or connected to) a major airport, so that attendees can get to the meeting site and return home quickly and economically. On the other hand, a sales meeting meant to motivate salespeople to exceed their quotas in the year ahead and reward them for their past year's performance is frequently held at a resort in a warm climate (Hawaii and Florida are popular destinations). Cruise ships are also popular for such meetings.

**Scheduling.** The next issue to address is the amount of time needed to achieve the meeting's objectives. The dates of the meeting are also important. A toy show must occur early enough in the year for retailers to place their orders in time for Christmas. Boat shows are held in the spring, just before the boating season begins. Television executives gather every January to show off new programs to advertisers and stations so that the fall season programming can be finalized. Meeting planners should be careful to pick a time that does not conflict with another meeting that might require the presence of or attract the same delegates. Planners should also avoid religious and national holidays. Exhibit 3 breaks convention scheduling down by month.

**Format.** Once the length of the meeting and the dates have been established, it is time to make decisions about the meeting's format. The format is the overall schedule of events—what is going to happen during the meeting and in what order? When will the meeting start and finish? What will be the times and lengths of meals? coffee breaks? social events? How many general sessions, round-table discussions, and workshops will there be? If there is a trade show, when will it open and close? How many exhibitors will be involved and how much time will they need to accomplish their objectives? If there are tours, when will they occur and how long will they take?

**Exhibit 3   Convention Scheduling by Month**

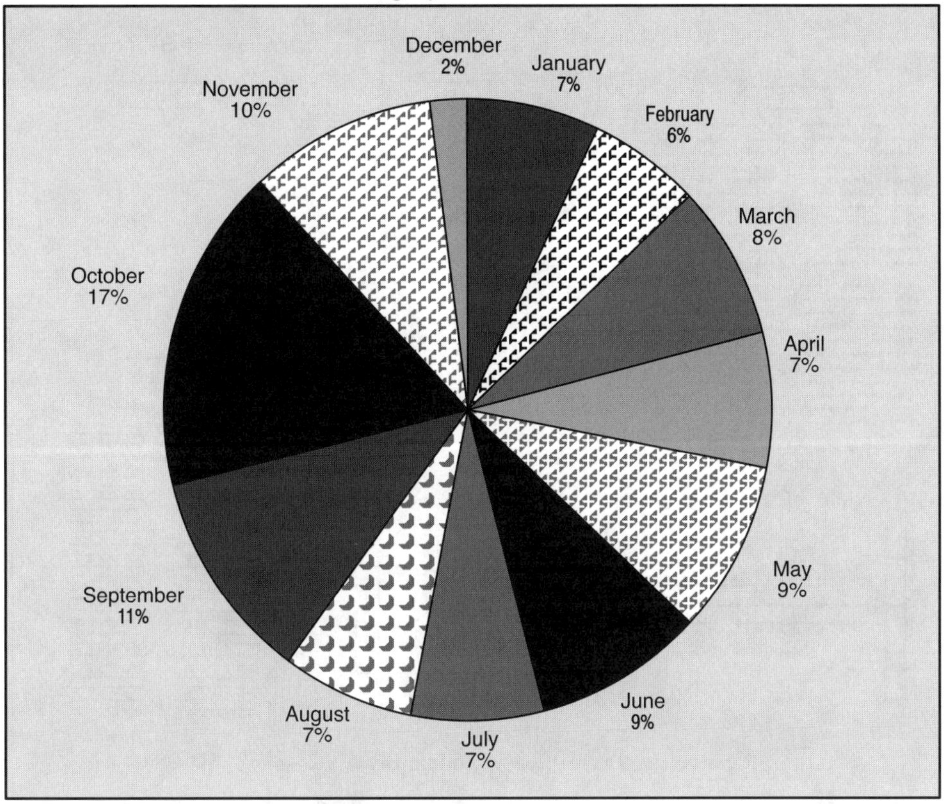

- December 2%
- January 7%
- February 6%
- March 8%
- April 7%
- May 9%
- June 9%
- July 7%
- August 7%
- September 11%
- October 17%
- November 10%

Source: *Meetings & Conventions,* August 1996, p. 77.

## Choosing a Location

Some meeting locations are predetermined. Many corporations hold their meetings at their own headquarters, for example. Other organizations change the meeting site from year to year to ease the travel costs for delegates from different geographic areas. Location is also affected by the nature of the organization. One would not expect a religious group to meet in Las Vegas or Atlantic City, where many of the leisure activities available are not compatible with the group's values. The transportation logistics involved are also a consideration. How accessible is the meeting site to airports? In Europe, where trains are used extensively for intercity travel, accessibility to the train station can be a major consideration.

## Choosing a Facility

Once the location has been chosen, a facility must be selected. Will it be a resort, a center-city hotel, a conference center, or a cruise ship? Size and cost are two of the major considerations here.

**Exhibit 4  Sample Meeting Room Setups**

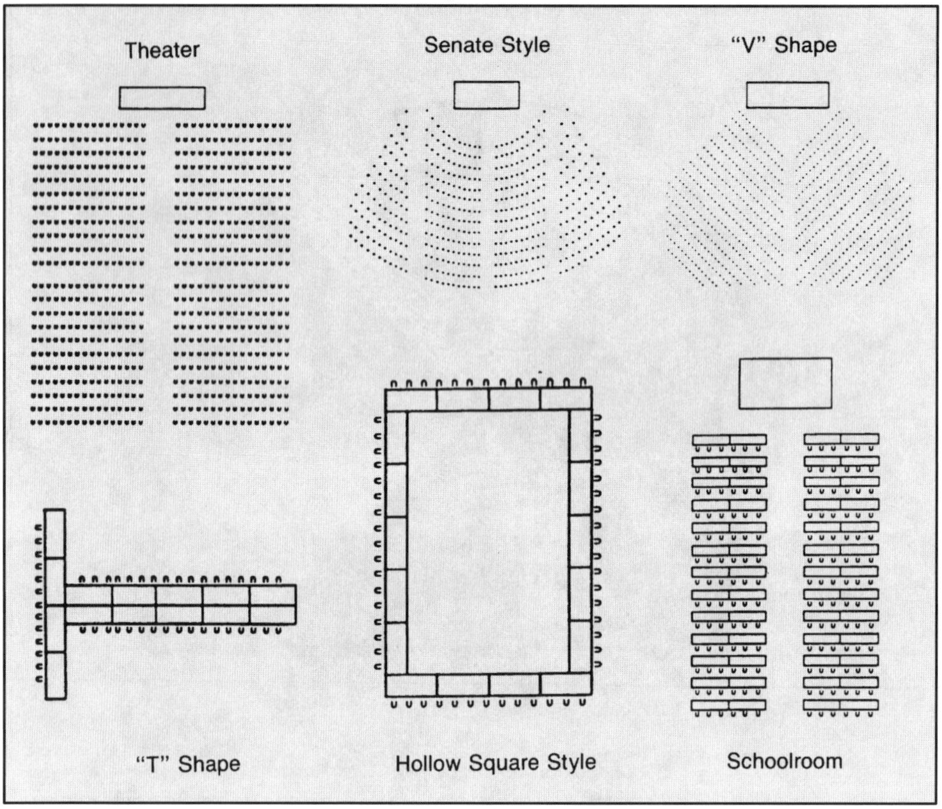

Source: Adapted from *The Convention Liaison Council Manual,* 4th ed.

In terms of size, a facility must have enough guestrooms, meeting rooms, and exhibit space. Factors to consider when choosing a facility include the following:

- Are the guestroom accommodations adequate? Are there a sufficient number of suites for VIPs and hospitality functions? What about the availability of smoking and no-smoking rooms?

- Can the meeting rooms be set up in a variety of styles? Theater, schoolroom, and hollow square are some of the basic styles (see Exhibit 4).

- What types of amenities and recreational facilities are offered? This can be very important for meetings where relaxation is an objective. Some groups insist on resorts with golf courses, tennis courts, and spas; others want hotels located in or near scenic attractions.

- Are the meeting rooms adequately soundproofed? Meetings and activities in adjoining rooms should not intrude on each other.

- Does the resort, hotel, or cruise ship offer adequate audiovisual facilities? Is there a good sound system, especially for large rooms? What about the lighting? State-of-the-art lighting facilities include track lighting and theatrical lighting equipment. What kind of projection equipment is available? A group can rent much of this equipment from suppliers other than the hotel, but the hotel's meeting rooms must have enough outlets and electrical power to accommodate it.

- How far are the meeting rooms from the guestrooms? Can the meeting rooms be reached without climbing stairs? Are there a sufficient number of conveniently located elevators or escalators? These access issues have taken on added importance since the passage of the Americans with Disabilities Act.

Of course, an association or corporation's budget is an important determining factor in where the meeting will be held. Some industry groups, such as the American Association of Advertising Agencies, can afford to meet regularly at five-star resorts where delegates are likely to spend $250 a day or more. Other groups have more modest budgets. The price of many items is a matter of negotiation between the hotel and the meeting's sponsor. Questions for negotiation include whether there will be a charge for meeting room space, what the functions will cost, whether the hotel is willing to pay for a function (such as a manager's reception), what the guestrooms will cost, and how many guestrooms will be provided on a complimentary basis. Exhibit 5 lists several important variables that influence meeting planners' facility choices.

## Meetings Industry Careers

Persons who plan, organize, and coordinate meetings, conventions, and trade shows may have various job titles. Only in the largest associations are such people engaged full time in meeting planning and have titles such as "meeting planner," "meeting coordinator," or "exhibits manager" (see Exhibit 2). Many **meeting planners** have job titles that relate to other activities they perform, such as sales, marketing, or administration. For example, the marketing manager of a company may also be its convention manager or meeting planner. For the purposes of this discussion, however, we will refer to all those who plan and organize meetings, conventions, and trade shows as meeting planners.

As mentioned earlier, persons who are actively engaged in meeting planning can be found in associations, corporations, governments, and travel agencies. There are also association management companies that include meeting planning among the management services they provide to clients. Independent meeting planners not associated with a company are another type of meeting planner. While these independent professionals are known as "meeting planners" in North America, in other parts of the world they are called professional conference or congress organizers (PCOs). Associations for meeting planners include Meeting Planners International, the Professional Convention Management Association, the American Society of Association Executives, and the Society of Government Meeting Planners.

### Exhibit 5  Important Variables Influencing Choice of Facility

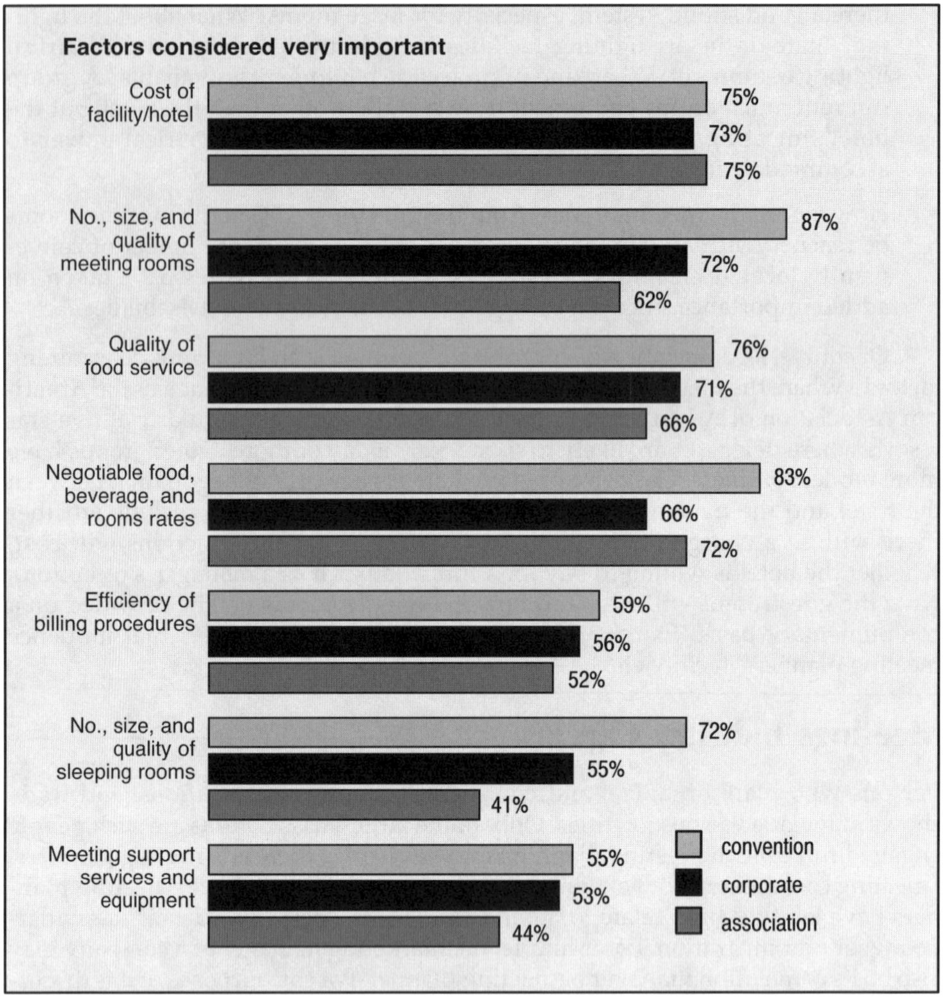

**Factors considered very important**

| Factor | Convention | Corporate | Association |
|---|---|---|---|
| Cost of facility/hotel | 75% | 73% | 75% |
| No., size, and quality of meeting rooms | 87% | 72% | 62% |
| Quality of food service | 76% | 71% | 66% |
| Negotiable food, beverage, and rooms rates | 83% | 66% | 72% |
| Efficiency of billing procedures | 59% | 56% | 52% |
| No., size, and quality of sleeping rooms | 72% | 55% | 41% |
| Meeting support services and equipment | 55% | 53% | 44% |

Source: *Meetings & Conventions*, August 1996, p. 70.

There are a number of tasks that meeting planners routinely perform and must be skilled at. The Convention Liaison Council in Washington, D.C., which certifies meeting planners and awards the designation of Certified Meeting Planner (CMP), lists 25 tasks meeting planners should be able to perform. Among the most important of these are:

- Establishing meeting objectives
- Selecting meeting sites and facilities
- Negotiating with facilities

# An Introduction to the Meetings Industry 295

**Something many meeting planners look for in a facility is adequate exhibit space.** (Photo courtesy of Las Vegas Hilton, Las Vegas, Nevada)

- Budgeting
- Handling reservations, housing, and food and beverage issues efficiently
- Choosing from transportation options (air and ground)
- Planning programs
- Planning meeting room setups
- Managing exhibits
- Selecting guest speakers
- Booking entertainment

In order to perform these tasks successfully, meeting planners must be superb negotiators and diplomats. The organizations they work for and the persons who attend the meetings expect them to choose the best sites and arrange for the best accommodations and transportation at the lowest prices. They want their food and beverage service and their social events to be superior—and they expect all of this to happen without any mishaps or delays. Meeting planning is a difficult job, requiring a high degree of specialized knowledge.

During the actual meeting, the planner is usually busy and under a great deal of pressure to keep things moving and resolve problems that come up. Meeting planners often arrive at a site a day or two in advance, to ensure that all of the elements they have negotiated and contracted for are in place. Are the hotels prepared to receive the delegates? Is transportation in place? Are the meeting rooms arranged as they should be? Have the arrangements for guest speakers been confirmed? Are there any problems with setting up the trade show? Cellular telephones and shortwave radio communications are often required to keep the planner in touch with the hotel staff in different parts of the hotel (and in touch with various hotels within the city, in the case of a large convention).

Even when things are going well, unanticipated events can threaten a convention's success. Speakers can fail to show up, hurricanes and snow storms can disrupt transportation arrangements, and fires, strikes, or demonstrations can occur. Good meeting planners devise contingency plans to handle all of these situations.

After a meeting is over, the meeting planner must still deal with a number of crucial tasks. Equipment and exhibit booths must be packed and shipped. Invoices from hotels, restaurants, and other facilities must be checked and settled. Equally important, the meeting must be evaluated from the point of view of the attendees, the sponsor, and the exhibitors. This information provides feedback for future meeting planning.

## Travel and Tourism Careers Associated with Meeting Planning

Up to this point, we have discussed the meeting planners that the hospitality industry serves—the part-time or full-time meeting planners in associations, corporations, or other groups. Now let's look at some of the careers within the travel and tourism industry that may involve you in the meetings market.

**Careers in Hotels.** Many hotel careers touch the meetings industry or involve meeting planning. The hotel's sales manager is usually instrumental in bringing meetings business to the property. Some hotel salespeople specialize in meetings business. These salespeople usually spend many years cultivating relationships with professional meeting planners and learning about their businesses or activities. They often know as much or more about professional meeting planning than their clients. Many of them have built a "following," and when they move to a new property they sometimes bring their clients with them.

In small hotels, the person who sells a meeting or convention to a group is responsible for coordinating the meeting as well. At large hotels that do a lot of convention business, once the sale is made, the job of working with the group is turned over to a **convention services manager (CSM),** a relatively new position in the hotel business. The convention services manager sees to it that everything the hotel promised the group, whether in the contract or orally, is delivered. In some hotels this job is quite important, and the CSM reports directly to the hotel's general manager and has a department staffed by several persons.

Another key hotel staff member involved in meeting and convention planning is the catering manager. The catering manager is the person in charge of banquets and other food and beverage operations that are not connected with room service or the hotel's restaurants and lounges. In addition to preparing some of the food for large conventions, many catering departments do their own marketing, and solicit and handle the arrangements for small meetings such as weddings, monthly meetings of a business or civic club, and dinners honoring elected officials.

**Careers in Convention and Visitors Bureaus.** Since the CVB for a destination is the entity responsible for marketing that destination to meeting planners, it follows that the job of the CVB's chief executive is a marketing one. In many instances the CVB also handles tourism development and visitor information services as well. CVBs usually have a sales department that works closely with the area's hotels and exhibition facilities to bring business to the destination. Associations often will contact a CVB and ask for the names of hotels in the area that meet certain criteria for their meetings. For example, an association meeting planner might ask for a list of downtown hotels with 100 rooms available from March 5–8, and 10,000 feet of exhibit space. The CVB will usually tell all of their members about this inquiry so that those who are interested can contact the meeting planner directly. CVBs almost never book hotel rooms for meeting planners, but in some cities they also serve as the marketing and sales arm for the city's convention center. CVBs also place advertising on behalf of their destinations, produce brochures and films, research potential markets, and provide maps and other materials to visitors who request them.

**Careers in Tourism Departments.** As mentioned earlier, many states, countries, and other political and geographic entities have their own Department or Ministry of Tourism.

Some tourism departments are well-funded and spend significant amounts on advertising and promoting their destinations. Tourism departments maintain overseas offices with salespersons who call on travel agencies and tour operators to persuade them to promote their destination. In some destinations, the Department of Tourism stages or helps fund events such as festivals, golf or tennis tournaments, sailing regattas, and even dog shows. Typically these departments employ nationals of their country to attend trade shows and create and coordinate events designed to entice travelers to visit their countries. Career opportunities consist of positions in sales and administration.

**Careers as Exhibitors or Exhibit Designers.** There is an entire category of professionals who do nothing but design, promote, and manage exhibits and trade shows. **Exhibitors** and **exhibit designers** have their own trade association, the International Exhibit Association. They even have their own annual trade show, where they learn about the newest ideas and designs in exhibit building. The firms in which these professionals work may hire exhibit halls, rent space to exhibitors, and promote shows directly to the trade or to the public. Sometimes when a trade show is connected to a convention, the convention organizers will contract out the promotion and management of the show to an exhibitor rather than handle it themselves.

Designing and building exhibits, shipping them, and erecting them on-site is another large industry. Some of this work is done by full-service exhibit houses, some by custom designers. There are also a number of advertising agencies that are skilled in helping their clients design and build trade exhibits. Finally, there are manufacturers of "off-the-shelf" exhibits that come in modular form and can be customized to fit any exhibit situation. All of these firms have career opportunities for specialists who sell, design, and produce exhibits.

## Chapter Summary

A meeting is any group of people who gather together for a specific purpose. A meeting can consist of a few people in a conference room. A convention might have 100,000 delegates at a major convention center using a dozen or more hotels in a large city. Many specialized services, facilities, and technologies may be used.

Meetings are held by associations, corporations, and governments. There are also trade shows and expositions that may be a part of or independent from a meeting or convention.

The four kinds of trade shows are: industrial shows, wholesale and retail trade shows, professional and scientific exhibitions, and public or consumer shows.

Conventions and visitors bureaus are nonprofit organizations that market the destinations in which they are located. Governments may play a similar role.

Almost any kind of facility can be used to hold a meeting. Meetings have been held at amusement parks, football stadiums, and castles. However, most meetings are held in hotels and motels. Conference centers, universities, and cruise ships also serve as popular meeting venues.

One of the first questions a meeting planner needs to address is the objectives of the meeting. Some meeting locations will obviously be more appropriate than others, once objectives have been set. The next question that must be addressed is the amount of time needed to achieve the stated objectives. The dates of the meeting are also important. Once the length of the meeting and the dates have been established, it is time to make some decisions about the format. The format is the overall schedule of events: what is going to happen during the meeting and in what order?

Some meeting locations are predetermined. Many corporations hold their meetings at their own headquarters. Other organizations move their meetings around to ease the travel costs for delegates from different geographic areas. Once the location has been established, a facility must be chosen. Size and cost are two of the major considerations here. Other considerations include guestrooms, meeting rooms, amenities and recreational facilities, soundproofing, audiovisual systems, adequate access, and budget.

Meeting planners may hold a variety of job titles within an organization. Few do it full time. Persons who are actively engaged in meeting planning can be found in associations, corporations, governments, and travel agencies. There are also association management companies and independent meeting planners.

Meeting planners are involved in everything from establishing meeting objectives and selecting sites to budgeting, selecting guest speakers, and booking entertainment. The best meeting planners are superb negotiators and diplomats. During the actual meeting the planner is usually very busy and under a great deal of pressure to keep things moving and resolve problems that come up. After a meeting is over there are still a number of crucial tasks left for the meeting planner. Evaluation for future planning purposes is one of the most important of these.

Many of the travel and tourism industry careers associated with serving the meetings market are found in hotels. Hotel sales managers and their staffs, convention service managers, and catering managers all play key roles.

Convention and visitors bureaus employ marketing staffs to handle tourism development and sell their destinations to meeting planners. Tourism departments, which are usually branches of governments, do the same but often on a global basis.

Finally, there is an entire category of professionals who do nothing but design, promote, and manage exhibits and trade shows. Some exhibit design work is done by full-service exhibit houses, some by custom designers. There are also a number of advertising agencies that are skilled in helping their clients design and build exhibits. There are manufacturers who produce "off-the-shelf" exhibits that come in modular form and can be customized to fit any exhibit situation. All of these firms have career opportunities for people who want to sell, design, and produce exhibits.

## Endnotes

1. The Convention Liaison Council, "The Economic Impact of Conventions, Expositions, Meetings, and Incentive Travel," 15 October 1995, Deloitte & Touche Consulting Group.
2. The Convention Liaison Council.
3. *Introduction to Meeting Management* (Birmingham, Ala.: The Education Foundation of the Professional Convention Management Association, 1988), pp. 31–33.
4. Denney G. Rutherford, *Introduction to the Conventions, Expositions, and Meetings Industry* (New York: Van Nostrand Reinhold, 1990), pp. 44–45.
5. Rutherford, p. 44.
6. Rutherford, p. 44.
7. Rutherford, p. 44.

## Key Terms

**convention and visitors bureau (CVB)**—A nonprofit service organization that promotes a destination and sometimes offers personnel, housing control, and other services for meetings and conventions.

**convention services manager (CSM)**—A member of a hotel or resort's staff who is responsible for all aspects of a convention.

**exhibit designer**—Someone who designs a display booth or area to show products or services to prospective buyers.

**exhibitor**—The company or organization sponsoring an exhibit booth.

**exposition**—An exhibit of products and services that is usually closed to the public. Also called a trade show.

**meeting**—A planned event in which a group of people gather together to accomplish something.

**meeting planner**—Someone who plans meetings for an association, a corporation, or some other group.

**meetings industry**—An industry that comprises meetings (small meetings, conventions, trade shows, etc.), meeting planners, meeting sponsors (associations, corporations, etc.), and meeting suppliers (facilities as well as firms that supply services for meetings—audiovisual firms, exhibit design companies, and so on). Also referred to as the conventions, expositions, meetings, and incentive travel industry (CEMI).

**trade show**—An exhibit of products and services that is usually closed to the public. Also called an exposition.

## Review Questions

1. What types of meetings do associations typically hold?
2. Why is it important for large associations to select meeting sites years in advance?
3. What types of meetings do corporations typically hold?
4. How is planning an association meeting different from planning a corporate meeting?
5. What are the various types of trade shows?
6. What role do civic and government organizations play in the meetings industry?
7. Where are association and corporate meetings typically held?
8. What are some factors a meeting planner must consider when choosing a facility?
9. What are some of the tasks meeting planners should be able to perform?
10. What are some of the travel and tourism careers associated with the meetings industry?

## Internet Sites

For more information, visit the following Internet sites. Remember that Internet addresses can change without notice. If the site is no longer there, use a search engine to look for additional sites.

*Associations*

American Society of Association Executives
www.asaenet.org

Association of Destination Management Executives
www.adme.org

Hospitality Sales and Marketing Association International
www.hsmai.org

International Association for Exposition Management
www.iaem.org

International Association of
Convention & Visitor Bureaus
www.iacvb.org

Professional Convention Managers
Association
www.pcma.org

*Publications*

*Meetings & Conventions*
www.meetings-conventions.com

# REVIEW QUIZ

When you feel you have covered all of the material in this chapter, answer these questions. Choose the *best* answer.

1. What percentage of the hotel industry's operating revenue is generated by the meetings industry?

    a. 11%
    b. 36%
    c. 52%
    d. 67%

2. Compared with association meetings, corporate meetings generally require _____ lead time.

    a. much less
    b. somewhat less
    c. about the same amount of
    d. even more

3. Which of the following is *not* one of the four kinds of trade shows?

    a. public or consumer shows
    b. educational shows
    c. professional or scientific exhibitions
    d. industrial shows

4. Which segment of the meetings industry generates the most business?

    a. conventions and expositions
    b. stockholders meetings
    c. sales meetings
    d. incentive travel

5. Which of the following is a typical function of a convention and visitors bureau?

    a. conducting feasibility and market studies for new or prospective convention hotels
    b. booking hotel rooms for meetings
    c. producing films that promote the destination as a meeting site
    d. placing advertising for specific meeting facilities

6. The position of "convention services manager" is:

    a. found mainly in big hotels.
    b. responsible for booking convention groups.
    c. a relatively new one within the hotel industry.
    d. a and c.

## REVIEW QUIZ *(continued)*

7. Which of the following is a point that a meeting planner typically negotiates with a hotel?
   a. Will there be a charge for the meeting room space?
   b. How much will the hotel charge the group for guestrooms?
   c. Is the hotel willing to pay for a function, such as a manager's reception?
   d. All of the above.

**Answer Key:** 1-b-C1, 2-a-C1, 3-b-C1, 4-a-C1, 5-c-C2, 6-d-C2, 7-d-C2

Each question is linked to a competency. Competencies are listed on the first page of the chapter. An answer reading 3-b-C4 translates to:

   3: the question number
   b: the correct answer
   C4: the competency number

## Chapter 10 Outline

Early Cruises
    Transportation and Immigration
    New Passengers and New Directions
The Birth of Modern Cruising
    Carnival Is Born
    The Cruise Industry Today
Cruise Ship Organization
    The Captain
    The Hotel Manager
A Case Study in Quality Management
    Emphasizing Service
    The Importance of Service Delivery
      Systems
    Specific Operations Procedures
    Passenger Comments Are Taken
      Seriously
    Everyone Is Involved
    Opportunities
    Problems
    Passengers Expect Customized Service
    Empathy Is an Important Factor
Chapter Summary

## Competencies

1. Summarize the beginnings of the cruise industry, describe the birth of modern cruising, and describe the cruise industry of today.

2. Explain how a cruise ship is organized.

3. Explain how Seabourn Cruise Lines got started, and describe its approach to providing quality service to passengers.

# 10
# Floating Resorts: The Cruise Line Business

JUST A DECADE AGO, texts on hospitality management did not address the cruise ship industry. The reasons were simple. There were few cruise ships, they did not carry many passengers, and their crews were all recruited from emerging nations. In addition, their land-based infrastructure was small. Hospitality students were not recruited for positions either at sea or on land, and if they had applied for them they would have probably been rejected. Openings at sea were for jobs like captains, first mates, pursers, and stewards; no hospitality schools trained students for those kinds of positions. Moreover, salaries were far below American standards, and living conditions aboard ships were Spartan. On land, jobs were limited to telephone reservation clerks and marine operations.

The situation is dramatically different today. Altogether the International Council of Cruise Lines estimates that almost 600,000 jobs in the United States can be attributed to the industry today. That figure includes workers in transportation, manufacturing, wholesale and retail trades, and agriculture. These jobs created by the cruise industry generated approximately $19 billion in 1997.[1]

More than 100 cruise ships call at a dozen U.S. ports. These ships are floating vacation resorts—some carrying as many as 3,000 guests and costing $500 million or more. They generate revenues of $10 billion annually.[2]

The ships are managed by hotel managers, many of whom come from fine hotels and hospitality schools—executive chefs, maîtres d'hôtel, chief housekeepers, and cruise directors. A majority of these managers are recruited from North America and Europe and are offered salaries competitive with land-based resorts. Even on land there are many positions now available. Carnival Cruise Lines, the world's largest, employs 17,500 people—16,000 at sea and 1,500 people on land in hotel and food service operations, sales and marketing, entertainment and casino management, itinerary planning, finance, information systems, marine operations, and new building.

Yet cruise lines are still in their infancy. Only seven percent of Americans have ever taken a cruise. So far cruising has captured only two percent of the hotel/cruise vacation market in North America. It is, however, the fastest growing of all segments in the hospitality industry, and it appears to generate the highest rates of customer satisfaction. Between 1996 and 2000, 27 new cruise ships will be launched with an average of 1,716 berths per ship. This represents a growth of 35 percent. Eighty-four percent of all passengers report that they were very satisfied

**This modern cruise ship passes the tip of Miami Beach as it heads toward Caribbean ports of call. The 855-foot-long, $275 million floating resort can carry more than 2,000 passengers.** (Courtesy of Carnival Cruise Lines)

or extremely satisfied with their most recent cruise, and 74 percent rated it a good or excellent value for the money.[3]

In this chapter we will explore the evolution of this business from steamship transportation to floating vacation resorts, cruise line management, and career opportunities for those who are interested in this exciting and dynamic business.

## Early Cruises

If you define a cruise as going to a number of ports for the purpose of sightseeing, and then ending up back where you started, then the first person to take one and tell about it was the noted English novelist William Makepeace Thackeray. In 1844 the Peninsula and Oriental Steam Navigation Company, popularly known as the P&O, invited Thackeray to travel on board its ships to Greece, the Holy Land, and Egypt. His book *Notes of a Journey from Cornhill to Grand Cairo* told of the trip. Thackeray reported getting seasick; complained about the prices, bugs, and lack of pretty women in Athens; and objected to the beggars he encountered while climbing the pyramids in Egypt. Even so, he said he had a good time and recommended that others consider taking the journey.

The first American-origin cruise was probably the 1867 voyage of the paddle wheel steamer *Quaker City*, with a similar itinerary except that it started from New York. Among the passengers was the American humorist Mark Twain, who chronicled his adventures in *The Innocents Abroad*. Twain, too, became a cruising

An example of early cruise line advertising for the Holland America Line.

enthusiast. He described how every evening after dinner guests would promenade the deck, sing hymns, say prayers, listen to organ music in the grand saloon, read, and write in their journals. Sometimes dances were held on the upper deck accompanied by music that Twain did not particularly enjoy. "However," he wrote, "the dancing was infinitely worse than the music." When the ship rode to starboard, "the whole platoon of dancers came charging down to starboard with it, and brought up in mass at the rail; and when it rolled down to port, they went floundering down to port with the same unanimity of sentiment. The Virginia reel, as performed on board the *Quaker City*, had more genuine reel about it than any reel I ever saw before."[4]

## Transportation and Immigration

From the time of the *Quaker City* up to the late 1950s, far more people crossed the Atlantic for necessity rather than pleasure. This was the period of immigration, and travel conditions for most passengers crossing the Atlantic were miserable.

Even for those traveling first class, it was often uncomfortable because the voyages were long and there were no ports to stop at. Ship builders tried their best to make people forget that they were at sea. The English architect Arthur Davis, who designed some of the great Cunard liners, put it this way:

> The people who use these ships are not pirates, they do not dance hornpipes; they are mostly sea sick American ladies, and the one thing they want to forget when they are on the vessel is that they are on a ship at all. If we could get ships to look inside like ships, and get people to enjoy the sea, it would be a very good thing; but all we can do as things are is to give them gigantic floating hotels.[5]

The other objective, of course, was to make the ships go as fast as possible so that the voyages would last only a few days instead of two weeks. On the whole this strategy worked, and passengers began to regard steamships as both luxurious and unsinkable. This situation was dramatized when on a clear spring night, April 15, 1912, on her maiden voyage, one of the most luxurious ships afloat, the White Star liner *Titanic*, struck an iceberg in the North Atlantic and sank. This 46,329-ton liner (less than half the size of today's largest ships) carried 2,228 passengers and crew. In two hours and forty minutes, 1,523 perished. They were mostly second class passengers and immigrants, who were trapped because the twenty lifeboats could only carry half of those on board. At first, because most passengers were convinced that the ship would not sink, they did not rush to fill the boats. Confusion and unpreparedness compounded the problem; 40 percent of the available lifeboat seats stayed empty as the boats were lowered. Boat number one was launched with only five passengers and seven crew. It had a capacity of forty! The sinking of *Titanic* was one of the saddest nights in history. Stories of courage and cowardice survive to this day. For example, Isidor Straus, co-owner of Macy's Department Store, and his wife, Ida, were returning home from a vacation on the French Riviera. Mrs. Straus refused to board a lifeboat without her husband. "I will not be separated from my husband," she said. "As we have lived, so shall we die. Together." Historians tend to blame Captain Edward Smith (who went down with his ship) and White Star's Managing Director Bruce Ismay (who was on board but managed to escape), because allegedly they were anxious to run on schedule and arrive at the announced time when the press would be waiting. Even though they were advised there were icebergs in the area (another ship, the *California*, just twenty miles away, had stopped for the night because of the same warnings), the ship did not slow down.

After the *Titanic* disaster, ships were moved to a more southerly route, more lifeboats were added, 24-hour wireless watches at sea were required, and other safety measures were implemented.

## New Passengers and New Directions

By the 1920s, the transatlantic business was booming again until the United States curtailed its open-door immigration policy. Since the lines earned most of their revenue from this source, a new kind of passenger had to be found. Fortunately World War I had created an interest in Europe among Americans. Immigrants' accommodations were turned into "tourist class," and soon they were filled with teachers, students, and sightseers who wanted to see London, Paris, and Rome, or visit some of the famous battlegrounds they had read about. There was another incentive as well. Prohibition had dried up America in 1920. Those who enjoyed a martini or scotch and soda could get as many as they wanted on an ocean voyage!

Soon spending a week at sea became the fashionable thing to do. The press ran frequent articles about the lavish and expensive first-class lifestyles, where people dined, danced, and partied all night with exciting, interesting, and often rich companions. Going to Europe on a transatlantic liner was the best of all travel experiences.

Nineteen twenty-nine was the beginning of the Great Depression. Many people could no longer afford to go to Europe for their vacations. As a result, steamship lines started to offer cheaper alternatives. These included short, inexpensive vacation/party cruises to Nova Scotia, Nassau, and Bermuda. The ships that were utilized for these cruises had been designed for transatlantic traffic and were not really suited for cruising—especially in warm waters. They were not air-conditioned, and their lack of outdoor deck space and pools did not give the feeling of a resort at all. As the cruising market grew, however, new and more luxurious ships were deployed, and with them more expensive and longer itineraries. Ships became lighter colored, more open, and more resort-like. Posters showed passengers dressed in leisure clothes around an outdoor pool instead of dressed in business suits strolling around an enclosed deck.

Up to World War II, the major steamship lines were owned by European interests. When the war started, almost all of the vessels were converted into troop ships or stayed in port. This situation continued until 1945 when the rebuilding of Europe once again spurred a growing demand for ocean liners. For the first time the United States recognized that it might need its own troop ships and subsidized the building and operation of new vessels. The *United States*, launched in 1951, was designed to be the fastest ship afloat. On her very first crossing she set a new world record of 3 days, 10 hours, and 40 minutes, beating *Queen Mary* by a full 10 hours.

The post-war boom marked the last days of the great steamship liners. Besides the *United States* and *Queen Mary*, there were the *Queen Elizabeth*, the French Line's *France*, Holland America's *Rotterdam*, and a host of sleek Italian liners built for warm-water cruising in the Mediterranean. These ships crossed the Atlantic, cruised to exotic ports, and circled the globe.

Everything started to come apart in 1958. That was the year that Pan American World Airways offered its first nonstop, transatlantic crossing on a Boeing 707 jet. Steamships were effectively out of business as a means of transportation. Some ships were moth-balled, such as the *United States*. Others were scrapped. The *Queen Mary* became a landlocked hotel in Long Beach, California. The *France* was converted to a cruise ship, and it continues to sail today as the *Norway*.

## The Birth of Modern Cruising

There were no real cruise lines until the early 1960s, when Miami entrepreneur Leslie Frazer chartered two ships, the *Bilu* and *Nili*, and marketed them exclusively for cruises.

The S.S. *France* plies the seas again as the cruise ship *Norway*.

In 1966, Ted Arison, a young Israeli from Tel Aviv who had started and lost two air cargo businesses, joined with Norwegian Knut Kloster to bring the *Sunward*, the first new vessel built especially for cruising, into the market. They formed a cruise line called Norwegian Caribbean Lines to market the vessel. By 1971 the NCL fleet had added three more ships, the *Starward, Skyward,* and *Southward*. NCL was successful in transforming South Florida contemporary cruising from a regionally marketed collection of old transatlantic liners to a nationally marketed cruise line featuring brand-new vessels designed for Caribbean cruising.

At the same time, a former Miami Beach hotelier named Ed Stephan had dreams of starting his own cruise line. After producing some designs and plans, he traveled to Norway and enlisted the help of prominent shipping executives. Thus another industry giant, Royal Caribbean Cruise Lines (now Royal Caribbean International), was born. RCCL quickly launched a modern fleet based on Stephan's innovative designs of ships with a sleek, yacht-like profile and an observation lounge located in the ship's funnel, high above the superstructure, which was inspired by Seattle's Space Needle. By 1972 the RCCL fleet consisted of the *Song of Norway,* the *Nordic Prince,* and the *Sun Viking*. By then, the cruise business was not limited to Florida.

A Seattle businessman, Stanley McDonald, founded Princess Cruise Lines offering cruises to the Mexican Riviera. It was an instant hit, and by 1972 Princess had four vessels. At the same time a former bush pilot, Chuck West, was building a seasonal cruise business along Alaska's Inside Passage. West's cruise line was part of his overall tour operation, which he called Westours.

"The Love Boat" television series featured adventure, comedy, and romance—and popularized cruise travel—during its 1977–1986 run on ABC Television.

In 1977 Princess scored a coup that would forever change the image of cruising. Most people had no idea what taking a cruise was like. A television production company, Aaron Spelling Productions, decided to use a luxury cruise ship as the location for a major TV series. Princess made two of their vessels, the *Island Princess* and the *Pacific Princess,* available for the filming. The series was called *The Love Boat* and in 10 years of production it featured stories of people who fell in love, solved personal problems, or just had a great adventure. There is little doubt that the program popularized the idea that a cruise was a mass market vacation—not just for the rich and famous.

## Carnival Is Born

Partnerships do not always work out well, and in 1971 the most successful of all of them, between Ted Arison and Knut Kloster, broke up. Arison decided to leave Norwegian Cruise Lines and start his own business. With the help of a friend, Meshulam Riklis, Arison bought a laid-up ocean liner, the *Empress of Canada,* renamed it the *Mardi Gras,* and founded Carnival Cruise Lines.

What is now the world's largest cruise line did not have a very auspicious beginning. When the *Mardi Gras* entered service on March 7, 1992, she ran aground at the tip of Miami Beach shortly after leaving the dock. She sat there for a full 24 hours while tourists gazed at her in amazement before she was refloated. It did not help that Carnival's only ship was an old one competing in a sea of new vessels. Carnival's marketing director, Bob Dickinson (now Carnival's president), mulled over the problem. He concluded that people were not really looking for a specific ship or port when they went on a vacation; what they really wanted was to have fun. Dickinson's solution was to provide more activities and entertainment onboard than Carnival's competitors and call their ship "The Fun Ship." This was a total reversal of cruise marketing. Up to that time, cruise promotion had been destination driven. Dickinson determined to make the ship itself the destination. Because it was an old ship, the company was forced to offer very low prices which in turn attracted a younger crowd. Until then, cruises had been viewed as suitable only for wealthy older people. This was a whole new market. The younger age and informality of the passengers added to the "fun" on the ship and Carnival was able to deliver on its promise. By 1975 the line was profitable and started adding more ships to the Carnival fleet. Dickinson's strategy, which changed consumers' perception of cruising from a pastime for the rich to a vacation for the masses, was probably the defining event in the development of the modern cruise industry.

## The Cruise Industry Today

In North America there are 35 cruise lines. Between 1970 and 1996, 57 million passengers took cruises from North American ports. In 1996 alone the figure was 4.6 million, of which 44 percent were first-time cruisers. Cruise Lines International Association (CLIA) estimates that the number of North American cruisers annually will be just under seven million by 2000. This figure represents about 65 percent of the estimated potential world market.

Cruise lines are divided into various market segments by CLIA. The largest category by far is the contemporary/value segment, which are the popular-priced, mass-market lines. These lines tend to get a lot of their business from first-time cruisers. Carnival, Norwegian, and Royal Caribbean are all part of this segment. The premium cruise lines charge more and carry fewer passengers per **ton** of space. (In the shipping business, the tonnage of a ship refers to the volume, not the weight.) Celebrity, Holland America, and Princess are in this category. The luxury segment is the top of the line. Typical of this segment is Seabourn, which charges an average of $800 per day per person. Crystal, Cunard, Silversea, and Windstar are also luxury lines. The final segment is called "specialty" lines. These vessels specialize in a single destination and include American Hawaii Cruises and Delta Queen Steamboat.

There are three giant players in the industry. The largest of these is Carnival. Carnival owns Carnival Cruise Lines, Holland America Line-Westours, Windstar, and has controlling interests in Seabourn and Costas, as well as joint ventures in Europe and the Far East. Between all of its brands, Carnival accounts for an estimated 28 percent of the North American passenger capacity.[6] Next is Royal Caribbean International, which also owns Celebrity Cruise Lines. The third largest

# Industry Innovators

Robert H. Dickinson
President
Carnival Cruise Lines

In 1973 when Bob Dickinson joined Ted Arison, who was trying to start a cruise line, it was a very small business. Cruising was a limited vacation option for most travelers, and the industry did nothing to dispel its stodgy reputation as only for the "newly wed or nearly dead."

Dickinson came from a background of finance and corporate planning at Ford Motor Company and RCA. With little experience in marketing or sales, he recognized that Carnival had to change not just the rules of the game but the whole playing field if Carnival were to succeed. Although their "golden fleet" consisted of one tired old ship, Dickinson boldly repositioned the entire cruise experience from a pastime for the rich to a vacation for the masses. Carnival's "fun ships" were the first to become destinations themselves instead of transportation, and that remarkable insight turned the cruise industry into one of the fastest growing segments of the hospitality business today.

After 25 years in the business, Dickinson continues to innovate to the point where observers have commented that "when Carnival sneezes, the cruise industry catches a cold."

Carnival ships were the first to utilize entertainment architecture—the fun is not simply in the activities but in the way the ship is put together. For example, on a Carnival ship one might enter a cocktail bar themed to resemble an Egyptian catacomb or a library copied from the movie *Gone with the Wind* (complete with a realistic wax Scarlett O'Hara standing by the fireplace).

In 1982 Carnival was the first to offer free air travel with its cruises, thus making them affordable for the mass market. In 1997, having introduced what by then had become a standard industry feature, Dickinson recognized that air cost structures had changed dramatically in the intervening years: he was the first to unbundle the very package he had created and competitors quickly followed.

Carnival was the first to offer a vacation guarantee: passengers who don't like their cruise can request their money back and get it—along with a ticket back to the point of embarkation—if they ask before the ship reaches the first port. It was also the first to launch a completely smoke-free ship, *Paradise*, built in a smoke-free atmosphere!

Dickinson is a highly visible manger who spends much of his time on his ships and with travel agents. He has an open door and holds regular meetings called "Share the Vision," in which small groups of employees kick around ideas with him. He is proud of the fact that Carnival has one of the lowest turnovers of any company in the business. "The ones we have lost," he says, "were not positive people." Carnival's management team includes a number of women in senior positions. Just about everyone is expected to pay their dues by coming up through

*(continued)*

> **Industry Innovators** (continued)
>
> the ranks. "We're a large corporation with a far flung work force," Dickinson says. "I think it's important that we personalize the company and continue to nurture the family atmosphere started by Ted."
>
> Dickinson is not shy. He frequently prods travel agents publicly to think of themselves as professional retail sales people. He frequently talks about changing the way cruises are sold and has suggested that Carnival might open their own "vacation stores" to beef up sales. He co-authored a book on travel marketing in which he laid out a blueprint for travel agents to "maximize their long-term profits instead of teetering on the edge of insolvency."* Carnival's sales force, which is almost evangelical in its enthusiasm for cruising, has been named by *Sales and Marketing Magazine* as one of the three top sales forces in the United States in any industry.
>
> Dickinson says he likes his job "because we're in the happiness business." He enjoys mentoring his employees and watching them succeed. Indeed, Mickey Arison, Carnival's chairman and Ted's son, credits Dickinson with being one of his principal mentors. Dickinson believes that "those who *can* help *should*" and is frequently honored for his contributions to numerous charitable boards.
>
> *Bob Dickinson and Andy Vladimir, *Selling the Sea: An Inside Look at the Cruise Industry* (New York: John Wiley & Sons, 1997).

player is P&O, which owns Princess Cruises and Princess Tours in the United States, as well as the P&O line in the United Kingdom.

The average cruise passenger is 51, has a household income of $64,000, and pays $200 a day for an all-inclusive vacation that includes a cabin, four to five meals a day, and entertainment.[7]

## Cruise Ship Organization

As we have said, cruise ships today are floating vacation resorts. In some ways they are very similar to a hotel as far as organization. While each line has its own unique organization, in general they follow a pattern. Exhibit 1 shows a ship organizational chart from the Holland America Line. At the top is the captain, who has three persons reporting to him: the chief officer, the chief engineer, and the hotel manager. Under the hotel manager are a purser, food and beverage manager, chief housekeeper, physician, cruise director, and other smaller departments that may be combined with these major ones on other lines.

### The Captain

Although a cruise ship can be compared to a hotel, it is in fact a vessel at sea and is therefore first and foremost operating under maritime laws. It is under the command of the **captain**, who is responsible for its operation and the safety of all of those aboard. It is his job to see that all company policies and rules are followed, as

**Exhibit 1  Ship Organizational Chart**

```
                            SHIP'S STAFF
                              Captain
        ┌─────────────────────┼─────────────────────┐
   Chief Officer         Chief Engineer         Hotel Manager
   Deck Department       Engine Department      Hotel Department
                                                   as below
   Navigation Officers   Engineers
   Radio Officer         Electricians
   Security Officer      Spec Service Engr
   ┌──────────┐          ┌──────────┐
   Boatswain  Carpenter  Foreman Engine   Engine Mechanic
   Asst Bosun Locksmith  Fireman/Greaser  Machinist
   Fireguards Upholsterer Wiper           Plumber
   Quarter Master                         Elec Technician
   Sailor AB/OS                           Refr. technician

                        HOTEL DEPARTMENT
                          Hotel Manager                                continued
   ┌──────────┬──────────────────┬──────────────────────────────────────────┐
   Purser         Guest Relations Mgr              Food & Beverage Mgr
   ┌──────────┬──────────┐         ┌──────┬──────┬──────┬──────┬──────┐
   Human Resources Off. Information Services Off. Front Desk Supervsrs  Asst F&B Mgr  Executive Chef  Maitre  Bar Manager  Storekeeper
   Clerk                Clerk                     FDA's
                                                  Foreman Kitchen  2nd Exec Chef    2nd Maitre     Bar Supervisors  Asst Storekeeper
   Printer                                        GPA Kitchen      Sous Chef        Head Stewards  Barman           GPA Stores
                                                  Foreman SA       Baker            Stew Rest      Stewards BLD
                                                  GPA SA           Butcher          Gpa F&B        Stewardess BLD
                                                  GPA Sanitation   Patissier                       Wine Stewards
                                                  GPA Messroom     Chef De Parties                 GPA Deckboys
                                                                   Demi Chef de P.                 GPA Crewbars
                                                                   Aide Cuisine
                                                                   Asst Cooks
                                                                   Personnel Cook
                                                                   Asst Pers Cook
                                                                   GPA Crew Kitchen
                                                                   Foreman Pantry
                                                                   GPA Pantry

                         Hotel Manager
continued
   ┌──────────┬──────────────────┬──────────┬──────────────┬──────────────┬──────────────┐
   Controller Chief Housekeepr   Physician  Shorex Manager  Cruise Director  Concessionaire Mgr
   Asst Controller  Asst Housekeeper  Laundry Supervsr  Nurses  Asst Shorex Mgr  Asst Cruise Dir   Musical director  Concessionaire Staff
   Clerk            Housekpng Supervsrs  Laundry Staff         Port Lecturer    Hostess          Musicians
                    Steward Cabins                                              Cruise Staff     Pianist
                    Steward Night                                               Youth Counselor
                    GPA Bellboys                              Tailors           Stage Manager
                    GPA Captain                                                 Cast
                    GPA Officers                                                TV Technician
                    Foreman HK                                                  Film Operator
                    GPA HK
```

Courtesy of Holland America Line

well as national and international laws. He has legal authority to enforce these laws granted to him by the country the ship is registered in.

Vessels also must comply with the laws of the ports they sail from and to. For example, both the U.S. Coast Guard and the U.S. Centers for Disease Control and Prevention inspect all ships sailing to and from U.S. ports for safety and sanitation on a regular basis.

Reporting to the captain are the **chief officer** (called the staff captain on some lines), who is second in command and also the captain's deputy; the chief engineer,

**Specialty lines focus on cruises to a single destination.** (Courtesy of American Hawaii Cruises)

who is in charge of the physical plant; and the hotel manager. These persons and their staffs are officers and wear uniforms with appropriate stripes indicating their rank and department. To some extent a ship is a paramilitary organization. Rank, regulations, and discipline are taken very seriously. All officers have duties they must perform. Otherwise they are subject to discipline. Unlike hotel or restaurant employees, officers and crew members cannot walk off the job or refuse to obey commands.

## The Hotel Manager

Among the senior officers reporting to the captain, the hotel manager has the largest staff. His or her crew are the people directly responsible for creating the vacation

> **Flags of Convenience**
>
> The laws under which a ship operates depend upon where it is registered. The choice of country depends on many factors, including the financing of the vessel, the cost of operation, and/or the route the vessel sails. The flag-of-convenience tradition dates back to the early days of naval warfare when merchant ships, to avoid being attacked, carried the flag of a neutral nation, thus protecting their passengers and cargo from the ravages of war.
>
> Staffing considerations play an important part in the decision about a ship's flag state. Many countries, including the United States, Norway, and Britain, have strict regulations concerning unionized labor, which create a high labor cost. Countries such as Panama, Liberia, Bermuda, and the Bahamas do not have such laws and thus many cruise ships are registered there.
>
> Unions are not the only issue. The British, Italians, Greeks, Dutch, and Norwegians are all known for their nautical skills, rigorous training, and strict licensing standards. Just about every major cruise line recruits from this group. Similarly French, German, and Austrian food service personnel are in high demand. No cruise ship could provide the same kind of experience that has been so successful if they operated under other flags. The United States, for example, requires that all ships registered in the U.S.A. use only licensed American officers and that three-quarters of the unlicensed crew be U.S. citizens. Also, the ships themselves must be built in the United States, despite the fact that many of the best shipyards in the world are in Europe. Other countries have similar regulations.

experience that the line offers. Today many hotel managers have been recruited from land-based resorts. (Both Carnival and Royal Caribbean recruit at schools of hospitality management for entry-level positions in the hotel department.)

This job has some similarities but also many differences to a manager's job in a hotel. One major difference is that there is no sales or marketing staff to supervise. Nor does anyone have to check in on board the ship. These functions are all performed on shore. Besides the food and beverage and room services, the hotel manager may be responsible for medical care, entertainment, and shore excursions. In addition, there are casino operations, the beauty salon, health spa, gift shops, photography, and more. On some cruise lines many of these services are concessions. For instance, the beauty and spa services typically are provided by Steiner-Transocean, a London-based company. The larger lines run their own food and beverage operations, but some of the smaller ones use outside caterers, known as ship's chandlers, to provide both the food and the personnel. In these cases, the hotel manager is responsible for only the housekeeping and social activities.

Princess Cruise Lines, in the British tradition, calls its hotel manager the chief purser. On some lines the doctor reports to the captain. The duties of each position vary somewhat by line. Some hotel managers are given more autonomy than others. There are vessels where virtually every decision is made on shore in advance or via satellite telephone while at sea.

Typically hotel managers on board ships spend four months at sea, followed by two months off. Many have families who join them occasionally on short cruises. Salaries are competitive with land-based jobs. Indeed, considering that all housing and food is supplied, as well as medical expenses, they often pay better.

**The Purser's Office.** One of the most important departments in the hotel division is the purser's office. The chief **purser** is the ship's banker, information officer, human resource director, and complaint handler. The purser is also second in command of the hotel department and is in charge whenever the hotel manager is off the ship. The purser's office runs the front office and clears the ship at foreign ports. In some ways it is similar to the rooms division of a hotel.

Most cruise ships use a credit system to handle guest accounts. Checks and/or cash are not accepted for transactions onboard. After passengers board they are asked to come to the purser's office and register their credit card. All charges incurred on board are then billed to that card. If they don't have a credit card, they are asked for a cash deposit. When the deposit is used up, credit is cut off. Ships do not accept checks because there is no feasible method for clearing them while at sea or in a foreign port. Technology makes it possible for the ships to issue an all-purpose, magnetic-coded card that serves as identification, door key, and charge card, and also shows cabin number, dining time, and table assignment (see Exhibit 2).

The purser also holds all of the money on the ship—usually in a large safe. Passengers convert travelers checks to get cash for the casino and duty-free shopping. The purser holds all of the casino funds and payroll for the crew as well. The amount of cash a large ship carries can be substantial; more than $500,000 is not unusual.

The purser's staff also handles passenger problems like lost luggage, broken plumbing, and cabin upgrades, when they are available. The job is considered attractive. Living conditions are good, and pursers are allowed to mingle with passengers in specified public areas when they are off duty.

**The Food and Beverage Department.** Research shows that one of the most important components of every cruise, from the passengers' point of view, is the food. It is the thing people are most likely to remember and talk about. Over the years, cruises have built a reputation for serving very good food and a lot of it. It goes back to the early days of steamship travel when Caesar Ritz designed a Ritz-Carlton restaurant for the Hamburg-Amerika line. While food is included in the price of every cruise, beverages are not (except on the most luxurious of ships), and they are the largest single source of onboard revenue for all of the major lines. These two factors make the job of the food and beverage manager the linchpin of every successful cruise. In addition to feeding the passengers, the food and beverage department is also responsible for feeding the crew—a challenging task because they are onboard for months at a time, represent many different cultures and nationalities with different tastes, have nowhere else to go, and must be satisfied if they are to satisfy guests.

Reporting to the food and beverage manager typically are the assistant food and beverage manager, executive chef, the maître d' (dining room manager), the bar manager, and the provision master (storekeeper).

Food and beverage managers who come from a hotel background describe their job as being very different aboard a ship. Dedrick Van Regemorter, a 15-year

Floating Resorts: The Cruise Line Business  **317**

**Exhibit 2   Onboard Identification Card**

**This all-purpose card lists name, cabin assignment, dinner sitting, and other important cruise information.** (Courtesy of Princess Cruises)

Marriott veteran and now a food and beverage manager with Princess Cruises, makes these observations:

> There is a tremendous difference between food and beverage services in a hotel and onboard a ship. The ship is a very closed environment. You live with the people you work with, so it's extremely important to develop good interpersonal skills. Also, the number of stripes you carry on your shoulders is very important. It makes a big difference in the amount of attention you get from others.
>
> My responsibilities are also different. While I do all of the ordering as far as items and quantity, I don't get involved with the financial details.

The elegant reception foyer aboard the Regal Princess is surrounded by a shopping gallery and specialty bars serving coffee, pastries, wine, and caviar. (Courtesy of Princess Cruises)

Highlighted by a marble foyer, glass elevators, circular staircase, and stained-glass dome, the Sun Princess's four-story Grand Plaza atrium is a main social area on the ship. (Courtesy of Princess Cruises)

> In a hotel, I had to control wages, overtime, and other costs, as well as generate income. I do have a consumption budget, but I don't worry about food costs. I don't even know what it costs to feed a passenger.
>
> Serving tables on a cruise ship is very different from a hotel as well. The group being served stays the same for a whole week. This enables the waiter to develop a relationship with the guests and learn their preferences. After the first night, experienced servers remember whether guests like coffee, tea, or espresso, regular or decaffeinated, with or without sugar and cream. In a hotel waiters have other concerns, such as handling cash and the number of people they have to serve at one time.
>
> Another difference is the way we do our cooking. The majority of our galley crew are trained cooks. The levels and positions are different. We still use the traditional French culinary setup. We use a lot more labor, which in part accounts for the high quality of our food. We do everything from scratch. We bake our own bread daily. We make our stock from bones. We buy a whole hindquarter and cut it down. Nothing goes to waste. We don't have leftovers. We have a limited storage capacity and no trucks come by to take away what we don't use. We know exactly how many people are coming and what they will order. That's because even though we have a lot of choices, we serve the same menu on every cruise.
>
> Our passengers expect quite a bit when it comes to food. They don't expect the same things they would have at home or even in an ordinary restaurant. I like to compare the food we serve daily to what you might order when you go to that extraordinary restaurant for a special occasion. That's why lunch is four or five courses, and dinner six or seven. If you feel like eating lobster or rack of lamb, price is no consideration because you've already paid for it.
>
> On land it's not possible to give 800 people a quality dining experience in an hour and forty minutes. But I have 107 people in our galley and they don't have to worry about what people are going to order or when to prepare it. All they have to worry about is taking orders from 108 waiters and cooking them individually. Having a ship that's consistently full removes a lot of uncertainty and allows us to produce really fine food and serve it in style.[8]

There are several points that Van Regemorter makes that are important to note. Safety, sanitation, and health are the most important considerations on any ship. That means that the **galley,** the shipboard equivalent of a kitchen, is a very highly disciplined operation. Everything must be done according to regulation; there can be no exception. There are many instances where one small error has caused hundreds to get sick. As Van Regemorter points out, one of the ways this discipline is achieved that is very different from in a hotel or restaurant is that everyone is taking orders from a person who has not just economic power over them but legal power. Not obeying orders from an officer on a ship is a form of mutiny. In reality, everyone strives very hard to get along because it is not practical to quit in the middle of the ocean thousands of miles away from home! Food and beverage managers need even better people skills—including tact and diplomacy—than land-based managers: they are with their people 24 hours a day for months at a time.

Another important difference that should be noted is that the food and beverage department on a ship does not deal with food costs at all. The cruise industry calculates costs very carefully, but this is done by land-based personnel. The luxury cruise lines spend $25–$30 per day per passenger on raw food costs, premium lines spend $12–$18, and mass market lines spend $8–$11. That includes breakfast, lunch, dinner, midmorning snacks, afternoon tea or ice cream, a late buffet, and 24-hour room service. One of the reasons for the low prices is the enormous economies of scale that are possible.

Carnival Cruise Lines uses 24,500 dozen eggs 52 weeks a year, as well as 29,800 pounds of tenderloin, 47,000 pounds of chicken, and 4,970 cases of wine (including champagne). This kind of ordering and the resulting cost savings are only possible because Carnival, like all the major lines, serves the exact same menu on all of their ships all year long. To make this possible, these lines tend to build several ships of the same size, which allows them to have similar galleys and passenger counts. Predictable demographics and ship itineraries make accurate forecasting possible. Royal Caribbean knows that when it puts escargot on the French evening menu, which occurs on the fifth night out, after visiting Jamaica, 22 percent of the 1,800 passengers will most likely order it. Standardization is everything.

Serving is another very different matter on a cruise ship. The problem is time. Except for the smaller luxury ships, none of today's vessels has enough main dining room seats to handle more than half of the passengers at the same time. There are two **sittings**—one usually at 6 P.M., the other at 8:30 P.M. The trick is to serve everyone a complete dinner—appetizer, soup, salad, entrée, dessert—one course at a time, and get them out of the dining room with enough time to clean up and reset the tables before the next sitting. On the menu there is always a choice of four or five appetizers, a couple of soups and different salads, four or five entrées, and several desserts. (It is, in fact, this abundant choice that helps creates the feeling of fine dining as opposed to banquet service.) Many people order wine as well. Because the dining experience is such an important part of the cruise vacation, no one must feel that they are being rushed or receiving banquet style service. To the contrary, they expect their server to know them by name, be aware of their preferences, discuss each menu item with them, and exchange it for another if it doesn't meet their expectations; since the server's compensation comes almost entirely from tips, it is important that he or she do so. The average food server's base salary is less than $100 monthly plus room, board, and medical. But their tips (on the major lines, passengers tip an average $3–$4 per person, per day, in the dining room and the same to room stewards) make it possible to bring home salaries of $24,000 a year—tax-free in most cases and with virtually no expenses!

The cruise lines have adopted several strategies to handle the dining situation without passengers feeling rushed. For instance, there are two shows each evening, one after each sitting. Passengers who want a good seat for a show, or intend to go to a movie in the theater after dinner, leave promptly. To respond to the demand of guests who do not want to eat at specified times and may want to spend more or less time dining, some ships have alternative dining rooms that have no additional charge but serve a different menu and require reservations. Others have opened their **lido deck** dining room (the lido deck is the one with the main swimming pool), which ordinarily just serves lunch for informal dining at night. Some have 24-hour pizzerias.

Multiple dining rooms—featuring different menus—help cruise ships deliver a high-quality dining experience for every passenger. (Photos courtesy of Seabourn Cruise Lines)

Just as the passengers need to be fed at all hours, so do the officers and crew. Dining facilities are usually open for them many hours of the day, with cooks on duty.

Finally, students should understand that as important as the food is to the passengers, beverages are even more important. Beverages are the single largest source of onboard revenue on every major cruise ship. As a rule, ships generate more bottom-line profit selling drinks than they do at the casino or shops. For this reason drinks are served in almost every part of the ship at any time when a particular area is likely to be in use. Moreover, because passengers are often on some kind of a schedule (cocktails before dinner or a drink before the show starts, for example) drinks must be served promptly. This requires a substantial commitment of well-trained personnel who can mix and serve a large number of drinks fairly rapidly. This staff needs to be well supervised. Those who have seen reruns of "The Love Boat" TV series know that Isaac Washington, the bartender, is one of the most important characters on the ship.

**The Chief Housekeeper (Steward's) Department.** The **steward's department** is very similar to the housekeeping department of any hotel. It is responsible for the cleaning and general maintenance of all cabins and interior areas on a ship. It is also responsible for passenger laundry and dry cleaning, as well as cleaning of all the crew's uniforms, linen, sheets, and towels. Cabin stewards are also responsible for cabin food service, and for loading and unloading luggage and delivering it to passengers' cabins.

The most important difference between housekeeping on shore versus at sea is that in hotels guests rarely interact on a regular basis with the persons who clean their rooms. On ships they always do. Cabins on a ship are regularly serviced twice a day—generally while passengers are having breakfast and again while they are at dinner. In addition, cabin stewards are on duty a good part of the morning and evening (70 hours a week is normal for this position) and assist passengers with other matters such as lifeboat drills, wheelchairs, pressing clothes for the captain's party, etc. Like food servers, their compensation depends largely on tips, so they learn their guests' names and generally find as many ways as they can to be helpful. Good cabin stewards can be crucial to a guest's total cruise experience.

The busiest day for this department is **turnaround day.** This is the day a ship finishes a cruise and starts another one. A typical 70,000-ton vessel may have six hundred or more cabins, with an average of two persons in each cabin. Each cabin may have two to three pieces of luggage. That's 2,400–3,600 pieces to be unloaded and loaded in a single day! Moreover, passengers are usually off the ship between 9 and 10 A.M. and by noon new passengers begin to arrive. The ship often sails by 5 P.M. That means all those cabins must be completely cleaned, linens changed, and all major lounges and other public spaces vacuumed and polished—all in three or four hours.

**The Cruise Director and Staff.** The **cruise director's** staff is one of the most visible parts of the crew from the passengers' point of view. Members of this department are the entertainers, musicians, and children's counselors, and they direct all of the guest activities.

An important part of the cruise staff's job is to sell and coordinate the shore excursions. **Shore excursions** are a significant part of onboard revenue for any cruise line. In Alaska, passengers go white-water rafting, walk on or fly over glaciers, and attend salmon bakes. In the Caribbean there are snorkeling expeditions, beaches, tours of old sugar plantations, visits to Mayan ruins, rain forests and volcanoes, opportunities to play golf, see nightclubs, go shopping, and more. In the Mediterranean there are tours to the Acropolis in Athens, gondola rides in Venice, and visits to Pompeii in Naples. Typically these tours are contracted from local tour operators. They are sold in advance on the ship so that when it arrives in port a sufficient number of tour buses and guides are available for each activity. It is important that tours run as scheduled since ships spend a limited amount of time in port. This can be a logistical problem when you are handling five or six different tours for more than a thousand passengers.

Before a ship arrives in port, a member of the cruise staff usually gives a destination and shopping talk. All of the large cruise lines recommend certain shops whose merchandise they know to be fairly priced and reliable. These shops pay a promotional fee to the line, in return for which their location and merchandise are promoted by the line. Often the cruise line guarantees that if there is any problem with a purchase and the shop will not make a necessary adjustment, the line itself will.

Another important duty of the cruise staff is to prepare the daily activity calendar. Every day the ship publishes this schedule for all of the passengers. It is distributed in their cabins the night before. If the ship is going to be in port, the schedule shows its arrival and departure times, tour departure times, when the meals are served and where, what activities there will be for those who are staying on the ship, library hours, the times of the movies, and other entertainment. When a ship has a day at sea, the cruise staff usually is very busy running a myriad of activities. There are aerobic classes, bingo, tennis tournaments, dancing lessons, carved ice and cooking demonstrations, talks on finance, health, the history and politics of the region the ship is sailing in, art auctions, bridge lessons, and more. All of these need to be scheduled, promoted, and run by the cruise department.

Finally, the cruise director is responsible for monitoring the quality of the shows and other entertainment that are offered nightly to passengers. The revues and other acts are cast, rehearsed, and produced by others. In most instances they are the work of independent producers and agents. Carnival Cruise Lines is an exception; it produces and stages all of its own entertainment. Royal Caribbean produces some of its own entertainment and subcontracts the rest. In some cases the cruise director or a member of the cruise staff acts as the master of ceremonies. The cruise director is also responsible for providing feedback to the home office concerning audience reaction. Obviously the demographics of the passengers, which vary by season and itinerary, affect the suitability of the entertainment.

**The Medical Department**. In the hotel business, when a guest gets sick, a doctor is called in. If they need medical attention they are rushed to a hospital. Since this is not possible on a ship at sea, all cruise ships carry a physician and at least one nurse.

The nature of the business makes this a critical department on any ship. Despite the fact that the age of the average cruise passenger ranges between 49 and 51 industry-wide, cruise ships get a good number of older and disabled passengers.

The *Carnival Destiny* has 25 disabled cabins; Holland America's *Rotterdam VI* has 23. All modern cruise ships are completely accessible, which also makes them attractive for older passengers or those with arthritis or other mobility problems. Considering that cruise ships are not subject to the Americans with Disabilities Act because they sail under flags of convenience, they appear to be way ahead of the hotel industry in this matter. The reasons are simple. The disabled market is a large one (49 million Americans reported suffering from some kind of disability in 1997), targeting it is a sound marketing strategy, and it produces profits. Moreover it's the right thing to do. Princess is part of P&O, which is chaired by Lord Jeffery Sterling, who heads Motability, a large United Kingdom charity dedicated to causes relating to the disabled. Princess has created the "Love Boat Access Program," including a brochure that highlights the features for the disabled on each ship, many of which were suggested by passengers. They include wheelchair gangways, Braille elevator buttons, phone amplifiers, and visual smoke detectors. Princess also developed tenders (launches that run between the ship and shore) that are designed to board wheelchairs, as well as gangway crawlers that carry persons in wheelchairs and others who find ascending steep stairways difficult. Most ships accommodate Seeing Eye dogs for the blind and other service animals.

Ships, however, need more than accessible facilities, a doctor, and a few nurses. Modern cruise ships are equipped with state-of-the-art medical care centers. Physicians onboard ships have emergency-room training, and their equipment includes cardiac defibrillators, x-ray machines, operating tables, hospital beds, and enough prescription drugs to stock a small pharmacy! The object of medical care is to treat minor injuries and stabilize major medical conditions until patients can be evacuated. Operators don't like to talk about it, but ships have morgues as well.

Princess Cruise Lines' fleet medical officer is Dr. Allister Smith, who points out that only three percent of passengers may become critically ill and that his medical staff treats more crew than guests. Smith says practicing medicine at sea is not the same as on shore:

> Time, which is one of the main tools doctors use, is taken away from you at sea. If a patient has certain symptoms ashore, you can wait and see what happens. But with a passenger, if the ship is in port and the patient perhaps seriously ill, a decision must be made on the spot to put him ashore.

Forty percent of Princess's doctors are women. All of them are U.K. registered with extensive maritime experience.

## A Case Study in Quality Management

Up to now we have been focusing on the mass-market cruise lines whose ships carry between 1,000 and 3,000 passengers. To get a closer look at the way a cruise ship is managed, how the different departments described above work together, and how the cruise vacation experience is produced, let us turn to one of the smaller quality lines. Seabourn Cruise Lines, with only three ships with a much smaller capacity, is consistently ranked by consumers, travel agents, and journalists as being the best cruise line in the world. It has won the *Condé Nast Traveler* reader's choice poll four times, and it gets "5 stars+" from Berlitz Travel Guides and others.[9]

Seabourn was founded by a Norwegian industrialist and entrepreneur, Atle Brynestad, a self-made man who started his first business at 16 by knitting and marketing his own line of Norwegian sweaters. From sweaters, Brynestad took an interest in real estate, hotels, and department store glassware and acquired Norway's oldest crystal company, the Hadeland Glassworks, which today creates some of the world's finest crystal.

Sensing that there was a growing market for cruises and that Norwegians seemed to have a knack for running them well, Brynestad decided to develop a new concept for cruising. He was attracted to the premium end of the market because of his personal lifestyle and experience. By the mid 1980s there were several concepts of luxury cruising in the market. Cunard's *Queen Elizabeth 2 (QE2)* was a 66,000-ton dual-purpose vessel built for both transatlantic crossings and cruising. At the opposite end of the scale was a Norwegian company, Sea Goddess Cruises, with two ships that were designed to have the ambiance of large luxury yachts. At 4,253 tons each, they had a passenger capacity of only 116. In between was Royal Viking, another Norwegian line. Brynestad recruited the founder of Royal Viking, Warren Titus, to help him.

The two men felt that while Royal Viking's facilities and services were the finest afloat, their ships were too large to provide the kind of intimate and exclusive quality of service that the premium market wanted. While Sea Goddess was able to satisfy this expectation for the most part, their ships were so small that they lacked many of the amenities that the market expected and, moreover, didn't behave as well in choppy waters as a larger ship might.

Their solution was to design a new kind of ship—10,000 tons—that would accommodate 204 people, all of them in 106 suites of 277 to 575 square feet each. Competitive Royal Viking ships had some cabins as small as 138 square feet, while Sea Goddess suites ranged from 205 to 475 square feet. This new Seabourn design, they felt, could offer both the intimacy of a small yacht and the amenities and spaciousness of a larger ship. Other considerations were that this size ship could accommodate a large enough galley to prepare all meals on an "a la minute" basis rather than banquet style and a large enough crew to provide a high crew/passenger ratio (two crew members for every three passengers).

## Emphasizing Service

From the beginning Brynestad recognized that he was not selling a cruise but a unique vacation experience. Because of Seabourn's size and high service levels, it would have to be priced at the very top of the market. Seabourn's Mediterranean cruises would cost $800 to $1,000 a day and most cruises would last 14 days. That meant that the average couple would spend at least $20,000 per cruise. With that kind of price tag come extremely high expectations. Market studies show the average household income of Seabourn's clientele is $200,000. According to Brynestad, "Our clientele doesn't need to save up money to go on one of our cruises. They are not determined to have a good time, no matter what happens or how they are treated. To satisfy them, we need to win their hearts." After every voyage all Seabourn clients receive a tangible expression of Seabourn's heart—a dozen roses in one of Brynestad's Norwegian crystal vases.

**Seabourn's Type A suite offers wood panelling, tasteful decorations, and a large picture window.** (Courtesy of Seabourn Cruise Lines)

Seabourn begins to win its passengers' hearts long before they board the ship. Passengers receive a questionnaire after they have booked passage asking for their preferences in liquor and food. Documentation arrives in a leather wallet packed in a gift box. When passengers arrive the night before a cruise they are housed in a luxurious hotel, such as the Cirigan Palace in Istanbul (a former nineteenth-century sultan's palace). All embarkation procedures are completed in the hotel before departure of the ship, so that when guests finally arrive at the ship (usually after a complimentary sightseeing tour of the city) they are handed a glass of champagne at the foot of the gangway. Then they are escorted aboard, where they are greeted by name by a white-gloved hotel manager and his staff and escorted directly to their suite, where an iced bottle of champagne waits. There is no hassle, no waiting, no lines, and no formalities.

Unlike a hotel room, or even an ordinary cruise line cabin, Seabourn accommodations do require some orientation. The standard 277-square foot suite seems more like a small studio apartment. Special amenities include personalized monogrammed stationery, and a bar and refrigerator stocked with guests' favorite brands of liquor, wines, beer, and sodas. TVs all have VCRs and there's even a videotape entitled, "Welcome to Your Suite."

Room service is provided 24 hours a day, including all the caviar and champagne one can consume. During meal hours, complete dinners from the dining room menu are served by dining room waiters, one course at a time, for those who wish a private candlelight dinner or simply don't want to dress up. For those who wish to be served in the main dining room, passengers can come in anytime they want without reservations and sit with whomever they wish. There are plenty of tables for two for couples who wish to dine alone, as well as larger tables for groups who wish to sit together. No one ever sits alone; single passengers are invited to join other guests or dine at tables with officers and senior hotel staff members. There is also a Verandah Café with indoor and outdoor seating for more casual dining.

The ship has three public lounges where entertainment consists solely of small musical groups with a soloist and other cabaret-style entertainers. There is also an enrichment lecturer who is familiar with the area; sometimes these are well-known authors or commentators.

Other shipboard amenities include a spacious gym, sauna and steam baths, beauty salon, three whirlpools and a swimming pool, a jogging track, and a library stocked with over 200 videotapes and a selection of recently published fiction and nonfiction. There is even a self-service laundry for guests who don't wish to use the ship's regular service.

More than most companies, Seabourn recognizes that in the hospitality business the passengers are part of the physical product; guests expect each other to behave and dress in a certain way. Consequently, there are very strict dress codes—casual, informal, and formal. The ship's program lists the dress acceptable in public areas after 6 P.M. Guests understand that this is not a matter of personal choice, since they are free to dine in their cabin and watch a movie or read. On formal nights all male guests wear tuxedos. On one cruise a passenger complained to the hotel manager when a guest at another table removed his dinner jacket during a meal. The headwaiter politely asked him to put it back on.

## The Importance of Service Delivery Systems

Seabourn's philosophy of how you achieve superior service is based on two main tenets. The first is that you have to take care of your internal guests (your employees) before you can expect them to take care of your external guests (the passengers). The second is that guests are Seabourn's most important asset. Therefore it is the staff's job to find out very quickly what the guests expect and make certain they get that and more. Only by doing this, the company feels, can guests successfully differentiate Seabourn cruises from the ordinary and be able to articulate those differences when they get home. Larry Rapp, vice president of hotel operations, puts it this way: "In order to provide superior service, each employee must feel absolutely secure in his or her position. He or she has to feel, from a psychological standpoint, free to take whatever decision needs to be taken to satisfy the guests without constraint from a company system, a budget plan, or an organization plan. The crew member who is speaking to a guest has to have the power to provide satisfaction, and no hierarchy should get in the way of that." Every employee has a copy of a document called *Twelve Points of Seabourn Hospitality*, which is also posted in the hotel manager's office. The points include:

- Any crew member who receives a guest complaint "owns" that complaint. He or she is responsible for ensuring guest satisfaction.

- Always remember the importance of teamwork and service to co-workers.

- Communicate guest problems to fellow employees and management.
- Take responsibility for your own behavior.
- Do not be afraid to make a mistake as long as your efforts are sincerely intended to do your job in a better way.

## Specific Operations Procedures

To make certain there is no misunderstanding, before signing on with a ship, all supervisors receive written instructions on supervision of hotel employees. Their contract states that their performance evaluations will be based on their ability to accomplish specific tasks. These include (1) finding a way to motivate his or her team to find out what each guest wants and give it to them and (2) encouraging open communication by creating in their employees self-confidence, empathy, and respect.

Seabourn has a specific management style it expects supervisors to follow, and it is written in the operations manual to help them meet their goals. It is very explicit:

1. I will support front line employees, not try to control them.
2. I believe every employee wants to do the best job he or she can.
3. I fully realize that my employees' attitudes and feelings affect their performance, and that my supervision can affect those attitudes and feelings.
4. I will give positive feedback to my colleagues as often as possible.
5. When I need to give negative feedback, I will refer only to facts—not to people. I will say, "This ashtray needs cleaning." I will not say, "You don't take proper care of ashtrays," or, even worse, "You are a sloppy person."
6. I will listen to the ideas of my employees and give them full credit when they contribute to success.
7. I will give each of my colleagues all the respect that is their right as a human being. This means treating them as they want to be treated.

## Passenger Comments Are Taken Seriously

On the *Seabourn Spirit* Mediterranean cruise from Istanbul to Venice that was studied to develop this case, there was a waiters' meeting after the dining room closed at 11 P.M., during which guest comment cards from the previous week were reviewed. In attendance were Johannes Moser, hotel manager; Harald Lange, maître d', who chaired the meeting; Chef Jurg Inniger; and all 17 waiters from 10 countries. The meeting began with Chef Inniger reading aloud the negative comments from the previous week concerning the food. He stated first that the negative comments were not negative but constructive. "We want to maintain our reputation for the best food," he told the group.

The first comment he had was that the "pasta was not done correctly." A waiter pointed out that this comment was from an Italian family. Italians are very particular about their pasta. But the same comment card went on to say that "the food improved the second week." The waiter added, "By the second week, we knew

**The dining room of a Seabourn ship.** (Courtesy of Seabourn Cruise Lines)

this family. They liked spicy food and we gave it to them." Lange complimented the waiter for being on his toes.

Another comment stated that "the pastry needs improvement." A member of the group commented that he had tasted the croissants that morning and they were horrible. The chef agreed and noted that the baker had become ill in Istanbul and left the ship. A new one was due the next day. The only other negative food comment was that "the menu was too Americanized." Chef Inniger told the waiters he needed more feedback from them as to what their European clientele liked.

Then some of the positive comments were reviewed. They included "great selection," "superb meals," "good cuisine and variety—better than before," "my kind of food," "I blame you for the weight I gained," and "all our special requests were handled with no problem." Overall, the score on cuisine was 9.81 out of a possible 10. Inniger noted that 87.3 percent of the responses gave the cuisine a perfect 10 and no one gave it below an 8.

**Evaluating Wait Service.** Maître d' Lange then reviewed the comments on the waiters' service. There were only three negatives. The first dealt with slow dinner service on the Verandah. Lange recommended that waiters concentrate more on their stations. Another guest mentioned that his wine glass had been removed before the end of the meal and said this was not a good idea; there was always the possibility that someone would want more. Everyone thought this was a good comment. "From now on we won't do it," said one of the waiters. Finally, a guest wanted to know why he couldn't order full room service by the pool but had to return to his suite to get it. Lange noted that in truth they didn't have enough staff on board to offer this. "But," he added, "people paying $35,000 ought to be able to get it." A discussion was held in which several waiters contributed ideas. It was decided that the full room service menu would be offered from one of the bars on deck and that trays of sandwiches would be passed around at lunch time so guests would not feel the need to order room service.

Lange also read the positive comments they had received. "You have given a new meaning to class and superb service. We are used to traveling on a private yacht, but we like this cruise so much we're spending an extra $25,000 to stay another week. All your waiters are as adorable as my two sons." Several waiters were mentioned by name and the others applauded or cheered whenever one of these comments was read.

The meeting ended with a review of the known likes and dislikes of the guests boarding in Athens in a couple of days. One liked certain cheeses, and a note was made to check with the provision master to be sure they would be onboard. Another liked bran cereal and skim milk for breakfast every day. One was known to like fresh fruit juice brought to him while exercising on the treadmill. Everyone made notes so they would remember. The meeting was highly participative. After every negative comment there were several suggestions as to how to improve things. No one was criticized directly and there were no recriminations.

There was a similar meeting in the housekeeping department. Every negative comment was reviewed and the tone of the meeting was always, "How can we solve this problem?" never, "People don't understand that we can't do this." The amazing thing is that these meetings are held weekly. Seabourn is constantly refining and improving its service.

## Everyone Is Involved

"The whole secret is getting everyone involved in producing the product," says Hotel Manager Moser, who was part of the original group who developed the Seabourn concept and started as their first food and beverage manager. "Then it becomes theirs, and they own it and are proud of it. I not only solicit their ideas, I try them out when I can. If they work, I adapt them." When asked how he could do this with such a demanding clientele where mistakes can be fatal, his answer was, "We hire good people we can trust and then we train them. 'God is in the details,' said Frank Lloyd Wright."

Training goes on continually at all levels. Hotel managers have been supplied with a series of management tapes used in business schools and training seminars; they are shown and discussed on a voluntary basis regularly. The company also offers all supervisors the opportunity to attend courses at any hotel school of their choice when they are off the ship on vacation. The wine steward gives monthly tastings and lectures on wines and the regions they come from; the chef briefs the waitstaff every night before dinner by presenting the dishes that are on the menu and giving a short lecture on the recipes and how they are prepared. Waiters regularly are quizzed in writing to improve their knowledge of food and wine. In keeping with Seabourn's nonthreatening, nurturing atmosphere, the quiz, along with the answers, is posted a week in advance so everyone has a chance to study and learn the answers before the test.

## Opportunities

Moser doesn't see the *Seabourn Spirit* as a cruise ship at all, but a small hotel that floats. The exact same sentiment was echoed later in the voyage by another crew member. "I would never work on a cruise ship," he said scornfully. Compensation for service personnel aboard Seabourn ships is unique. There is no tipping permitted. The hotel staff is compensated by a salary plus a revenue sharing plan that is based on the number of guests onboard for each cruise. The theory, says Moser, is, "If we do a good job, people will take more cruises and tell their friends. If they do that, the company makes more money and so the people responsible for creating that experience should share in it."

Seabourn's method of getting everyone involved in producing the product, combined with eclectic itineraries where different ports are visited every week, offers some unique opportunities as well as problems. The most important opportunity is the one to forge a lasting personal relationship between the customers and the company. The morning after the *Seabourn Spirit* sailed from Istanbul with 90 new passengers onboard, the dining room waiters met to examine pictures of all the new people who had joined the ship and memorize their names. In the lounges and dining room whenever crew members recognized someone, they repeated their names out loud so that other crew members could hear. They also then greeted the guest by name. The payoff becomes most obvious in the dining room where, even if a passenger sits at a different table every night with a different waiter, he or she is greeted by name.

Rapp points out another opportunity to provide a unique experience. That is Seabourn's cuisine, where the policy is to buy fresh regional products at ports where they are available. On the voyage, Chef Inniger had purchased fresh strawberries in Odessa, fish in Istanbul, and goose liver in France. During a stop in the Greek Islands the chef and provision master headed off to the local fish market to buy some of that day's catch; that appeared on the menu the next evening. Freshness is an obsession onboard. Orange juice is squeezed fresh daily; yesterday's fresh juice is consumed by the crew. Even the wine steward and head bartender buy many of the wines used on the ship in their countries of origin. "Because I am involved in the wine selection, I can explain them and sell them enthusiastically," Head Bartender Norbert Fuchs said.

## Problems

The problems are most likely to occur in the area of shore excursions. Unlike a seven-day Caribbean cruise where the ship visits the same port every week, a Seabourn ship may visit some ports only a few times a year. That means they have to work harder to get the best equipment and tour guides for shore excursions since the infrastructure is dominated by the larger vessels that call more regularly. In addition, things change often; some museums and other sites close for renovations, new ones open, and the recommended shopping and dining venues are different. Guests expect and want superior and unique excursions, and they are hard to come by—especially if the tour manager hasn't been there for six months.

Courtesy of Seabourn Cruise Lines

But the real problem is that ships cannot run their own shore excursions; that is reserved for the local community virtually everywhere. The implication of this is that guests are off the vessel and interacting with persons who are not company employees—even though the tours, like the airline flights, are perceived as part of the Seabourn vacation experience.

Seabourn's way of dealing with this is to differentiate their version of what is offered as much as possible. Buses that could hold 49 passengers are only half filled, and every bus gets not only a local guide but a member of Seabourn's own cruise staff. Bottles of water and soft drinks are carried onboard, and a complimentary refreshment stop is included.

The company tries very hard to audition the specific guides who will be used and specifically requests them whenever possible. Very explicit written contracts are given to all tour operators that specify, among other things, that all admissions are to be included, that there will be no tipping solicited or permitted, that the buses will arrive and depart at set hours at each stop, and that special requirements may be set, such as, "After lunch the guide will be stationed by the bell tower on the square to answer questions."

At some destinations it is possible to offer unique tours not available at all on other ships. These tours are usually quite expensive and only available when enough passengers sign up, but they often do. One example might be a balloon trip over vineyards in France. In Venice, guests willing to pay $390 were offered "an unforgettable evening in eighteenth-century Venice." The evening consisted of a five-course dinner in a restored Venetian Palazzo. Period Venetian dishes were served after a "Degustation of Wine," and entertainment was provided by a trio of musicians in period costumes playing ancient instruments, and a group of actors from La Commedia Dell 'Arte. There was also a private tour of the Guggenheim Museum for $85 hosted by one of its curators after closing hours, with wine being served. These tours are often the creation of the ship's travel office, which gives them a feeling of ownership and thus an internal mandate to see that they succeed.

## Passengers Expect Customized Service

Seabourn's success can be attributed to a complex and carefully orchestrated corporate culture based on values shared among the management, employees, and guests. President Larry Pimentel, a former travel agent himself, likes to tell agents in sales seminars that they should "sell what counts, not discounts." That is precisely the point. On a Seabourn cruise everyone seems to understand what counts. The passengers who are paying more than $800 per diem know they are buying a unique and personal experience, and that's what counts for them. They expect uniqueness and customized service; indeed, they demand it. The company shares the same value. "It is those very qualities that make the difference," says Pimentel.

It doesn't matter what you want; the company will get it for you. People frequently bring their own recipes, which the chef is glad to prepare. In some cases, special ingredients have been flown to the ship to fulfill these requests. Pimentel points out that Seabourn is not simply an expensive cruise, but an entirely different experience. "Buying Seabourn is a lifestyle decision," he says. "To provide that experience, the company relies on highly trained and motivated people, people who are motivated not by money, although they are well paid, but rather by a genuine pride in what they do."

This pride is reinforced regularly. When Seabourn won the Condé Nast award the first time, owner Brynestad sent every crew member a piece of his crystal as a present. After a spectacular party on this particular cruise, the following memo was sent to every manager on the ship and posted in the crew quarters:

> To Everyone Involved in the Fourth of July BBQ Yesterday:
>
> Thank you all for the effort you have put in to make this special day a success. Many guests commented how much they appreciate your hard and professional work. Some people dream of worthy accomplishments, while you stay awake and do them.
>
> Congratulations,
>
> Johannes Moser
> Hotel Manager

## Empathy Is an Important Factor

Another key is Atle Brynestad's "heart." The company shows genuine respect and empathy in dealing with its employees on every level. The only way to lose one's job at Seabourn is to lack that empathy for fellow employees and for guests. If there was a company song, it would be that old vaudeville number "You Gotta Have Heart." *Heart* translates into a recognition that everyone on the ship is literally in the same boat, and that it is a special boat where dreams come true for the guests and the employees.

Finally, there is empowerment. Seabourn is not purely a creation of Brynestad, Titus, and Pimentel. Indeed, 50 percent of the company is now owned by Carnival Cruise Lines. (Like other Carnival brands, it is profitable.) Clearly, Carnival's management team, like Seabourn's, understands that what drives the company is that it is a creation of the people on the front line who interact with the guests and together shape the experiences for the benefit of all parties. Larry Rapp adds:

> Everybody in this industry talks about moments of truth. There is no place on earth where a company has more moments of truth than on a cruise ship. They wake up in the morning; they meet their stewardesses. They go to breakfast and see our waiters. From there they go to a lecture on the next port of call or to an aerobics class. Every time they turn around, they encounter a member of our staff. There are hundreds of moments of truth every day. And obviously every one of those has to be positive or we lose.

There are lessons to be learned from this case study as a service experience that apply not only to the cruise industry but to other hospitality organizations as well. They are simple to enumerate but difficult to accomplish:

- Affluent guests don't buy rooms or food or seats. They buy experiences. The more personal the experience provided, and the more unique it is, the more customers are willing to pay for it. Value is not merely a function of dollars. Satisfaction is an equally important dimension.

- Employees should be treated with the same kind of respect one expects to receive. It goes without saying that managers need to understand what respect means.

- Employees should be involved in shaping the product and empowered to deliver it, so that they share in the pride and rewards that come with accomplishment. Give them constant feedback so they can see how they are doing.

People want to work in an organization because they want to accomplish more than they can alone. Companies that can mesh the personal goals of employees with an organization's overall goals will succeed and prosper.

## Chapter Summary

More than 100 cruise ships call at a dozen U.S. ports. These ships are floating vacation resorts—some carrying as many as 3,000 guests and costing $500 million or more. They generate revenues of $10 billion annually. The passenger services aboard these ships are managed by hotel managers, pursers, food and beverage directors, executive chefs, maîtres d', chief stewards, and cruise directors, many of whom come from fine hotels and hospitality schools. Only seven percent of Americans had ever taken a cruise by 1998.

Modern cruising was born in the early 1970s with the formation of Carnival Cruise Lines, Norwegian Caribbean Lines, Royal Caribbean Cruise Lines, and Princess Cruise Lines. Carnival's strategy, which changed consumers' perception of cruising from a pastime for the rich to a vacation for the masses, was probably the defining event in the development of the modern cruise industry.

Cruise lines are divided into four market segments by Cruise Lines International Association (CLIA): contemporary/value, premium, luxury, and specialty lines. The average cruise passenger is 51 years old, has a household income of $64,000, and pays $200 a day for an all-inclusive vacation that includes cabin, meals, and entertainment.

The laws under which a ship operates depend first upon where it is registered. The flag of that country is called a flag of convenience.

Cruise ships are very similar to hotels in their organization. At the top, the captain, who is responsible for the ship's operation and the safety of all those onboard, has three persons reporting to him: the chief officer, the chief engineer, and the hotel manager. The hotel manager oversees a purser, food and beverage manager, chief housekeeper, physician, cruise director, and other smaller departments and concessions; functions such as sales and marketing and reservations are carried out on shore. The hotel manager may also be responsible for providing medical care, entertainment, and shore excursions.

The chief purser is the ship's banker, information officer, human resource director, and complaint handler.

The food and beverage manager oversees the assistant food and beverage manager, executive chef, the maître d'hôtel, the bar manager, and the provision master. Because of safety and sanitation requirements—as well as passenger expectations—food and beverage operations are highly disciplined operations. Beverages are the single largest source of onboard revenue on every major cruise ship.

The steward's department is responsible for cleaning and general maintenance of all cabins and interior areas on a ship. The way cabin stewards interact with passengers often becomes a key component of guest satisfaction.

The cruise director's staff directs all guest activities and includes entertainers, musicians, and children's counselors. They also sell and coordinate shore excursions and prepare the daily activity calendar.

Modern cruise lines pay a great deal of attention to medical care. All ships carry at least one physician and a nurse. A determined devotion to accessibility makes ships attractive vacations for handicapped and older persons.

The Seabourn case illustrates how carefully cruise ships orchestrate the entire cruise vacation experience. Employees are highly trained and treated with respect. Very little is left to chance. Guest comments are taken seriously and acted upon almost instantly. These methods produce a high level of satisfaction and repeat business.

## Endnotes

1. International Council of Cruise Lines, 1997 estimates based on Price Waterhouse studies.
2. International Council of Cruise Lines, estimated 1998 figure.
3. Cruiser Segmentation Study, Cruise Lines International Association, 1995.

4. Much of the information cited in this chapter was originally researched and developed by Bob Dickinson and Andy Vladimir in *Selling the Sea: An Inside Look at the Cruise Industry*, (New York: John Wiley & Sons, 1997).
5. John Maxtone-Graham, *The Only Way to Cross* (New York: Macmillan, 1972), pp. 112–113.
6. Cruise Lines International Association—1996 North American Passenger Capacity.
7. Estimated 1997 figures compiled from various trade sources.
8. Dickinson and Vladimir, pp. 88–92.
9. The material in this case study first appeared in the Spring 1995 *FIU Hospitality Review* ( A School of Hospitality Management Publication, Florida International University). The study was prepared by Associate Professor Andrew Vladimir, who spent two weeks behind the scenes aboard the *Seabourn Spirit* from Istanbul to Venice and conducted additional extensive interviews with the line's major executives at Seabourn's headquarters in San Francisco.

## Key Terms

**captain**—The person on a ship who is responsible for its operation and the safety of all of those aboard. The captain sees that all company policies and rules, as well as national and international laws, are followed.

**chief officer**—The captain's second in command and deputy. Also called the staff captain on some lines.

**cruise director**—Oversees a staff responsible for managing a ship's entertainers, children's counselors, and guest activities, including selling and coordinating shore excursions.

**flag of convenience**—The flag of the country where a cruise ship is registered and under whose laws it must operate.

**galley**—The shipboard equivalent of a kitchen.

**lido deck**—The deck of the ship containing the main swimming pool. It is usually a center for many onboard activities.

**purser**—The second in command within the hotel department and a cruise ship's banker, information officer, human resource director, and complaint handler.

**shore excursions**—Specially arranged trips, tours, and activities that occur off the ship. They are a significant part of onboard revenue for any cruise line.

**sitting**—The time allotted for serving one complete meal to a group of diners. Most of today's vessels have enough dining room space to serve only half of the passengers at the same time. To compensate, there are two sittings—one usually at 6:00, the other at 8:30. The trick is to serve everyone a complete dinner and get them out of the dining room with enough time to clean up and reset the tables before the next sitting.

**steward's department**—Similar to the housekeeping department in a hotel. This department is responsible for cleaning, general maintenance of cabins and public spaces, and laundry.

**ton**—The unit for measuring the volume of a cruise ship, as opposed to measuring the weight.

**turnaround day**—The day when a cruise ship finishes one cruise and starts another one.

## Review Questions

1. What was the primary reason for transatlantic travel prior to the late 1950s?
2. What were some of the factors affecting the rise in the number of transatlantic passengers in the 1920s?
3. What three major cruise lines were born in the mid-to-late 1960s?
4. What characteristics distinguished cruise ship travel prior to the creation of Carnival Cruise Lines?
5. What unique characteristics did Carnival introduce to the cruise line industry?
6. How would you describe the average cruise passenger?
7. What are some of the responsibilities of a cruise ship captain?
8. Which departments are overseen by a cruise ship hotel manager?
9. What important duties are overseen by the cruise director's staff?
10. What is meant by the term "flag of convenience"?

## Internet Sites

For more information, visit the following Internet sites. Remember that Internet addresses can change without notice. If the site is no longer there, use a search engine to look for additional sites.

*Cruise Lines*

American Hawaii Cruises
www.cruisehawaii.com

Carnival Cruise Lines
www.carnival.com

Cunard Cruise Lines
www.cunardline.com

Disney Cruise Lines
www.disneycruise.com

Holland America Westours
www.hollandamerica.com

Norwegian Cruise Line
www.ncl.com

Princess Cruise Lines
www.princesscruises.com

Royal Caribbean International
www.rccl.com

Seabourn Cruise Lines
www.nobhilltravel.com/seaindex.htm

Silversea Cruise Lines
www.asource.com/silversea

Windstar Cruise Lines
www.windstarcruises.com

**Other Cruise Resources**

Cruise Lines International Association
www.cruising.org

*Cruise Trade* Magazine
www.traveltrade.com/cruisetrade/index.html

General Cruise Travel
www.travelpage.com/cruise.htm

"The Love Boat" Unofficial Home Page
www.asb.com/usr/indtvprd/loveboat/lbp1.htm

*Porthole Magazine*
www.porthole.com

The *Queen Mary*
www.queenmary.org

*Titanic* Links
www.mollybrown.com/links.html

# REVIEW QUIZ

When you feel you have covered all of the material in this chapter, answer these questions. Choose the *best* answer.

1. Which of the following statements about the cruise industry of the 1980s is *true*?

    a. There were few cruise ships.
    b. The cruise industry had a large land-based infrastructure.
    c. Hospitality students were not recruited to fill cruise jobs.
    d. a and c.

2. The defining event in the development of the modern cruise industry was probably:

    a. when the *Queen Elizabeth* was built.
    b. Carnival Cruise Lines' strategy of adding on-board activities and entertainment, making the ship itself the "destination."
    c. when immigrant accommodations on the old transatlantic liners were turned into "tourist class" cabins.
    d. Royal Caribbean International's decision in 1951 to introduce gambling—blackjack, roulette, baccarat, and so on—to cruise ships.

3. A cruise ship is under the command of the:

    a. captain.
    b. hotel manager.
    c. cruise director.
    d. chief officer.

4. The single largest source of onboard revenue on every major cruise ship comes from the sale of:

    a. food.
    b. gift shop merchandise.
    c. beverages.
    d. chips or "markers" (for gambling).

5. A typical medical department on a cruise ship:

    a. can dispense drugs but cannot perform operations.
    b. does not employ nurses.
    c. has enough prescription drugs to stock a small pharmacy.
    d. does not have a morgue.

6. Seabourn Cruise Lines was founded by:

    a. Atle Brynestad, a Norwegian industrialist and entrepreneur.
    b. Ted Arison, a young Israeli from Tel Aviv.
    c. Miami entrepreneur Leslie Frazer.
    d. a Seattle businessman named Stanley McDonald.

## REVIEW QUIZ (continued)

7. Seabourn's philosophy of how you achieve superior service is based on two main tenets:

   a. quality is free; and employees are our most important asset.
   b. take care of your internal guests (your employees); and guests (passengers) are Seabourn's most important asset.
   c. improve constantly and forever the system of production and service; and drive fear of failure out of the workplace.
   d. focus on the guests (passengers) at all times; and follow the Seabourn continuous-quality-improvement process.

**Answer Key:** 1-d-C1, 2-b-C1, 3-a-C2, 4-c-C2, 5-c-C2, 6-a-C3, 7-b-C3

Each question is linked to a competency. Competencies are listed on the first page of the chapter. An answer reading 3-b-C4 translates to:

- 3: the question number
- b: the correct answer
- C4: the competency number

## Chapter 11 Outline

The Story of Gaming
Gaming in America
    Gaming in Nevada and New Jersey
    Riverboat and Offshore Gambling
    Indian Gambling
    Industry Size
Casino Games
    Table Games
    Slot Machines
Casino Operations
    Casino Terminology
    Casino Employees
    Casino Customers
Casino Marketing
    Future Marketing Trends
Casino Controls and Regulation
Career Opportunities in Casino Hotels
    Casino Hotel Operation
    The Importance of Food and Beverages
    Service Demands in Casino Hotels
Chapter Summary

## Competencies

1. Summarize the history of gaming around the world and in America, and describe the major casino games played today.

2. Explain the casino terminology used for games, employees, and customers.

3. Describe in general terms the marketing approaches, regulations, controls, and operations in place at a modern casino hotel.

4. Describe the career opportunities available in casino hotels.

# 11

# Gaming and Casino Hotels

THIS CHAPTER IS about gambling, or *gaming*, which is what it has come to be called in the industry. The two words are interchangeable. For the most part we will focus on gaming within hotels, although free-standing casinos, riverboats, offshore gaming junkets, and even Internet gambling are proliferating. We will start with a brief history of gaming, discuss the growth of the industry, types of games, terminology, security, and casino hotel operations.

## The Story of Gaming

No one knows when gambling first started. The first recorded account dates back to early Chinese dynasties in 2300 B.C. Some of the earliest pieces of gaming evidence we have comes from ancient Egypt; dice have been found by archeologists in pyramid excavations. (As near as we can tell, gamblers back then faced the same problems that they do today. People who couldn't pay their gambling losses were punished and made to work off their debts!) Ancient Greeks considered gambling immoral but it occurred anyway; historians tell us that Greek soldiers played dice before the offensive against Troy. Both the Old and New Testaments mention gambling. Indeed, Roman centurions gambled for Christ's robes following his crucifixion. While there were laws barring gambling in the early part of the Roman Empire, it was later embraced and became a popular diversion for Roman citizens. Romans enthusiastically bet on gladiators, on the lions against the Christians, chariot races, and other blood sports held in venues like the Coliseum.

After the Crusades (circa A.D. 1200–1300), gambling spread through Europe. In fact, games that evolved into dice, roulette, and blackjack had their roots in medieval times. Craps, for instance, began as a game called hazard that was played by English knights. By the seventeenth century, forms of roulette and blackjack had been introduced.

The elegant casinos of Baden-Baden, Germany, and Monaco in Monte Carlo were built in the mid-nineteenth century and became a favorite of European royalty and the aristocracy. Gambling was legalized in Great Britain in the 1960s to assist churches in collecting funds. Today, Austria, Egypt, Poland, Turkey, Russia, Macao, Australia, New Zealand, and the Philippines, among others, have popular gambling facilities. At least 22 jurisdictions in the Caribbean have casinos. In many countries, casinos are owned or controlled by the government.

At New York-New York Hotel & Casino, guests can shop along Park Avenue, ride a roller coaster, and visit a 150-foot-tall replica of the Statue of Liberty. (Courtesy of New York-New York Hotel & Casino)

## Gaming in America

Following Columbus's discovery of the New World, Spanish and Portuguese sailors brought dice and cards with them on the first expeditions—along with their horses, which they raced in leisure moments. Indians shaped their own dice from fruit pits and joined in the games.

Early American colonists developed a taste for gambling as well. (It was one way, for example, to raise needed funds to fight the Revolutionary War.) They justified their popular lotteries by using the money raised to fund other worthy causes, such as municipal projects, colleges, and universities. Columbia, Dartmouth, Harvard, and Yale were all partially funded by lotteries. Card games, too, were widely played.

By the early nineteenth century some places had established reputations as favorite gambling destinations. The most prominent of these was New Orleans, conveniently situated on the Mississippi River and a major port. By 1810 the city was said to have as many gambling halls as the four largest American cities put together. But gambling attracted criminals as well as average citizens. Riverboats were known to be home to cardsharps and professional gamblers, and there were many instances of travelers being cheated out of all of their money.

Prior to 1861 and the start of the Civil War, there was a move to prohibit gambling in most states. In the latter part of the nineteenth century, lotteries were outlawed by the federal government. However, other forms of gambling continued to survive in a few places including riverboats plying the Ohio and the Mississippi Rivers, as well as the states that were on those rivers.

## Gaming in Nevada and New Jersey

By the early twentieth century, gambling had become illegal in most states. Even Nevada, which had allowed it since 1868, outlawed it in all forms in 1910. But, in 1931, during the Great Depression, the state legislature of Nevada decided to revive it as a means to economic recovery. Almost all forms of gambling were permitted.

The first casinos were mostly in converted stores, but by 1935 clubs began to appear, first in Reno, and later in Las Vegas. In 1946 the Flamingo Hotel and Casino opened—the first elegant casino hotel that included entertainment. Opening night featured a bevy of Hollywood movie stars as performers and guests who would return regularly, giving Las Vegas a reputation as a glamorous vacation spot.

In 1976 legalized casino gambling was allowed in depressed Atlantic City, New Jersey, mainly for many of the same economic reasons that appealed to Las Vegas. The first casino hotel was built by Resorts International (which had already developed Paradise Island in the Bahamas).

Today, gambling of one form or another is permitted almost everywhere in the United States. Hawaii and Utah are the only two states that prohibit all forms of gambling.

## Riverboat and Offshore Gambling

By 1997 six states had legalized riverboat gambling, giving it a firm foothold. Laws concerning their operations, however, vary considerably. For example, in Iowa the boats are required to leave the shore and make cruises that can last from 90 to 120 minutes. In Illinois, cruises last for approximately two hours. In Mississippi the boats are not allowed to leave the dock at all and guests can gamble as long as they wish.

Major hospitality companies have taken an interest in riverboat operation.

In coastal states such as Florida, Georgia, and Texas, offshore gambling is gaining in popularity. Large tour boats and even a few small, obsolete cruise ships offer gambling "cruises to nowhere." These boats sail three miles offshore before they open their casinos, and they stay out an average of three or four hours.

## Indian Gambling

With the passing of the Indian Gaming Regulatory Act (IGRA) in 1988, Congress made it legal for Native Americans to open casinos on their property in states where gambling was allowed. The purpose of the act was to promote tribal economic development, protect Indian gaming from organized crime, and establish an appropriate regulatory body. Today Connecticut and Minnesota are two states with major casino operations on reservations, although there are many others.

It should be noted that the largest casino in the world is located on an Indian reservation. It is called Foxwoods Resort Casino in Ledyard, Connecticut. Foxwoods is run by the Mashantucket Pequot Tribal Nation. Besides two hotels, there is a casino with more than 4,000 slot machines and a 3,200-seat bingo hall.

## Industry Size

In 1996 the gross amount wagered or bet (known as the "handle") on all forms of legal gambling in the United States was more than $586.5 billion. About 75 percent was wagered at land-based, riverboat, and cruise ship casinos. Gambling on Indian reservations scored the second largest handle: $65.1 billion (11.1%). Of course, there are other forms of gambling that are very popular, including horse racing, bingo, and lotteries.

Of the total amount gambled in non-Indian casinos, $47.6 billion was **gross gambling revenue** (GGR). Gross gambling revenue is the amount that is retained by the gambling business. It is considered the net receipts of the operation and the amount that is taxed by the government bodies. The retention percentage for casinos was 4.4 percent. The gross gambling revenue (GGR) for Indian casinos was $5.4 billion or 8.2 percent of the handle.

The states with the highest handle were Nevada with $222.2 billion and New Jersey with $89.4 billion.

## Casino Games

There are basically two types of casino games, those classified as table games and slot machines. The most common table games include baccarat, blackjack, craps, and roulette (see Exhibit 1).

### Table Games

*Baccarat* was named after an Italian word meaning "zero." It went from Italy to France in the fifteenth century where it was known as *Chemin de Fer*. The object of the game is to come as close as possible to the number 9, which is known as a natural. (Scoring an 8 is the second-best hand and is also known as a natural.) It is played with eight complete decks of cards. The cards are shuffled by the croupier (dealer), cut, and placed in a special box referred to as the "shoe." The shoe is passed to a player who becomes the banker. The first and third cards dealt from the shoe constitute the player's hand; the second and fourth cards are the banker's hand. Face cards and 10 count as 0, aces count as 1, and all other cards count at face value. The hand with the highest point total closest to 9 wins.

*Blackjack* is played at a table seating 5 to 8 players across from a dealer. Here the object is to get closer to 21 than the dealer. If anyone goes over 21, they automatically lose. The shoe can contain between one and eight decks. The dealer gives each player two cards face up; the dealer gets one card face up and one card face down. Kings, queens, jacks, and 10s each count as 10. Aces count as 1 or 11, as the player wishes. All other cards count at their face value. Additional cards may be distributed, if the player desires, until a player or the dealer is declared a winner.

*Craps* is considered by many players to be the most exciting game in any casino. In its many varieties of betting, craps can be a complicated game. It is played on a rectangular table covered with green felt. The table is marked with all of the possible bets that can be made. A pair of dice are thrown by one of the players designated as

**Exhibit 1  Table Game Layouts**

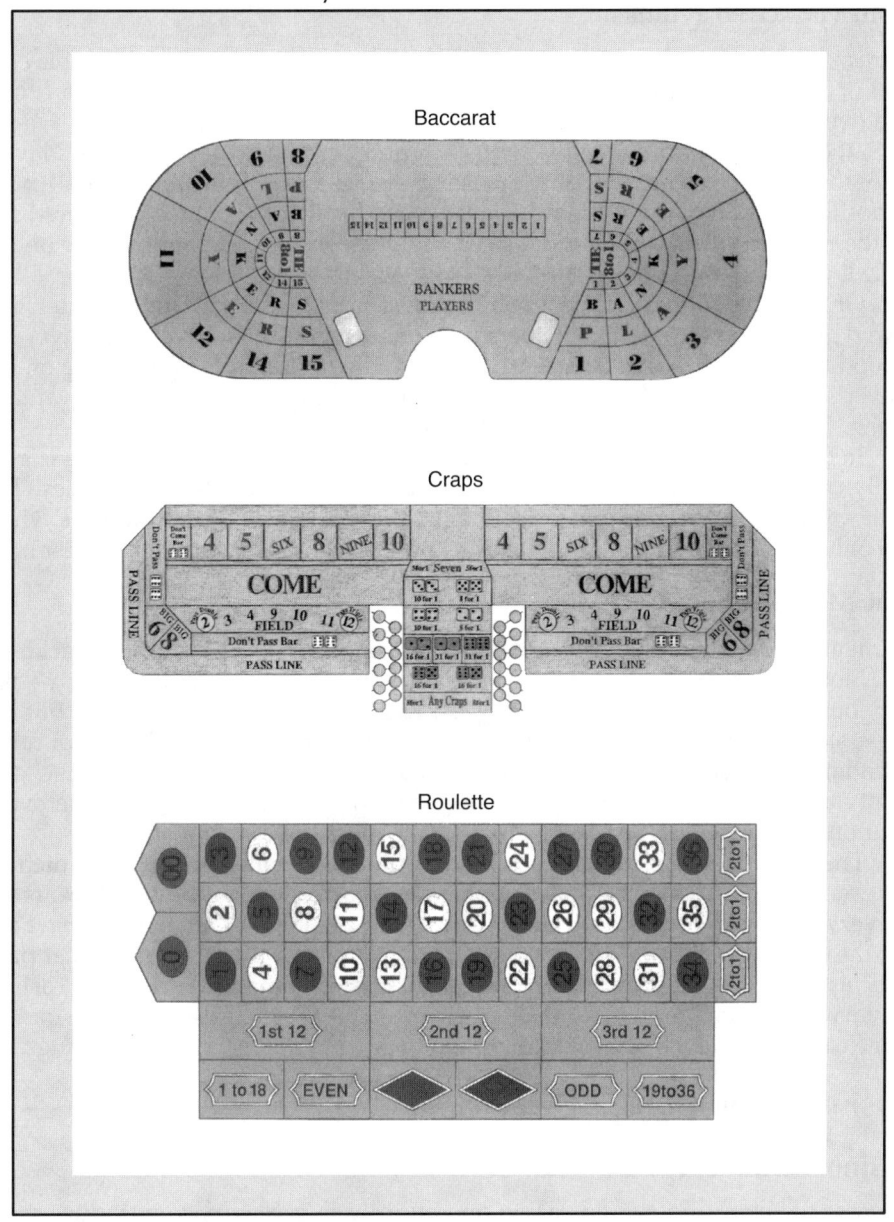

*Baccarat*

*Craps*

*Roulette*

the "shooter." Other players bet with or against the shooter by putting their chips on sections of the table that are marked *pass* line, *don't pass* line, *come* field etc.

In the most basic bet, players who bet on the pass line win if the shooter rolls a 7 or 11; they lose if he rolls "craps," which is 2, 3, or 12. Of course there are many other ways to win and lose and the action moves very fast—which is why the game is often perceived as difficult.

*Roulette* is the simplest table game of them all. In American roulette the table consists of a revolving wheel in which there is a ball and slots numbering from 1 to 36 and two symbols, 0 and 00 (in most other countries there is only one zero). On the table there is a diagrammed area with each number and symbol marked. Players place their chips on a number or symbol and the dealer spins the roulette ball in the opposite direction of the spinning wheel. When the ball falls into a numbered slot on the roulette wheel, the dealer places a marker on the winning number on the table layout and pays the winning bet.

Of the table games, blackjack is the most popular in the United States, followed by craps and roulette. People who gamble regularly know that a player has a good chance of winning in blackjack, where the house odds (depending on the player's skill level) can be less than two percent. With craps, the house advantage is only 1.4 percent. In American roulette the house advantage is 5.26 percent.

In European casinos, where roulette is the most popular game, gaming is generally considered more of an entertainment than a way of winning money. The odds are a little better for players of French roulette, however, because the wheel has only one 0. With French roulette, the house advantage is only 2.63 percent.

## Slot Machines

As mentioned earlier, much of the gaming in American casinos is in slot machines.

Slots are by far the most profitable games from a casino's point of view—not only because the percentage of money the casino keeps is high (usually), but because slots are the least labor-intensive of all games, requiring no dealers or other attendants, except for employees who maintain the machines, make change, and empty and refill the hoppers. There are also a high number of bets made every hour on a slot machine, and the more bets, the more the casino makes.

The amount of money slot machines pay out is controlled in every jurisdiction. For example, in Atlantic City, slot machines must pay back 83 percent, or 83 cents out of every dollar bet; the house keeps 17 cents. Nevada does not regulate the payback but the Gaming Control Board, as a policy, does not approve any game that pays back less than 75 percent. In order to attract business in competitive markets, casinos may pay back more, hoping to make their profit on the increased betting volume. Some casinos in Nevada have been known to pay back 99 percent in winnings.

# Casino Operations

## Casino Terminology

In order to better understand casino operations it is necessary to introduce some key definitions used in casino management.

**Markers. Markers** are printed or written forms that look like bank checks extending credit to a player. They are IOUs and can be given to dealers in exchange for chips instead of cash. They have no cash value; they refer simply to the amount of credit that the casino is willing to extend. Typically the casino agrees not to cash

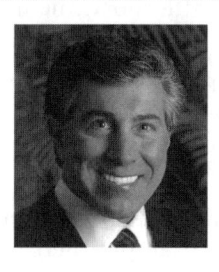

# Industry Innovators

Stephen A. Wynn
Chairman & CEO
Mirage Resorts

Although Steve Wynn is generally credited for igniting the spark that turned Las Vegas, Nevada, into the glittering wonder it has become today, he does not gamble. "If you want to make money in a casino, own one," he is widely quoted as saying. Wynn knows what he's talking about. His father was a compulsive gambler who ran bingo parlors. When he died leaving huge debts, Wynn and his wife took over the parlors and the debts. It took them years to pay off creditors while running the games themselves.

His father had always wanted to open a casino in Las Vegas, and in 1967 Wynn moved there with his family to fulfill his father's dream. He bought an interest in the Frontier Hotel and became the slot manager. Unknown to him, the hotel was owned by Detroit mobsters. When he found out, he sold his shares.

Wynn's next venture was a profitable real estate deal that made enough money so he was able to invest in a rundown casino, the Golden Nugget. By the time he was 31, he took control and became the youngest casino owner in Nevada history. At that time, almost all casinos were dimly lit, smoke-filled rooms with questionable clientele. Wynn changed that by transforming the Golden Nugget into a sparkling, bright game hall that attracted legitimate high rollers.

Using his Las Vegas property as collateral, Wynn then opened the Golden Nugget in Atlantic City. In 1987, he sold his operations to the Bally Corporation and used the proceeds, along with money raised by issuing bonds, to build the Mirage resort, which opened in 1989.

The Mirage was the first of a new kind of Las Vegas hotel—designed to be a family attraction. Guests enter through a lush, tropical atrium filled with 60-foot palm trees and waterfalls. Behind the front desk is a 20,000-gallon, coral-reef aquarium stocked with sharks and other large fish. The Mirage is also home to two unique animal habitats: a dolphin habitat and the Secret Garden, where six rare white lions and tigers live.

Next to the Mirage, Wynn opened Treasure Island in 1993. The theme here is pirates, and every hour there is a very realistic battle that includes the complete destruction and sinking of a nearly 100-foot British frigate.

In 1998, Wynn opened the Bellagio, a $1.4 billion, 3,000-plus room property that he says is the "most romantic hotel in the world." The resort features $60 million in original art by famous artists. Resorts in Biloxi, Mississippi, and Atlantic City are also on the way.

Wynn is known for being politically active—especially for environmental causes. He personally led a measure to ban all personal watercraft (jet skis) from Lake Tahoe where he lives, arguing that they were polluting the lake. He has also taken the lead in fighting for laws to control erosion and traffic and air pollution in Las Vegas. He is a member of the board of trustees of his alma mater, the University of Pennsylvania, and the George Bush Presidential Library.

these checks for 30 or 45 days, giving the player time to deposit the money in his or her bank account.

**Cashier's Cage.** The **cashier's cage,** generally referred to simply as the cage, is where chips and cash are stored, where checks are cashed, where credit cards are accepted, and where markers are approved. It is the control center for the flow of chips to and from tables.

**Pit.** A grouping of tables within a casino that defines a management section is called a **pit.** These can be the same game or a combination. For example, there may be four craps tables and four roulette tables in one pit, or simply eight craps tables. The manager of the group is called the **pit boss.**

**Fill and Credit Slips.** Each table has an inventory of chips. At the end of each shift the inventory at each table is restored to the original amount. If the inventory is depleted, then a **fill slip** is completed and additional chips are issued from the cage. If there is an excess of chips, a **credit slip** is completed and the extra chips are returned to the cage.

In modern casinos these pieces of paper have been replaced by a computer network so that requests can be transmitted electronically from the pit. If there is no computer system, security guards are utilized to carry credit and fill slips back and forth to the cage.

**Drop Box.** Each table is equipped with a box that locks in place beneath the table. Cash and markers received from players are deposited through a slot into the **drop box.** At the end of a shift, boxes are removed from the table and brought to a count room. At specific times they are opened and the contents counted carefully under strict supervision. When boxes are removed from the table, the slot is automatically locked and can be reopened only by keys that are under the control of the account team.

**Table Drop. Table drop** is the amount of money and markers that is placed in a drop box at a gaming table in exchange for chips. It may or may not represent the amount placed on bets at that table since players often carry chips from one table or game to another, or cash them in. The table drop, however, is a good measure of gaming activity within the casino.

**Slot Drop.** Unlike the table drop, where all money and markers deposited are counted, **slot drop** represents the amount of money put into a slot machine *less the amount paid out*. For example, if $100 is put into a slot machine and $90 is paid out, the drop is $10 or 10 percent.

**Table Win.** The **table win** is the amount bet minus the amount that is paid back to the players. It is calculated as follows:

|   | Opening chip inventory |
|---|---|
| + | Fill slips |
| − | Credit slips |
| − | Closing chip inventory |
| TOTAL = | Total chips missing from the table |

Once the total missing chips are determined then a second calculation is required:

$$\begin{array}{rl} & \text{Table drop} \\ - & \underline{\text{Total chips missing from the table}} \\ \text{TOTAL} = & \text{Table win} \end{array}$$

**Hold Percentage.** The **hold percentage** is a calculation to determine the percentage of chips purchased at a table by a customer that is won back by the casino. It is calculated as follows:

$$\text{Win} \div \text{Drop} = \text{Hold}$$

For example, if the win is $1,400 and the drop is $4,000, then the hold is 35 percent. In other words, the casino won (kept) 35 percent purchased at that table.

## Casino Employees

Casinos are staffed by **croupiers**, or dealers, whose job it is to conduct the table games. Casino managers expect dealers to be fast and friendly. Manual dexterity and math skills are also important. Like all casino employees, dealers are carefully screened for honesty. They are also under constant electronic and personal surveillance. Some U.S. dealers earn as much as $50,000 per year if they deal in high-action games; the average salary is $25,000 to $30,000. Dealers may earn large sums in tips. Some players not only tip dealers generously, they place a bet for the dealer at the same time they place one for themselves (for good luck).

**Floor people** are casino employees who supervise dealers. They are trained to enforce good dealing procedures, resolve disputes, and watch for cheaters. Today's cheaters are often extremely sophisticated, using computers and other electronic devices. A floor person will usually supervise two to four tables and reports to a pit boss.

A pit boss manages a larger group of tables and pays special attention to tables with high action. A big part of a pit boss's job is to make sure that gamblers placing large bets are happy. Often pit bosses act as hosts for these gamblers.

The person in charge of the casino at any given time is the shift manager. Shift managers work six to eight hours at a time. Under the shift manager is the games manager, who is responsible for all of the table games.

All of these employees have high-pressure jobs because they are responsible for so much cash. In a large casino it is not unusual for betting activity to reach $1 million an hour. Many casinos win $1 million for their owners in an 18-hour day.

## Casino Customers

Casinos often divide their customers into two broad groups: Grind players and high-end players. Both are vital to the long-term health of a gaming establishment.

**Grind players** generally enter a casino with a budget. They have decided to play $25, $200, or some other relatively modest amount. When their budget is gone

**The Crystal Palace Casino, Nassau, Bahamas.** (Courtesy of Carnival Cruise Lines)

or when they have won enough to make them feel lucky, they happily leave. Gaming for them is a form of entertainment, and their losses are viewed as the price of that entertainment.

**High-end players** (often called "high rollers" or "high-stakes players") are a different breed of gambler. Gaming for them represents a chance to experience a meaningful risk, a big thrill, for which they are prepared to put down a large amount of money. It is difficult to estimate how much a high-end player will bet, because it depends on a casino's particular market. A player with $5,000 to spend in a weekend of gambling would typically be considered a high-roller. Some high-end players bet much more than that, however—sometimes as much as $500,000 on a single bet!

High-end players play regularly and expect to suffer big losses at times. They minimize their losses by negotiating with the casinos where they play regularly. Rebates, gifts, free guest rooms, and free food are three common ways casinos help ease the sting of losing. Often the value of these rebates for losses and complimentary items can reach as high as 25 to 50 percent of what the player lost. These rebates are most common in baccarat, where typically the highest sums are wagered, and are negotiated in advance.

Casino managers have been known to present Rolex watches to high-end players and their spouses when they arrive at the hotel. These players may leave with Cadillacs if their losses (the casino's winnings) are significant enough.

Some high-end players have "personal representatives" who approach the casino's managers before the players arrive to negotiate terms. This representative asks questions like the following:

- What kind of action are you expecting? (How much money do you expect my client to play?)
- How many hours a day do you expect my client to play?
- What percent of the loss will you cover through complimentary items?
- How long will you hold my client's marker?
- Will you give my client a discount if he or she pays off the marker immediately?
- Will you offer a suite and food and beverages for some of my client's friends and relatives who don't gamble but would like to stay at your hotel?

A personal representative usually receives a commission of 10 percent of the money the casino wins from the client.

## Casino Marketing

There are three separate markets that casinos generally target. The *high-end*, as we have discussed, is made up of those people who are willing to gamble $5,000 or more on every visit to a casino. Since they are, for the most part, experienced gamblers who play regularly and make credit arrangements in advance, they are well known to operators. This kind of gambler is recruited through agents and friends. Marketing to them consists mainly of offering rebates, complimentary lodging, food and entertainment, and often gifts as well.

The *middle-range* customer can be described as the person who spends between $3,000 and $5,000 per trip. Many casinos call this segment their core market. The key to marketing to them is first to be able to identify them—a task that has become much easier with the advent of technology. Modern casinos use an automated rating system that tracks frequency of play, amount of time played, the particular games played, and the size of the average bet to assign a theoretical value or a certain number of points to players. With this information a direct-mail campaign can be created offering everything from junkets to room discounts and special events for those who qualify. What is offered is calculated very carefully based on how much a player is expected to (or agrees to) play. The rule of thumb in the industry is to offer to comp up to 50 percent against expenses—win, lose, or draw. This sum is applied against the room, food and beverages, and entertainment charges that the guest has incurred.

Casino junkets are sometimes advertised or organized by brokers. Junkets are all or partially paid trips to a casino. Guests generally agree, in advance, to play a certain amount of money over a certain period of time—usually four hours a day.

The Mirage in Las Vegas uses its Web site to highlight a wide range of entertainment options that would appeal to vacationing families. (Courtesy of Mirage Resorts)

Casino personnel monitor the action carefully. These junkets often lure first-time visitors who may then be invited back based on their observed performance.

Once a casino has identified one of these valuable players, it may send them a regular newsletter and invitation to play in special tournaments, join their VIP club, and attend parties or events organized around special holidays.

*Low-end* players are very important for the health of any casino. Because their game of choice is often slot machines, they help create a busy ambiance and can be very profitable, since the house odds on slots are significantly better than with other games. Bus tours, which are particularly popular in Atlantic City because of its proximity to New York City and Philadelphia, are the major marketing tool for this market. These tours operate on regular schedules. Players on a tour are usually refunded the amount of the bus fare in the form of vouchers good for free meals, show tickets, and rolls of quarters or tokens for playing the slots.

Typically, low-end players on bus tours spend about six hours in town. To keep players in a particular casino—so they won't wander off to visit a competitor down the boardwalk—casinos may offer free cocktails and hold frequent drawings for automobiles and cash.

### Future Marketing Trends

As gaming continues to grow, gamblers have become more sophisticated. Casinos that cater to the grind market have been forced to offer complimentary items to grind players who've learned that part of the game is to recover some of your losses. Many casinos in Las Vegas have formed slot clubs. These clubs cost nothing to join. Members are issued electronic cards, which they enter into slot machines before starting to play. The cards record the volume of play, and players are awarded points based on how much they bet. These points can be exchanged for food, beverages, guest rooms, or gifts.

## Casino Controls and Regulation

Because of the high volume of cash and credit transactions, casino controls must be stringent. There are many opportunities for customer and employee dishonesty. Because money is not earned by tangible products or services such as rooms and food, there is no way of measuring what has been "sold." Nor is it practical to record every single gambling transaction. So how does a casino make certain it keeps all of the cash it earns?

There are three kinds of controls that casinos use: accounting controls, equipment controls, and human controls.

- Accounting controls include sophisticated formulas to calculate expected profitability by the game, by the table, and by the shift. As we have mentioned, there are numerous credit and cash control procedures that are carefully recorded.

- Equipment controls are electronic surveillance cameras, safes, lock boxes, etc.

- Human controls are at every level—from pit bosses to security guards. There are on-site inspectors, both human and electronic, monitoring every part of the casino and every transaction.

Casinos are carefully regulated by the governments that sanction them. This is necessary to ensure that the government collects its share of the proceeds, as well as to discourage organized criminal activities. Legislation usually dictates the casino's size, types of games permitted, investigation and licensing of employees, hours and days of operation, marketing activities, and type and size of public space.

While regulations differ everywhere, the Nevada model of gaming control is widely copied. Nevada has two bodies that deal with gaming and report directly to the governor: the Gaming Commission and the Gaming Control Board. The Gaming Commission is charged with enacting necessary gaming regulations, issuing licenses, and handling disciplinary matters. The Gaming Control Board investigates applicants, enforces regulations, and audits the books and control systems of casinos.

## Career Opportunities in Casino Hotels

Students who are just interested in a career in gaming usually get specialized training and experience, which is available at gaming institutes. These are private schools that teach the skills needed to fill jobs such as croupiers and casino managers.

The majority of hospitality students, however, are drawn to the hotel and food and beverage operations, which are extensive in the gaming industry. Career tracks in the rooms division, food and beverage, and sales and marketing—all leading to general management positions—are possible at casino hotels.

The best way to understand casino hotels is to think of them not as hotels with casinos attached, but rather as casinos with guest rooms, restaurants, shopping arcades, and even theme parks attached. A description of what casino hotels are like appeared in award-winning humorist Dave Barry's syndicated newspaper column:

> We stayed at Caesars Palace, a giant hotel-casino decorated to look exactly the way the Roman Empire would have looked if it had consisted mainly of slot machines. Caesars also features roughly four zillion flashing lights, huge toga-clad statues that move, cocktail waitresses designed by Frederick's of Rome, and a bar on a large indoor boat that is actually floating. ("Mom, I think maybe you've had enough, you might...." SPLASH. "MAN OVERBOARD!")
>
> In other words, by Vegas standards, Caesars is very understated. It's a traditional Amish farm settlement compared to the casino next door, the Mirage, which has real dolphins, albino tigers, an indoor rain forest, and an outdoor volcano that erupts on schedule. (You're going to see more and more hotels installing volcanoes in response to demand from the business traveler.) Also, right behind the front desk is a giant aquarium containing sharks. So you definitely should not mess with the Mirage. ("Were you planning to pay for those hotel towels in your suitcase, Mr. Furbitt? Or would you prefer to *take a little swim?*")[1]

Hilton is a major player in the casino hotel business. It was the first big hotel chain to enter the gambling business when it purchased Las Vegas's Flamingo Hotel in 1971. It is now Nevada's largest employer, with 11,000 employees working in five properties. Hilton also operates casinos in Australia and Turkey.

Many Las Vegas hotels today have elaborate theme-park attractions as well as entertainment on their properties to attract more family business. Mirage's 3,000-room hotel has a volcano that erupts every 15 minutes from dusk to midnight, spewing smoke and fire 100 feet above the lagoons below. There is a 20,000

**Many casinos list numerous career opportunities on their Web pages, including current openings and internships.** (Courtesy of Trump Hotels & Casino Resorts)

**The MGM Grand.** (Courtesy of MGM Grand, World's Largest Hotel, Casino & Theme Park, Las Vegas, Nevada)

gallon aquarium stocked with sharks, rays, and exotic fish; a tropical rain forest; a dolphin environment housing a family of Atlantic bottlenosed dolphins; and a white-tiger habitat that exhibits the animals used by entertainers Siegfried and Roy in their show.

The Treasure Island Hotel and Casino offers a 24-hour show with live actors in a simulated cannon battle between the pirate ship *Hispaniola* and the British warship *HMS Sir Francis Drake*. At New York-New York Hotel & Casino, guests can stroll through Central Park, ride the Manhattan Express roller coaster, shop along Park Avenue, and visit a 150-foot-tall replica of the Statue of Liberty.

The $1 billion MGM Grand is, for the moment, the world's largest hotel. Besides 5,005 guest rooms, 751 suites (with a total of 7,778 beds to be made), seven restaurants, and the world's largest casino (the size of four football fields) with

**Exhibit 2  Casino and Hotel Departments**

```
                            President
     ┌──────┬──────┬──────┬──────┬──────┬──────┐
  V.P.    V.P.   V.P.    V.P.   V.P.          V.P.
  Casino  Hotel  Admin-  Mar-   Finance       Loss
  Opera-  Opera- istra-  keting               Preven-
  tions   tions  tion                         tion
                   │       │      │      │      │
               Personnel Controller Credit Collection Dir. of
                                    Manager Manager   Surveillance
                           │          │
                         Case      Rating Clerks
                         Manager
                           │
                         Pit Clerks
```

slots from five cents to $500, the hotel boasts an adjacent 33-acre theme park with a tour of a simulated Hollywood studio back lot, the world's tallest SkyCoaster, and two wedding chapels for couples who want to get married during their stay.

## Casino Hotel Operation

The most striking difference between a casino hotel and other types of hotels is in the organization and management of the facility. The importance of this point cannot be over emphasized, because it changes completely the way casino hotels are operated compared to traditional resorts. In casino hotels the hotel operation is subordinate to the gambling operation. The vice president of hotel operations is not in complete control but reports to a higher resident authority who usually holds the title of president of the hotel. There is also on the property a vice president of casino operations who is as important as the hotel manager when it comes to making decisions about almost everything. That's not all. Other vice presidents also make a lot of decisions that are usually handled as part of hotel operations. In Exhibit 2, note that there are a total of six vice presidents reporting to the president. There's also a vice president of administration who handles human resources, a vice president of marketing, a vice president of finance, and a vice president of loss prevention (security).

Why have these departments been removed from the hotel operation? Because decisions affect the casino as well. For instance, security is an important consideration. That means that not just the people working in the casino need to be selected for their honesty and integrity—all employees do, no matter who they work for. Moreover, an entirely different kind of security force is required in a casino hotel than in a regular one. There is casino surveillance and building security.

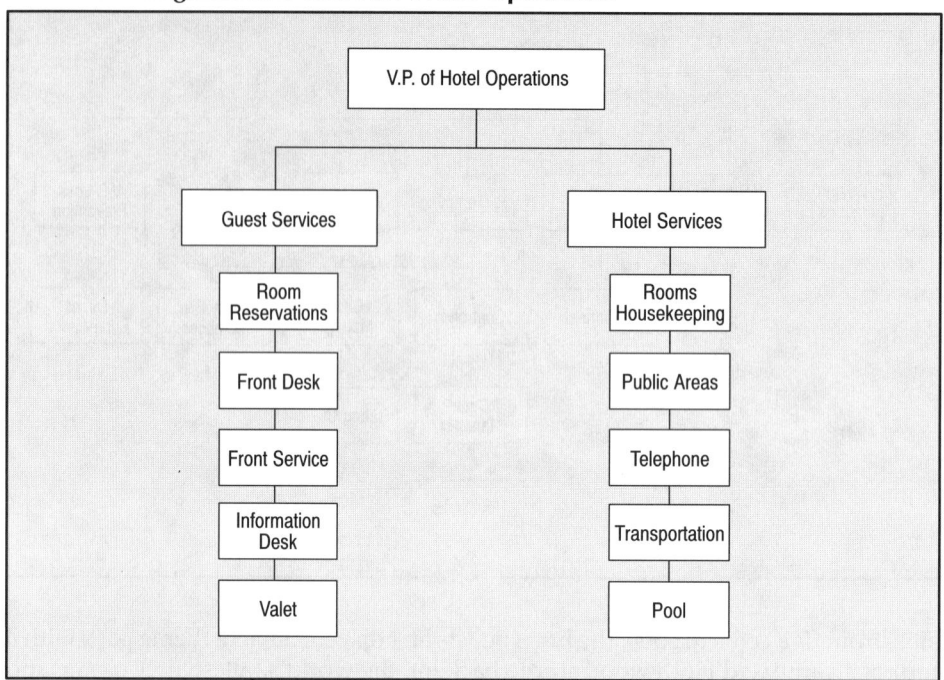

**Exhibit 3    Organization Chart for Hotel Operations**

```
                        V.P. of Hotel Operations
                                 │
              ┌──────────────────┴──────────────────┐
         Guest Services                       Hotel Services
              │                                     │
      Room Reservations                     Rooms Housekeeping
              │                                     │
         Front Desk                           Public Areas
              │                                     │
        Front Service                          Telephone
              │                                     │
       Information Desk                       Transportation
              │                                     │
           Valet                                  Pool
```

Thus there are two separate departments, administration and security, that are independent. Controls, credit, and the management of cash also are not simply matters for either the hotel manager or the casino manager to determine. Decisions about them affect both entities. Marketing, too, is unique. Gamblers are one audience; resort and convention guests another. But they're all at the same property at the same time.

The bottom line here is that the vice president of hotel operations in many large Las Vegas and Atlantic City casino hotels is basically just in charge of the rooms department and hotel services such as the spa, transportation, and pool (see Exhibit 3).

## The Importance of Food and Beverages

While food and beverage operations are key to any resort operation, in casino hotels they play an added role. They make gaming convenient by "fueling" the players. It isn't necessary to wander far or leave the premises in order to get any kind of dining experience—from a pastrami sandwich to a Châteaubriand.

The food and beverage department is operated as a separate division under its own vice president. At the Mirage, this division, which has 14 food outlets, is the largest of all in terms of number of employees.

A closer look at the food and beverage operations of the MGM Grand shows the scope and variety of dining experiences that are offered. The MGM Grand has seven fine-dining restaurants—all of them imaginatively decorated—as well as a variety of other outlets, including a 24-hour café and a New York-style deli.

The fine dining operations are:

- Gatsby's. French and California cuisine specialties, including farm-raised ostrich and Colorado rack of lamb, and three separate wine cellars.

- Wolfgang Puck Café. Famed chef Wolfgang Puck has created a series of signature pizzas and other items for this restaurant.

- Mark Miller's Coyote Café and Grill Room. Southwestern specialties like jerk chicken tacos and blue-corn enchiladas, margaritas and blended rum drinks.

- The Brown Derby. Another re-creation of this famous Hollywood landmark—the home of Cobb salad.

- Emeril Lagasse's New Orleans Fish House. Creole/Cajun cooking from a famous New Orleans chef.

- Franco Nuschese's Tre Visi and La Scala. Italian regional specialties.

- Dragon Court. Chinese cuisine.

## Service Demands in Casino Hotels

Service operations in casino hotels are unique as well. Both entertainment and food are important components of the gambling experience. They provide opportunities for winners to celebrate and losers to console themselves. Because of all the services they provide, casino hotels are even more labor-intensive than other kinds of hotels. Elaborate and extensive entertainment and multiple dining facilities with all-night service mean that the number of employees per hotel room may be three or four times higher than in conventional hotels and resorts.

Despite the complexity of operating casino hotels, they are tremendously attractive cash cows to knowledgeable operators who have experience in running them. Although not all casino hotels have been financially successful, those that are generate profits far in excess of other hotels.

Because the casino books must be kept separately, and in order to offer rebates and other incentives to important guests, casino managers must keep careful track of the amount of money played. One typical source of tension that may arise between casino managers, hotel managers, and food and beverage managers is how much money the casino will be charged for complimentary rooms and food and beverages.

Another source of tension between the casino division and the rooms division involves guest room inventory. Research has shown that most people take gambling trips—especially to Nevada and Atlantic City—on impulse, planning them no more than 48 hours in advance. This means that a casino hotel must keep a certain number of guest rooms available at all times for this last-minute traffic. On the other hand, popular resort hotels with casinos tend to fill their guest rooms five or six weeks in advance, especially around holidays. Enough rooms must be held open so that the hotel is not forced to turn away gamblers—its most profitable source of revenue—due to lack of rooms. However, if too many rooms are held, the

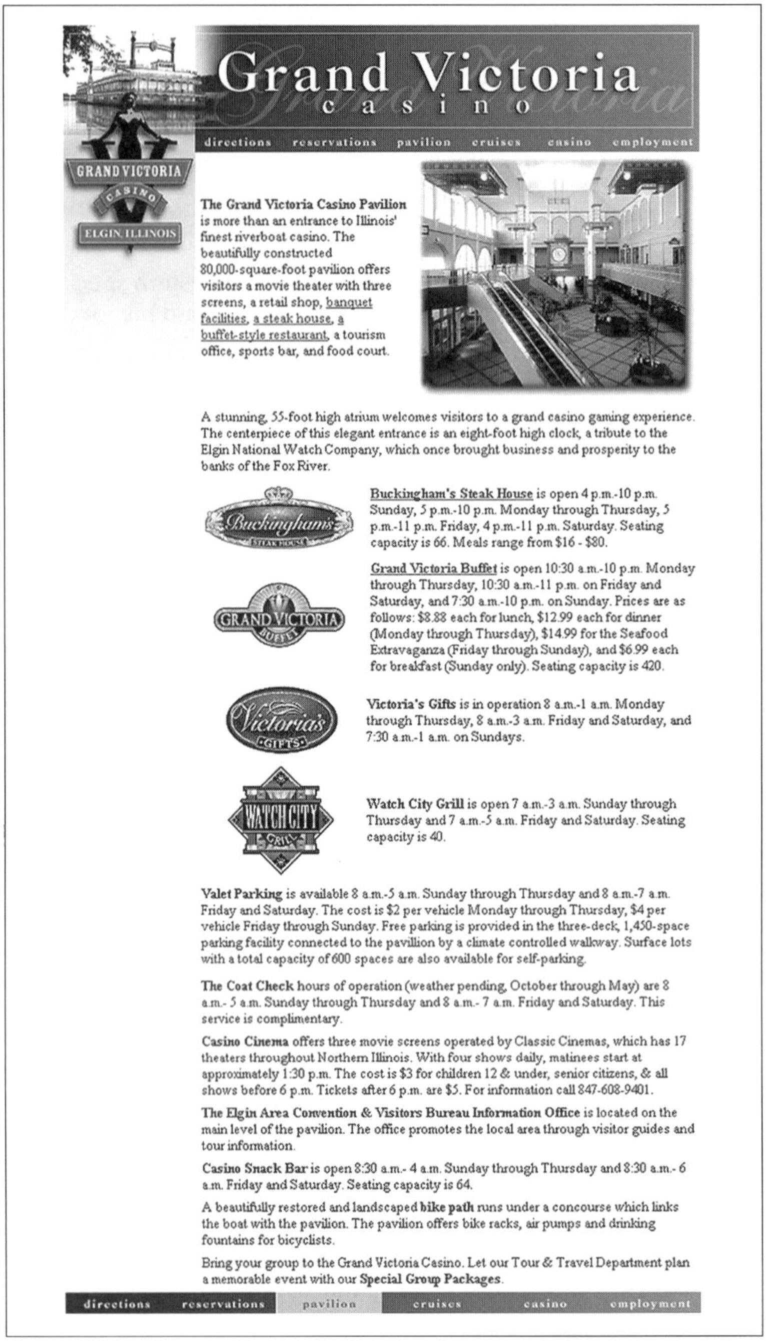

# Grand Victoria Casino

directions    reservations    pavilion    cruises    casino    employment

**GRAND VICTORIA CASINO — ELGIN, ILLINOIS**

The Grand Victoria Casino Pavilion is more than an entrance to Illinois' finest riverboat casino. The beautifully constructed 80,000-square-foot pavilion offers visitors a movie theater with three screens, a retail shop, banquet facilities, a steak house, a buffet-style restaurant, a tourism office, sports bar, and food court.

A stunning, 55-foot high atrium welcomes visitors to a grand casino gaming experience. The centerpiece of this elegant entrance is an eight-foot high clock, a tribute to the Elgin National Watch Company, which once brought business and prosperity to the banks of the Fox River.

**Buckingham's Steak House** is open 4 p.m.-10 p.m. Sunday, 5 p.m.-10 p.m. Monday through Thursday, 5 p.m.-11 p.m. Friday, 4 p.m.-11 p.m. Saturday. Seating capacity is 66. Meals range from $16 - $80.

**Grand Victoria Buffet** is open 10:30 a.m.-10 p.m. Monday through Thursday, 10:30 a.m.-11 p.m. on Friday and Saturday, and 7:30 a.m.-10 p.m. on Sunday. Prices are as follows: $8.88 each for lunch, $12.99 each for dinner (Monday through Thursday), $14.99 for the Seafood Extravaganza (Friday through Sunday), and $6.99 each for breakfast (Sunday only). Seating capacity is 420.

**Victoria's Gifts** is in operation 8 a.m.-1 a.m. Monday through Thursday, 8 a.m.-3 a.m. Friday and Saturday, and 7:30 a.m.-1 a.m. on Sundays.

**Watch City Grill** is open 7 a.m.-3 a.m. Sunday through Thursday and 7 a.m.-5 a.m. Friday and Saturday. Seating capacity is 40.

**Valet Parking** is available 8 a.m.-5 a.m. Sunday through Thursday and 8 a.m.-7 a.m. Friday and Saturday. The cost is $2 per vehicle Monday through Thursday, $4 per vehicle Friday through Sunday. Free parking is provided in the three-deck, 1,450-space parking facility connected to the pavillion by a climate controlled walkway. Surface lots with a total capacity of 600 spaces are also available for self-parking.

**The Coat Check** hours of operation (weather pending, October through May) are 8 a.m.- 5 a.m. Sunday through Thursday and 8 a.m.- 7 a.m. Friday and Saturday. This service is complimentary.

**Casino Cinema** offers three movie screens operated by Classic Cinemas, which has 17 theaters throughout Northern Illinois. With four shows daily, matinees start at approximately 1:30 p.m. The cost is $3 for children 12 & under, senior citizens, & all shows before 6 p.m. Tickets after 6 p.m. are $5. For information call 847-608-9401.

**The Elgin Area Convention & Visitors Bureau Information Office** is located on the main level of the pavilion. The office promotes the local area through visitor guides and tour information.

**Casino Snack Bar** is open 8:30 a.m.- 4 a.m. Sunday through Thursday and 8:30 a.m.- 6 a.m. Friday and Saturday. Seating capacity is 64.

A beautifully restored and landscaped **bike path** runs under a concourse which links the boat with the pavilion. The pavilion offers bike racks, air pumps and drinking fountains for bicyclists.

Bring your group to the Grand Victoria Casino. Let our Tour & Travel Department plan a memorable event with our **Special Group Packages**.

directions    reservations    pavilion    cruises    casino    employment

The Grand Victoria Casino Riverboat in Elgin, Illinois, features three restaurants and a snack bar, in addition to a sports bar and food court.
(Courtesy of the Grand Victoria Casino)

hotel is stuck with empty guest rooms that could have been sold. As you can see, hotel managers must perform a fine balancing act to plan correctly.

## Chapter Summary

The first recorded account of gambling dates back to early China. Today, casinos exist everywhere. In many countries, they are owned or controlled by the government.

Gambling was accepted early on in regions of the United States, and riverboats became popular venues. But by the early twentieth century, gambling had become illegal in most of the country. In 1931 it was revived in Nevada and in 1976 became legal in New Jersey. Today, gambling exists in most states in one form or another—if not throughout the state, it can be found on Indian reservations, riverboats, and offshore. Gambling is an enormous business generating almost $600 billion annually.

There are basically two types of casino games: table games and slot machines. The most common table games include baccarat, blackjack, craps, and roulette. Of the table games, blackjack is the most popular in the United States, followed by craps and roulette. Slots are the most profitable games because of the percentage of money the casino gets to keep and the low labor requirements.

Casino employees include croupiers (dealers), floor people, pit bosses, and shift managers. From an operational point of view, casinos often divide their customers into two broad groups: grind players and high-end players. While those are the two kinds of customers playing, from a marketing point of view there are three separate markets that casinos generally target with their promotional activities: high-end, middle-range, and low-end. Different strategies are used to attract each group. There are three kinds of controls that casinos use: accounting controls, equipment controls, and human controls. Casinos are carefully overseen by the governments that sanction them. While regulations differ, the Nevada model of gaming control is widely copied.

The best way to understand casino hotels is to think of them not as hotels with casinos attached, but rather as casinos with guest rooms, restaurants, shopping arcades, and even theme parks attached. In casino hotels, the hotel operation is subordinate to the gambling operation. As a result, many management activities that are usually associated with non-casino hotels such as food and beverage and marketing are separated from the hotel manager's duties. This may cause some tension between hotel managers and casino managers.

## Endnotes

1. Dave Barry, *Tropic Magazine*, *The Miami Herald*, 31 January 1993.

## Key Terms

**cashier's cage**—Generally referred to simply as the cage, this is where chips and cash are stored, where checks are cashed, where credit cards are accepted, and where markers are approved. It is the control center for the flow of chips to and from tables.

**credit slips**—Forms that state the amount of excess chips at each table at the end of a shift. Extra chips are returned to the cage along with the credit slips.

**croupier**—An attendant or dealer at a gaming table who collects and pays bets.

**drop box**—A locked box beneath each table into which cash and markers received from players are deposited. At the end of a shift, boxes are removed from the table and brought to a count room, where they are opened and the contents counted under strict supervision.

**fill slips**—Forms that state the amount of chips short at each table at the end of a shift.

**floor people**—Casino employees who supervise dealers. They are trained to enforce good dealing procedures, resolve disputes, and watch for cheaters.

**grind players**—Players who budget a modest amount for play and leave when that amount is used up. They view gaming as entertainment, and their losses are viewed as the price of that entertainment.

**gross gambling revenue (GGR)**—The net receipts of a gaming operation.

**high-end players**—Players who play regularly, are prepared to gamble a large amount of money, and expect to suffer big losses at times. Often called "high rollers" or "high-stakes players," high-end players may bet as much as $500,000 on a single bet.

**hold percentage**—A calculation to determine the percentage of chips purchased at a table by a customer that is won back by the casino. It is calculated as follows: Win ÷ Drop = Hold. For example, if the win is $1,400 and the drop is $4,000, then the hold is 35 percent. That is, the casino won (kept) 35 percent purchased at that table.

**markers**—Printed or written IOUs that extend credit to a player and can be given, instead of cash, to dealers in exchange for chips. Typically the casino agrees not to cash these checks for 30 or 45 days, giving the player time to deposit the money in his or her bank account.

**pit**—A grouping of tables within a casino that defines a management section. These can be the same game or a combination. For example, there may be four craps tables and four roulette tables in one pit, or simply eight craps tables.

**pit boss**—The manager who oversees a pit.

**slot drop**—The amount of money put into a slot machine, less the amount paid out. For example, if $100 is put into a slot machine and $90 is paid out, the drop is $10 or 10 percent.

**table drop**—The amount of money and markers that is placed in a drop box at a gaming table in exchange for chips. The table drop is a good measure of gaming activity within the casino.

**table win**—The amount bet minus the amount that is paid back to the players.

# Review Questions

1. When did the gaming industry first start?

2. When and why was gambling revived?
3. What is the Indian Gaming Regulatory Act (IGRA)?
4. What are the two basic types of casino games?
5. Which games are the most profitable and why?
6. What are some of the key definitions used in casino management?
7. Why are casino employees considered to have high-pressure jobs?
8. What two broad groups of customers are vital to the long-term health of a gaming establishment?
9. What types of benefits can be given to high-end, experienced gamblers?
10. Why are casino operations carefully regulated?
11. Why are hotel casinos not thought of as hotels with casinos attached?
12. How does the operation of a casino hotel differ from that of a traditional resort?

## Internet Sites

For more information, visit the following Internet sites. Remember that Internet addresses can change without notice. If the site is no longer there, use a search engine to look for additional sites.

*Casinos*

Ballys Casinos
www.ballys.com

Caesars Palace
www.caesars.com

Casino Magic
www.casinomagic.com

Circus Circus Las Vegas Casino
www.circuscircus.com

Cliff Castle Casino
www.cliffcastle.com

Colorado Belle Casino
www.coloradobelle.com

Connecticut/Rhode Island Casinos
www.ct-casinos.com

Excalibur Casino
www.excalibur-casino.com

Foxwoods Resort Casino
www.foxwoods.com

Golden Nugget Casino
www.goldennugget.com

Harrahs Casino
www.harrahs.com

Imperial Palace Hotel/Casino
www.imperialpalace.com

Island Casino
www.islandcasino.com

Las Vegas Hilton
www.lv-hilton.com

Luxor Casino
www.luxor.com

MGM Grand Casino
www.mgmgrand.com

Mirage Casino
www.themirage.com

Monte Carlo Casino
www.monte-carlo.com

Nevada Gambler
www.elguru.com

New York-New York Casino
www.nynyhotelcasino.com

Orleans Casino
www.orleanscasino.com

Prima Donna Casino
www.primadonna.com

Taj Mahal Casino
www.trumptaj.com

Treasure Island Casino
www.treasureislandlasvegas.com

Tropicana Casino
www.tropicana.lv.com

Trump Castle Casino
www.trumpcastle.com

Virtual Vegas (Internet gaming)
www.virtualvegas.com

Windsor Casinos
www.windsornights.com

# REVIEW QUIZ

When you feel you have covered all of the material in this chapter, answer these questions. Choose the *best* answer.

1. The first recorded accounts of gambling come from:

    a. cave paintings near the Dead Sea.
    b. the book of Genesis in the Old Testament.
    c. early Chinese dynasties in 2300 B.C.
    d. pyramid excavations in Egypt.

2. Three modern casino games that have their roots in medieval times are:

    a. blackjack, craps, and poker.
    b. blackjack, dice, and roulette.
    c. baccarat, bridge, and pass.
    d. *Chemin de fer*, dice, and roulette.

3. Nevada legalized nearly all forms of gambling in 1931 primarily as a means to:

    a. increase tourism to the state.
    b. aid economic recovery during the Great Depression.
    c. raise money for improved education.
    d. fund the Nevada State Highways project.

4. "Gross gambling revenue" is:

    a. tax-free income for an individual casino.
    b. the total revenue of all U.S. casino operations.
    c. the amount of revenue retained by a gambling business.
    d. the same thing as the "handle" amount.

5. A "table drop" refers to:

    a. the amount of money and markers placed in a drop box at a gaming table.
    b. a box locked in place beneath a gaming table.
    c. the number of chips placed at a gaming table at the start of an employee's shift.
    d. a printed or written form that extends credit to a player.

6. The person who conducts the table games at a casino is known as a:

    a. casino manager
    b. floor boss
    c. croupier
    d. gaming supervisor

## REVIEW QUIZ *(continued)*

7. The game of choice for low-end players is:

    a. blackjack.
    b. slot machines.
    c. baccarat.
    d. craps.

8. Casinos use three kinds of controls:

    a. management, service, and personnel.
    b. accounting, practical, and ethical.
    c. transaction, credit, and security.
    d. accounting, equipment, and human.

9. In many large casino hotels, the vice president of hotel operations:

    a. may only be in charge of the rooms department and various hotel services.
    b. oversees all functions related to hotel operation.
    c. oversees the vice president of casino operations.
    d. b and c.

10. To maintain a high level of service, the number of employees per room at a casino hotel is:

    a. twice as high as a conventional hotel or resort.
    b. variable, based on seasonal occupancy levels.
    c. two or three times higher than in a conventional hotel or resort.
    d. increased during major trade shows and conventions.

**Answer Key:** 1-c-C1, 2-b-C1, 3-b-C1, 4-c-C2, 5-a-C2, 6-c-C2, 7-b-C3, 8-d-C3, 9-a-C4, 10-c-C4

Each question is linked to a competency. Competencies are listed on the first page of the chapter. An answer reading 3-b-C4 translates to:

3: the question number
b: the correct answer
C4: the competency number

# Part III

# Hospitality Management

## Chapter 12 Outline

A Manager's Job
    Management Tasks
The Evolution of Management Theories
    The Classical School
    The Behavioral School
    The Quantitative School
    The Systems School
    The Contingency School
    The Quality Focus School
Reengineering
    Reengineering in the Hotel Business
The Importance of Leadership
    Strategy I: Attention through Vision
    Strategy II: Meaning through Communication
    Strategy III: Trust through Positioning
    Strategy IV: Self-Development
    Service Organizations and People Power
Conclusion
Chapter Summary

## Competencies

1. Describe the basic goals and tasks of managers, and trace the development of management theories, beginning with the first management theorist, Robert Owen, and continuing with the classical school and the behavioral school of management.

2. Explain the quantitative, systems, contingency, and quality focus schools of management.

3. Describe reengineering, summarize four basic strategies of effective leaders, and explain the concept of employee empowerment.

# 12

# Managing and Leading Hospitality Enterprises

THIS CHAPTER BEGINS by defining the task of managers. It traces the evolution of management theory and discusses six schools of management thought—the classical, behavioral, quantitative, systems, contingency, and quality focus schools. The chapter then turns to modern service management techniques before discussing the competencies needed by today's hospitality managers and the importance of leadership.

## A Manager's Job

It is usually easy to single out the managers in a hotel, restaurant, or club. Managers have titles. They usually have nice offices. Often their jobs come with perks such as company cars, country club memberships, and expense accounts. But what exactly do managers do? This question cannot be answered precisely or easily. Managers in different businesses do different things, and the entire field of management is changing rapidly as America moves from a manufacturing-based to a service-based economy.

Peter Drucker, probably America's greatest management theorist, says a manager has two broad goals. The first is "creation of a true whole that is larger than the sum of its parts, a productive entity that turns out more than the sum of the resources put into it."[1] Drucker compares a manager to a conductor of an orchestra who is able to pull together the music played by each musician into a beautiful symphony. The Four Seasons hotel company, in its statement of operating philosophy, compares its general managers to orchestra conductors. Managers are told that their role is to "keep all of the various pieces playing in proper tempo and harmony so the performance is pleasing to the customer."[2] Unlike conductors, who have a composer's score in front of them and only have to interpret it, managers must do more, says Drucker. They must write their own score, and in that sense managers are composers as well as conductors.

The second broad goal of a manager is to "harmonize in every decision and action the requirements of [the] immediate and long-range future."[3] In other words, a manager must consider not only the needs of today but also the needs of next year and beyond. "He not only has to prepare for crossing distant bridges—he has to build them long before he gets there."

These two goals separate managers from supervisors. Supervisors are generally concerned with implementing established policies. Although supervisors may act like orchestra conductors at times—that is, lead and direct their employees—it is not their job to compose the music as well; that has already been done by higher-level managers. Nor do supervisors worry about the long-range future; their job is to take care of what is going on today.

This is not to imply that a manager does not do supervisory work. Managers do other things besides manage (see Exhibit 1), but they always focus their activities on creating and harmonizing—or should, if they want to be effective managers.

## Management Tasks

According to Drucker, a manager has five basic tasks:

- Setting objectives
- Organizing
- Motivating and communicating
- Measuring performance
- Developing people[5]

Let's take a look at each of these in turn.

**Setting Objectives.** A manager sets objectives. Unlike a worker or supervisor, a manager must decide what goals and objectives his or her department or organization should strive to achieve. The manager then decides what work must be done to reach those objectives and, lastly, directs and communicates with his or her employees to get the work done.

In 1992 the Ritz-Carlton hotel won the Malcolm Baldrige National Quality Award, an award established by the United States Congress to recognize U.S. companies that have achieved excellence through adherence to quality-improvement programs. Ritz-Carlton has a set of "Gold Standards" that embody the service objectives of its managers (see Exhibit 2). The "Gold Standards" card, a pocket-size card that all staff members must carry with them while at work, clearly states the company's objective to create a certain kind of hotel:

> The Ritz-Carlton Hotel is a place where the genuine care and comfort of our guests is our highest mission.
>
> We pledge to provide the finest personal service and facilities for our guests who will always enjoy a warm, relaxed yet refined ambience.
>
> The Ritz-Carlton experience enlivens the senses, instills well-being, and fulfills even the unexpressed wishes and needs of our guests.

**Organizing.** A manager organizes. A manager must analyze the work that his or her department is responsible for, divide that work into various jobs, and assign the jobs to employees, some of whom might have to be trained. All the classic management texts emphasize that managers must know how to delegate. According to author Weiss Roberts, even Attila the Hun, a brilliant fifth-century leader who forged a conglomeration of 70,000 barbarians into a well-disciplined army, understood this concept. Attila is credited with having these ideas:

**Exhibit 1  Hospitality Management Skills**

Here are some of the skills top hospitality managers should possess.

**Management Skills**

Hospitality managers must be able to:

- Plan and organize work in a timely and efficient manner
- Select and train subordinates
- Make decisions correctly and effectively
- Adapt their leadership styles to the needs of workers
- Recognize the organizational structure and chain of command
- Understand, interpret, and apply company policies and rules
- Understand, interpret, and apply local, state, and federal laws and ordinances
- Apply current technology to problem-solving situations
- Supervise subordinates

**Human Resources Skills**

Hospitality managers must be able to:

- Function in stressful situations
- Establish functional relationships with superiors, peers, and subordinates
- Show sensitivity to employees' differences in age, sex, race, creed, national origin, and physical abilities
- Balance the needs and wants of employees and guests
- Establish a positive work environment
- Maintain objectivity in resolving differences within their work groups
- Accept criticism and use it constructively
- Convey to employees that following personal grooming, health, and safety rules is essential for effective performance
- Take personality differences into account when making decisions
- Think creatively

**Marketing Skills**

Hospitality managers must be able to:

- Understand the concept and purpose of marketing
- Know how to generate or locate marketing data
- Know proper research methods
- Create a marketing strategy
- Write a marketing plan
- Develop and implement media advertising
- Develop a media mix and schedule
- Create and implement public relations programs
- Understand sales techniques
- Plan and implement promotional activities

**Accounting and Finance Skills**

Hospitality managers must be able to:

- Understand the nature and limitations of the accounting system used at the firm
- Understand tools and techniques used to interpret financial statements
- Understand the importance of cash planning for business purposes
- Understand economic conditions affecting the hospitality environment
- Understand financing alternatives available to the hospitality industry
- Use ratio analysis for comparative purposes and assess the firm's weaknesses and strengths
- Implement internal control measures
- Understand budgeting as a management tool
- Understand the firm's goals and objectives, including the significance of profit-and-loss analysis
- Use accounting information in making business decisions
- View accounting as a management information system

Source: An industry survey conducted by Professor Joseph Gregg, Florida International University.

## Exhibit 2  Ritz-Carlton's Gold Standards

### THREE STEPS OF SERVICE

1. A warm and sincere greeting. Use the guest name, if and when possible.

2. Anticipation and compliance with guest needs.

3. Fond farewell. Give them a warm good-bye and use their names, if and when possible.

---

*"We Are Ladies and Gentlemen Serving Ladies and Gentlemen"*

---

### THE RITZ-CARLTON

### CREDO

The Ritz-Carlton Hotel is a place where the genuine care and comfort of our guests is our highest mission.

We pledge to provide the finest personal service and facilities for our guests who will always enjoy a warm, relaxed yet refined ambience.

The Ritz-Carlton experience enlivens the senses, instills well-being, and fulfills even the unexpressed wishes and needs of our guests.

---

### THE RITZ-CARLTON BASICS

1. The Credo will be known, owned and energized by all employees.

2. Our motto is: "We are Ladies and Gentlemen Serving Ladies and Gentlemen." Practice teamwork and "lateral service" to create a positive work environment.

3. The three steps of service shall be practiced by all employees.

4. All employees will successfully complete Training Certification to ensure they understand how to perform to The Ritz-Carlton standards in their position.

5. Each employee will understand their work area and Hotel goals as established in each strategic plan.

6. All employees will know the needs of their internal and external customers (guests and employees) so that we may deliver the products and services they expect. Use guest preference pads to record specific needs.

7. Each employee will continuously identify defects (Mr. BIV) throughout the Hotel.

8. Any employee who receives a customer complaint "owns" the complaint.

9. Instant guest pacification will be ensured by all. React quickly to correct the problem immediately. Follow-up with a telephone call within twenty minutes to verify the problem has been resolved to the customer's satisfaction. Do everything you possibly can to never lose a guest.

10. Guest incident action forms are used to record and communicate every incident of guest dissatisfaction. Every employee is empowered to resolve the problem and to prevent a repeat occurrence.

11. Uncompromising levels of cleanliness are the responsibility of every employee.

12. "Smile — We are on stage." Always maintain positive eye contact. Use the proper vocabulary with our guests. (Use words like — "Good Morning," "Certainly," "I'll be happy to" and "My pleasure").

13. Be an ambassador of your Hotel in and outside of the work place. Always talk positively. No negative comments.

14. Escort guests rather than pointing out directions to another area of the Hotel.

15. Be knowledgeable of Hotel information (hours of operation, etc.) to answer guest inquiries. Always recommend the Hotel's retail and food and beverage outlets prior to outside facilities.

16. Use proper telephone etiquette. Answer within three rings and with a "smile." When necessary, ask the caller, "May I place you on hold." Do not screen calls. Eliminate call transfers when possible.

17. Uniforms are to be immaculate; wear proper and safe footwear (clean and polished), and your correct name tag. Take pride and care in your personal appearance (adhering to all grooming standards).

18. Ensure all employees know their roles during emergency situations and are aware of fire and life safety response processes.

19. Notify your supervisor immediately of hazards, injuries, equipment or assistance that you need. Practice energy conservation and proper maintenance and repair of Hotel property and equipment.

20. Protecting the assets of a Ritz-Carlton Hotel is the responsibility of every employee.

---

This is a reproduction of a small six-sided card all Ritz-Carlton staff members are expected to carry whenever they are working, to remind them of the importance of serving customers well. (Courtesy of the Ritz-Carlton Hotel Company, Atlanta, Georgia)

**Managers must know how to communicate effectively both orally and in writing.**

- Chieftains should never delegate responsibilities necessitating their direct attention.
- Those actions that don't require a chieftain's direct handling are appropriately delegated to the one most able to fulfill the assignment.
- Realize that a chieftain cannot accomplish every responsibility of his office by himself. Should he prove otherwise, a leader should understand that he is, in fact, chieftain over little or nothing at all.[6]

**Motivating and Communicating.** A manager must turn a group of individuals into a team that works together. To do this, managers must have excellent "people skills." They must be good at listening to employees with problems and helping them work out solutions. They must make wise and fair decisions regarding compensation and promotions. They must instinctively understand how to encourage and reward superior performance.

At Lettuce Entertain You Enterprises (LEYE), the Chicago-based restaurant company that operates 35 restaurants with many different concepts, owner Richard Melman believes keeping people happy is one of the most important reasons for LEYE's success. LEYE has 25 partners, all of whom are granted an equity stake. All 3,000 employees qualify for such benefits as divorce therapy, while getting married earns you a $50 bonus. New parents get a $100 check and a silver spoon from Tiffany's.[7]

Above all, managers should know how to communicate—both orally and in writing—with their superiors and peers as well as with the people who report to them. The need for communication skills is often not recognized by those who want to become managers. Because of the nature of their jobs, managers have to "sell" their ideas to others. Selling an idea requires abilities ranging from writing a convincing memo or report to standing in front of a group and making a well-organized presentation. Communication skills can be developed through training and practice.

**Measuring Performance.** Managers decide what factors are important to the success of their organizations and then establish standards against which to measure individual or group performance. Domino's Pizza measures performance weekly by calling back a number of consumers who ordered pizzas from them. Store managers at Taco Bell spend most of their time out front where they can hear customer comments about the quality of their operations.

Managers at Marriott, besides regularly taking a scientific sampling of guests and non-guests, pay a great deal of attention to what is known as the "GSI"—Guest Satisfaction Index. This index is compiled from in-room survey forms that guests voluntarily fill out. As J. W. "Bill" Marriott, Jr., chairman of Marriott Corporation, puts it: "Measurement of customer perception causes a lot of focus just where we want it, on the customer."[8] Ritz-Carlton reports that giving customer complaints a high priority has reduced the number of complaints by 27 percent in the past three years. "Our goal is 100 percent complaint resolution prior to departure," says President Horst Schulze.[9]

To measure performance, managers must collect statistical, financial, and qualitative data on how an organization or a department is doing, and then analyze and interpret the data for subordinates, superiors, and colleagues.

The Xerox Corporation pioneered a measurement technique that has been adapted by service companies in many industries, including hotel and restaurant chains. Xerox calls it **"competitive benchmarking"**:

> Competitive benchmarking is the continuous process of measuring our products, services, and practices against our toughest competitors or those companies recognized as leaders. Benchmarking is a structured approach for looking outside our organization by studying other organizations and adapting the best outside practices to complement our internal operations and creative new ideas. It is an ongoing management process that requires constant updating and the integration of competitive information, practices, and performance into decision-making and communication functions at all levels of our business.[10]

Companies like Ritz-Carlton, Marriott, McDonald's, and Taco Bell all use benchmarking as a regular measurement tool. This is one reason for managers to acquire a sound knowledge of marketing research techniques, statistical analysis, and communication skills.

**Developing People.** A manager develops people, including himself or herself. Continual learning enables people to move ahead. Along with outside seminars and educational programs, ongoing on-the-job training is one of the main tools managers use to develop their employees.

Successful managers recognize that the people who work for them are their most important resource. They also know that setting an example is the surest and best way to develop people. It is by following a good leader that people learn how to become leaders themselves. "What a manager does can be analyzed systematically," Peter Drucker said. "What a manager has to be able to do has to be learned (though perhaps not always taught). But [there is] one quality [that] cannot be learned, one qualification that the manager cannot acquire but must bring with him. It is not genius; it is character."[11] J. Willard Marriott, founder of the hotel chain bearing his name, believed the same. In a letter to his son when Bill Jr. took over the reins of the company, Marriott senior wrote, "A leader should have character, be an example in all things. This is his greatest influence."[12]

# The Evolution of Management Theories

Although discovering the best way to manage people and work has been a concern dating back thousands of years, it was not until the nineteenth century, after the Industrial Revolution in England and the industrialization of other countries had begun, that the subject of management was systematically studied and written about.

Probably the first modern management theorist was a Scottish cotton mill manager, Robert Owen (1771–1858). Owen thought that a manager's job was to institute reform. He believed that the way to motivate his workers and increase their productivity was to treat them better. He reduced the length of the standard working day to $10^{1}/_{2}$ hours, refused to hire children under the age of 10, and created an incentive pay system based on daily evaluations of an employee's work.

After Owen, other industrialists and theorists contributed their views about management. Over the years, six schools of thought on management have emerged:

- The classical school
- The behavioral school
- The quantitative school
- The systems school
- The contingency school
- The quality focus school

## The Classical School

The founder of the **classical school** was Fredrick W. Taylor (1856–1915), an American industrial engineer who managed the Midvale Steel Company in Philadelphia. Taylor revolutionized the manufacturing process by coming up with scientific principles of production. According to Taylor's theories of scientific management, there was one best way to do every job; if managers analyzed what needed to be done to perform a job, they could come up with that best or most efficient way of performing it. Taylor believed that workers should be trained to do their jobs using only the "best way" that had been devised by management, and paid according to how fast and how well they performed. He suggested using a "differential rate system of piece work," under which one of two rates would be paid for a job: "a high price per piece, in case the work is finished in the shortest possible time and in perfect condition, and a low price, if it takes a longer time to do a job, or if there are any imperfections in the work."[13] Taylor also advocated "discharging workers and lowering the wages of the more stubborn men who refused to make any improvement." In 1912, in testimony taken by a committee of the House of Representatives investigating the practicality of using the "Taylor System" in government, Taylor compared workers to horses and said that just as a trotting horse was a "first class" horse not suited for hauling coal, so there were "first class" men who were better suited for some jobs than other men and so should be given those jobs.[14]

While Taylor's methods were widely hailed, many thought his approach was too hard-nosed and rational and criticized him for comparing people to horses and for failing to take into account the needs of workers. Because they felt that pushing workers to produce more was in some cases irrational and might ultimately result in fewer jobs, both unions and workers were critical of Taylor's ideas. In a strike at the Watertown Arsenal, government workers refused to adhere to what they called Taylor's "Stopwatch System" on the grounds that "it is not a question of what a job is worth, but is based upon the quickest time that one can make."[15] Taylor defended his point of view by saying that if labor and management cooperated, his system would work.

A one-time associate of Taylor's, Henry Gantt (1861–1919), added to Taylor's thinking by devising a control system for production scheduling so that managers could forecast how much work should be expected from each employee. His Gantt Chart, which identifies work progress and deadlines in a visual form, is still used today.

Frank Gilbreth (1868–1924) and his wife, Lillian Gilbreth (1878–1972), contributed much to the classical school of management. Frank was an efficiency expert; Lillian was an industrial psychologist. By doing a series of motion studies, Frank was able to reduce the number of motions needed to lay a brick from 18 to 5. If bricklayers were trained to lay bricks using Gilbreth's five-step system, their productivity would triple. Gilbreth's research was a logical continuation of Taylor's idea that a "best way" could be found for every job. Lillian concentrated her efforts on studying worker fatigue. She advocated standard work days, lunch periods, and regular breaks for all employees. The Gilbreths also developed what they called a **"three position plan of promotion,"** in which workers would do their own jobs while at the same time preparing themselves for promotion by learning the next higher job, and also training workers below them to take over their job when the promotion actually came. That way every worker would always be looking forward to, and preparing for, a better job.

While one group of classical management theorists was developing systems to increase worker efficiency and productivity, another group was concerned with organizational theory—that is, defining the duties and functions of managers. The leader in this area was Henri Fayol (1841–1925), a French engineer and the manager of a large coal mining enterprise. Fayol was interested in what managers contributed to a business and how businesses were organized. From his studies, Fayol came up with a number of management principles. Fayol believed that these principles could be applied to any situation. Much of what we consider to be general management theory today was first articulated by Fayol in his 14 principles of management (see Exhibit 3). In Fayol's view, the manager's primary role was to be a regulator and integrator, taking all of an organization's rules, structures, and traditions and making them work together.

In summary, theorists of the classical school were mostly concerned with productivity. According to these theorists, workers were rational people interested primarily in making money. The classical school of management emphasizes satisfying employees' economic needs (pay them better for doing more work) and physical needs (don't tire them out) but ignores their social needs for respect and

## Exhibit 3  Fayol's 14 Principles of Management

1. **Division of work.** In Fayol's words, specialization leads to "more and better work with the same effort." This concept eventually led to the modern assembly line. Fayol believed specialization applied to managers as well as workers.
2. **Authority and responsibility.** Fayol defined authority and responsibility as "the right to give orders and the power to exact obedience." Managers need both authority and responsibility to accomplish things.
3. **Discipline.** Discipline is a function of leadership. Poor leadership produces poor discipline. Managers should enter into fair agreements with employees, and then both sides must respect and adhere to all the rules. When the rules are violated, managers must, for the well-being of the business, apply certain sanctions.
4. **Unity of command.** "For any action whatsoever an employee should receive orders from one superior only," said Fayol.
5. **Unity of direction.** Those activities in an organization having the same objective should be under the direction of one person with a single plan. In other words, one person should be in charge of sales, another finance, and so forth.
6. **Subordination of individual interest to general interest.** The interests of a single employee or group of employees are less important than the interests of the whole organization.
7. **Payment of personnel.** Workers should be paid at a rate that is fair and affords satisfaction to both employers and employees. Fayol advocated (1) paying workers by either time or piece or by the job, (2) giving bonuses, and (3) providing for employee welfare through better working conditions. He did not favor profit sharing except for senior managers, on the grounds that it was impractical.
8. **Centralization.** "The issue of centralization or decentralization is a simple question of proportion; it is the matter of finding the optimum degree of centralization for the particular concern." Managers must centralize things enough so that they can maintain control, but they also must give workers some authority so that they can perform their jobs. This balance will vary in different organizations, so managers must be flexible and seek the best degree of centralization.
9. **Scalar chain.** This is "the chain of superiors in a firm ranging from the ultimate authority to the lowest ranks." Generally, Fayol felt it was a mistake to deviate from this without reason, but he also believed that there were times when this might be necessary.
10. **Order.** "There must be a place appointed for each thing and each thing must be in its appointed place." Similarly, "there must be an appointed place for every employee....As in the case of orderly material arrangement, charts or plans facilitate the establishment and control of human arrangements."
11. **Equity.** Managers must be impartial and at the same time understanding in dealing with their employees. Fayol advocated both kindliness and justice.
12. **Stability of tenure of personnel.** A high employee turnover rate is not good for any organization. Organizations should have policies and plans that help them retain workers.
13. **Initiative.** Employees must be encouraged to show initiative on the job. "Thinking out a plan and ensuring its success are two of the keenest satisfactions that an intelligent person can experience," said Fayol. While some mistakes might occur, allowing employee initiative injects zeal and energy into an enterprise.
14. **Esprit de corps.** "Union is strength." Promoting team spirit is a key factor in good management. "Dividing enemy forces to weaken them is clever, but dividing one's own team is a grave sin against the business." Fayol also advocated oral communications rather than written ones because written ones might be misunderstood.

Adapted from Henri Fayol, *General and Industrial Management*, revised by Irwin Gray (New York: Institute of Electrical and Electronic Engineers Press, 1984), pp. 61–82.

recognition. While many of the ideas developed by Taylor and his followers are still used today, we recognize now that scientific management ignores the human desire for job satisfaction. In service businesses such as hotels and restaurants, this human factor can make the difference between providing a good product and a bad one.

## The Behavioral School

In recent years, many managers have recognized that the classical approach to management has serious limitations, especially when applied to service industries. To begin with, the relatively stable and predictable business environment enjoyed by the classical theorists is a thing of the past. In today's business world, turbulence and ambiguity are the norm. This means that rigid systems and rules no longer work as well as they used to. Managers must be more flexible and adaptable. In service industries especially, regulations and formal procedures may interfere with an employee's ability to satisfy consumer expectations. In addition, employees today are better educated and want to make their own decisions as much as possible.

For these and other reasons there has been a movement towards a human relations or **behavioral school of management.** Behaviorists attempt to find ways of motivating workers besides using the rules, systems, and wages proposed by classical management thinkers.

One of the first behaviorists was Chester I. Barnard (1886–1961), president of the New Jersey Telephone Company. Barnard believed that only when the goals of employees as well as employers were being satisfied could an organization grow and prosper. People want to work within an organization, said Barnard, because they want to accomplish more than they can do alone. Therefore, if management can mesh the personal goals of its employees with the organization's overall goals, a company should be successful.

A landmark in the development of behavioral management theory occurred when George Elton Mayo (1880–1949), a Harvard Business School professor, evaluated some studies on human behavior in work settings performed at the Western Electric Company's plant in Hawthorne, Illinois. Conducted between 1924 and 1933, these **"Hawthorne studies"** revolutionized the way managers looked at human relations problems. The Western Electric company designed and conducted the experiments to assess the effects of lighting conditions on workers. In the first experiment (which spanned three years), two groups of workers were segregated from the rest and each group was placed in its own "test room." Each test room started out with the same amount of light, with both groups performing the same task. For one group the light level was gradually increased over a period of time and, as expected, the group's productivity increased. Next the light level was gradually lowered and, to the surprise of the researchers, productivity increased again. Moreover, in the other test room, where the light remained constant, productivity also increased! The company's puzzled researchers decided that there must be other factors at work besides the amount of light.

At that point the researchers started a second series of experiments, this time looking at other variables that might be affecting productivity. Five workers were placed in a separate test room and given varied rest periods, shorter work days, a

*The Hawthorne studies revealed that one of the most important ways for managers and supervisors to help motivate employees is to establish a good relationship with them.*

shorter work week, and higher wages. The researchers acted as supervisors in this set of experiments and allowed the workers a say in deciding when and how long their rest periods would be. On the whole, performance improved, but there were unexpected variations.

In the midst of these experiments, Mayo and his associates became involved, and they began to suspect that the real agent of change was the human factor:

> The records of the test room showed a continual improvement in performance of the operators regardless of the [experimental] changes made during the study. It was also noticed that there was a marked improvement in their attitude toward their work and working environment. This simultaneous improvement in attitude and effectiveness indicated that there might be a definite relationship between them. In other words we could more logically attribute the increase in efficiency to a betterment of morale than to any of the...alterations made in the course of the experiment....Comment after comment from the girls indicates that they have been relieved of the nervous tension under which they previously worked. They have ceased to regard the man in charge as a boss...[and] they have a feeling that their increased production is in some way related to the distinctly freer, happier, and more pleasant working environment.[16]

Subsequently, 21,126 workers of the plant were interviewed over a period of three years to check the findings of the test group. Mayo and his associates eventually determined that their findings were valid. The employees worked harder and more efficiently when they knew that management was interested in them and that they had the ear of a sympathetic supervisor. This was far more important in motivating them than was the level of lighting or even the amount of money they were paid. This finding—that there was a clear link between supervision, morale, and productivity—was subsequently labeled the **Hawthorne effect,** and Mayo's book, *The Human Problems of an Industrial Civilization,* became a bestseller in business circles.

The idea that managers should concentrate on employee motivation was developed further by Abraham Maslow (1890–1970).[17] Maslow's idea was that we all have a system of priorities in our needs. Maslow defined a hierarchy of needs and theorized that we try to satisfy our needs progressively—that is, we satisfy one group of needs first because they are the most basic (or strongest), then go on to the second group, and so forth.

Group I needs are physiological. These are our most powerful needs, and until they are satisfied we are not interested in anything else. They are our needs for water, food, and shelter.

Group II needs are the safety needs—our needs for protection and security. As soon as we are satisfied that we have a roof over our heads and something to eat, these needs emerge as primary.

Social or belonging and love needs are in Group III. Once we have food and security, the next thing we hunger for is love, affection, and a feeling that we belong to a community or group. These needs are all part of a need to relate to others around us.

Group IV needs are esteem needs. All of us need to think well of ourselves and have others think well of us. We want to achieve some degree of independence, and be recognized and appreciated for our work.

Self-actualization needs make up Group V. These are needs for fulfillment—to express ourselves and reach our full potential. These needs are the highest of all and they emerge only after all other needs are met.

Another theory of how human beings are motivated was suggested by Douglas McGregor (1906–1964), a professor of psychology at Massachusetts Institute of Technology. McGregor said managers tend to believe one or the other of two basic sets of assumptions about human nature and behavior, and these assumptions governed a manager's behavior and management style.

McGregor labeled the first set of assumptions **Theory X**, and said they represented the "traditional view of direction and control." Theory X assumptions are:

- The average human being has an inherent dislike of work and will avoid it if possible.

- Because people dislike work, most people must be coerced, controlled, directed, and threatened with punishment to get them to put forth adequate effort toward the achievement of organizational objectives.

- The average employee prefers to be directed, wishes to avoid responsibility, has relatively little ambition, and wants security above all.[18]

McGregor thought that while most managers believed these assumptions, they were really nothing more than self-fulfilling prophecies. In fact, McGregor said, if more managers would change their assumptions to **Theory Y**, which is based on a whole different set of ideas, workers would behave entirely differently. The assumptions of Theory Y are:

- Working is as natural as playing or resting. The average human being does not inherently dislike work.

- External control and the threat of punishment are not the only means of encouraging employees to work towards organizational objectives. Employees will exercise self-direction and self-control in the service of objectives to which they are committed.

- Commitment to objectives is a function of the rewards associated with achieving those objectives. The most significant of such rewards—the satisfaction of ego and self-actualization needs—can be direct products of effort directed toward organizational objectives.

In the final analysis, McGregor believed that managers who did not try to control their employees through formal structures, but instead tried to motivate them by encouraging and challenging them, would be the most successful.

## The Quantitative School

While the behavioral school of thought founded by Barnard and Mayo influenced a great number of managers, there were still some unanswered questions. For one thing, not all companies that improved working conditions achieved the expected results. It turned out that in many instances the corporate culture, salary levels, or the way the company was organized played a more important part in determining motivation and productivity. In other words the problem of how to motivate workers turned out to be much more complex than was realized by any of the early behavioral researchers.

A new approach that would integrate the management ideas of the classical and behavioral schools was needed. To many, the answer lay in a mathematical approach to management problems, using models created during World War II when scientists developed radar, missiles, and the atomic bomb. This approach depended on two cornerstones, *operations research (OR)* and *management information systems (MIS)*. Managers trained in the **quantitative school** use complex mathematical decision-making models based on consumer research to determine the probability of success for a new restaurant location or to project the optimum number of guestrooms for a given hotel site. From this they are able to determine the cost of construction, the number of employees needed to operate the property, and the expected return on investment for the owners. Management information systems give hotel and restaurant managers the information they need to make decisions. For example, reservation systems project occupancy rates and income for future periods of time so that hotel managers can modify their marketing activities accordingly. Property management systems report how income and expenses change on a daily basis.

A major problem with quantitative management is that it tends to direct a manager's attention to short-term goals such as achieving the lowest possible costs and the highest profits. Doing this often results in ignoring such critical factors as employee morale, employee turnover, and—most important—customer satisfaction. Moreover, important activities such as training and research and development are often put on the back burner because they don't make an obvious contribution to the bottom line. In recent years MBA programs at major universities have modified their curriculum to de-emphasize the role of quantitative methods in decision-making. While quantitative methods remain an important management tool, they should be regarded as just one weapon in a manager's arsenal of techniques.

## The Systems School

According to the **systems school,** a company is a system composed of many interrelated departments, which in turn is part of a larger external environment (made up of such things as competing companies, the economy in general, societal values) that influences its behavior. Managers cannot act independently—what they can or cannot accomplish depends on other managers inside their company and on outside environmental factors. For example, the decisions made by a hotel's food and beverage director as to what kind of food will be served and at what price will affect the types of groups that the sales department can attract to the hotel. Similarly, the number of rooms the sales department sells to groups affects the number of rooms that the rooms department has to sell to individual travelers. All of these decisions are affected by the external environment—how many other hotels are nearby, what their rates are, how strongly they are competing for each other's business, and consumer needs and wants.

Managers who favor the systems school view their organizations in terms of *internal systems* and *external systems.* Internal systems are not individuals or departments, but rather a means by which a service is delivered. For example, for a guest to check into a hotel, several different departments are involved. The housekeeping department is responsible for seeing that the room is clean and ready on time. The front desk is responsible for checking in the guest and assigning a room. Someone from the uniformed service department escorts the guest to the room. This is a process involving many functions and several departments. The output is the guest settling down comfortably in his or her room.

External systems are those outside the hotel that the manager has no control over. These include economic conditions, government regulation, and actions by competitors. Suppliers, too, are part of external systems.

Internal and external systems are connected, and when they interact and cooperate with each other they can often produce *synergy,* which simply means that the sum of their actions may be greater than their parts. For example, hotels working together with each other and the local government may be able to reduce crime in an area and thus make it a safer and more attractive tourist destination.

Systems managers understand that they must view their organizations as a whole, not in parts. This is similar to the environmentalist view that we all live on Spaceship Earth and mutual cooperation is necessary for our survival. Managers who think this way not only look at the trees but see the forest. They understand that the quality of service their facility produces is the result of every input that is involved in the final output, which means every person's work has an impact on the final outcome. From this, as we will see, comes an important concept in the achievement and management of quality.

## The Contingency School

The **contingency school,** sometimes referred to as the **situational management school,** recognizes that every situation is different and every manager is different. Contingency theorists suggest that there are few management principles that are as universal as Taylor, Fayol, and Mayo believed. Managers must be pragmatic and decide what is likely to achieve the needed results in any given situation. The solution may use classical, behavioral, or quantitative management ideas, depending on what the problem is and what resources are available to the manager to solve it. Managers must constantly adapt to changing circumstances, and the way to do this is to be flexible, keep an open mind, and change one's own behavior to fit the situation at hand.

Managers who are comfortable with the contingency theory are often especially adept in managing diverse work groups that contain people with different ethnic backgrounds. They can also do well working in foreign countries, where they are likely to be placed in situations where traditional management approaches don't work. These managers are often comfortable with change because they are willing to experiment and try new approaches.

One example of this kind of outlook might be found in U.S. managers who have tried to understand and borrow from Japanese management techniques. For example, Japanese managers and employees believe in the concepts of *kawaiso* and *kaizen*. *Kawaiso*, literally translated, means "pathetic" or "pitiable," but in management it refers to the obligation of a manager to take care of his or her employees much as fathers or mothers are obligated to protect and care for their children. *Kaizen* refers to the Japanese belief that it is a worthy and important objective to continually search for a better way to do things and to thereby improve one's self. These two beliefs imply a reciprocal agreement between managers and workers. Managers are obliged to help and protect their employees, and employees are expected to help managers get the job done better by seeking better ways to do it and by improving their own skills.

## The Quality Focus School

In the early 1980s, at the same time the contingency school was gaining popularity, U.S. managers began to focus their attention on quality management. It was a logical step, since the systems approach had highlighted the idea that service was a process, not a function, and that meant that the chain of events that constituted the process could be no stronger than its weakest link. Moreover, the success of Japanese management techniques, especially in the automobile industry, turned American eyes westward to more closely examine the reasons behind Japanese success.

What they found was that the Japanese had been enormously influenced by the work of two Americans, both in their 80s, whose ideas had received little attention in the United States. These two unsung quality management champions were

W. Edwards Deming and Joseph Juran. A third American, Philip Crosby (who had started his own quality consulting business after working for ITT as vice president of quality), was also preaching the importance of quality and getting a considerable amount of attention. Each of these men had their own distinctive approach to quality management.[19]

Deming, an electrical engineer who first visited Japan in 1950, introduced the revolutionary concept that consumers were not only a part of any production line, they were the most important part. Furthermore, he told his audiences that the way to make a profit in business was to attract repeat customers who would tell others about your product or service. Deming summarized his views in a 14-point program that told managers what they needed to do if they expected to run quality operations:

> To begin, managers had to put aside their preoccupations with today to make sure there was a tomorrow. They had to orient themselves to continuous improvement of products and services to meet customers' needs and stay ahead of the competition. They had to innovate constantly and commit resources to support innovation and continuous quality improvement. They had to build quality in. They had to break down department and worker-supervisor barriers. They had to rid themselves of numerical targets and quotas and instead had to concentrate on improving processes, giving workers clear standards for acceptable work, as well as the tools needed to achieve it. Finally, they had to create a climate free of finger-pointing and fear, which blocks cooperative identification and solution of problems.[20]

Deming believed that, if managers did all of these things, not only would they achieve quality, but productivity would increase as well, because by building in quality you got the job done right the first time and thus had none of the costs associated with having to do it over or having to replace lost customers.

Joseph Juran, who first visited Japan in 1953 (just three years after Deming), told his audiences that the definition for quality was "fitness for use." In other words, said Juran, people said that a product or service had quality if they could be sure it would do what they expected it to do, the way they expected it to be done. The way quality was achieved was by utilizing a comprehensive approach that touched everything a company did—from designing its product or service, to developing the delivery system, to its relations with customers and even suppliers. Juran developed a cost-of-quality (COQ) accounting system. He identified four different kinds of quality costs:

- Internal failure costs (from defects identified before the product or service was delivered)

- External failure costs (from defects discovered after the product or service was delivered)

- Appraisal costs (for assessing the condition of the ingredients or materials used)

- Prevention costs (for keeping the defects from occurring in the first place)

In a restaurant, for example, an internal cost might be food that was improperly cooked in the kitchen and had to be replaced. External costs might be the cost of replacing an order that was improperly recorded, leading a server to give french fries to a guest who ordered a baked potato. Appraisal costs could be the costs associated with checking ingredients that did not meet specifications for quality, size, or amount. Examples of prevention costs are the costs of training and communicating with employees and suppliers so that defects in quality don't occur in the first place. Juran believed that it was not economically feasible to achieve zero defects because at some point the costs associated with doing so would become too high. He advocated an approach that would achieve optimal quality on a continuing basis.

Philip Crosby liked to argue that "quality is free." Crosby defined quality as "conformance to requirements" and believed that any product which consistently reproduced its design specifications was of high quality. Ultimately, the goal of quality improvement was zero defects, to be achieved through prevention, rather than after-the-fact inspection.[21] Crosby believed that, to achieve quality improvement, top management had to change its thinking. If managers expected imperfection, they would get it, for workers would understand that managers expected and tolerated it. But if managers set zero defects as their goal and communicated that standard to everyone that worked for them, then it would be possible to achieve perfection. To achieve perfection, companies had to focus on changing their corporate culture so that employees would become involved in and commit themselves to the idea of delivering the perfect product or service every time, no matter what it took. Unlike Juran, who focused on statistical and analytical tools for measuring the cost of quality, Crosby said if you focus on people instead of numbers you can achieve zero defects. Prevention costs will always be lower than the costs of correcting mistakes and losing customers, Crosby believed. Therefore, quality always costs less than controlling and correcting errors.

Ritz-Carlton officials have said that the ideas of Deming, Juran, and Crosby influenced them when setting up their own quality program.[22] Ritz-Carlton managers created a system for problem-solving that employees are expected to use:

1. IDENTIFY the problem you need to solve and determine why it is important to solve.
2. SPLIT the problem by pinpointing where it does and does not occur—WHERE, WHEN, WHAT KIND & HOW MUCH, WHO.
3. VERIFY the causes of the problem. Don't fix anything until you know what to fix. (Don't chase ghosts.)
4. DEVISE changes that will eliminate the causes of the problem (or reduce the impact) permanently. This is called an ACTION PLAN.
5. IMPLEMENT the changes (action plan).
6. EVALUATE the implementation of the action plan.
7. EVALUATE the effectiveness of the action plan. The problem or the causes must be eliminated or reduced.
8. STANDARDIZE the effective changes. Include the standard procedure, method, material, person type, or environment in our policies.

Note the emphasis in this sequence on eliminating the problem. Ritz-Carlton strives for "100 percent compliance to customer requirements." Computerized guest profiles showing the preferences of 240,000 repeat visitors are kept on file. Managers receive daily quality production reports based on data from 720 work areas in each hotel. All workers are directed to continually identify defects throughout the hotel and are expected and empowered to solve guest problems as soon as they hear about them, doing "whatever it takes"—even if the problem involves a different department than the one they work for. No matter what their normal duties are, other employees must assist if aid is requested by a fellow worker who is responding to a guest complaint or wish.

Stories about the lengths the staff will go to satisfy guests abound. Nancy and Harvey Heffner of Manhattan were quoted in the *New York Times* as saying, "They can't do enough to please you." When the couple's son became sick in Naples, the hotel staff brought him hot tea with honey at all hours of the night. When Mr. Heffner had to fly home on business for a day and his return flight was delayed, a driver for the hotel waited in the lobby most of the night.[23]

Ritz-Carlton is just one of many companies that have embraced the **quality focus school**. In 1982, two McKinsey & Company consultants, Thomas H. Peters and Robert A. Waterman, Jr., wrote *In Search of Excellence,* a study of 43 excellent, large companies. In summarizing their findings, Peters said, "In the private or public sector, in big business or small, we observe that there are only two ways to create and sustain superior performance over the long haul. First, take exceptional care of your customers . . . via superior service and superior quality. Secondly, constantly innovate. That's it. There are no alternatives in achieving long term superior performance, or sustaining strategic competitive advantage, as business strategists call it."[24]

Peters and Waterman turned the management spotlight onto customers and suggested that while all of the various management theories and systems had their place, managers must never forget that they are in business to satisfy customers, and all the systems in the world to motivate employees and organize them using scientific principles will not succeed unless the final outcome is a satisfied customer. Although quantitative management theorists generally recognized the importance of the external environment—including customers—Peters and Waterman said that customers should be the *most* important consideration when managers decide how to run their business. Peters, in fact, suggested that companies start drawing their organization charts upside down with customers at the top and presidents on the bottom![25] Under the Peters and Waterman model of excellent management, the principles of scientific management apply only so long as they help the company please the customer, and even wages should be tied to customer satisfaction. We have come a long way from Fredrick Taylor, who believed in paying workers according to how well they met their manager's expectations, not their customers'.

## Reengineering

**Reengineering** has become a buzzword in American business in recent years. Many companies have tried it; some have succeeded, others have failed. Its importance as a management concept, however, is firmly established. Michael Hammer and James Champy are the acknowledged founders of reengineering. Their ideas came to national attention in 1993 with the publication of their best-selling business book *Reengineering the Corporation: A Manifesto for Business Revolution*.[26] Because of the interest it stirred up, both Hammer and Champy wrote more books by themselves and with others.[27] Soon books and articles on how to reengineer proliferated.

The ideas they expressed are a logical extension of everything that has gone before. Hammer and Champy argue that modern management practices have evolved from the now obsolete ideas of Frederick Taylor, Henri Fayol, and others who concentrated on the best ways to get things done. While everyone agrees that the customer should be the focus of all management, you can only go so far if you continue to adhere to organizational structures that favor such ideas as the division of labor and decentralization. These ideas may have had merit when they were introduced, but over time it has been found that they add layers of workers and management. To produce real results you have to make dramatic—not incremental—changes. A change of 10 percent is an incremental change. Reengineering can improve results by 40 percent or more. That is revolutionary.

Reengineering is defined as *the fundamental rethinking and radical redesign of business processes to achieve dramatic improvements in critical, contemporary measures of performance such as cost, quality, service, and speed.* "Business processes" are the key words here. Processes are a company's meat and potatoes—the way it produces, sells, and serves its customers. Processes generally involve the work of people in more than one functional department. For instance, a convention in a hotel involves, at the minimum, people from the sales and marketing department, rooms division, and food and beverage department. Hammer and Champy believe that work organized around functions or tasks can never achieve the dramatic results that organizing around outcomes can. To accomplish this, functional departments should be replaced by process teams. After all, what customers care about is the outcome—not the work that goes into producing it.

An example of how reengineering works is the insurance company that used to take 24 days to issue a policy. The actual amount of work took 10 minutes. The rest of the time was needed to move paperwork between 14 departments. The company reorganized to allow one person to complete all of the necessary tasks. Now the process takes only a few hours. Henry Ford was a pioneer of specialization with the moving assembly line. Each worker had to complete only one task. In a radical reengineering of their procurement process by requiring fewer documents, Ford was able to combine the work of three departments into one, dramatically accelerating the process and simultaneously reducing the number of people involved from 500 to 125.

These kinds of examples have led to the characterization of reengineering always involving downsizing (shrinking the workforce) and the replacement of people with computers. Hammer and Champy insist that downsizing, restructuring, and quality improvement are not the same and will continue whether or not companies reengineer. Reengineering means starting all over. Doing that, of course, means changing the status quo and there is bound to be resistance from

**386**   *Chapter 12*

(DILBERT© United Feature Syndicate. Reprinted by permission)

workers who are concerned about their jobs. When Delta Air Lines reengineered itself, its shares of stock, which had been declining, turned around, and by 1997 Delta had the highest operating margin of any major carrier. Not only was it making money, but it was filling its airplanes. But Delta had always been a worker-friendly culture, a place where employees were nurtured in a family atmosphere. Reengineering and the accompanying downsizing changed all that. While chairman Ron Allen justified the downsizing as the price of survival, Delta's board did not agree and Allen was forced to resign.

In his best-selling book *The Dilbert Principle,* cartoonist Scott Adams says:

> Reengineering has a tendency to reduce the number of employees needed to perform a function. That unfortunate side effect causes fear and mistrust in the employees whose participation is vital to making reengineering a success. You might think fear and mistrust would sabotage the effort, but that doesn't have to be the case. There are many example of processes that work just fine even when there's plenty of fear and mistrust. Examples:
>
> - Capital punishment
> - Presidential elections
> - Multilevel marketing
>
> Pity the poor slob who is assigned the task of reengineering the company: insufficient management support from above, treachery from below. It's possible to succeed but the odds are against it. The odds are approximately the same if you bet on a race horse who has not won on a muddy track and it suddenly starts pouring rain. And the horse has a cast on two legs. And it's dead.[28]

Despite such incidents and comments, reengineering has gained a substantial foothold in current management thinking.

## Reengineering in the Hotel Business

The hotel business is a classic example of an enterprise organized along functional lines. Departments are focused on specific areas—food and beverage, rooms, sales and marketing. Career paths usually stay within the same area because skills are not transferable. Consequently, communication and cooperation between departments is often difficult. Since different departments have different goals, agreement often involves compromise, which in turn leads to a lower level of customer service. "We can't do this because of the way we do that" is often heard in one form or another.

Professors Nebel, Rutherford, and Schaffer have studied the situation. In an article published in *The Cornell H.R.A. Quarterly* they enumerate the problems that make hotel operations difficult. Some of them are:

- Central decision making. Authorization for purchases often must be signed by GMs, slowing down the response time for special needs. Because authorization to set room rates usually rests at the top, all negotiations generally must go through the GM.

- Difficulty of cross-functional coordination. Problems include conflicts between room service and housekeeping departments over whose responsibility it is to remove dishware from guest rooms; guest service problems with restaurant cashiers who report to the controller's office, not to the food and beverage department; kitchen equipment maintenance, which is the responsibility of the engineering department instead of being under the authority of the executive chef.

- Unclear responsibility for overall performance. The specialization of sales effort (i.e., business and leisure) leads to difficulty in determining overall responsibility and commissions.

- Limited opportunities for general management training. Empirical evidence shows that hotel general managers in the United States follow career paths mostly within one department during their rise to GM. Because of a lack of cross-training within hotels, young managers have a thorough knowledge only of the major department in which they have worked.

- Stifled innovation. Central decision making and coordination often result in a bureaucracy that focuses power in the hands of one or only a few people at the top of the organization. For example, while airlines have developed sophisticated reservation systems that include seat reservations, special meals, and confirmed pre-boarding passes, guests at most hotels must still stand in line to check in, even if they hold a reservation.[29]

Hotels, too, can reengineer themselves if they are willing to stop asking, How can we improve what we are doing, and instead ask, How can we do things differently so that the outcome for the guests will be better. Indeed, many already have. Some hotel chains have combined jobs by clustering hotels regionally so that a group of hotels may have one general manager, one controller, and one director of sales, instead of a separate one for each hotel. Others have eliminated front office managers or consolidated responsibilities, for example, combining the positions of director of catering and food and beverage manager. Many corporate and regional staffs have been downsized.

An example of how one hotel business process might be developed and how, as a result, a hotel's organization can begin to change is given by Nebel, Rutherford, and Schaffer. They suggest that hotels which attract sufficient numbers of conven-

## Exhibit 4  Group-Business Process Map

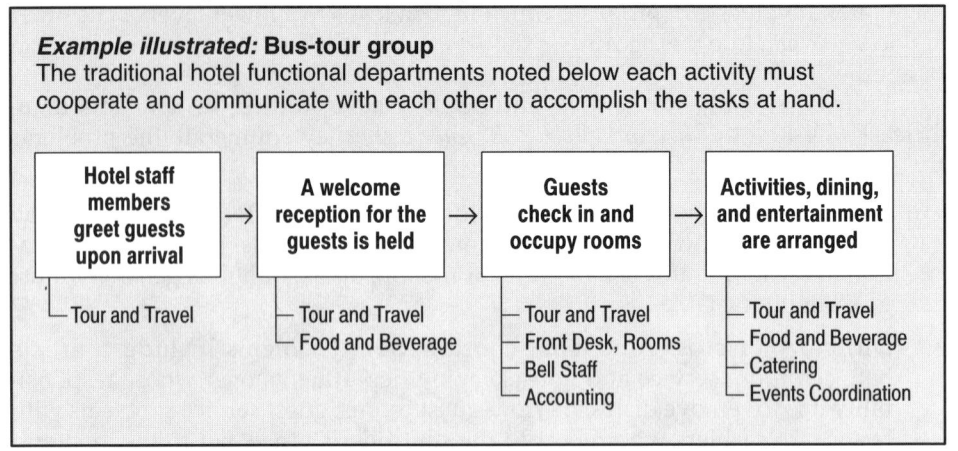

**Example illustrated: Bus-tour group**
The traditional hotel functional departments noted below each activity must cooperate and communicate with each other to accomplish the tasks at hand.

| Hotel staff members greet guests upon arrival | → | A welcome reception for the guests is held | → | Guests check in and occupy rooms | → | Activities, dining, and entertainment are arranged |
|---|---|---|---|---|---|---|
| — Tour and Travel | | — Tour and Travel<br>— Food and Beverage | | — Tour and Travel<br>— Front Desk, Rooms<br>— Bell Staff<br>— Accounting | | — Tour and Travel<br>— Food and Beverage<br>— Catering<br>— Events Coordination |

Source: Eddystone C. Nebel III, Denney Rutherford, and Jeffrey D. Schaffer, "Reengineering the Hotel Organization," *The Cornell H.R.A. Quarterly,* October 1994.

tions and large-group meetings consider reorganizing around the actual work that needs to be done to host those guests successfully, rather than around traditional functional departments.

The first step is to appoint a reengineering team. The team then develops a "process map" (see Exhibit 4). This map (part of Hammer and Champy's model) clearly shows that nearly every hotel department is involved in group business in one way or another.

Then the team needs to reevaluate the hotel's known performance shortcomings that may result in inconsistent customer satisfaction.

The next step is to revise job descriptions throughout the hotel; this allows the hotel to organize people into large-group business process teams. Ideally these teams will be as small as possible so several jobs can be combined into one. Decisions will be made by the people on the team who know the most about the process—not by department heads. Teams will be able to coordinate events without outside intervention. Team performance would be measured by results that are customer-oriented rather than task-based. One major benefit of this kind of approach is that executives become facilitators and leaders rather than checkers and arbitrators.

## The Importance of Leadership

Throughout this chapter we have referred to the persons who manage an organization as "managers." This is perhaps misleading. In 1985, Warren Bennis—an industrial psychologist, an advisor to four American presidents, and a man who has been called the father of the leadership theory—wrote a landmark book (together with Burt Nanus) called *LEADERS: The Strategies for Taking Charge.* Bennis and Nanus interviewed 60 successful CEOs, all presidents or chairs of boards, and 30 outstanding leaders from the public sector. Bennis concluded that these people succeeded not by being managers, but by being *leaders*. While Bennis acknowledged that both management and leadership were important, he said there was a profound difference between the two:

> To manage means to bring about, to accomplish, to have charge of, responsibility for, to conduct. Leading is influencing, guiding in direction, course, action, opinion. The distinction is crucial. *Managers are people who do things right and leaders are people who do the right thing.* The difference may be summarized as activities of vision and judgment—*effectiveness*—versus activities of mastering routines—*efficiency*.[30]

To make the distinction clear, Bennis quoted from an advertisement for United Technologies, headlined "Let's Get Rid of Management," that ran in the *Wall Street Journal*. Here is what the advertisement said:

> People don't want to be managed. They want to be led. Whoever heard of a world manager? World leader, yes. Educational leader. Political leader. Religious leader. Scout leader. Community leader. Labor leader. Business leader. They lead. They don't manage. The carrot always wins over the stick. Ask your horse. You can lead your horse to water, but you can't manage him to drink. If you want to manage somebody, manage yourself. Do that well and you'll be ready to stop managing. And start leading.[31]

After their research was complete, Bennis and Nanus concluded that all of the 90 leaders they interviewed employed four basic strategies:

- Strategy I:     Attention through vision
- Strategy II:    Meaning through communication
- Strategy III:   Trust through positioning
- Strategy IV:    Self-development

We'll discuss each of these strategies in the following sections.

## Strategy I: Attention through Vision

Leaders create a focus for their organization. Ray Kroc of McDonald's told Bennis, "Perhaps [the ability to lead] is a combination of your background, your instincts, and your dreams." Leaders have clear ideas of what they want their organizations to be like and they are good at instilling their ideas in their employees. Before the first load of concrete was poured, Walt Disney knew what Disneyland would look like, how people would feel after spending a day there, and how he would get them to feel that way. That was his vision. Kemmons Wilson dreamed of a network of roadside inns no more than 100 miles apart that would have special facilities for children. Leaders have a vision of what their organization will be like when everything is in place and working right.

## Strategy II: Meaning through Communication

Bennis and Nanus point out that dreaming is not enough. Successful leaders are able to translate dreams into reality by getting others to share their dreams, commitment, and enthusiasm:

> How do you capture imaginations? How do you get people aligned behind the organization's overarching goals? How do you get an audience to recognize and accept an idea? Workers have to recognize and get behind something of established identity. The management of meaning, the mastery of communication, is inseparable from effective leadership.[32]

Effective leadership is accomplished partially through effective communication. Some leaders write inspiring memos. Others hold meetings complete with models, drawings, and charts to get their ideas across. Many use analogies, comparing what they want things to be like to something that everyone already understands. Bennis points out that such communication has little to do with facts—rather, it concentrates on direction. The idea is to get everyone in the organization to share the same ideas and dreams so that they will all hear the same music and play the same tune—based not on having a song book in front of them, but because they just know instinctively what the tune should sound like.

## Strategy III: Trust through Positioning

Leaders not only have a vision and communicate that vision in a way that gets everyone behind it, they know how to steer a constant and steady course in the direction they have laid out. People who work for effective leaders trust their reliability. They know that their leaders are going to do what they have said they are going to do, whatever it takes. Ritz-Carlton's managers expect their employees to satisfy guests—whatever it takes—and every employee knows that they mean it. When Bennis and Nanus entered Ray Kroc's office, he showed them an elaborately framed statement that he said was his favorite inspirational message. The same message was in every other executive's office at McDonald's, in a place where no visitor could miss it. The statement, originally written by former U.S. President Calvin Coolidge, reads:

> Nothing in the world can take the place of persistence.
> Talent will not; nothing is more common than unsuccessful men with great talent.
> Genius will not; unrewarded genius is almost a proverb.
> Education will not; the world is full of educated derelicts.
> Persistence and determination alone are omnipotent.

Effective leaders hold on to their principles, ideas, and visions and are not deterred by obstacles, no matter how insurmountable they seem. The people who work for them know this and trust them to carry out their vision. In this respect they are no different from the legendary generals in military history, whose soldiers knew that they would fight until they achieved victory and thus were willing to fight alongside them.

## Strategy IV: Self-Development

Bennis believes that effective leaders are out on the front line leading the charge most of the time. "Our top executives spent roughly 90 percent of their time with others and virtually the same percentage of their time concerned with the messiness of people problems."[33] He calls this "the creative deployment of self." Leaders know what they are good at and they are constantly using their personal strengths to achieve their goals. At the same time, they understand their weaknesses and compensate for them. If they believe they can't compensate for their weaknesses (by surrounding themselves with a competent staff in the areas in which they do not excel, for example), they typically do not take the job.[34] "It's the capacity to develop and improve their skills that distinguishes leaders from followers," Bennis says. Leaders generally do this without being prodded. They have a strong feeling of self worth—who they are and what they can do—and they act based on that confidence in themselves and their own abilities.

At the same time, leaders value and respect others. They understand that you can't get others to follow you willingly unless it feels good to them. Leaders seldom criticize others. The head coach of the Los Angeles Rams football team told Bennis and Nanus that he

> never criticizes his players until after they're convinced of his *unconditional* confidence. *After* that's achieved he might say (if he does spot something that can help a player), "Look, what you're doing is 99 percent terrific, but there is that 1 percent factor that could make a difference. Let's work on that."[35]

The Wallenda family was and still is the most famous international group of circus acrobats. They have performed their daring tightrope and high-wire acts in every major circus all over the world. Their daring and skill are unmatched. Bennis and Nanus quote Karl Wallenda as saying, "Being on the tightrope is living, everything else is waiting."[36] Karl Wallenda died in front of an audience of thousands in San Juan, Puerto Rico, trying to walk a wire between two high buildings. The Wallendas still walk the tightrope because they don't think about falling. They expect to win, not to lose.

James Burke, retired CEO of Johnson & Johnson and one of the most successful leaders of a global enterprise, likes to tell about the time as a young manager he made a terrible error that cost his company several million dollars. He was called by General Johnson, who he expected would fire him. Instead, Johnson praised him and told him that he admired managers who were willing to take risks and make mistakes. Even today at Johnson & Johnson, managers who refuse to take risks and never make mistakes hardly ever get promoted.

Leaders are not afraid to make mistakes. They believe that making mistakes may be the best way to learn—not only about themselves but about their employees. This is where the key principle of **empowerment** comes from. Leaders empower their employees to solve problems. They expect that in doing so some will make mistakes. Some of these mistakes may even be costly. But employees who make mistakes learn from them and become better at doing their jobs. It makes their jobs more rewarding because they are given a chance to act like a leader—to climb on the tightrope and walk it and take responsibility for their own actions. Sure, there are risks, but there are also rewards. Companies that encourage their employees to take risks, to fail, and to be rewarded when they succeed develop a strong group of well-trained leaders who also know how to follow. In the best companies all employees are encouraged to become leaders by taking customer problems into their own hands and solving them. They are empowered to solve them by being given the resources—whether it is money or the assistance of other people. This requires great trust on the part of their leaders—and a well-trained group of people as well, so they *can* be trusted—but, as Bennis points out, leaders who trust themselves understand instinctively that it is necessary to trust others.

### Service Organizations and People Power

In successful service firms, the employees who deal with customers are encouraged and empowered to take responsibility for customer satisfaction. At Delta, for example, gate agents are empowered to upgrade passengers and even give them free airline seats if they have been bumped or needlessly delayed.

According to the *Wall Street Journal,* many of the nation's largest hotel chains are cutting costs and improving service by empowering employees to better serve customers. "Empowerment is the recognition that employees are not as dumb as employers thought they were," says Darryl Hartley-Leonard, the president of Hyatt Hotels Corporation.[37] At the Fairmont Hotel in San Francisco, Keith Hanlon, a bellperson who helped a couple celebrating their 50th wedding anniversary to their room, sent up a bottle of iced champagne with his business card. At the Hampton Inn in Greensboro, North Carolina, Tonya Greene, a room attendant, saw a guest change rooms twice because of a cold draft, so she arranged for him to get the $54 per night room for free. Hampton has been implementing a company-wide program in which customers are given a free night's stay if they are not completely satisfied.[38]

As Peters and Waterman observed and as Heskett confirms, successful service companies have relatively small executive groups at the top that meet frequently and informally. Managers spend a good deal of their time out of their offices, managing by walking around (MBWA). The idea is to have as few levels of management as possible between the top of the organization and the bottom, so that people will be encouraged to work together, not prevented from doing so by layers of management and numerous closed doors. Given the importance of people and their relationships in service organizations, selecting, training, and promoting the right people is of paramount importance.

## Conclusion

In this chapter we have tried to illustrate that in the management of hospitality organizations there is no single model or style of managing that is appropriate in all circumstances or for all organizations. Managers have different personalities, and thus any two managers are likely to adopt different solutions to the same problem. There are no absolutely right or wrong ways of doing things. There are, however, certain management principles involving market segmentation, operations strategy, and human resources that are used in excellent companies and that seem to produce the best results. In order to apply those principles, managers must be able to do certain things, many of which cannot be taught in a classroom but must be learned by experience. Four management professors—Robert E. Quinn, Sue R. Faerman, Michael P. Thompson, and Michael R. McGrath—have put together eight managerial/leadership roles and their key competencies (see chapter appendix). Managers and aspiring managers would do well to keep these various management roles in mind and try to develop their skills in them as they pursue their careers.

## Chapter Summary

A manager's job is similar to that of a conductor of an orchestra, in that he or she must take all of the individual parts of a company and harmonize them into a whole. The manager must also compose the music that the orchestra is going to play. Managers have five basic tasks to perform. They are: setting objectives, organizing, motivating and communicating, measuring performance, and developing people.

The classical school of management was founded by Fredrick Taylor, who advocated scientific management. Taylor believed there was a best way to perform every job. Frank and Lillian Gilbreth looked for new ways to make people more efficient and studied worker fatigue. Henri Fayol developed 14 principles of management that included division of labor, unity of command, and centralization, among others. His work is the basis of the current systems approach used in industrial management today.

The behavioral school was founded by Chester Barnard, who believed in satisfying the needs of both employers and employees, and George Elton Mayo, who was a researcher involved in the Hawthorne studies. Mayo found that when managers paid positive attention to employees, employees worked harder and had better morale. Abraham Maslow identified a hierarchy of needs, starting with basic physiological needs and ranging up to needs to know and understand. Douglas McGregor developed Theory X and Theory Y, which represent opposing views about how people are motivated to work.

The quantitative school attempted to integrate the management ideas of the classical and behavioral schools. Managers using quantitative techniques apply mathematical decision-making models to management problems. A problem with the quantitative approach is that it tends to focus management attention on meeting short-term financial goals at the expense of employee morale, research and development, and other factors.

The systems school holds that all organizations are a system and therefore events or decisions that occur in one part affect every other part. Managers cannot act independently—what they can and cannot accomplish depends on other managers within the company and on outside environmental factors such as the state of the overall economy.

The contingency school proposes that every situation is different and every manager is different and thus there are no universal principles of management. Managers must be pragmatic and determine for each situation what actions are likely to achieve the results they want.

The quality focus school of management became popular in the 1980s, with the success of Japanese automobile companies. The Japanese were influenced by three Americans—W. Edwards Deming, Joseph Juran, and Philip Crosby—who were little known in the United States until their ideas helped Japanese companies achieve success. Deming emphasized that managers must look to the future, strive for continuous improvement in their products, and break down barriers between employees and managers. By building in quality, a company saved the costs associated with product recalls and lost customers.

Joseph Juran defined quality as "fitness for use." Consumers think they have a quality product if it performs what they expect it to perform, the way they expect it to perform. Juran believed that it was not possible to achieve zero defects, because at some point costs would become too high.

Philip Crosby argued that quality is "free," because the costs associated with preventing defects would always be lower than the costs of correcting mistakes and losing customers. He believed that if managers expected imperfection, that is what they would get; therefore they should expect perfection. They could achieve perfection by increasing employee involvement in improving work processes and gaining their commitment to make perfect products.

Reengineering is defined by Hammer and Champy as "the fundamental rethinking and radical redesign of business processes to achieve dramatic improvements in critical, contemporary measures of performance such as cost, quality, service, and speed." Hotels that are organized according to functional lines may be good candidates for reengineering certain processes such as large-group business.

Managers above all should be leaders. Successful managers know what they want their business to accomplish, clearly communicate that vision to their employees, are good at overcoming obstacles, and are out front leading the charge most of the time. They aren't afraid to make mistakes, and strive to improve themselves and their skills. Leaders also empower their employees to solve problems and become leaders themselves. Effective service organizations believe in people power and managing by walking around (MBWA). They focus a lot of attention on selecting, training, and promoting the right people.

There are eight managerial/leadership roles that a manager must play. These are director, producer, coordinator, monitor, mentor, facilitator, innovator, and broker. To increase their chances for success, managers and aspiring managers should develop their skills in each of these roles.

## Endnotes

1. Peter F. Drucker, *Management: Tasks, Responsibilities, Practices* (New York: Harper & Row, 1974), p. 398.
2. Ronald Zemke and Dick Schaff, *The Service Edge* (New York: New American Library, 1989), p. 43.
3. Drucker, p. 399.
4. Drucker, p. 399.
5. Drucker, pp. 400–401.

6. Weiss Roberts, *Leadership Secrets of Attila the Hun* (New York: Warner Books, 1990), pp. 74–75.
7. Janet Denefe, "Melman's Magic," *F&B Magazine,* July/August 1993, p. 24.
8. Zemke and Schaff, p. 48.
9. All of the quotes and references to Ritz-Carlton in this chapter were supplied to the authors by Patrick Mene, corporate director of quality for the Ritz-Carlton Hotel Corporation, Atlanta, Georgia, in the form of a series of articles, speeches, presentations, and other documents. The authors wish to acknowledge the generous assistance of Mr. Mene and Ritz-Carlton for sharing this material.
10. *Competitive Benchmarking: The Path to a Leadership Position* (Xerox Corporation, 1992).
11. Drucker, p. 402.
12. Robert O'Brien, *Marriott: The J. Willard Marriott Story* (Salt Lake City: Deseret Book Company, 1987) p. 265.
13. Fredrick W. Taylor, "A Piece Rate System," *Scientific Management,: A Collection of the More Significant Articles Describing the Taylor System of Management,* edited by Clarence Bertrand Thompson (Cambridge: Harvard University Press, 1914), p. 637.
14. "The Taylor System of Shop Management at the Watertown Arsenal," *Scientific Management,* p. 755.
15. "The Taylor System of Shop Management," p. 743.
16. George Elton Mayo, *The Human Problems of an Industrial Civilization* (Boston: Macmillan, 1933), pp. 75–76.
17. This discussion of Maslow's theories is distilled from A. H. Maslow, *Motivation and Personality* (New York: Harper & Row, 1970).
18. Daniel A. Wren, *The Evolution of Management Thought* (New York: Wiley, 1979), p. 484.
19. The following discussion of Deming, Juran, and Crosby has been abstracted and paraphrased in part from "A Note on Quality: The Views of Deming, Juran, and Crosby," by Artemis March, associate for case development, under the supervision of Professor David A. Garvin of the Harvard Business School, 1986 (9-687-011), and from a teaching note by research associate Norman Klein and Professor David A. Garvin on the same subject, 1990 (5-691-022). Both documents are the property of the President and Fellows of Harvard College and are available from the Publishing Division of the Harvard Business School, Boston, Massachusetts 02163.
20. March, p. 2.
21. March, p. 7.
22. Edwin McDowell, "Ritz-Carlton's Keys to Good Service," *New York Times,* 31 March 1993.
23. McDowell.
24. Tom Peters and Nancy Austin, *A Passion for Excellence* (New York: Random House, 1985), p. 4.
25. Peters and Austin, p. 34.
26. Michael Hammer and James Champy, *Reengineering the Corporation: A Manifesto for Business Revolution* (New York: HarperCollins, 1993).
27. Hammer authored *The Reengineering Revolution: A Handbook* with Steven A. Stanton (Harper Business, 1995) and *Beyond Reengineering: How the Process-Centered Organization Is*

*Changing Our Work and Our Lives* (HarperCollins, 1996). Champy wrote *Reengineering Management: The Mandate for New Leadership* (HarperCollins, 1994) and co-edited *Fast Forward: The Best Ideas on Managing Business Change* (Harvard Business School Press, 1996) with Nitin Nohria.

28. Scott Adams, *The Dilbert Principle* (New York: Harper Business, 1996), pp. 276–277.
29. Eddystone C. Nebel III, Denney Rutherford, and Jeffrey D. Schaffer, "Reengineering the Hotel Organization," *The Cornell H.R.A. Quarterly,* October 1994, pp. 88–95.
30. Warren Bennis and Burt Nanus, *LEADERS: The Strategies for Taking Charge* (New York: Harper & Row, Perennial Library Edition, 1986), p. 21.
31. Bennis and Nanus, p. 22.
32. Bennis and Nanus, p. 33.
33. Bennis and Nanus, p. 56.
34. Bennis and Nanus, p. 60.
35. Bennis and Nanus, p. 64.
36. Bennis and Nanus, p. 69.
37. James S. Hirsh, "Now Hotel Clerks Provide More Than Keys," *Wall Street Journal,* 6 March 1993, p. B-1.
38. Hirsh, p. B-1.

# Key Terms

**behavioral management school**—Management theorists who sought to develop better ways to motivate workers than the rules, systems, and wages proposed by the classical management theorists.

**classical school**—A school of management thought in which workers are seen as rational people interested primarily in making money. This management approach addresses an employee's economic and physical needs, but not his or her social needs or need for job satisfaction.

**competitive benchmarking**—A phrase coined by the Xerox Corporation that refers to the continuous process of measuring products, services, and practices against those of a business's toughest competitors or other companies recognized as leaders.

**contingency school**—According to this school of thought, every management situation is different and every manager is different. Therefore, there are few universal management principles. Also known as the situational management school.

**empowerment**—A management technique whereby front line employees are authorized to solve customers' problems and make some other decisions that were once made only at higher levels within the organization.

**Hawthorne effect**—The phenomenon that employees work harder and more efficiently when they know their managers are interested in them and their work.

**Hawthorne studies**—Studies of workers at the Western Electric Company's plant in Hawthorne, Illinois, involving Harvard Business School professor George Elton

Mayo. The studies were originally designed to assess the effects of lighting conditions on worker productivity, but subsequently were broadened to include other working conditions, such as rest periods and type of supervision.

**quality focus school**—A school of management thought that emphasizes the importance of quality over all other aspects of management. Its founders were Deming, Juran, and Crosby.

**quantitative school**—A school of management that tries to integrate the management theories of the classical and behavioral management schools.

**reengineering**—The fundamental rethinking and radical redesign of business processes to achieve dramatic improvements in critical, contemporary measures of performance such as cost, quality, service, and speed.

**situational management school**—This school of thought believes that every management situation is different and every manager is different. Therefore, there are few universal management principles. Also known as the contingency school.

**systems school**—This school of management thought proposes that a company is a system of many interrelated parts. The company, in turn, is part of a larger external environment (system). Therefore, managers cannot act independently; what they can accomplish depends on factors inside and outside the company.

**Theory X**—A traditional set of assumptions some managers make about human nature that governs their management style. According to Theory X, the average employee (1) dislikes work and must be directed and threatened with punishment in order to put forth adequate effort, and (2) avoids responsibility and values security above anything else.

**Theory Y**—A set of assumptions some managers make about human nature that governs their management style. According to Theory Y, (1) the average employee does not inherently dislike work, (2) external control is not necessary if employees are committed to the organization's objectives, and (3) commitment to objectives is achieved by association rewards with the attainment of those objectives.

**three position plan of promotion**—A plan developed by Frank and Lillian Gilbreth in which workers not only perform their jobs but also (1) learn the next higher job and (2) train a worker below them to take over their present job when they are promoted.

## Review Questions

1. Managers must perform which five basic tasks?
2. Who are the founders of the classical school of management?
3. What are Taylor's and Fayol's contributions to management theory?
4. What are the Hawthorne studies?
5. What are Maslow's and McGregor's contributions to management theory?
6. How is the systems school different from the contingency school?

7. Can the principles of management developed by industrial managers apply as well to service managers? Why or why not?
8. Explain reengineering.
9. What are four basic strategies of successful leaders?

# Internet Sites

For more information, visit the following Internet sites. Remember that Internet addresses can change without notice. If the site is no longer there, use a search engine to look for additional sites.

## Hotel Companies/Resorts

Fairmont Hotels
www.fairmont.com

Hampton Inn
www.hampton-inn.com

Hyatt Hotels Corporation
www.hyatt.com

Lettuce Entertain You Enterprises
www.cyberchicago.com/Clients/lettuce/lettuce1.html

Marriott International
www.marriott.com

Ritz-Carlton Hotels
www.ritzcarlton.com

## Organizations, Resources

Business Process Reengineering and Innovation
www.brint.com/BPR.htm

The Malcolm Baldrige Award
www.quality.nist.gov/nqpwsmap.htm

Reengineering Resource Center
www.reengineering.com

## Publications

*Inc.* Online
www.inc.com

*Strategy & Business*
www.strategy-business.com

## Restaurant Companies

McDonald's
www.mcdonalds.com

Taco Bell
www.tacobell.com

# Chapter Appendix
## Eight Managerial/Leadership Roles

### Director Role

As a director, a manager must be a decisive initiator who defines problems, establishes objectives, generates rules and policies, and gives instructions. A manager directs by taking charge of a situation, focusing on results, and making things happen. As directors, managers must also set goals and define the action plans that will be needed to reach them. Finally, managers must know how to delegate effectively by recognizing that they cannot accomplish much by themselves. It is only through the work of others that things get done.

### Producer Role

As producers, managers are expected to be task-oriented, work-focused, and highly interested in the task at hand. Managers must be able to motivate themselves to a high level of productivity, respond to challenges in a positive manner, and have the drive and ambition to continuously improve their performance.

Just as managers must motivate themselves, they must also motivate others by understanding that what they expect of their employees and how they treat them largely determines their employees' performances and career progress.

In the role of producer, a manager must also learn how to cope with and minimize the effects of negative stress that occurs regularly in many hospitality jobs, because often there are slow periods followed by peaks of frenzied activity.

### Coordinator Role

As a coordinator, a manager makes sure that work flows smoothly and that activities are carried out according to their relative importance, with a minimum amount of conflict among individuals, departments, or groups of workers. This is accomplished by planning the use of financial and human resources to ensure the most effective delivery of services.

Managers must establish standards and priorities and schedule work by task and by employee. Managers must also establish lines of authority by clarifying who reports to whom and who is supposed to perform which jobs.

Finally, as coordinators, managers must learn to use controls as effective mechanisms that provide feedback on whether actual performance is consistent with planned performance and whether customers are actually receiving the level of service intended.

### Monitor Role

As monitors, managers are expected to know what is going on and make sure people are complying with rules and producing as expected. Managers must be able to keep track of facts such as food costs or occupancy rates, analyze them, and decide what is important. To do this, managers must be good at handling paperwork, reading memos, and taking notes at meetings. Managers must also know how to make effective use of information by keeping an open mind and using good judgment. To solve problems, managers must be able to discover and weigh all possible factors and then decide which solution is likely to produce the desired result(s). This requires clear analytical thinking. Managers must also be able to present information to others by writing effective memos, proposals, and letters.

### Mentor Role

As a mentor, a manager is expected to be helpful, considerate, sensitive, approachable, open, and fair. Managers do this by understanding themselves and others, by interpersonal communication—including developing active listening skills—and by developing employees through performance evaluation and training.

### Facilitator Role

In the facilitator role, a manager fosters collective effort, builds cohesion and morale, and manages interpersonal conflict. This can be accomplished through team building. Effective managers are first of all team players. They believe that working together is better than working alone. They are able to get others to share that belief. Managers who are facilitators practice participative decision-making. When an important decision comes up, they involve the individuals whose work lives are affected by the decision. Furthermore, they are skillful in conflict management, which research shows may take between 20 and 50 percent of a manager's time. These managers know how to use collaborative approaches to resolve disputes.

### Innovator Role

In today's rapidly changing environment, the ability of managers to initiate and implement change so that they can keep up with the times is an essential survival skill. Nowhere is change more evident than in the hospitality field, where new life-styles and demographic profiles are constantly affecting how and where people travel as well as their diets and tastes. Managers must deal with changes that are unplanned and sometimes unwelcome. Doing this requires the creativity to generate new ideas and solutions. Innovative managers know how to plan for and manage change. They welcome new technology, new ideas, and are willing to take risks to find new and better ways of doing things.

### Broker Role

In organizations, good ideas work only if people see a benefit in adopting them. Managers must be brokers who know how to build and maintain a power base, negotiate agreement and commitment, and present ideas effectively. Managers who are good brokers understand that power and authority are not the same thing. Real power doesn't come from a title or a position, but from the shape and impact a person's presentation of self has on others—the personal characteristics that people find attractive or influential or persuasive. Power can also be gained through the expertise a manager may possess in special areas like food preparation or computers. Managers who are effective brokers are good negotiators and know how to get agreement among groups or individuals with opposing ideas. They are also competent public speakers and know how to communicate not only on a one-to-one basis but to an audience.

## REVIEW QUIZ

When you feel you have covered all of the material in this chapter, answer these questions. Choose the *best* answer.

1. Which of the following is a tenet of the behavioral school of management, as expressed by Chester Barnard?

   a. Managers should try to mesh the personal goals of employees with the organization's overall goals.
   b. What managers can or cannot accomplish depends in part on outside environmental factors.
   c. There is one best way to do every job.
   d. The consumer is the most important part of the production line.

2. The management task of motivating and communicating involves all of the following *except:*

   a. listening to employee problems.
   b. making fair decisions regarding employee compensation.
   c. deciding who should be promoted and when.
   d. analyzing operational reports.

3. According to Peter Drucker, one of the broad goals of a manager is to:

   a. make sure that all policies implemented have the authorization of executive management.
   b. analyze every aspect of production so that potential productivity increases can be realized.
   c. consider both immediate and long-range needs in every decision.
   d. formulate and refine the company's mission statement so that the customer is always the first consideration.

4. Managers who are comfortable with the _____ school of management often are especially adept at managing diverse work groups.

   a. systems
   b. behavioral
   c. contingency
   d. quality focus

5. Quantitative management tends to direct a manager's attention to _____ rather than _____.

   a. employee morale and turnover; profitability
   b. customer satisfaction; productivity
   c. research and development; cost reduction
   d. short-term goals; the long-term health of the organization

## REVIEW QUIZ *(continued)*

6. Which of the following statements about leaders is *false?*

    a. Leaders are afraid to make mistakes.
    b. Leaders have a vision about what their organizations should be like.
    c. Leaders are effective communicators.
    d. Leaders are not deterred by obstacles.

7. Which of the following statements about reengineering is *true?*

    a. Reengineering aims at improving results by as much as 25 percent.
    b. Reengineering means changing the status quo.
    c. Reengineering always entails downsizing.
    d. a and b.

**Answer Key:** 1-a-C1, 2-d-C1, 3-c-C1, 4-c-C2, 5-d-C2, 6-a-C3, 7-b-C3

Each question is linked to a competency. Competencies are listed on the first page of the chapter. An answer reading 3-b-C4 translates to:

- 3: the question number
- b: the correct answer
- C4: the competency number

## Chapter 13 Outline

Labor Trends
    Changing Demographics
    High Turnover
    Legislation
Human Resources Programs
Chapter Summary

## Competencies

1. Identify current labor trends affecting the hospitality industry.
2. Describe elements of a good human resources program.

# 13

# Managing Human Resources

IT HAS BEEN said that a manager can be compared to a conductor, whose job it is to instruct and direct all of the various musicians so that they perform well together. But before a conductor can direct a beautiful performance, all of the individual musicians must be able to play their instruments well. What kind of performance could you expect if the violinists did not know how to play their instruments or the flutists could not read music?

So it is in the hospitality industry. Before a manager can direct and shape employees' individual contributions into an efficient whole, he or she must first turn employees into competent workers who know how to do their jobs. Employees are the musicians of the orchestra that the members of the audience—the guests—have come to watch perform. If employees are not skilled at their jobs, then the performance they give will get bad reviews. Just as an orchestra can have a fine musical score from a great composer and still perform poorly because of incompetent musicians, so a hotel or restaurant can have the finest standard recipes, service procedures, and quality standards and still have dissatisfied guests because of poor employee performance.

That is why properly managing human resources is so important. No other industry provides so much contact between employees and customers and so many opportunities to either reinforce a positive experience or create a negative one. In this chapter we will talk about the shortage of workers, high turnover rates, and labor-related legislation—elements contributing to what can only be called a labor crisis. We will then turn our attention to the chief strategy used by hotel and restaurant managers to combat this crisis: good human resources programs designed to help managers hire, train, motivate, and retain employees.

## Labor Trends

By any measure, one of the most serious problems the hospitality industry faces today is a shortage of labor. Many industry leaders feel that a shortage of workers and the poor quality of workers are the biggest problems facing the industry, even ahead of overbuilding and foreign competition concerns. The problems managers face include: (1) fewer applicants for jobs, (2) jobs staying vacant longer, (3) turnover edging upward, and (4) lack of qualified applicants. There are a number of factors that contribute to the labor crisis:

- Changing demographics
- High turnover
- Legislation

Opportunities to make a positive impression on guests abound in the hospitality industry. (Left photo courtesy of The Dusit Thani Hotel, Bangkok, Thailand)

## Changing Demographics

Most observers agree that there are at least six demographic trends that will have a significant impact on the American work force and consequently on all U.S. businesses in the next decade.

**The Growth in Population.** In the 1950s the U.S. population was growing at a rate of as high as 2 percent annually. Today's population growth rate is only slightly more than .9 percent, and the rate is projected to gradually decrease in the future. While the country has experienced an unexpected boom in births and a high increase in immigration, there was a record number of deaths. Between 1990 and 1995, the number of immigrants to the United States was almost 1 million annually. In future years, as the birth rate continues to decrease, the number of deaths will rise due to an aging population base. That means that immigration will play an ever more important role in shaping the American work force.

**The Middle-Aging of America.** In 1985, 50 percent of American workers were between the ages of 16 and 34, 38 percent were between 35 and 54, and the remaining 12 percent were over 55, according to the U.S. Bureau of Labor Statistics. But by the year 2000 the situation will have changed dramatically. It is estimated that by 2000 the number of workers within the 16-34 age bracket will have declined by 12 percent, so that the total for this group will be only 38 percent; while the number of workers between the ages of 35 and 54 will have increased 13 percent, from 38 percent to 51 percent. The number of workers over 55 will decline to 11 percent in the same period. There is good news and bad news in these statistics. The good news is that middle-aged workers are usually more experienced and dependable than their younger counterparts. The bad news is that there will be fewer young workers available to start at the bottom and work their way up.

**The Increase in Women Workers.** Because of the rising cost of living and the increase in the number of single family households, the number of U.S. women joining the work force has been growing steadily since the middle of the century. In 1955 only 35 percent of women worked outside the home, but the Hudson Institute

**The number of women employed in the hospitality industry continues to grow.**

estimates that this figure will reach 60 percent by 2000. Already, two-thirds of all U.S. mothers are in the work force, and more than half of all women work. The growing number of working women is a boon for the restaurant business, since these women have less time for homemaking and they (and their families) eat out more. Employers who wish to recruit women must understand and possibly help to resolve the issue of dependent care, which was not necessary in the past when they dealt with a predominantly male work force.

**The Shifting Population.** For years, the population in the United States has been moving away from the Northeast and Midwest and settling in the Sunbelt and western states. More than 80 percent of population growth will be in these two areas of the country until 2020, according to projections by the U.S. Bureau of the Census.

Virtually every state in New England has lost population. Eight of the ten fastest growing states have been in the West. In addition, there has been a large influx of immigrants from the Caribbean and Central and South America who have settled in Southern and Western states. This means that there will be a labor shortage in some areas of the country, but not in all. This is especially true since job growth will be confined to service industries such as hospitality. The number of new jobs in manufacturing has decreased dramatically in the past decade and is expected to continue to decline because of reengineering, downsizing, and the growth of technology.

**The Growth in Education Levels.** While the rate of college enrollments has been increasing, most American adults have still never been to college. Moreover, there is some evidence that literacy has been decreasing in some regions due to the large number of non-English-speaking immigrants entering the country every year. However, as the demand for skilled workers increases, more adults are expected to seek degrees of some sort—either from a university, junior college, or technical school.

**The Diversity of the Work Force.** In 1960 only 10 percent of Americans belonged to a minority group. Today, 25 percent of all Americans are nonwhite. By the year 2050, Blacks, Hispanics, Asians, and Native Americans will represent more than 50 percent of the U.S. population. Non-Hispanic whites will become the new minority. Clearly, as more and more managers and employees from diverse races and cultures are mixed together in the workplace, there will be an increasing need for diversity training.

## High Turnover

High turnover rates are another labor problem that hospitality managers must cope with. According to the National Restaurant Association, median turnover for the restaurant industry is between 90 percent and 130 percent annually, depending on the type of restaurant. One hotel operator reports that most departing employees are room attendants, food servers, and bus help, and nearly half of them leave during the first two weeks of employment. One result of this high turnover rate is that many hotel and restaurant employees are not well trained or experienced enough to provide the quality of service customers expect.

It is difficult to pin down all of the reasons for the industry's high turnover rates, but there are a few that may be universal:

- *Inefficient hiring systems.* Because it is so difficult to find employees, managers hire many individuals without screening them or fully explaining what their jobs involve. For example, a hotel is open and must be staffed 24 hours a day, seven days a week. New employees often don't understand what it is like to work all night, or on holidays or weekends, and that they are likely to be called on to fill some of those shifts. When they discover what a hospitality job can entail, they often get discouraged and look for other work.

- *Limited opportunities for advancement.* Most people want to better themselves. Few people are satisfied with minimum-wage employment at a hotel or restaurant if they can find a better job. Often they can. Another problem is that many hotels and restaurants have no training programs where entry-level workers can learn skills that will make them promotable within the company. A worker who wants to get ahead may have to quit and go somewhere else.

- *Lack of training and supervision.* People hired for entry-level positions should be trained to do their jobs. Many receive inadequate training, make mistakes, get discouraged, and quit. While on-the-job training may be the cheapest form of training, it is also the most traumatic for employees.

## Legislation

It is important for hospitality managers to understand legislation that will have an impact on the way they manage their businesses. In 1938 the U.S. Congress passed the Fair Labor Standards Act (FLSA), which established laws concerning wages and overtime. Employees of service industries were exempt until 1967, and it was not until 1979 that all of the provisions were in force. The law addressed such issues as the employment of minors and equal pay for both sexes performing the same kind of work.

A number of other federal and local laws have influenced human resources practices. The Civil Rights Act of 1964 bans discrimination on the basis of race, sex, religion, or national origin. One result of this law was the formation of the Equal Employment Opportunity Commission (EEOC), which oversees the enforcement and administration of this law. In recent years the EEOC has expanded its horizons to cover sexual harassment cases.

The Occupational Safety and Health Act (OSHA) of 1970 spells out what constitutes safe working conditions. In addition, it requires employers to make sure that workers have necessary safety equipment while on the job, and that equipment such as meat slicers and ladders conform to safety standards.

The Americans with Disabilities Act of 1990 is designed to protect the civil rights of persons who have physical or mental disabilities. Employers may not deny jobs to disabled persons who are capable of performing them, and must provide reasonable access to the workplace for them (such as special parking spaces and ramps for wheelchairs).

The Family and Medical Leave Act of 1993 provides that employees must be given up to twelve weeks off a year without pay if they need it for childbirth, adoption, or illness of the employee or a family member.

## Human Resources Programs

A sound human resources program typically contains the following elements:

- It starts with "Who we are and what we believe"
- It defines the job
- It recruits the most suitable candidates
- It selects the best applicants
- It incorporates a continual training program
- It motivates employees
- It evaluates the program

**Who We Are and What We Believe.** There is a growing recognition among managers in service industries that you can't expect employees to treat customers any better than they themselves are treated. Ritz-Carlton refers to its employees in its mission statement as "internal customers," and believes that in order for its employees to offer quality service to guests, Ritz-Carlton must first offer it to employees. The company promotes a corporate culture that encourages employees to stop their day-to-day routine to help fellow employees. This helps build stronger teams and eliminate internal competition.

At McDonald's, teenage employees are given a handbook that tells them that "working part-time is an excellent way for you to learn about the real world. But it's more important for you to make education Priority #1. At McDonald's, our commitment is to help students explore the best of both worlds."[1] This communicates to employees McDonald's belief in the importance of education.

Both of these companies recognize that when they talk about being in the "people business," they mean the people who work for them as well as the people who buy from them. Successful human resources programs recognize that people are the most valuable resource they have, and ensure that every step within the program takes into account the basic worth of individuals, their sensitivities and vulnerabilities. These companies say, in effect, "We are employers who care about the people who work for us."

**Defining the Job.** Before the right person can be hired to perform a particular job, managers must understand exactly what the job involves so that an applicant's skills and the requirements of the job can be matched accurately.

The task of analyzing a job is somewhat more complicated in the hospitality industry than elsewhere. The job of a spot welder, for example, is the same whether the welding takes place on top of a skyscraper or in a machine shop. But a food server's job can vary tremendously, depending on the time of day, the operation's physical layout and design, whether he or she is working at a local diner or a fine-dining restaurant, the operation's equipment, and the guests' expectations. Even merchandising techniques can affect a food server's job: in most restaurants, guests order off a printed menu; in others, servers are expected to show a blackboard to diners or memorize the daily specials.

Since the same job can differ from property to property, independent hotels and restaurants must perform their own job analyses in order to understand how jobs are done at their particular properties. Hotels and restaurants that belong to chains do not typically perform their own job analyses; this task is done at corporate headquarters. Days Inn's franchise division commissioned the School of Industrial and Systems Engineering at the Georgia Institute of Technology to prepare an analysis of Days Inn's room-cleaning procedures. The Georgia Tech analysts concluded that all major tasks in room cleaning fall into "natural groupings" or job blocks, and recommended that Days Inn adopt the room cleaning sequence shown in Exhibit 1.

Once a job has been analyzed, then a number of documents can be prepared to help employees understand and learn the job, among them job lists, job breakdowns, and job descriptions.

## Exhibit 1  Sample Guestroom Cleaning Sequence

**Preliminary**

The room attendant enters the room, turns on the light, and opens the curtains. He/she places the in-room cart at the side of the vanity. He/she then makes a forward sweep through the room, dumping ashtrays in the trash can bags, picking up these bags, and picking up room trash. He/she deposits the trash in the main cart outside the door and returns to the room, picking up ashtrays and washing them in the sink or leaving them there to soak if necessary.

**Block 1**

From the vanity, the room attendant makes a second sweep through the room, gathering all dirty terry, placing terry on the used bed, and wrapping the dirty linen around it. If two beds are used then he/she places the ball on the second bed, wrapping the dirty linen from that bed around it. Note that the procedure eliminates stuffing linen and terry into a pillow case. This is a time-consuming procedure. The room attendant takes the ball and places it in the main cart outside the door.

**Block 2**

From the main cart, he/she takes all necessary clean linen, re-enters the room, and makes the bed(s).

**Block 3**

From the beds he/she goes directly to the vanity and performs all necessary work, including terry re-stocking. He/she does not need to move away from the vanity due to the convenience of the in-room cart.

**Block 4**

He/she moves the in-room cart next to the bathroom. Here he/she performs all bathroom cleaning tasks.

**Block 5**

He/she makes a circuit of the room to dust. Returning to the in-room cart, he/she moves it next to the desk, cleans the desk mirror, replaces the trash can bag, re-stocks necessary stationery supplies, and replaces the desk ashtray. Then, moving the in-room cart toward the door, he/she replaces the air conditioner ashtray, and takes the in-room cart outside the room.

**Block 6**

Removing the vacuum (or other carpet cleaning tool) from the main cart, he/she vacuums the room.

This is only part of the job analysis of a typical room attendant position. The complete description might also cover the room attendant's responsibility for stocking the in-room cart with sheets, pillowcases, towels, glasses, soap, toilet paper, stationery, and other items, as well as more detail on how beds should be made, toilets cleaned, and so on.

**Exhibit 2    Sample Job List**

```
                                              Date: xx/xx/xx
                        JOB LIST
Position: Housekeeping Room Attendant
Tasks: Employees must be able to:
  1. PARK in designated area.
  2. WEAR proper uniform.
  3. PUNCH in.
  4. PICK up clipboard and keys.
  5. MEET with supervisor.
  6. OBTAIN supplies.
  7. PLAN your work.
  8. ENTER the room.
  9. PREPARE the room.
 10. MAKE the beds.
 11. GATHER cleaning supplies.
 12. CLEAN the bathroom.
 13. DUST the room.
 14. CHECK/REPLACE paper supplies and amenities.
 15. CLEAN windows.
 16. INSPECT your work.
 17. VACUUM the room.
 18. LOCK the door and mark your report.
 19. TAKE breaks at designated times.
 20. RETURN and restock cart.
 21. RETURN to housekeeping with clipboard and keys.
 22. PUNCH out.
```

As the name implies, a **job list** is simply a list of the tasks that must be performed by the individual holding that particular job (see Exhibit 2). Job lists are useful as training tools and can serve as reminders for new employees.

Job lists are the foundations for **job breakdowns**—specific, step-by-step procedures for accomplishing a task (see Exhibit 3). The first column in Exhibit 3 shows a task (7) from the job list shown in Exhibit 2. The second column breaks down the task by identifying the steps that an employee must take to accomplish the task. These steps are written as performance standards. The third column, "Additional Information," explains why each step of the task is performed and may also include such information as desired attitudes when performing the step, safety tips, or pointers on how to reach the performance standard. In column four, managers can record information for quarterly performance evaluations. As you can see, a job breakdown can be as useful in evaluating employees as in training them.

Once a job list and a job breakdown have been developed for a particular job, a **job description** can be written that outlines (1) the title that goes with the job, (2)

## Exhibit 3 Sample Job Breakdown

**POSITION:** Housekeeping Room Attendant, morning shift
**NAME:**
**SUPERVISOR:**

| JOB LIST | PERFORMANCE STANDARDS | ADDITIONAL INFORMATION | 1st Qtr Yes/No | 2nd Qtr Yes/No | 3rd Qtr Yes/No | 4th Qtr Yes/No |
|---|---|---|---|---|---|---|
| 7. PLAN YOUR WORK. | A. STUDY your assignment sheet. | Early service requests, rush rooms, check-outs, VIPs and no-service requests will be noted on your chart. | | | | |
| | B. CLEAN check-outs first, whenever possible. | Cleaning check-outs first gives the front desk rooms to sell. | | | | |
| | C. CLEAN early service requests as noted on your report. | | | | | |
| | D. CLEAN VIP rooms before lunch, whenever possible. | A VIP is our most important guest. | | | | |
| | E. LOCK your cart room door and proceed to your section. | | | | | |
| | F. HONOR "do not disturb" signs. | We must honor the privacy of guests. Many guests like to sleep in. Never knock on a door that has a "do not disturb" sign. | | | | |
| | G. CHECK rooms marked c/o and then check the rooms which are circled on your report. These are rooms due to check out. | Rooms marked c/o have already checked out at the front desk. Check-out time is noon. | | | | |
| | H. PLAN your work around early service requests. | If you have early service requests, be sure to clean these rooms at the proper time. | | | | |

the person to whom the employee reports, (3) the work to be performed (in general terms), and (4) the education or skills the employee must have (see Exhibit 4). A job description can be useful in a number of ways. It can be used as a recruiting tool to show prospective employees the nature of the work to be performed; it is an excellent training tool; supervisors can use it to monitor work in progress; and it can be used as the basis for employee evaluation. Job descriptions can also ease employee anxiety because they specify in writing the person to whom the employee reports and the responsibilities of the employee.

**Productivity Standards.** A good human resources program has **productivity standards.** Productivity standards tell managers how long it should take employees to complete tasks using the best methods management has devised, and how much work can be performed in a given time period. Productivity standards are often

**Exhibit 4  Sample Job Description**

---

**JOB DESCRIPTION**

JOB TITLE:   Executive Housekeeper

IMMEDIATE SUPERVISOR:   Resident Manager/Assistant Resident Manager

**JOB SUMMARY**  Supervises all housekeeping employees, has the authority to hire or discharge, plans and assigns work assignments, informs new employees of property regulations, inspects housekeeping personnel work assignments, and requisitions supplies.

**DUTIES**  Supervises all housekeeping employees, hires new employees as needed, discharges employees when necessary, and writes warning notices when policy has been violated. Evaluates employees in order to upgrade when openings arise.

Plans the work for the Housekeeping Department and distributes assignments accordingly. Assigns Housepersons, Inspectors, and Linen Room Attendants to their regular duties, or any special assignments that need to be accomplished. Schedules employees and assigns extra days off according to the occupancy forecast. Maintains a time log record book of all employees within the department.

Informs new employees of regulations. Trains and assigns new employees to work with experienced help. Checks on the work of these employees occasionally and observes the reports made by the Inspector or Section Housekeeper.

Inspects the housekeeping staff periodically to determine if they are on duty and checks the quantity and quality of their work, checking places likely to be overlooked.

Approves all supply requisitions, such as spreads and bathroom rugs. Maintains a lost and found department and is responsible for all lost and found items. Determines the rightful owner and mails to appropriate address.

**PREREQUISITES**   Education         High school required.

Experience        Minimum three (3) years as an Assistant Housekeeper or Inspector.

Skills            Ability to plan and implement housekeeping programs and policies and to work and communicate with management, associates, and subordinates.

Approved _____  Date _____

---

based on a manager's personal experience, the business's historical records, and industry standards.

In order to know if productivity standards are being met, employee productivity must be measured. Productivity can be measured in dollars or units produced or served.

When productivity is expressed in dollars, it can be calculated by two different methods. The first consists of dividing sales by payroll costs:

$$\frac{\$10{,}000{,}000 \text{ (sales)}}{\$2{,}500{,}000 \text{ (payroll)}} = \$4$$

In this example, every $1 of payroll expended produced $4 of sales.

The second method of calculating productivity using dollars consists of dividing sales by the number of **full-time-equivalent (FTE) employees:**

$$\frac{\$10{,}000{,}000 \text{ (sales)}}{280 \text{ (FTE employees)}} = \$35{,}714 \text{ (rounded)}$$

In this example, $35,714 was generated for every FTE employee.

Units produced or served divided by the number of employees also yields a measure of productivity. For instance, suppose a restaurant with ten FTE employees serves 500 **covers,** or meals, on a particular evening:

$$\frac{500 \text{ covers (units produced or served)}}{10 \text{ (FTE employees)}} = 50$$

In this example, 50 covers were served per FTE employee.

Fifty is the number of covers that were actually served that evening, but fifty covers might or might not meet the work productivity standard for the restaurant. The restaurant's standard might be that 65 covers should be served for every FTE employee, in which case the 10 FTE employees should have served 650 covers. Managers then have several options. They can investigate why employees served fewer covers that evening. It could be that guests at many tables stayed longer than average, so that the restaurant didn't seat enough guests to meet the productivity standard. Or it could be that several new food servers were scheduled that evening and they did not serve guests as quickly as the more experienced servers. Depending on the circumstances, managers might then decide to re-train the new servers or conclude that they just need a little more experience. Or managers might wait to see if an investigation is really necessary. Managers may decide not to investigate what happened that evening at all, but to keep a close eye on the covers per FTE employee for the next week or two. Only if covers per FTE employee stay below the standard for a significant period would they take the time to investigate the causes.

Productivity standards are not only essential for payroll control, they are also important in job analysis and as measures of expectation when recruiting, training, or evaluating an employee.

Managers should never assume that high productivity equals guest satisfaction and business success. While managers of service businesses must watch their productivity measures carefully in order to achieve their economic goals, they must also remember that success in business has qualitative as well as quantitative dimensions. In other words, successful businesses base their productivity standards in part on guest expectations, not on profitability or efficiency objectives alone. For example, the Bob Evans restaurant chain bases many of its productivity standards on its guests' expectations, and carefully measures how well it meets those expectations. Guests should not have to wait for a table for more than 15 minutes; after guests are seated, an employee should come by with water and a greeting within 60 seconds; food should arrive at the table no longer than 10 minutes after the guests order it; and a vacated table must be readied for new guests within 5 minutes.

**Recruiting Suitable Candidates.** Once the various jobs have been defined and productivity standards established, recruiting workers becomes the top priority for managers. A major goal of recruiting is to find the best workers available who are willing to work for the wages offered by the business. This task is complicated by the fact that in the hospitality industry work skills alone are not a sufficient measure of a person's suitability for a job. Personality must also be taken into consideration if the position involves guest contact.

To a large extent, whether an operation can recruit people who have the personality and skills to fit into a service-oriented business depends on the labor market in which it is functioning. Market areas differ as to levels of unemployment, diversity of the work force, and competitive industries. Hotels and restaurants might have trouble recruiting good employees in locales with a low level of unemployment and a number of large businesses with high wage scales. Even in some areas with high levels of unemployment, there may not be a wide selection of people with the basic skills and temperament to work in a hospitality organization. In some unfavorable market areas, employees must be transported daily from nearby towns to their place of work—a costly procedure. When McDonald's opened a new restaurant in Boca Raton, Florida—a town where the leading employer is IBM—it found it necessary to transport workers by bus from Miami, 50 miles away! The Hyatt Regency Hotel in Greenwich, Connecticut, assists workers who commute to the area by train from places like Mt. Vernon, New York, or Stamford, Connecticut. The hotel leased a van and hired two full-time drivers to pick up employees at the train station, ensuring that the workers get to work on time and saving them taxi fare.

**Internal and external sources of employees.** All sources of new employees fall into one of two categories: internal or external. Of these, internal sources are the least costly and often the most reliable. One internal source consists of recruits recommended by current employees. Since employees have a good understanding of the nature of the work involved, and since they tend to be careful about whom they recommend, employees often bring in recruits who do very well. Bulletin boards and company newsletters are ways of getting the news of job openings to employees.

Often employees will suggest friends and relatives for positions. Some operators have rules prohibiting family members from working together. These rules are typically a result of previous negative experiences, or of fears that if one member of a family leaves the company, other members may leave as well. While these concerns are sometimes justified, there are many examples of family members working for the same employer, at the same time, quite successfully.

Another internal source of applicants for a vacant job is the current staff. Promoting from within establishes the operation as a good place to work—one in which opportunities are available for those who want them and work hard for them. In fact, a strong internal-promotion policy is in itself a valuable recruiting tool, and many companies spell out career ladder progressions as part of their recruitment program. For example, just about all of the Domino's Pizza franchisees were once store managers—owning your own store is part of the career track that is offered as a recruitment incentive. A full 30 percent of Marriott's managers started out as hourly employees.

There are also some potential problems associated with internal promotion. An employee-applicant who loses a position to another employee (or to an outside applicant) might turn his or her disappointment into negative actions, such as not performing up to standards or complaining on the job (which could affect the morale of others). In general, employers who use internal promotion effectively also have strong employee counseling programs.

External sources for employees can be informally tapped. Managers and supervisory staff often are able to locate new personnel through their social and professional contacts. In many cases this procedure involves recruiting from competitive operations. Companies find that being heavily involved in local community affairs makes them more approachable, and that a larger number of people apply for job openings than would otherwise.

Classified advertising and direct mail are examples of formal external recruiting methods. Classified advertising can be placed in local daily newspapers, in industry journals, and even on radio stations. Direct mail to schools, colleges, and seniors' groups is also a good way to reach job candidates. An advantage of advertising and direct mail is that they generally produce a large number of applicants—everyone looking for a job is likely to apply for what sounds like an attractive position. A disadvantage of the direct mail recruiting method is that many applicants are not qualified and must be screened out by the human resources department. This can be time-consuming and expensive.

Other formal external sources that are often used to recruit employees are state government employment offices and private employment agencies. People who are out of work and wish to receive unemployment compensation are usually required to register with state employment offices, so these offices usually have sizable lists of candidates. Many of these individuals may not be qualified for hospitality jobs, however, and must be screened carefully. There are some private employment agencies that charge a fee for placing an individual with a company; the fee is paid by either the employee or the employer. These agencies are mostly used to find supervisory and management personnel.

In some communities, atypical external sources can provide recruits. The city school systems in New York City and Miami, Florida, have their own "Academies of Tourism." These academies help high school students gain an awareness and understanding of the hospitality industry. All of the students work in an internship in their senior year; some continue into hospitality programs in college, and others go directly into the work force. In many communities, students in hospitality programs offered by junior colleges and four-year institutions are eager to gain work experience while in school.

The National Restaurant Association (NRA) has identified some population groups that can answer the needs of the restaurant industry and other hospitality organizations. These groups include minorities, disabled workers, senior citizens, and workers with limited skills. The NRA points out that some individuals within these groups might need help in improving their English-speaking skills. Special job trainers or equipment might be needed for handicapped workers, and new career ladders might be needed for older workers.

**Recruiting supervisors and managers.** Since most of you reading this text are supervisors or managers, or aspire to be in the future, in this chapter we concentrate on how supervisors and managers recruit, select, hire, and train workers for hourly staff positions. However, in this section we'd like to say a brief word about how you might be recruited for a supervisory or management position.

A good deal of recruiting is done by companies at colleges that teach hospitality management. A hotel or restaurant chain may offer graduates an opportunity to enter a management training program that, upon completion, qualifies them for a supervisory position in one of its properties. Or graduates may receive direct placement offers. With these, graduates are put directly into supervisory or management positions and are given on-the-job training. Often, direct placement recruiting is done by independent companies and clubs that do not offer full-scale management training programs.

Some hotels and food service companies employ the services of executive recruiters or "headhunters." Companies usually engage these recruitment firms to find people for senior management positions. Executive recruiters receive substantial fees for their services.

Another recruitment technique is popularly called "networking." With networking, individuals either contact or are contacted by friends, classmates, and former associates about a job opening. Most observers agree that most management positions are filled via networking rather than through advertising.

Of course, many graduates from hospitality programs—and supervisors and managers already employed in the industry—find their own positions by directly contacting the companies they would like to work for.

**Selecting the Best Applicants.** Selecting the right employees has long been considered one of the keys to operating a successful hospitality business. As mentioned earlier, personality must be considered as well as skills. Almost 100 years ago, Ellsworth Statler told his hotel managers to "hire only good-natured people." That is still a good idea today.

Selecting an employee to fill a position involves five steps:

- Receiving and processing applications
- Interviewing applicants
- Evaluating applicants
- Checking references
- Hiring the selected person

These steps should not be taken lightly. Top-notch companies go about hiring people for even the lowest-paid positions carefully. Selectivity is the watchword. At the Walt Disney Corporation no one is hired on the basis of one interview or on the recommendation of one interviewer; at least two are required.

**Receiving and processing applications.** Most hotels and restaurants use exactly the same application form whether they are hiring unskilled or skilled personnel. It is considered a good practice to have applicants fill out these forms on-site. This is to make sure that the applicant fills out the form him-or herself, because the completed application serves as an indication of the applicant's neatness and literacy.

Applications generally cover an applicant's name, address, telephone number, work experience, references, and education, as well as some other miscellaneous items. Some applications also contain a clause in which the applicant agrees, upon accepting the job, to submit to a drug-screening test at any future time should the employer request it. After someone is employed, whether he or she can be tested is a matter for negotiation. Most employers believe it is better to secure permission up front so they can administer the tests on an as-needed basis.

Human resources managers are often more interested in a person's intellect and attitude than in his or her specific skills. With today's sophisticated training techniques, almost any entry-level job can be learned in a matter of weeks, so the key factors that managers look for are a person's adaptability to a job, enthusiasm, and willingness to learn. That means a job application, at least in the hiring of entry-level employees, is a pre-screening tool more than anything else—it helps weed out people not suitable for a position, rather than identify the best candidates. Paul Breslin, resident manager of the 1,224-room Atlanta Hilton and Towers and former director of human resources for the Fontainbleau Hilton in Miami Beach, puts it this way: "We are no longer looking for people with five years' experience to be a front office clerk. They can learn the job with two weeks of training and two weeks of practical, hands-on experience. What we want are people who can adapt to a new environment and retain what they are taught."[2]

**Interviewing applicants.** Once an application is filled out and submitted, the applicant is often given a short screening interview by someone in the human resources office. In this interview, the interviewer reviews the facts on the application and notes the applicant's personal grooming and language skills. In small operations this interview can be extended to cover all aspects of the candidate's history, because the person doing the interviewing will also do the hiring. In large operations the human resources department only does the screening and first interviews; there is usually a second interview by the manager for whom the new employee will work.

Breslin has some advice about interviewing prospective employees: "Don't ask them any questions you don't need to know the answer to, such as 'Are you married?' or 'How many children do you have?'"[3] As far as handicapped individuals are concerned, Breslin says, "Focus on what the person can do rather than what they cannot do."[4]

Some areas should be avoided altogether, since questions relating to them may be interpreted as violations of the applicant's rights. Topics to avoid during an interview include an applicant's birthplace, age, race or color, religion or creed, height, weight, marital status, national origin, citizenship, membership in lodges and religious or ethnic clubs, and arrest record. The general rule of thumb is: Don't ask a question unless it has a direct bearing on whether the candidate can successfully perform the job in question. Since the standards for what constitutes discriminatory or otherwise unlawful questions vary from state to state and year to year, interviewers must keep abreast of current federal and state laws.[5]

**Evaluating applicants.** The goal when evaluating applicants is to fit the person to the job. Don't put someone in a position where there's a lot of guest contact if he or she is more suited to a back-of-the-house position. Room attendants in hotels must bend over to make a bed or scrub the bathroom floor or tub; obviously, someone with a bad back would not be suitable for this kind of work.

Pick the most interested candidate who enjoys the kind of work that must be done. Make sure that he or she has the necessary language, writing, and physical skills, and (of course) look carefully at cleanliness and personal grooming. Beyond these traits, having an enthusiastic and optimistic attitude and the ability to function as part of a team are paramount.

One interesting technique used in some quarters to help managers evaluate applicants is video-assisted testing. Hospitality authors Casey Jones and Thomas A. Decotiis advocate "work sampling" as a method of predicting the performance of employees in guest-contact positions before they are hired. Work sampling tests employees by presenting them with situations simulating the actual job. Working with a major hotel company, Jones and Decotiis developed a video-based work-sample test that could be administered easily to large numbers of applicants and scored quickly.[6] Forty guest-service simulations based on actual guest/employee incidents were filmed. After each simulation is presented, a prospective employee is asked to choose among four possible responses to the guest's behavior. Here is a typical simulation:

> The scene is the front desk, where a single front desk agent is on duty, checking out a guest. Several other guests are in line to check out. Suddenly, another guest rushes to the desk and says, "Hey, I'm going to miss my plane. I need to check out right now or I'm going to miss it." The frame freezes. The agent should: (A) ask the people in line if it's okay to check out the guest ahead of them; (B) say, "I'm sorry, sir, but I'll get to you as soon as I finish with Mr. Steinberg here," (C) say, "Yes sir, right away," or (D) look for a supervisor.
>
> Action B is the best. It acknowledges the guest's special need by serving him next, but allows the agent to continue serving the guest who is at the head of the line (and may also have a time problem). Action A would shift the problem to the other guests, and if one of them objected, an embarrassing situation would arise. Action C would be viewed as extremely inconsiderate to guests in line and the guest being served. Action D is a last resort; supervisors should be called for help only in very difficult situations.[7]

According to the researchers, a work-sample test such as this one has proved valid as a predictor of job performance. It also has proven to be especially useful to applicants for whom English is a second language, because they can both see and hear the test problem.

**Checking references.** Before offering someone a position, always check the person's references. Checking references is one of the most important steps in the hiring process, according to Breslin and other experts. "Calling references can really give you greater insight into the applicant's previous overall job performance," says Breslin. "In addition, applicants usually know when you have called and that sends the message to them that they are important to you and that you are hiring them for the long term."[8] Of course, a former employer of the applicant may only confirm that the applicant worked for the organization from date X to date Y and decline to say anything more. Even that much information is useful, since it will help you check the accuracy of the candidate's application or résumé.

Some companies have a third party such as a detective agency do a further check on candidates for certain positions. If the candidate is interviewing for a position that involves being responsible for large amounts of money, you may want to run a credit check. If the applicant is seeking a hotel position as a parking attendant or as a driver of a courtesy van, you may run a check on the applicant's driver's license. You must be careful, however. Such checks are unlawful unless they clearly relate to the job the candidate is applying for.

**Hiring the selected person.** The key points to keep in mind when hiring applicants is to make sure they clearly understand the position they are being offered; what they will be required to do; what their hours will be; whom they will report to; their vacation and other benefits; the dress code or uniform requirements (if applicable); how much pay they will be getting to start; and when and under what circumstances they can expect a pay increase. If managers do not make these matters absolutely clear to applicants, misunderstandings can occur that could permanently spoil manager/employee relationships before they even get off the ground.

**Implementing Continual Training Programs.** Training is one of the most crucial parts of a human resources program, but it is more often talked about than practiced. When an operation gets busy, training is often overlooked or temporarily suspended because of a lack of time or a lack of trainers.

Training is enormously demanding. It should be an ongoing process for all current employees; for new employees the training process or program has to be started all over again at square one. Training is also expensive, for employees who are learning are not fully productive. For these reasons, there is a great temptation to take shortcuts in training procedures. Managers often rationalize their negligence by telling themselves that current employees don't need to be trained, or on-the-job training is good enough for new hires. Yet without training at all levels within the organization, there can be no consistency of product and service. Training is the process that teaches trainees the knowledge and skills to operate within the standards set by management. Training also attempts to develop within employees a positive attitude toward guest service.

Poor training contributes to high turnover and substandard job performance. Employees should feel comfortable in their jobs and be able to do them well so that they do not become discouraged and quit. To train their employees well, many companies use such modern technology as the video-assisted testing described earlier for new job applicants. At Domino's, McDonald's, and Wendy's, front-line training is accomplished through videotapes sent to individual stores and played on an on-site VCR. These videos introduce new items and emphasize product consistency and control standards. Sonesta International Hotels uses a board game that all of its employees play to sensitize themselves to guest needs. You advance

**THE ORIENTAL**
BANGKOK

Dear Guest:

I would like to inform you that we have formulated and put into operation the first fully professional training programme for hotel staff in Thailand. Called "The Oriental Hotel's Apprenticeship Programme"—OHAP for short—its hundred students may be observed putting theories into practice in various departments of the hotel. You may come across one or more of these young people during your stay with us and if they should fall short in any way of the standards of service you have come to expect from The Oriental, we ask your kind and good-natured forbearance.

This programme has been devised in response to a pressing need for well-trained hotel personnel in Thailand. It is part of our continuing effort to do the best we can for the future service offered to visitors by our hotel and by Thai tourist industry as a whole.

Thank you for your attention.

Yours sincerely,

Kurt Wachtveitl
General Manager

This letter, placed in each guestroom of the Oriental hotel in Bangkok, informs guests of a training program taking place at the hotel and asks for their patience should any student/trainee fall short of the hotel's service standards. (Courtesy of The Oriental, Bangkok, Thailand)

on the board by giving the right answers to guests and lose spaces by giving the wrong answers.

According to Lewis C. Forrest, Jr., author of *Training for the Hospitality Industry*, the basic steps in the training process are:

1. Establish a training policy
2. Define training needs
3. Plan the training

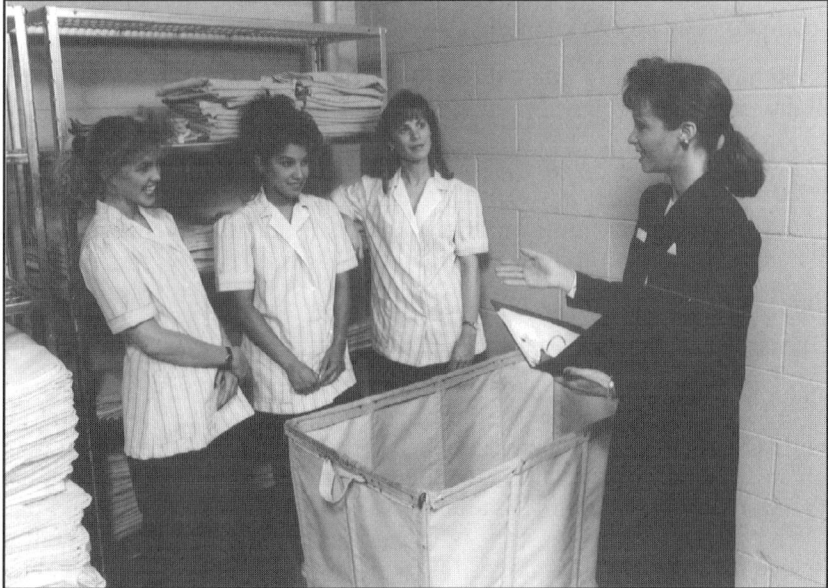

**Training helps give employees confidence.**

4. Prepare the employees
5. Conduct the training
6. Evaluate the training
7. Follow through with ongoing coaching[9]

Training should be continuous and ongoing. A company with an active training program expresses a commitment to its employees. A training program should define who will be trained (ideally, all categories and levels of employees), who will be responsible for training (corporate staff, on-site managers, supervisory personnel), and the training aids and techniques that should be used (see Exhibits 5 and 6).

Regular, ongoing training on basic job tasks is necessary at all levels of an organization. Unless continuing positive reinforcement is provided, employees tend to forget some of what they learned. In addition to ongoing training in employees' regular duties, it is often necessary to hold extra training sessions on topics such as sanitation, fire safety, CPR, and terrorist threats.

One hotel that takes training seriously is Washington D.C.'s 128-year-old Sheraton Carlton, located two blocks from the White House. This historic landmark reopened in 1988 after a $16 million renovation. According to *Lodging* magazine, the hotel spent $500,000 on training before the first guest arrived.[10]

In developing its training program, Sheraton Carlton's management focused on a single theme that could guide managers and line employees: "Bring the guest back." Once the theme was established, management relied on Sheraton's Guest Satisfaction System (SGSS) for implementation. Whatever job employees were assigned to do, they would be trained to do it with four points in mind:

- Every time they saw a guest they would smile and offer an appropriate hospitality comment.

- They would speak to guests in a friendly, enthusiastic, and courteous tone and manner.

- They would answer guest questions and requests quickly and efficiently, or take personal responsibility for getting the answers.

- They would anticipate guests' needs and solve any problems that arise.[11]

After establishing the theme, management drew up job lists for 58 positions with accompanying procedures for meeting SGSS standards. The front desk agent had 137 tasks, for example, while the busperson's list contained 25 tasks. First, all employees had to be trained to accomplish each of their job tasks. The hotel's managers were given a three-day seminar in effective training techniques. Two weeks before the hotel opened, all 200 employees attended a special orientation where SGSS standards were taught through guest speakers, skits, role-plays, and videos. Skill-training sessions for individual employees and groups of employees were established. Employees learned how to perform a task, and were then observed performing the task by the manager/trainer and other employees. In guest-contact situations, other employees played the guest roles. Some sessions were videotaped; the videotapes were then critiqued by the employees involved as well as their trainers. After the training sessions were completed, each employee received a certificate of completion signed by the manager/trainer and the employee, certifying that the employee had the knowledge to perform effectively in his or her position.

While most training focuses on knowledge and skills, there are other issues that directly affect employees' job satisfaction and attitudes that are equally important.

**Exhibit 5  Sample Training Aid**

## TRAINING ACTIVITY OUTLINE

**TASK:** ADMINISTER GUEST MAIL

**OBJECTIVE:** Upon completion of this training activity the learner will be able to record, send up or store guest's mail according to the procedure in effect at the Front Office.

**STANDARD:** Proper handling of guest's mail requires receiving all mail which arrives prior to their stay at the time of registration, notifies in-house guests of mail on the day it arrives, delivering telexes within thirty minutes of arrival, and stamping all messages with the time received.

**RESOURCES:** Computer system (if available), mail log, handouts, mail slots.

| METHOD OF TRAINING | TRAINING STEPS | TIME |
|---|---|---|
| LECTURE | Trainer notes when mail arrives, when mail is collected, and the process to follow when mail, telexes or other messages for a guest are received by the hotel. | 10 min. |
| DEMONSTRATION | Trainer takes learner through a step-by-step series of instructions to show how to time-stamp messages, record mail received and notify a guest mail is being held. | 15 min. |
| REVIEW | One-on-one discussion of the job skill learned to determine the degree of comprehension. | 5 min. |
| TEST | Trainer administers the test provided on the following page. | 10 min. |
| | | 40 min. |

---

## TRAINING ACTIVITY LIST

EMPLOYEE _____ DATE _____

**TASK:** ADMINISTER GUEST MAIL

**INSTRUCTIONS:** Respond to the following questions in writing:

1. Why is it important to time-stamp all guest messages?

2. Telexes received are forwarded to a guest: (Circle the best answer.)
   A. within 30 minutes
   B. on the same day received
   C. within one hour
   D. other

3. Fill in the blanks:
   A. Mail arrives at the hotel at _____ a.m. and at _____ p.m.
   B. Mail departs the hotel at _____ a.m. and at _____ p.m.
   C. Stamps can be purchased at _____.

4. Under what circumstances would guest mail be delivered to a guest room:

5. What should you do with guest mail addressed to a guest who will not arrive at the hotel for five days?

6. How does a guest know mail is being held at the Front Office?

7. What should you do if a letter arrives at the hotel for a guest who has already checked out?

---

These pages are from a training manual developed by the Sheraton hotel chain. A series of training activity outlines within the manual show the manager/trainer what should be covered when training an employee to perform a particular task, and the approximate time training should take. Once the training is completed, the trainee takes a test to see how well he or she has learned. (Courtesy of the Sheraton Hotel Corporation)

### Exhibit 6  Sample Training Aid

| | | | NEW EMPLOYEE<br>TRAINING PROFILE | | | EMPLOYEE<br>GUEST SERVICE AGENT -2-<br>POSITION | | |
|---|---|---|---|---|---|---|---|---|

| PRIMARY TASK | PERFORMANCE STANDARD | TRAINING METHOD | HOURS PROFILE | HOURS ACTUAL | EMPLOYEE'S SIGN-OFF / TRAINER'S SIGN-OFF | DATE / DATE |
|---|---|---|---|---|---|---|
| 3. Register Guest (cont.) | e) Hands pen to guest with point facing employee.<br>f) Verifies payment, obtains signature and confirms registration. (Travel Vouchers are verified in the Sheraton Travel Voucher Manual). | | | | | |
| | g) Uses upselling techniques to obtain higher revenue.<br>h) Accepts cash for payment after obtaining identification from guest. "No Posts" the account to ensure no outstanding balance.<br>i) Ensures registration card is time stamped and dated. | | | | | |
| | j) Listens attentively to guest.<br>k) Becomes familiar with names of V.I.P., complimentary, and pre-registered guests at the start of each shift by reviewing report provided by Front Office Management. | | | | | |
| | l) Assists in pre-keying and pre-registering guest rooms.<br>m) Treats each guest as an individual. | | | | | |
| 4. Room the Guest | a) Guest Service Agent selects a room within the specified room category. | Introduce task, provide handout | 60 min. | | | |

Here is an example of how job breakdowns can be used in training. The job task is listed in the extreme left column; the second column lists the performance standards of the hotel. Column three shows the manager/trainer which training method should be used. Column four shows (1) the suggested or target time for training ("Profile"), and (2) the actual training time. Then there is space for the manager/trainer and the employee to sign off, indicating that the employee's performance meets the property's standards. (Courtesy of Sheraton Hotel Corporation)

Many of these issues fall under the broad heading of diversity. **Diversity training** programs seek to make all workers feel comfortable in the work atmosphere—no matter what their race, culture, sex, or age. Diversity programs are not the same as affirmative-action programs. Affirmative-action programs were created as a result of government mandates to eliminate discrimination based on gender and race. By their very nature, they have accelerated more diversity among workers. The problem of course is how to handle this diversity. Some believe that the answer lies in teaching people to "celebrate their differences." Experience has shown, however, that this approach is not always effective.

Gene Monteagudo, director of diversity of Hyatt Hotels and Resorts, likes to quote George Washington Carver: "How far you go in life depends on your being tender with the young, compassionate with the aged, sympathetic with the striving, and tolerant of both the weak and the strong, because someday in life you will have been one or all of these." Monteagudo believes, "A better approach than celebrating differences is to celebrate similarities. The best cultural diversity programs help people see that humans are much more alike than different. All have basic needs for dignity, survival, and social contact. Helping participants see that they share common goals encourages them to set aside the barriers that prevent them from working together to achieve that goal."[12]

**Motivating Employees.** Finding a way to motivate workers is perhaps a manager's most difficult challenge. The importance of having employees who are motivated is clear. The present shortage of workers demands that individual workers increase their productivity. How can managers increase productivity? According to a National Science Foundation report that reviewed three hundred studies of productivity, pay, and job satisfaction,

> increased productivity depends on two propositions. First comes motivation: arousing and maintaining the will to work effectively—having workers who are productive not because they are coerced, but because they are committed. Second is reward. Of all the factors that help to create highly motivated and highly satisfied workers, the principal one...appears to be that effective performance be recognized and rewarded in whatever terms are meaningful to the individual—financial, psychological, or both.[13]

The message is clear. Motivation is a matter of commitment. A manager can only motivate employees to do their best at what the manager wants them to do if it is something the employees want to do as well. Bill McClean, former CEO of a major bank, puts it this way: "You need not read further concerning motivation unless you genuinely understand that to get employees to perform minimum duties, one only needs to drive them. To gain their top performance, one must inspire them to drive themselves."[14]

**Techniques.** There are four techniques managers can use to create a self-motivational environment for employees.

*Remove the fear of failure.* Hospitality enterprises are busy and occasionally stressful places. For workers to function well, they must be well-trained and secure in the fact that they are valued and that they can count on keeping their jobs. Delta Airlines is known for doing all it can to avoid laying anyone off for economic reasons. Employees who are respected and aware of their importance to the company are not afraid of taking risks to do their best. Many hospitality companies don't even refer to their workers as "employees." At McDonald's they are crew members; at the Walt Disney Corporation they are cast members. These terms are intended to give workers a sense of importance.

*Pay a fair wage.* Employees who are worrying about how they're going to pay next month's rent or a big car-repair bill aren't usually in the mood to take care of other people's problems—they're too worried about their own. In a best-selling

Here a room attendant/butler is learning through role playing to understand the responsibilities of a floor supervisor. (Courtesy of New World Hotels International Limited)

book on management called *Leadership Secrets of Attila the Hun,* the author attributed this management advice to Attila: "Grant your Huns the benefit of your interest in the welfare of their families and the condition of their stores; share your riches with those who are loyal and stand in need. They will be certain to willingly follow you into the mouth of Hell, should the occasion arise."[15] Many excellent companies view themselves as an extended family. Thomas Peters and Robert Waterman, Jr., the authors of *In Search of Excellence,* reported that "we found prevalent use of the specific terms 'family,' 'extended family,' or 'family feeling' at [such successful companies as] Disney, McDonald's, [and] Delta."[16]

Offer incentives and rewards for performance. People like to be rewarded. It makes them feel good. The more rewards and awards a company gives, the more motivated its employees are likely to be. Incentives do not have to be monetary to be important. Peters and Waterman put it this way:

> We were struck by the wealth of non-monetary incentives used by excellent companies. Nothing is more powerful than positive reinforcement. Everybody uses it. But top performers, almost alone, use it extensively. The volume of contrived opportunities for showering pins, buttons, badges, and medals on people is staggering at McDonald's, Tupperware, IBM, and many other top performers. They actively seek out and pursue endless excuses to give out rewards.[17]

**It pays to have fun!**

# JOIN THE FAMILY.

**APPLICATION ON INSIDE.**
Always, An Equal Opportunity/Affirmative Action Employer.

This tabletop tent card asks job seekers to join the McDonald's "family." (Courtesy of McDonald's Corporation, Oak Brook, Illinois)

At Delta Airlines the employee magazine, *Delta Digest*, always includes a section called "Above and Beyond" that reports awards given to employees for exceptional service to passengers. Recognition and celebration are another way of letting employees know they are important to the company, which helps make the company important to them.

*Operate with an open-door policy; keep everyone informed about everything.* Companies with highly motivated employees have few secrets. Communication is a two-way street in these companies. Everyone at the bottom knows what everyone at the top is thinking about important issues, and vice versa. When Ed Carlson was president of United Airlines, he said: "Nothing is worse for morale than a lack of information down in the ranks. I call it NETMA—Nobody Ever Tells Me Anything—and I have tried to minimize that problem."[18] United has always been known as a company that communicates with all of its employees all of the time. It publishes a daily *Employee Newsline* and a monthly employee newspaper. It also issues *Supervisors Hotline* every other week. At Walt Disney World, employees receive weekly newsletters called *The EYES & EARS* and *Resort Report,* which focus

Rewards can help motivate employees and managers alike.

on cast (employee) recognition and resort information. Walt Disney World managers also get *Five Star Team*, a monthly newsletter that discusses current management issues and management development. Finally, Disney has designed a series of property-specific employee handbooks.

Besides using newsletters and newspapers, effective managers communicate with their employees via regular meetings, bulletins, and even paycheck stuffers. Operating results are posted where everyone can see them. A variety of techniques are used to make sure management at the top knows what workers on the front line think. Bill Marriott, Jr., still spends nearly half of his time in the field, first listening and then talking to employees (the sequence is important). In addition to other forms of communication, the Marriott company conducts annual attitude surveys of all employees. One Marriott executive calls it "our early warning system."[19]

To keep the lines of communication open, top executives at Shoney's (frequently cited as one of the best limited-menu chains in the industry) regularly visit Shoney's restaurants. Operations managers are expected to spend as much as four days a week in the field. And they do more than listen and talk: Chairman Ray Danner has been known to clean out a dirty washroom himself—then clean the collective clocks of the restaurant crew that let it get that way.[20]

Many companies practice the open-door policy—literally. At Delta Airlines the doors of the executive offices have always been open to any Delta employee. Pilots, mechanics, flight attendants—anyone can walk in and say what's on his or her mind or ask for help.

To ensure communication continues right to the end, excellent companies almost invariably hold exit interviews with departing employees. Hospitality companies generally regard such interviews as a necessary evil to help prevent possible lawsuits from disgruntled former employees. According to professors Robert H. Woods and James F. Macaulay, writing in the *Cornell Quarterly*, "this is neither the intended use of exit interviews nor their most common use outside of the hospitality industry. Most companies use exit interviews to collect information on why employees leave. Correctly used, these interviews point to problems that cause turnover."[21]

**Evaluating the Program.** Although we are discussing evaluation last, it should be clear by this time that evaluation occurs in almost every part of a human resources program, from selection and hiring to training and motivating. Companies that do a good job in retaining, developing, and motivating employees recognize that where there are problems, they are often the result of a flawed system instead of a flawed person. For example, when a room service breakfast order is delayed too long, you can't blame the server if the only service elevator is tied up by the housekeeping department eager to get the rooms cleaned. However, the fact remains that most employees like to know how they are doing and be rewarded when they achieve extraordinary results. "Ritz-Carlton values are reinforced continuously by daily 'lineups,' frequent recognition for extraordinary achievement, and a performance appraisal based on expectations explained during the orientation, training, and certification processes," according to the *Cornell Quarterly*.[22]

**Performance reviews** are typically held every three, six, or twelve months. New employees are usually reviewed more frequently than experienced employees. The purpose of performance reviews is not to confront employees with their shortcomings. The performance review is a natural step that follows selection, training, and motivating. It lets employees know how well they have learned to do what the company expects of them, and it lets managers know how well they are doing in hiring the right people and training them. Performance reviews are also coaching tools that managers can use to improve employee performance.

Good performance reviews are specific and objective. Some managers fill out a review form before meeting with an employee, on which they can rate the employee's knowledge, skills, and personal attributes—often on some kind of numerical basis. During the review the manager shares these ratings with the employee and gives him or her a chance to comment on them. Some companies have the employee fill out the same form before the review meeting so that the manager and the employee can compare ratings. The manager can recommend follow-up training, coaching, and counseling if this seems called for. Some companies have the manager and the employee draw up a joint goal-setting agreement in which the two agree as to (1) what will be done on both sides to improve the employee's performance in his or her current job, and (2) what the manager and employee will do to prepare the employee for a more rewarding position.

## Chapter Summary

The hospitality industry is facing a labor crisis. There are fewer applicants for jobs, jobs are staying vacant longer, turnover is increasing, and there is a lack of qualified applicants. This crisis is largely a result of changing demographics, although some businesses make the situation worse by using inadequate hiring procedures, offering employees few opportunities to advance, and improperly training and supervising employees.

Other issues that have an impact on the hospitality industry include unions and legislation such as the Fair Labor Standards Act, the Civil Rights Act, and the Americans with Disabilities Act.

As part of their strategy to deal with the shortage of employees, many hospitality companies have developed human resources programs. A human resources program typically involves a corporate philosophy embodying the worth of the employees. It also includes job analyses, productivity standards, and employee recruitment, selection, training, motivation, and evaluation programs.

Jobs should be analyzed to establish the best way to perform them. Once jobs are understood, job lists, job breakdowns, and job descriptions can be prepared. These are helpful in training and recruiting employees.

Productivity can be expressed in dollars or in units produced or served. But productivity standards cannot be based on numbers alone—they must take into account quality goals and guest expectations as well.

Effective recruiting demands an understanding of the local labor market. The goal of recruiting is to find the best workers available for the wages the business can pay. Recruiters can use internal sources (current employees and people recommended by employees) and external sources (those recruited through advertising, community involvement, and employment agencies). Groups that can help answer the hospitality industry's labor needs include minorities, disabled workers, senior citizens, and workers with limited skills. There are many job programs in place to help hospitality businesses find and train potential employees in these groups.

Selecting an employee to fill a vacancy involves five steps: receiving and processing applications, interviewing applicants, evaluating applicants, checking references, and hiring the selected person.

Training is one of the most crucial parts of a human resources program. Unfortunately, training is often neglected. Basic steps in the training process are: establishing a training policy, defining training needs, planning the training, conducting the training, and evaluating the training. Today many companies supplement traditional training methods with interactive videotapes and games.

A manager who wants motivated workers must gain their commitment to the company and its goals. There are four techniques managers can use to accomplish this: (1) remove the fear of failure, (2) pay a fair wage, (3) offer incentives and awards for performance, and (4) operate with an open-door policy—keep everyone informed.

Evaluation is the final step in a human resources program. Employees need to know how they are doing. Regularly scheduled performance reviews help accomplish this. Companies that do a good job of retaining, developing, and motivating employees recognize that where there are problems, they are often the result of a flawed system instead of a flawed person.

## Endnotes

1. From a letter by Edward H. Rensi, president, McDonald's U.S.A., printed as an introduction to "Ingredients for Success: Food for Thought on Finding Your First Job," produced in conjunction with the American School Counselor Association. Copyright 1993, McDonald's Corporation.

2. From a personal interview with Paul Breslin, resident manager, Atlanta Hilton and Towers, Atlanta, Georgia, 30 July 1997.

3. Breslin interview.

4. Breslin interview.

5. Adapted from David Wheelhouse, *Managing Human Resources in the Hospitality Industry* (East Lansing, Mich.: Educational Institute of AH&MA, 1989), pp. 89, 93.

6. Casey Jones and Thomas A. Decotiis, "A Better Way to Select Service Employees: Video Assisted Testing," *Cornell H.R.A. Quarterly*, August 1986.

7. Jones and Decotiis.

8. Breslin interview.

9. Lewis C. Forrest, Jr., *Training for the Hospitality Industry*, 2d ed. (East Lansing, Mich.: Educational Institute of AH&MA, 1990), p. 5.

10. Kathleen Keenan, "A Cool Half Million for Training Creates Warm Luxury," *Lodging*, December 1989, p. 25.

11. Keenan, p. 25.

12. Richard Bruns, "Diversity: From Top Management to the Front Line," *Lodging*, November 1994, p. 73.

13. Ron Zempke and Dick Schaff, *The Service Edge* (New York: New American Library, 1989), p. 72.

14. J. W. McClean, *So You Want to Be the Boss* (Englewood Cliffs, N.J.: Prentice-Hall, 1990), p. 44.

15. Weiss Roberts, *Leadership Secrets of Attila the Hun* (New York: Warner Books, 1990), p. 79.

16. Thomas H. Peters and Robert J. Waterman, Jr., *In Search of Excellence* (New York: Harper & Row, 1982), p. 261.

17. Peters and Waterman, p. 269.

18. Peters and Waterman, p. 267.

19. James L. Heskett, *Managing in the Service Economy* (Boston: Harvard Business School Press, 1986), p. 127.

20. Zempke and Schaff, pp. 286–287.

21. Robert H. Woods and James F. Macaulay, "R for Turnover: Retention Programs That Work," *Cornell Quarterly*, May 1989, p. 84.

22. Charles G. Partlow, "How Ritz-Carlton Uses 'TQM,'" *Cornell H.R.A. Quarterly*, August 1993, p. 19.

## Key Terms

**covers**—The actual number of meals served at a food function or during a meal period.

**diversity training**—Training that seeks to make all workers feel comfortable in the work atmosphere—no matter what their race, culture, sex, or age.

**full-time-equivalent employee (FTE)**—A measure used for statistical purposes in which two or more part-time employees whose hours add up to 40 hours a week (the number of hours one full-time employee would work) equal one full-time-equivalent (FTE) employee. For example, four part-time employees who each work ten hours a week would, for statistical purposes, be recorded as one FTE employee.

**job breakdown**—The specific, step-by-step procedures for accomplishing each task of a particular job.

**job description**—A recruiting and training tool that outlines for a particular job (1) the title that goes with the job, (2) the person to whom the employee reports, (3) the work to be performed (in general terms), and (4) the education or skills the employee must possess.

**job list**—A list of the tasks that must be performed by the individual holding a particular job.

**performance review**—A meeting between a manager and an employee, to (1) let the employee know how well he or she has learned to meet company standards, and (2) let the manager know how well he or she is doing in hiring and training employees. Typically held every 3, 6, or 12 months, depending on the employee's performance and experience.

**productivity standards**—Measurements that tell managers how long it should take an employee to complete tasks using the best methods management has devised, and how many tasks an employee can perform in a given time period. This measurement differs according to the task the employee is performing.

## Review Questions

1. What factors contribute to the labor crisis?
2. What five demographic trends will have a significant impact on U.S. businesses within the next decade?
3. What are some common reasons for the hospitality industry's high turnover rates?
4. What are the differences between job lists, job breakdowns, and job descriptions?
5. What are some internal and external sources of employees?
6. What steps are involved in filling a vacant position?
7. What should an interviewer keep in mind when interviewing job candidates?
8. Why is training important?
9. What are some techniques for motivating employees?
10. Performance reviews serve what purpose?

## Internet Sites

For more information, visit the following Internet sites. Remember that Internet addresses can change without notice. If the site is no longer there, use a browser to look for additional sites.

*Associations*

Educational Institute of the
American Hotel & Motel Association
www.ei-ahma.org

National Restaurant Association
www.restaurant.org

## Organizations, Resources

Americans with Disabilities Act
Document Center
janweb.icdi.wvu.edu/kinder/

HR On-Line
www.hronline.com

Human Resources Law Index
www.hrlawindex.com

Occupational Safety and Health
Administration (OSHA)
www.osha.gov

Society for Human Resource
Management
www.shrm.org

U.S. Department of Labor
www.dol.gov

*Workforce* Online
www.workforceonline.com

## Publications

*HRMagazine*
www.shrm.org/docs/
HRmagazine.html

*Workforce*
www.workforceonline.com/workforce

## REVIEW QUIZ

When you feel you have covered all of the material in this chapter, answer these questions. Choose the *best* answer.

1. Which of the following is a major reason for the U.S. hospitality industry's high turnover rates?

    a. increase in women workers
    b. limited opportunities for advancement
    c. labor legislation
    d. middle-aging of the U.S. population

2. Which of the following laws addresses the employment of minors?

    a. Civil Rights Act of 1964
    b. Occupational Safety and Health Act
    c. Family and Medical Leave Act of 1993
    d. Fair Labor Standards Act

3. Which of the following statements about employee training is *false*?

    a. It is not necessary to constantly train and retrain employees on basic job tasks.
    b. Training is expensive.
    c. Training can be used to help employees develop positive attitudes about guest service.
    d. Managers must define their company's employee-training needs.

4. Specific, step-by-step procedures for accomplishing a task are given in job:

    a. lists.
    b. specifications.
    c. breakdowns.
    d. descriptions.

5. Most management positions are filled through the use of:

    a. advertising.
    b. college recruitment programs.
    c. executive recruiters.
    d. networking.

6. It is possible to measure productivity in units produced or served by dividing:

    a. payroll costs by covers.
    b. covers by FTE employees.
    c. payroll costs by sales.
    d. sales by FTE employees.

## REVIEW QUIZ (continued)

7. The more employee awards a company gives, the:
   a. more competition there is among employees.
   b. less effective they are as motivators.
   c. more motivated its employees are likely to be.
   d. less attention the employees pay to them.

**Answer Key:** 1-b-C1, 2-d-C1, 3-a-C2, 4-c-C2, 5-d-C2, 6-b-C2, 7-c-C2

Each question is linked to a competency. Competencies are listed on the first page of the chapter. An answer reading 3-b-C4 translates to:

3: the question number
b: the correct answer
C4: the competency number

## Chapter 14 Outline

The Marketing Concept
    The Four Ps of Marketing
Developing a Marketing Plan
    Situation Analysis
    Objectives
    Strategies
    Tactics
    Controls
Sales Management and Personal Selling
    How to Be a Successful Salesperson
    Basic Qualities of a Salesperson
Making the Sales Call
    Prospecting and Qualifying
    Preparation
    Presentation
    Overcoming Objections
    Asking for the Sale
    Follow-Up
Selling Through Travel Agencies
    Types of Travel Agencies
    What Travel Agencies Do
    How Travel Agents Are Trained
    How Travel Agents Are Paid
Chapter Summary

## Competencies

1. Distinguish marketing from selling, identify and explain the Four Ps of Marketing, and describe how a marketing plan is developed.

2. Describe how hotels organize their sales departments, summarize the characteristics and qualities salespersons should possess, describe four customer personality types (and give examples of sales strategies salespersons can use for each of them), and summarize the steps of a sales call.

3. Explain how travel agencies began, describe types of travel agencies, explain what travel agencies do, and describe how travel agents are trained and paid.

# 14

# Marketing and Selling Hospitality

THIS CHAPTER DISCUSSES the marketing concept, marketing plans, and personal selling. It concludes with a section on selling through travel agencies.

## The Marketing Concept

The purpose of a business is to get and keep customers, for without customers there is no business.

Professor Theodore Levitt points out that:

> customers are constantly presented with lots of options to help them solve their problems. They don't buy things, they buy solutions to problems....No business can function effectively without a clear view of how to get customers, what its prospective customers want and need, what options its competitors give them, and without explicit strategies and programs focused on what goes on in the market place.[1]

That is what marketing is: the effort to determine and meet the needs and wants of current and potential customers.

There is an important distinction between selling and marketing that many students fail to recognize. This is due to confusing terminology that is commonly used in business. Often, people whose jobs are in sales are called "marketing representatives." The title suggests that the words "sales" and "marketing" are interchangeable; they are not. **Marketing** is a much broader term that includes sales and a great deal more. The difference between the two has often been stated this way: selling is getting rid of what you have; marketing is having what people want.

Some marketers look at it this way: marketing is the art of *buying from* customers, which is exactly the opposite of *selling to* customers. In other words, customers have money in their pockets that you, the salesperson, want to "buy." How can you buy the customer's money? By paying for it with a product or service. This marketing approach to selling can help you sell in two ways. First, your focus is on the customers rather than on your products. Instead of focusing on the attributes of your products, you focus on persuading customers to "sell" you their money—which usually leads you to study your customers and their needs and wants. Second, you have a different attitude toward customers—you value them more and approach them more carefully because you realize you are trying to convince them to give up something of value.

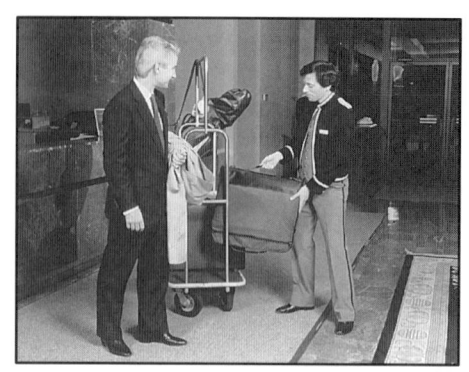

Not all hospitality products are tangible. A hospitality product can be a service or a property's business concept. (Photo on right courtesy of La Quinta Motor Inns, Inc.)

## The Four Ps of Marketing

The list of activities that can be included in the efforts to get and keep customers is quite extensive. For a restaurant, the things that influence whether customers eat there include the location, decor, menu, quality and presentation of food, type of service, and prices. All of these are marketing decisions first and foremost. To make these decisions, a restaurant's managers must determine (1) what their current and potential customers need or want, (2) how to provide it, and (3) how to persuade current and potential customers to patronize the restaurant. These activities break down into four basic responsibilities that are popularly called the "**Four Ps of marketing**": product, place, price, and promotion.

How businesses allocate their resources among product, place, price, and promotional efforts varies widely, depending on the objectives of each business. In a sense, the Four Ps are like the ingredients in a recipe for success, and the relative proportion of resources allocated to each effort and the way these four marketing efforts are combined is often referred to as the **marketing mix.**

**Product: What Do You Sell?** The term "product" as used in the hospitality field can have several meanings. Obviously, a product can be a meal or some other tangible item that a hotel or restaurant provides to guests. A hospitality product can also be an intangible service, such as a food server serving a meal. Product can also refer to a hotel or restaurant's concept—as in, "A La Quinta motel is an economy product designed specifically to appeal to 'road warriors' (traveling business-persons)." In this case, product refers to all the things that make the experience of staying at a La Quinta what it is—its philosophy, facilities, amenities, level of service, and the tangible products it sells to guests.

For many small hospitality business owners, determining the concept for a hotel or restaurant was not considered a marketing decision. For example, many ethnic restaurants in the United States got their start because immigrant families from such countries as Italy, Greece, and France decided to open eating establishments offering the kind of food they knew how to prepare. Since these families generally opened their restaurants in neighborhoods where other people of the same origin lived, their restaurants enjoyed a built-in market. It was not necessary for the owners to be marketing-oriented—they simply sold what they knew how to make, and as long as they did it well there were plenty of customers.

This approach no longer works, because those built-in markets have, for the most part, disappeared. While it is still true that people who have the same tastes and lifestyles are likely to live in the same neighborhood, consumers today have so many different choices that simply opening a business in a location, no matter how good that location, cannot ensure success. This is especially true in the hospitality field, where there are no revolutionary new developments that are likely to convince customers to give up their old buying habits and form new loyalties. People have been eating and sleeping the same way for thousands of years. While the surroundings have gotten nicer, the basic services offered by dining and lodging establishments have not changed. And yet, surprisingly enough, many hotels and restaurants still market themselves as if they were offering something truly unique in a marketplace without competitors. They first decide what they are going to sell and then wrestle with the problem of how to sell it.

A hotel or restaurant's concept—the type of establishment it is or will be—should be first and foremost a marketing decision that is based on providing a better solution to a customer's problem—which might be anything from finding a place for a quick bite to eat, to searching for a site to hold a wedding reception for 300 people. To come up with a successful concept for a hospitality business requires a clear understanding of what people are looking for and what competitors already offer them. Only a business that understands what problems consumers are hoping to solve—and can offer better solutions—has a hope of succeeding.

This reinforces what Professor Levitt of the Harvard Business School says about people never buying a product, but rather the utility they expect to receive from it. In a speech for the American Association of Advertising Agencies at the Greenbriar in White Sulphur Springs, West Virginia, Levitt put it this way: "When you go into a hardware store you do not buy a quarter-inch drill, you buy the expectation of a quarter-inch hole."

It all comes down to what we pointed out earlier in this section—hospitality businesses do not simply sell rooms, meals, spas, airplane seats, or even rental cars. What they sell is a service that uses those physical objects the same way a play in the theater uses a stage, sets, costumes, and props to put on a performance. Indeed, there are many similarities between service delivery and the theater, and it is useful to think about these similarities when looking at hospitality marketing from a customer's point of view.

First of all, there is the matter of the **front of the house** and the **back of the house**, terms used in the hotel business to describe the areas that the guests see (the front desk, for example, is in the front of the house) and the areas that the guests do not see (the kitchen and other behind-the-scenes areas). Theaters also have a front of the house (the seats for the audience and the stage on which the performance takes place) and a back of the house (dressing rooms, lighting booths, and so on). The front of the house in both hotels and theaters is designed to create an impression. Like actors in a play, hotel employees are given roles to play—front desk agent, dining room manager, housekeeper. The audience comes to a play to be entertained or distracted from their normal concerns in the same way people check into hotels or go to restaurants to get away from their familiar surroundings. There are many more comparisons that can be made, but for our purposes it is enough to remember that, as Hamlet pointed out in Shakespeare's tragedy, "the play's the thing." When people enter a hotel or restaurant, they expect to be transported to a place where everything looks beautiful and clean, and smiling people are friendly and want to help them and take care of them. They want a performance, and that is what managers must be prepared to offer them.

**Place: Where Do You Sell It?** "Place" also has several meanings in hospitality marketing. To begin with, it clearly refers to the physical location of the business, which, as we have seen previously, can be crucial to its success.

Place can also have a profound effect on marketing methods. For instance, the fact that a large number of Holiday Inns are located all over America means that people are reminded of the Holiday Inn name wherever they go, so when they are in a strange town the Holiday Inn there is a familiar place. Moreover, because Holiday Inn is everywhere, its corporate management can advertise on national television or in national magazines, which would be too costly and inefficient for many of its competitors.

Place has another meaning as well, which is the physical location not of the hotel but of the site where the reservation for the hotel is made. This can be via telephone at a central reservation system office, at a travel agency, or even on a home computer. Obviously, the more places from which it is possible to buy a hotel room, the easier it will be to fill up that hotel.

**Price: What Do You Sell It For?** Too often, hotels and restaurants set their prices on a cost-plus basis. It is assumed that food costs, for example, should be 30 percent of the menu item's total cost to a guest. But this orientation ignores how guests feel about what they are getting and what they are willing to pay for it. The basic flaw with **cost-plus pricing** is that guests don't care what your costs are. Moreover, it doesn't take into account a notion that almost all retailers understand: that some items are **loss-leaders**—items that are not profitable in themselves but which attract customers to stores where they may buy other items that are profitable. Typically, bars and lounges that offer a free or nominally priced buffet during happy hour are purposely sacrificing the low profit margin on their food in order to gain higher profits from beverage sales.

Cost-plus or product-driven pricing is used by many businesses to set prices, but ultimately consumers decide whether they will pay for what is being offered, and if they won't pay the price set by management, the price must be adjusted or the product or service must be dropped. Therefore, **consumer-based pricing** is a much more realistic method of setting prices. With consumer-based pricing, companies first determine what customers want, what they are willing to pay for it, and then figure out a way to deliver that product and service at the desirable price.

There are many other methods of pricing besides cost-plus and consumer-based pricing. One is **competitive pricing**. With competitive pricing, hotels base room rates on what competitors charge. This strategy can work only as long as consumers see all of the hotels in the area as being equal. If there is a perceivable difference (such as one hotel being brand-new while the others are much older), then competitive pricing will favor the hotel that appears to offer the most, the newest, or the nicest facilities. Another problem with competitive pricing is that your competitors may be willing to lose money, or have lower costs, and can therefore make money charging prices that would mean losses for you.

Most businesses practice customer-based pricing. This is a pricing method based on what the customer perceives to be a good value. Hotels and restaurants that use this system try to give customers what they expect (or more than they expect) for the price being charged. Businesses that set prices with the customer in mind also recognize that consumers may perceive a larger difference between $9.95 and $10 than there actually is, and so try to keep their prices at the lower figure. There is another psychological factor at work in pricing—the assumption that quality costs money, and that you must pay more to get better quality. Many people are willing to pay more, and refuse to stay in the cheapest motel. These customers believe that there are no free lunches and you always get what you pay for. Restaurants that have a real quality advantage over competitors in terms of product or service also have a definite pricing advantage. Even if it costs them less than it costs their competitors to produce a meal, they can charge more and their sales will actually increase, since many people believe that extra quality is worth more money.

Hospitality authors Robert Lewis and Richard Chambers observe that:

> foodservice in convenience stores owes a good part of its growth to the raising of food prices in fast-food restaurants. Even supermarket business increased because of the raising of restaurant prices. Consumers traded down and down until many, and not just at the lowest level, decided to stay home and eat. Many who preferred higher-quality restaurants maintained that quality level by eating better at home.[2]

In economics, this phenomenon is known as **elasticity of demand**—the response by customers to changes in price. In the Lewis and Chambers example, restaurants have been steadily increasing their prices. Some consumers have responded by refusing to pay the higher prices, turning instead to other alternatives, such as convenience store food or preparing food at home.

Elasticity of demand is important to understand, because if demand for a product or service is elastic, then managers can raise or lower consumer demand through various strategies, including raising or lowering prices. If demand for a product or service is low at one price, then lowering that price may increase the demand. For example, in New York City, rates for hotel rooms are high during the week because business travelers will pay high prices for the rooms. Those same guestrooms may go unoccupied on weekends, however, when demand from business travelers drops off significantly. The rooms may be sold if the prices for them are lowered enough so that they appeal to a different guest group—families or singles wanting a weekend getaway package, for example.

If demand is inelastic, then demand will vary little if at all, no matter what type of adjustments are made. This is the experience of resorts in areas such as Bermuda (in the winter when it is too cold) and Palm Springs, California (in the summer when it is too hot), where lowered room rates and special promotional advertising have not been entirely successful in raising room occupancies to an acceptable level during the off-season. Many people do not want to go to Bermuda or Palm Springs during the off-season, no matter how attractive the price.

Some critics charge that the hotel industry has been unwilling to accept the reality of elasticity of demand, and that the low occupancy rates, which are still endemic in many parts of the country, are not a result of overbuilding, but rather of a failure of hotel managers to recognize that when prices are above what consumers perceive is a good value, they will find something else to do or somewhere else to go.

Students interested in pricing should recognize that for the purposes of this introductory text we have simplified this subject considerably. For example, today many hotels use **yield management** computer programs to set their prices. Yield management programs seek to optimize the revenue a hotel receives in any given period by adjusting the rates that are offered to different market segments, based on the projected supply of rooms and the demand for them. It is a system originally developed by the airlines to allocate the number of seats on each flight that would be available for each of the different fares that the airline offers. These numbers change constantly as reservations come in and the forecasts are adjusted accordingly. In addition, Professor William Quain has developed a method for analyzing sales-mix profitability that looks at prices from the point of view of profit analysis by segment (PABS).[3] Quain suggests that judging performance based on the average daily rate (ADR) is "a mistake that occurs when hotels have a sales plan, not a marketing plan."[4] Quain's work suggests that the cost of making a sale is a key component in setting room prices. For example, it may be cheaper to sell a block of 100 rooms to one meeting planner rather than processing 100 individual reservations, so room prices can be set lower for the meeting planner. The amount of money a guest is likely to spend in the hotel should also be taken into consideration when setting rates. Guests attending meetings tend to have all of their meals on the property, so 100 meeting attendees may be more profitable than 100 individual guests, even if the meeting attendees are charged less for their guestrooms.

Christopher W. Nordling and Sharon K. Wheeler developed a market-segment accounting model for the Las Vegas Hilton that restructures the traditional approach of viewing each hotel department as a profit center and then using that information to account for revenues, costs, and profits, which in turn lead to pricing decisions.[5] Nordling and Wheeler point out that "managers have always gone after what they believed to be the highest profit segment based on which type of guest pays the highest average room rate. But few operators have measured *all* of the attendant costs of servicing each segment and the non-room profit (or loss) produced by the segment."[6] They believe that only this kind of an analysis, which shows the relative value of each market segment, can correctly help managers set prices that will produce optimal revenues for a property.

**Promotion: How Do You Spread the Word?** The fourth P in marketing stands for **promotion.** It is placed last because promotional decisions ideally should be made after product, place, and price decisions have been made. Promotion consists of all the ways an enterprise uses to persuade people to buy its products and services. All promotional activities fall into one of six categories:

- Personal selling
- Advertising
- Public relations and sponsorship marketing
- Sales promotion
- Direct marketing communications
- Point-of-purchase communications

Personal selling is discussed in this chapter.

Traditionally, companies have looked at these functions separately. It is not uncommon for a hotel to use different people (either their own employees or outside agencies) to coordinate sales, public relations, direct marketing, and point-of-purchase merchandising. For example, advertising might be designed and placed by the advertising agency who works with the general manager. Personal sales and public relations may be handled by different people within the hotel. Direct response programs might be initiated by the marketing department, and point-of-purchase materials might be supplied to the food and beverage department by a local graphic designer or printer.

There is a new school of thinking, however, that says that all of these tasks are various forms of *marketing communications* and that to be effectively managed they should be integrated. **Integrated marketing communications** has become the new model that many firms use in organizing their marketing activities. All activities, whether they involve personal sales calls, advertising programs, or tent cards for the dining room, are coordinated. This ensures that the organization sends out messages to its employees, customers, the press, and others that are consistent and directed at achieving the overall mission of the organization.

However, while these various forms of marketing communications should be integrated, each has unique strengths and weaknesses. Personal selling is used as the primary way to attract corporate and group business. Advertising is often targeted at leisure travelers (who cannot be reached by direct sales), or designed to build an image for a brand name such as Hilton or Sheraton. Public relations often has a much wider audience and attempts to influence individuals and groups not reached by traditional personal selling or advertising—employees, community opinion leaders, financial institutions, unions, and others. Sales promotion is used to quickly boost sales.

To succeed, a hotel or restaurant must know how to use promotional activities and how to organize and combine them so they work together to produce a synergistic effect—one where the whole is greater than the sum of its parts. The principal tool used to accomplish this is the marketing plan.

## Developing a Marketing Plan

All business activities should be planned. Although this rule seems obvious, it is often ignored. Managers sometimes feel that planning takes too much time. They argue that it is better to go out and do something than sit around and figure out how to do it. Nevertheless, in the case of marketing, where the expense involved can be astronomical, planning may be regarded as a survival tool. Companies like McDonald's spend more than $1 billion a year on marketing and advertising activities. If those funds were not spent effectively and did not produce the desired results, McDonald's would suffer severe losses. Even a small restaurant owner with a marketing budget of $25,000 must make those dollars return themselves quickly in the form of increased revenue, or the dollars available for marketing will disappear in no time at all.

A marketing plan is a blueprint for organizing, in the most efficient way possible, a business's marketing strategies and activities. New marketing plans are usually created on a regular basis. Many businesses create one every year, others may create marketing plans every two years, three years, or five years. Good plans are always reviewed and often revised on a quarterly basis to take current conditions into account. A good marketing plan has several parts:

- Situation analysis
- Objectives
- Strategies
- Tactics
- Controls

Developing a marketing plan may sound like an intimidating procedure, but it is relatively uncomplicated and follows a series of logical steps.

## Situation Analysis

The first step in developing a marketing plan is the situation analysis. A marketing department's situation analysis is in some ways similar to feasibility studies prepared for proposed restaurants or hotels, except that the marketing department's situation analysis is prepared for an already existing property and is even more marketing oriented.

A situation analysis prepared by a marketing department typically consists of a marketplace analysis, a competition analysis, a review of internal data, a target audience profile, and a problems and opportunities section. The situation analysis is often called a SWOT analysis. SWOT stands for strengths, weaknesses, opportunities, and threats.

**Marketplace Analysis.** Before we can do anything about a situation, we must understand it. Therefore, the first thing a situation analysis contains is a description of the marketplace. If we were doing a situation analysis for a hotel, our first step would be to write down the important data that is likely to affect hotel occupancy in our area in the year ahead. Are businesses opening or closing? Is the economy growing? What is the outlook for tourism? Is the state or city planning any major new campaigns to attract tourists? Is the airport projecting more traffic or less?

**Competition Analysis.** Marketplace information is very general. It concentrates on overall or big trends that are likely to affect your business in the years ahead. In addition to this kind of information, the situation analysis should include a competition

> **Sources for Travel and Tourism Marketing Information**
>
> The following organizations publish the latest travel and tourism statistics and research. The books and reports they produce are available for fees varying from $25 to $200.
>
> Cruise Lines International
>   Association (CLIA)
> 500 5th Avenue, Suite 1407
> New York, NY 10110
>
> Pacific Asia Travel Association
> 1 Montgomery Street
> Telesis Tower, Suite 1750
> San Francisco, CA 94104
>
> Travel and Tourism Research
>   Association and Business
>   Research Division
> University of Colorado
> Campus Box 420
> Boulder, CO 80309
>
> World Tourism Organization
> Capita Haya, 42
> E-Madrid 20
> Spain
>
> International Air Transport
>   Association
> Montreal 2000, Peel Street
> Montreal, Quebec
> Canada
> H3A-2R4
>
> Travel and Tourism Research
>   Association
> 1133 21st Street, N.W.
> Washington, D.C. 20036
>
> U.S. Travel Data Center
> 1133 21st Street, N.W.
> Washington, D.C. 20036
>
> World Travel & Tourism Council
> P.O. Box 6237
> New York, NY 10128

Source: Somerset R. Waters, *Travel Industry World Yearbook: The Big Picture, 1993–94* (New York: Child & Waters, Inc., 1993), p. 158.

analysis. The competition analysis seeks to pinpoint who your competitors are. These are not always easily spotted. For example, the Greenbriar Hotel in White Sulphur Springs, West Virginia, competes with the Boulders Resort in Carefree, Arizona, for conventions. As we pointed out earlier, fast-food establishments compete with convenience stores and supermarkets for market share.

Besides simply listing competitors, it is important to get down on paper a description of the competitors' establishments and how they compare with your facility, both in terms of the physical plant and the quality of service. The prices competitors charge should be compared with the prices you charge (or plan to charge). A competition analysis for a hotel also includes the number of hotel rooms or beds in the market, average occupancy rates, and the kinds of properties found in the area—resorts, city hotels, motels, and so on. If the market is overbuilt, it should be noted. Finally, the analysis should include a careful look at who the competitors' guests are, where they come from, and whether you can reasonably expect to lure them away from your competitors. New business (except in the cruise industry, which attracts a high number of first-time cruisers annually) almost always comes from the customer-base of competitors, customers who either are unsatisfied or believe that you can offer them something superior.

**Internal Analysis.** The object of this section of the situation analysis is to compile data from internal operating sources that will be useful in formulating marketing strategies and tactics. This kind of data should include information on sales mix, such as the percentage and amount of revenue that comes from room sales, food, beverages, catering, and other activities. Finances should be taken into account as well—the capital and resources available, cash flow, and budgets. Human resources policies and operations data such as how well the reservation system is functioning belong in this section.

**Target Audience Profile.** The most important part of the situation analysis is the target audience profile. You should begin with the demographics—that is, what you know about the ages, income, family size, and geographic location of your guests. You should also know as much as you can about your guests' lifestyles. How often do they travel or eat out? Where do they eat? Who makes the decision? This information will help you organize your sales efforts and select advertising media.

Ideally, a target audience profile should help you identify your current or potential heavy users. Are they businesspeople grabbing a quick breakfast on the way to work, or mothers with young children meeting friends for lunch? A restaurant's heavy users sometimes represent only 25 percent of the guest base but as much as 75 percent of sales because they come in regularly several times a week. The same is true in hotels, where a small base of corporate guests can easily represent more than half of a hotel's total sales.

**Problems and Opportunities.** This section is the one in which the strengths and weaknesses of the company are most often identified. Once you have completed the fact-finding phase of the situation analysis, the work really begins. Now you have to interpret what those facts mean. Does the fact that there are no Greek restaurants in your neighborhood mean that there is an opportunity to convert yours to one, or does it simply mean that people in the area do not like Greek restaurants? Does the fact that all of the hotels in your city are mid-price mean that there is a market for a luxury one? There may indeed be a market, but it may be so small that upgrading your property to go after it would not be a profitable venture. Many restaurateurs start a catering service, believing that their food service expertise is sufficient to attract customers and earn profits. This is an illusion. There may already be several competent caterers in the area with established reputations and a loyal customer base. In such a situation it can be a long and costly process to start a new catering operation, and it might never succeed unless there is a real point of difference between the established caterers and the new operation. Even then, success is not guaranteed. To paraphrase the old proverb, "The man who built a better mousetrap and then waited for the world to beat a path to his door starved to death."

The problems and opportunities section is the place to list, as objectively as you can, the problems that stand in the way of significantly increasing your sales or your market share. For example, if you operate a downtown dinner restaurant in a city where fewer and fewer people are coming downtown for dinner in the evening, put that down on paper. You have a genuine problem. You also may have an equally genuine opportunity to open a second restaurant in the suburbs, or open for lunch in your city location.

Similarly, with airline deregulation, many carriers found themselves faced with new competition on routes that previously had been exclusively theirs. That was a problem. But, in turn, they were free to seek out new and profitable markets previously denied them and thus could develop their own new opportunities. Remember, however, not all new opportunities should be pursued. It was mainly the overbuilding of new hotels in the 1980s that caused so many hotel bankruptcies and foreclosures.

## Objectives

Once facts about the current business situation have been gathered and analyzed, managers can create marketing objectives. Marketing objectives are clear and concise descriptions of exactly what managers want the marketing program to accomplish. These objectives are usually specific and measurable.

A business usually has several different types of objectives. A financial objective is usually first. Most companies base their company-wide expense budget on expected income; expected income is stated in the marketing plan as monthly profit goals. Then there are usually growth objectives. Objectives to significantly increase your sales or expand into new markets are growth objectives. Sometimes financial objectives and growth objectives conflict with each other—building a new wing onto the hotel may diminish profits temporarily, for instance. Quality objectives are important in the marketing plans of service organizations. Quality objectives may encompass introducing new amenities or improving existing products or services. Finally, there are philosophical objectives that may address issues such as better working conditions for employees, more environmentally conscious waste management, or support of local charities and cultural programs.

## Strategies

After marketing objectives are established, marketing strategies can be devised. Strategies are simply descriptions of how the marketing objectives will be achieved. For example, suppose one of your objectives is to raise the amount of leisure business at your hotel from 20 percent to 30 percent in six months. Your strategies to do this might include:

- Generating support from more travel agents
- Increasing consumer advertising expenditures
- Developing special honeymoon and other travel packages

To be sure that these strategies are realistic, projected cost figures should be attached to each of them. How much money is going to be spent on generating support from more travel agents, on advertising, and on developing the new travel packages? If a strategy costs too much, it can be eliminated, modified, or replaced with a less expensive one.

## Tactics

Strategies are general in nature. How are you going to "generate support from more travel agents"? Are you going to invite travel agents to visit your property on familiarization (fam) tours? Are you going to offer them special rates? Are you going to visit them in their offices and leave brochures? How many visits will you make? Who will make them? Which travel agencies will you visit? When will this be done?

The answers to all of these questions help managers develop tactics or action plans for achieving marketing objectives. Without tactics, a marketing plan is a useless document. It is not a plan at all. A real marketing plan contains tactics for every strategy, so that anyone with a copy knows what to do and how to do it.

### Controls

Control is as important in marketing as it is in operations. If marketing's tactics are specific, you should be able to tell what is supposed to happen every month and how much it is expected to cost. Results can be anticipated too. Advertising a special honeymoon package ought to produce a number of reservations by honeymooners. If it doesn't, something is wrong. Marketing plans should not be inflexible—they should be reviewed on a regular basis and revised when necessary. That is the function of controls—to monitor and correct deviations from the plan.

## Sales Management and Personal Selling

Some hotel and restaurant chains have millions of dollars to spend on advertising, public relations, and sales promotion, but most hotels and restaurants have limited marketing budgets. Therefore, personal selling by the owners, managers, or sales force is the business-building tool hotels and restaurants most frequently employ.

Most hotels have a marketing and sales or a sales department. Some of these departments are quite sophisticated. Salespersons generally report to a sales manager, who may in turn report to the director of marketing and sales (remember, sales is only one of the functions of marketing). In mid-size to small hotels, the director of marketing and sales and the sales manager are often the same person, although the functions of each job are different. Most clubs, restaurants that have private meeting rooms, and caterers have at least one full-time salesperson on staff (unless the owner or manager takes on this function, which is usually not a good idea).

The sales manager is in charge of the sales office and is responsible for overseeing the sales staff. Some sales managers assign salespersons according to source of business. There may be a salesperson in charge of selling corporate programs targeted at individual business travelers, for example; another in charge of booking meetings and conventions business; and a third in charge of tour business. Other salespersons may be in charge of travel agency sales, military and government sales, and catering sales. Or, sales managers may use a regional approach—there may be an eastern salesperson, a western salesperson, and even an international salesperson, depending on the size and nature of the business. According to James Abbey, author of *Hospitality Sales and Advertising*, the general goals of a sales manager include:

- Increasing property revenue through personal sales calls, telephone calls, and correspondence

- Establishing guidelines for the number of personal sales calls, telephone calls, and sales letters required from each salesperson
- Assisting the general manager with obtaining the maximum sales effort from all employees
- Holding weekly and monthly sales meetings
- Maintaining sales reports and establishing a sales filing system to insure that all files are processed and kept up to date[7]

In order to accomplish these tasks, a sales manager must first recruit and train salespersons. The ability to be an effective salesperson can be learned; it is not a skill that is inherited or based purely on natural talent. Nevertheless, some people are better at it than others.

There are individuals who do not like the idea of selling to someone else. They consider it to be manipulative or unethical behavior. To be sure, unethical salespersons are a part of American folklore. Some early American salespersons were peddlers whose wares included snake oil, charms, and fake antiquities, all of which required a certain amount of deception to sell. Even today, surveys show that used-car salespersons are some of the least-trusted of all individuals, and salespersons as a group are considered less trustworthy than most other professionals. Nevertheless, sales can be an honorable and rewarding career, and, as often as not, today's salesperson is regarded as an important partner, counselor, and helper. At IBM, for example, the mission of the sales team is to help companies solve problems, which is different from selling them computers. However, because IBM salespersons are good problem solvers, they also sell a great many computers.

## How to Be a Successful Salesperson

There are certain characteristics that successful salespersons share, according to Professor Charles Garfield, a clinical professor of psychology at the University of California. Garfield, who has studied super-achievers in all areas, says that exceptional salespersons are similar in these ways:

- They are always taking risks and making innovations to try and surpass previous levels of performance.
- They have a powerful sense of mission and set short-, intermediate-, and long-term goals to fulfill that mission. Their personal sales goals are higher than those set by their managers.
- Super-salespersons are more interested in solving problems than in placing blame or bluffing their way out of situations. Because they view themselves as professionals, they are always upgrading their skills.
- Super-salespersons see themselves as partners with their customers and as team players rather than adversaries. They believe their task is to communicate with people.
- Super-salespersons do not take rejection personally; rather, they treat it as information they can learn from.

- Like other peak performers Garfield has studied, such as athletes and entertainers, super-salespersons use mental rehearsal. Before every sale, they review it in their mind's eye, from shaking the customer's hand when they walk in to discussing his or her problems and asking for the sale.[8]

How does one become a good salesperson? One characteristic is essential in sales: intelligence. Derek Taylor, a successful hotel sales director in England for more than 30 years, puts it this way:

> Sales…is a cerebral occupation. It takes a great deal of thought, for in trying to convince a client to buy the product, you are trying to influence his mind. I have often been asked what book a prospective hotel salesperson should read to understand his job; my answer remains Freud's *Two Short Accounts of Psychoanalysis*. It is a nice simple book that tells you the rules of the game. The capacity to outthink the client who is not all that keen on buying your hotel is the vital difference between success and failure.[9]

**Four Types of Personalities.** Most professional salespersons would agree with Taylor that an understanding of how people think and how to relate to them is the most important characteristic of any salesperson. The idea that extroverted, sociable people make better salespersons than those who are quiet and introverted has little basis in fact. They make different types of salespersons, but studies have shown that there is no difference in sales effectiveness between people who are outgoing and sociable and those who are quiet and reserved. The key is the ability to relate to other people, to be able to listen to them, and then to communicate with them in terms that they understand and in a manner that they can empathize with. In other words, the first step in successful sales is to recognize the kind of person you are dealing with and then use that information to decide how to sell to him or her.

One useful way of doing this that was originally developed by sales consultant Tony Alessandra is to think of all personalities as falling somewhere on a grid consisting of two dimensions (see Exhibit 1). One dimension defines personalities as ranging from high responsiveness to low responsiveness, the other from high assertiveness to low assertiveness. High-responsive people are very open; they are relaxed and warm and are willing to share personal feelings. Low-responsive people tend to hide personal feelings and be formal and guarded. Highly assertive people are willing to take risks, are impatient, extroverted, and express opinions readily. People with a low degree of assertiveness are supportive, easygoing, and reserve opinions.

As can be seen from Exhibit 1, depending on where on the grid a person falls, he or she can be characterized as an Amiable, an Expressive, a Driver, or an Analytical.

**Amiables.** People who are Amiables consider personal relationships to be of utmost importance. They are interested in buying from people with whom they have established a personal relationship. Amiables are easy to recognize because their conversation often deals with relationships they have with others. They also tend to be indirect and slow-paced.

Most Amiables are hesitant to talk business until they feel comfortable with a person, and thus a salesperson who tries to come to the point quickly will not make a favorable impression on them. Amiables are particularly susceptible to buying

## Exhibit 1  Four Personality Types

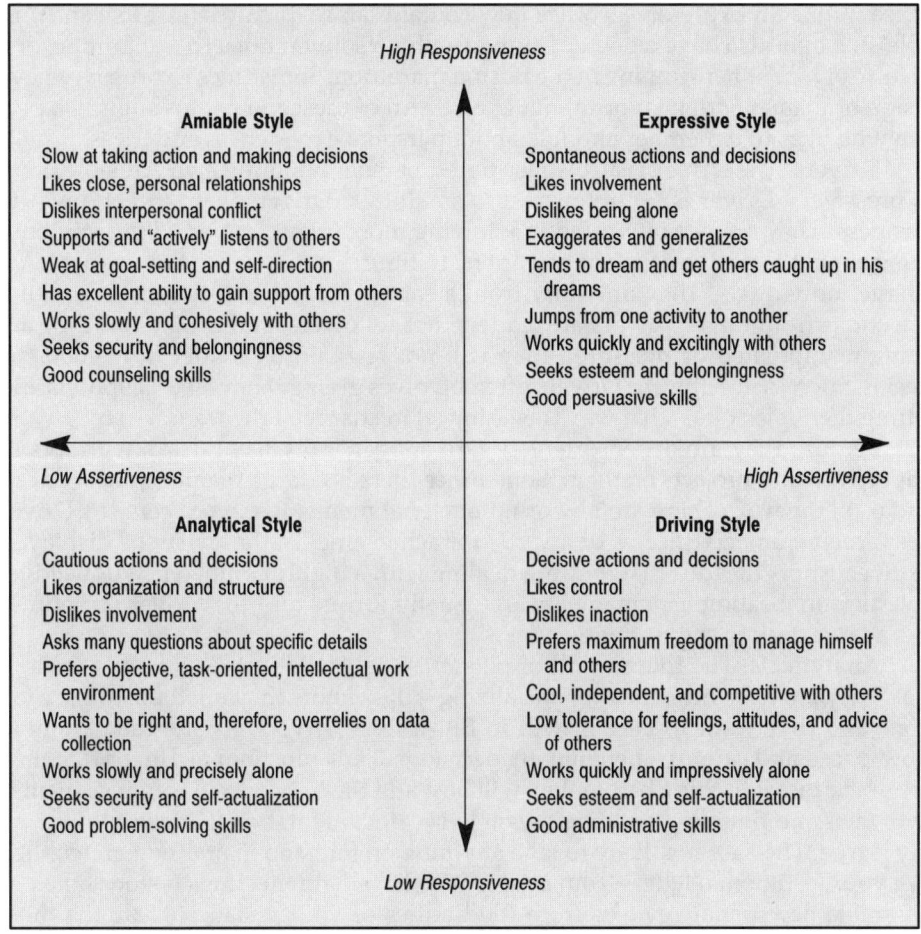

*High Responsiveness*

**Amiable Style**

Slow at taking action and making decisions
Likes close, personal relationships
Dislikes interpersonal conflict
Supports and "actively" listens to others
Weak at goal-setting and self-direction
Has excellent ability to gain support from others
Works slowly and cohesively with others
Seeks security and belongingness
Good counseling skills

**Expressive Style**

Spontaneous actions and decisions
Likes involvement
Dislikes being alone
Exaggerates and generalizes
Tends to dream and get others caught up in his dreams
Jumps from one activity to another
Works quickly and excitingly with others
Seeks esteem and belongingness
Good persuasive skills

*Low Assertiveness* ←→ *High Assertiveness*

**Analytical Style**

Cautious actions and decisions
Likes organization and structure
Dislikes involvement
Asks many questions about specific details
Prefers objective, task-oriented, intellectual work environment
Wants to be right and, therefore, overrelies on data collection
Works slowly and precisely alone
Seeks security and self-actualization
Good problem-solving skills

**Driving Style**

Decisive actions and decisions
Likes control
Dislikes inaction
Prefers maximum freedom to manage himself and others
Cool, independent, and competitive with others
Low tolerance for feelings, attitudes, and advice of others
Works quickly and impressively alone
Seeks esteem and self-actualization
Good administrative skills

*Low Responsiveness*

Source: Anthony J. Alessandra, Ph.D., and Phillip S. Wexler, *Non-Manipulative Selling* ©1979, p. 22. Reprinted by permission of Prentice-Hall, Englewood Cliffs, New Jersey.

from individuals who went to the same school as they did, belong to the same club, or live in the same neighborhood. Often you can tell when you are sitting in an Amiable's office by the way it is decorated or arranged. An Amiable's desk typically has family pictures or personal items on it, and usually the seating arrangement is open and informal.

**Expressives.** An Expressive is also open and interested in relationships, but, unlike an Amiable, an Expressive moves faster and is much more direct. Expressives do not hesitate to open up and tell you about themselves and their ideas and opinions. To successfully sell to Expressives, you must respond to what they say in a lively and interesting manner, so that they will feel they are dealing with someone who is really interested in them.

Again, one way to recognize an Expressive quickly is to look around his or her office. While an Expressive's office may contain family pictures (just like an Amiable's), it may also have a golf or fishing trophy, a souvenir of a trip to Europe, or a picture of him or her running in the Boston marathon. Sometimes Expressives have a sign or plaque with a favorite saying on it. All of these mementos suggest a person who likes to remember and talk about personal experiences and ideas.

**Drivers.** The Driver is also a fast-paced person, but, unlike an Amiable or an Expressive, a Driver is not interested in small talk. Drivers want to get down to business. They are not interested in knowing more about you or telling you anything about themselves; they only want facts, figures, and results. Drivers are take-charge individuals. They only buy from a salesperson whom they feel is taking directions from them. Drivers are leaders, not followers, and if they feel they are being manipulated or pressured they will not respond no matter how good the deal is. Success in selling to Drivers often involves giving them several options and letting them pick one—that way they can feel in charge of the transaction.

Because they are action-oriented, Drivers generally have desks with lots of paperwork and projects on them. Sometimes there is a large planning sheet or calendar on the wall. There are few or no personal mementos to be seen. If a Driver has received any certificates or awards for achievements, these may be displayed to give visitors the idea that they are dealing with a highly competent, knowledgeable person. Seating arrangements are usually formal and the Driver sometimes has a large desk to suggest power.

**Analyticals.** The fourth kind of person is the Analytical. Analyticals are logical. They too have little time for socializing—they know they are there to get a job done and they want to get on with it. But unlike Drivers, Analyticals are more slow-paced and careful when making decisions. They must be convinced that they are doing the right thing before they will buy, and the only way to convince them is with facts and figures. Analyticals want to see documentation that everything you say is true. They are not likely to take anything on faith, no matter how much they like you. Testimonial letters from people who have held meetings in your hotel, or favorable newspaper reviews from food critics of your restaurant, are the most convincing things you can show Analyticals.

An Analytical's office usually contains nothing distracting in it; it is all business. It often contains business and reference books, charts, and graphs that can be consulted if necessary.

**Sales strategies based on personality types.** Clearly, we cannot neatly categorize everyone and say that he or she is an Amiable, an Expressive, a Driver, or an Analytical. All of us have some of each of these personality styles within us. But, generally speaking, we tend to fit into one of these personality types more than the others. Successful salespersons take time before they start selling to establish which kind of personality they are dealing with. From that point on it is a question of modifying their own behavior so that it matches that of the person on the other side of the desk.

If you are selling to an Amiable, for example, the conversation might start with a question about how long he or she has been in that job or in the city. This may be followed by sharing some similar information about yourself to see if common ground can be established. If you are dealing with an Expressive, you might briefly comment on his or her tennis trophy. A Driver wants you to come to the point quickly—tell him or her why you are there and what you hope to accomplish. Analyticals want to see pictures, plans, and facts supporting your sales presentation, and will take the time to go over these support materials carefully.[10]

## Basic Qualities of a Salesperson

Besides inherent intelligence, an interest in people, and an ability to relate to them, a prospective salesperson needs some other qualities. The late DeWitt Coffman, international hotel consultant and author of *Hospitality for Sale* and other sales and marketing books, pointed out that nearly all textbooks about personal selling emphasize the following basic qualities:

- Courtesy
- Deportment
- Appearance
- Knowledge of product or service
- Willingness to work
- Personality[11]

Let's look at each of these characteristics more closely.

**Courtesy.** According to Coffman, courtesy is best defined as "a combination of friendliness and politeness, tempered by conservatism and reserve. It is the use of 'please' and 'thank you' and all the other terms for showing appreciation. It is consideration and respect and interest in the other person's comfort, pleasure, and deportment." Without courtesy, a salesperson is doomed from the start. While you may accept service from a discourteous food server in a restaurant where you are already seated, you are not likely to entrust the planning of your next meeting to a person who strikes you as being rude or uncaring.

**Deportment.** Deportment is related to physical posture. Individuals who deport themselves well stand tall, sit erect, and look alert, pleasant, and enthusiastic.

**Appearance.** Appearance can make a big difference in a person's sales success. Appearance in this context refers to personal grooming and dress, not physical attractiveness. (Incidentally, there is no evidence that beauty or handsomeness offers the slightest advantage in making a sale. Indeed, some salespersons report that being physically attractive has actually hindered their sales efforts, because their prospects are distracted!)

Sales training programs constantly refer to presenting a "professional" image. What is a professional image? For one thing, it is conservative. There is nothing wrong with choosing clothes for your personal wardrobe that make a statement about what kind of person you are, but when you are selling, the objective is to get the prospect to concentrate on your product or service, not on you. That is why

**Salespersons dress conservatively so that their clothes do not distract potential customers from the sales message.**

almost all salespersons avoid dressing too colorfully, displaying the latest fashions, or wearing large rings, bracelets, or earrings.

*Forbes* magazine interviewed top executives on how they projected leadership to their staff and customers.[12] Their answers offer some interesting insights about how they regard clothing and appearance:

> I'm not looking for anything other than fitting in when I'm selling. In New York, I could always play a little bit more because it's a free, fun city. I have long red nails and bleached blonde hair that's down around my shoulders. I wear a good, sassy, fairly short skirt. But if I go to the South or Midwest, I'll wear long pants and a darker color. If I'm on my way to Alabama, I pull my hair back, wear a pair of glasses, because that's how they do it.
>
> Janet Tweed
> CEO, Gilbert Tween Associates
> An executive search firm

A professional image is enhanced by neat grooming, pressed clothes, and shined shoes. Clothing alone cannot project leadership or a professional image. If a sales person looks shoddy and unkempt, prospects generally assume that the company he or she represents is the same.

> I just hired somebody in a very high paying position and he comes to work in frayed shirts. It irritates me. It's not corporate.
>
> Lillian Vernon
> CEO, Lillian Vernon Corp.

Clothes and grooming are not the only things that can affect your professional image.

> If you are overweight, especially if you are a woman, forget about moving up. You may be a fabulous professional, but your obesity has absolutely topped off your career. You will go no further unless you're prepared to take on that problem.
>
> Paula Rosput
> President, Pan Energy Power Services

**Knowledge of Product or Service.** A knowledge of your product or service is essential. Says Coffman:

> the salesman promoting banquet business should know exactly the seating capacity of the various rooms in his establishment under all possible set-ups. He should know the complete price range of menus available and all the additional services available such as music, loud speakers, and flowers. The waiter or waitress should know every item on each day's menu and the general type of preparation of each of these items. The room clerk should have a mental image of every room, or every type of room, he is selling. All of the personal charm in the world cannot overcome ignorance or lack of knowledge.[13]

Knowledge of the prospect's needs is equally important. There is no point in going to a meeting ready to discuss how well your property handles banquets when the prospect wants to talk about his or her company's annual training meeting.

**Willingness to Work.** Willingness to work sounds like an obvious qualification, but it is not. Salespersons often get discouraged because most of the calls they make do not produce immediate business. The truth is that sales is a game of numbers. The more calls you make, the more sales you will make. But on the way to making those sales, you will receive a large number of rejections because it is hard to locate good prospects. In the insurance industry it takes nine prospect calls to create one customer. Selling computers to businesses is even harder: 125 phone calls to prospects may produce 25 interviews that lead to 5 sales presentations and 1 sale.[14] Hanging tough requires a lot of determination, or what Derek Taylor calls tough-mindedness. Taylor says he likes to hire salespeople who are considered "stubborn, difficult, awkward, or bloody-minded. These are the ingredients professional salespeople need to bolster their persistence and fuel their determination to get the account."[15]

**Personality.** The final quality a successful salesperson needs is personality. This frightens some people who would otherwise be interested in a sales career. "I don't have the right personality," they tell themselves, "I'm not interesting enough as a person," or "I'm too shy." The secret of personality is to come across as being interested in others, not yourself. Which friends of yours have a winning personality? The ones who come to mind are usually the ones who are interested in what you have to say. Sometimes we confuse liveliness and playfulness with personality. They are not the same. Anyone who is courteous, friendly, and a good listener is judged by most others to have a good personality.

## Making the Sales Call

An effective sales call consists of six steps:

1. Prospecting and qualifying
2. Preparation
3. Presentation
4. Overcoming objections
5. Asking for the sale
6. Follow-up

Let's discuss each of these steps in sequence.

### Prospecting and Qualifying

Even experienced salespersons often waste a lot of effort calling on people who are not legitimate prospects. One reason is that many companies establish quotas for the number of calls a salesperson is expected to make in a day or a week. There isn't any doubt that the only way to sell is to make a large number of calls, but the more carefully the prospects are selected, the greater the return will be.

There are several good sources of leads for hospitality enterprises besides the inquiries that come in through the mail and on the telephone daily. To begin with, current guests are often the best source of new leads. Other excellent sources are the companies you do business with—your vendors, suppliers, bankers, insurance people, and accountants. All of these people have other clients who might be interested in using your facilities. Trade publications and newspapers are excellent sources of leads. Many hotels, restaurants, and caterers look in their local newspapers for people who are getting married and contact them promptly. Many cities have a convention and visitors' bureau that develops leads for meetings and conventions and distributes them to all local hoteliers. Airlines have group sales departments that are constantly negotiating rates with groups such as the Rotarians that will have a large number of people flying to a convention location. Airlines will often contact hotels to seek their cooperation in creating flight/hotel packages.

### Preparation

There are two parts to the preparation process. The first is to decide exactly what you hope to accomplish with the sales call. "Make the sale" is not a good objective

**Salespersons spend a lot of time prospecting for potential customers.**

because actually making a sale is not the objective of most sales calls. It usually takes several calls to close a sale. A hotel salesperson's objective for a first sales call might only be to "introduce our property" or "gather information about the prospect's annual meeting so we can make a proposal." Only after another meeting or two might the objective become "make the sale."

Equally important to the preparation process is to research the prospect and his or her company so that everything that might be needed is at hand during the meeting. On a first call, it is important to know as much about the company as possible beforehand. What are its products or services? How well is it doing? Who are its competitors? A well-informed salesperson can ask specific and intelligent questions that will assure the prospect that the salesperson is really interested in his or her company. Effective salespersons are truly interested in their prospects' companies—that is what makes them effective!

## Presentation

By the time a salesperson is in a face-to-face meeting with a prospect, he or she should already know what the prospect is interested in buying. If the prospect hasn't told you what he or she might be interested in buying, ask. Without this information, a sale is not possible. Let prospects tell you about their problems and then you can suggest some ways in which you might help solve them.

In a good presentation, the salesperson always focuses on benefits, not features. The prospect is interested in benefits—"What's in it for me?"—not in what you are selling. For example, one of your convention hotel's features may be its ten lighted tennis courts. But if you merely mention this fact, the prospect might think, "So what?" The benefit should be spelled out clearly. Rather than saying "We have ten lighted tennis courts," you should say something like: "With ten lighted tennis courts, there are always enough courts available for your delegates to use after their meetings, no matter what time they finish."

Successful presentations almost always employ the use of visual aids. However, don't make them the focus of the presentation. They are simply there to reinforce what you are saying.

## Overcoming Objections

Even with the best of presentations, you can expect a prospect to raise some objections. It is normal for people to ask tough questions or try to put off decisions, especially if they fear making a mistake. You should not be discouraged by objections. An objection often signals that the prospect is interested, but that you haven't correctly identified the prospect's needs or clearly pointed out how your hotel or restaurant can fill them. You should respond to an objection with further questioning to determine what the prospect is really looking for.

There will be many instances when objections can't be overcome. A prospect may simply not be interested in what you have to sell. For example, your property may not have a golf course and a golf tournament may be the highlight of your prospect's annual meeting. In that case, the best strategy is to end the presentation, thank the prospect for his or her time, and withdraw gracefully. By doing so, you can retain your positive relationship with the prospect, and you may do business with him or her in the future.

## Asking for the Sale

This is the part of selling that inexperienced salespersons fear most. No one wants to be rejected, and asking for the sale and not getting it can be discouraging.

Timing is everything in closing. Experienced salespersons seldom get rejected, simply because they don't ask for the sale until they sense that the prospect is ready to buy. Signs that a prospect is ready to buy are usually obvious to a careful observer. The prospect nods in agreement throughout the presentation. He or she looks relaxed. At the end of the presentation he or she asks you to confirm some of the details of your proposal. That is the time to ask for the sale. Salespersons should not be tentative at this point; the prospect expects you to ask. Often experienced salespersons simply assume that the sale has been made and ask questions

**Repeat sales depend on a trusting relationship.**

such as, "How many rooms shall I reserve for you?" or "When can we expect your deposit?"

## Follow-Up

It is an established principle of salesmanship that the sale really begins once the order is signed. This is especially true in the hospitality industry, where good service and word-of-mouth recommendations are keys to increasing business. Careful follow-up can keep the customer sold and lead to repeat bookings.

The follow-up process typically starts with a letter sent to the client within a day or two after your last meeting, thanking him or her for the sale and confirming the details. But that is only the beginning. Professional salespersons stay with the client every step of the way. They check to make sure that everything that happens is exactly what the client wants and, if possible, sees that he or she gets more than was expected. Sales depend on a continuing relationship, where the client comes to view the salesperson as a partner and friend.

## Selling through Travel Agencies

One of the most prominent trends in the travel industry in recent years has been the growing importance of travel agencies in the distribution of travel products. This is quite a change from the early days of travel, when travelers had to arrange for transportation and accommodations on their own.

The first travel agent was Thomas Cook. In the mid-1850s, Cook recognized that with the emergence of railroads and steamships there was a need for someone willing to make arrangements for people who wished to explore England and the

**This trade ad was designed to run in publications read by travel agents.** (Courtesy of the Danish Tourist Board, McCartin & Kunin, Inc., and KLM Royal Dutch Airlines)

Continent, but were nervous about traveling on their own to foreign places. Soon Cook had established himself as a sales agent for these new and convenient forms of transportation, and in 1856 he offered his first "Grand Tour" of Europe.

About the same time (1850), the American Express Company was formed in the United States. Originally started with the purpose of shipping merchandise and money across America and then to Europe, the company soon grew to the point where it also offered travelers checks and dispensed information on foreign destinations. Not until 1915, however, did the company decide to go into the business of handling tourist travel and offering tours.

Modern travel agencies represent airlines, hotels, car rental firms, cruise lines, and wholesale tour operators. As representatives, their job is first and foremost to dispense information about these various services to the public at large. In this sense they are information brokers. However, because travel agents buy airline tickets, make hotel reservations, and make other travel arrangements for clients, they are also distributors and salespersons and, as such, they receive commissions from the organizations whose products they distribute and sell.

Today there are more than 33,000 travel agencies in the United States. They sell 80 percent of all airline tickets. This is more than double their number a decade ago, when fewer than 15,000 agencies sold only 40 percent of airline seats. Airline tickets account for 61 percent of their total sales, the rest coming from hotels, car rentals, tours, cruises, and other travel services.

Most travel agencies are small businesses with average annual sales in the neighborhood of $3 million. Fifty-nine percent of agency locations have yearly revenues under $2 million, while 41 percent have revenues of more than $2 million. Only 11 percent of locations exceed $5 million. Most travel agency business still comes from domestic travel, which represents 69 percent of all sales. The largest portion of that (49%) is leisure-related travel. The average agency employs 5.9 persons.[16]

## Types of Travel Agencies

There are various types of travel agencies, and new variations spring up all the time because of new technology and the ease of entry into the business. The most common travel agencies are full-service, commercial, in-plant, and group and incentive.

**Full-Service.** Although **full-service agencies** handle all types of travel, in most cases a little more than half of their business comes from vacationers booking airline tickets and hotel rooms. Before airline deregulation, air fares did not vary much from airline to airline, and many travelers—especially business travelers—called the airlines directly to make their travel arrangements. Agencies were used more for convenience than for any other reason. However, with today's complicated and competitive airline fare structures, it is a formidable task for anyone without a computer to figure out which airline offers the best fares and the most convenient schedules. This has led many more travelers to buy their airline tickets through travel agencies.

**Commercial.** **Commercial agencies** specialize in commercial business and frequently have little or no walk-in clientele. Travel agents at these agencies deal with corporate customers on the telephone and book primarily airline tickets, hotel rooms, and car rentals. Often they handle meeting arrangements for their clients as well. Rosenbluth Travel in Philadelphia is an example of a highly sophisticated commercial agency with a separate meeting planning facility.

**In-Plant.** **In-plant agencies** are located in the offices of large corporate clients so that ticketing and other arrangements can be booked instantly and in person. In-plant agencies are branch offices of commercial agencies.

In some cases, commercial agencies do not need to open an in-plant office staffed with an agent, but instead install **satellite ticket printers (STPs)** in clients' offices. Under this arrangement, the client calls the agency to arrange travel, but instead of the agency printing the ticket in its office and then delivering it or mailing it to the client, the ticket is printed on the satellite ticket printer in the client's office.

**Group and Incentive.** **Group and incentive agencies** specialize in creating customized travel programs for groups and corporations. Many companies reward their top salespersons with trips to exotic places. Others hold annual conventions in Hawaii or the Caribbean for all managers and their spouses. Then there are church groups that wish to visit religious sites such as the Vatican, or veterans groups who wish to return to the beaches of Normandy. Group and incentive agencies specialize in this kind of business.

**Other Agencies.** In addition to the travel agencies just mentioned, there are several less common types of agencies that should be noted.

**Direct-response agencies.** **Direct-response agencies** do not have walk-in offices, but market their products through the mail, usually to senior citizens or other special groups such as disabled persons or alumni associations. Many direct-response agencies offer extended-stay options for clients who, for example, may wish to spend a month in Spain in their own apartments. In addition, there are direct-response agencies that operate with 800 numbers and offer no travel advice, but instead provide rebates to clients who make their own airline reservations and simply call the agency to issue the ticket(s) that they have already reserved.

**Tour operators.** Although travel agencies represent many tour operators, in many cases **tour operators** sell directly to the public, thereby acting as their own travel agents. Tours are frequently sold by mail and are often advertised in magazines such as *Travel & Leisure* and *The New Yorker*. Many "adventure" vacations, such as African safaris, treks to Nepal, and trips to the Galapagos Islands, are marketed in this fashion. Companies like Perillo and Tauk Tours are good examples of tour operators.

**Cruise-only agencies.** For travel agents, an essential part of selling cruises is knowing the layout of as many cruise ships as possible, so that the agents can recommend the best cabins (the ones with the best views, least noise, and least motion) to their clients. Understanding which ports of call offer the most interesting attractions is also important. Because of these complications, almost all cruise tickets are sold through travel agents. As a practical matter, most travel agents simply do not have enough experience or have not inspected enough ships to be able to give authoritative advice on cruises. For this reason, many travel agencies have been formed in recent years to handle cruise business only. **Cruise-only agencies** go to extra lengths to train their agents to become familiar with cruise ships, their menus, on-board services, and ports of call. Since the cruise business is growing rapidly (today there are 100 cruise ships operating out of American ports alone), these agencies tend to do very well in markets where cruises are popular.

**Consolidators. Consolidators** are travel agencies that have negotiated special arrangements with certain airlines that allow them larger commissions on certain routes and flights, or simply have been able to obtain more favorable fares or larger commissions based on unsold seats or other marketing considerations. For example, an airline may have 50 unsold seats on a particular flight a few days or weeks before departure. It may then call a consolidator and say, "We'll pay you a 25 percent commission on every unsold seat you can move for us. Although we sell the seats for $200, you can sell them for $125, because we'd rather get a lower profit than nothing at all." Sometimes there is a catch: the airline will try to sell the 50 unsold seats at the airline's $200 price right up until a day or two before the flight leaves, and only at the last moment let the consolidator know how many seats are still available at the $125 price.

Some consolidators sell to individual clients and advertise regularly in the Sunday travel sections of major metropolitan newspapers. However, most consolidators do not deal directly with the public—they purchase seats at bulk rates and then re-sell them to travel agencies. Many travel agencies refuse to deal with consolidators, despite the fact that they can obtain cheaper fares, on the grounds that they can't offer an adequate level of protection for their clients. This is because many flights booked through consolidators may not be confirmed until a few days or even a few hours before departure.

**Travel clubs.** Travel clubs charge an annual fee (usually $35 to $50), and in return offer their members packaged vacations at special prices. These vacations are usually developed on short notice by the clubs, working with tour operators that have unsold airline seats and hotel rooms and are willing to sell them to clubs at substantial discounts.

**Internet agencies.** Technology is changing the face of the travel agency business rapidly. Companies who were never in the travel business before, notably Microsoft, have entered and appear to be gaining market share and momentum. Virtually all other types of agencies are scrambling to keep up. Chairman Bill Gates has stated publicly that the company intends to dominate the travel agency business using the Internet as a tool.

Microsoft's Expedia, which calls itself "a travel agency in your computer," reported sales of $1 million a week in 1997. Expedia's features include *Mungo Park*, an online adventure travel magazine; Fare Trekker, a search engine for the lowest airfares; and World Guide—which lists attractions and includes pictures and street maps of lodging facilities, along with rates, room availability, and car rental information. Everything can be booked online, with instant confirmation.

While figures are still sketchy, it is estimated that 21 percent of U.S. travel agencies were online in 1997, and about half of those reported getting some bookings. Nevertheless, as consumers become more aware of their ability to make their own travel arrangements online—not only through agencies, but directly with airlines, hotels, and other travel suppliers—and as home computers proliferate, it is almost certain that technology's impact on travel marketing will be felt forever.

## What Travel Agencies Do

We have mentioned the principal products sold by travel agencies in the previous sections. Some of these products need further elaboration and clarification. The four products travel agents sell that we will discuss in this section are airline tickets, hotel rooms, cruises, and tours.

**Sell Airline Tickets.** Airline tickets make up more than two-thirds of sales for most travel agencies. In order to sell tickets for all major airlines throughout the world, agencies must be accredited by the Airlines Reporting Corporation and the International Airlines Travel Agent Network. Monies that travel agencies collect from clients are forwarded weekly to these organizations through area settlement banks, which then distribute the money to the airlines.

Ninety-five percent of all travel agencies subscribe to one or more of the four computer reservation systems. The major systems are Apollo, SABRE, SystemOne, and WORLDSPAN. Of these computer reservation systems, SABRE and SystemOne are the most widely used. In addition, there are two major multinational European systems—AMADEUS and GALILEO—owned by a group of European carriers; and a Far Eastern system called Abacus, owned by Singapore Airlines. All of these airline systems are linked together. This makes it possible for a travel agent to compare schedules, fares, and seat availabilities from different airlines, make an instant reservation, issue a ticket, and in some cases issue a boarding pass as well. Agencies with computers use them to book 95 percent of the domestic airline tickets they sell and 82 percent of the international airline tickets they sell. Seventy percent of the car rentals and 52 percent of the hotel reservations they sell are booked electronically as well.

Computer systems are a major expense for travel agencies. An agency with $2 million in annual sales typically has five computer reservation terminals per location and spends more than six percent of its gross income on computer rentals and supplies. However, computer rental fees charged by airlines are negotiable, depending on the volume of business or the market share that an agency is able to generate for the airline supplying the system.

**Sell Hotel Rooms.** Some hotels can have their guestrooms booked through the airline computer systems that travel agents use. However, these are only hotels in the major chains. On the whole, the lodging industry has not kept up with the airlines or travel agents in computer technology. Many hotels still do not have computerized property management systems. Even those that do have such systems do not, in most cases, have hardware and software that is compatible with the airline reservation systems.

Industry analysts expect this to change, however. As travel agencies become more involved in making hotel reservations for their clients, the lodging industry is expected to accelerate programs to interface with travel agency computer systems.

In the meantime, just about every travel agency subscribes to the *Official Hotel & Resort Guide, Hotel & Travel Index*, or a similar publication from which they draw their information about guestroom rates. Guestrooms are booked by telephone, or—especially in the case of foreign countries—by mail, telex, or fax. Some hotels are represented by hotel representatives (or "reps") who can instantly confirm reservations on behalf of the hotels they represent.

Travel agencies and hotels have not yet established an entirely satisfactory business alliance. Despite the fact that travel agencies book the majority of airline seats and virtually all cruises, travel agencies account for only 25 percent of guestroom reservations at hotels. There are two principal reasons for this. In the past, many hotel chains have bypassed agents in their marketing efforts, urging consumers via TV, radio, and magazine advertising to call the hotels directly for reservations using a toll-free 800 number. Travel agencies have opposed this practice because it deprives them of commissions. The second reason is that some hotels have developed a reputation among travel agencies for not paying travel agents the commissions they owe them. According to Eric Friedheim, chairman and editor-in-chief of *Travel Agent* magazine:

> Tardy remittances or refusals to pay still plague the agency/hotel relationship, already strained by persistent bypass....Only chains, hotel reps, and top flight establishments aggressively solicit agency support with fam trips, advertising seminars, overrides, and other incentives....Careless or cumbersome accounting procedures by hoteliers more often than not deprive the agent of rightful compensation.[17]

*Marketing and Selling Hospitality* **463**

# Want a hotel that rewards you, pays commissions on time, and really wants to get to know you?

## Swissôtel to the rescue.

We'll rescue you from the ordinary with extraordinary programs like these:

- **Win Swisstakes And Win The World:** Book through GDS and you can win a 3-week trip for two to your choice of Swissair/Swissôtel destinations and $1,000 spending money. Plus thousands of other prizes weekly.

- **New Centralized Commission:** With Hotel Clearing Corporation, you now get an entire month's commission the way you want it—in one check, on time, and in the currency of your choice!

- **Getting-To-Know-You Fam Trips:** Qualified agents can visit any Swissôtel worldwide for just $75* (or equivalent in local currency) per night. We'll even ask you what you think, so we can serve you and your clients better.

For more information, call **1-800-63-SWISS**.

GDS Chain Code: SL

*Swissôtel to the rescue.*

**swissôtel**

Part of the Swissair experience

*New York $125. Based on availability.

ATLANTA • BOSTON • CHICAGO • NEW YORK
AMSTERDAM • BANGKOK • BASEL • BEIJING • BRUSSELS • CAIRO • DÜSSELDORF
HANOI' • ISTANBUL • JAKARTA' • MONTREUX • SEMARANG' • SEOUL • ZÜRICH
'Swissôtel Worldwide Partner Hotel

**This Swissôtel ad highlights benefits for travel agents to spur business.** (Courtesy of Swissôtel)

Hoteliers have made significant strides responding to these challenges, although much still needs to be done. *Travel Weekly's* 1996 travel survey showed that 77 percent of agents consider ease of collecting commissions a "very important" factor in choosing a hotel. Only a hotel's reputation for honoring reservations (90%) and reputation and service of the hotel (83%) rank higher. Many major hotel chains have established toll-free travel agent help desks to straighten out commission problems. Most have introduced a centralized commission policy, whereby agents receive one check at the end of the month, along with a detailed statement from the chain representing all of its properties (in the past, travel agents used to collect individually from each hotel). Many problems still remain with small independent properties who do not keep good records or are negligent in making payments.

As far as advertising is concerned, many hotels encourage travelers to call their travel agents for reservations. Marriott has a written policy that all sales brochures, public relations materials, and radio and television advertising should contain the phrase "Or call your travel agent."

Since consumers are expected to place as much as 50 percent of all their hotel reservations through agencies in the next decade, both agencies and hoteliers continue to explore ways in which the two can work together on a fair and equitable basis.

Several chains, including Hilton and Hyatt, have implemented a number of policies to increase travel agent incentives and loyalty. These include:

- Joining a centralized electronic commission payment service, such as Hotel Clearing Corporation (HCC)
- Creating special reservation telephone lines with reservationists trained to work with travel agents
- Increasing capability of agents to book all available inventory at lowest rates through their central reservation system (CRS)
- Introducing special rates and other incentives to encourage agents to visit their hotels on familiarization (fam) trips
- Creating travel agent advisory boards to provide feedback for the companies' travel agent programs

**Sell Cruises.** The cruise industry may well be the most exciting growth category in the entire leisure market. Since 1970 the industry has had a compound annual growth rate of 10 percent. About 95 percent of all cruises are sold by travel agents. Cruise sales are now second (after airline ticket sales) in generating revenue and profits for many agents.

Travel agents often favor selling cruises over other vacations, because cruises produce high levels of client satisfaction, are easy to sell, and often yield higher commissions than land-based vacations. A typical land-based travel package takes 66 minutes to sell and produces an average commission of $98. A cruise, on the other hand, takes an average of 43 minutes to sell and produces an average commission of $142 (in part because meals, entertainment, and transportation are all included and arranged for by the travel agent).

One study by the Cruise Lines International Association shows that, among people who have taken both a cruise vacation and a resort vacation in the past five years, cruising gets higher marks for pampering by staff, organization, pleasurable dining experiences, and value for money.

**Sell Tours.** Tours are another popular product with travel agents. Like cruises, tours are often all-inclusive. Basically, tours fall into three classifications: escorted, independent, and package.

An **escorted tour** is a group of travelers traveling with a guide who has travel experience and has set up an itinerary for the group. Escorted tours appeal to people who are inexperienced travelers or who do not enjoy traveling alone. However, some experienced travelers—who recognize that escorted tour operators are able (through volume discounts) to secure airline seats and hotel rooms at a far lower cost than they can—book these tours simply to take advantage of the low prices that companies like Cosmos (one of the largest escorted bus-tour operators) can offer. Some escorted tours are very expensive, however. For example, Lorraine Travel in Miami offers escorted tours around the world on a Concorde jet that cost $40,000 and up per person.

**Independent tours,** known in the trade as **FITs (foreign independent tours),** are tours created for families or individuals who walk into the travel agency and tell an agent what country or area they would like to visit and what they would like to see and do there. Independent tours are usually tailored exactly to the needs of the client and require agents to do a good deal of detail work. The travel agent must arrange for transportation, work out daily itineraries, make hotel reservations, and set up sightseeing excursions or buy theater tickets. Many agencies charge a special fee for this kind of careful planning, in addition to the regular commissions they earn.

**Package tours** are similar to independent tours in that travelers who buy a package tour travel by themselves rather than with a large group. The difference is that travelers do not put their own tours together—they buy a tour that has been planned by a packager or tour operator. Certified Vacations in Ft. Lauderdale, Florida, is such a packager. It assembles its own tours as well as the "Dream Vacation" tours for Delta Airlines. When agents or customers call the Delta Dream Vacation desk, they actually get a Certified Tour travel agent, who books a Dream Vacation tour for them for a package price that is considerably lower than if the elements of the tour (airline tickets, hotel rooms, and so on) were purchased separately.

## How Travel Agents Are Trained

Many travel agents start their careers by attending one of the many vocational training schools that teach the basic skills required. While these schools (which offer courses lasting anywhere from a few weeks to several months) will not guarantee placement, many travel agencies recruit from the graduates of these schools. Community colleges also offer travel agent training programs. Courses in these colleges generally focus on the technical skills needed to make airline reservations and issue tickets, as well as on basic geography, since many students have not had the opportunity to travel.

**Familiarization tours allow travel agents to get acquainted with all of a destination area's hotels, restaurants, and sights. This is an open market in Jerusalem.** (Courtesy of Moriah Hotels Ltd., Tel Aviv, Israel)

Travel suppliers have learned that the best way to train agents is to give them an opportunity to see the places they are asked to sell. Two travel agency trade associations, the American Society of Travel Agents (ASTA) and the Association of Retail Travel Agents (ARTA), sponsor numerous meetings and events where agents can learn to improve their skills. So does the Cruise Lines International Association (CLIA), which runs the CLIA Sales Institute and the CLIA Management Institute, where agents learn to sell cruises and improve their agency management skills. Airlines offer agents a 75 percent discount on fares and hotels; tour operators and cruise lines all have special rates so agents can become familiar with their products. Many times, destinations and tour operators or airlines will get together to offer (for a low price) a group of agents a familiarization trip in which they are taken to a particular place and given a chance to inspect all of the hotels and other sights. These are working trips—it is not unusual for agents to visit more than a dozen hotels, plus a couple of restaurants and a sightseeing attraction, in a single day. Most agents take careful notes and are often expected to write reports for other agents in their office when they return. In addition to all of these methods, there are numerous trade shows in the industry such as those run by ASTA at their world congresses, and the traveling Henry Davis shows, where many travel suppliers put up booths and distribute literature about their hotels and destinations. Also, airlines, tour operators, and destinations frequently hold in-depth training seminars for agents.

There is a formal certification program for travel agents as well, run by the Institute of Certified Travel Agents. Agents who complete this five-year study program earn the designation of CTC (Certified Travel Counselor), considered the most prestigious in the industry.[18]

# Earn 15% Commission

**Book Alamo now!** Rentals of five days or more on any compact car or above anywhere in the United States, Canada, and Europe. Good for rentals picked up and completed between now and Dec 15, 1996.

*Chevy Cavalier*

Simply request **Rate Code RE**, when booking weekly rentals on a compact car or above between now and Dec 15, 1996, and earn **15% commission**.

For reservations, use your GDS, access us at http://www.goalamo.com or call

## 1-800-4-AGENTS.

**Alamo**

*Alamo features fine General Motors cars like this Chevy Cavalier.*

**Travel agents are paid commissions from travel suppliers. The standard commission is 10 percent, although commissions can be higher or lower.**
(Courtesy of Alamo Rent-A-Car, Inc.)

## How Travel Agents Are Paid

Many travel agents advertise that "our services are free." This is not exactly correct. While services are generally free to consumers, agents are paid a commission, as noted earlier, from all major travel suppliers. In some cases, consumer activists have noted that this may cause a conflict of interest for travel agents. Commissions may influence the agent's advice, which is supposed to be impartial. To compound this problem, in recent years many agencies have banded together into "consortiums"—groups of agencies that use their combined strength to negotiate lower rates for their clients and higher commissions for their agencies. Two such associations are Worldwide Travel Trust and Hickory. One result of this is that sometimes agencies may be tempted to suggest airlines, hotel chains, or cruise lines that are not the best choice for their clients, but with whom they have negotiated higher commissions. Good agents adamantly refute any charge that they might be tempted to do this. They say their first interest must be their client, or else they will not get any repeat business. Nevertheless, many consortiums have "preferred suppliers" and instruct their agents to offer the products of these suppliers before any others, simply because they are more profitable to sell.

In recent years, as airline commissions have been reduced, many agencies have imposed some transaction fees on airline tickets. These fees are sometimes waived for good customers.

## Chapter Summary

There is a real difference between selling and marketing. Selling is getting rid of what you have; marketing is having what customers want. The marketing concept can be defined as the effort to determine and meet the needs and wants of current and potential customers.

The Four Ps of marketing are: product, place, price, and promotion. The concept of a restaurant or hotel is first and foremost a marketing decision. To make it correctly requires a clear understanding of what consumers are looking for and what competitors already offer them to satisfy their needs. People almost never buy a product—they buy the utility they expect to receive from a product.

"Place" refers to the physical location of a property. It also refers to the place where a sale of a guestroom is made, which can be over the telephone or at a travel agency.

There are four methods of pricing commonly used in the hospitality industry. These are cost-plus pricing, competitive pricing, market-demand pricing, and customer pricing.

Promotion decisions are made after the other marketing Ps are established. Promotion consists of all of the ways a business uses to persuade consumers to buy its products and services. All promotional activities fall into one of six categories: personal selling, advertising, public relations and sponsorship marketing, sales promotion, direct marketing communications, and point-of-purchase communications.

To properly allocate marketing resources, a company should begin with a marketing plan. A good marketing plan consists of several parts: situation analysis, objectives, strategies, tactics (or action plans), and controls.

Hotel sales department personnel are often assigned to specific types of travelers or given specific regions. The sales manager is in charge of sales efforts. He or she is expected to increase property revenues through sales calls, establish guidelines for selling, assist the general manager with obtaining maximum sales efforts from all employees, hold weekly and monthly sales meetings, maintain sales reports, and establish a sales filing system.

Successful salespersons have certain characteristics in common. The main ones are an ability to understand how people think and an ability to relate to them.

To do this, it helps to understand and be able to recognize four basic personality types: Amiables, Expressives, Drivers, and Analyticals. Effective salespersons learn to recognize each personality type and interact with prospects in the way that makes them most comfortable.

Salespersons need certain basic qualities in order to succeed. These are courtesy, deportment, a neat and conservative appearance, knowledge of product or service, willingness to work, and personality.

A sales call consists of six steps: (1) prospecting and qualifying, (2) preparation, (3) presentation, (4) overcoming objections, (5) asking for the sale, and (6) follow-up.

Travel agencies help hospitality businesses such as hotels and cruise companies in their sales efforts. Modern travel agencies act as representatives of airlines, hotels, car rental firms, and wholesale tour operators. There are several types of agencies: full-service agencies, commercial agencies, in-plant agencies, group and incentive agencies, direct-response agencies, tour operators, cruise-only agencies, consolidators, and travel clubs.

Travel agencies use airline reservation computer systems to book airline tickets, hotel rooms, and car rentals. Agencies also obtain information on hotels through hotel representatives and directories.

Travel agents obtain training in several ways: by attending special schools, through trade association programs, and by taking familiarization (fam) tours. They also attend trade shows and may participate in a certification program.

Agents are paid on a commission basis by the travel businesses they represent.

## Endnotes

1. Theodore Levitt, *The Marketing Imagination* (New York: Macmillan, 1983), pp. xii–xiii.
2. Robert C. Lewis and Richard E. Chambers, *Marketing Leadership in Hospitality* (New York: Van Nostrand Reinhold, 1989), p. 354.
3. William J. Quain, "Analyzing Sales-Mix Profitability," *Cornell H.R.A. Quarterly*, April 1992, pp. 56–62.
4. Quain, p. 58.
5. Christopher W. Nordling and Sharon K. Wheeler, "Building a Market-Segment Accounting Model to Improve Profits," *Cornell H.R.A. Quarterly*, June 1992, pp. 29–36.
6. Nordling and Wheeler, p. 30.
7. James R. Abbey, *Hospitality Sales and Advertising*, 2d ed. (East Lansing, Mich.: Educational Institute of the American Hotel & Motel Association, 1993), p. 79.
8. Philip Kotler and Gary Armstrong, *Marketing: An Introduction*, 2d ed. (Englewood Cliffs, N.J.: Prentice-Hall, 1990), p. 444.
9. Derek Taylor, *Sales Management for Hotels* (New York: Van Nostrand Reinhold, 1987), p. 23.
10. These sections on personality styles were adapted from Anthony J. Alessandra and Phillip S. Wexler, *Non-Manipulative Selling* (Englewood Cliffs, N.J.: Prentice-Hall, 1979), pp. 13–41.
11. C. Dewitt Coffman, *Marketing for a Full House* (Ithaca, N.Y.: School of Hotel Administration, Cornell University, 1984), p. 183.
12. Scott Bistayi, "Image," *Forbes*, 16 June 1997, p. 22.

13. Coffman, p. 183.

14. Vincent L. Zirpoli, "You Can't Control the Prospect, So Manage the Presale Activities to Increase Performance," *Marketing News,* 16 March 1984, p. 1.

15. Taylor, p. 25.

16. *Travel Weekly*—Annual Travel Agency Survey, 1996.

17. Eric Friedheim, "Agents Continue Hunt to Capture Elusive Hotel Commissions," *Travel Agent,* 30 April 1990, p. 96.

18. For more information on the Certified Travel Counselor certification program, write to the Institute of Certified Travel Agents, 148 Linden Street, P.O. Box 812059, Wellesley, Massachusetts 02181-0012.

## Key Terms

**back of the house**—The areas of a hotel or restaurant in which personnel have little or no direct guest contact, such as kitchen areas and the accounting department.

**commercial agency**—A travel agency that specializes in commercial business and usually has little or no walk–in clientele.

**competitive pricing**—Basing prices on what competitors charge.

**consolidator**—A travel agency that has negotiated special arrangements with certain airlines that allow it larger commissions on certain routes and flights, or that simply has been able to obtain more favorable fares or larger commissions based on unsold seats or other marketing considerations.

**consumer-based pricing**—Pricing based on what consumers are willing to pay.

**cost-plus pricing**—Determining a price by taking the total cost of providing a product or service and adding to it (1) a percentage to cover overhead or fixed expenses, and (2) a predetermined gross profit margin.

**cruise-only agency**—A travel agency that sells only cruises.

**direct-response agency**—A travel agency that markets its products exclusively through the mail, usually to senior citizens.

**elasticity of demand**—A measure of customer responsiveness to changes in price.

**escorted tour**—A group of travelers traveling with an experienced guide who has set up an itinerary for the group.

**foreign independent tour (FIT)**—A tour created for individuals or families who walk into a travel agency and tell an agent what country or area they would like to visit and what they would like to see and do there. Also called an independent tour.

**four Ps of marketing**—The four basic marketing responsibilities: product, place, price, and promotion.

**front of the house**—The areas of a hotel or restaurant in which employees have extensive guest contact, such as the front desk (in hotels) and the dining room(s).

**full-service agency**—A travel agency that handles all types of travel for consumers.

**group and incentive agency**—A travel agency that specializes in creating customized travel programs for groups and corporations.

**independent tour**—A tour created for individuals or families who walk into a travel agency and tell an agent what country or area they would like to visit and what they would like to see and do there. Also called a foreign independent tour (FIT).

**in-plant agency**—A branch office of a travel agency typically located in the offices of large corporations.

**integrated marketing communications**—A marketing model in which all marketing activities are coordinated, ensuring that all corporate messages are consistent and directed at achieving the organization's overall mission.

**loss-leaders**—Items sold at or below cost in order to attract customers to a business, where they may buy other items that are profitable.

**marketing**—(1) A system of interacting activities formulated to help managers plan, price, promote, and make available services or products to potential customers or guests in a particular target market. (2) The effort to determine and meet the needs and wants of present and potential customers. Marketing includes sales and a great deal more.

**marketing mix**—The mixture of marketing activities a business engages in.

**package tour**—Similar to an independent tour, in that travelers who buy a package tour travel by themselves rather than with a large group, but the travelers do not put their own tour together—they buy a tour that has been planned by a tour packager or operator.

**promotion**—All the ways a business uses to persuade people to buy its products and services.

**satellite ticket printer (STP)**—A travel agency's ticket printer located in a client's office.

**tour operator**—A business that puts together travel tours and sells them directly to individuals or through travel agencies.

**travel club**—A travel agency that charges an annual fee to its members and in return offers packaged vacations to members at reduced prices.

**yield management**—A hotel pricing system adapted from the airlines that uses a hotel's computer reservation system to track advance bookings and then lower or raise prices accordingly—on a day-to-day basis—to yield the maximum revenue. Before selling a room in advance, the hotel forecasts the probability of being able to sell the room to other market segments that are willing to pay higher rates.

# Review Questions

1. What is the difference between marketing and selling?
2. What are the Four Ps of marketing?
3. Which four methods of pricing are commonly used in the hospitality industry? How do they differ from one another?

4. Promotional activities fall into which four areas?
5. What are the differences between marketing objectives, strategies, and tactics?
6. How do the four personality types proposed by sales consultant Tony Alessandra differ from one other?
7. What basic qualities should a good salesperson possess?
8. A sales call consists of what six steps?
9. What are the four most common types of travel agencies?
10. Why do many hotels and travel agencies have strained business relationships?

## Internet Sites

For more information, visit the following Internet sites. Remember that Internet addresses can change without notice. If the site is no longer there, use a browser to look for additional sites.

### Computer Reservation Systems (CRS)

Abacus
www.abacus.com.sg

The SABRE Group
www.sabre.com

Aerotech Systems, Inc.
www.multires.com

WORLDSPAN
www.worldspan.com

Apollo Products
www.apollo.com

### Hotel Companies/Resorts

Hilton Hotels
www.hilton.com

La Quinta Hotels
www.laquinta.com

Holiday Inn Worldwide
www.holidy-inn.com

### Organizations, Resources

Cruise Lines International Association
www.cruising.org

Microsoft Expedia
www.expedia.msn.com

Easy SABRE Travel Planner
www.easysabre.com

Traveler.net
www.traveler.net

Institute of Certified Travel Agents
www.icta.com

Travelocity
www.travelocity.com

Internet Travel Network
www.itn.com

*Marketing and Selling Hospitality* **472-a**

# REVIEW QUIZ

When you feel you have covered all of the material in this chapter, answer these questions. Choose the *best* answer.

1. How businesses allocate their resources among product, place, price, and promotional efforts depends on the:

    a. amount of profit needed.
    b. quality of the product.
    c. skills of the sales force.
    d. objectives of each business.

2. Managers can raise or lower consumer demand through various strategies if demand for a product or service is:

    a. static.
    b. elastic.
    c. dynamic.
    d. inelastic.

3. Individuals who consider personal relationships of utmost importance, are interested in buying from people with whom they have a personal relationship, and tend to be indirect and slow-paced are called:

    a. Amiables.
    b. Expressives.
    c. Drivers.
    d. Analyticals.

4. To be a good salesperson, an individual must:

    a. have an outgoing personality.
    b. be courteous and friendly and be a good listener.
    c. not be shy.
    d. be lively and playful.

5. Which of the following statements about making a sales call is *false*?

    a. Even experienced salespersons waste time calling on people who are not legitimate prospects.
    b. Successful sales presentations almost always include visual aids.
    c. When prospects raise an objection during a sales presentation, that usually signals that they are not interested in buying.
    d. An established principle of salesmanship is that the sale really begins once the order is signed—in other words, proper follow-up to the sale is crucial.

## REVIEW QUIZ *(continued)*

6. Which of the following statements about how travel agents are paid is *true*?
    a. The services of travel agents are free.
    b. Travel agents are paid commissions from travel suppliers.
    c. Individuals who ask travel agents to help them plan their travel pay the travel agents directly.
    d. None of the above.

7. "A group of tourists accompanied by a guide who has travel experience" describes a(n) _____ tour.
    a. package
    b. independent
    c. escorted
    d. consolidated

**Answer Key:** 1-d-C1, 2-b-C1, 3-a-C2, 4-b-C2, 5-c-C2, 6-b-C3, 7-c-C3

Each question is linked to a competency. Competencies are listed on the first page of the chapter. An answer reading 3-b-C4 translates to:

3: the question number
b: the correct answer
C4: the competency number

## Chapter 15 Outline

Advertising
    Definition of Advertising
    What an Advertiser Needs
    Advertising Agencies
    Creating Effective Advertising
Choosing Advertising Media
    Newspapers
    Magazines
    Radio
    Television
    Direct Marketing
Public Relations
Publicity
Sales Promotion
Chapter Summary

## Competencies

1. Define and describe advertising, including what an advertiser needs, advertising agencies, and how to create effective advertising.

2. Summarize factors involved in choosing advertising media; describe newspapers, magazines, radio, and television as advertising media; and explain direct marketing.

3. Explain the role and importance of public relations, publicity, and sales promotion for hospitality businesses.

# 15

# Managing Marketing Communications

> The codfish lays a thousand eggs
> The homely hen lays one
> But the codfish never cackles
> To show what she has done.
> And so we praise the homely hen
> The codfish we despise
> Which clearly shows to you and me
> It pays to advertise!
> Anonymous

THERE ARE FOUR basic components to the marketing mix: product, price, place, and promotion. Promotion can be further broken down into personal selling, advertising, public relations, publicity, and sales promotion. In this chapter we will cover advertising, public relations, publicity, and sales promotion.

All these forms of communication have one important difference from personal selling: they communicate with many people at the same time. Personal selling talks to one person at a time, making it the most effective form of sales. You can tailor your message to fit each prospect's needs, watch the prospect react to the message, and make any changes to the sales presentation that might be necessary. Unfortunately, every business has far more prospects than it has salespersons, and in most cases many of the prospects are unknown. Therefore it is necessary to find a way to broadcast your sales message to a wider audience—to talk to not one person at a time but to hundreds or thousands of them.

## Advertising

**Advertising** is a substitute for personal salesmanship. Through advertising, we attempt to talk to those prospects who, for one reason or another, will never get a personal sales call, as well as to prospects who never directly communicate with an advertiser. Advertising also has some unique advantages over personal selling. For instance, advertising can get into offices and homes where a salesperson can't. Many companies use advertising for exactly that reason—to get a "salesperson" past a closed door.

Another advantage of advertising is that it can be repetitive. Once we've seen a salesperson and heard his or her pitch, we are not likely to listen to the pitch again, but print and broadcast ads can reach us many times. This is an important feature, for many people need repeated exposures to sales messages before they understand and remember them.

Advertising can, and often does, increase the value of products and services in the customer's eyes. It does this in several ways; one way is by inspiring consumer confidence. Consumer confidence in a product or service can take a number of forms. A customer wants the security of knowing that he or she is not wasting money; a brand name—made familiar through advertising—can provide that through the assurance of consistent quality. A plain two-story building doesn't stand for much until we put two words on it—Holiday Inn. Now, even though you don't know exactly what the inside looks like, you know that you'll get a clean room, reliable service, and well-thought-out amenities at a reasonable price. Other hotel brand names such as Four Seasons, Hyatt, Sheraton, Hilton, and Marriott all assure travelers that they are going to get whatever quality or value they have been promised. These companies understand that they risk everything if too many guests are disappointed, so they are careful to provide consistent products and services, and truthfully advertise them.

Another form of confidence is developed when a product is advertised in a way that boosts the consumer's self-esteem, telling a person that using the product will make him or her feel more successful, more important, or more self-confident. Travelers who stay at hotels like the Regent in Hong Kong, the Ritz-Carlton in Boston, Lé Bristol in Paris, and the Cipriani in Venice know that they are paying for the best that money can buy. When businesspeople stay in a hotel that has achieved the reputation of being for top executives, it makes them feel successful and it signals their status to associates in that city. Advertising can let large groups of people know what status a hotel or restaurant has earned.

What advertising adds to the value of a product is known as **added-value.** The American Association of Advertising Agencies cites Dr. Thomas S. Wuster, vice president of the Boston Consulting Group:

> Chickens, water, and payment systems are all considered commodities. But Perdue has used advertising and quality controls to change chicken from a commodity into a product with distinct features; Perrier has used attractive packaging and advertising to make water into a drink of choice; American Express has continued to upgrade its brand value added through its gold- and platinum-card introductions. In each case a company has added something of value to consumers.[1]

Many hotel and restaurant managers say that, while stressing the value of what they offer is an interesting concept, they get better results by featuring low prices in their advertising. Wuster thinks otherwise:

> Many believe that advantage based on lower costs is more real and lasting than advantage based on higher price realization and "elusive" concepts of superior consumer value. In fact, however, our experience and research suggest that the opposite is true: Value-based advantage is even more enduring than cost-based advertising.[2]

The bottom line, according to the Boston Consulting Group, is that "loyalty is a longer-lasting competitive barrier than low cost," and that companies that use advertising to make their name stand for quality will be able to hold on to their customers longer than those who compete by lowering their prices. Someone can always offer a lower price or a newer hotel, but a name that stands for superior value or service will outlast them.

To illustrate this, the Boston Consulting Group pointed out that in 19 of 22 consumer categories, the leading brand in 1925 was still the leader 60 years later. For instance, in 1925 Kellogg was the leading cereal brand, and it still is. Gillette razors, Hershey's chocolate, Wrigley chewing gum, Nabisco crackers, Ivory soap, Campbell's soup, Coca-Cola soft drinks, and Colgate toothpaste are other examples of leading brands that have held on to their position by competing on the basis of quality and value rather than price.

Although the Boston Consulting Group did not study hotels and restaurants, the same inferences for the most part can easily be drawn. The Plaza Hotel in New York City, the Greenbriar in White Sulphur Springs, West Virginia, and The Ritz-Carlton Laguna Niguel in California are hotels that have never competed on the basis of price. Nor have such famous restaurants as Le Cirque in New York, Joe's Stone Crab in Miami, or the Tour D'Argent in Paris. These establishments have transformed themselves into institutions that cannot be displaced by newer or more trendy offerings.

Research shows that advertising is crucial for consumer products of all kinds. A study by the Strategic Planning Institute indicates that brands that advertise much more than their competitors average a return on investment (ROI) of 32 percent, while brands that advertise much less than their competitors average only 17 percent ROI. According to the Institute, "relative advertising influences relative perceived quality, market share, and relative price. These in turn influence profitability and growth."[3]

The need for hospitality managers to understand the role of advertising is underscored by the significant amounts of money invested in advertising by hospitality enterprises. For example, in 1996 McDonald's spent $1,074,600,000 on advertising, making it the twelfth largest advertiser in America. The Marriott Corporation spent $148,300,000, but this was spread over all of their hotel brands and restaurant operations so that no single brand ranked among the top advertisers.[4]

No discussion of the role of advertising would be complete without mentioning the social concerns that are sometimes raised when advertising is discussed. Critics frequently charge that advertising makes people buy things they do not need and cannot afford. This is not true. Consumers' wants and needs are determined by society, not by advertising. Most advertisers have learned through experience that it is very difficult to change consumers' buying behavior. Usually, therefore, advertising is used to get them to choose between competing brands in a category in which they have already decided to buy something.

Critics also say that advertising is sometimes tasteless, it reinforces undesirable stereotypes, it exerts an unhealthy effect on social values, and it influences the character of the media. It would be naive to say that advertising is not guilty of these charges some of the time. However, most economists believe that advertising is, on the whole, a good thing for society because it supports a highly diverse media structure at a low cost to consumers. For example, usually only one-third of the cost of publishing a newspaper is paid for by its subscribers. The rest is covered by advertising. In the United States, commercial television programs are free to the public and paid for entirely by advertisers. In countries where advertising is restricted, television programs are subsidized by the government, which collects taxes from the public to pay for them.

## Definition of Advertising

According to Professors Charles H. Patti of the University of Denver and Charles F. Frazer of the University of Colorado at Boulder, advertising has a number of characteristics that distinguish it from other forms of communication. Some of these are:

- *It is paid for by the sponsor rather than run at the discretion of the medium.* This distinguishes advertising from publicity—publicity is not paid for and is run at the discretion of the medium.
- *It is impersonal.* Advertising is disseminated to a mass audience. This distinguishes it from personal selling.
- *It identifies the sponsor of the message.* Advertising is distinguished from propaganda in that the source of the message is identified within the message itself.
- *It is persuasive.* Advertising is rarely designed to tell all sides of the story about a product or service; it is not designed to be objective information. Advertising is a tool organizations use to persuade people to accept products, services, or ideas.[5]

In short, Patti and Frazer define advertising as "planned communication activity in which messages in mass media are used to persuade audiences to adopt goods, services, or ideas."[6]

Many people say, "I depend on word-of-mouth advertising to promote my business." These people do not understand what advertising is. Word-of-mouth is not a message a sponsor pays to place in mass media, it is not planned, nor does it necessarily persuade. It does help promote a business and thus is a legitimate form of marketing communications, but it is not advertising.

## What an Advertiser Needs

Advertising does not work equally well for all products and services under all conditions. To produce an effective advertising campaign, an advertiser needs:

- A competitive advantage
- Unique positioning
- A segmented market

**Competitive Advantage.** One of the key factors for advertising success is product differentiation—in other words, there must be a clear difference between what you sell and what your competitors offer. Produce wholesalers, for instance, do not need to advertise their lettuce or tomatoes to restaurants because most wholesalers sell similar grades and quality of produce. But if one wholesaler has a demonstrable difference, such as guaranteed fast delivery or lower prices, that is another matter. Advertising works best when a business has a demonstrable competitive advantage that it wants to communicate to consumers. This advantage might be superior service, lower prices, or higher quality.

The advantage must not only be demonstrable—that is, one that can be seen or experienced—it must be one that satisfies an important consumer need. For example, Hyatt Hotels, in promoting its weekend getaway packages in major cities, offered an 8 P.M. check-out on Sundays instead of the industry's usual 12 noon check-out time. This was an important difference to guests, because the 8 P.M. check-out allowed them to spend Sunday afternoon at the beach or pool and even have dinner at the hotel before checking out. Another important competitive advantage in the hotel business can be location and price. The Doral Inn in Manhattan ran an effective ad with the headline, "What Separates The Doral Inn From The Waldorf Astoria? Forty Feet And About $100" (see Exhibit 1).

Too often, advertisers ignore the principle of featuring an important difference and instead advertise features that consumers don't care about. One survey of the nation's most frequent travelers found that large numbers of travelers don't care much about in-room bars, computerized travel directions, or other new gimmicks. What they really want are simple pleasures—quiet hotel rooms, clean rental cars, comfortable airline seats. Having newspapers delivered to rooms, which many hotels don't bother with, appeals far more to travelers than a health club.

Sometimes a business may have an important feature that competitors have as well, but if no one has advertised it, the first business that does can gain an advantage. In an airfare war, all airlines may cut their prices to the same level, but the one that advertises the fare reduction first usually gets the lion's share of the business. Almost 80 percent of hotels offer a "kids-stay-free" plan, but many don't advertise it. The ones that do are more likely to get family business.

**Unique Positioning.** Another factor that contributes to effective advertising is **positioning.** This theory, first articulated by two advertising agency owners, Al Reis and Jack Trout, asserts that because of the number of products available in the marketplace today and the amount of "clutter" or marketing noise caused by the large number of messages we are exposed to every day, most people do not remember (nor are they interested in remembering) what advertisers have to say. In short, advertising messages do not "get through" into the consumer's mind. Companies that aspire to offer everything in their advertising messages in reality don't offer anything of value or importance because people don't remember what they are saying. The secret, according to Trout and Reis, is to get inside the prospect's mind. "You concentrate on the perceptions of the prospect. Not on the reality of the product."[7]

According to Trout and Reis, an advertiser gets into our minds by linking its message to information we already know, not by getting us to remember new information. For example, in the classic case of Avis car rentals, Avis succeeded by telling consumers that "We Try Harder." At the time they ran this campaign, Hertz was the number-one car rental company and no one had even heard of Avis. By associating themselves with this fact (without even mentioning the name of their competitor) they were able to quickly establish a "position" in their prospects' minds that was unique and compelling. To help position itself in prospects' minds

**480** Chapter 15

**Exhibit 1    Advertisement Emphasizing a Competitive Advantage**

### WHAT SEPARATES THE DORAL INN FROM THE WALDORF ASTORIA?

### FORTY FEET AND ABOUT $100.

Come enjoy a Waldorf location at the Doral Inn EXCL Executive Club. For as little as $138 per night, per room, take the elevator directly to our private sixth floor welcoming lounge. And enjoy complimentary continental breakfast and evening hors d'oeuvres. An exclusive executive lounge for cocktails and relaxing. Free use of personal computer and copier. An on-site fitness center with squash courts. And deluxe accommodations on two private floors. Reserve the EXCL Executive Club Level by calling 1-800-22-DORAL or (212) 755-1200. And discover Doral value in a Waldorf location.

**Doral Inn**
541 Lexington Avenue at 49th Street
New York, New York 10022

Doral Hotels & Resorts · Florida: Doral Ocean Beach Resort · Doral Resort and Country Club · Doral Saturnia International Spa Resort
New York: Doral Court · Doral Inn · Doral Park Avenue · Doral Tuscany · Doral Arrowwood · Colorado: Doral Telluride Resort and Spa

In this newspaper ad, the Doral Inn tells readers it has a great location—and doesn't charge guests as much for it as its nearby competitor. (Courtesy of Doral Inn, New York, New York)

as a resource for frequent business travelers, Westin Hotels & Resorts linked itself to the *Wall Street Journal* in a magazine ad (see Exhibit 2).

Of course, the name of your product can help position it. Few wanted to vacation at Hog Island in the Bahamas until the late Huntington Hartford bought it and changed its name to Paradise Island. That new position attracted a host of new

## Exhibit 2  Example of Positioning

### If The Wall Street Journal were a hotel, it would be a Westin.

A Westin is more than a luxury hotel, it's a business resource designed for frequent travelers like you. Every service we offer is geared to help you work as comfortably and efficiently on the road as you do back at the office. If there's a smarter way to get things done, you'll find it first at Westin. For reservations, call your travel consultant or (800) 228-3000.

*Westin's business amenities include computers, voice mail, full-sized desks, fax machines and express checkout.*

**WESTIN HOTELS & RESORTS**

MCI   Westin Hotels & Resorts use MCI Vnet,™ a virtual private network, for their internal communications.

**This ad for Westin Hotels & Resorts clearly positions Westin as a luxury hotel for frequent business travelers.** (Courtesy of Westin Hotels & Resorts)

resorts and visitors. Pictures can create a position as well. Bermuda's advertising has shown pink beaches, mopeds, horse-and-buggies, and British traffic bobbies in its advertising for the past 20 years. Hawaii is known for its tropical foliage, which it features in almost all of its ads.

Here are some other positions of hospitality and travel businesses that you may be familiar with:

- McDonald's—Have You Had Your Break Today?
- Hyatt Hotels & Resorts—We've Thought of Everything

- Renaissance Hotels and Resorts—Relax. You're at a Renaissance.
- Motel 6—We'll Leave the Light On for You
- Courtyard by Marriott—The Hotel Designed by Business Travelers
- Carnival Cruise Lines—The Fun Ships
- Princess Cruise Lines—The Love Boats
- British Airways—The World's Favourite Airline
- Delta Air Lines—On Top of the World

Advertising slogans sometimes reflect positioning, but not always. Slogans may only be catchy phrases that have nothing to do with a company's positioning strategy.

**Segmented Market.** This brings us to the third factor that boosts advertising's effectiveness: a segmented market. **Market segmentation** refers to a company's ability to identify different segments of its market and separately promote its products and services to these segments. This is also called target marketing. Companies that practice **target marketing** make different products for each market segment and then create different advertising campaigns.

The Marriott Corporation practices market segmentation very thoroughly. Marriott's Fairfield Inns aim for the economy segment of the market—that group of consumers who buy based on price and look for a room for under $50 a night. Courtyard by Marriott is aimed at business travelers willing to pay for mid-price rooms. Residence Inn, which offers mini-suites with cooking facilities, is targeted at business travelers who must spend an extended period of time in one location. Marriott Suites are full-service properties for travelers who want a larger-than average guestroom. Then there are traditional Marriott Hotels and Resorts, targeted at the upscale segment of the market.

Marriott has different names and different advertising campaigns for each of these products. Instead of viewing their market as just "people who go to hotels," they have segmented their market into smaller groups that they can identify, designed products with features that appeal to those groups, and then communicated those different features.

Almost all hotels practice some form of market segmentation. City hotels seek to appeal to traveling businesspersons on weekdays and tourists on weekends. Hotels in Bermuda advertise water sports to families in the summer months, but offer golf and tennis packages in the winter when it is too chilly to go swimming. Resorts may go after affluent consumers at the height of their season, then try to attract other groups by advertising lower prices in the off-season.

Price is only one way to segment customers. American Express segments its travel agency customers into different groups according to how they react to different travel products. With help from the Gallup organization, American Express identified five basic travel customer types:

- *Indulgers* are wealthy and confident people willing to pay for their comfort. They like to be pampered. These people prefer cruises and resorts that feature health spa programs. Twenty-seven percent of American travelers are Indulgers.

**Marriott designed Residence Inn properties to appeal to business travelers on extended stays.** (Courtesy of Marriott Hotels and Resorts)

- *Dreamers* read and talk a great deal about travel but lack confidence in their travel skills. They like to go to places recommended in guide books and tend to buy tried-and-true travel packages. Dreamers represent 24 percent of the market.

- *Economizers* see travel as an outlet for stress and a chance to relax. They scrimp on services and amenities even when they can afford them. Economizers are interested in price and value.

- *Adventurers* are young, confident, and independent. They prefer new experiences, cultures, and people. Many are interested in trips to the South Pacific and the Orient. Forty-four percent of Adventurers are between 18 and 34 years old.

- *Worriers* are afraid to fly and have little confidence in their decision-making while on the road. Half of them are over 50. Worriers need well-traveled, experienced agents to help them choose a destination and tell them how to get there.[8]

By dividing their markets into small market groups, advertisers can tailor an advertising campaign to fit the wants and needs of each group and place ads in the media that appeal to each group. (More about this later in the section on media selection.)

## Advertising Agencies

The first decision hospitality business owners or managers encounter when putting together an advertising campaign is: Should they attempt to take care of their advertising themselves, or hire an advertising agency? Advertising agencies help clients create and place advertising. Agencies employ marketing strategists, artists, writers, production managers, and media selection experts. Agencies generally work on a commission basis of 15 percent, so that an advertiser who spends $100,000 on an ad campaign pays $15,000 for advertising agency services and $85,000 for space in the media where the advertising runs. Agencies bill their clients for the cost of media space or airtime and then—after receiving full payment from the client—are allowed by the media involved to deduct 15 percent from the client's payment before distributing the balance to the media. Sometimes agencies work for a fee when a 15 percent commission is not enough for the work involved, or, conversely, when the work the agency is expected to perform does not justify a 15 percent commission.

Many advertisers opt to handle their advertising themselves by hiring freelance writers and artists to design their advertising, and then negotiating with the media directly for space and time. For a small advertiser this can mean considerable savings, since agency retainers plus fees for writing and designing ads can sometimes be substantial. On the other hand, many advertisers have found that there can be a big difference between customer response to a good ad and a bad one, and argue that even small advertisers will get better results by using an agency instead of doing it themselves. While this may be true, there are some freelancers who can and do create outstanding ads (many freelancers are hired by ad agencies for certain projects), and therefore much depends on the nature of the advertising to be created, the freelancers available in an area, and the media to be used. Sometimes media prices are negotiable, and advertising agencies are in a better position to obtain the most favorable rates.

There are a wide variety of books and articles on how to choose an advertising agency, but one of the best ways is to simply take note of the advertising you like and then find out who did it by calling the advertiser or the media. Most agencies do not accept competing accounts unless they are located in different market areas.

## Creating Effective Advertising

Movies and television shows have created an oversimplified and glamorous impression of how advertising is produced. Typically, writers and artists are shown as becoming suddenly inspired with an idea for an ad campaign—almost as if a bolt of lightning has come down from above. The truth is far more mundane. Good campaigns are based on marketing plans, which in turn are based on thorough market research. Effective advertising is almost always the product of a rational, methodical process. Most ads reflect a position that has been carefully worked out in advance, and are written to appeal to a specific target market. The people who create the ads are not geniuses who pull great ideas out of thin air. There is no doubt that talent is involved, but it is a special kind of talent that includes sorting out and synthesizing facts. Indeed, it is not uncommon to find advertising copywriters with strong backgrounds in research. Most professional advertising copywriters thrive on research reports, profiles of target audiences, demographics, and psychographics.

Think of the inventor Thomas Edison. He did not sit in his laboratory with his feet on his desk until the idea for a light bulb popped into his head. The idea grew out of years of collecting information about the properties of electricity and conductors. So it is with good advertising.

**The Anatomy of a Print Ad.** Print advertisements consist of three basic elements: headline, body copy, and signature.

The **headline** is the heading or the title of the ad. It is similar to the headline of a newspaper story. The purpose of the headline is to draw readers' attention and get them to read the rest of the ad. Effective headlines often contain the main promise of the ad. Some advertisements contain a sub-headline that spells out the promise made in the headline.

The **body copy** is the main portion of an ad. This is text that usually contains an amplification of the promise or benefit offered in the headline.

Finally, ads usually contain **signatures** or logotypes. A "signature" is the name of the advertiser; a **logotype** or **"logo"** is "a unique trademark, name, symbol, signature, or device to identify a company or other organization."[9] McDonald's golden arches are an example of a logo; so is the unique type that Coca-Cola uses to spell its name.

There are few rules as to what works and what doesn't in advertising. Since advertising is an art and a craft as much as a science, advertisers are always trying new techniques for getting and holding consumers' attention and persuading them to buy. However, over the years many advertising studies have been done by independent research companies, advertisers, and agencies, which have led to some general guidelines that most advertisers follow.

**Print advertising guidelines.** Every ad should contain a promise. The promise can be stated or merely implied, but it is there, usually in the headline—the first thing most people read. Five times as many people read the ad's headline as read the body copy. That means that unless a headline sells, the advertiser has wasted most of its money.

Why does an ad need a promise? To attract readers. People won't remember an ad just because an advertiser wants them to, no matter how eloquently or clearly it is written. To be remembered, messages must include something that has personal meaning for readers. Consumers don't care about your hotel's features per se—they care about how those features can benefit them. Holiday Inn promises reasonable family prices in some ads (see Exhibit 3).

If you are advertising something that is only available to certain groups, it is a good idea to put something in the headline to flag them down. When Marriott advertises discounts available only to members of the American Association of Retired Persons (AARP), it usually puts a banner across the top of the ad that says "AARP Members Only."

There is conflicting evidence on how long a headline should be. While some studies show that headlines with less than ten words do better than longer ones, other studies show that people will read long headlines as well as long advertisements if

## Exhibit 3  Effective Advertising Highlights Specific Benefits

**Vacations are much more fun when you don't have to spend his college tuition.**

Holiday Inn SunSpree® Resorts put a great vacation within everybody's reach. Families and couples alike can swim, ski, golf, hike, bike or do just about anything else. All for less than they ever imagined. To learn more, call the Resort Desk at 1-800-HOLIDAY. See? Even the call saves you money.

*Holiday Inn SunSpree Resorts*
www.holiday-inn.com

**Call 1-800-HOLIDAY and ask for the Resort Desk or access HI in your GDS.**

**ARIZONA**
SCOTTSDALE—tennis, golf, volleyball, fishing, croquet
**FLORIDA**
CLEARWATER—golf, beach volleyball, shuffleboard, beach
DAYTONA BEACH—tennis, golf, beach, volleyball, racquetball, sailing
FORT MYERS—tennis, golf, water volleyball, basketball, beach
HOLLYWOOD—tennis, golf, shuffleboard, biking

JACKSONVILLE BEACH—tennis, golf, beach volleyball, snorkeling
KEY LARGO—deep-sea fishing, snorkeling, scuba
LAKE BUENA VISTA—tennis, golf, theme parks
PALM BEACH—beach, golf, kayaking, snorkeling, beach volleyball, biking
PANAMA CITY BEACH—beach, tennis, golf, beach volleyball, sailing

**MAINE**
BAR HARBOR—tennis, golf, croquet, beach, deep-sea fishing, horseback riding, sailing
**MINNESOTA**
ELY—tennis, golf, table tennis, paddleboats, lake, fishing, skiing, canoeing, hiking
**MONTANA**
WEST YELLOWSTONE—golf, hiking, fishing, rafting, cross-country skiing and snowmobiling
**NEW YORK**
LAKE PLACID—tennis, golf, skiing, fishing

**NORTH CAROLINA**
ASHEVILLE—tennis, basketball, volleyball, golf, rafting
**SOUTH CAROLINA**
MYRTLE BEACH—beach, golf, tennis, beach volleyball, badminton, snorkeling
**TENNESSEE**
GATLINBURG—ice skating, rafting, horseback riding, skiing, tennis, golf, fishing
**TEXAS**
CORPUS CHRISTI—tennis, golf, deep-sea fishing
SOUTH PADRE ISLAND—tennis, golf, volleyball, snorkeling, basketball, deep-sea fishing, horseback riding

**VIRGINIA**
VIRGINIA BEACH—tennis, golf, volleyball, badminton, horseshoes, bike rentals
**WISCONSIN**
OCONOMOWOC—golf, skiing, racquetball, tennis, fishing, volleyball
**CANADA**
OSOYOOS, BRITISH COLUMBIA—skiing, golf
WHISTLER, BRITISH COLUMBIA—tennis, golf, lake, mountains, skiing
**CARIBBEAN**
MONTEGO BAY, JAMAICA—tennis, golf, paddleboats, basketball, beach, kayaking

**MEXICO**
MAZATLAN—tennis, golf, beach, deep-sea fishing, volleyball, shuffleboard

**Opening Soon**

**FLORIDA**
ST. PETERSBURG—golf, tennis, sailing
**HAWAII**
KAUAI—tennis, golf, snorkeling, hiking, horseback riding
**OKLAHOMA**
AFTON—golf, tennis, sailing

Free sports activities are selected by the resort and may vary by location. Additional sports activities may be offered by independent operators at an additional charge. Some activities may be offered off-site. ©1997, Holiday Hospitality Corporation. All rights reserved. Most hotels are independently owned and/or operated.

(Courtesy of Holiday Inn Worldwide)

they are interested in what the advertiser is saying. David Ogilvy, who founded Ogilvy & Mather Advertising and went on to be elected to the Advertising Hall of Fame, wrote one of the most famous automobile ads of all time for Rolls-Royce. The 17-word headline—"At 60 miles an hour the loudest sound you can hear is the ticking of the clock"—was followed by 607 words of factual copy. Hilton Hotels uses a 14-word headline and long copy to explain the benefits for business travelers of staying in one of its airport hotels (see Exhibit 4).

Jim Johnston, chairman and co-founder of Jim Johnston Advertising, in an advertisement run by the *Wall Street Journal,* says this about headlines and advertising copy:

> Headlines *can* be visuals; words can stop readers. They can attract, intrigue, provoke—and pull the reader into the copy. But that's only the beginning. Copy is no task for tyros. It must work word for word, line for line. Effective copy is *simple* but not *simplistic;* intelligent but not obtuse; interesting but not frivolous. People *will* read long copy. They won't read dull, confusing copy, no matter how short.

In the body copy of the ad, advertisers should try to "make the sale"—that is, present the reasons why you should buy their product, stay at their hotel, or eat at their restaurant. The Regency Hotel in New York uses a headline to focus on its location: "As Preferred as Park Avenue." The body copy amplifies this promise: "Located in one of the world's most exclusive neighborhoods, it promises an enclave of quiet elegance. Here are superb accommodations, a restaurant, lounge, fitness center and select meeting facilities…and of course, uncompromising service."

The final part of an ad should contain a call to action. In most cases ads don't make sales—salespersons make sales. The purpose of most ads is to interest the reader and put him or her in touch with a salesperson. "Call this number for reservations," "See Your Travel Agent," or "Send For Our Free Brochure" are typical calls to action. Salespeople who don't ask for the sale aren't successful; neither are ads that don't include a call to action.

An ad should always contain the signature or name of the advertiser and the advertiser's logo (if it has one). Sometimes advertisers are reticent about making their name too large—as if they are ashamed of who they are. But if the signature is not large and clear, people could miss it entirely. Often the only thing people see in an ad is the headline, picture (if any), and signature. This is why some advertisers always try to put their name in the headline. Readership studies show that many ads succeed in attracting attention and getting readership, but fail entirely in getting prospects to remember what company placed it. The Hong Kong Tourist Association puts its name in the headline as well as in the bottom of its ads, where it invites readers to take action.

Finally, there is an old proverb, "One swallow doesn't make a spring." One advertisement doesn't make a campaign, either. A campaign consists of a number of advertisements that bear a family resemblance in both style and content but are different enough to attract new attention from readers who may have already read a previous advertisement. The advertising campaign for Bullard's restaurant in the Sheraton Needham Hotel in Massachusetts is a good example of an effective print campaign for a restaurant (see Exhibit 5). This award-winning campaign, created by

**Exhibit 4  Long Headlines Can Be Effective Advertising Tools**

## Why Is An Airport Hilton The Best Place To Land?

**Because We Mean Business.** Not only do we understand the needs of the business traveler, we cater to them. Like picking you up from the airport and checking you in quickly with Zip-In Check-In? And if you're hungry, you can always get something to eat at an Airport Hilton 24 hours a day. Plus, members of Hilton HHonors® Worldwide can earn both airline miles toward flights on 19 major airlines and HHonors points at more than 400 Hiltons in 50 countries worldwide. With reasons like these, it's no wonder business travelers are choosing an Airport Hilton as their final destination. You can make reservations online at www.hilton.com or by calling your professional travel agent or 1-800-HILTONS.

*Hilton*

(Courtesy of Hilton Hotels)

### Exhibit 5  An Award-Winning Restaurant Print Campaign

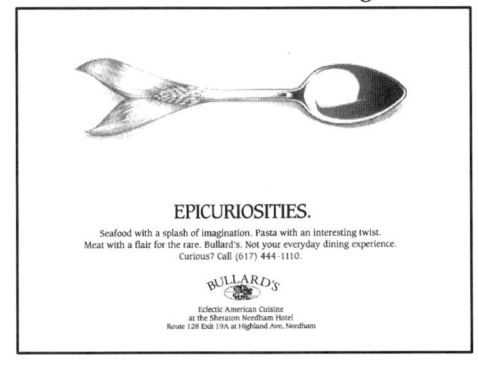

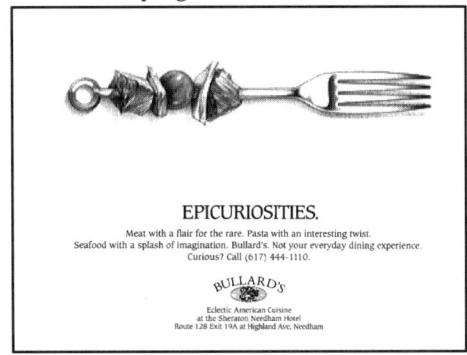

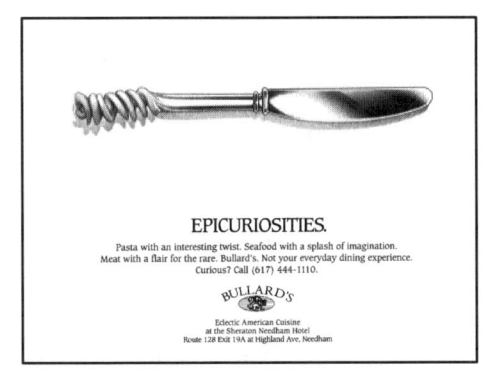

**EPICURIOSITIES.**
Seafood with a splash of imagination. Pasta with an interesting twist. Meat with a flair for the rare. Bullard's. Not your everyday dining experience. Curious? Call (617) 444-1110.

BULLARD'S
Eclectic American Cuisine
at the Sheraton Needham Hotel
Route 128 Exit 19A at Highland Ave, Needham

**EPICURIOSITIES.**
Meat with a flair for the rare. Pasta with an interesting twist. Seafood with a splash of imagination. Bullard's. Not your everyday dining experience. Curious? Call (617) 444-1110.

BULLARD'S
Eclectic American Cuisine
at the Sheraton Needham Hotel
Route 128 Exit 19A at Highland Ave, Needham

**EPICURIOSITIES.**
Pasta with an interesting twist. Seafood with a splash of imagination. Meat with a flair for the rare. Bullard's. Not your everyday dining experience. Curious? Call (617) 444-1110.

BULLARD'S
Eclectic American Cuisine
at the Sheraton Needham Hotel
Route 128 Exit 19A at Highland Ave, Needham

**This ad campaign won the Hospitality Sales and Marketing Association International's Adrian Gold Award.** (Courtesy of Bullard's, Sheraton Needham Hotel, Needham, Massachusetts; and Irma S. Mann, Strategic Marketing, Inc., Boston, Massachusetts)

the Boston advertising agency ISM, follows all of the guidelines discussed earlier. The ads all use the same layout and the same headline, "Epicuriosities." The illustration for each ad is different, however, and the copy focuses on different entrées. The headline arouses curiosity and there is an implied promise that the food at Bullard's is unique. The illustration supports that idea. The body copy is simple but further reinforces the single-minded message that Bullard's food is unique and imaginative. At the end, the ad asks for the order by suggesting the reader call the restaurant.

**Using Broadcast Media Effectively.** Unlike print media, in which a consumer chooses to read advertisements that are of interest, ads in broadcast media are intrusive. Listeners and viewers have tuned in to a program, and in the middle of that program they are interrupted by a commercial that they may not be interested in. Newspapers and magazines are primarily informational media, but radio and television are entertainment media. Commercials interrupt that entertainment. Therefore, broadcast advertisers often seek to entertain in order to make their messages more palatable.

One way to entertain consumers is through humor (see Exhibit 6). However, using humor requires great skill because commercials are surrounded by professional entertainment and amateurish commercials stick out like a sore thumb. Moreover, a

## Exhibit 6  Humorous Radio Ads

**SAWGRASS    Radio    :60**

*(office sounds in background)*

WOMAN #1: Stella, you notice anything weird about Mr. Hastings?
STELLA: Ahhh, you mean like wearing sunglasses in the office?
WOMAN #1: Well, ya.
STELLA: Mmmm, mmm.
WOMAN #1: And look at his feet.
STELLA: He's wearing golf shoes.
WOMAN #1 Right.
STELLA: Uh!
WOMAN #1: You know at the coffee area, he asked me if he could play through.
STELLA: Oh, well, listen, I caught him at his desk, hanging ten, yelling
BOTH WOMEN: Surf's up!
WOMAN #1: I know, I heard that.
STELLA: Mmmm, mmm.
WOMAN #1: Well, at least he's still wearing a tie.
STELLA: Ya, but with a tennis outfit?
ANNOUNCER: People all over Jacksonville are driving themselves to distraction. A beautiful distraction. Sawgrass. With our Commuter Vacation Package, you can go from desk to dunes in 30 minutes or less. Stay in the Sawgrass Resort Village, play golf, tennis or just relax on the beach after work and be back in the office the next day. Give your family a week or weekend at Sawgrass, complete with supervised programs for the children. Call 285-2261 and say you want to drive yourself to distraction. No one at work will know you're on vacation, unless you get carried away.

*(office sounds in background)*

WOMAN #1: Stella, what's he doing in the secretarial pool?
STELLA: I don't know. Looks like a half gainer.

*(springboard)*

STELLA: Stand back.

*(splash)*

**PIER 66    Radio    :60**

TOM: Boy, it's good to be home again. I wonder who called?
*SFX: (Click, rewind phone message machine)*
RAY: *(telephone voice, beep)* Tom. It's Ray. I'm going to spend the weekend at Pier 66. Meet me there. They've got this great Get Acquainted Summer Deal. Just 25 bucks a day if we share the room.
JONI: *(second message; SFX/Beep)* Tom, this is Joni, Sally's friend. Meet me at the Pier Top Lounge at Pier 66 Friday night. Bye.
RAY: *(third message; SFX/Beep)* Tom, Ray again. Sunday night. Where have you been?! You missed a great weekend at Pier 66. I met this terrific gal named Joni.
DON PARDO: *(SFX soap opera music)* Will Ray find out about Tom and Joni? Will Joni find out about Tom and Ray? Find out at Fort Lauderdale's Pier 66 Hotel and Marina, the 22-acre island resort on the Intracoastal. They'll be talking about it around the pool, on the courts, in the jacuzzis, at the restaurants and high above it all in the revolving Pier Top Lounge. Make your reservations now. Call 525-6666. So long for now from Pier 66.

Source: *The Art of Hotel & Travel Advertising: A Look at the Past—A Guide to the Future* (Washington, D.C.: Hotel Sales & Marketing Association International, 1987), pp. 53–54.

commercial needs "staying power" so listeners will enjoy hearing it or viewing it more than once, and unless it is well done they will tune out fast.

Some advertisers use a local broadcast personality in markets where the personality has a strong following. Local TV talk-show hosts or radio DJs often have a great deal of credibility with their listeners, especially when they endorse restaurants or other establishments that they personally patronize.

Music, too, can be effective in broadcast ads when it is correctly used. Music is not suitable for telling the whole message—commercials that are sung in their entirety are seldom remembered (with a few exceptions, such as the award-winning "I'd Like to Buy the World a Coke" TV commercial from the 1970s)—but music can enhance the ad's theme. McDonald's still uses the memorable music to its "You Deserve a Break Today" jingle although it has since changed its slogan. Super 8 Motels made an effective television commercial using the popular song, "Oh, What a Beautiful Morning," from Rodgers and Hammerstein's musical *Oklahoma* (see Exhibit 7). Targeted at business travelers, this commercial tries to evoke the feelings of tranquillity many business travelers seek on the road.

**What Works and What Doesn't.** *Fortune* magazine interviewed some of the top minds on Madison Avenue and their clients to get an idea of what kind of advertising appealed to consumers entering the 21st century. They found three cutting-edge strategies that can reach out and grab today's consumer:

- *Make 'em laugh.* Cliff Freeman, president of Cliff Freeman and Partners, whose firm is known for its comic "Pizza-Pizza" campaign for Little Caesar's Pizza, believes that humor and satire are the keys to many successful commercials. "The truth is, there is so little to say about a lot of products. So the marketing becomes about association, leaving people with a simple idea. And if you do humor well, people will love the brand."

- *Make 'em bond.* Many smart marketers now build campaigns around concepts that emphasize individual values. No advertisers, say top marketers, do this better than Coca Cola, which links its soda to some vague, worldwide social movement, and Nike, which emphasizes achievement and rebellion. By transforming their brands into icons, both Coke and Nike have blown away their competitors and shown others how to break out of the "ours is better and cheaper" box. Companies should constantly redefine their image in the marketplace to keep up with shifting consumer attitudes.

- *Find out what they really like.* Consumers are developing strong loyalties to certain media brands—from the Discovery Channel to ESPN to Howard Stern. By separating the media titles that draw strongly loyal fans from those that attract mostly casual viewers, an advertiser with a relatively small ad budget can reach more desirable customers. Loyal viewers of a typical TV show are 30 percent more likely than casual viewers to buy the products of the show's advertisers, according to research by DDB Needham Advertising.[10]

## Choosing Advertising Media

In planning an advertising campaign, once the message is decided on the next important decision an advertiser needs to make is where to run it. Should the advertising be

**492** *Chapter 15*

**Exhibit 7   Music Works**

"Businessman's Beautiful Morning" :30

MUSIC: LUSH ORCHESTRAL ARRANGEMENT OF "OH, WHAT A BEAUTIFUL MORNING".

ANNCR (VO): For those whose romance with the road is rekindled with each sunrise...

beautiful mornings begin at 8.

Super 8 Motels.

**Super 8 Motels' TV spot using "Oh, What a Beautiful Morning" is a good example of the effective use of music in television advertising.** (Courtesy of Super 8 Motels, Aberdeen, South Dakota)

| Winner Ads | Loser Ads |
|---|---|
| Commercials with humor | Hidden-camera testimonials |
| Commercials with children | Company CEOs |
| Product demonstrations | Commercials with celebrities |
| Real-life situations | Brand comparisons |
| Commercials with pets | Musical commercials |

The top results of an annual survey of the most popular television commercials in the country conducted by New York-based advertising research firm Video Storyboard Tests.

placed entirely in local newspapers? What about magazines? Radio? Television? Direct mail? There are many considerations in answering this basic question. One way to approach the problem is to consider whether what you are advertising is a planned purchase. If so, newspapers are probably the best medium. Because their very nature is informational, newspapers are good places for any advertising message whose real thrust is information. The consumer can study it, reread it, and even tear it out and carry it around. Airlines advertise new fares in newspapers; restaurants can print their menus and specials in a newspaper.

But what about an item that is not a planned purchase—one the consumer has to be motivated to buy? Or an image-building campaign to attract younger customers to a new restaurant? In these cases, the excitement and immediacy of broadcast media can make a real difference. An iceberg in Alaska's Glacier Bay, the colorful tropical fish at the Great Barrier Reef in Australia, and storybook castles in Europe all look much more enticing on television than they would in a black-and-white newspaper ad.

Ideally, an advertiser should use more than one medium to sell anything. There's a synergistic effect in advertising that has been proven time and time again: the use of any two media together is more powerful than the sum of the same media used independently.

Budget is also a powerful consideration when choosing media. The more people an advertiser attempts to reach, the less frequently it will be able to reach them. The campaign might end up selling to no one. The purpose of an advertising campaign is to persuade people to buy, and even 5 fully persuaded people who become customers are better than 500 half-persuaded people who buy nothing. Most advertisers cannot afford to advertise to everyone in every market. They invest their money in key markets in which they are already drawing customers, rather than advertising in new markets where they are unknown. And they run their campaigns long enough to have an impact. Here's what Thomas Smith, a British advertiser writing in the nineteenth century, had to say on the subject:

> The first time a man looks at an advertisement he does not see it.
> The second time he does not notice it.
> The third time he is conscious of its existence.
> The fourth time he faintly remembers having seen it before.
> The fifth time he reads it.
> The sixth time he turns up his nose at it.

The seventh time he reads it through and says, "Oh, bother."
The eighth time he says, "Here's that confounded thing again."
The ninth time he wonders if it amounts to anything.
The tenth time he thinks he will ask his neighbor if he has tried it.
The eleventh time he wonders how the advertiser makes it pay.
The twelfth time he thinks it may be worth something.
The thirteenth time he thinks it must be a good thing.
The fourteenth time he remembers he has wanted such a thing for a long time.
The fifteenth time he thinks he will buy it some day.

Mr. Smith may have overstated the case a bit, but the principle is as sound today as it was then: it takes more than 1 exposure to reach anyone via advertising. The available evidence indicates the average is probably around 3 exposures, and that by 6 exposures 80 to 90 percent of the target market is probably aware of our message. By the time we have reached 10 exposures we are probably at 99+ percent in most cases.

## Newspapers

Despite the growth of electronic media, newspapers remain America's largest advertising medium, representing over 23 percent of total advertising expenditures.[11] Fifty-nine percent of American adults read a daily newspaper weekdays. Seven out of ten adults also read a Sunday newspaper. The average newspaper reader spends 62 minutes reading the Sunday newspaper and 45 minutes reading one or more newspapers on a weekday.

Newspapers have many different rates for different kinds of advertisers and for different editions. Local advertisers generally pay lower rates for ad space than national advertisers. In addition, most metropolitan newspapers offer "zoned" editions that carry news and advertising of interest to a single suburb. This makes it possible for a suburban restaurant, for example, to buy advertising space targeted directly at people who live in the immediate area. Finally, newspapers offer different rates for different kinds of advertising. Classified advertising is the least expensive. Usually there are rates for travel agencies, movie theaters, hotels, and restaurants that are lower than the rates paid for the regular display advertising that department stores and other advertisers run.

Most newspaper space is sold on a **run-of-paper (ROP)** basis. This rate, which is the lowest, allows the paper to place the advertising anywhere it wants in the paper. For a higher price, advertisers can specify the section in which they want their ads to appear. Hotels and restaurants often use several different sections of a newspaper for maximum effectiveness. The entertainment section is used for restaurant advertisements. In some papers there is a special weekend section, which can be useful for restaurant ads, since readers who consult this section are looking for places to go and things to do. Meeting facilities are sometimes advertised in the business section. In December many hotels and restaurants advertise private rooms for office holiday parties.

Businesses that do a lot of newspaper advertising can buy ad space on a contract basis. For this, the advertiser agrees to buy a certain amount of space in a year and in return gets a volume discount, depending on how much space has been ordered.

## GRAND OCCASION

Birthdays are just life's way of reminding you to have dinner at The Renaissance.

**For Reservations Call**
**474-7474**

*The Renaissance*
LINCOLN'S PREMIERE DINING EXPERIENCE
333 South 13th Street • at The Cornhusker

No matter what the occasion, mention this ad when making reservations and receive a complimentary gift.

**This newspaper ad for The Renaissance restaurant seeks to position the restaurant as a place to celebrate a "Grand Occasion," such as a birthday.** (Courtesy of The Renaissance, Lincoln, Nebraska)

**Advantages.** Newspapers appeal to a large spectrum of people and thus have a broad audience. On the whole newspaper readers tend to be somewhat more affluent, better educated, and older than the general population. There is no difference in newspaper readership between the sexes, however—an equal number of men and women read newspapers. Most Americans who read newspapers also watch TV, listen to the radio, and read magazines. People who want to be informed use many sources.

One of the great advantages of newspapers is their sense of immediacy. Newspapers contain information about what happened yesterday, what is happening today, and what will happen tomorrow. While television reporting is mostly concerned with what has already happened, newspapers print the exact time and place where movies are playing tonight, what is going on sale in the next few days, and calendars of events for the upcoming weekend. This quality of immediacy makes newspapers especially good for the kind of advertising that calls for an immediate response—a Thanksgiving or Easter "getaway weekend" package at a hotel, for example, or a Mother's Day champagne brunch at a restaurant.

Newspapers also invite involvement. Consumers react to newspapers differently than they do to radio and television, where they are passive and information is thrown at them. Newspaper readers decide what they are going to read and how much time they are going to spend reading it. It is involvement that helps make newspapers powerful persuaders.

Newspapers offer other advantages that cannot be matched by other media. They are flexible. An ad can usually be placed just a day before publication—in some cases, less than a day before. That means the information in them is usually "hot."

Newspapers carry local news and are written for local audiences. That makes them ideal for local businesses to display their addresses and telephone numbers, and include maps showing their locations. Newspapers also carry coupons, many of which are unavailable elsewhere. Many shoppers value these coupons and plan their purchases to take advantage of them.

Newspaper advertising is also relatively inexpensive on a per-insertion basis, especially for local advertisers, who advertise consistently and thus earn a volume discount and get a lower rate than national advertisers.

**Disadvantages.** Newspapers also have some major disadvantages. They are the least selective of all media. Because they are a mosaic of information of interest to everyone, their circulation is composed of a broad spectrum of the population. Because newspaper rates are based on their total audience, advertisers pay to reach a lot of readers who are not prospects for their products.

Newspapers are printed on newsprint, which has poor reproduction qualities—especially when it comes to photographs. In addition, newspapers have a short readership "life," ranging from a day to less than an hour. As a well-worn cliché states, there is nothing as useless as yesterday's newspaper.

Finally, advertisers have limited control over where their advertising will appear in a newspaper, and what it will appear next to. A restaurant ad can appear next to a critic's review panning that same restaurant. Contrary to the belief held by those who think advertisers influence what appears in a newspaper, at large daily papers the editorial department and the advertising department have little or no contact, and editorial policy is rarely influenced by advertising considerations.

## Magazines

In the years before radio and television, magazines were the only national advertising medium. Unlike newspapers, which were local in scope, magazines allowed an advertiser to reach broad groups of people not only in the United States but internationally. Today magazines are still a major international advertising medium—*Readers Digest, Time,* and even *Ladies Home Journal* have international editions that go to every corner of the globe.

However, on the domestic front magazines can serve a different purpose for advertisers. Whereas newspapers carry information that is of interest to a broad spectrum of people, most magazines target their audiences very narrowly. In other words, within one newspaper we might find news items and features about travel, food, entertainment, and sports, but each of those subjects alone is the focus of a host of magazines. Would-be travelers can read *Travel & Leisure* and *Condé Nast Traveler.* Those interested in food can choose from *Gourmet, Food and Wine,* and others. There are magazines for stereo enthusiasts, sailors, apartment dwellers, single people, golfers, homemakers, beekeepers, soap opera fans, entrepreneurs, and dog breeders. Of course, some of these groups are larger than others. *TV Guide* has a circulation of 13 million people.

**Advantages.** The main advantage of magazines is their ability to advertise to only those people who are likely to be interested in and perhaps buy your product or service. Not everyone who reads *Travel & Leisure* travels; some are armchair travelers. But all *Travel & Leisure* readers are interested in travel, all are interested in the travel advertising that appears in that magazine, and a large percentage of the readers do take frequent trips. Some types of specialized magazines fare very well with lodging advertisers because their readers are prone to choose resorts that appeal to their special interests. Bob Stein—of Gardner, Stein, and Frank advertising in Chicago—puts it this way:

> The tennis player, reading a tennis magazine, is influenced in his choice of vacation resorts (he may, for example, choose to vacation at a certain hotel solely because an advertisement in the magazine focuses on the hotel's first-rate tennis courts)....The newly engaged young woman, in planning her wedding, consults bridal magazines that advertise honeymoon retreats (idyllic scenery, heart-shaped tubs, mirrored ceilings, 24-hour room service) that may also interest her. In short, hospitality marketers can expect a better response from readers who regularly turn to magazines for information on subjects in which they have a particular interest than they can from a mass-media audience.[12]

Another advantage of magazine advertising is that it is long-lasting. Television and radio messages are fleeting. If you don't catch them at the moment they are broadcast, you lose them until they come on again. Newspaper ads may last a day or so, then they are destroyed or recycled. But magazines stay around for weeks, even months, and continue to build an audience. Daniel Starch's 30-year study covering 12 million inquiries generated by magazine ads found that, for monthly magazines, 54 percent of all inquiries that an ad generates are likely to come in the first month after publication, 22 percent more come in the second month, and by the sixth month 94 percent of the expected return is in. In other words, a hotel that places a coupon ad in a January magazine issue offering a free brochure can still expect to receive some coupons as late as June. Because magazines have a long life they also have a lot of readers—about 3.6 adults read a single copy of the average magazine. For this reason, the measure of a magazine's readership or audience is as important as its circulation numbers.

Finally, magazines offer superb reproduction to advertisers (see Exhibit 8). Because they are printed on high-quality paper with sophisticated four-color presses, magazines can reproduce pictures with a clarity and brilliance unavailable in any

**498** *Chapter 15*

**Exhibit 8    A Targeted Magazine Ad**

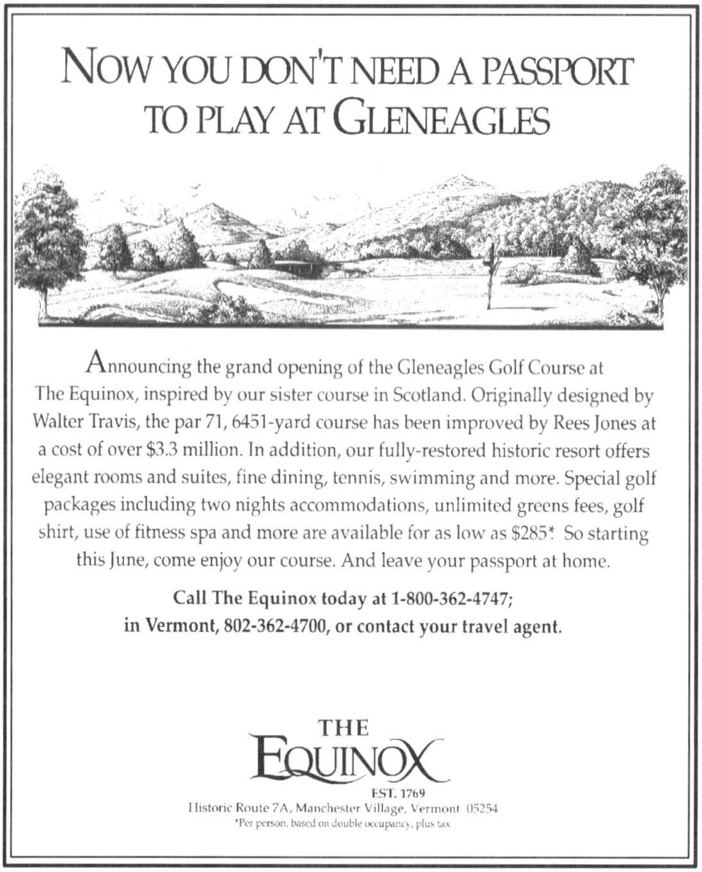

> # NOW YOU DON'T NEED A PASSPORT TO PLAY AT GLENEAGLES
>
> Announcing the grand opening of the Gleneagles Golf Course at The Equinox, inspired by our sister course in Scotland. Originally designed by Walter Travis, the par 71, 6451-yard course has been improved by Rees Jones at a cost of over $3.3 million. In addition, our fully-restored historic resort offers elegant rooms and suites, fine dining, tennis, swimming and more. Special golf packages including two nights accommodations, unlimited greens fees, golf shirt, use of fitness spa and more are available for as low as $285.* So starting this June, come enjoy our course. And leave your passport at home.
>
> Call The Equinox today at 1-800-362-4747;
> in Vermont, 802-362-4700, or contact your travel agent.
>
> **THE EQUINOX**
> EST. 1769
> Historic Route 7A, Manchester Village, Vermont 05254
> *Per person, based on double occupancy, plus tax

**The Equinox Resort targets golfers in this ad especially suitable for golf magazines.** (Courtesy of The Equinox, Manchester Village, Vermont, and The Gleneagles Group, A Guinness Company)

other media. Magazines like *Travel & Leisure* and *National Geographic* are as valued for their photographs as for their articles.

**Disadvantages.** In spite of their many advantages, magazines also have some serious disadvantages. For one thing, magazines have long **closing dates.** In other words, the date on which a magazine "closes"—when all advertising for the issue in question must be submitted—is usually two months or more in advance of the publication date. In addition, color advertisements often take many weeks to prepare, so that it is not unusual for an advertiser who wishes to run an ad in September to put it together in May. It is not possible to cancel an ad or change it after the closing date.

Another disadvantage of magazines is that their circulation, which is generally national in scope, often does not match the regions advertisers are most interested in. Some magazines have regional editions, but most don't. Because hotels have fixed locations, most of their business is not equally divided around the country but comes from a few areas. Resorts in Las Vegas get most of their business from California. It makes little sense for these resorts to advertise in a publication like *Gourmet*, for example, which carries a substantial amount of travel advertising but has many readers in New England and the South, areas that contribute relatively few tourists to Las Vegas.

Finally, magazines are an expensive advertising medium on an absolute dollar basis. The **cost per thousand (CPM)** readers is sometimes as much as ten times higher than for other media. This cost is often justified in that most magazines reach a specific audience.

**Trade Magazines.** Besides consumer magazines, there is a classification of magazines called trade or business publications in which companies advertise to each other. *Lodging* magazine, published by the American Hotel & Motel Association, and *Restaurants USA*, published by the National Restaurant Association, are two such publications. Magazines like these have controlled circulations; they go to members of these associations only. They are good advertising media for businesses that wish to sell products such as furniture and kitchen equipment to hotels and restaurants. *Hotel & Travel Index, Travel Weekly*, and *Travel Agent* are the principal magazines used by airlines, hotels, cruise lines, and destinations to reach travel agents. The trade advertising that appears in these magazines often differs from consumer advertising in that the advertising is more detailed and informational in nature. This is because a trade magazine's audience is interested in the products advertised—indeed, they often read a trade magazine to keep up with the latest products in their field.

## Radio

More than 99 percent of all homes in America have radios. In fact, the average home has 5.5 radios located all over the house—living room, bedrooms, kitchen. Moreover, 95 percent of all cars are equipped with radios and those radios are on 90 percent of the time the car is in use. The average adult American listens to radio 3 hours and 45 minutes every weekday.

Some groups of people listen to radio more than others. For example, 99.4 percent of young people ages 12-17 listen to the radio weekly. College students have an unusually high allegiance to radio. One study showed that radio for this group accounts for 49 percent of total time spent with radio, TV, newspapers, and magazines combined.

Hospitality enterprises use a large amount of radio because barter is common in both businesses. Unsold hotel rooms and unsold radio spots are perishable commodities. A spot on the six o'clock news that is not sold is worth nothing after 6:01 P.M. Since there are always some unsold spots—just as there are always some unsold hotel rooms—radio stations and hotels often enter into a barter arrangement in which the radio stations exchange airtime for rooms and meals at the hotels. The stations use these credits to entertain guests, hold station parties, or give away hotel products and services to listeners as prizes in contests. For the most part these arrangements are advantageous to both parties, and by using them hotels and restaurants can increase the size of their advertising budgets substantially.

The standard unit of radio-ad airtime is the 60-second commercial, generally referred to as a "spot." Most stations offer 30-second spots as well, but since 30-second spots are often priced at 80 percent of the cost of a 60-second spot, they are seldom used.

It is a good idea to use a professional advertising agency when buying radio time, because the cost of ad spots is highly negotiable. Stations have many package plans, bonus spots, and other complicated deals that make it difficult for an amateur to obtain the best prices.

**Advantages.** One of radio's unique characteristics is that it is a very personal medium. It speaks to one listener at a time and is a private form of communication that evokes different responses in each of us. Unlike media that supply a picture to go along with the words, radio gives us no visual clues at all. This can be an advantage, because radio asks us to use our imaginations, to add our own mental pictures to the words. Thus it is a more involving medium.

To demonstrate the power of radio to stir the imagination, comedian Stan Freberg created a radio commercial for the Radio Advertising Bureau. Here is part of it:

> Okay, people, now when I give the cue, I want the 700-foot mountain of whipped cream to roll into Lake Michigan, which has been drained and filled with hot chocolate. Then the Royal Canadian Air Force will fly overhead, towing a ten-ton maraschino cherry which will be dropped into the whipped cream, to the cheering of 25,000 extras.

Effective radio commercials invite people to create a picture in their mind's eye of what the announcer is saying.

Another advantage of radio is that it is highly selective. Because radio stations have different formats, they attract different types of audiences. According to Arbitron, a service that measures radio and television audiences, here are the formats currently in use at AM and FM radio stations:

- Contemporary Hit
- News/Talk
- Adult-Oriented Rock
- Easy Listening/Beautiful Music
- AM Adult Contemporary
- FM Adult Contemporary
- Country
- Urban Contemporary/Black
- Classical
- Nostalgia/Big Band
- Religious
- Spanish

Each of these formats attracts listeners with different demographics. For example, adult-oriented rock stations attract the largest number of adults in the 18–25 and the 25–34 age brackets. Only a small percentage of the listeners of news/talk stations fall in this age group; the largest groups of listeners to these stations are in the 35–49 and 50–64 age brackets. More teenagers listen to contemporary hit radio than any other format, and seniors constitute the bulk of listeners to nostalgia/big band stations.[13] A restaurant featuring fine dining with moderate to expensive prices would do best advertising on a classical or an AM adult

> One of the most successful campaigns using radio is Motel 6's "We'll leave the light on for you," created by the Richards Group in Dallas, Texas. This award-winning campaign features the distinctive voice of writer and radio personality Tom Bodett and a well-established musical theme. Using humor, it carries the idea of using your imagination to the extreme.
>
> **"Niagara Falls"**
>
> MUSIC: (SWEEPING ORCHESTRAL)
>
> TOM: Don your galoshes and travel with me now to the glorious rushing torrent that is...Niagara Falls. Its awesome power and grandeur make it one of North America's most spectacular natural wonders, attracting nearly ten million visitors every year.
>
> MUSIC: (MOTEL 6 THEME)
>
> Reminds me of the glorious spectacle that is Motel 6. The fact we're renovatin' nationwide has everbody flockin' to see us. And why not—after all, we do have guest laundry and data ports in most places. And as for rushing torrents of water, well, we're proud to say the plumbing works just fine. And best of all, the price won't leave you over a barrel—it's still the best of any national chain. For reservations, call 1-800-4-MOTEL-6, and we'll leave the light on for you.
>
> **"Temples of Nepal"**
>
> MUSIC: (MONKS CHANTING)
>
> TOM: Close your eyes. Breathe deeply. Project with me now as we travel to the remote corners of Asia. Land of the great Temples of Nepal. For the devout monks who inhabit these ancient shrines, all of life is a journey that leads to a higher plain of existence.
>
> MUSIC: (MOTEL 6 THEME)
>
> Kinda reminds me of Motel 6. We're on a journey to a higher plain, too. I mean, we're renovatin' nationwide. So while you enjoy our snappy new look, you can also expand your mind watching a free in-room movie. Then raise your level of consciousness with a free cup o' morning coffee. As for the answer to that greatest of questions, yes, Grasshopper, the price is still the best of any national chain. For reservations, call 1-800-4-MOTEL-6, and we'll leave the light on for you.

**A sample of Motel 6 radio advertising.** (Courtesy of Motel 6)

contemporary station. These stations attract large numbers of 35- to 49-year-old adults, the most frequent users of restaurants of this kind. On the other hand, restaurants such as T.G.I. Friday's and Bennigan's would get the most responses from adult-oriented rock and FM adult contemporary stations, which draw listeners in the 25–34 age group.

For restaurants, radio has the advantage of reaching a large part of their potential customers when they are literally in the market ready to buy. The highest radio listenership takes place during "drive time," when people are driving to and from work. It is the ideal time to suggest a good place to have breakfast this morning, lunch today, or dinner this evening.

**Disadvantages.** Despite these strong advantages, radio does have some disadvantages that make it less than an ideal medium. First of all, there are a huge number of AM and FM stations in almost every market. Because there are so many stations, listeners are fragmented into many groups, and if an advertiser wishes to reach a large segment of the population it must buy spots on many different stations.

Also, radio listenership at any given moment is small—an advertiser who wishes to reach all of a radio station's listeners has to buy many spots at different times on different days. Because people's habits vary, some of a radio station's listeners only hear it when they are driving; others hear it after school or after work. Some listen to a station while they are working, but never at home. The bottom line is that while the cost of an individual radio spot might be low, it requires a lot of spots on many radio stations for an advertiser to **"cume"**—that is, accumulate a large audience—and that can turn an inexpensive medium into an expensive one.

Moreover, radio signals cover a large area. When a local restaurant uses radio it must recognize that many of the people who listen are not legitimate prospects because they live too far away. Of course, for those restaurants that draw patrons from a large geographic area, this can be an advantage. Finally, if it is necessary to include telephone numbers or directions in an ad, radio is not the best medium, because most people will not remember them and it is often not convenient to write them down.

## Television

Television has become the most powerful and persuasive of all advertising media. In Japan, the most TV-oriented society in the world, the average time per day spent watching television is 9 hours and 12 minutes. The United States comes a close second with 7 hours of television viewed on the average in every American household. Citizens of other countries watch considerably less. In Canada, the average is only 3 hours, 24 minutes, while in Germany and France about 2 $1/4$ hours are average.[14]

**Advantages.** It is television's large reach and powerfully persuasive nature that make it so attractive to advertisers of all kinds. Television is the only medium that appeals to our eyes and ears at the same time. It allows an advertiser to show and demonstrate the product or service right in the prospect's living room. Moreover, most Americans believe television is more exciting, interesting, and entertaining than other media.

There is no doubt that well-done television sells. Television mirrors all of our hopes, fears, and values in its commercials and programming, and thus captures our attention. When relations between the United States and the former Soviet Union were at a low point, Wendy's ran a commercial that reflected the American view of Soviet society at the time. The commercial featured a Soviet fashion show where there was only one kind of garment to choose from, and contrasted this with the large number of choices on a Wendy's menu. The commercial won many awards and boosted the awareness of Wendy's tremendously.

The Wendy's commercial is also an example of the effective use of humor in TV advertising. Research shows that humor can sell on television, but only if it's well done. David Ogilvy cautions advertising copywriters: "I must warn you that very very few writers can write funny commercials which *are* funny. Unless you are one of the few, don't try."[15]

When Florida wanted to demonstrate that there was more to see in Florida than Walt Disney World, it created a commercial that showed other attractions and urged viewers to "See Florida Coast to Coast." Another technique that works well in television is what is called "slice of life." Slice-of-life commercials show actors simulating a real-life situation. American Express uses this to sell their traveler's checks by showing visitors being robbed of a purse or wallet in a foreign country.

**Disadvantages.** Despite the advantages of television, up to now television advertising has been confined to advertisers who have substantial budgets. Television is an expensive medium. On prime time—8 P.M. to 10 P.M., when most sets are in use—a typical network spot can cost $150,000 for 30 seconds of airtime, and even on daytime television a $25,000 price tag for 30 seconds is not unusual. A single 30-second spot in the 1998 Super Bowl cost $1,300,000! Local spots that run in a single market are of course much less expensive. A few hundred dollars will buy a 30-second commercial next to the evening news in most areas, but still—like advertising placed in other media—a good TV ad campaign requires several spots per week for a number of weeks, so even a modest campaign is likely to cost $10,000 or more to run in one market on a single station.

In addition, television commercials are costly to produce. The average cost of producing a 30-second national TV commercial was $278,000 in 1996, according to the American Association of Advertising Agencies. Some advertisers have been known to spend three or four times that much to produce a single 30-second spot.

As with radio stations, television stations generally base their prices for airtime on the expected number of people who will be exposed to the ad during its time slot. This is determined by rating services such as Arbitron that measure listenership by means of viewer diaries and electronic meters placed in people's homes. Just as with prices for radio airtime, prices for TV airtime are highly negotiable.

Even for advertisers that have the funds to advertise on television, there exists a serious question as to TV advertising's effectiveness in the face of ever-increasing **"clutter."** Clutter refers to the proliferation of commercials, which reduces the impact of individual commercials. In the United States, for example, up to 18 minutes of every broadcast hour is used for advertising (and remember, each spot is typically only 30 seconds in length). The problem is much less severe in other countries. German television shows only 2 minutes and 45 seconds of commercials every hour, while both France and Japan average less than 1 minute each hour![16]

An even bigger problem that television is facing is audience segmentation. The proliferation of cable television has fractionalized the audience so that the large networks no longer enjoy the huge audiences they once did. Television is moving away from being a mass-market medium to a niche-market one—much like magazines and radio. From the point of view of small advertisers, this is a boon, for it makes the medium much more affordable. But it also makes it much more difficult to reach a broad audience and assure that dollars are being used efficiently.

## Direct Marketing

**Direct marketing,** also known as direct response advertising, is the fastest-growing segment in the marketing communications field. By definition, direct marketing encompasses those activities that seek to sell goods and services by communicating directly with consumers. Many businesses keep extensive customer records that aid them in their direct marketing efforts. (The process of collecting and storing, in a computer data base, information about past, present, and prospective customers so that they can be communicated with directly is called **database marketing**.) Direct mail, telemarketing, and the new field of interactive media are all forms of direct marketing.

**Direct Mail.** The most widely used form of direct marketing is direct mail (see Exhibit 9). Advertisers can get mailing lists from various sources. First of all, many hotels maintain lists of previous guests. Travel agencies that issue airplane tickets, book cruises, and book hotel rooms also have the names and addresses of customers who have used their services. Many corporate directories list companies in an area, the names of their owners and principal officers, and the number of their employees. Then there are companies that compile lists from various sources and sell them. These companies buy lists of car owners from car dealers, or lists of credit card holders, magazine subscribers, people who send for various catalogs in the mail, and so forth. Mailing list companies "rent" these lists to customers by supplying them with a complete set of mailing labels.

Aside from the mailing list, the most important part of a direct mail campaign is to have a good offer that is properly packaged in an attractive and interesting direct mail piece, so that it will be read and not thrown away.

**Advantages.** Direct mail advertising offers some unique advantages:

- *Direct mail is highly selective.* Advertisers can direct their messages to people who live in specific neighborhoods or even on selected city blocks, or select recipients by other characteristics—profession, income, life-style, or possessions (such as cars or boats).

- *Direct mail enhances response.* A direct mail piece can include a postage-paid card or envelope to encourage responses.

- *Direct mail is a personal medium.* Computerized letters have made it possible to personalize a direct mail piece to each individual reader. Recipients handle direct mail pieces one at a time, which means they get the advertiser's message without any competition at the moment it is read.

- *Direct mail offers flexibility of timing and format.* Material can be timed to go out exactly when it will produce the greatest impact and can be easily varied by region.

- *Direct mail can be measured.* Advertisers can measure exactly how many responses a particular direct mail piece produces and relate that to the cost of creating and mailing the piece. This is one medium where you can tell exactly what you get for your money.

**Exhibit 9  Sample Direct Mail Piece**

# LITTLE PALM INTERNATIONAL TRIBUNE & FINANCIAL TIMES

"Hot Topics From The Tropics"

### Club Plans Coming Along

We are moving forward with our study of becoming a member-owned private club. If you have already called about this we should have something for you soon. If you would like information please call and leave your name with Ben Woodson. The club would allow the members to use Little Palm for a nominal nightly fee.

Laurence & Jo Kemmish, of London, enjoying the beach.

Cliff Robertson, Paul and Robin Cardamone, Robert Culp.

### Billfish Tournament Winner

Susan Troubetzkoy of Palm Beach Gardens, Florida was this year's winner of the LPI Billfish Tournament aboard Scuka III, a 48' Viking. She caught two bills within the allotted time. There were eight boats in the fleet and every boat caught at least one. It was a jovial and competitive gathering. Everyone said they would be back next year. Sorry we didn't get a picture, Susan, but if they don't know what you look like you can sneak up on them again next year.

### Three Cheers For Genetic Engineering

After years of guerilla warfare against the loveable, cute, dwarf, endangered, protected, nuisance Key Deer which graze unashamedly on plants, herbs and bathing suits, a breakthrough has been made. Through a tip from frequent visitor, Hobie Stovall, Clarksdale, Miss., we have found the answer. Pierce Ledbetter, son of Limited Partner Scott Ledbetter, manufactures...er, collects a deer repellant called Zoo Doo. This wonderful repellant is nothing but elephant and rhino droppings from the zoo. Well, it is a little more complicated than that but not much. Zounds, it works. If you have a similar problem, call Pierce at 1800-I LUV DOO. Isn't this what the alchemists were trying to do, turn you-know-what into gold? Pierce claims he is an entremanure. Cut the jokes, Pierce, that's my department.

### New Activities

First, we have added a fascinating trip to the reef. This trip goes to the reef in late afternoon. The idea is to dive the reef in daylight, come to the surface for the Keys sunset, and then resubmerge to see the coral bloom and all the creatures that travel at night such as lobsters, stone crabs, eels etc. It is a spell-binding trip, and you are back in plenty of time for dinner. The second addition is water skiing with Capt. Hunter. Also, we are now offering facials, manicures and pedicures. All of these events can be arranged through the quaterdeck.

### Gore's Visit

Vice-President Albert Gore and his family came to Little Palm for a few days for a rest after the election. They were a delight to have and we hope they return often. In fact they were so nice I will even vote for him next time.

**This newsletter helps former guests remember Little Palm Island Resort.** (Courtesy of Little Palm Island, Little Torch Key, Florida)

Direct mail is used extensively in the hospitality business. Airlines and hotel chains use direct mail to build loyalty among frequent flyers and repeat guests. Writing in *Lodging* magazine, Michael D. Sena, president of Alvin B. Zeller Inc. in New York, says:

Guest segmentation is a must for today's hotel marketer. Managing your property's [guest] mix has never been more important. Direct mail enables you to do both. For example, if your objective is to increase midweek meetings business, you might target corporations within your surrounding zip codes, and select those with more than 100 employees and individuals that carry the title of VP sales or marketing. Similarly, you could select clubs, associations, or fraternal groups with prescribed limits.[17]

Many restaurants also use direct mail programs extensively. Restaurants often mail coupons to homes. Exhibit 10 is an example of a letter written by the new manager of a restaurant, announcing the restaurant's renovation. Regina's, a San Francisco restaurant, uses its theater-district location as bait to lure customers in. By extending its operating hours, Regina's attracts a theater-going crowd, and its excellent newsletter provides theater schedules alongside its restaurant news. Each mailer includes a tear-off section for making a reservation.[18] Miller also cites the newsletter produced for the American Festival Cafe in New York City's Rockefeller Plaza. The stories relate to restaurant activities and menus and tie in with timely themes. "For example, when the circus came to town, a circus-and-cooking promotion was the restaurant's featured event, and the newsletter's lead story profiled the ringmaster and his interest in cooking along with his recipes."[18]

**Disadvantages.** Many people are wary of direct mail offers and shy away from shopping for anything through the mail. Unfortunately, their skepticism is somewhat justified. In the travel business, scams that advise consumers that they have been "selected to receive" or have "won" a vacation, as well as other scams that promise unbelievably low air fares or hotel rooms, are still common.

Direct mail can be costly. Direct mail marketers have become much more sophisticated, using computer technology to develop extensive data bases of clusters of people within zip codes based on purchasing behavior, life-styles, and census data. This system of geo-demographic target marketing, while extremely effective, is also expensive. Companies like Claritas Inc. in Alexandria, Virginia, compile and sell data describing these neighborhoods and predicting buying behavior. Their system is known as PRIZM (Potential Rating Index for Zip Markets), and by using it, marketers can determine the names and addresses of people who are most likely to eat in expensive restaurants, visit resorts, and take cruises. Companies that try the old shotgun approach of sending out mail to everyone in a given area are finding it harder to compete.

Other problems with direct mail, besides its credibility and cost, include the speed with which mailing lists become out of date (usually within six months, because of the high percentage of people who move) and the costs of putting together an effective direct mail package and mailing it, costs that continue to escalate.

**Telemarketing.** Telemarketing—the use of a telephone for marketing communications—is undoubtedly the most pervasive form of direct marketing. One study shows that executives spend an average of 14 weeks a year engaged in business calls.

Telemarketing can be divided into two classes: inbound and outbound. Hotel and airline reservation systems, which are fueled by newspaper and magazine ads with toll-free numbers to call, are examples of inbound telemarketing. Companies

## Exhibit 10  Sample Direct Mail Letter

**CAFFE BACI**

NINO PERNETTI

To all our friends ......

For the past three years, I have enjoyed my position as the manager of Caffe Abbracci. I was delighted when Nino asked me in May to become the new general manager of Caffe Baci. It is not every day that something like this happens.

The beautifully renovated Caffe Baci is something to be proud of. **Some things never change...Caffe Baci just got better.** As you enter the charming foyer, you will enjoy the ambiance of our new marble wine bar. Next you will want to be seated in the "Il Giardino Room" that has been decorated in unique Italian bisque tiles and accented by a magnificent vaulted skylight. The center of attraction is an imported Tuscany wood burning oven. During the day we serve an executive lunch as well as a variety of thin-crust pizzas. At dinner, we still serve the same wonderfully classic Italian cuisine that made Caffe Baci famous. We have also introduced creative specialties, prepared in the Tuscany oven. To tempt your palate I have enclosed a copy of the menu.

I trust that you will find these new changes a welcome addition for your dining pleasure. I look forward to greeting you soon.

Ciao,
Paolo

AMERICAN EXPRESS **Cards**
We Welcome The American Express® Card

**VALET PARKING NOW AVAILABLE**

2522 Ponce de Leon Blvd.   •   Coral Gables, FL 33134   •   442-0600   •   Fax 442-0061

**This letter from Caffe Baci's manager informs readers that the restaurant's renovation is complete. A menu was enclosed with the letter.** (Courtesy of Caffe Baci, Coral Gables, Florida)

---

like Burger King, with customer comment and complaint lines, also use inbound telemarketing to build loyalty and resolve disputes.

Outbound telemarketing is similar to face-to-face selling. Here the seller calls the prospect to gain an appointment for a personal sales call, to determine potential interest, or to make a sale directly. Sometimes computers are programmed to make hundreds of these calls hourly, using recorded messages. This method has been severely criticized by people who find being called by a computer annoying, but in certain circumstances—for example, when useful information is being offered and consumers are simply being asked to indicate whether they would like to have a brochure mailed to them—it has proven effective.

**Interactive Media.** The most exciting development in marketing communications is by far interactive media. **Interactive media** refers to marketing communications that are delivered via:

- The World Wide Web
- Online services
- CD-ROM
- Electronic kiosks
- Interactive phone

**The impact of the Internet.** By 1997 there were an estimated 30 million people using the Internet. As an advertising medium, it has been called a marketer's dream. Internet users are young, well educated, and have above average income. While exact figures are hard to come by (a major problem for this media), the Interactive Advertising Bureau (IAB), an industry association that promotes advertising on the Web, estimates that 58 percent are men, 42 percent women, and their average age is 35—a figure that has been increasing steadily. Sixty-five percent of households who use the Internet have incomes of $50,000-plus, and 75 percent have attended college. Like other kinds of advertising, the purpose of interactive media in most cases is not to make sales but, rather, to stimulate them. Surveys by the IAB of its members show these reasons for use:

- Information (72.1%)
- Promotion (48.2%)
- Public relations (45.8%)
- One-to-one marketing (37.2%)
- Electronic commerce (17.6%)[19]

There are three basic choices advertisers have in deciding what form their ads should take. The first is to build a *destination site* on the World Wide Web. These sites have home pages that provide information and entertainment, often with high production values so that visitors are encouraged to return repeatedly. These sites are the most expensive to produce and maintain. Next are *micro-sites,* which are small clusters of brand pages hosted by content sites or networks. Finally, there are *banners,* which work best for brand names that consumers are familiar with. With all three, the goal of the advertiser is to get site visitors to click through to read more of the message and get involved or interact with the company.

Is Internet advertising effective? If the advertiser has realistic goals, it can be. Some products and services lend themselves better to interactive media than others. Those that can easily be sold online and shipped economically or delivered digitally are obviously better candidates. So are considered purchases where

## Table of Contents

Need Help? | Find | Go to Contents

Home | Travel Agent | Magazine | Maps | Resources | Communicate | About Expedia

**Click to see the new Expedia Travel Channel**

Travel Info Delivered to Your Desktop — Add Active Channel

Active Channels require Internet Explorer 4.0

### Travel Tip

*"The best way to see **Antigua** is by taxi tour. We were able to barter with a driver for a $20, 2-hour tour that went to all of the historic sites, with plenty of opportunities for pictures—well worth the money."*

*Tanis K., British Columbia*

### ▸ Travel Agent

*Research, reserve, and buy your travel online. Simple step-by-step wizards make it fast and easy to book flights, hotels, and rental cars. As soon as you register to become an Expedia member, you can start to enjoy the 10 benefits of membership.*

YOUR ITINERARIES
Access all your personal trip plans

FARE COMPARE
Look up the lowest published airfares quickly and easily

FARE TRACKER
Receive free e-mail alerts on low fares to your favorite destinations

### ▸ Expedia Travel Network

*Shop for cruises, vacation packages and more...*

CRUISES
Plan your next vacation with sea, sun, sumptuous food, and exotic ports of call

VACATION PACKAGES
Investigate all-inclusive vacations for the ultimate in planning convenience

RESORTS
Explore a selection of world-class resorts with pure indulgence in mind

### ▸ Expedia Magazine

*See what's new on the travel scene in our changing mix of travel news and opinion, vacation ideas, and expert advice*

FULL CIRCLE
Take 360° Surround Video tours of top destinations. Don't miss the Full Circle Archives

TRAVEL NEWS
Get the latest news for travelers like you

EXPerts
Sample opinions, expertise, and savvy travel advice from our columnists. More insightful information in Archives

FEATURES
Explore fresh travel ideas for places both new and familiar. Check the Features Archives for more inspiration

MUNGO PARK LEGENDS
An archive of multimedia expeditions

### ▸ Resources

*Dip into our databases and use our tools to learn where, when, and why to go*

WORLD GUIDE
Find trip-planning info in our 14,000-page virtual guidebook with links to thousands of sites around the Web

*(continued)*

> | | |
> |---|---|
> | **SPECIAL INTEREST VACATIONS**<br>Follow your personal passion to help arrange your next vacation | **HOTEL DIRECTORY**<br>Choose from more than 38,000 properties worldwide |
> | **TRAINS, BUSES, & CHARTERS**<br>Charter your transport or reserve seats for a different sort of getaway | **WORLDWIDE LINKS**<br>Explore the globe via our index of 10,000 selected sites |
> | **SHOPPING PLAZA**<br>Browse for travel accessories, books, and much, much more ... | **CURRENCY CONVERTER**<br>Convert Andorran pesetas to Zambian kwachas—or any of 200 other currencies in our database |
> | ▸ **Expedia Maps**<br>*Complete your itinerary with a map of your destination* | **WEATHER WATCH**<br>Check conditions and forecasts around the globe |
> | **ADDRESS FINDER**<br>Locate addresses in the U.S. | **FLIGHT INFO**<br>Get the current status of a flight |
> | **WORLDWIDE PLACE FINDER**<br>Find a place anywhere in the world | |
> | **BUSINESS FINDER**<br>Find a business by name or location | |
> | **DRIVING DIRECTIONS**<br>Map your way from city to city in North America | |
>
> © 1998 Microsoft Corporation and/or its suppliers. All rights reserved.

Online resources such as Microsoft Corporation's *Expedia* (www.msn.expedia.com) offer opportunities for savvy marketers. (Courtesy of Microsoft Corporation)

consumers can check specifications or details. Airline tickets and hotel reservations would appear to meet these criteria. However, some constraints need to be kept in mind. Everyone doesn't own a computer that is connected to the Internet, and everyone doesn't like to shop digitally. Many people may prefer to shop in stores or over the telephone with a live person at the other end.

The final constraint is that there are thousands of sites on the Internet—and the numbers keep growing. To turn this media from a passive one to an active one requires that sites be marketed so that people know they exist and can find them. That means the use of other media. In other words, interactive media is another valuable part of the total media mix and does best when it is part of an integrated marketing communications campaign.

## Public Relations

A company does not function in a vacuum, but rather as part of a society that consists of the people who work for it, the people and companies who do business with it, the public at large, and the government that regulates and taxes it. These groups are known as a company's "publics." In order for a company to effectively deal with these publics, a relationship of trust must exist. Employees will not cooperate with or put forth their best efforts for a company that they do not trust or that they feel is taking advantage of them. The public will not buy services or products from a company that, in their estimation, is not responsible or trustworthy: if they can't trust the company or its owners, how can they trust the products or services it sells? And the government, as the protector of the society it governs, is especially vigilant in dealing with a company that it regards as not operating in the public interest. Given these circumstances, every hotel, restaurant, travel agency, tour company, and other hospitality business should give some thought to the relationships it has with all of the various publics it interacts with. The techniques that a company uses to improve these relationships are known as **public relations**, or "**PR.**"

The goal of public relations is usually to improve the climate or atmosphere in which a company operates. Here are some results a company might expect from a successful public relations campaign:

- Its products and services are better known
- Its relationship with employees has improved
- Its public reputation has improved

A successful public relations campaign can get people to do something that will help a company, stop them from doing something that might hurt it, or at least allow the company to proceed with a course of action without criticism. "An organization with good public relations has a favorable image or reputation, perhaps as a result of public relations activities," says Richard Weiner, an award-winning public relations counselor and the author of *Webster's New World Dictionary of Media and Communications.*[20]

In developing and implementing public relations plans, companies often use a simple five-step process:

1. *Research or fact-finding.* The purpose of research or fact-finding is to identify the attitudes of the publics, who the key opinion leaders are, and what must happen to change bad perceptions or reinforce good ones.

2. *Planning.* A public relations strategy is devised that will produce the desired outcome(s).

3. *Action.* Action steps are taken to implement the strategy.

4. *Communication.* The company's actions are communicated to the interested publics.

5. *Measurement or evaluation.* The results of the public relations campaign are studied to see if the desired outcomes have been achieved or if more action is needed.

McDonald's is a classic example of a hospitality company that practices good public relations (see Exhibit 11). It has always been important to McDonald's to be

**Exhibit 11  Public Relations at McDonald's**

McDonald's uses booklets, posters, and other public relations materials to inform its customers of the many ways in which it tries to be socially responsible. (Courtesy of McDonald's Corporation, Oak Brook, Illinois)

known as a company that values cleanliness. Indeed, founder Ray Kroc emphasized cleanliness along with quality, service, and value as being the four most important things in any McDonald's operation. For that reason Kroc instructed the first McDonald's franchisees to pick up all litter within a two-block radius of their stores, whether it was McDonald's litter or not.[21] However, by the mid-1970s McDonald's had grown so large that its discarded packages were found everywhere, from nearby city streets to campgrounds and beaches miles from the nearest restaurant. As public consciousness grew about the importance of not polluting, more and more critics pointed to McDonald's as a leading culprit, and the company realized it needed to take further action.

In 1976, McDonald's commissioned the Stanford Research Institute to do an environmental impact study comparing the paperboard packaging McDonald's was using at the time with polystyrene packages, an economical alternative that also offered some other product benefits. The study concluded that polystyrene was better from an environmental perspective when all aspects of the problem were taken into consideration. "Paper and paperboard used with food have to be coated, making them 'mixed materials' that are nearly unrecyclable. Polystyrene uses less energy than paper in its production, conserves natural resources, represents less weight and volume in landfills, and is recyclable."[22] McDonald's accepted the study's recommendations and switched to polystyrene wherever it could.

But in the 1980s new questions were raised. Environmentalists pointed out that the manufacturing process for polystyrene released halogenated chlorofluorocarbons into the earth's atmosphere, which harmed the ozone layer. By 1987 McDonald's had directed all of its packaging suppliers to eliminate these dangerous chemicals from the manufacturing process. At the same time it reduced by 29 percent the thickness of its containers, and by 20 percent the weight of plastic straws. It used a lighter paper for wrapping sandwiches and began using recycled paper for napkins and tray liners. At the same time the company launched a new investigation into recycling programs.

To make sure that everyone knew what it was doing, McDonald's made its concern for the environment the theme of its 1989 annual report and printed the report entirely on recycled paper generated from paper waste from its offices and restaurants worldwide.[23] This was followed in 1990 by the announcement of McRecycle USA, a program in which McDonald's committed itself to buy $100 million in recycled materials for use in building and remodeling its restaurants.

Despite all of these positive actions, many critics continued to question whether McDonald's was really an environmentally friendly company. So in November 1990 the company made a decision to turn back the clock by phasing out polystyrene packaging and returning to paper while investigating other alternatives.

It is important to understand the role public relations has played in all of these decisions. McDonald's has always been socially responsible and extremely concerned about its image. These two facts are part and parcel of its public relationships. To McDonald's, public relations activities go much deeper than simply sending out press releases and having corporate officers serve on various charitable boards. The company understands that real public relations means taking significant actions first, then announcing them to the public. Without the first step, the second would be meaningless. Many companies do not understand this basic principle: if you want to make news, you must first do something newsworthy.

## Publicity

Public relations and publicity are often confused with each other, but they are not the same thing. Richard Weiner defines **publicity** as "a public relations technique in which information from an outside source—usually a public relations practitioner—is used by the media. A message is developed and distributed, without specific payment to the media, through selected outlets (magazines, TV, and so on) to further particular interests of the clients."[24]

Publicity is sometimes called free advertising, but this is a misnomer. Advertising is paid for and advertisers control the message in their ads. Publicity is not paid for by the advertiser, and the media—not the advertiser—control the message, because they are writing or broadcasting stories that they consider newsworthy, which just also happen to mention a company or be about a company. Because publicity is not paid for by an advertiser, it has more credibility with consumers than an ad. Unfortunately, publicity can be unfavorable as well as favorable. A newspaper article about a restaurant's discrimination in hiring or a TV story about a hotel fire are examples of bad publicity.

New hotels and restaurants usually work hard to publicize their grand openings and often receive a good deal of attention and publicity. Press kits are the most common publicity materials prepared by a property. These kits generally consist of a series of fact sheets about the property; some news releases about the building, the architects, the general manager, and other key property personnel; and several glossy black-and-white photos that can be reproduced in newspapers.

However, grand openings occur only once and businesses need publicity throughout their lives. Newspapers receive thousands of press releases every week and generally discard most of them. Therefore it is often necessary to stage special events or create new products or services to focus the media's attention and give them something newsworthy to write about. One of Richard Weiner's most celebrated publicity stunts was the Texas Armadillo Race he created for Lone Star Beer. Weiner recruited "professional" armadillo racers and had them compete against one another. The cost was minuscule but the armadillo race (and Lone Star) appeared on several network TV shows.

Another example of a special event created to generate publicity is a promotion by New York's famous Rainbow Room restaurant in Rockefeller Plaza. The Rainbow Room decided in 1989 to tie in with the 50th anniversary of the 1939 New York World's Fair, which was being commemorated with a series of events in the city. The Rainbow Room invited curators of museums and other exhibits to meet the press and talk about their upcoming commemorative events at a press conference sponsored by the restaurant. At the same time they displayed their own memorabilia of the fair and served food from the original menus of the World's Fair pavilions. Renowned chef Pierre Franey, who first came to America to cook at the French Pavilion, was the restaurant's spokesman for reporters' questions related to food. As you might expect, the Rainbow Room received considerable PR mileage out of this community service event.[25]

Hotels and restaurants often try to stimulate publicity by inviting travel editors and writers to visit. Sometimes these invitations are arranged by publicists who organize all-expenses-paid press tours. However, while freelancers often accept invitations to go on these tours, many of the top newspapers and travel magazines will not publish anything that a freelancer writes while enjoying a free trip, because they believe he or she is likely to be biased. Their editors and writers usually pay for everything when they visit a hotel or restaurant, and report on both the positives and the negatives they encounter.

## Sales Promotion

Unlike advertising and public relations, which aim to achieve results over time, **sales promotion** consists of sales tools and techniques to encourage immediate action—not only by consumers, but by others in the trade. Extra commissions paid

> **CLUB MED NEWS**
>
> CONTACT: Edwina R. Arnold                                    FOR IMMEDIATE RELEASE
>
> ### VALUE COMES FIRST WITH A CLUB MED FAMILY VACATION
>
> **KIDS FREE AT FOUR RESORTS MAY 5–JUNE 16 & SEPT. 8–DECEMBER 15: AT IXTAPA THEY'RE FREE FROM MAY 5–DECEMBER 15**
>
> It's not just that kids can vacation for free, it's what they get for free that makes **Club Med the best value in family vacations.** Among the latest innovations at Family Villages: a brand-new look in Eleuthera complete with a kid-size sailing fleet and a Pony Club at St. Lucia.
>
> At four Club Med villages — Sandpiper, St. Lucia, Punta Cana and Eleuthera — kids between the ages of 2 and 5 stay free May 5–June 16 and September 8–December 15. At Sandpiper, babies aged 4–23 months are also welcome at no charge. **Ixtapa,** however, welcomes 2–5 year olds free from May 5 right through to December 15. And at all family-oriented resorts except Sandpiper, air-inclusive packages for kids and their parents are also available.
>
> Today, there are **38 Mini Clubs and 13 Baby Clubs** dotted around the world from Bali to Brazil, from Japan to the U.S.A. And, **a total** of **115,000 youngsters** under the age of 12 **spent their vacation at Club Med** in 1989. Close to home, family villages with Mini Clubs are located at **St. Lucia** (island of St. Lucia), **Ixtapa** (Mexico), **Punta Cana** (Dominican Republic) and **Eleuthera** (Bahamas). **Club Med–Sandpiper** (Florida) boasts
>
> ...More...
>
> 40 WEST 57 STREET, NEW YORK, N.Y. 10019, PHONE: (212) 977-2100, TELEX: 422183, CABLE: MEDCLUBINC, N.Y.

This news release announces special family vacation packages. (Courtesy of Club Med)

to travel agents, cooperative advertising, contests, and familiarization trips for agents are all examples of hospitality industry sales promotions directed at the trade. For many years Carnival Cruises has run a mystery-shopper program in which travel agents are handed $1,000 in cash on the spot for recommending a Carnival Cruise to someone who asks about a Caribbean vacation.

Probably the most widely used form of sales promotion directed toward consumers is a loyalty marketing program, such as Marriott's Rewards, Hyatt's Gold Passport, and American Airlines AAdvantage frequent-flyer program. All of these programs reward people who travel frequently and do repeat business with these companies. Such programs stimulate additional travel by offering incentives to fly and stay at hotels. Free travel is a common form of sales promotion (see Exhibit 12.)

Tie-ins are a form of sales promotion in which marketers of diverse products or services team up to create consumer awareness and generate sales. Delta Airlines and Polaroid ran one successful sales promotion in which, in exchange for proof of purchase of a Polaroid 600 camera, customers received a certificate good for a free round-trip ticket to anywhere Delta flew (when they bought a ticket of equal or greater value).

Sweepstakes are a popular form of sales promotion. Faced with a decrease in trans-Atlantic traffic due to fear of terrorism, British Airways created an ambitious and successful "Go For It America" sweepstakes. Launched in June with entry blanks printed in newspapers, British Airways offered 5,200 readers free round-trip tickets for two to London with free first-night lodging. The July prize was 100,000 British pounds; in August the winner received a five-year London townhouse lease; and in September the prize was a new Rolls-Royce. The airline also included travel agents in this promotion—agents got an opportunity to win prizes every time they booked a passenger on British Airways.

Promotions are used extensively by restaurants to get publicity and stimulate business. For example, *Food Arts* magazine reported that "what started as a gesture of hospitality to the Democratic National Convention in New York City ended up as a staggering sales success in a sluggish economy." The promotion was called "The Summer of $19.92" and was originally conceived by New York '92 Host Committee restaurateur Joseph Baum and publisher Tim Zagat. The promotion included a luncheon for convention delegates for a prix fixe of $19.92 during the four days of the July convention; 108 of the city's top restaurants participated.[26] The promotion was so successful that many restaurants kept it going through Labor Day and into the fall.

"Wine and Dine" promotions, where restaurants tie in with vineyards for special meals, are common (see Exhibit 13). One of the best known of these is New York Wine Week, held by Alan Stilman's New York Restaurant Group, which owns the Park Avenue Cafe, Smith & Wollensky, and the Post House, as well as other New York City eateries. During New York Wine Week, customers pay regular lunch prices but are treated to free-flowing wine from the finest vineyards in France and California. The participating vintners pour over 100 wines during the week-long promotion.[27]

At Kaspar's by the Bay in Seattle, Washington, chef Kaspar Donier combines cooking classes with a prix fixe dinner once a month for about 60 customers who are members of "The Recipe Club." Customers arrive at 7 P.M., and after Donier runs through a demo, they're served a $25 four-course dinner. After that, Donier provides the recipes and answers questions.[28] The *Wall Street Journal* reported that a few New Jersey restaurants have tapped a new market by providing funeral-goers with meals after the services. "Called repasts, mercy lunches, or funeral brunches, the meals are gaining in popularity among the bereaved in Bergen and Hudson counties" according to the *Journal*.[29] Demand by local restaurants to advertise these brunches prompted the *Observer*, a weekly newspaper in Kearny, New Jersey, to create a "Funeral Brunches" section on its obituary page.

*Managing Marketing Communications* **517**

**Exhibit 12**  Advertisment Promoting Travel Incentives

# Introducing Marriott Rewards.

## It's never been easier to earn points.
*(You're welcome)*

## Or harder to decide where to use them.
*(Sorry)*

**Marriott** HOTELS·RESORTS·SUITES   **COURTYARD**   **FAIRFIELD INN**   **Marriott VACATION CLUB** Vacation Villas   **TownePlace Suites** Marriott   **Marriott** CONFERENCE CENTERS

Now you can earn points at nearly a thousand different hotels in the Marriott family, so free vacations come quicker than ever. Redeem your points for free stays at our hotels, or choose from cruises, airline miles or other great rewards. For more information click over to our Web site (www.marriottrewards.com), or pick up the phone and **call 800-249-0800 to enroll.**

**VISA**   Here's an offer exclusively for VISA® cardholders:
**Pay for your stays with your VISA card and get 10% bonus points** now through November 15th.

**Marriott REWARDS**℠

©1997 Marriott International, Inc.

(Courtesy of Marriott International, Inc.)

### Exhibit 13  A Tie-In "Wine and Dine" Promotion

**Mark's Place — The Hess Collection**

**WINE MEETS ART!**

The Hess Collection Winery has been one of the best kept secrets in the Napa Valley. For over ten years, Hess Vineyards on Mt. Veeder has concentrated on quietly establishing itself as an exceptional producer of premium Cabernet Sauvignon and Chardonnay grapes. This decade long story began when Swiss entrepreneur and art collector Donald Hess visited the Napa Valley and discovered the magical taste of California's premier wine producing region. Mr. Hess was drawn immediately to the prospect of being part of this beautiful valley's growing reputation as a world-class wine region. After considerable reflection and personally conducted research, Donald Hess found himself on the steep slopes of Mt. Veeder. Hess knew that he needed an experienced hand to work with the grapes, so he hired on Randle Johnson, who has toiled on Mt. Veeder since 1977, when he began with the renowned Mayacamas Vineyards.

Today Hess has established a tremendous reputation for all of its wines and has built a beautiful winery with a world-class art collection to match! Some critics maintain that the Hess Collection Reserve Cabernet is unsurpassed (we heartily agree) by any produced in California. Join us when we taste these wonderful wines with winemaker Randle Johnson. Along with the winery's new 1990 Chardonnays, one of the highlights will be the Florida debut of the 1989 Hess Collection Cabernet (a wine we thought was stunning from barrel). The grand finale will be a **very, very** rare treat: the 1987 Hess Collection Reserve Cabernet poured from Magnums - the only time large format bottles of this legendary Cabernet have ever crossed Florida state lines.

Mark will be preparing seven special courses matching our cuisine with these great wines. In order to preserve the intimacy of the evening, seating is limited to 75 people. Come taste some great wines from one of Napa's new cult wineries, and enjoy it all while Mark dazzles you with some exciting new culinary creations. The Hess Collection Wines and Mark's Place Cuisine...sure to be a memorable evening when wine meets art.

The Hess Collection
$150 Per Person
(All Inclusive)
Tuesday Nov. 17, 1992
7:00 PM Sharp/By Reservation Only
☎ (305)-893-6888

---

**HESS COLLECTION WINERY**
*WINEMAKER DINNER*
November 17, 1992

ASSORTED PASS AROUNDS
*Select Chardonnay 1991*

AMUSE
Sweet corn fritter with caviar
*Select Chardonnay 1991*

FIRST COURSE
Kumomoto, Malapeque and Hog Island oysters mignonette
*Collection Chardonnay 1990*

SECOND COURSE
Ingrid's crispy potato and spinach wrapped sea scallops with brown butter vinaigrette
*Collection "Mt. Veeder" Chardonnay 1990*

MAIN COURSE
Texas antelope chop with autumn mash, roast shallot and cabernet sauce
or
Grilled breast of Moullard duck with foie gras and wild mushrooms
*Collection Cabernet 1988*
*Collection Cabernet 1989*

CHEESE COURSE
Selection of cheeses and Timmy's homegrown organic greens
*Reserve Cabernet 1987 from Magnum*

SELECTION OF HOMEMADE CHOCOLATE DESSERTS
Gianduja chocolate triangles
Warm petit chocolate decadence
Chocolate truffles
Chocolate sorbet
Served with raspberry coulis and a trio of chocolate sauces

2286 NE 123rd STREET, NORTH MIAMI, FLORIDA 33181  ☎ 305-893-6888

This tie-in promotion was co-sponsored by Mark's Place in North Miami and the Hess Collection Winery in Napa Valley, California. (Courtesy of Mark's Place, North Miami, Florida)

## Chapter Summary

Advertising acts as a substitute for a personal salesperson. Advertising is valuable because it is repetitive and thus helps consumers understand and remember sales messages. It increases the value of products and services by adding value to the name and reputation of a company.

Some critics charge that advertising leads people to buy things they don't want or need, but in fact most advertising is used to influence the brand choice of something that consumers have already decided to purchase.

Advertising is paid for by the sponsor, is impersonal, identifies the sponsor, and is persuasive. It is a planned communication activity in which messages in mass media are used to persuade audiences to adopt goods, services, or ideas.

There are certain factors that favor the use of advertising. These include a demonstrable competitive advantage, unique positioning, and market segmentation. Positioning consists of getting inside the prospect's mind by linking the message the advertiser wishes to convey to something the prospect already knows. Market segmentation refers to a company's ability to identify different segments of its market and separately promote its products and services to these segments.

Some hospitality advertisers employ an advertising agency. Advertising agencies consist of marketing strategists, artists, writers, production managers, and media selection experts. Agencies generally work on a 15 percent commission. Whether a company should use an agency depends on the nature of the company's advertising, the advertising agencies or freelancers available in an area, and the media to be used. Sometimes media prices are negotiable, and advertising agencies are in a better position to obtain the most favorable rates.

Effective advertising is not only inspired; it is almost always the product of a rational and methodical process.

Print advertisements consist of several elements. Usually there is a headline; some advertisements also contain a sub-headline. The main portion of an ad is called the body copy. Finally, ads usually end with a signature and a logotype ("logo").

There are some general guidelines that most print advertisers follow: (1) put a promise in the headline, (2) "make the sale" in the body copy, and (3) close with a call to action. A successful print campaign consists of a series of advertisements that bear a family resemblance in both style and content but are different enough to attract new attention from readers.

Broadcast advertisers seek to entertain because commercials interrupt the entertainment provided by the medium.

Once the ad message is decided on, an advertiser must determine where to run it. Any advertising message whose real thrust is information works well in newspapers. For image-building campaigns and purchases that are not planned, the excitement and immediacy of broadcast media can make a real difference. Ideally, an advertiser should use more than one medium to sell something.

Budget is a consideration when choosing media. The more people an advertiser attempts to reach, the less frequently the advertiser will be able to reach them. It takes more than one exposure to persuade anyone via advertising.

Despite the growth of electronic media, newspapers remain America's largest advertising medium. Newspapers appeal to a large spectrum of people. One of the great advantages of newspapers is their sense of immediacy. Newspapers are also flexible, local, and relatively inexpensive for local advertisers. Newspapers have disadvantages too. They are the least selective of all media. They have poor ad reproduction capabilities and a short readership life. Advertisers have limited control over where their advertising will appear in a newspaper.

Whereas newspapers carry information of interest to a broad spectrum of people, magazines target their audiences very narrowly. The main advantage of magazines is their ability to reach a particular market segment. Another advantage is that magazines have a long life—magazine ads continue to build an audience for weeks and even months. Finally, magazines offer superb ad reproduction. Disadvantages of magazines include long closing dates, limited circulation flexibility, and high advertising costs.

More than 99 percent of American homes have radios. Radio is a very personal medium that invites listeners to use their imaginations. Because radio stations have different formats, they attract different types of audiences. Radio's disadvantages include the large number of radio stations in most markets, the small listenership of a station at a given moment, and the difficulty of using phone numbers and directions effectively in a radio ad.

Television is by far the most powerful and persuasive of all advertising media. It is the only medium that appeals to our eyes and ears at the same time. But high costs and declining ad effectiveness due to "clutter"—the sheer number of commercials on TV—have kept some advertisers away from the medium.

There are a variety of forms of direct marketing or direct response advertising. Direct mail is the most widely used. Direct mail advertising has some unique advantages. Direct mail is highly selective, encourages a response, is a personal medium, offers flexibility of timing and format, and can be measured. The two most important parts of an effective direct mail program are the mailing list and the offer. Direct mail's disadvantages include its credibility, the need to use sophisticated data-based list generation, high cost, and list obsolescence. Other direct response techniques include inbound and outbound telemarketing and interactive media.

Interactive media appeals to young, affluent, and educated consumers. Advertisers use it predominantly to communicate information using World Wide Web destination sites, micro-sites, and banners.

Every hotel, restaurant, travel agency, tour company, and other hospitality enterprise should give some thought to its public relationships—that is, the relations it has with all of the various "publics" it interacts with. The techniques that a company uses to improve these relationships are known as "PR" or public relations. In developing and implementing public relations plans, companies often use a simple five-step process: research or fact-finding, planning, action, communication, and measurement or evaluation.

Publicity is a public relations technique in which information from an outside source—usually a public relations practitioner—is used by the media. Hotels and restaurants often receive a lot of publicity at their grand openings. The need for publicity continues throughout the life of the business.

Sales promotion consists of sales tools and techniques to encourage immediate action by consumers or the trade. Probably the most widely used sales promotions directed toward consumers are loyalty marketing programs such as Marriott's Honored Guest, Hyatt's Gold Passport, and American Airlines AAdvantage frequent-flyer program.

Restaurants also use sales promotion to generate publicity and stimulate business. Sales promotions may include special commemorative events or tie-ins with wine producers. Tie-ins are a form of sales promotion in which marketers of diverse products or services team up to create consumer awareness and generate sales. Sweepstakes are widely used as a form of sales promotion among travel and hospitality companies.

## Endnotes

1. *The Value Side of Productivity* (New York: American Association of Advertising Agencies, 1989), pp. 17–18.
2. *Value Side of Productivity,* p. 18.

3. Bradley T. Gale, "How Advertising Affects Profitability and Growth for Consumer Businesses," in *Value Side of Productivity,* p. 35.
4. *Advertising Age,* 9 September 1997.
5. Charles H. Patti and Charles F. Frazer, *Advertising: A Decision-Making Approach* (New York: Dryden Press, 1988), p. 4.
6. Patti and Frazer, p. 5.
7. Al Reis and Jack Trout, *Positioning: The Battle for Your Mind* (New York: Warner Books, 1981), p. 8.
8. "Profiles in Travel," *Travel Agent Magazine,* 16 October 1989, p. 40.
9. Richard Weiner, *Webster's New World Dictionary of Media and Communications* (New York: Simon & Schuster, 1990), p. 272.
10. Edward A. Robinson, "Frogs, Bears, and Orgasms: Think zany if you want to reach today's consumers," *Fortune,* 9 June 1997, pp. 154–156.
11. Many of this section's facts about newspapers were compiled from the Newspaper Association of America's Web site at www.naa.org.
12. Bob Stein, "Reaching Your Audience through Special-Interest Magazines," *Cornell H.R.A. Quarterly,* November 1982, p. 37.
13. J. Thomas Russell and W. Ronald Lane, *Kleppner's Advertising Procedure,* 11th ed. (Englewood Cliffs, N.J.: Prentice-Hall, 1990), p. 217.
14. Michael Wolf, Peter Rutten, Albert F. Bayers III, and the World Research Team, *Where We Stand* (New York: Bantam Books, 1992), pp. 68–69.
15. David Ogilvy, *Ogilvy on Advertising* (New York: Crown Publishers, 1983), p. 105.
16. Wolf, Rutten, and Bayers, pp. 68–69.
17. Michael D. Sena, "Leaping Direct-Mail Hurdles: A Hassle-Free Approach," *Lodging,* May 1990, p. 62.
18. Jessica Miller, "Marketing Communications," *Cornell H.R.A. Quarterly,* October 1993, p. 51.
19. Miller, p. 51.
20. Internet Advertising Bureau, www.iab.net, 1997.
21. Weiner, p. 381.
22. Scott Hume, "The Green Revolution," *Advertising Age,* 29 January 1991, p. 32.
23. Hume, p. 32.
24. Hume, p. 32
25. Weiner, p. 380.
26. Miller, p. 52.
27. "Build It," *Food Arts,* October 1992, p. 64.
28. "Build It," p. 66.
28. "Build It," p. 66.
29. Eleena de Lisser, "House Wines From These Brunches, Of Course, Will Be From Graves," *Wall Street Journal,* 8 March 1993.

## Key Terms

**added-value**—What advertising adds to the value and reputation of the product, service, or company being advertised.

**advertising**—Planned communication activity in which messages in mass media are used to persuade audiences to adopt goods, services, or ideas.

**body copy**—The main text of an ad.

**closing date**—The day when all copy and other ad components must be delivered to the media if the ad is to appear on its scheduled date.

**clutter**—The proliferation of commercials in media. Clutter reduces the impact of any single ad.

**cost per thousand (CPM)**—The cost to reach 1,000 people one time. CPM is a measure of audience used to price advertising space.

**"cume"**—To accumulate an audience. It is the number of unduplicated people or households that is achieved by an ad or advertising schedule over a period of time.

**database marketing**—A marketing system that stores information about past, current, and prospective customers in an electronic database (computer). This information can be used to construct individual profiles containing demographic, geographic, and psychographic data, allowing marketers to communicate with customers individually and develop continuing relationships with them.

**direct marketing**—Those activities that seek to sell goods and services by direct communication with consumers. Direct marketers frequently use direct mail, telemarketing, and other advertising media to effect a measurable response or buying action at any location (such as the home). Also called direct response advertising.

**headline**—The most prominent part of a print advertisement, in which a promise or benefit is often expressed. It is used to get attention.

**interactive media**—Marketing communications delivered via the World Wide Web, online computer services, CD-ROMs, electronic kiosks, etc. It allows individuals to decide what they want to see, when they want to see it. They can purchase marketed goods and services at the click of a button or choose to view more information on their screen before they buy.

**logotype (logo)**—A unique trademark, name, symbol, signature, or device used to identify a company or other organization.

**market segmentation**—The process by which customers are classified into groups or segments, based on a variety of factors (depending on which factors prove most useful from a marketing point of view). Market segments can be based on demographic information (age, income), geographic information (where customers are located), psychographic information (life-styles, social class), or a combination of these.

**positioning**—A marketing term used to describe how consumers perceive the products and services offered by a particular advertiser in relation to similar products and services offered by competitors. Positioning strategies attempt to establish in the minds of consumers a particular image of an advertiser's products and services.

**publicity**—The editorial mention in the media of an organization's people, products, or services.

**public relations (PR)**—A systematic effort by a business to communicate favorable information about itself to various internal and external publics in order to create a positive impression.

**run-of-paper (ROP)**—The basis on which most newspaper advertising space is sold, in which the newspaper staff picks the ad's position.

**sales promotion**—Sales tools and techniques such as contests, extra commissions, familiarization tours, and loyalty marketing programs that are designed to generate an immediate response.

**signature**—The name of the advertiser as it appears at the bottom of a print ad.

**target marketing**—Marketing that is designed to appeal to a specific consumer group.

## Review Questions

1. What are the advantages of advertising?
2. What factors favor advertising?
3. What are some guidelines for creating print ads?
4. How can advertisers use broadcast media effectively?
5. What advice does David Ogilvy give advertisers?
6. What are the advantages and disadvantages of newspaper advertising? magazine advertising?
7. What are the advantages and disadvantages of radio advertising? television advertising?
8. What are direct mail's advantages and disadvantages?
9. What are the differences between public relations and publicity?
10. What is sales promotion?

## Internet Sites

For more information, visit the following Internet sites. Remember that Internet addresses can change without notice. If the site is no longer there, use a browser to look for additional sites.

*Airlines*

American Airlines
www.aa.com

British Airways
www.british-airways.com

*Airlines*

Delta Air Lines
www.delta-air.com

*Cruise Lines*

Carnival Cruise Lines
www.carnival.com

Princess Cruise Lines
www.princesscruises.com

*Hotel Companies/Resorts*

Club Med
www.clubmed.com

Motel 6
www.motel6.com

Four Seasons Hotels
www.fshr.com

Ritz-Carlton Hotels
www.ritzcarlton.com

Hilton Hotels
www.hilton.com

Sheraton Hotels
www.sheraton.com

Holiday Inn Worldwide
www.holiday-inn.com

Super 8 Motels
www.super8motels.com

Hyatt Hotels
www.hyatt.com

Westin Hotels
www.westin.com

Marriott International
www.marriott.com

*Organizations, Resources*

American Association of Advertising Agencies
www.aaaa.org

Internet Advertising Bureau
www.iab.net

American Hotel & Motel Association
www.ahma.com

National Restaurant Association
www.restaurants.org

Boston Consulting Group
www.bcg.com

Newspaper Association of America
www.naa.org

*Publications*

*Advertising Age*
www.adage.com

*LODGING*
www.ei-ahma.org/webs/lodging/

*Fortune*
www.pathfinder.com/fortune/

*Restaurants USA*
www.restaurantsusa.com

*Hotel & Travel Index*
www.traveler.net

*Travel Weekly*
www.traveler.net

*Restaurant Companies*

McDonald's
www.mcdonalds.com

T.G.I. Friday's
www.tgifridays.com

# REVIEW QUIZ

When you feel you have covered all of the material in this chapter, answer these questions. Choose the *best* answer.

1. Which of the following is *not* a characteristic of advertising?

    a. It is paid for by the sponsor rather than run at the discretion of the medium.
    b. It is impersonal.
    c. It attempts to tell all sides of the story about a product or service.
    d. It is persuasive.

2. According to the Strategic Planning Institute, brands that advertise much more than their competitors average a return on investment (ROI) of _____ percent.

    a. 5
    b. 16
    c. 24
    d. 32

3. An advantage of advertising in magazines is that:

    a. magazine ads are long-lasting.
    b. when judged on a cost-per-thousand basis, magazine advertising is relatively inexpensive.
    c. magazines have long "closing" dates.
    d. most magazines serve a broad audience.

4. One of radio's disadvantages as an advertising medium is that:

    a. it is a very personal medium.
    b. radio listenership at any given moment is small.
    c. listeners have to use their imaginations.
    d. radio is highly selective.

5. Which of the following is *not* an advantage of direct mail?

    a. Direct mail can be easily measured.
    b. Direct mail is a personal medium.
    c. Direct mail is inexpensive.
    d. Direct mail is highly selective.

6. Which of the following statements about publicity is *true*?

    a. Publicity is free advertising.
    b. Publicity is more credible with consumers than an ad.
    c. Just as with advertising, publicity is controlled by the advertiser.
    d. Public relations and publicity are the same thing.

## REVIEW QUIZ *(continued)*

7. The aim of sales promotion techniques is to:
    a. gradually increase sales over time.
    b. encourage others in the industry—travel agents, for example—to take immediate action.
    c. encourage consumers to take immediate action.
    d. b and c.

**Answer Key:** 1-c-C1, 2-d-C1, 3-a-C2, 4-b-C2, 5-c-C2, 6-b-C3, 7-d-C3

Each question is linked to a competency. Competencies are listed on the first page of the chapter. An answer reading 3-b-C4 translates to:

- 3: the question number
- b: the correct answer
- C4: the competency number

## Chapter 16 Outline

Why Management Companies Exist
The Evolution of Management Companies
Management Contracts
    Contract Provisions
    Advantages and Disadvantages
Chapter Summary

## Competencies

1. Identify unique characteristics of the hotel business, explain why hotel management companies came into existence, and summarize the history of management companies.

2. Describe a hotel management contract.

# 16
# How Management Companies Manage Hotels

**T**HIS CHAPTER COVERS hotel management companies and their methods of operation. First it explains the beginnings of management companies and continues by describing their history and evolution. It then focuses on management contracts between hotel owners and management companies, identifying and explaining major contract provisions and the reasons for them. Finally, the chapter describes the opportunities and risks for hotel owners and management companies when entering into a management contract.

## Why Management Companies Exist

The growth and prosperity of hotel management companies, and the unique and changing nature of their relationships with hotel owners, underscore the fact that hotels are a special kind of real estate. They are very different from office buildings and shopping malls, for example.

To begin with, unlike most other businesses, hotels operate 24 hours a day. Moreover, unlike 24-hour operations such as all-night gas stations or drugstores, hotels must provide a multitude of readily available specialized services. At full-service properties, guests expect that food and beverage service will be provided—in some cases on a 24-hour basis. Rooms must be cleaned daily. Full-service hotels may also offer laundry and valet services, meeting and convention rooms and services, fitness clubs, tennis courts and golf courses, airport limousines, concierge services, business centers, and secretarial services. The number and range of facilities and services a lodging property offers depends on the property's biggest guest group, which may be business travelers, tourists, or conventioneers.

In fact, a hotel is a miniature self-sustaining society. Managers of large hotels often compare what they do to running a small city. Many large hotels have their own energy-generating facilities, security forces, and shopkeepers. Guests sleep, eat, work, play, and sometimes die in hotels. The hotel is the guests' headquarters—their office and home, the center of their daily business and social life. Because a hotel can be so many things, managing it can be complex and extremely demanding. Managers and their staffs must be prepared to cope with a variety of activities and emergencies while maintaining and controlling the hotel's physical plant.

Managing a hotel requires special expertise. Buying a franchise is one way inexperienced hotel owners can try to acquire that expertise. When they buy a franchise, they buy an established image, a tested and successful operating system, employee training programs, marketing and advertising programs, and reservation systems.

However, while a franchise may provide systems, programs, and training, it does not provide the cadre of experienced managers and employees necessary to run a hotel. For this reason, when hotel chains such as Hilton and Sheraton first expanded, they managed every new property themselves rather than sell franchises. They understood that they could not write down everything they knew in training manuals, and that mastery of the science of running a hotel could not be easily acquired in a short training course.

Rather than buy a hotel franchise, some inexperienced owners decided the best way to make sure their hotel was profitable was to hire professional hotel managers from established hotel chains or independent management companies. The hotel management company was born.

## The Evolution of Management Companies

For hundreds of years hotels were started and operated by hoteliers, just as restaurants were started by chefs. These hoteliers were professionals who knew how to manage a hotel.

But as the lodging industry grew in the last half of the twentieth century, a new breed of owners appeared. These new owners were entrepreneurs who regarded the buildings and land they occupied as attractive investments, or they were real estate developers who felt that a hotel would be the best use for a piece of property they owned. These new owners, who knew nothing about the hotel business and usually were not interested in it, had several options for running their hotels. Many hired professional hotel managers and operated their hotels as independent properties. In order to generate business and name recognition they sometimes tied in with a referral service such as Best Western or a marketing group like Preferred Hotels.

Another option was to turn management of the property over to a hotel company. Hotel companies such as Hilton were receptive to the idea because it was a way to expand their earning base without the financial risk of developing a hotel from the ground up.

From the standpoint of these new owners—who were real estate investors, not hoteliers—the most logical way to employ a hotel company was a lease, an instrument that they were very familiar with. Under this arrangement, a hotel owner or developer—which might be an individual, a company, or even a government—would simply rent out a structure to a hotel company either as a fully developed and furnished turnkey operation or, more likely, as an unfurnished building that had to be outfitted by the hotel company. For instance, the government of Bermuda constructed the town of Saint George's first hotel, expecting the hotel would bring tourists to that part of the island. The building was then leased to the Holiday Inn Corporation. Subsequently the hotel has been leased to several other operators.

Under early lease arrangements, the hotel company was responsible for hiring and managing the entire staff of the hotel, collecting all the revenues from sales, and paying all operating costs. They also paid rent to the owners for the use of the facility. In return they received a share of the hotel's gross operating profit. Gross operating profit was determined by deducting operating costs from total revenue. Obviously, the hotel's fixed charges—such as depreciation, interest on borrowed capital, and real estate taxes—were paid by the owner of the building. For a few leased hotels, the rental agreement was based on a percentage of total sales. Sometimes the rent was based on a combination of a percentage of sales as well as a share of the gross operating profit.

Another typical arrangement was the two-thirds/one-third lease. Here, two-thirds of the gross operating profit went to the owner and one-third went to the hotel company. This kind of arrangement was the basis of the contract made in 1954 between Hilton Hotels and the Puerto Rican government, the lessee and lessor, respectively, of the Caribe Hilton Hotel in San Juan, Puerto Rico. Hilton used the same formula to expand to Turkey, Mexico, and Cuba. It was in Cuba, after Castro's takeover and the disruption of operations because of the revolution, that Hilton recognized the potential for losses due to circumstances beyond their control. According to Charles A. Bell, former executive vice president of Hilton International, "That is why Hilton converted their profit-sharing lease agreement into management contracts under which the owners took the risk of operating losses, as well as debt service, and had the ongoing responsibility of supplying working capital."[1]

While Hilton was growing by leasing new properties and creating new types of leases, the Inter-Continental Hotel Corporation (IHC) was pioneering the management contract. In the early 1950s, IHC signed its first management contracts with the respective owners of the Techendama in Bogota, Colombia, and the Tamanaco in Caracas, Venezuela, while the hotels were still under construction. Instead of paying rent and keeping the hotels' profits, IHC did not pay rent and received from each owner a management fee (which originally was based on a fixed fee per room) and an "incentive fee." The incentive fee was a percentage of the hotel's gross operating profit, plus reimbursement of IHC's overhead—specific expenses incurred by IHC in managing the property.

Incentive fees are now a regular part of management contracts, but in the 1950s this concept was a real innovation. The term **"incentive fee"** describes that portion of the management fee that is based on a percentage of a negotiated level of profitability. For example, one basis is a percentage of operating cash flow after debt service (CFADS). It is called an incentive fee because it is designed to motivate the hotel company to produce maximum profit for the owners, so the hotel company can collect the maximum incentive fee. As it gained more experience with this concept, IHC switched from a fixed fee per room to a percentage of gross revenue plus a percentage of gross operating profit with no reimbursement of company overhead. At first, IHC made a small investment in each of the hotels it managed, to entitle it to a director on the boards of the companies that owned the hotels. Later, in Europe and the Far East, IHC invested as much as one-third of the project cost.

One of the pioneers of management companies in the United States was Robert M. James, CHA, former president (retired) of Regal-AIRCOA, now Richfield Hotel Management Inc. When James started his company in 1971, few U.S. hotels were operating under management contracts. In 1970 there were fewer than 10 management companies operating 22 properties.

Since contracting with a hotel owner to manage the hotel for him or her was virtually a new field, there was little information or experience to guide the first U.S. management companies. To help remedy this situation, James started the International Council of Hotel and Motel Management Companies—a committee of the American Hotel & Motel Association—which enabled management company representatives to meet with one another and learn more about management contracts.

As a result of the economic recession in the early 1970s, management companies' services were in great demand. They could provide professional management for U.S. hotels that had been taken back by the investors—many of them insurance companies. The number of management companies has grown to the point where there are approximately 1,700 hotels operated by the 20 top management companies (see Exhibit 1).

## Management Contracts

A hotel **management contract**, as defined by Professor James Eyster of Cornell's School of Hotel Administration, is "a written agreement between an owner and an operator of a hotel or motor inn by which the owner employs the operator as an agent (employee) to assume full responsibility for operating and managing the property."[2] The operator (management company) can be a hotel chain with a familiar name and market image, such as Hyatt or Sheraton. It can also be an independent management company. Independent management companies operate franchise hotels as well as independent hotels. For example, Carnival Hotels and Resorts manages 82 properties under various franchises such as Sheraton, Westin, and Hampton Inns, as well as many independent resorts such as the five-star Grand Bay Hotel in Miami and the Pier House in Key West, Florida. (Carnival Hotels and Resorts, excluding casino hotels, was purchased by Patriot American Hospitality, the Dallas-based REIT, in early 1996.)

Under the earliest management contracts, the operator was simply regarded as a company hired to perform a service, much as an architectural firm might be hired to draw the plans for a hotel. The management company got paid for performing those services, but took no financial risk and therefore was not entitled to any profits. However, as noted previously, that basic concept has evolved over time. Management companies now typically own a piece of the hotels they manage, thereby assuming a share of the financial risk. Other changes to the basic concept are as follows:

- Twenty years ago, most financing of lodging facilities in the United States was done by insurance companies and lending institutions. They invested for the long term, hoping to realize both profits and appreciation on the value of the property. Since the late 1980s, however, the situation has been changing. Current investors include "the operators themselves, and pools of money from Wall Street and Real Estate Investment Trusts," according to Thomas F. Hewitt, president and chief operating officer of Carnival Hotels and Casinos.[3] (A **Real Estate Investment Trust [REIT]** is like a mutual fund; it allows individuals

Exhibit 1    Top 20 Management Companies

| Rank | Management Company Headquarters | Rooms | Hotels |
|---|---|---|---|
| 1 | Interstate Hotels Co.<br>Pittsburgh, PA | 45,329 | 223 |
| 2 | Bristol Hotel Co.<br>Dallas, TX | 28,799 | 101 |
| 3 | Capstar Hotel Co. Corp.<br>Washington, DC | 24,287 | 121 |
| 4 | Prime Hospitality<br>Fairfield, NJ | 19,513 | 140 |
| 5 | Tharaldson Property Management<br>Fargo, ND | 15,829 | 250 |
| 6 | Unihost<br>Mississauga, Ontario | 14,400 | 132 |
| 7 | American General Hospitality<br>Dallas, TX | 13,398 | 65 |
| 8 | Ocean Hospitalities<br>Portsmouth, NH | 13,026 | 77 |
| 9 | Richfield Hospitality Services Inc.<br>Englewood, CO | 12,989 | 55 |
| 10 | Westmont Hospitality Group<br>Houston, TX | 12,912 | 63 |
| 11 | Remington Hotel Corp.<br>Dallas, TX | 11,500 | 70 |
| 12 | Winegardner & Hammons<br>Cincinnati, OH | 10,228 | 49 |
| 13 | Beck Summit Hotel Management Group<br>Boca Raton, FL | 10,000 | 60 |
| 14 | Lane Hospitality<br>Northbrook, IL | 9,708 | 53 |
| 15 | Sage Hospitality Resources<br>Denver, CO | 8,103 | 56 |
| 16 | Barrington International Hospitality<br>Ft. Lauderdale, FL | 7,800 | 34 |
| 17 | Hostmark Management Group<br>Rolling Meadows, IL | 7,385 | 33 |
| 18 | Amerihost Properties<br>Des Plaines, IL | 7,112 | 89 |
| 19 | Davidson Hotel Co.<br>Memphis, TN | 7,000 | 28 |
| 20 | WestCoast Hotels<br>Seattle, WA | 6,906 | 32 |

Source: *Hotel & Motel Management,* March 2, 1998.

**The Ritz-Carlton, Palm Beach is operated under a management contract.** (Courtesy of the Ritz-Carlton Hotel Company)

to combine their resources to invest in income-producing properties or lend funds to developers or builders.) In Europe and the Pacific Rim, financial institutions still play an important role in financing hotels, while in countries such as Mexico, Venezuela, and Argentina, governments often provide needed funds.

- The relationship between owners and operators has dramatically shifted. Writing in the *Cornell Quarterly*, Eyster says that there has been a significant change in management contracts in the 1990s due to (1) increased competition among operators, (2) the more active role of owners in management of their investment, and (3) low hotel demand.[4]

- Environmental concerns have also slowed development in the United States and abroad. Today it is recognized that hotels and resorts might damage

Thomas F. Hewitt, President and Chief Operating Officer of Carnival Hotels and Casinos.

ecologically sensitive areas, so it is harder to get approval to build. Often the cost of meeting environmental requirements can substantially increase the capital required to develop a new property.

Because of these reasons, hotel owners have become even less willing than they were before to take all of the financial risk by themselves. The stakes have gotten too high. Moreover, some management companies have grown in size and power to the point where it makes economic sense for them to own all or part of the properties they manage. As part owners, they can take a share of the hotel's profits in addition to collecting their management fees. "I don't think there's a pure management contract that is written in the industry any more, at least not among the major companies," says Hewitt. "[The management contracts] all involve some degree of ownership, lending, or something that involves risk [for the management company]."

## Contract Provisions

The provisions of a management contract are important not only to the owner and the operator, but also to the lenders who finance the project. Lenders want assurance that the hotel owner and the management company operating the hotel have a reasonable opportunity to make a profit. They also want to be sure that differences between the owner and the management company have been resolved in advance; otherwise, the viability of the project may be jeopardized.

Contract provisions detail the exact terms that the parties have agreed upon. Although the basic provisions of all management contracts are similar, there can be significant differences from contract to contract. These differences include the amounts invested by the owner and the management company; the nature and amount of control exercised by each party; and fee structures, including the incentive arrangement.

In the following sections, we discuss some of the major terms and provisions often addressed in hotel management contracts.[5]

**Operating Term.** The **operating term provision** defines the length of the initial term of the contract and its renewal options. The management company (hereafter referred to as the "operator") usually prefers a long initial period, while the owner usually prefers a shorter one. Eyster explains that while a long-term contract offers stability for both parties, it is a disadvantage to the owner if the owner wants to remove the operator before the contract comes up for renewal. Operators generally favor long-term contracts because such contracts give them more time to recover a return on their investment. The lenders' concern is that the term of the contract and the term of the loan coincide, making it probable that the hotel will be run by only one operator throughout the loan's payback period. Such a stable situation makes it more likely that there will be an uninterrupted flow of revenues and profits to cover debt payments.

The length of the contract is often a serious negotiating point. Although the industry standard was once 20 years, it now varies from 1 year to 20 years. Eyster's research shows that 12 years is the median contract term for a chain operator with some equity in the hotel it is managing. However, for independent hotel operators that do not have established brand names, the median contract length is 3 years.[6]

**Fee Structure.** The **fee structure provision** outlines the fees the owner must pay to the operator for managing the property. This is one of the most important contract provisions because it affects both the owner's and operator's profits. The fee structure is negotiable, and will vary from contract to contract depending on the bargaining power of the parties. Eyster categorizes the payments owners make to operators into three areas.

**Technical assistance fees** cover the time and expertise of the operator as a consultant in the design of the facilities. Architectural and interior design are the services most commonly rendered, although equipment selection and help with security concerns such as lighting and locking systems are often involved as well.

**Pre-opening management fees** are similar to technical assistance fees in that they cover work done by the operator before the hotel opens. Pre-opening management activities include planning, staffing, training, marketing, budgeting, and other activities that the operator must perform before the property is ready to receive guests. These activities are very important—especially for hotel owners with no previous experience—since they may well influence the hotel's long-term success.

**Post-opening management fees**, also known as simply "management fees," are the fees paid to the operator for managing the property. In the case of a chain operator such as Hilton or Westin, the fee also covers the use of the established brand name. As has been noted, an independent management company does not bring a recognizable name to the negotiating table. If the owner wants a franchised name like Hampton Inn or Embassy Suite, or wants the property to be part of a referral reservation system like that of Best Western, he or she must deal directly with the franchisor or reservation system. That cost is distinct and separate from the management fee. This is the main justification for a chain operator's higher management fee; a chain operator gives the owner's hotel an already established name.

Post-opening management fees are almost always based on some kind of formula. It is typically a basic fee plus an incentive. The important thing in determining an equitable management fee is to relate the fee to the services received and to define the level of profit upon which the incentive fee is based. According to Eyster's study of management fee structure, in those companies he surveyed between 1993 and 1996, the basic fee for chain operators ranged from 1 percent to 6 percent of gross revenue and 1 percent to 5 percent for independent operators (see Exhibit 2).[7] The incentive fee is a negotiated figure and there are a number of ways to calculate it. One method utilizes a percentage of operating cash flow after debt service (CFADS). As Exhibit 2 shows, there are other similar methods that allow the owner to cover debt service before the operating company receives incentive fee distribution. Although exact contract details are proprietary information, Hewitt indicated that for his company, which is an independent operator, incentive fees range from 2 percent to 5 percent of income before fixed charges. "Good operators have the opportunity to make more money under today's incentive system," Hewitt says. "We look for a profit based on a percentage of gross revenues, or income, or cash flow. It's very dependent on the property, the revenue mix the property has, the project's financing, and so forth. There are different provisions in each contract, but we try to include all of these considerations in most contracts."[8]

Eyster says that in some contracts negotiated in the mid-1990s, owners have set a maximum percentage on the basic and incentive fees combined. His study shows a maximum that ranges from 4.5 percent to 5.5 percent of gross revenue.[9]

**Operator-reimbursable expenses** are incurred when a management company's corporate office provides centralized reservation systems, bulk purchasing, national advertising campaigns, accounting expenses, and travel costs of corporate staff who supervise the hotel. Each managed property reimburses the operator for its share of these costs.

**Reporting Requirements.** The **reporting requirements provision** defines the types of reports and the frequency with which they are to be provided by the operator to the owner. These reports include budgets, financial statements, variance reports between budget and actual performance, market plans, audited statements, and—in some cases—weekly and daily activity reports.

**Exhibit 2  Management-Fee Structures**

| | Basic fee (percentage of gross revenues) | | | Incentive fee range (bases actual or negotiated) | |
|---|---|---|---|---|---|
| | Low | Median | High | | |
| **Chain operators** | | | | | |
| Full-service, no equity | 1% | 2.25% | 3.5% | 10–32% | CFADS |
| | | | | 12–40% | CFADS & ROE |
| | | | | 15–22% | Improved IBFC |
| | | | | 8–12% | IBFC** |
| Full-service, equity | 2% | 2.5% | 3.5% | 8–20% | CFADS |
| | | | | 10–20% | CFADS & ROE |
| | | | | 5–8% | IBFC** |
| Limited-service* | 3% | 5% | 6% | 0–15% | CFADS & ROE |
| Caretaker*** | 2% | 2.5% | 3% | 10–25% | Improved IBFC |
| **Independent Operators** | | | | | |
| Full-service, no equity | 1% | 1.5% | 3% | 8–12% | CFADS |
| | | | | 10–28% | CFADS & ROE |
| | | | | 12–15% | Improved IBFC |
| | | | | 5–8% | IBFC** |
| Full-service, equity | 2% | 2.5% | 3% | 5–10% | CFADS |
| | | | | 5–10% | IBFC** |
| Limited-service* | 3% | 4% | 5% | 0–10% | CFADS |
| Caretaker*** | 1.5% | 2% | 3% | 8–20% | Improved IBFC |
| | | | | 10–25% | Improved property value |

CFADS = cash flow after debt service; ROE = return on equity; IBFC = income before fixed charges
* Includes properties with no operator equity participation and those with operator equity.
** Payment of incentive fee is usually subordinated to a negotiated cash-flow amount; subordinated fees are usually waived rather than deferred; no interest is charged on deferred fees.
*** Basic fee is sometimes a guaranteed minimum-dollar amount.

Source: James J. Eyster, "Hotel Management Contracts in the U.S.," *Cornell Quarterly,* June 1997, p. 25.

**Approvals.** Since the management contract is an agreement between the hotel's owner and operator, decisions about the hotel's development or operation generally require input from both parties, or at least an approval from one party of the other's decision. The agreement should have an **approval provision** that defines in what areas approvals are necessary. It is common for a contract to call for the owner's approval of the general manager, the controller, and the director of sales and marketing, according to Hewitt. Even lenders are no longer entirely passive, and have become more interested in reviewing budgets.[10] In many cases owners are concerned about restaurant concepts and marketing and pricing strategies as well.

Some owners want to be much more involved than others. According to Hewitt, "In the seventies and eighties a management company presented a marketing program and then told the owner, 'We'll see you next year.'" He says things are dramatically different today. "We insist when we write a contract that the owners should have a degree of participation, sometimes weekly, maybe quarterly. Our regional and divisional people communicate with owners on a regular basis. The day-to-day decisions are of course left to management."[11]

Contract provisions relating to owner input have given owners and lenders, or their representatives (referred to as asset managers), more of a voice in operational decisions. According to James Eyster, involvement has increased considerably in operational decisions: the hotel's operating policies, the budgeting process, and personnel selection.

Although the operating companies continue to set standards, owners—through on-site representatives or representation on policy-making committees—take part in the decision-making process. In the past, the operator was responsible for developing and following the operating budget. Today, in most cases, owners provide input and have the right to approve the budget. Also, owner control over capital replacement or improvement budgets has increased significantly. Line staff members are sometimes employees of the owner under the relationship established by some management contracts, with the executive staff employed by the operator. Owners now have a greater say in the selection of the general manager and other key department heads.[12]

Even when communication between the owner and the operator is good, they may not always agree, so the contract should contain provisions for settling disputes. A number of management contracts contain an arbitration provision, specifying that the arbitration come from a qualified person or firm.[13]

**Termination.** All management contracts contain a provision that allows either party to terminate the management agreement under certain conditions:

- Non-performance of a contract provision by the other party
- One of the parties filing for bankruptcy
- One of the parties causing licenses to be suspended or revoked[14]

Some contracts include other reasons for termination. These relate to the damage or loss of the property or the sale of the property. Sometimes there is a "termination without cause" provision. If a contract is terminated without cause, the owner must pay a penalty fee to the operator to compensate for the loss of profits anticipated by the operator.

**Operator Investment.** Operators or management companies are in the business of managing, and sometimes investing. On the other hand, owners prefer a good-faith investment on the part of the operator. Today, more operators are investing in the properties they manage, usually in the form of loans or equity. When an operator loans money to an owner, the management contract specifies the amount in the **operator investment provision**; how the loan will be used (initial working capital, or to cover negative cash flows); the term of the loan; and the interest rate. When the investment is an equity contribution, it may be in the form of cash, free technical services, waived pre-opening management fees, or even conversion of incentive fees.[15]

**Operating Expenses.** In addition to the normal costs of operating a hotel, an operator will incur expenses in its home office or on the premises of the property itself. Expenses such as centralized advertising, reservation systems, and computer and accounting services are typical of the costs that an operator sometimes charges to the hotel's owner. The operator should clearly state the operating expenses it will pass on to the owner in the **operating expenses provision**—this helps avoid challenges by the owner later on. In recent years, "owners have demanded and received both a clearer definition of system-reimbursable expenses in their contracts and a better method of verifying those expenses than formerly."[16]

**Other Provisions.** Other provisions of most management contracts include those that:

- Restrict the operator from competing in the same market area by operating another property within the area (unless approved by the owner)
- Specify the methods of transferring ownership or management interests to others by either party through a sale or a lease
- Stipulate exclusive rights to work with each other on future hotels
- Define the rights of each party in case the property is damaged or condemned
- Provide indemnification for the adverse performance of the other party
- Lay out a plan for a cash reserve for the replacement of furniture, fixtures, and equipment

## Advantages and Disadvantages

Management contracts have advantages and disadvantages for each of the parties involved.

One of the primary disadvantages for owners is that while a management contract relieves them of day-to-day operating responsibilities, they still have to carry all or most of the financial burden. Although operators have increasingly provided loans and equity investments in recent years, owners are still primarily responsible for funding their properties. They must make up for losses or insufficient revenues to cover operating costs. In addition, management fees reduce owner profits.

Owners do, however, benefit from management contracts. The primary advantage is that they buy the services of an established hotel operator with a proven track record and a good reputation. Although a management fee must be paid, the potential for profit is increased. An experienced operator can offer marketing expertise and systems of cost control that would otherwise not be available to the owner.

At first it may appear that operators have few serious disadvantages in a management contract arrangement. One of the greatest advantages, from an operator's point of view, is that it can control a large number of properties with a relatively limited investment. The operator's financial risk is much lower than the owner's.

Nevertheless, there are disadvantages to a management contract for operators as well. An operator's reputation is on the line every day at every hotel it manages. The operator must look to the owner for funding when there is a shortfall in revenues. If the owner refuses to supply it or doesn't have it, the resulting sub-standard services and facilities will reflect on the operator. In addition, today the operator's real opportunity for profit lies in the incentive fee. An operator dealing with a difficult or poorly financed owner will probably never realize the anticipated profits.

A further disadvantage is that, unless the operator has provided equity, the owner may make decisions regarding the property's development or sale without the operator's input. The owner can also dismiss the operator or not renew the contract at the end of its term, possibly damaging the operator's reputation and taking away its opportunity to realize profits from the work it has done. A hotel is rarely an overnight success; it usually takes years to realize an operating profit, and only those who are in it for the long haul are likely to reap the rewards.

On the whole, management contracts are carefully crafted so that all parties are well protected. But even with the best intentions, sometimes there are serious disagreements between owners and operators. An example of what can happen surfaced publicly when the Ritz-Carlton Hotels (49% owned by Host Marriott Corporation) removed its name overnight from four properties it operated that were owned by a Los Angeles-based holding company with Saudi investors, Al Anwa. Ritz-Carlton alleged that the owner owed $4 million in unpaid management fees and other costs, and said the hotel never received promised renovations and enhancements to operating systems and that it needed to protect its reputation. In response, the owners alleged that the company was mismanaging the hotel by exploiting expense accounts. When negotiations between the two parties reached an impasse, Ritz-Carlton removed its name overnight—and without warning—from four hotels in New York, Houston, Washington, D.C., and Aspen. According to the *Wall Street Journal*, "Ritz-Carlton conducted a midnight raid of sorts, sending crews through the back doors of the four landmark hotels to remove company files, gold-framed award plaques, photographs, and computers. The company then unceremoniously lowered its blue-and-gold with the famous lion and crown, ferried the goodies off to nearby rented rooms, and evacuated about 200 corporate staff members. Guests paying up to $1,500 a night awoke to find a letter slipped under their door informing them that they were no longer staying at a Ritz-Carlton."[17]

While this kind of incident is highly unusual, it does happen occasionally, and it illustrates the necessity of both parties understanding what they get and what they give up in a management contract.

## Chapter Summary

Hotels are a special kind of real estate. They are small, self-sufficient communities, and they need people with hotel expertise to operate them. In the last half of the twentieth century, inexperienced hotel owners such as investors and real estate developers began to acquire hotel properties. These owners realized that the best way to gain hotel management expertise was to bring in experienced hotel operators by (1) leasing the hotel to them, or (2) signing a management contract with them that allowed them to run the hotel.

With the first leasing agreements, the operator paid rent for the building but kept whatever profits were made. With the first management contracts, operators did not pay rent and did not keep all of the hotel's profits—they received a basic fee to cover their overhead costs plus a share of the profits or an incentive fee.

A management contract is a written agreement between an owner of a hotel and a hotel management company (operator) in which the owner employs the operator as an agent to assume full responsibility for managing the property. The operator can be a hotel chain with an established brand name or an independent management company.

Management contracts are still evolving, for several reasons. Most new hotel owners are only interested in short-term involvement. Hotel development has slowed because the tax structure and business climate have changed and environmental concerns have become more important. In addition, owners are no longer willing to take all of the financial risks by themselves; operators are now sharing some of the risks.

The most important provisions in a management contract are those dealing with the operating term, the fee structure, reporting requirements, approvals, termination of the contract, operator investment, operating expenses, and employees.

From an owner's point of view, the advantage of hiring a management company is that it relieves him or her of the burden of running the hotel and provides the hotel with experienced management personnel and operating systems. The disadvantages are that the owner is still responsible for paying the bills even though the management company operates the hotel, and management fees reduce the owner's profits.

Hotel management companies benefit from management contracts because the companies can grow without putting up large amounts of capital, keeping their financial risk low. However, difficult or under-financed owners can damage an operator's reputation and deprive it of profits it has earned. The owner can also dismiss the operator who built the business, even if the hotel is showing a profit.

## Endnotes

1. Charles A. Bell, "Agreements with Chain-Hotel Companies," *Cornell Quarterly*, February 1993, p. 28.

2. James J. Eyster, *The Negotiation and Administration of Hotel and Restaurant Management Contracts*, 3d rev. ed. (Ithaca, N.Y.: School of Hotel Administration, Cornell University, 1988), p. 4.

3. Thomas F. Hewitt, personal interview, 29 July 1997.

4. James J. Eyster, "Hotel Management Contracts in the U.S.," *Cornell Quarterly*, June 1997, p. 14.

5. These provisions and some of the comments about them are adapted from Stephen Rushmore, "Make Sure Management Contracts Contain These Terms," *Lodging Hospitality*, April 1988. The authors also wish to acknowledge their debt to Professor James J. Eyster. Many of the observations and comments relating to these provisions are based on Eyster's *The Negotiation and Administration of Hotel and Restaurant Management Contracts*.

6. Eyster, "Hotel Management Contracts in the U.S.," p. 21.
7. Eyster, "Hotel Management Contracts in the U.S.," p. 25.
8. Hewitt interview.
9. Eyster, "Hotel Management Contracts in the U.S.," p. 26.
10. Hewitt interview.
11. Hewitt interview.
12. Eyster, "Hotel Management Contracts in the U.S.," p. 15.
13. Eyster, "Hotel Management Contracts in the U.S.," p. 33.
14. Eyster, *Negotiation and Administration.*
15. Eyster, "Hotel Management Contracts in the U.S.," p. 22.
16. Eyster, "The Revolution in Domestic Hotel Management Contracts," *Cornell Quarterly,* February 1993, p. 21.
17. "Ritz-Carlton Checks Out of Four Key Hotels," *Wall Street Journal,* 4 August 1997, B1.

# Key Terms

**approval provision**—The provision of a hotel management contract specifying which operator decisions require management approval. The mechanism for settling owner/operator disputes is sometimes included in this provision.

**fee structure provision**—A provision in a contract between a hotel owner and a hotel management company that outlines the fees the owner must pay to the management company for managing the property.

**incentive fee**—That portion of the management fee (paid by hotel owners to hotel management companies) that is based on a percentage of income before fixed charges (also known as gross operating profit), or on a percentage of cash flow after debt service.

**management contract**—A written agreement between an owner and an operator of a hotel or motor inn by which the owner employs the operator as an agent (employee) to assume full responsibility for operating and managing the property.

**operating expenses provision**—The provision in a hotel management contract that outlines the expenses the management company will pass on to the hotel's

**operating term provision**—The provision of a hotel management contract that defines the length of the initial contract and its renewal options.

**operator investment provision**—The provision of a hotel management contract outlining the details of the operator's investment in the property.

**operator-reimbursable expenses**—Expenses a hotel management company's corporate office incurs in providing services (bulk purchasing and national advertising campaigns, for example) to its managed properties. Each managed property reimburses the management company for its share of these costs.

**post-opening management fees**—Fees paid by an owner to a management company for managing the property. In the case of a chain management company, the fees also cover the use of the established brand name.

**pre-opening management fees**—Fees paid by an owner to a management company for work done before the opening of the hotel, including planning, staffing, training, marketing, budgeting, and other activities that the management company must perform before the property is ready to receive guests.

**real estate investment trust (REIT)**—An investment instrument, somewhat like a mutual fund, that allows individuals to combine their resources to invest in income–producing properties or lend funds to developers or builders.

**reporting requirements provision**—The provision of a hotel management contract that stipulates the types of reports the management company must provide to the owner and how often they must be submitted.

**technical assistance fees**—Fees paid by an owner to a management company covering the time and expertise of the company as a consultant in the design and plan of the facilities.

## Review Questions

1. How can a hotel owner who is not a hotelier ensure that the property is managed effectively?
2. What is an incentive fee?
3. What three provisions are common to almost every management contract?
4. What are the differences between a lease and a management contract?
5. What are some of the industry-wide changes responsible for the evolution of management contracts?
6. In negotiating a management contract, which party prefers a long-term contract and which party prefers a short-term contract? Why?
7. What are four types of fees owners pay to operators?
8. What do the "approvals" and "termination" provisions of a management contract cover?
9. What are the advantages and disadvantages of management contracts, from both the owner's and operator's points of view?

## Internet Sites

For more information, visit the following Internet sites. Remember that Internet addresses can change without notice. If the site is no longer there, use a search engine to look for additional sites.

## Hotel Companies/Resorts

Best Western
www.bestwestern.com

Doubletree Hotel Corporation
www.doubletreehotels.com

Hilton Hotels
www.hilton.com

Host Marriott Corporation
www.hostmarriott.com

Interstate Hotels Corporation
www.ihc-hotels.com

Preferred Hotels & Resorts
www.preferredhotels.com

Richfield Hospitality Services
www.richfield.com

Ritz-Carlton Hotels
www.ritzcarlton.com

Sheraton Hotels
www.sheraton.com

Starwood Lodging
www.starwood.com

## Organizations, Resources

The Franchise Network
www.bison1.com/main.html

## REVIEW QUIZ

When you feel you have covered all of the material in this chapter, answer these questions. Choose the *best* answer.

1. Buying a franchise does *not* provide a hotel owner with:

    a. employee training programs.
    b. marketing programs.
    c. experienced managers and employees.
    d. a tested and successful operating system.

2. Hotel management companies came about because:

    a. early lease arrangements between hotel owners and independent hotel managers proved inadequate.
    b. individuals who didn't know much about hotels, such as developers or real estate investors, built hotels and wanted experienced people to run them.
    c. the Tax Reform Act of 1986 made it more advantageous for hotel owners to hire hotel management companies rather than buy a franchise or run the hotel themselves.
    d. a and c.

3. It is common for a management contract to give the owner approval of the:

    a. controller.
    b. resident manager.
    c. executive chef.
    d. chief of security.

4. With respect to management contracts, lenders tend to:

    a. want assurance that the hotel owner and the management company have a reasonable opportunity to make a profit.
    b. act as disinterested parties during negotiations.
    c. dictate approval terms for restaurant concepts and marketing and pricing strategies.
    d. negotiate for significant influence in day-to-day operational decisions.

5. A management company usually prefers a _____ initial contract term, and a hotel owner usually prefers a _____ initial contract term.

    a. long; long
    b. long; short
    c. short; long
    d. short; short

## REVIEW QUIZ (continued)

6. Which of the following is usually considered an operator-reimbursable expense?

    a. security lighting and locking systems
    b. architectural design fees
    c. franchise fees
    d. national advertising

7. One of the disadvantages a management contract has for hotel owners is that:

    a. the management company may sell the hotel without the owner's input.
    b. incentive fees typically must be paid to the hotel management company even if the hotel does not show a profit.
    c. they still must carry all or most of the financial burden.
    d. none of the above.

**Answer Key:** 1-c-C1, 2-b-C1, 3-a-C2, 4-a-C2, 5-b-C2, 6-d-C2, 7-c-C2

Each question is linked to a competency. Competencies are listed on the first page of the chapter. An answer reading 3-b-C4 translates to:

   3: the question number
   b: the correct answer
   C4: the competency number

## Chapter 17 Outline

What Is a Franchise?
    Types of Franchises
The History of Franchising
    Product or Trade-Name Franchising
    Business Format Franchising
How Franchising Works
    Initial Investment
    Franchise Regulations
Owning a Franchise
    Advantages
    Disadvantages
    Advantages and Disadvantages for Franchisors
Franchising Issues
Chapter Summary

## Competencies

1. Explain what a franchise is, describe types of franchises, summarize the history of franchising, and explain how franchising works.

2. State common reasons individuals give for wanting to buy a franchise, outline the advantages and disadvantages to owning a franchise, list advantages and disadvantages for franchisors, and summarize other franchising issues.

# 17

# Franchising Is Big Business

THIS CHAPTER DEALS with franchising in the hospitality industry. It covers the history of franchising, the reasons for its popularity, the advantages and disadvantages of owning a franchise, and how franchising works. Finally, there is a brief look at the future of franchising.

## What Is a Franchise?

In its simplest form, the word *franchise* refers to the authorization given by a company to another company or an individual to sell its unique products and services. Franchising is a marketing or distribution system: the franchisor grants an individual or company the right to conduct business according to the franchisor's guidelines for a specified time and in a specified place.

Franchising is big business. According to the International Franchise Association, there are approximately 558,000 franchise outlets in the United States, and the number continues to grow. These outlets produced about $803 billion in sales. Franchise units employed eight million people.[1] Franchising has grown all over the world. For example, there are about 190,000 franchisees in Japan, 26,400 in Britain, and 19,000 in Mexico.[2]

Let's review the following terms, which will be used throughout the chapter:

- **Franchise**—In addition to the meaning mentioned earlier, franchise can also refer to the name of the business format or product that is being franchised. The Marriott Corporation grants Residence Inn franchises as well as Courtyard by Marriott franchises.

- **Franchising**—The major trade association in franchising, the International Franchise Association, defines franchising as "a continuing relationship in which the franchisor provides a licensed privilege to do business, plus assistance in organizing, training, merchandising, and management in return for a consideration from the franchisee."

- **Franchisor**—The franchise company that owns the trademark, products, and/or business format that is being franchised.

- **Franchisee**—The individual or company granted the right to do business under the franchisor's name. A person who buys a Dairy Queen franchise is a franchisee.

Franchise rights vary. Most franchisors grant franchisees the right to use the franchise name and its distinctive trademark, logo, architecture, and interior

545

**Courtyards are Marriott franchises.** (Courtesy of Marriott Corporation)

design. Some franchisors also sell their method of operation, or designate territories in which the franchisee may operate. In some cases, the franchisor may grant the franchisee the right to sell the franchisor's product(s); for example, Starbuck's has the right to sell Starbuck's coffee.

## Types of Franchises

There are two types of franchises: the product or trade-name franchise and the business format franchise.

The **product or trade-name franchise** is a supplier-dealer arrangement whereby the dealer (franchisee) sells a product line provided by the supplier (franchisor) and, to some degree, takes on the identity of the supplier. This is the type of franchise that exists in the automobile, gasoline service station, and soft drink industry. The majority of total franchise sales in the United States are from product or trade-name franchising.

**Business format franchises**, which include fast-food restaurants and lodging chains, are characterized by an ongoing business relationship between franchisor and franchisee that includes not only the product, service, and trademark but the entire business concept itself.

The majority of the growth in franchising has been in the business format franchise category. Besides food service operations and hotels, this category includes non-food retailers, personal and business services, real estate services, and other service businesses.

Restaurants make up the majority of business format franchises. See Exhibit 1 for the top twenty restaurant chains.

See Exhibit 2 for the top ten hotel chains.

**Exhibit 1  The Top 20 Restaurant Franchise Chains**

| | |
|---|---|
| 1. McDonald's | 11. Hardee's Hamburgers |
| 2. Subway | 12. Dunkin' Donuts |
| 3. Pizza Hut | 13. Arby's |
| 4. Burger King | 14. Blimpie Subs & Salads |
| 5. Taco Bell | 15. Sonic Drive-In |
| 6. KFC | 16. Denny's |
| 7. Dairy Queen | 17. Long John Silver's |
| 8. Wendy's | 18. Jack in the Box |
| 9. Domino's Pizza | 19. Eatery Express (Kmart snack bars) |
| 10. Little Caesar's Pizza | 20. Papa John's Pizza |

Source: *Nation's Restaurant News*, June 23, 1997, p. 118.

## The History of Franchising

Franchising is not a new concept. A precursor of modern franchising occurred in Roman times, when private citizens bid for the right to operate tax-collecting "franchises" for the government. These "franchisees," called "publicans," kept a percentage of the taxes they collected for themselves. It was a lucrative business—especially for the unscrupulous—and publicans were generally detested, as the Biblical phrase "publicans and sinners" reminds us.[3] This form of franchising existed in the Middle Ages as well when royalty and church officials rewarded important citizens with the right to collect revenues in return for "various services or considerations."[4]

### Product or Trade-Name Franchising

All of the early franchises were product or trade-name franchises that allowed individuals or companies willing to put up their own capital to sell and, in some cases, make the product of the franchisor. The only restrictions on franchisees were on what they sold and the territory where they sold it.

In 1851, I. M. Singer & Company used franchising to develop a network of sewing-machine dealers throughout the United States. Under the Singer concept, a dealer was allowed to open a Singer Sewing Machine store in return for an agreement to sell only Singer machines and supplies. Since people did not know how to use these new sewing machines, the dealers also provided service in the form of sewing lessons and classes. This was the beginning of modern franchising systems.

Because the Singer company had a unique product that was in demand, and one that dealers could not obtain unless they agreed to open a Singer Sewing Machine store, the company did very well. However, franchising did not catch on in a big way until the early 1900s, with the production of automobiles and soft drinks.

Just as in the case of Singer sewing machines, automobiles were new and complicated mechanical devices requiring service and repair. No one was willing to buy a horseless carriage unless there was someone nearby who could fix it if it broke down. Automobile manufacturers, most notably General Motors at first,

**Exhibit 2  The Top 10 Hotel Franchise Chains**

| | |
|---|---|
| 1. Hospitality Franchise Systems | 6. Carlson Hospitality Worldwide |
| 2. Choice Hotels International | 7. Accor |
| 3. Holiday Inn Worldwide | 8. ITT Sheraton Corporation |
| 4. Promus Companies | 9. Hilton Hotels Corporation |
| 5. Marriott International | 10. Best Western International |

Source: *Hotels*, July 1997, p. 46.

came up with a solution similar to the Singer company's: they established dealerships to sell and service their cars. Because dealers were located in the communities where the cars were sold, they were trusted neighbors who could be relied on to back up the promises made by the automobile manufacturers. Not surprisingly, the petroleum companies that grew along with the automobile dealers adopted the same form of distribution. Even today gas stations are, for the most part, individually owned small businesses that have the right to use a company's trade name and sell its products.

The first Coca-Cola franchise was granted in 1899. Franchising was necessary because Coca-Cola was packaged in a unique glass bottle that consumers paid a deposit for and returned to the company. Handling the bottles required local bottling companies that could pick them up, wash them, and re-use them. Moreover, it was expensive to ship bottled drinks all over the country from the company's headquarters in Atlanta, Georgia. In order to expand, Coca-Cola gave franchisees the right to build Coca-Cola bottling plants in return for purchasing Coca-Cola's bottles and syrup. Coca-Cola also agreed to train its bottlers in production techniques and marketing. Soon Coca-Cola bottling plants were established all over America.

Each Singer or General Motors franchise involved a relationship between the manufacturer (franchisor) and the retailer (franchisee) who sold the manufactured product(s) directly to the public. Note that in both cases the retailer performed a service (product servicing and repair) for the franchisor in addition to just selling the product. This was one reason why franchising was the most efficient form of distribution for these products. In the case of Coca-Cola, the relationship was between the manufacturer/franchisor and a wholesaler (franchisee). Coca-Cola's wholesalers did not sell directly to the public, but delivered Coca-Cola to retail soda fountains and grocery stores. Again, however, the franchisee (wholesaler) performed a service for the franchisor: in this case, bottling the product. These new products—sewing machines, cars, and soft drinks—required the seller to provide services as well as the product itself, making franchising necessary and practical.

## Business Format Franchising

The first person to pioneer the idea of the business format franchise was Howard Dearing Johnson, founder of the Howard Johnson Company. Johnson started his chain in 1925 with a drug store that he successfully converted into an ice cream parlor. By 1928 he had two thriving ice cream parlors and decided to open a third that would serve food as well. This was his first restaurant. A friend offered

Johnson some land so Johnson could build a second restaurant. Johnson had no more capital to invest, however, and convinced his friend to build the restaurant. Johnson would provide him with a franchise to sell Howard Johnson ice cream as well as assist in the design and supervision of the restaurant.

The friend's restaurant was an instant success, and Johnson realized that he had found a way to expand his business without investing any money of his own. Johnson decided to continue with the strategy of encouraging others to build Howard Johnson restaurants, which would sell Howard Johnson ice cream and other products that he would supply. He continued to assist in the design and management of these new restaurants so that he could help make them a success. Johnson did not ask for a royalty on sales for these extra services; his sole profit came from the sale of Howard Johnson products. By the end of 1936 there were 61 Howard Johnson's restaurants, most of which were franchises; by 1939 there were 107 restaurants operating in a half dozen states.[5] In 1954 Johnson entered the lodging business by franchising his first motor lodge in Savannah, Georgia. By 1969 there were 391 lodges, 90 percent of which were franchises. After 11 more years of continued growth, Howard B. Johnson, son of the founder, sold Howard Johnson's to Imperial Group Ltd., a British corporation. Imperial sold the company to Marriott in 1985. Marriott kept a few of the bigger hotels and quickly sold the rest of the lodging properties to Prime Motor Inns; Marriott then sold the free-standing Howard Johnson's restaurants to various buyers over the next few years. The hotel name was later acquired by HFS.

In spite of Johnson's success, franchising did not catch on with the rest of the hospitality industry until the early 1950s. Lodging's most notable early franchising success was Holiday Inn. Kemmons Wilson and a partner owned three successful Holiday Inn motor hotels in the early 1950s and wanted to expand nationwide. They decided to finance their expansion by selling Holiday Inn franchises to franchisees who would build their Holiday Inns according to a set format and contribute some money from each guestroom for advertising. The rest is history.

The beginning of the franchise giant McDonald's was a drive-in self-service restaurant in San Bernardino, California, built in 1948 by two brothers, Maurice and Richard McDonald. In 1954, Ray Kroc, a milkshake-machine salesman, called on the McDonald brothers to deliver eight of his Multimixer machines. What he found was an efficient octagonal assembly-line operation turning out beverages, french fries, and 15-cent hamburgers. As Kroc tells it, "When I saw it working that day in 1954, I felt like some latter-day Newton, who'd just had an Idaho potato caromed off his skull."[6] Kroc understood what made the restaurant a success. In his book, *Grinding It Out: The Making of McDonald's*, he explained what went through his mind:

> I've often been asked why I didn't simply copy the McDonald brothers' plan. They showed me the whole thing and it would have been an easy matter, seemingly, to pattern a restaurant after theirs. Truthfully the idea never crossed my mind. I saw it through the eyes of a salesman. Here was a complete package. I could get out and talk up a storm about it... Besides, the brothers did have some equipment that couldn't be readily copied. They had a specially fabricated aluminum griddle for one thing, and the set up of all the rest of the equipment was in a very precise step-saving

**This is typical of the kind of unit the McDonald's Corporation franchises today.** (Courtesy of McDonald's Corporation, Oak Brook, Illinois)

pattern. Then there was the name. I had a strong intuitive sense that the name McDonald's was exactly right. I couldn't have taken the name. But for the rest of it, I guess the real answer is that I was so naive or honest that it never occurred to me that I could take their idea and copy it and not pay them a red cent.[7]

The McDonald brothers, who drove Cadillacs and lived together in a luxurious home, were not interested in expanding. They were happy with what they had achieved and did not want to work any harder. They granted Kroc an exclusive ten-year franchise. He agreed to put up buildings exactly like the one their architect had drawn up, complete with the golden arches. The McDonald brothers inserted contractual clauses that obligated Kroc to follow their plans down to the last detail—even to signs and menus. And there was a clause that prohibited Kroc from doing anything differently without a registered letter of permission from the two brothers. It was agreed that Kroc could charge franchisees 1.9 percent of their gross sales and that he would give .5 percent of that to the McDonalds. Kroc was also allowed to charge a franchise fee of $950 to cover the expenses he incurred in finding a suitable location for each franchise and a landlord who would build to the McDonalds' specifications.

Kroc brought in Harry Sonneborn to assist him, and the two planned the future of their new enterprise. They realized that for their franchise to succeed they had to do more than simply sell prospective franchisees a name and a menu.

Besides, a hamburger—ready-made according to the franchisor's specifications—could not be sold to a franchisee like Howard Johnson's ice cream; franchisees would have to cook their own hamburgers. Kroc writes:

> We agreed that we wanted McDonald's to be more than just a name used by many different people. We wanted to build a restaurant system that would be known for food of consistently high quality and uniform methods of preparation. Our aim, of course, was to ensure repeat business based on the system's reputation rather than on the quality of a single store or operator. This would require a continuing program of educating and assisting operators and a constant review of their performance. It would also require a full-time program of research and development. I knew in my bones that the key to uniformity would be in our ability to provide techniques of preparation that operators would accept because they were superior to methods they could dream up for themselves.[8]

Here Kroc expresses the heart of the concept of modern franchising: a franchise company's reputation depends on the quality and consistency of all of its franchises, and quality and consistency are maintained by ongoing training and development. In 1961 Kroc bought out the McDonald brothers for $2.7 million. Now there are more than 20,000 McDonald's units in 89 countries.

## How Franchising Works

In order to obtain a license from a franchisor, a franchisee must pay a fee for the privilege of using the franchisor's name, identity, business systems, operating procedures, marketing techniques, and (in the case of hotels) reservations system. The typical franchise fee arrangement has two parts: (1) an initial franchise fee, payable upon signing the franchise agreement, and (2) ongoing fees.

Initial franchise fees vary. They are calculated by assigning a monetary value to the following:

- The franchisor's goodwill
- The value of the new franchise unit's trading area or territory
- The average cost of recruiting a franchisee
- The cost of training a franchisee
- The cost of signs, ads, plans, and other aids

The goodwill of a business—the reputation or prestige it enjoys among customers—is an intangible asset that is easier to estimate for an established franchisor such as McDonald's than for a new franchisor. Although intangible, goodwill can be calculated by relating it to the franchisor's profits, profits being one measure of the amount of goodwill a franchisor enjoys. For example, if a franchisor's franchises average $150,000 in profits per year, the value of the goodwill for a new franchise might be $2^{1/2}$ times that, or $375,000. A percentage of the goodwill charge—anywhere from 4 percent to 12 percent—could be part of the initial franchise fee. Franchisors differ in how they calculate goodwill and how they charge it to their franchisees.

Some territories are more valuable than others, due to their demographic makeup and the propensity of their residents to eat out. Therefore, a new franchise's location would be considered in setting the initial franchise fee.

The value of recruiting, training, and other aids is easier for the franchisor to calculate since it can refer to actual costs.

Restaurant franchisors generally charge a flat franchise fee for one unit; some franchisors charge a reduced rate for additional units. On the other hand, hotel franchisors base their initial franchise fees on the number of guestrooms the franchisee builds, with a minimum fee for those franchisees whose hotels fall below a certain number of rooms. Here are some examples of initial franchise fees:

| | |
|---|---|
| Subway | $10,000 |
| Domino's Pizza | $6,500 |
| McDonald's | $22,500 |
| ITT Sheraton | $30,000, plus $150 for each room over 100 |
| Hilton Garden Inns | Conversion: $200 per room for the first 100; $100 per room thereafter<br>New: $250 per room for the first 100; $150 per room thereafter |
| Hampton Inns | $450 per room; $45,000 minimum |

Ongoing franchise fees vary. All franchisors charge a royalty fee, usually calculated on a percentage of the franchisee's sales. As with initial franchise fees, royalties are related to the value of the franchise. Examples of typical royalty fees are as follows:

| Franchisor | Percent of Gross Revenues |
|---|---|
| Comfort Inns | 5% |
| Hilton Garden Inns | 5% |
| Subway | 8% |
| McDonald's | 12%–14.5% |
| KFC | 4% or $600 per month, whichever is greater |

Some hotel franchisors operate a central reservations system and charge franchisees a fee to cover the cost of operating the system. The calculation of this fee varies. It is usually a percentage of rooms revenue, an amount per available room per month, or an amount per reservation.

## Initial Investment

Although most restaurant franchises are still considered small businesses, the initial investment required to establish a successful franchise is creeping up, due (among other factors) to the increasing cost of real estate, construction, and property taxes. The total investment to open a McDonald's ranges from $465,000 to

$600,000. The land is owned by McDonald's and the rent is included in the continuing royalty fee of 12 percent to 14.5 percent. (McDonald's also has a leasing plan for new franchisees who cannot afford the total investment required to purchase a unit.) It costs from $641,000 to $1,410,000 to open a Wendy's—including the land, building, equipment, and signs.

Hotel franchises cost even more. Because of the high cost of franchises, franchisors want to be sure that their franchisees will have enough capital to operate their units until they start making a profit. For this reason, some franchisors require their franchisees to have a minimum personal net worth. This amount varies from franchisor to franchisor. Choice Hotels created a loan program that allows developers to secure construction and long-term financing.

## Franchise Regulations

Franchising is regulated in the United States by the Federal Trade Commission and a number of states. In those states with special regulations, a franchisor must register with the proper state authority before offering a franchise for sale within the state. State and local restrictions take precedence if they are more demanding than federal requirements.

All franchisors must comply with Federal Trade Commission Rule 436.1, which requires that a prospective franchisee be given a prospectus—the **Uniform Franchise Offering Circular (UFOC)** (see Chapter Appendix). This prospectus is a disclosure document that informs the franchisee about certain vital aspects of the franchisor and the franchise agreement before the agreement is signed. This disclosure statement must be in the hands of the prospective franchisee ten business days prior to signing the franchise agreement, so that the franchisee will have ample time to study it and understand the risks involved. The UFOC covers everything from the franchisor's history and financial condition to the detailed terms of the sales agreement. Franchisees should study the UFOC carefully before buying a franchise. See the Chapter Appendix for more information on what a UFOC must contain.

# Owning a Franchise

Franchising has not only been a boon to companies seeking to expand quickly; it is one of the safest ways for individuals to have their own business. Ray Kroc considered it the quickest way to capture the American dream and was proud of the fact that people credited him with making many of his associates millionaires.

Starting a business from scratch is risky. According to the International Franchise Association, franchises are more successful than independent new businesses. However, success depends on the franchisor. More experienced companies are more likely to provide the kind of advice and support that translates into profitability.

Franchising gives an individual entrepreneur a chance to compete in the marketplace against giant companies. It provides some insurance for success, for when franchisees buy a franchise, they buy (1) a format and formula that has already been tested, and (2) the experience of the franchisor, who is expected to teach them what they need to know to succeed.

The Development Group, a consulting firm that sells franchises for its clients, asked prospective franchisees why they wanted a franchise. Their answers were revealing:

- Self management was the most important reason given: 73 percent of applicants saw owning a franchise as a way to be their own boss.
- Financial independence was a close second: 69 percent of applicants thought owning a franchise was a better way to ensure financial security than depending on a paycheck from someone else.
- Career advancement ranked third (53% of applicants). If you own your own franchise you don't have to wait for someone else to promote you. You can move as fast as you are able.
- New skills/training was cited by 49 percent as their main reason for buying a franchise. Many people, for example, would like to own their own hotel or restaurant but simply don't know how. Good franchise companies provide training and assistance.
- A franchise was seen by 32 percent as a long-term investment that would appreciate in value.

## Advantages

There are many advantages to owning a franchise in addition to those just cited, including:

- Site selection assistance
- Easier credit
- Construction expertise
- Fixtures and equipment assistance
- Good training
- Opening support
- Promotional assistance
- Economies of scale
- Ongoing support

**Site Selection Assistance.** The first advantage for franchisees is that their franchisor will help them select a good site for their business. Almost all successful franchisors know exactly what kinds of sites work best for their franchises. In many cases the franchisor selects the site, buys or leases the land, puts up the building, and then leases it to the franchisee. In other instances, the franchisees do all of this for themselves, but even then, franchisors almost always approve sites based on their experience of the amount and kind of population needed in an area, traffic patterns, and other considerations.

Choice International, which franchises Sleep Inn, Comfort, Quality, Clarion, Rodeway, Econo Lodge, and Mainstay Suites, offers prospective franchisees help

# Industry Innovators

Henry R. Silverman
President/CEO
Cendant Corporation

Many people never have heard of Henry Silverman, although they have stayed in one of his hotel franchises, driven one of his rental cars, or vacationed at one of his timeshare resorts. There's a good chance that they bought their house through one of his companies as well.

Cendant is the world's largest franchisor of hotels, rental car agencies, and vacation timeshares, as well as residential real estate brokerage offices. Silverman was the founder and the largest shareholder of Hospitality Franchise Systems (HFS), which he merged with direct-marketing giant CUC International to form Cendant.

A graduate of Williams College and the University of Pennsylvania Law School, Silverman joined the navy and then practiced law for a few years before deciding he wanted to be an investment banker. He became interested in corporate takeovers and acquisitions and soon became hooked on the art of making a deal. His first hotel deal was Days Inn, which he bought through Reliance Insurance. By 1990 Silverman concluded that there was a fortune to be made in franchising service industries. He founded HFS and started acquiring companies that could offer attractive franchises.

HFS's business strategy was simple: Build a network of thousands of franchisees who would pay royalties and fees in return for the right to use one of their brand names. Support services would include training, national advertising, and discounts on products from Coca-Cola to IBM computers. The first were in the hotel field—Days Inn, Howard Johnson, Park Inn, Super 8, Knights Inn, Ramada Inns, Wingate Inn, Village Lodge, Travelodge, and others. By this point, his company was public and Silverman recognized that continuing growth was the only way to keep stockholders interested in HFS.

By 1997, HFS had acquired a franchising empire that included Avis car rental, Value Rent-a-Car, Century 21 real estate, Coldwell Banker real estate, and Resorts Condominiums. In a story headlined "HFS Stands for Growth," *Time* magazine said, "Dealmaker Henry Silverman has made this little-known company franchising's fastest flyer."[*] Then, just about the time when industry watchers wondered what kind of a deal Silverman would come up with next, he announced that HFS would merge with CUC International, a company that specializes in telephone shopping services, in a $10.9 billion deal. "By combining HFS's brands and our consumer reach of more than 100 million customers annually with CUC's direct-marketing expertise, powerful club membership delivery system, and 68 million memberships worldwide, we will create tremendous new opportunities," Silverman said.

Silverman is known as a tough and persistent manager who demands quality from his franchisees. "We terminate over 30,000 rooms a year. Virtually all for

*(continued)*

> **Industry Innovators** (continued)
>
> quality," he says. To pressure franchisees to improve their properties, HFS provides an array of renovation programs, training programs, and incentives. If that doesn't work they try to persuade the franchisees to make improvements. "We have reams of data that show that the top 10 percent of our system do $8,000-a-room better per year in revenue, which is virtually all profit, than the bottom 10 percent. So we say, 'Look, you have a 100 room property. You're going to increase your revenues by $800,000 a year, and your bottom line by that.' Some people say, 'I don't have the money, I don't want to get the money, I don't want to borrow the money'—and some do it. It's a slow process."[**]
>
> Silverman works long hours and expects the same from his employees. Managers are given the people and resources to do their jobs, but if they don't perform up to expectations they are fired. "People are accountable in our business," he says. "In many businesses, no one ever gets fired. They get transferred. The round pegs are put in square holes. We don't have lateral moves at HFS. You either move up or you move out. It's very simple. Either you perform or you're gone. That really sharpens one's focus."[†] Those who perform are richly rewarded. "Our employees, including me, are very well compensated, we all are very well incentivized, and we should work hard because the shareholders, the board, have enabled most of us to become wealthy far beyond our wildest dreams," Silverman told one reporter. "Because literally we have people in midlevel management in their 30s worth many millions of dollars saying, 'This is great. How did it happen?' It happened because everyone worked hard, we worked together, and we created a lot of value. And we've all participated in it."[††]
>
> ---
>
> [*] John Greenwald, "HFS Stands for Growth," *Time,* 17 March 1997.
> [**] Tony Giovanetti, "Henry Silverman: Mixing Luck and Skill to Build Franchising Empires," *Hotel Business,* 7–20 November 1996.
> [†] Giovanetti.
> [††] Giovanetti.

with not only site selection but also site acquisition and site and market assessment. Restaurant franchisors do the same. In its franchise-offering circular, filed with the Federal Trade Commission in Washington, D.C., the Subway sandwich chain states:

> The location of the store must be approved by the franchisor and the franchisee. The franchisor, or a corporation it designates, will then endeavor to lease the approved site and sublet the premises to the franchisee at cost. The responsibility for finding a site rests solely with the franchisee, and the franchisor will not unreasonably withhold approval of a location found by a franchisee. In rendering its assistance, the franchisor considers the population in the area of the site.

While Subway requires franchisees to find their own locations, McDonald's prefers to pick locations for its franchisees, based on sophisticated airplane and helicopter surveys and demographic studies.

**Easier Credit.** Obtaining credit is often easier for a franchisee than for individuals starting their own business. Banks and other lenders are reluctant to loan money for starting small businesses because of their high failure rate. Franchises are a much better risk. Few national franchises fail, because franchisors work hard to keep their franchises going, and so lenders are usually more willing to make capital available.

Some franchisors may help provide financing to qualified applicants. This can be in the form of loans, guarantees, locating potential lenders, or preparing a loan package or business plan that can be shown to a bank or other potential lender. Some franchisors have been known to accompany franchisees in their visit to the lender. Many people have been able to get into the franchise business by using all kinds of creative financing plans and more than one source of capital. These include lines of credit, Small Business Administration loans, Employee Stock Options (ESOPs), credit unions, insurance policies, venture capital, and trade credit (from suppliers). Some franchisors even have lease programs that allow prospective franchisees to lease units with an option to buy them.

**Construction Expertise.** Virtually all franchisors supply franchisees with architectural and floor plans for the franchise building. Choice International has plans available for three different styles of two-story 100-unit Sleep Inns, and furnishes all interior and exterior designs and site plans, including landscaping. McDonald's and Burger King have a large variety of building interior designs to choose from, depending on the market and the amount the franchisee is able to invest.

Some franchisors also help the franchisee employ the builder and supervise the construction. Since most franchisees do not have experience in this area, the assistance of a construction professional can mean considerable savings. Choice International provides preliminary and code-modified working drawings, elevations, and floor plans, as well as all structural, mechanical, plumbing, and electrical drawings necessary to complete the project. When the hotel is finished, a Choice International representative conducts a final site inspection to make sure that everything was done properly.

**Fixtures and Equipment Assistance.** Franchisors help franchisees select, purchase, and install fixtures and equipment. The Subway chain has an equipment-leasing program for franchisees who do not have sufficient capital to purchase necessary fixtures. Sheraton has a division called the Sheraton Supply Company, a one-stop shopping center for all of the items needed to open a new Sheraton or refurbish an existing one. The company issues a product catalog as well as a guestroom design catalog with different interior design schemes that fit the Sheraton image.

**Good Training.** Classroom and on-the-job training is a major part of most franchise programs. As noted earlier, 49 percent of all franchisees list training as their main reason for buying a franchise. Most franchisors have extensive training programs because it is in their best interests to see that franchisees meet franchise standards.

KFC offers an intensive three-week training program at the company's headquarters in Louisville, Kentucky. Tuition is included in the initial franchise fee, but attendees are responsible for most of their own travel expenses. An allowance for meals and lodging is provided. The curriculum covers every aspect of operating a

**McDonald's trains managers at Hamburger University in Oak Brook, Illinois.**
(Courtesy of McDonald's Corporation, Oak Brook, Illinois)

KFC restaurant, from bookkeeping to sanitary systems. In addition, a KFC representative visits every restaurant on a regular basis to troubleshoot and offer guidance. McDonald's has a four- to eight-week program at Hamburger University in Oak Brook, Illinois. A unique aspect of the McDonald's franchise training program is that prospective franchisees must successfully complete the training program *before* being considered for a franchise. Holiday Inn provides its franchisees with an intensive two-week training program. The curriculum includes hotel organization, daily operations, food and beverage control, back office systems, marketing, promotion, and personnel administration. The program is supplemented by a staff of field advisors who work with franchisees at their properties.

A set of operations manuals and training videos is a part of most franchise packages. Some operations manuals are very detailed. The Dunkin' Donuts manual instructs franchisees in everything from how to make donuts to how to interview prospective job applicants. It also has sections on marketing, bookkeeping, and equipment operation. Sheraton gives each Sheraton franchisee a set of manuals outlining Sheraton's basic policies and procedures. Topics include preopening, food and beverage operations, advertising, sales, budgeting and forecasting, housekeeping, front office procedures, and security.

**Opening Support.** Just about all franchisors help their franchisees prepare and open their franchise units for business. International Tours, a travel agency franchise headquartered in Tulsa, Oklahoma, sends a company representative to each new franchise. This representative oversees the first few days of operation to make sure that everything runs smoothly. He or she also attends the grand opening

**Franchisors help franchisees by producing merchandising materials such as this tray liner.** (Courtesy of Wendy's, Dublin, Ohio)

party. The grand opening usually consists of a party and a series of other events to introduce the franchise to the local community. McDonald's opens its restaurants with a series of champagne receptions for local politicians and families of the crew. In 1990, when McDonald's opened its first Russian franchise on Pushkin Square in Moscow, 700 people attended a champagne and caviar reception!

**Promotional Assistance.** Promotional assistance—that is, help with advertising, sales, and public relations—is one of the main strengths a franchisor can offer a franchisee. Most franchisors charge franchisees a marketing or advertising fee that is used to purchase television time, radio spots, newspaper ads, and produce other promotions such as coupons, sweepstakes, or contests. Burger King charges each franchisee an advertising royalty of 4 percent of monthly sales. This money is used for newspaper and magazine advertisements, mailers, promotional displays, and television and radio commercials. The company also helps franchisees with cooperative advertising plans, offers ongoing sales incentives, and sponsors periodic awards for superior sales and quality. Wendy's charges 2 percent of gross sales for national advertising, and another 2 percent for local advertising efforts.

Advertising and sales efforts in the lodging industry can be complicated. For Choice International Comfort Inns and Suites, an advertising and marketing fee of 1.3 percent of gross rooms revenue plus 28 cents per room per day is charged. A

A franchisor's regional representatives give franchisees ongoing support.
(Courtesy of McDonald's Corporation, Oak Brook, Illinois)

monthly fee for use of the Choice International reservations system is levied that costs 1.75 percent of gross rooms revenue plus $1 per night per reservation made through the system. In return, franchisees receive advance reservation services; listings in travel directories; participation in trade shows; the services of Choice's meeting sales department; direct mail, telemarketing, and other sales programs; as well as sales seminars, workshops, and blitzes. Sheraton established a Group Rates Availability Bank (GRAB) and staffed it with professional salespeople who sell for hotels throughout the Sheraton system. These salespeople handle group reservations of ten or more rooms and confirm arrangements to clients on a same-day basis. In addition, Sheraton has a special toll-free number for frequent travelers, travel agents, tour operators, and corporate and industry accounts.

**Economies of Scale.** Because they are part of a franchise chain, franchisees receive the advantages of economies of scale in purchasing supplies, equipment, and advertising.

**Ongoing Support.** The franchisor remains available to the franchisee on an ongoing basis after the franchise unit becomes operational. All franchisors have regional representatives and district managers who regularly meet with franchisees. Franchisors help franchisees with merchandising and day-to-day problems. As members of a franchise organization, franchisees have access to many types of specialists that they would otherwise have to hire.

## Disadvantages

Despite all of the advantages of franchising, there are problems that have caused some franchisees to regret their decision to purchase a franchise. Disadvantages include:

- Restrictions
- Unwanted products or procedures
- Unwanted advertising
- Unprotected territories
- Cancellation
- Inadequate training

**Restrictions.** A major disadvantage of franchising is that most franchise contracts restrict franchisees a great deal. A franchisor's success depends on having consistent quality throughout the system. When people check into a Holiday Inn anywhere in the United States, they expect to find the same kind of room, similarly priced and furnished, with the same kind of amenities. A Big Mac or a Whopper is expected to taste exactly the same, whether it is purchased in Los Angeles, California, or London, England. This means that franchisors must strictly enforce their standards. Operators of Holiday Inns *must* furnish and maintain guestrooms in a certain way; Holiday Inn kitchens *must* adhere to certain standards and staffing *must* be at required levels. A McDonald's franchisee *must* throw away unsold hamburgers after ten minutes no matter how much it costs, and a Dunkin' Donuts franchisee *must* make new donuts every four hours. All of these franchisors run regular and unannounced inspections, and franchisees who fail to adhere to standards run the risk of having their franchise canceled. This is not an idle threat. Every year some franchisees have their contracts canceled for failure to follow company guidelines.

These restrictions mean that some franchisees cannot be as creative as they'd like to be. They can't come up with their own advertising campaigns or introduce new menu items on their own. Restaurant chains are especially strict about their menus. Franchisees cannot add or subtract anything from menus or change recipes in any way without permission, and permission is seldom granted. There are rare occasions when a franchisee will get an idea approved, however. McDonald's likes to point out that many of its menu items evolved from the ideas of its operators. Ray Kroc credited franchisee Lou Groen with inventing Filet-O-Fish to help him in his battle against the Big Boy chain in the Catholic parishes of Cincinnati. Jim Delligatti in Pittsburgh came up with the idea for the Big Mac. Herb Peterson in Santa Barbara created the Egg McMuffin; and Harold Rosen in Enfield, Connecticut, came up with the Shamrock Shake, a special green milkshake served around St. Patrick's Day.[9]

**Unwanted Products or Procedures.** When new products or procedures are introduced, franchisees must embrace them whether they want to or not. Originally, many McDonald's operators did not want to open for breakfast—it meant dramatically increased labor costs and a whole new shift. They doubted that they would sell enough breakfasts to make it pay. But when the company decided to introduce breakfast on television, every franchisee was forced to open at 6:00 A.M., even in areas where there was no business. Breakfast is still a losing proposition for some McDonald's franchisees.

**Unwanted Advertising.** A franchisor's advertising program can be another cause of franchisee dissatisfaction. When Burger King decided a few years ago to launch a television campaign featuring "Herb the Nerd," many franchisees did not like it. They felt it actually drove away customers. Nevertheless, they were forced to accept it and pay for it until the company itself decided the campaign was not effective and canceled it. In some cases, franchisees feel the franchisor's national campaign does not help them, although it may benefit franchisees elsewhere.

**Unprotected Territories.** Another area of dispute between franchisors and franchisees involves territories. Many franchisors do not grant specific territories. This means they allow a franchisee to establish a new unit as close as a mile or two away from an existing unit if business in the area warrants it.

There have been a number of suits brought against franchisors by franchise operators over this issue. In Iowa, the legislature responded to franchisee anger by passing a law banning any new fast-food outlet within three miles of an existing franchise from the same system or within a population radius of 30,000.[10]

According to a report in the *New York Times*:

> McDonald's negotiates compensation agreements for some owners faced with encroachment from a new store or minimizes the potential for conflict by offering them a new franchise. In general, though, it argues that extending the chain also stimulates people to eat more often at existing restaurants, offsetting encroachment concerns.[11]

Legislation to protect franchisees' rights, and the formation of a number of franchise owners groups, are restricting the power of franchisors to control their operators' destinies. In many cases, these groups now have a voice in determining company policies on encroachment into their territories, as well as input on new product introductions and advertising campaigns.

**Cancellation.** Franchisees are not always guaranteed that they will be able to renew their franchise after the initial 20-year period (the usual length of a franchise contract). If a franchisee has not been adhering to the standards set by the company, for example, the franchisor may decide not to renew the franchise. The franchisor may also decide not to renew for reasons outside the franchisee's control. Theoretically, a franchisee might spend a lifetime building a business and then be unable to pass it on to his or her children because the franchise contract expired and was not renewed.

**Inadequate Training.** Not all franchisors provide high-quality training programs to their franchisees. Sometimes a franchisor's salespersons misrepresent the training franchisees will receive.

## Advantages and Disadvantages for Franchisors

Franchising has advantages and disadvantages for the franchisor as well. Little to no capital is required for expansion, because the franchisees provide the funding. Franchisors can expand quickly, while transferring the investment risk to the franchisees. A company can develop rapidly through franchising without the need of a large system of corporate administrators and staff. Because a franchise unit is owned by a local individual or company, the franchisor gains an involved and motivated on-site manager who is a member of the community. This means the franchisee is likely to be accepted by the local community, and the franchise is in the hands of someone who knows local authority and ordinances.

The downside is that the franchisor gives up the profits generated by its franchise units, settling for royalties instead. Also, the franchisor surrenders a certain amount of control to the franchisees. In a company-owned unit it is easier to make changes in operating procedures and marketing approaches and get feedback from unit managers.

## Franchising Issues

Franchising will continue to be a major force in the expansion of the hospitality industry. There are problems, however, that strain franchisor/franchisee relations. The most common areas of disagreement include encroachment, financial violations such as unpaid royalty charges, and contract violations.

Some segments of the hotel and restaurant business have reached a mature stage of growth. For example, there is one quick-service restaurant for every 1,400 people in the United States. Outside of the United States, the proportion is one for every 100,000.[12] New concepts are more difficult to come by, and franchise chains and individual franchisees are competing for market share with each other.

Franchisors, however, have not been taking these signs of a mature market lying down, but they have instead reached out to penetrate new markets. The strategy for a number of restaurant chains is to establish outlets in nontraditional locations such as supermarkets, convenience stores, airports, schools and colleges, ballparks, and hospitals. Pizza Hut offers room service in a number of Choice Hotels nationwide. Several California high schools offer fare from Pizza Hut and Taco Bell. Taco Bell has even installed carts along the Moscow subway to sell to the roughly nine million Russians who ride the subway each day.

In the lodging industry, too, franchising is in transition. As a result of oversupply of full service and luxury brands, there are few in that segment being developed in the late 1990s in the United States and in some parts of Asia and Europe. Instead, hotel chains have introduced new economy and budget brands under their trade name or a new name. As a result of these expansion strategies, some franchisees have been accusing franchisors of encroachment. Franchisors have countered with impact studies and defined geographic areas for each franchisee to allay their fears. For example, Blimpie International uses a software mapping program that pinpoints every location—not only to cite competition but to recognize an encroachment problem.

## Chapter Summary

Franchising is a marketing or distribution system. In its simplest form, the term "franchise" refers to the authorization given by one company to another to sell its unique products and services.

There are two types of franchises: the product or trade-name franchise and the business format franchise. The product or trade-name franchise is a supplier-dealer

## Get on BOARD!

### Now the industry leader can be your partner!

In today's hotel franchise market, it pays to work with a winner. And in all regards, that winner is Choice. With more than 4,000 hotels open and under development in more than 33 countries, Choice Hotels International is the world's leading hotel franchise company. With brand names that are recognized the world over, systems that deliver bottom-line profits, and a commitment to driving total revenue, Choice is your ideal lodging partner. And, as you will see, we have a franchise product to match any business strategy.

### Unsurpassed Support

When you become a member of the Choice lodging family, you will also discover a host of benefits designed to improve your bottom line, including a nationwide marketing program, innovative conversion packages, an advanced reservations system, and much more.

### Financing Programs

Choice offers financing programs in conjunction with respected companies to help our franchise partners refinance or acquire capital for development, acquisitions and renovations.

### Choice 2001

Thanks to this advanced reservation system, franchise partners realize several key benefits, including a brand-specific toll-free number, Internet reservations capability, and a global distribution system link to travel agents. A unique advantage of the CHOICE 2001 system is that each hotel is listed by geographic location and by proximity to major attractions and events. As most customers choose a hotel based on location, followed by price, the CHOICE 2001 system gives franchise partners and their properties a true competitive advantage.

### RevPAR

At Choice, we are dedicated to generating maximum revenue per available room (RevPAR) for our franchise partners through proven success systems, comprehensive support services, worldwide reservations, and brand-specific marketing.

### Award-winning National Advertising

National television advertising, complemented by consumer and trade print ads and an aggressive publicity effort, ensure top-of-mind awareness for Choice franchise properties with the traveling public, particularly corporate travelers.

### We Work For You

Today, Choice chains are among the best known in the world. But more important, we work consistently for our franchise owners. In repeated independent surveys, an overwhelming majority of our general managers and owners said that they would recommend Choice as a franchising company to their business associates. Developers select Choice because of its proven ability to deliver strong results, and because Choice creates a positive, working partnership based on open communication, dignity, and respect.

Ready to make the right choice? Then call the Choice development office today toll-free for more information, 800-547-0007, or contact them by email here.

Back to Franchise Opportunities

**At The Choice Hotels Web site, interested professionals can learn about franchising opportunities.** (Courtesy of Choice Hotels International) arrangement whereby the dealer (franchisee) sells a product line provided by the supplier (franchisor) and to some degree takes on the identity of the supplier. Business format franchises are ongoing business relationships between franchisors and franchisees in which franchisors sell their product(s), service(s), trademark, and the business concept itself to franchisees in return for royalties and other franchise fees.

Franchising is not a new concept. In 1851, I. M. Singer & Company used franchising to develop networks of sewing-machine dealers all over the United States. The first person to pioneer the idea of the business format franchise was Howard Johnson, founder of the Howard Johnson Company.

The evolution of franchising was driven by the desire of some companies to expand their business, coupled with the desire of entrepreneurs like McDonald's founder Ray Kroc to take a successful idea and build on it, rather then risk starting from scratch. Franchising also provided companies with an alternative method of financing growth other than through company-owned units.

Franchising is one of the safest ways for individuals to run their own businesses. Compared to the national failure rate for small businesses, very few franchises fail. When people buy a franchise, they buy (1) a format and formula that has already been tested, and (2) the experience of the franchisor, who will teach them what they need to know to succeed. One study showed that prospective franchisees had the following reasons for wanting their own franchise: self management, career advancement, new skills/training, and long-term investment.

There are many other advantages to owning a franchise. Franchisors help franchisees with site selection; credit; construction; fixtures and equipment; training; pre-opening and opening activities; and advertising, sales, and public relations.

Franchising is not for everyone, however. Many franchisees do not like the restrictions imposed on them by their franchise agreement. Franchisors have tough standards and usually do not hesitate to cancel the franchises of operators who will not adhere to those standards. Franchisees must also go along with the franchisor's advertising and marketing program whether they agree with it or not. Sometimes there are disputes over territories.

Franchising has disadvantages for the franchisor as well. While little or no capital is required to expand (because funding is provided by the franchisee), the franchisor gives up the profits generated by the franchise units, settling for royalties instead. Also, the franchisor surrenders a certain amount of control to the franchisees.

The typical franchise fee arrangement has two parts: (1) an initial franchise fee, payable upon signing the agreement, and (2) ongoing fees, which consist of royalties (based on monthly gross sales) and advertising and marketing fees. In addition to these fees, there is an initial investment required to purchase the physical facility, equipment, and supplies necessary to operate the franchise.

Before selling a franchise, franchisors are required by the Federal Trade Commission to submit a Uniform Franchise Offering Circular (UFOC) to the prospective franchisee. The UFOC must contain the sections shown in the Chapter Appendix.

There is no doubt that franchising will continue to be a major force in the expansion of the hospitality industry. But there are many upheavals taking place, due to the expansion strategies of franchisors.

# Endnotes

1. *Franchise Fact Sheet*, International Franchise Association, Washington, D.C., 22 December 1993.
2. *Worldwide Franchising Statistics*, Arthur Andersen, LLP (Chicago, 1995).
3. N. G. L. Hammond and H. H. Scullard, eds., *The Oxford Classical Dictionary* (Oxford England: Clarendon Press, 1979), pp. 613, 898–899.
4. Charles L. Vaughn, *Franchising* (Lexington, Mass.: Lexington Books, D. C. Heath and Company, 1974), p. 11.
5. Vaughn, pp. 15–17.
6. Ray Kroc and Robert Anderson, *Grinding It Out: The Making of McDonald's* (New York: Berkeley Books, 1978), p. 71.
7. Kroc, pp. 72–73.
8. Kroc, p. 86.
9. Kroc, pp. 173–174.
10. "Indigestion at Taco Bell," *Business Week*, 14 December 1992, p. 67.
11. Barnaby J. Feder, "McDonald's Finds There's Still Plenty of Room to Grow," *New York Times*, 9 January 1994, p. F-5.
12. "Franchising," *International Herald Tribune*, 21 April 1995, p. 17.

# Key Terms

**business format franchise**—An ongoing business relationship between a franchisor and a franchisee in which the franchisor sells its products, services, trademark, and business concept to the franchisee in return for royalties and other franchise fees.

**franchise**—Refers to (1) the authorization given by one company to another to sell its unique products and services, or (2) the name of the business format or product that is being franchised.

**franchisee**—The individual or company granted a franchise.

**franchising**—A continuing relationship in which the franchisor provides a licensed privilege to do business, plus assistance in organizing, training, merchandising, and management in return for a financial consideration from the franchisee.

**franchisor**—The franchise company that owns the trademark, products, and/or business format that is being franchised.

**product or trade-name franchise**—A supplier/dealer arrangement whereby the dealer (franchisee) sells a product line provided by the supplier (franchisor) and to some degree takes on the identity of the supplier.

**Uniform Franchise Offering Circular (UFOC)**—A prospectus that outlines certain vital aspects of a franchisor and the franchise agreement. By law, the UFOC must be given to a potential franchisee before the franchisee signs the franchise agreement.

## Review Questions

1. What is the difference between a franchisor and a franchisee?
2. What are two types of franchises?
3. How did I. M. Singer, General Motors, and Coca-Cola contribute to franchising?
4. How are initial franchise fees calculated by the franchisor?
5. What is the Uniform Franchise Offering Circular?
6. According to a poll by the Development Group, why do franchisees purchase a franchise?
7. From a franchisee's point of view, what are the advantages and disadvantages of franchising?
8. Why do franchisors hold franchisees to such strict standards?
9. From a franchisor's point of view, what are the advantages and disadvantages of franchising?
10. What issues in the industry affect the future of franchising?

## Internet Sites

For more information, visit the following Internet sites. Remember that Internet addresses can change without notice. If the site is no longer there, use a search engine to look for additional sites.

### Hotel Companies/Resorts

Accor
www.accor.com

Best Western
www.bestwestern.com

Carlson Companies, Inc.
www.carlson.com

Choice Hotels International
www.choice-hotels.com

Hilton Hotels
www.hilton.com

Holiday Inn Worldwide
www.holiday-inn.com

ITT Sheraton
www.sheraton.com

Marriott International
www.marriott.com

Promus Hotels
www.promus-inc.com

### Restaurant Companies

Blimpie Subs & Salads
www.blimpie.com

Burger King
www.burgerking.com

Dairy Queen
www.dairyqueen.com/dairyque.htm

Domino's Pizza
www.dominos.com

KFC
www.kfc.com

McDonald's
www.mcdonalds.com

Pizza Hut
www.pizzahut.com

Subway
www.subway.com

Taco Bell
www.tacobell.com

Wendy's International
www.wendys.com

*Associations*

American Association of
Franchisees and Dealers
www.aafd.org

International Franchise
Association (IFA)
www.franchise.org

*Organizations, Resources*

Franchise Handbook Online
www.franchise1.com

FranInfo
www.franinfo.com

# Chapter Appendix

## Uniform Franchise Offering Circulars

All franchisors must comply with Federal Trade Commission Rule 436.1, which requires that a prospective franchisee be given a prospectus—the Uniform Franchise Offering Circular (UFOC). The purpose of a UFOC is to inform the franchisee about certain vital aspects of the franchisor and the franchise agreement *before* the franchisee signs the agreement. A UFOC must contain the following:

1. **Background.** The franchisor's background, including the franchisor's personal and business background and financial history, must be disclosed. Franchisors must state if they have any previous experience operating the kind of business they propose franchising. However, they are not required to disclose background that is not connected with their current enterprise.

2. **Key associates and managers.** The franchisor must identify and give the backgrounds of directors, trustees, partners, principals, and other managers of the franchising company.

3. **Litigation.** The franchisor must disclose any criminal or civil action involving unfair business practices, fraud, or violations of the franchise law. In those states where laws forbid revealing criminal records, only civil actions are revealed.

4. **Bankruptcy.** The statement must reveal whether the franchisor, partners, officers, or predecessors in the business have declared bankruptcy in the last 15 years.

5. **Initial Fee.** This section describes the initial franchise fee and how it must be paid. The refund policy must also be stated.

6. **Other fees and ongoing royalties.** Here the franchisor states the amount of monthly royalty plus advertising, marketing, reservation, and other fees the franchisee must pay. If the franchisor charges for training or for the time and expenses of its field representatives, such charges must be disclosed.

7. **Initial investment broken down into components.** In this section the amount of investment needed to open the franchise is stated. This includes the cost of the real estate, equipment, and supplies. If the amount is likely to vary due to local conditions, a range must be stated. In some cases, these figures do not include a figure for working capital, but anyone considering a franchise should add this to cover the period until the business starts making a profit.

8. **Designated suppliers.** The franchisor must state whether the franchisee is required to purchase or lease products, services, and equipment from a spec-ified source. Generally this practice is frowned upon—and in some cases, is unlawful—except in certain instances. For example, the franchisee may be required to lease the building and land from the franchisor and buy certain signs from the franchisor.

9. **Obligation to purchase supplies according to franchisor specifications.** Franchisors cannot force a franchisee to buy from them or suppliers they designate (except as noted above), but in most cases it is reasonable to expect that the supplies a franchisee buys must meet franchise specifications. In the case of fast-food franchises, the specifications for all products to be used are often contained in the operating manuals. In lodging franchises, typical specifications include such items as size and quality of furnishings and construction materials.

10. **Financing.** In cases where financing assistance by the franchisor or others is offered, details of the parties involved and conditions should be set forth.

11. **Obligations of the franchisor.** Here the franchisor must describe all of the services promised to a franchisee after the agreement is signed. These include services provided before and after opening, such as site selection and training. If a franchisee is expected to pay for personal travel and living expenses while being trained at the franchisor's headquarters, this must be disclosed.

12. **Exclusive territory.** In many cases, the territory of the franchise is limited to the actual location. In others, protection may extend to a certain geographical area or be described in terms of population density. In any case, the franchisor must disclose what protection, if any, is offered to the franchisee. Even when the franchisor forbids another franchise unit from being built within the franchisee's territory, the franchisor cannot protect the franchisee from other franchisees who may wish to solicit business within the franchisee's territory. For instance, several franchised travel agencies with different owners located in different parts of a city may compete with each other by advertising the same tours in the same newspaper.

13. **Trademarks, logotypes, and commercial symbols.** Since a franchisee often is buying the use of a recognized name, the franchisor is obligated to state whether that name is fully protected, and, if not, what steps are being taken to register and protect it. It should be noted that names of particular products served as well as that of the establishment can be protected. For example, McDonald's has registered not only its name and its golden arches but also names like "Big Mac."

14. **Patents and copyrights.** Some franchisors have unique, patented equipment or designs as part of their franchise. If this is part of the franchise, it must be disclosed.

15. **Obligation of the franchisee to participate in the conduct of the business.** If the franchisor requires the franchisee to personally operate the business, such a requirement must be stated. Some franchisors allow absentee ownership; others forbid it.

16. **Restrictions on goods and services.** Almost all restaurant franchisors restrict the variety of menu items that franchisees can sell. Lodging franchises usually limit the sales of goods and services on the premises to those that are normally incident to the operation of the facility.

17. **Renewal, termination, repurchase, and assignment.** This section covers the rights of both of the parties to renew, terminate, or assign the franchise. It is often the clause that is most litigated, because franchises can be terminated for non-performance and because franchisees sometimes wish to sell or otherwise terminate their franchise.

18. **Arrangements with public figures.** Some franchises are named after real people or use the names of celebrities in their promotions. If there is a formal arrangement with one or more public figures to use their name or reputation, the details and compensation must be disclosed.

19. **Projected earnings.** If franchisors project earnings, they must disclose the formula used in the calculation process. Names and addresses of units that have achieved these earnings are sometimes given. However, most franchisors do not project any sales or profits, since these figures can easily be misleading or misinterpreted and lawsuits can be filed for misrepresentation.

20. **Information regarding the franchises of the franchisor.** Franchisors are required to list the number of franchises they have sold as well as the franchises' addresses and the names of their owners. Prospective franchisees are well-advised to contact current owners for information before purchasing their own franchises.

21. **Financial statement.** An audited financial statement of the franchisor that is no more than six months old must be a part of the UFOC.

22. **Contracts.** The franchise agreement and any other agreements—such as a lease that the franchisee will be required to sign—must be attached to the UFOC.

## REVIEW QUIZ

When you feel you have covered all of the material in this chapter, answer these questions. Choose the *best* answer.

1. There are _____ franchise outlets in the United States.

    a. a little over a half million
    b. about a million
    c. about two million
    d. a little over three million

2. The founder of Holiday Inn was:

    a. Ray Kroc.
    b. Kemmons Wilson.
    c. I. M. Singer.
    d. Howard Johnson.

3. Franchisors charge a royalty fee that is usually calculated on:

    a. a sliding-scale percentage of the franchisee's total expenditures.
    b. the franchisee's net revenue before fixed charges.
    c. the franchisee's average after-tax income, based on the last three years' tax returns.
    d. a percentage of the franchisee's sales.

4. The Uniform Franchise Offering Circular must be in the hands of the prospective franchisee _____ signing the franchise agreement.

    a. ten business days prior to
    b. thirty days prior to
    c. within one week after
    d. within the first 60 days after

5. When they were asked why they wanted to buy a franchise, *most* prospective franchisees said they:

    a. thought owning a franchise was a good way to advance their careers.
    b. wanted to learn new skills.
    c. wanted to be their own boss.
    d. thought owning a franchise was a good way to achieve financial independence.

6. Which of the following statements is *not* one of the advantages of owning a franchise?

    a. construction expertise
    b. guaranteed profits
    c. promotional assistance
    d. site selection assistance

## REVIEW QUIZ *(continued)*

7. The usual length of an initial franchise contract is:
   a. 6 months.
   b. 1 year.
   c. 10 years.
   d. 20 years.

**Answer Key:** 1-a-C1, 2-b-C1, 3-d-C1, 4-a-C1, 5-c-C2, 6-b-C2, 7-d-C2

Each question is linked to a competency. Competencies are listed on the first page of the chapter. An answer reading 3-b-C4 translates to:

3: the question number
b: the correct answer
C4: the competency number

## Chapter 18 Outline

What Is Ethics?
Social Responsibility and Business Ethics
    How We Arrive at Our Values
    Is Business Like Poker?
    Is Honesty Always the Best Policy?
    The Search for a Common Moral Ground
Ethical Issues in Hospitality
    Environmental Issues
    Discrimination
    Sexual Harassment
    AIDS in the Workplace
    Advertising Claims
    Truth-in-Menu Laws
Must There Be a Code of Ethics?
    Some Ethical Litmus Tests
Chapter Summary

## Competencies

1. Define ethics, distinguish social responsibility from business ethics, describe six kinds of moral reasoning, and compare the ethical standards of business and poker.

2. Explore whether honesty is always the best policy, give examples of different viewpoints concerning morality, contrast deontology with utilitarianism, and explain the concept of ethical relativism.

3. Describe ethical issues in the hospitality industry, explain the need for a code of ethics for hospitality businesses, define the term "stakeholder," and identify three questions individuals should ask themselves when making a decision.

# 18

# Ethics in Hospitality Management

**I**N THIS CHAPTER we define and discuss ethics in the hospitality industry. The chapter distinguishes ethics from social responsibility and explores how values are arrived at. Concepts such as whether it is ever right to lie are examined. Ethical issues in hospitality such as discrimination, AIDS, advertising claims, and truth-in-menu laws are discussed. Finally, an ethical litmus test is offered.

## What Is Ethics?

There is a children's story about a group of blind men from "Indostan" who, by touching an elephant, attempt to describe to each other what it is like. The first man, falling against the elephant's side, says the elephant is like a wall. The second, feeling the elephant's tusk, tells the others that the elephant is like a spear. The third, with the animal's trunk in hand, says the elephant is like a rope. The fourth is certain an elephant is like a tree, having touched a leg, while the fifth blind man feels the elephant's ear and concludes elephants are like fans. The sixth, seizing its tail, pronounces that an elephant is like a snake:

> So these men of Indostan
> Disputed loud and long
> Each in his own opinion
> Exceedingly stiff and strong;
> Though each was partly in the right
> And all were in the wrong![1]

Trying to describe ethics is similar to the blind men describing the elephant. Depending on how we approach the question and our own system of values, we can come up with very different answers.

**Ethics** is a set of moral principles and values that we use to answer questions of right and wrong. Ethics can also be defined as the study of the general nature of morals and of the moral choices made by individuals in their relationships with others.

There is evidence that many people have forgotten the true meaning of ethics. Today we tend to think of ethics in pragmatic terms—our choices are based on what seems reasonable or logical to us according to our own personal value system. This is called "ethical relativism" because it casts ethics in the role of being relative to what the situation is or how we feel about it.

In truth, ethics is something different. The very concept of ethics suggests that there is a real distinction between good and bad, right and wrong, and that it is our obligation to do our best to distinguish between these and then always try to do what is right. Although we all have different personal values and morals, we should recognize that there are some universal principles that virtually all religions, cultures, and societies agree upon. These principles form the basis of ethical behavior. The foundation of all of these principles is the belief that other people's rights are as important as our own, and that it is our duty not to harm others if we can avoid it. In fact, it is our duty to help them whenever possible. This idea is at the heart of the value system of most societies, tribes, and organizations. Without it, we would not find it possible to live and work together.

## Social Responsibility and Business Ethics

It is important to distinguish between social responsibility and business ethics. The concept of social responsibility suggests that "at any one time in any society there is a set of generally accepted relationships, obligations, and duties between the major institutions and the people. Philosophers and political theorists have called this set of common understandings 'the social contract.'"[2] This contract differs among societies and may change over time. For example, today we expect that businesses will take care (1) not to pollute the air we breathe or the water we drink, (2) not to damage the ozone layer, (3) to offer fair wages and employee benefits, (4) to provide a satisfactory product or service at a reasonable price, and (5) to in some way participate in making the community in which they operate a better place. These are not ethical considerations—they are part of a "deal" that says that we as consumers expect companies to act in this manner because they are a part of the society we all share (see Exhibit 1).

Many companies recognize this and have stated publicly their belief that it is good business to be a good citizen. They support local arts, build parks, raise funds for charities, and try to put back some of their profits into the community that has made their success possible. For example, Domino's Pizza formed SCORE, its Strategic Committee on Respecting the Environment. A joint committee of company officials and franchisees, SCORE oversees an environmentally responsible agenda that includes recycling, supplying non-toxic cleaning agents to franchise units, and forming a non-profit wildlife habitat.[3] *Time* magazine singled out McDonald's as being an outstanding example of a company that understands the meaning of social responsibility in an article entitled, "'America's Hamburger Helper': McDonald's gives new meaning to 'we do it all for you' by investing in people and their neighborhoods."[4] According to *Time*:

> McDonald's stands out not only as one of the more socially responsible companies in America, but also as one of the nation's few truly effective social engineers. Both its franchise operators, who own 83 percent of all McDonald's restaurants, and company officials sit on boards of local and national minority service organizations, allowing the company to claim that its total involvement in everything from the Urban League and the NAACP (National Association for the Advancement of Colored

**Exhibit 1    Social Responsibility and McDonald's**

### The Planet We Share

Every McDonald's restaurant is committed to protecting our environment. Not just for this generation, but for generations yet to come. That's the idea behind McDonald's Earth Effort.

### McDonald's Earth Effort™

McDonald's Earth Effort is a far-reaching program that starts with the three waste reduction principles: reduce, re-use, recycle; then goes beyond to include our policy of not using beef raised on rain forest land. Using energy-efficient equipment. Developing educational programs for schools. And more.

### McRecycle USA

For recycling to really work, there have to be people who want to buy recycled products. That's why we started McRecycle USA. It's the most visible part of McDonald's Earth Effort—a commitment that McDonald's will buy at least $100 million worth of recycled products every year for the building, operating, and equipping of our restaurants.

McDonald's is the largest user of recycled paper products in our industry. Our carryout bags are made from recycled corrugated boxes and newsprint. And our take-out drink trays are made from recycled newspapers.

But our use of recycled materials goes far beyond paper products. Your local McDonald's may have walls built of insulated concrete blocks made with recycled photographic film. Or roofing tiles made from used computer casings. Or a soft, colorful McDonald's Playland surface made from recycled automobile tires.

The really good news is that in just two years, we've bought $400 million worth of recycled products through the McRecycle program—twice our goal.

### We're Cutting Down on Our Trash

It's called "source reduction," and it's the most effective way to combat the garbage problem. So when a leading environmental group—the Environmental Defense Fund—asked us to form a joint task force on the subject, we agreed. Together, we've found lots of ways to reduce McDonald's solid waste.

One good example is our switch from foam packaging to paper wraps for our sandwiches, like our Quarter Pounder With Cheese sandwich. That Earth Effort reduced the volume of our sandwich packaging by 90%. We've also reduced waste in other areas, from napkins to Happy Meal bags to shipping boxes.

### We Don't Use Beef Raised on Rain Forest Land

It's a simple but important part of McDonald's Earth Effort. Tropical rain forests play a vital role in the Earth's ecology. Therefore, McDonald's does not, has not, and will not permit the destruction of tropical rain forests for our beef supply. Nowhere in the world do we purchase beef raised on rain forest (or recently deforested rain forest) land. And everywhere, we continue monitoring our beef suppliers to make sure this policy is strictly enforced.

### More Efforts for Our Earth

Over two decades ago, McDonald's began looking for ways to conserve energy in each individual restaurant. That effort continues today, with most of our restaurants using the latest energy-efficient equipment.

*(continued)*

**Exhibit 1** *(continued)*

> For the last 20 years, we've also developed educational programs for local schools on ecology and other environmental topics. Local McDonald's restaurants have also sponsored tree-plantings and litter-pickup drives.
>
> Our environmental efforts were recognized by the White House with one of the first-ever President's Environmental and Conservation Challenge Awards. McDonald's has also received the National Recycling Coalition's Award for Outstanding Corporate Leadership.
>
> **We Live Here, Too**
>
> That's the real power behind McDonald's Earth Effort. The people who work in your McDonald's restaurant also live in your community. And they're as dedicated as you are to making sure that the neighborhood—as well as the planet—we share is as clean and healthy as possible. For all of us.

**This material appeared in a small take-away booklet placed in McDonald's restaurants (printed on recycled paper), to let customers know about McDonald's "Earth Effort."** (Courtesy of McDonald's Corporation, Oak Brook, Illinois)

People) to the U.S. Hispanic Chamber of Commerce may constitute the biggest volunteer program of any business in the nation.[5]

Ethical behavior is a whole different matter. During the savings and loan scandals that erupted in the United States in the 1990s, it was revealed that many savings and loan organizations that lavishly contributed funds to United Way and other charities, sponsored symphony and ballet performances, and generally acted in a socially responsible manner were at the same time stealing millions of dollars from depositors. These companies were trying to create an aura of social responsibility, but were entirely lacking in ethics because, while they were contributing to society with one hand, they were stealing with the other.

## How We Arrive at Our Values

Author Hunter Lewis says that there are six ways in which we arrive at our values—our personal beliefs about what is "good" and "just." The six kinds of moral reasoning are:

1. *Authority.* Beliefs can be derived from an authority. Here we take someone else's word, such as that of the Bible or the church.

2. *Deductive logic.* Deductive logic is another basis for our beliefs. Here is a simple example of deductive logic: If all chocolate is fattening, and if this dessert is chocolate, then this dessert must be fattening.

3. *Sense experience.* Often beliefs are arrived at through sense experience. In these cases we gain direct knowledge through our five senses. We decide that something is true because we heard it; can see it with our own eyes; or can touch it, taste it, or smell it.

4. *Emotion.* Emotion can dictate our beliefs. We may "feel" that something is true. Sometimes our emotions concerning others influence our ideas about them. For example, if we love someone we tend to idealize him or her. Violent criminals might have parents who say, "He's a nice boy" or "But she's really a good girl."
5. *Intuition.* Intuition is another way to arrive at knowledge. Here we use our unconscious or intuitive mind to process information and discover the solution to a problem. Sometimes we refer to our intuition as our "gut feeling."
6. *Science.* Science is the basis of some beliefs. When we use the scientific method we use our senses to collect facts, our intuition to develop a hypothesis, our logic to experiment, and our senses again to complete the test. Physicians use this process to arrive at their beliefs about the causes of disease and what cures to prescribe.[6]

Although we may use all six techniques of moral reasoning at one time or another, Lewis believes that each of us has a dominant or primary technique. To discover your dominant technique, Lewis suggests you ask yourself whom you would confide in if you had a serious personal issue on your mind and wanted advice.

If your answer is a priest, a minister, a rabbi, or another religious leader, your primary mode may be to use authority as the basis for your beliefs. If you would ask a professor of philosophy to help you, you would be looking for someone who could think through your problem in a highly structured or logical way. If your confidant were a professor of history and literature who is also a good friend, you might be relying on his or her own personal sense experience plus the experience of Western culture as contained in its history and literature. Suppose you turn to a family member or close friend. Here your dominant reasoning style could be characterized as emotional. Clearly you are looking for empathy from a member of your peer group. Some people would seek an answer from a Buddhist or guru of immense calm and unspoken wisdom. They would be hoping to use meditation and other tools to unlock their powers of intuition. If you don't recognize yourself in any of these groups, perhaps you would consult a psychiatrist who could offer an appraisal based on social science methods and principles.[7]

The point is that we are all likely to have a different set of values or ethics depending on which moral reasoning technique is our dominant one. To many of us, some actions are wrong because the Bible or the Torah or the Koran says so. To others, actions are wrong only if our friends and family would condemn them. Some believe that anything is okay "so long as it isn't against the law" or even "so long as you don't get caught." Nearly everyone agrees that it is a good idea to tell the truth, and that stealing from others is wrong.

## Is Business Like Poker?

There is a school of thought that recognizes that honesty is the best policy and it is never right to lie or steal, but holds that the rules of business are different and that behavior that is unacceptable elsewhere is legitimate in the business world.

Business writer Alfred Carr attracted a good deal of attention by comparing business to a poker game:

> No one expects poker to be played on the ethical principles preached in churches. In poker it is right and proper to bluff a friend out of the rewards of being dealt a good hand. Poker's own brand of ethics is different from the ethical ideals of civilized human relationships. The game calls for distrust of the other fellow. It ignores the claim of friendship. Cunning, deception and concealment of one's strength and intentions, not kindness and open-heartedness, are vital in poker. No one thinks any worse of poker on that account. And no one should think any the worse of the game of business because its standards of right and wrong differ from the prevailing traditions of morality in our society.[8]

While Carr's argument might seem to make sense at first glance, Robert Solomon and Kristine Hanson—authors of *It's Good Business*, a book about business ethics—point out that it shows a misunderstanding of both poker and business:

> Bluffing isn't lying, which is as forbidden in playing poker as it is in business. Most business is conducted in conversation where truth and mutual trust are essential...A poker game involves only its players; business is essential to the well-being of the entire society. The rules of poker protect the game and its players; the rules of business protect everyone else too. Carr's suggestion ignores that core of ethics that does not vary from community to community—which we call 'morality.' Morality consists of those basic rules which are not merely a matter of a single game or practice, but provide the preconditions of every game, every practice. Carr may be trivially correct when he says the rules of poker are different from the rules of other games and practices, but he is quite wrong when he suggests that this constitutes a divergence from morality.[9]

Solomon and Hanson point out that the ultimate goals of business are to promote a good life for every individual and wealth for the nation as a whole. The goal of poker is to redistribute the wealth among a small group of players. Because the goals are different, and because in the business world much more is at stake, the rules of poker and business should and must be different.

## Is Honesty Always the Best Policy?

According to some moral philosophers, honesty is the only acceptable policy. They argue that all lying, whether "little white lies" or vicious falsehoods, injures both the liar and the person lied to, and may injure society as well. When someone lies to Congress about the extent of the United States' military involvement in an area, or the cost of a weapon or social welfare program, the result is that our elected officials do not have the information they need to protect our interests, which is what we have elected them to do.

The principle involved here is described by Sissela Bok, author of *Lying: Moral Choice in Public and Private Life*, who writes, "All our choices depend on our estimates of what is the case; these estimates must in turn often rely on information from others. Lies distort this information and therefore our situation as we perceive it, as well as our choices."[10] When we lie to others, Bok argues, we take away their right to make their own choices and instead manipulate them by giving them false information on which to base their decisions. In a real sense we are taking away their freedom. Unless we have a very strong reason for doing so, lies cannot and should not be tolerated.

Liars like to believe that their reasons for lying are sound. Most liars do not believe anyone ought to lie to them, but justify their own behavior on the grounds that they are protecting someone else's feelings or confidences, or that their lie is necessary to protect their business or their employees. But according to Bok, when we lie—for any reason—we run risks that we may be found out and our credibility will be damaged. Even worse, few lies are solitary ones. The first lie "must be thatched with another or it will rain through."[11] Eventually

> psychological barriers wear down; lies seem more necessary, less reprehensible; the ability to make moral distinctions can coarsen; the liar's perception of his chances of being caught may warp…For all these reasons, I believe that we must at the very least accept as an initial premise Aristotle's view that lying is "mean and culpable" and that truthful statements are preferable to lies in the absence of special considerations. …Only where a lie is a last resort can one even begin to consider whether or not it is morally justified.[12]

Solomon and Hanson take a slightly more liberal view of lying. "Lying may always be wrong, but some lies are more wrong than others."[13] While they too believe that it is never right to lie, they suggest that sometimes it may be prudent or preferable to telling the truth. A sales representative, for instance, might understandably sound more enthusiastic about a product than he or she really is, and most people understand that salespeople present the favorable side of a product or service, not all sides. On the whole, however, they take the position that in business as in personal life, "telling a lie always requires extra thought and some very good reasons to show that this cardinal violation of the truth should be tolerated."[14]

Each person must decide for himself or herself what such a good reason would be. Clearly, if a robber walks into your business and asks for all your money and you say all you have is in the cash register, when in fact there is a considerable amount stored in the back room, this is a matter of self-preservation and one can justify lying. What about telling an employee whom you are letting go that you haven't got enough work, when in fact your real reason is that the person is incompetent? In this case it might be easier to lie, but one can argue that such a lie is easily seen through and it might be kinder in the long run to be honest with the employee, so that he or she can look for more suitable work. Each situation must be looked at individually, with our bias always on the side of telling the truth.

## The Search for a Common Moral Ground

Despite the fact that everyone may use a different set of values to determine what is ethical, many philosophers and educators who have spent their lives thinking about ethics have concluded that there are some universal moral imperatives or obligations that form the basis of civilized behavior and are necessary for any society to function. Michael Josephson is an attorney and founder of the Joseph and Edna Josephson Institute for the Advancement of Ethics, a non-profit institute that has been at the forefront of defining ethical behavior for businesses. In an interview with Bill Moyers on the Public Broadcasting System (PBS), Josephson said:

> History, theology, philosophy will show that every enlightened civilization has had a sense of right and wrong and a need to try to distinguish them. Now we may disagree over time as to what is right and what is wrong—but there has never been a disagreement in any philosophy about the importance of knowing the difference. The things that are right are the things that help people and society. They are things like compassion, honesty, fairness, accountability. They are absolute universal ethical values.[15]

Josephson points out that the Golden Rule, which says "Do unto others as you would have them do unto you," occurred in Greek culture and in Chinese culture thousands of years before Christ articulated his version.[16]

Josephson believes that most people have a built-in sense of what is right and wrong. The proof, he says, is that we feel guilt and shame when we do the wrong thing. Despite that knowledge, we often ignore our ideals about what constitutes proper behavior. There are a number of reasons for this. We have become a rights-oriented society. Sometimes we feel we have a right to certain things, but we have forgotten that with those rights come certain responsibilities. Too often, says Josephson, we measure our lives by what we get, what we acquire, and who we know. "It's the need to win, to be clever, and to be successful in other people's eyes that sometimes causes people to sacrifice the fundamental ideals," he says.

Ambassador Max Kampelman puts it this way: "There is a hole in our moral ozone layer. There is a vast difference between the right to do something, which is important, and doing something right, which is equally important."[17]

Sometimes businesspeople feel that the only way to be competitive and win is to be completely selfish—put their own interests above those of everyone else. Josephson tells the story of a lawyer who goes on a camping trip with a friend. They both are hiking with backpacks when suddenly they see a cougar about 20 yards away. The lawyer takes off his backpack, and the friend says, "What are you going to do?" The lawyer says, "I'm going to run for it." The friend says, "But you can't outrun a cougar." And the lawyer says, "I don't have to outrun the cougar. I just have to outrun you."[18]

Some justify the philosophy of putting our own interests ahead of everyone else's by saying that life is like having your hand in a bucket of water—when you remove it, the water settles down within moments and no one knew you ever lived. Therefore you should try to get everything you can for yourself, because it will make no difference to anyone else in the long run. There is another way of looking at the world and your place in it that holds that you can make a permanent and positive impact on society by doing what you can to make differences in the lives of the people you come in contact with. You can bring some of them happiness and joy, and help alleviate the pain and suffering of others.

Sometimes people argue that when you are dealing with unethical people, you have to be unethical, too, or you will be stepped on. Josephson says, "There is usually a choice of ethical and unethical behaviors. We tell people, unless you have three alternatives to every major problem, you haven't thought hard enough. As soon as you have three, you can find one that's ethical."[19]

Eventually most of us come to believe in the philosophy of helping people rather than taking advantage of them or using them for our own benefit, but the sad thing is that for many of us this occurs late in life, when we have learned that accomplishing a particular task or career goal did not bring us all the satisfaction we had hoped for. As Josephson observes, "We know that nobody on a deathbed says, 'I wish I had spent more time at the office.' People's values begin to change when they reflect upon how futile most of the flurry of activity was. And the fact is that a good conscience is the best pillow. Living a good life is the most important thing for us."[20]

**Deontology versus Utilitarianism.** There are two major traditions that dominate current thinking in moral philosophy: deontology and utilitarianism.[21]

**Deontology** holds that there are basic or universal ideals that should direct our thinking. Deontology is based on the beliefs of Immanuel Kant, an eighteenth-century German philosopher. Kant thought that the human mind could not possibly comprehend or arrive at the truth about God or the universe through pure logic or thought. He said that the only judgments we were capable of making were those based on evidence that we could see or prove the existence of. Kant believed in the existence of God, but said we have to take this on faith since we can't prove it by pure logic. Once one admits there is a God, then it is possible to make logical and reasonable assumptions about what is expected of us and how we are required to act. In short, there is a scientifically- arrived-at ideal that is necessary for humans to adhere to and for which adequate evidence exists, once one admits there is a God. Deontology proposes that ethical behavior is simply a matter of doing God's will. Since most of us believe that God is good, then goodwill or loving other human beings as God loves us is the universal principle on which all moral behavior must be based.

Along with the concept of goodwill goes a concept of duty to keep one's promises, which is known as Kant's **categorical imperative**—an absolute and universally binding moral law. Kant believed in always telling the truth because if we cannot believe what others tell us, then agreements and even conversations between people are not possible. Would you loan money to anyone if you knew that he or she had no intention of repaying it, even though he or she promised to? Deontology, in effect, says that the only way to measure whether an action is ethical is to ask whether we would be willing to live in a world where *everyone* routinely did the same thing. If our actions would be acceptable to us as a universal law, then they are correct and ethical.

Conversely, **utilitarianism** does not seek universal principles that can be applied to all situations, but instead says that ethical behavior consists of the greatest good for the greatest number. One determines this by "performing a social cost/benefit analysis and acting on it."[22] Robin and Reidenbach show that this philosophy is grounded in the ideas of Adam Smith, who said that "capitalistic systems, by providing the greatest material good for the greatest number, are considered ethical from a perspective of economic philosophy."[23] They point out, however, that there are some major criticisms of utilitarianism that should be considered. One is that an action might do a small amount of good for a large number of people while at the same time severely injuring a small group. For example, is it always ethical to build a mega-resort on a pristine beach in an underdeveloped country? Such a complex benefits tourism, but is often a disaster for the local community. A mega-resort introduces pollution, large numbers of visitors and noise to the area, and may lead to the destruction of the local culture. Moreover, utilitarianism suggests that each action should be judged on its own merits. When we do this there is a lack of consistency that opens the door to generalizations and excuses. One cannot say that anything is either moral or immoral, ethical or unethical, if "it all depends." For example, can an accountant embezzling company funds be excused because he or she believes the company is "ripping people off, so why shouldn't I?" Generally, we reject that kind of rationalization because it is entirely subjective.

**Ethical Relativism. Ethical relativism** suggests that there are no universal ethical principles at all; each issue must be considered in its situational or cultural context. For example, it might be unethical to bribe a government official in the United States to obtain a building permit or zoning variance, but quite acceptable in some other countries where bribes are a routine part of doing business. (Students should note that while one can debate whether bribing government officials is ethical or not, it is most definitely against U.S. law for any American corporation or citizen to do so.) This kind of reasoning is also known as **situational ethics**. It is a convenient ethical code for those who are not sure what their ethical values are or how they are arrived at, but, like utilitarianism, it provides little guidance for those who believe in a clear and consistent code of ethics.

## Ethical Issues in Hospitality

Each day hospitality managers are faced with a variety of business decisions with ethical overtones. Too often, managers ignore ethical considerations when making business decisions.

Here are a few examples of decisions that a hotel general manager or someone in a similar position at a club or restaurant might make in the ordinary course of business:

**New Menu**

You have just approved a new menu that retains many of your favorite high-calorie, high-cholesterol, high-sodium foods. There are no nutritious alternatives on the menu. You reason that hotel guests liked what was on the old menu and they will keep coming back.

**Bumped Reservation**

You have just been approached by an influential guest regarding a birthday party he would like to hold at the hotel two months from now. Unfortunately, just yesterday the hotel's meeting room was booked for that date. The guest asks you to bump the person who reserved the room. He suggests you tell that person the sales manager made a mistake in booking the room when it had previously been reserved. You agree to do so.

**Cashier's Integrity**

You decide to test a cashier's integrity. The cashier has been with the company ten years and has a flawless record. You slip a $50 bill in the register receipts. At the end of the day, the cashier shows a $5 overage. Upon questioning, the cashier admits to pocketing the $45 difference.

**Free Wine**

You recently purchased 20 cases of wine for the hotel from a new beverage supplier. Without your advance knowledge, the supplier delivered one free case of wine to your residence. You decide to keep the free case for your personal use, since it did not influence the purchase of the 20 cases for the hotel.[24]

In a *Lodging* magazine poll, 400 lodging managers were asked if they agreed with the ethics of the manager's decision in each of these hypothetical scenarios. The results of that poll are shown in Exhibit 2.

The "new menu" scenario considers how much responsibility each of us must take for the welfare of others. We may not consider ourselves our brother's keeper, but it can be argued that as hospitality professionals it is our duty to include low-calorie, nutritious meals on the menu.

We were told by one knowledgeable hotelier that meeting room reservations get "bumped" all the time. That may be so, but if we are going to respect the rights of others, the fair thing is to allow the person who made the reservation first to keep it. Moreover, it is wrong to lie and say the other reservation was made earlier when it was not. On the other hand, if we are ethical relativists, we might argue that if we do not go along with this influential guest we may lose a substantial amount of business, which could mean laying off employees and facing other consequences that might hurt others.

The case of the cashier's integrity also bears on the rights of others. Is it fair to put a loyal employee to a test of this nature without warning him or her in advance, especially when there is no evidence that anything is wrong? Would we like to be treated this way?

The free wine scenario poses the question of what constitutes honesty. The wine may have been delivered after the hotel's wine was ordered, but it still represents an unauthorized payment to the manager for "services rendered." The manager could return the free case and ask the supplier to show his or her appreciation for the order by giving the hotel an appropriate discount on its next wine purchase. Or the manager might give the extra case of wine to the hotel so that the hotel could profit from its sale. One test of whether it is ethical to keep this wine for personal use would be for the manager to ask how he or she would feel if other managers at the hotel found out about it.

Linda K. Enghagen surveyed 113 four-year colleges and universities on ethical issues in hospitality and tourism. While a total of 35 different issues were raised, the ten that received the most mentions were:

- Managing an ethical environment
- Relations with customers and employees
- Honesty
- Employee privacy rights
- Alcohol/drug testing
- Environmental issues

**Exhibit 2  Ethics Poll of Lodging Managers**

The *New Menu, Bumped Reservation, Cashier's Integrity,* and *Free Wine* scenarios (described in the text) were presented to lodging managers by *Lodging* magazine. When rating the manager's decision in each of the scenarios, the polled managers were asked whether they (a) strongly agreed, (b) moderately agreed, (c) were unsure, (d) moderately disagreed, or (e) strongly disagreed with the actions of the managers in the scenarios. Here are the results.

**New Menu**

| | | |
|---|---|---|
| (a) | Strongly agree | 6.1% |
| (b) | Moderately agree | 15.5% |
| (c) | Unsure | 8.9% |
| (d) | Moderately disagree | 24.9% |
| (e) | Strongly disagree | 44.6% |

**Comment:** The responses suggest a fairly high level of health consciousness among hotel managers.

**Bumped Reservation**

| | | |
|---|---|---|
| (a) | Strongly agree | 1.3% |
| (b) | Moderately agree | 5.1% |
| (c) | Unsure | 4.6% |
| (d) | Moderately disagree | 13.7% |
| (e) | Strongly disagree | 75.3% |

**Comment:** Clearly, managers believe that guest favoritism leads to guest dissatisfaction.

**Cashier's Integrity**

| | | |
|---|---|---|
| (a) | Strongly agree | 36.5% |
| (b) | Moderately agree | 25.6% |
| (c) | Unsure | 9.4% |
| (d) | Moderately disagree | 11.7% |
| (e) | Strongly disagree | 16.8% |

**Comment:** A minority of managers evidently believed that the test put too much pressure on the employee; however, 62.1% agreed with the manager's test.

**Free Wine**

| | | |
|---|---|---|
| (a) | Strongly agree | 7.4% |
| (b) | Moderately agree | 16.5% |
| (c) | Unsure | 10.6% |
| (d) | Moderately disagree | 17.5% |
| (e) | Strongly disagree | 48.0% |

**Comment:** 65.5% of respondents apparently felt that acceptance of the wine could influence future beverage purchases by the hotel.

Adapted from Raymond S. Schmidgall, "Hotel Scruples," *Lodging,* January 1991, pp. 38–40.

- Relations with foreign governments
- Codes of ethics and self-governance
- Employee abuse of alcohol/drugs
- Conflicts of interest[25]

## Ethics in Hospitality Management

These issues reflect the academic perspective. Industry leaders have cited many other ethical problems that concern them. These include:

- Sanitation
- Travel agent commissions
- Overbooking
- AIDS
- Employment discrimination by age, sex, or race
- Kickbacks
- Concealing income from the Internal Revenue Service
- Yield management
- Advertising claims
- Raiding of competition's staff
- Truth-in-menu laws
- Meeting the needs of disabled customers and employees
- Adequate safety and security measures

Let's take a closer look at some of these industry issues.

### Environmental Issues

Preserving and protecting the resources of tourist destinations has become a topic of major importance. Every time a hotel or an attraction is added to an area already crowded with visitors, there is a legitimate concern about its long-term impact on the environment. At an international symposium on ecology and tourism in Mazatlan, Mexico, James Speth, administrator of the U.N. Development Program, warned that "tourism and environmental protection are on a collision course." Speth urged that "rapid and forceful changes be made in the tourism industry to incorporate environmental protection policies."[26] At the same meeting, officials from the Mexican government said that Mexico was undertaking a major review of development plans at resorts like Huatulco and Los Cabos to stop the deterioration of coastal ecology.[27] Mexico's neighbor, Belize, is also taking steps to limit and control growth by keeping 80 percent of its land in tropical forest and turning down several proposals for resort development.[28]

Many destinations have already taken drastic steps to preserve their natural resources. In Bermuda, the number of hotel rooms has been restricted to 10,000 for a number of years, and cruise ship visits are restricted. In Egypt, officials have reduced the visiting hours at the Pyramids at Giza and limited the number of tourists who can visit at one time.

Much of the concern revolves around hotel and restaurant development, which is inevitable at popular tourist destinations because if visitors are allowed to visit a site they need to be accommodated while they are there. This dilemma is faced not only by developing nations, but also by highly developed industrialized countries where overbuilding has already caused major damage.

**Recognizing the value of environmental responsibility, many hospitality companies make a point of publicizing their progress.** (Courtesy of Inter-Continental Hotels and Resorts)

One hotel company that takes its environmental responsibilities seriously is Inter-Continental Hotels, which has prepared an Environmental Manual for use at all of its properties:

All of Inter-Continental's North American guestrooms are now fully stocked with environmentally conscious bath amenities. Items include pure vegetable-based soaps and liquid amenities in packaging made entirely from recycled soda bottles. The amenities and their paper packaging are tinted with water or vegetable-based biodegradable dyes and contain neither foil stamping or metallic inks, methods which are both costly and damaging to the environment.[29]

Walt Disney Resorts has implemented a substantial number of procedures to reduce waste as well. In a brochure placed in all its hotels, Disney asks guests to place such recyclable materials as beverage cans, bottles, and take-out boxes in a specially provided plastic bag (see Exhibit 3). At EPCOT Center in Orlando, Florida, Disney purchases paper towels and toilet paper in "jumbo" rolls rather than small packages, resulting in a source reduction of 813,000 packages a year. The size of the dispenser napkins in restaurants and snack bars has been reduced by 25 percent, which decreases food service waste by 263,085 pounds a year.

Many hotels in Germany urge guests to save water (the water used by the laundry) by re-using towels rather than asking for fresh ones every morning (see Exhibit 4). Modern cruise ships burn waste in on-board incinerators or compact and store it until it can be disposed of on land.

Burger King serves its sandwiches in "Earth-Happy Packaging" (paper wrap) (see Exhibit 5). McDonald's is the largest user of recycled products in the restaurant industry. Carry-out bags are made from recycled corrugated boxes and newsprint; takeout drink trays are made from recycled newspapers. Some new McDonald's units are constructed with insulated concrete blocks made with recycled photographic film and roof tiles made from used computer casings; children's play areas use recycled automobile tires.

You don't have to be big to be environmentally sensitive. In Ohio, Izzy's, a small deli-restaurant chain, encourages customers to bring in their own take-out packaging by charging customers $.11 extra for take-out orders packed by the restaurant. One small restaurant in Chicago has a successful recycling program despite the fact that it does not have room to store recyclable materials on-site. Its employees drop off bags of recyclables at recycling centers on their way home from work.[30]

## Discrimination

Even though it is unlawful, and a company may have policies forbidding it, discrimination of one sort or another can still occur, simply because some managers may have value systems that lead them to discriminate in certain instances, perhaps unconsciously. Because there are so many subtle forms of discrimination—based on age, race, religion, gender, sexual preference, nationality, or physical attributes—discrimination may be one of the most common violations of ethics found in the hospitality industry, and one of the most difficult to recognize. In many cases it is neither malicious nor intentional. That does not excuse it, however, and managers must know where they are likely to find it and how to eliminate it.

Almost all discrimination involves fear of one sort or another. We live in uncertain times; huge political and social upheavals have taken place. These

**Exhibit 3 Disney's Recycling Efforts**

> **RECYCLE IT!**
>
> We hope that you are enjoying your stay in the WALT DISNEY WORLD RESORT. To maintain the natural beauty of our World we ask your help in collecting recyclable materials. Please put all your beverage cans, polystyrene foam containers (cups, plates, take-out boxes, ice chests), and glass and plastic bottles (no caps or lids) in the attached plastic bag. Please stack newspapers separately beneath the recycling bag. Our housekeeping staff will do the rest. If you have any questions, please contact the Housekeeping Office. Thank you for your help.
>
> WALT DISNEY RESORTS

**This cardboard holder (printed with vegetable inks on recycled paper) contained a plastic bag and a brochure detailing Walt Disney World Resort's solid-waste reduction efforts.** (Courtesy of Walt Disney World Resort, Orlando, Florida)

changes are bound to make us uneasy. Many of us are afraid of losing our jobs. Others are afraid of losing power or prestige, or simply not "belonging" anymore. One way these fears manifest themselves is through discrimination. Discrimination allows us to express those fears and rationalize them by giving them faces and names. Unfortunately, many opportunists have made a career out of exploiting our concerns and thus have muddied the waters even more. Their ideas fuel our fears, and sometimes these fears express themselves in the workplace.

One of the most serious and blatant forms of discrimination still practiced in many parts of the world is racial. *Meetings & Conventions* magazine surveyed 50 members of the National Coalition of Black Meeting Planners, asking them how

**Exhibit 4    Sample Water Conservation Strategy**

> **VEREHRTER GAST,**
> können Sie sich nur vage vorstellen, wieviele Tonnen Hand- und Badetücher jeden Tag in allen Hotels und Kurbetrieben der Welt unnötig gewaschen werden - und welch ungeheure, unnötige Mengen von Waschmitteln dadurch unser Wasser belasten und verunreinigen?
>
> **BITTE ENTSCHEIDEN SIE UND HELFEN SIE MIT!**
> Handtücher auf den Boden heißt: »Bitte austauschen!«
> Handtücher zurück auf den Halter bedeutet: Ich verwende sie ein weiteres Mal
> » DER UMWELT ZULIEBE «
>
> — VIELEN DANK —

> **DEAR GUEST,**
> can you vaguely guess, how many tons of towels are unnecessarily washed everyday, in all Hotels in the World? This means enormous quantities of washing powder polluting and burdering our water!
>
> **Pleace decide yourself and help!**
> Towels on the floor means: »please change«
> Towels hung back on the rack means: »I will use it once more«
> »For the sake of our environment«
>
> — Thankyou —

**This notice (placed in guestrooms) asks guests to re-use towels in order to save water and avoid adding unnecessarily to the environmental problems caused by discharging chemical-laden laundry water into rivers and streams.** (Courtesy of Hotel an der Oper, Munich, Germany)

often incidents of racial discrimination occur in the meeting planning field. Four percent of respondents said they believe they always occur, 42 percent said they frequently occur, and 50 percent said they sometimes occur. No one answered "Never."[31] Yet when *Meetings & Conventions* then surveyed 100 meeting planners drawn from their own circulation list, 28 percent said that they believed incidents of racial discrimination never occurred in their profession.[32] According to the magazine:

> Midge Wilson, a professor of psychology and women's studies at Chicago's De Paul University and the co-author of *The Color Complex: The Politics of Skin Color Among African Americans,* sees the ability to ignore racism as one of the privileges of being white. "Not being aware of that sort of thing is fairly typical if you're a member of the dominant group," she says. "One of the privileges of membership in that group is that you don't have to concern yourself with what's happening to others. Whites simply don't have to recognize it."[33]

**Exhibit 5** Burger King's Earth-Happy Packaging

### New Earth-Happy Packaging

You'll probably notice that our sandwiches now come served in paper wrapping instead of a box. That's because we figure the world could probably use 15,000 less tons of trash a year. And less trash means less trucks to carry it. Which means less gas and a lot less air pollution. Not to mention the reduction in packaging the packaging has to be shipped in! All in all, it's just one of the ways we're trying to make the world a nicer place to eat.

This design appeared on Burger King sandwich bags. The bags were made with recycled newspapers; a toll-free number on the back of the bag invited customers to call with comments about Burger King's recycling efforts. (Courtesy of Burger King, Miami, Florida)

Many now believe that affirmative action may need to be taken to restore to minority groups the freedom and opportunities that have been denied them in the past. The hospitality industry faces the same challenges as the rest of society.

Discrimination also occurs in policies sometimes found in clubs and hotels that try to restrict the use of their facilities by certain racial and ethnic groups. Hotels have been known to discourage group business from certain groups of people because "our regular guests might feel uncomfortable." *Meetings & Conventions* magazine says "there are hoteliers who won't return the calls from predominantly minority organizations...or budge from the rack rates when they sit down to negotiate."[34] While some managers may think in these terms when making a business decision, ethical managers must ask if they can in good conscience be a party to a policy that clearly conflicts with ethical standards.

Many hospitality companies recognize the problem of racial discrimination and are doing something about it:

> Marriott points with pride to its selection as one of the 25 best employers for blacks in a readership poll conducted by *Black Enterprise* magazine. One of the reasons for that designation: The chain has had roughly a 50 percent increase in the number of minority hotel general managers in the last year, according to David Sampson, Marriott's vice president for human resources. In addition, Marriott has recently added a black woman, Floretta McKensie, a former District of Columbia schools superintendent, to its board of directors.
>
> ITT Sheraton sponsors scholarships for hospitality students at historically black colleges, including Grambling State University and Tuskegee Institute, and runs an internship program for minority students.[35]

Sex discrimination is another form of discrimination that must be addressed. For years, most male chefs believed that women had no place in professional kitchens, and even today that belief is widely held. Sometimes this is based on fallacies such as "it's a man's world" or "those large pots are too heavy for a woman to lift." But discrimination is not confined to the kitchen. Female hotel general managers are still relatively scarce when one considers that more than half of most hotels' employees are women. There are also questions of salaries and promotions. Male managers often assume that, since a married woman has a husband to help support her, she is in less need of a raise. Sometimes a female manager is not offered a promotion that involves a transfer to another city because it is wrongly assumed that her husband's job dictates where the family will live. Women have been denied sales positions because it was felt that men were better suited for traveling and going out drinking with clients. In other words, a female manager is just not "one of the boys." Discrimination on this basis is clearly unethical, as well as being unlawful in the United States.

Finally, no discussion of discrimination would be complete without mentioning age discrimination, a global problem. Companies under economic pressure to cut costs often look first to older workers, who often enjoy high earnings (due in part to their years of service) and may in the long run cost the company more if they stay employed until retirement and become entitled to a pension. Many companies favor younger applicants when considering new job applications.

While age discrimination is illegal in the United States, European employers legally can—and do—refuse to consider job applications from older people, reports the Wyatt Company (a consulting firm). Wyatt reports that many Europeans who lose their jobs after age 45 can only find short-term contract or temporary work. Employers in most European countries can also force employees to retire when they reach the normal age of eligibility for pensions—between 55 and 67, depending on the country.[36]

## Sexual Harassment

Another ethical problem in the workplace is sexual harassment. Men as well as women can be victims of sexual harassment by superiors of the opposite sex. Sexual harassment by employers includes asking their employees for dates, making sexual jokes or comments, touching employees inappropriately, or suggesting that sex will result in a promotion. The pressure to not complain when one's job and economic well-being are on the line is sometimes overwhelming. Companies cannot and should not allow anyone to believe for a moment that such behavior will go unnoticed or be excused.

The Federal Equal Employment Opportunity Commission (EEOC) has developed guidelines designed to prevent discrimination on the basis of sex. The guidelines detail the following three examples of misconduct that constitute sexual harassment:

- When submission to such conduct is made a term or condition of an individual's employment, either explicitly or implicitly;
- When submission to or rejection of such conduct by an individual is used as a basis of employment decisions; and
- When such conduct has the purpose or effect of unreasonably interfering with an individual's work performance or creating an intimidating, hostile, or offensive work environment.[37]

The third guideline, which cites a "hostile" work environment, should be of particular interest to managers, since it is a more subtle violation of the law and may not manifest itself in such obvious circumstances as employment or promotions. In 1986 the United States Supreme Court handed down a landmark decision, *Meritor Savings Bank* v. *Vinson*, that acknowledged the existence of a "hostile work environment" as a basis for a claim of sexual harassment.[38] The courts have, in a series of subsequent decisions, clarified the types of conduct that might support a claim of a hostile work environment. These include "treating women with less respect than men or being abusive to women but not men, and published images or remarks or spoken comments portraying women or men in a sexually demeaning manner."[39]

What this comes down to is that sexual harassment is largely subjective. If people feel that they are being sexually harassed, then they have a right to be protected from such behavior. Managers need to be extremely sensitive to the feelings as well as the behavior of employees.

## AIDS in the Workplace

AIDS is a good example of how prejudice and hysteria have affected some managers' ability to make fair and impartial decisions. Some people believe that carriers ought to be identified through testing, so that they can be informed and prevented from spreading the disease. But as columnist William Schneider points out, "What about their right not to be forced to learn whether they are under a probable sentence of death?"[40] There are other rights involved as well. Should employees who have tested HIV positive, but have not yet come down with AIDS (and may never come down with it), be promoted? One could argue that they should not be because they may not be able to stay in their new position long enough to benefit the employer, but no one knows how long a person in this situation will remain healthy, and to deny him or her a well-deserved promotion seems unfair by any standard. The issue is most often not one of promotion but simply of keeping one's job. It is illegal in the United States to discriminate against AIDS-infected workers, since (1) they are considered to be "disabled," and (2) their condition cannot be transmitted via food or casual contact, according to the latest scientific studies. Nevertheless, many hotel and restaurant operators have no written or expressed policy on the subject. A few operators are quite explicit about their attitudes. Fuddruckers, a hamburger chain based in Wakefield, Massachusetts, clearly states that "the company's policy is not to discriminate in any way against someone infected with AIDS, and if asked, to provide a list of AIDS-related social services."

## Advertising Claims

The purpose of advertising is to sell products and services. Most people understand this and therefore are skeptical about advertising claims. They are used to puffery and know that some restaurants that claim to serve "gourmet" meals may offer quite ordinary fare, and that resorts that offer "a luxury vacation" may in reality offer a mediocre one. Most people rely on recommendations from friends, relatives, and travel agents when making dining or travel plans, and take the claims made in brochures and advertising with a grain of salt.

There is a difference between puffery and outright deception. Resorts that advertise that they are "on the beach" should be on the beach and not across the street from it. Some resorts advertise that they offer golf, but neglect to mention that the course they use is 20 miles away and starting times are difficult to come by. If a rate is advertised, it should be one that is readily available.

In an unusual dispute that garnered a good deal of negative publicity for all concerned, Killington Ski Resorts of Vermont hired an engineering firm to measure its ski terrain and the terrain of nine other New England resorts. It then launched an advertising campaign charging its competitors with exaggerating their number of trails, the depth of their snow, snow conditions, and acreage of skiable terrain. The resort placed large advertisements in national newspapers that said "You can't ski on hype. This time of year, the hype on the trails is usually thicker than the snow." The ad then illustrated how much terrain Killington has that can be skied, and compared it with other resorts in the area.[41] In a related case, Sunday River Ski Resort in Maine filed a complaint charging Sugarloaf/USA with misleading advertising. In its advertising, Sugarloaf claimed that it was only 35 miles farther from Portland, Maine, than Sunday River. Sunday River said Sugarloaf is at least 42.6 miles farther. Sugarloaf changed its ads to say it was 39 miles farther.[42]

Unlike a television set, which can be returned if it is not satisfactory, a vacation is not returnable and represents an investment in time that cannot be replaced. Hoteliers have a moral duty to disclose all of the relevant details of their properties so that consumers can make a fair judgment as to whether their expectations are going to be met.

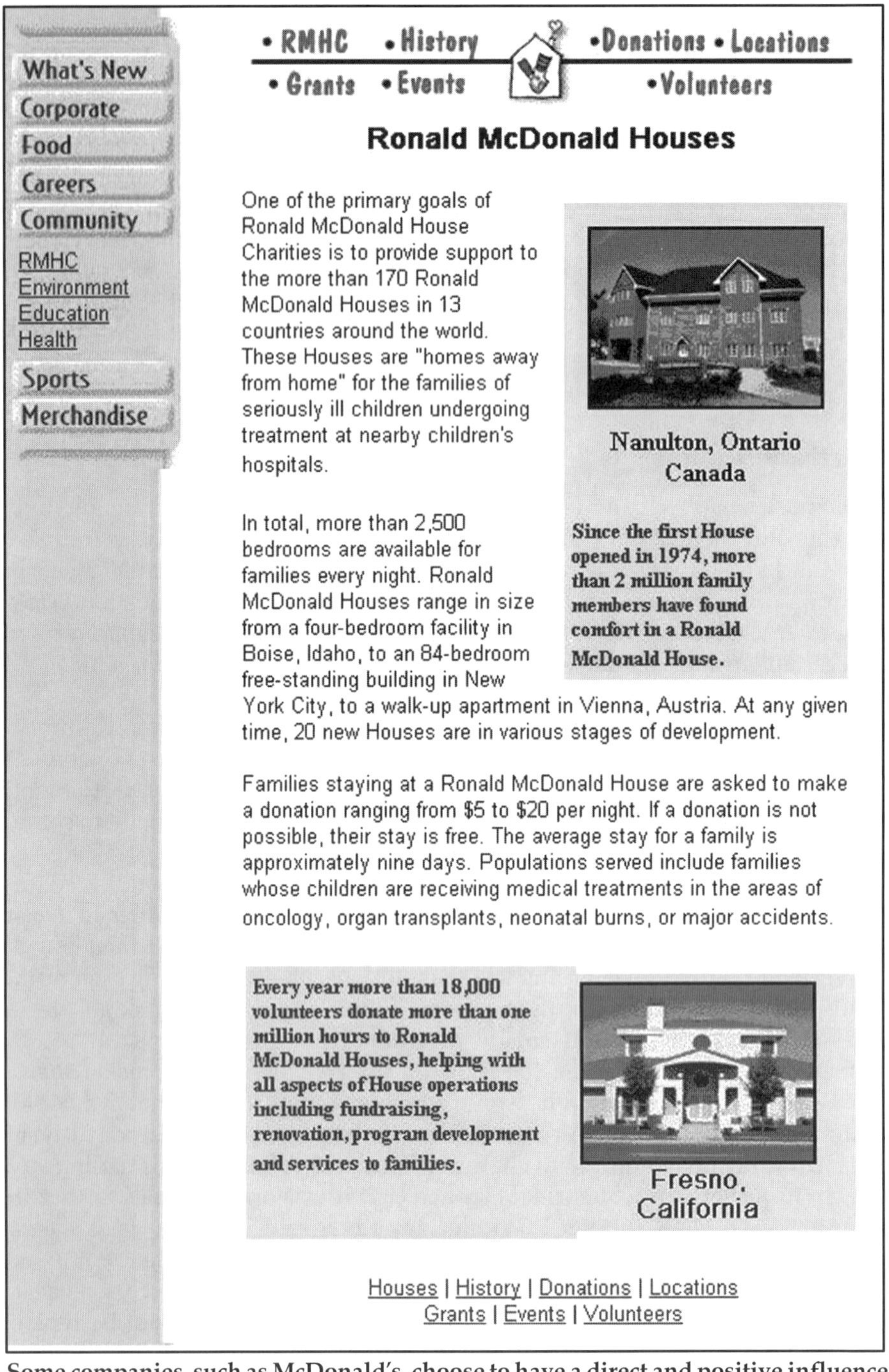

## Ronald McDonald Houses

- RMHC
- History
- Donations
- Locations
- Grants
- Events
- Volunteers

What's New
Corporate
Food
Careers
Community
RMHC
Environment
Education
Health
Sports
Merchandise

One of the primary goals of Ronald McDonald House Charities is to provide support to the more than 170 Ronald McDonald Houses in 13 countries around the world. These Houses are "homes away from home" for the families of seriously ill children undergoing treatment at nearby children's hospitals.

Nanulton, Ontario
Canada

In total, more than 2,500 bedrooms are available for families every night. Ronald McDonald Houses range in size from a four-bedroom facility in Boise, Idaho, to an 84-bedroom free-standing building in New York City, to a walk-up apartment in Vienna, Austria. At any given time, 20 new Houses are in various stages of development.

Since the first House opened in 1974, more than 2 million family members have found comfort in a Ronald McDonald House.

Families staying at a Ronald McDonald House are asked to make a donation ranging from $5 to $20 per night. If a donation is not possible, their stay is free. The average stay for a family is approximately nine days. Populations served include families whose children are receiving medical treatments in the areas of oncology, organ transplants, neonatal burns, or major accidents.

Every year more than 18,000 volunteers donate more than one million hours to Ronald McDonald Houses, helping with all aspects of House operations including fundraising, renovation, program development and services to families.

Fresno, California

Houses | History | Donations | Locations
Grants | Events | Volunteers

**Some companies, such as McDonald's, choose to have a direct and positive influence in local communities.** (Courtesy of McDonald's Corporation, Oak Brook, Illinois)

## Truth-in-Menu Laws

Many states have enacted truth-in-menu laws. In some states, fines can be as high as $500 for misrepresenting a menu item. But beyond legal obligations, there is a moral one to present what is being sold fairly and honestly. People have a right to know what they are eating, as well as to have enough information to make a fair evaluation about whether they are getting their money's worth. If a menu offers a 12-ounce sirloin steak, it ought to be 12 ounces every time it is served. Honest restaurateurs are proud of the fact that their gulf shrimp really comes from the Gulf of Mexico and their prime beef really is prime and not a lower grade. These may seem like minor points, but consumers have indicated that they are important to them.

Advances in the genetic engineering of food products have raised an interesting ethical question concerning truth-in-menu issues. After the Food and Drug Administration announced that it was not necessary to test or label genetically engineered (GE) fruits or vegetables that had been altered to extend their freshness or increase their size, a group of chefs protested. Rick Moonen, chef at the Water Club in New York City, put it this way:

> As a professional chef, I'm responsible for every plate of food that's served to every one of my patrons. And I must know what's on it. People come to your restaurant because of their confidence in you, because they feel you'll take care of them and their needs. If I'm serving GE foods, unlabeled and untested, I'm not fulfilling my obligation.[43]

Even if many patrons don't care if they are eating genetically engineered foods, it can be argued that they ought to know about it, especially since these products have not been sufficiently tested in the eyes of some critics.

## Must There Be a Code of Ethics?

Hospitality businesses that do not already have a code of ethics should develop one employees can live by and make decisions with while at work. Without such a code, how can a manager know what the company considers ethical or unethical? If every manager makes decisions based on his or her own ethical code, then a corporation may have no ethics at all, or a lot of different ethical codes depending on who is calling the shots. A company's ethics should reflect the company's mission and must be communicated to those who are responsible for carrying out that mission. Hospitality is a "people business"; ethics deals with our relationships with other people. For this reason, a code of ethics is almost mandatory for hospitality businesses whose managers want to achieve a unified direction and a satisfactory level of control over the conduct of business.

There is ample evidence to suggest that, without a code of ethics, some managers will make unethical decisions. According to a survey done by *Personnel Journal* magazine, middle managers—especially those 40 to 45 years old—are the most likely executives to do something unethical.[44] Some of these managers have a desire to "make it before it's too late," and strive to advance by shortcuts. In addition, they may have developed the attitude that "the company owes me" and therefore may be prone to cheating on expense accounts or making purchasing deals that benefit them.[45]

One business that has a strict and explicit code of ethics is the Sheraton Corporation. Sheraton's managers are expected to strictly comply with all the business ethics policies. The policies are quite lengthy and include the following:

### Conflicts of Interest

Employees are to exercise sound judgment, guided by the highest ethical standards of honesty and integrity, in all matters. No employee may abuse a corporate position for personal advantage or promote any actions contrary to stated ethical standards....

Employees and their immediate families shall not accept any gifts of cash or items of more than token value from third parties in connection with Sheraton business. All employees shall report immediately to their supervisors any offer or gift of more than token value.

### Quality

Our success as a corporation in fulfilling its obligation to shareholders is ultimately measured in terms of customer satisfaction. It is our policy to provide products and services that satisfy the needs and expectations of our customers; conform to appropriate specifications and contractual agreements, including reliability requirements; are safe for intended use and foreseeable misuse; and meet all applicable statutory requirements of local, regional, and national agencies.

Stephen S. J. Hall, a quality assurance consultant and the founder of the International Institute for Quality and Ethics in Service and Tourism (IIQEST), has proposed the ethics code for hotels shown in Exhibit 6.

## Some Ethical Litmus Tests

Even with laws and company policies and rules, ethical behavior is an intensely personal matter that every manager and employee must wrestle with. There are no easy guidelines that apply equally well in all circumstances. Ethical philosophers often talk about the moral duty of taking into account the interests of all stakeholders in arriving at a decision. A **stakeholder** is anyone who is affected by the outcome of a given decision. These could be your employees or your boss, the owners of the company you work for, the families of your employees, or the community in which the business operates. Sometimes managers or employees who are forced to implement unethical policies become whistleblowers and let other stakeholders know what is happening rather than be a silent part of an unethical action or plan.

In their book *The Power of Ethical Management*, Ken Blanchard and Norman Vincent Peale list three simple questions that they believe managers should ask themselves when making a decision:

1. *Is it legal?* Will I be violating either civil law or company policy?

2. *Is it balanced?* Is it fair to all concerned in the short term as well as the long term? Does it promote win-win relationships?

**Exhibit 6   Sample Code of Ethics for Hotels**

1. We acknowledge ethics and morality as inseparable elements of doing business, and will test every decision against the highest standards of honesty, legality, fairness, impunity, and conscience.
2. We will conduct ourselves personally and collectively at all times such as to bring credit to the service and tourism industry at large.
3. We will concentrate our time, energy, and resources on the improvement of our own products and services, and will not denigrate our competition in the pursuit of our own success.
4. We will treat all guests equally regardless of race, religion, nationality, creed, or sex.
5. We will deliver all standards of service and product with total consistency to every guest.
6. We will provide a totally safe and sanitary environment at all times for every guest and employee.
7. We will strive constantly, in words, actions, and deeds, to develop and maintain the highest level of trust and understanding among guests, clients, employees, employers, and the public at large.
8. We will provide every employee at every level all of the knowledge, training, equipment, and motivation required to perform his or her own tasks according to our published standards.
9. We will guarantee that every employee at every level will have the same opportunity to perform and advance, and will be evaluated against the same standard as all employees engaged in similar tasks.
10. We will actively and consciously work to protect and preserve our natural environment and natural resources in all that we do.
11. We will seek a fair and honest profit, no more, no less.

Source: IIQEST Ltd.

3. *How will it make me feel about myself?* Will it make me proud? Would I feel good if my decision were published in the newspaper? Would I feel good if my family knew about it?[46]

## Chapter Summary

Ethics is a set of moral principles and values that we use to answer questions of right and wrong. It focuses on moral choices and relationships with others. Although we all have different personal values and morals, there are some universal principles which virtually all religions, cultures, and societies agree upon. The basis of all of these principles is that other people's rights are as important as our own, and that it is our duty not to do anything to harm others.

Social responsibility is not the same as ethics, although the concepts are related. Companies have an unwritten social contract with society covering their rights and obligations. Ethics consists of "doing the right thing" in areas that may be entirely unrelated to that social contract, such as dealing with employees and customers.

There are six ways in which we arrive at our values about what is "good" and "just": authority, deductive logic, sense experience, emotion, intuition, and science. One of these ways is usually dominant within an individual and tends to influence the way he or she arrives at personal values. Although everyone is likely to have different values, on the whole most agree that it is a good idea to tell the truth whenever possible, and that stealing from others is wrong.

While some have argued that business is like poker and thus principles of ethical behavior do not apply in business, a careful examination shows that because businesses have different goals and there is much more at stake, the rules of business and poker must and should be different.

Honesty is always the best policy. When we lie we manipulate other people and impair their ability to make choices based on true information. People should think carefully before telling a lie, and have some very good reasons for violating this cardinal rule of ethics.

The most basic ethical rule is the Golden Rule: Do unto others as you would have them do unto you.

There are two major traditions that dominate current thinking in moral philosophy. These are deontology and utilitarianism. Deontology holds that there are basic or universal ideals that should direct our thinking. These include keeping one's promises (Kant's categorical imperative) and always telling the truth. Utilitarianism says there are no basic or universal ideals; ethical behavior consists of doing the greatest good for the greatest number. This philosophy is based on the ideas behind capitalism.

Many people who cannot choose between these two traditions prefer ethical relativism, also known as situational ethics. However, by definition situational ethics is ambiguous and thus cannot be incorporated into any management system.

Hospitality managers are faced with a variety of ethical decisions daily. What should be done to preserve and protect the environment has become an ethical question of major importance in the hospitality industry. Many destinations have already taken drastic steps to preserve their natural resources, and hotel and restaurant companies are implementing recycling programs.

One of the most serious ethical issues facing the industry is discrimination, not only in hiring and promotion, but in treatment of guests. Discrimination can be based on race, ethnicity, gender, or other characteristics.

Another ethical problem that must be addressed in the workplace is sexual harassment. Companies cannot and should not allow anyone to believe that sexual harassment will go unnoticed or will be excused.

AIDS is an issue that forces managers to make ethical decisions in regard to such things as testing and promotion policies. Advertising claims should not misrepresent the truth or create unrealistic expectations. Menus should honestly describe what is being sold.

Companies should adapt an ethical code such as the one suggested by IIQEST. A fair litmus test of an ethical decision is: (1) Is it legal? (2) Is it balanced? and (3) How will it make me feel about myself?

# Endnotes

1. John Godfrey Saxe, *The Blind Men and the Elephant* (New York: McGraw-Hill, 1963).
2. George A. Steiner, "Social Policies for Business," *California Management Review,* Winter 1972, pp. 17–24, cited by Donald P. Robin and Eric Reidenbach in "Social Responsibility, Ethics, and Marketing Strategy: Closing the Gap Between Concept and Application," *Journal of Marketing,* January 1987, p. 45.
3. "The Green Revolution," *Restaurant Hospitality,* September 1990, p. 30.
4. Edwin M. Reingold, "America's Hamburger Helper," *Time,* 29 June 1992, p. 66.
5. Reingold, p. 66.
6. Adapted from Hunter Lewis, *A Question of Values* (New York: Harper & Row, 1990), pp. 10–11.
7. Lewis, pp. 16–17.
8. Alfred Carr, "Is Business Bluffing Ethical?" *Harvard Business Review,* January/February 1968, cited by Robert C. Solomon and Kristine R. Hanson in *It's Good Business* (New York: Atheneum, 1985), p. 91.
9. Solomon and Hanson, pp. 90–93.
10. Sissela Bok, *Lying: Moral Choice in Public and Private Life* (New York: Random House, 1979), p. 20.
11. Bok, p. 26.
12. Bok, pp. 26–27, 32–33.
13. Solomon and Hanson, pp. 93–94.
14. Solomon and Hanson, p. 96.
15. Bill Moyers, "Ethical Dilemmas," *New Age Journal,* July/August 1989, p. 45.
16. Moyers, p. 45. The phrase Josephson is referring to appears in the New Testament: "Therefore all things whatsoever ye would that men should do to you, do even so to them: for this is the law and the prophets" (Matthew 5:12, King James Version).
17. Ambassador Max Kampelman, speaking at Florida International University's graduation ceremony, May 3, 1993, Miami, Florida.
18. Moyers, p. 97.
19. Moyers, p. 97.
20. Moyers, p. 97.
21. Robin and Reidenbach, p. 46.
22. Robin and Reidenbach, p. 46.
23. Robin and Reidenbach, p. 47.
24. Adapted from Raymond S. Schmidgall, "Hotel Scruples," *Lodging,* January 1991, pp. 38–40.
25. Linda K. Enghagen, "Ethics in Hospitality/Tourism Education: A Survey," supplied by the author. Professor Enghagen has been most helpful in the formulation of some of the ideas presented here.

26. "Hot Line," *TravelAge East,* 20 September 1993, p. 4.
27. "Hot Line," p. 4.
28. Eugene Sloan, "Belize Tries to Avoid the Eco-Tourism Trap," *USA Today,* 17 December 1992, p. 8-D.
29. "Inter-Continental Hotels Capture 'Greening of Tourism' Award," *Florida Hotel & Motel Journal,* October 1993, p. 12.
30. Susan M. Bard, "Conference Takes Look at Hotel Recycling," *Hotel & Motel Management,* 16 December 1991, p. 18.
31. David Ghitelman, "Racism: Let's Face It," *Meetings & Conventions,* November 1992, p. 53.
32. Ghitelman, p. 54.
33. Ghitelman, p. 54.
34. Ghitelman, p. 55.
35. Ghitelman, p. 58.
36. "Labor Letter," *Wall Street Journal,* 27 July 1993, p. A-1.
37. Arthur J. Hamilton and Peter A. Veglahn, "Sexual Harassment: The Hostile Work Environment," *Cornell Quarterly,* April 1992, p. 88.
38. Hamilton and Veglahn, p. 88.
39. Hamilton and Veglahn, p. 90.
40. William Schneider, "Homosexuals: Is AIDS Changing Attitudes?" *Public Opinion,* July/August 1987, p. 59.
41. Marj Charlier, "Resort Ads Caught Snowing the Ski Set," *Wall Street Journal,* 22 December 1992, p. B-1.
42. Charlier, p. B-1.
43. Julie Mautner, "Culinary Crusaders," *Food Arts,* December 1992, p. 29.
44. Study by *Personnel Journal,* November 1987, cited in "Survey: Middle Managers Most Likely to Be Unethical," *Marketing News,* 6 November 1987, p. 6.
45. "Survey: Middle Managers Most Likely to Be Unethical," p. 6.
46. Ken Blanchard and Norman Vincent Peale, *The Power of Ethical Management* (New York: Morrow, 1988), p. 27.

## Key Terms

**categorical imperative**—A moral obligation or command that is unconditionally and universally binding.

**deontology**—A system of ethics that assumes God exists and holds that there are basic or universal ideals.

**ethical relativism**—A philosophy that holds that ethical choices should be based on what seems reasonable or logical according to one's own value system. Also known as situational ethics.

**ethics**—(1) A set of moral principles and values that individuals use to answer questions of right and wrong; (2) the study of the general nature of morals and of the specific moral choices to be made by individuals in their relationships with others.

**situational ethics**—A philosophy that holds that ethical choices should be based on what seems reasonable or logical according to one's own value system. Also known as ethical relativism.

**stakeholder**—Anyone who is affected by the outcome of a given decision.

**utilitarianism**—A system of ethics based on the greatest good for the greatest number of people.

## Review Questions

1. What is ethics?
2. What is the difference between social responsibility and business ethics?
3. What are the six techniques of moral reasoning?
4. Is business like poker?
5. Is honesty always the best policy?
6. What is the difference between deontology and utilitarianism?
7. What is ethical relativism or situational ethics?
8. What are some typical ethical dilemmas hospitality managers must face?
9. Why should businesses have a code of ethics?
10. What three questions should managers ask themselves to test whether they are making an ethical decision?

## Internet Sites

For more information, visit the following Internet sites. Remember that Internet addresses can change without notice. If the site is no longer there, use a browser to look for additional sites.

### Hotel Companies/Resorts

Inter-Continental Hotels
www.interconti.com

Sheraton Hotels
www.sheraton.com

Walt Disney Resorts
www.disney.com

### Organizations, Consultants, Resources

The Better Business Bureau
www.bbb.org

Institute for Business and
Professional Ethics
www.depaul.edu/ethics

Institute for Global Ethics
www.globalethics.org

International Business Ethics Institute
www.business-ethics.org

## *Restaurant Companies*

Domino's Pizza
www.dominos.com

McDonald's
www.mcdonalds.com

# REVIEW QUIZ

When you feel you have covered all of the material in this chapter, answer these questions. Choose the *best* answer.

1. Political theorists have called the set of generally accepted relationships, obligations, and duties between society's major institutions and its people the:

    a. social contract.
    b. civil code.
    c. categorical imperative.
    d. moral compact.

2. Authors Robert Solomon and Kristine Hanson believe that the rules of poker and the rules of business should and must be different because:

    a. the goals of poker and the goals of business are different.
    b. there is much more at stake in the business world than there is in poker games.
    c. redistributing wealth is the business world's goal but it is not motivated by greed, as it is in poker.
    d. a and b.

3. Which of the following statements about deontology is *false*?

    a. Deontology is based on the beliefs of Immanuel Kant.
    b. The categorical imperative holds that everyone has a duty to keep his or her promises.
    c. According to deontology, each action should be judged on its own merits.
    d. According to deontology, ethical behavior is defined as doing God's will.

4. The philosophy that suggests that there are no universal ethical principles is called:

    a. the provincial doctrine.
    b. utilitarianism.
    c. ethical relativism.
    d. deontology.

5. AIDS-infected workers:

    a. should be separated from guests and other employees.
    b. are considered "disabled" according to U.S. law.
    c. can transmit AIDS via food.
    d. in the United States can legally be fired for having AIDS.

**602-b**  Chapter 18

## REVIEW QUIZ *(continued)*

6. Which of the following statements about sexual harassment is *true?*
    a. Making sexual jokes or comments is a form of sexual harassment.
    b. By definition, men cannot be sexually harassed.
    c. The U.S. government has not provided any guidelines for managers as to what constitutes sexual harassment.
    d. A sexual harassment claim will not be upheld if it merely cites a "hostile work environment."

7. According to a survey done by *Personnel Journal* magazine, _____ are the most likely executives to do something unethical.
    a. junior executives
    b. middle managers
    c. top managers
    d. senior executives

**Answer Key:** 1-a-C1, 2-d-C1, 3-c-C2, 4-c-C2, 5-b-C3, 6-a-C3, 7-b-C3

Each question is linked to a competency. Competencies are listed on the first page of the chapter. An answer reading 3-b-C4 translates to:

   3: the question number
   b: the correct answer
  C4: the competency number

# Appendix

## Hospitality Associations and Periodicals

The following is a list of some of the associations and periodicals that may be of interest to hospitality students, managers, and employees. Phone numbers are not included because they change somewhat frequently.

### ASSOCIATIONS

Associations are organizations of persons having a common interest or purpose. They can be a valuable resource for individuals seeking job opportunities, information about their profession, news of current trends, or just the camaraderie of individuals in similar fields with similar interests. What follows are representative associations related to the travel and tourism industry.*

American Bed and Breakfast Association (ABBA)
1407 Huguenot Road
Midlothian, VA 23113-2644

American Franchise Association (AFA)
10850 Wilshire, No. 700
Los Angeles, CA 90025

American Hotel & Motel Association (AH&MA)
1201 New York Avenue, NW, Suite 600
Washington, DC 20005

American School Food Service Association (ASFSA)
1600 Duke Street, 7th Floor
Alexandria, VA 22314

---

*All association names and addresses have been quoted from Deborah M. Burek, ed., *Encyclopedia of Associations* (Detroit, Mich.: Gale Research Company). This encyclopedia is updated each year.

American Society of Bakery Engineers (ASBE)
2 North Riverside Plaza, Room 1733
Chicago, IL 60606

American Society of Heating, Refrigerating and Air-Conditioning Engineers (ASHRAE)
1791 Tullie Circle NE
Atlanta, GA 30329

American Society for Hospital Food Service Administrators (ASHFSA)
c/o American Hospital Association
840 N. Lake Shore Drive
Chicago, IL 60611

American Society of Sanitary Engineering (ASSE)
P.O. Box 40362
Bay Village, OH 44140

American Society of Travel Agents (ASTA)
1101 King Street
Alexandria, VA 22314

American Travel Inns (ATI)
349 South 200 East, Suite 170
Salt Lake City, UT 84111

Association of Corporate Travel Executives (ACTE)
P.O. Box 5394
Parsippany, NJ 07054

Association of Group Travel Executives (AGTE)
c/o Arnold H. Light
The Light Group, Inc.
424 Madison Ave., Suite 705
New York, NY 10017

Association of Retail Travel Agents (ARTA)
1745 Jefferson Davis Hwy., Suite 300
Arlington, VA 22202-3402

Bed and Breakfast League/Sweet
 Dreams and Toast (BBL)
P.O. Box 9490
Washington, DC 20016

Center for Hospitality Research and
 Service (CHRS)
c/o Department of Hotel, Restaurant
 and Institutional Mgt.
Virginia Polytechnic Institute and State
 University
Blacksburg, VA 24061

Chinese American Restaurant Association (CARA)
173 Canal Street
New York, NY 10013

Club Managers Association of
 America (CMAA)
1733 King Street
Alexandria, VA 22314

Council on Hotel, Restaurant, and
 Institutional Education (CHRIE)
1200 17th Street, NW
Washington, DC 20036-3097

Cruise Lines International Association
 (CLIA)
500 5th Avenue, Suite 1407
New York, NY 10110

Food Industries Suppliers Association
 (FISA)
P.O. Box 2084
Fairfield Glade, TN 38557

Food Processing Machinery and
 Supplies Association (FPMSA)
200 Dangerfield Road
Alexandria, VA 22314

Food Service Marketing Institute
 (FSMI)
P.O. Box 1265
Lake Placid, NY 12946

Foodservice and Packaging Institute
 (FPI)
1025 Connecticut Ave. NW
Washington, DC 20036

Franchise Consultants International
 Association (FCIA)
5147 S. Angela Road
Memphis, TN 38117

Hospitality Lodging and Travel
 Research Foundation (HLTRF)
c/o Raymond C. Ellis, Jr.
American Hotel & Motel Association
1201 New York Avenue, NW,
 Suite 600
Washington, DC 20005

Hotel-Motel Greeters International
 (HMGI)
P.O. Box 20017
El Cajon, CA 92021

Hospitality Sales and Marketing
 Association International (HSMAI)
1300 L Street NW, Suite 800
Washington, DC 20005

Institute of Certified Travel Agents
 (ICTA)
148 Linden Street
P.O. Box 56
Wellesley, MA 02181-0503

International Association of Holiday
 Inns (IAHI)
3 Ravinia Drive, Suite 2000
Atlanta, GA 30346

International Association of Hospitality Accountants (IAHA)
Box 27649
Austin, TX 78755-2649

International Food Service Executive's
 Association (IFSEA)
1100 S. State Road, Suite 103
Margate, FL 33068

International Franchise Association
 (IFA)
1350 New York Ave. NW,
 Suite 900
Washington, DC 20005

International Society of Hotel Association Executives (ISHAE)
P.O. Box 1529
Tallahassee, FL 32302

Meeting Planners International (MPI)
1950 Stemmons Freeway
Infomart Building, Suite 5018
Dallas, TX 75207-3109

Mexican Food and Beverage Board (MFBB)
314 E. 41st Street
New York, NY 10017

Mobile Industrial Caterer's Association (MICA)
7300 Artesia Blvd.
Buena Park, CA 90621

National Association of Black Hospitality Professionals (NABHP)
P.O. Box 5443
Plainfield, NJ 07060-5443

National Association of Catering Executives (NACE)
304 W. Liberty Street, Suite 201
Louisville, KY 40202

National Association of Concessionaires (NAC)
35 E. Wacker Drive, Suite 1545
Chicago, IL 60601

National Association of Institutional Linen Management (NAILM)
2130 Lexington Road, Suite H
Richmond, KY 40475

National Association of Pizza Operators (NAPO)
P.O. Box 1347
New Albany, IN 47150

National Association of Restaurant Managers (NARM)
5322 N. 78th Way
Scottsdale, AZ 85250

National Bed-and-Breakfast Association (NB&BA)
P.O. Box 332
Norwalk, CT 06852

National Black McDonald's Operators Association (NBMOA)
c/o Mrs. Fran Jones
6363 W. Sunset Blvd., Suite 809
Los Angeles, CA 90028-7330

National Business Travel Association (NBTA)
1650 King Street, No. 301
Alexandria, VA 22314-2747

National Food Service Association (NFSA)
P.O. Box 1932
Columbus, OH 43216

National Restaurant Association (NRA)
1200 17th Street, NW
Washington, DC 20036

National Soft Serve and Fast Food Association (NSSFFA)
7321 Anthony Hwy.
Waynesboro, PA 17268-9736

Preferred Hotels Association (PHA)
1901 S. Meyers Road, Suite 220
Oakbrook Terrace, IL 60181

Roundtable for Women Food-Beverage-Hospitality (RWFBH)
145 W. 1st Street, Suite A
Tustin, CA 92680

Shakey's Franchised Dealers Association (SFDA)
5820 Wilshire Blvd., No. 500
Los Angeles, CA 90036

Small Luxury Hotels of the World (SLHW)
337 S. Robertson Blvd., Suite 202
Beverly Hills, CA 90211

Society for the Advancement of Food Service Research (SAFSR)
University of Nevada, Las Vegas
William F. Harrah College of Hotel Administration
Food and Beverage Department
4505 S. Maryland Parkway
Las Vegas, NV 89154-6022

Society of Corporate Meeting Professionals (SCMP)
2600 Garden Road, #208
Monterey, CA 93940

Society for Foodservice Management (SFM)
304 W. Liberty Street, Suite 201
Louisville, KY 40202

Tourist House Association of America (THAA)
RD 2, Box 355A
Greentown, PA 18426

Travel Industry Association of America (TIAA)
2 Lafayette Center
1133 21st Street, NW
Washington, DC 20036

Travel Industry and Disabled Exchange (TIDE)
5435 Donna Avenue
Tarzanna, CA 91356

Travel and Tourism Research Association (TTRA)
P.O. Box 58066
Salt Lake City, UT 84158

U.S. Travel Data Center (USTDC)
2 Lafayette Center
1133 21st Street, NW
Washington, DC 20036

## PERIODICALS

If you are interested in a periodical, the business section of your local library may carry it. If not, call information to obtain the phone number of the periodical's business office, call the office, and ask the representative to describe the publication or send you a sample copy. Subscriptions to these periodicals vary from a few dollars to a few hundred dollars. (Students: Many periodicals offer student rates—be sure and ask.) It is a good idea to make sure the periodical meets your needs before subscribing.

*Airline Companies*
American Business Directories, Inc.
5711 S. 86th Circle, Box 27347
Omaha, NE 68127-4146

*Airline Financial News*
Phillips Business Information, Inc.
1201 Seven Locks Road
Potomac, MD 20845-3394

*Airline, Ship & Catering Onboard Services*
International Publishing Co. of America Inc.
665 La Villa Drive
Miami Springs, FL 33166-6095

*Airliners Monthly News*
World Transport Press Inc.
Box 52-1238
Miami, FL 33152

*Airport Highlights*
Airport Council International—North America
1220 19th Street, NW, #200
Washington, DC 20036-2497

*Airports*
McGraw-Hill Aviation Group
1200 G Street, NW, Suite 200
Washington, DC 20005

*Annals of Tourism Research*
Pergamon Press, Inc.
660 White Plains Road
Tarrytown, NY 10591-5153

*Asia Pacific Foodservice Product News*
Young/Conway Publications, Inc.
1101 Richmond Ave., Suite 201
Point Pleasant Beach, NJ 08742-3094

*AsiaPacific Travel Magazine*
AsiaPacific Travel Co.
1540 Gilbrett
Burlingame, CA 94010-1605

*Asian Pacific Travel Facts*
6414 Kelly-Elliott Road
Arlington, TX 76017

*ASTA Notes*
American Assn. of Travel Agents
1101 King Street
Alexandria, VA 22314-2944

*ASTA Travel Agency Management*
1301 Carolina Street
Greensboro, NC 27401

*Bermuda Shorts*
Bermuda Department of Tourism
310 Madison Avenue, Suite 201
New York, NY 10017-6083

*Britainews*
British Tourist Authority
40 W. 57th Street, 3rd Floor
New York, NY 10019-4001

*Bus Tours Magazine*
National Bus Trader, Inc.
9698 W. Judson
Polo, IL 61064

*Business Travel Management*
Coastal Communications Corporation
488 Madison Avenue
New York, NY 10022-5772

*Business Travel News*
CMP Publications, Inc.
600 Community Drive
Manhasset, NY 11030

*Business Traveler International*
Business Traveler
51 E. 42nd Street, #1806
New York, NY 10017-5404

*CKC Report, The Hotel Technology Newsletter*
Chervenak, Keane & Co.
307 E. 44th Street
New York, NY 10017-4400

*Cameron's Foodservice Marketing Reporter*
Cameron's Publications
5325 Sheridan Drive, Box 1160
Williamsville, NY 14231-1160

*Canadian Hotel & Restaurant*
Maclean Hunter Ltd.
Maclean Hunter Building
777 Bay Street
Toronto, ON M5W 1A7
Canada

*Canadian Institutes of Travel Counsellors, Update*
3300 Bloor Street West, #2880
Etobicoke, ON M8X 2X3
Canada

*Canadian Travel Press Weekly*
Canadian Travel Press
Baxter Publishing Co.
310 Dupont Street
Toronto, ON M5R 1V9
Canada

*Caribbean Travel and Life*
8403 Colesville Road, #830
Silver Spring, MD 20910-3368

*Casino Magazine*
115 South State Street
Waseca, MN 56093

*Casino World*
Gramercy Information Services Inc.
Madison Square Station, Box 2003
New York, NY 10010-9998

*Casinos: The International Casino Guide*
B.D.I.T. Inc.
P.O. Box 1405
Port Washington, NY 11050

*Caterers*
American Business Directories, Inc.
5711 S. 86th Circle, Box 27347
Omaha, NE 68127-4146

*Cheers*
Jobson Publishing Corp.
100 Avenue of the Americas
New York, NY 10013-1678

*Chef Institutional*
Talcott
222 Merchandise Mart Plaza, Suite 1529
Chicago, IL 60654-1301

*Club Management*
Finan Publishing Co., Inc.
8730 Big Bend Blvd.
St. Louis, MO 63119-3730

*College/University Foodservice Who's Who*
Information Central, Box 3900
Prescott, AZ 86302-3900

*The Concessionaire*
National Association of Concessionaires
35 E. Wacker Drive, Suite 1849
Chicago, IL 60601-2202

*Condé Nast Traveler*
Condé Nast
350 Madison Avenue
New York, NY 10017-3136

*Convene*
Professional Convention Management Assn.
100 Vestavia Office Park, #220
Birmingham, AL 35216-3781

*Cooking for Profit*
CP Publishing Inc.
Box 267
Fond du Lac, WI 54936-0267

*Cook's Illustrated*
Natural Health Limited Partners
17 Station Street, Box 1200
Brookline, MA 02147

*Cook's Index*
John Gordon Burke Publisher, Inc.
Box 1492
Evanston, IL 60204-1492

*Cornell Hotel & Restaurant Administration Quarterly*
Elsevier Science Publishing Co.
Subscription Customer Service
655 Avenue of the Americas
New York, NY 10010

*Corporate & Incentive Travel*
Coastal Communications Corporation
488 Madison Avenue
New York, NY 10022-5772

*Corporate Travel*
Miller Freeman, Inc.
1515 Broadway
New York, NY 10036

*Correctional Foodservice*
International Publishing Co. of America Inc.
665 La Villa Drive
Miami Springs, FL 33166-6095

*Cruise & Vacation Views*
Orban Communications
60 E. 42nd Street, Suite 905
New York, NY 10165

*Cruise Industry News*
Nissen-Lie Communications
441 Lexington Ave., #1209A
New York, NY 10017-3959

*Cruise Trade*
Travel Trade Publications
15 West 44th Street
New York, NY 10036-6611

*Current Food Additives Legislation*
Columbia University Press
562 W. 113th
New York, NY 10025-8099

*Desserts!*
House of White Birches
306 E. Parr Road
Beme, IN 46711-9509

*Destinations*
American Bus Association
1015 15th Street NW, #250
Washington, DC 20005-2681

*Dietary Manager*
Dietary Managers Association
One Pierce Place
Itasca, IL 60143

*Directory of College and University Foodservice*
Chain Store Guide Services
3922 Coconut Palm Drive
Tampa, FL 33516-8321

*Directory of High Volume Independent Restaurants*
Chain Store Guide Services
3922 Coconut Palm Drive
Tampa, FL 33516-8321

*Directory of Restaurant and Fast Food Chains in Canada*
Maclean Hunter Ltd.
Maclean Hunter Building
777 Bay Street
Toronto, ON M5W 1A7
Canada

*FIU Hospitality Review*
School of Hospitality Management
Florida International University
North Miami Campus
3000 N.E. 145 Street
North Miami, FL 33181-3600

*F&B Magazine*
Hospitality Communications
1251 West Webster Street, Suite 2
Chicago, IL 60614

*F&B News*
Hospitality Communications
1251 West Webster Street, Suite 2
Chicago, IL 60614

*Food and Beverage Marketing*
Charleson Publishing
505 Eighth Avenue
New York, NY 10018-6505

*Food and Beverage Newsletter*
National Safety Council
1121 Spring Lake Drive, #558
Itasca, IL 60143-0558

*Food & Drink Daily*
King Communications Group
627 National Press Building
Washington, DC 20045

*Food Arts Magazine*
M. Shanken Communications, Inc.
387 Park Avenue South, 8th Floor
New York, NY 10016

*Food Broker Quarterly (FBQ)*
National Food Brokers Association
1010 Massachusetts Ave., NW
Washington, DC 20001-5499

*Food Business*
Putman Publishing Co.
301 E. Erie Street
Chicago, IL 60611-3059

*Food Business Letter*
Make It Tasty Spice Co.
Box 416
Denver, CO 80201

*Food in Canada*
Maclean Hunter Ltd.
Maclean Hunter Building
777 Bay Street
Toronto, ON M5W 1A7
Canada

*Food Chemical News*
CRC Press Inc.
1101 Pennsylvania Avenue
Washington, DC 20003

*Food Engineering*
Chilton Publishing
One Chilton Way
Radnor, PA 19089

*Food Engineering International*
Chilton Publishing
One Chilton Way
Radnor, PA 19089

*Food Facts*
National Research Bureau
Box 1
Burlington, IA 52601-0001

*Food Industry Futures—A Strategy Service*
C.R.S. Inc.
Box 430
Fayetteville, NY 13066-0430

*Food Industry Newsletter*
Newsletters Inc.
Box 2730
Bethesda, MD 20827-2730

*Food Industry Report*
Food & Nutrition Press Inc.
2 Corporate Drive, Box 374
Trumbull, CT 06611-1338

*Food Irradiation Update*
Technomic Publishing Co. Inc.
851 New Holland Ave., Box 3535
Lancaster, PA 17604-3535

*Food Management*
Penton Publishing
100 Superior Avenue
Cleveland, OH 44114-2518

*Food and Nutrition News*
National Livestock and Meat Board
444 N. Michigan Ave.
Chicago, IL 60611-3978

*Food Professional's Guide*
American Showcase
915 Broadway, 14th Floor
New York, NY 10010-7108

*Food Protection Report*
Charles Felix Associates
Box 1581
Leesburg, VA 22075-1581

*Food Safety Notebook*
LYDA Associates
Box 700
Palisades, NY 10964-0700

*Food Trade News*
119 Sibley Avenue
Ardmore, PA 19003

*Food World*
Best-Met Publishing Co., Inc.
5537 Twin Knolls Road, Suite 438
Columbia, MD 21045

*Foods—Carry Out*
American Business Directories, Inc.
5711 South 86th Circle, Box 27347
Omaha, NE 68127-4146

*Foodservice Director*
Bill Communications, Inc.
355 Park Avenue South, 3rd Floor
New York, NY 10010-1706

*Foodservice Equipment & Supplies Specialist*
Cahners Publishing
1350 East Touhy Ave.
Des Plaines, IL 60018-3358

*Foodservice & Hospitality Magazine*
Kostuch Communications Ltd.
980 Yonge Street, Suite 400
Toronto, ON M4W 2J8
Canada

*Foodservice Information Abstracts*
National Restaurant Association
1200 17th Street, NW
Washington, DC 20046-3097

*Foodservice Product News*
Young/Conway Publications, Inc.
1101 Richmond Ave., Suite 201
Point Pleasant Beach, NJ 08742-3094

*Gaming International Magazine*
Boardwalker Magazine Inc.
Box 7418
Atlantic City, NJ 08404-7418

*Gourmet News*
United Publications, Inc.
38 Lafayette Street
Box 1056
Yarmouth, ME 04096-1600

*Guide to Cooking Schools*
ShawGuides, Inc.
625 Biltmore Way, #1406
Coral Gables, FL 33134-7539

*Guide to Food & Beverage Industry Publications*
Food Processing Machinery & Supplies Association
200 Dangerfield Road
Alexandria, VA 22314-2884

*Guide to Hospitality Education*
CHRIE
1200 17th Street, NW
Washington, DC 20036-3006

*HSMAI Hotel Facilities Digest*
Hotel Sales and Marketing Association International
1300 L Street NW, #800
Washington, DC 20005-4133

*Healthcare Foodservice Magazine*
International Publishing Company of America, Inc.
665 La Villa Drive
Miami Springs, FL 33166-6095

*Healthcare Foodservice Who's Who*
Information Central
Box 3900
Prescott, AZ 86302-3900

*Hospitality and Automation*
2180 Pleasant Hill Road, Suite 5370
Duluth, GA 30136

*Hospitality Design*
Bill Communications, Inc.
355 Third Avenue South, 3rd Floor
New York, NY 10010-1706

*Hospitality Education and Research Journal*
CHRIE
311 First Street NW
Washington, DC 20001

*Hospitality Law*
Magna Publications
2718 Dryden Drive
Madison, WI 53704-3005

*Hospitality and Tourism Educator*
CHRIE
311 First Street NW
Washington, DC 20001

*Hospitality World*
International Food, Wine & Travel Writers Association
Box 1532
Palm Springs, CA 92263-1532

*HOSTEUR*
CHRIE
1200 17th Street, NW
Washington, DC 20036-3006

*Hotel Business*
ICD Publications
1393 Veterans Highway, #214N
Hauppauge, NY 11788

*Hotel & Motel Management*
Advanstar Communications
7500 Old Oak Blvd.
Cleveland, OH 44130

*Hotel & Resort Industry*
Coastal Communications Corporation
488 Madison Avenue
New York, NY 10022-5772

*Hotel and Travel Index*
Reed Travel Group
Subscription Department
P.O. Box 5820
Cherry Hill, NJ 08034

*Hotel/Motel Security and Safety Management*
Rusting Publications
402 Main Street
Port Washington, NY 11050

*Hotels*
Cahners Publishing
1350 East Touhy Ave.
Des Plaines, IL 60018-3358

*ICTA Update*
Institute of Certified Travel Agents
148 Linden Street, Box 812059
Wellesley, MA 02181-0012

*ID (Institutional Distribution)*
Bill Communications, Inc.
355 Third Avenue South, 3rd Floor
New York, NY 10010-1706

*Inn Business Magazine*
Zanny Publishing
11966 Woodbine Ave.
Gormley, ON L0H 1G0
Canada

*Inn Touch*
Wisconsin Innkeepers Association
509 W. Wisconsin Ave., #622
Milwaukee, WI 53203-2006

*Innkeeping*
P.A.I.I.
Box 90710
Santa Barbara, CA 93190-0710

*Innkeeping World*
Box 84108
Seattle, WA 98124-5408

*International Hotel Trends*
Pannell Kerr Forster
420 Lexington Avenue, Suite 2400
New York, NY 10170

*International Journal of Hospitality Management*
Pergamon Press, Inc.
660 White Plains Road
Tarrytown, NY 10591-5153

*International Gaming & Wagering Business*
BMT Publications, Inc.
7 Penn Plaza
New York, NY 10001-3900

*International Travel News*
Martin Publications, Inc.
2120 28th Street
Sacramento, CA 95818-1910

*Journal of College & University Foodservice*
Haworth Press
10 Alice Street
Binghamton, NY 13904-1580

*Journal of Ecotourism Development*
International Ecotourism Education Foundation
Box 676
Falls Church, VA 22040

*Journal of Foodservice Systems*
Food and Nutrition Press, Inc.
Corporate Drive, Box 374
Trumbull, CT 06611-1338

*Journal of Restaurant & Foodservice Marketing*
Haworth Press
10 Alice Street
Binghamton, NY 13904-1580

*Journal of Travel & Tourism Marketing*
Haworth Press
10 Alice Street
Binghamton, NY 13904-1580

*Journal of Travel Research*
Business Research Division
University of Colorado
Campus Box 420
Boulder, CO 80309-0420

*Just Go!*
1459 18th Street, #175
San Francisco, CA 94107-2801

*Lodging Hospitality*
Penton Publishing
1100 Superior Ave.
Cleveland, OH 44114-2518

*Lodging*
American Hotel & Motel Association
1201 New York Avenue, NW
Washington, DC 20005

*Lodging and Restaurant Index*
Restaurant, Hotel & Institutional
  Management Institute
Purdue University
3572 Young Graduate House,
  Room 101
West Lafayette, IN 47906-3572

*Lodging Outlook*
Smith Travel Research
P.O. Box 659
Gallatin, TN 37066

*Mature Group Traveler*
Meetings Info-Resources, Inc.
1000 Prospect Street, 1st Floor
Stamford, CT 06901-1640

*Meat Price Report*
National Provisioner, Inc.
15 W. Huron
Chicago, IL 60610-3812

*Meeting Manager Magazine*
Meeting Planners International
1950 Stemmons Freeway, #5018
Dallas, TX 75207-3109

*Meeting News*
Miller Freeman, Inc.
1515 Broadway
New York, NY 10036

*Meeting Planners Alert*
Darrells Graphic & Print
8554 Lorretto Ave.
Cotati, CA 94931-4471

*Meeting Planners Guide*
Worth International Communications
5979 NW 151st Street, Suite 120
Miami Lakes, FL 33014

*Meetings & Conventions*
Reed Travel Group
500 Plaza Drive
Secaucus, NJ 07096

*Meetings Monthly*
Publicom Inc.
CP 365 Place D'Armes
Montreal, PQ H2Y 3H1
Canada

*Mexico Update*
Travel Mexico Magazine Group
Box 188037
Carlsbad, CA 92009

*Military Club & Hospitality*
825 Old Country Road
Westbury, NY 11590

*Military Clubs and Recreation*
Club Executive, Inc.
Box 7088
Alexandria, VA 22307-0088

*Military Market*
Army Times Publishing Co.
6883 Commercial Drive
Springfield, VA 22159-0001

*Mobile and Industrial Catering*
Mobile Industrial Caterer's Association International
7300 Artesia Blvd.
Buena Park, CA 90621-1804

*Nation's Restaurant News*
Lebhar-Friedman, Inc.
425 Park Ave.
New York, NY 10022-3506

*Nevada Casino Journal*
3100 West Sahara Avenue, Suite 205
Las Vegas, NV 89102

*Organic Food Business News*
Hotline Publishing
Box 161132
Altamonte Springs, FL 32716

*Pasta Journal*
National Pasta Association
2101 Wilson Blvd., #920
Arlington, VA 22201-3055

*Pizza Today*
ProTech Publishing & Communications
Box 1347
New Albany, IN 47151-1347

*Recommend Magazine*
Worth International Communications
5979 NW 151st Street, Suite 120
Miami Lakes, FL 33014

*Report on Institutional Foodservice*
Information Central
Box 3900
Prescott, AZ 86302-3900

*Ron Paul's Future Foods Report*
Technomic Inc.
300 S. Riverside Plaza, #1940
Chicago, IL 60606-6613

*Resort Management*
Western Specialty Publications, Inc.
2431 Morena Blvd.
San Diego, CA 92110

*Resort Management Report*
Rouge Et Noir Inc.
Box 1146
Midlothian, VA 23113

*Restaurant Business*
Bill Communications, Inc.
355 Park Avenue South, 3rd Floor
New York, NY 10010-1706

*Restaurant Hospitality*
Penton Publishing
1100 Superior Ave.
Cleveland, OH 44114-2518

*Restaurant Merchandising News*
Mortimer Publishing
53 Sterling Road
Trumbull, CT 06611

*Restaurants & Institutions*
Cahners Publishing
1350 East Touhy Ave.
Des Plaines, IL 60018-3358

*Restaurants USA*
National Restaurant Association
1200 Seventeenth Street, NW
Washington, DC 20036-3097

*Russia & East Travel Newsletter*
Printing Consultants
Federal Square, Box 636
Newark, NJ 07101

*Sales & Marketing Management*
Bill Communications, Inc.
355 Park Avenue South, 3rd Floor
New York, NY 10010-1706

*School Food Service Journal*
American School Food Service Association
1600 Duke Street, 7th Floor
Alexandria, VA 22314

*School Foodservice Who's Who*
Information Central
Box 3900
Prescott, AZ 86302-3900

*Seafood Trend Newsletter*
Seafood Trend Association
8227 Ashworth Avenue, North
Seattle, WA 98103-4434

*Student Travels*
Student Travel Catalog
Council on International Educational
 Exchange
205 E. 42nd Street
New York, NY 10017-5776

*Successful Meetings*
Bill Communications, Inc.
355 Park Avenue South, 3rd Floor
New York, NY 10010-1706

*Survey of State Travel Offices*
U.S. Travel Data Center
1133 21st Street, NW
Washington, DC 20036

*Toll-Free Travel & Vacation Information
 Directory*
Pilot Books
103 Cooper Street
Babylon, NY 11702-2349

*Total Quality In Hospitality*
2718 Dryden Drive
Madison, WI 53791-9618

*Tour and Travel News*
CMP Publications, Inc.
600 Community Drive
Manhasset, NY 11030

*TravelAge East*
Official Airline Guide Travel
 Magazines
1775 Broadway, 19th Floor
New York, NY 10019

*TravelAge West*
Official Airline Guides
49 Stevenson, Suite 460
San Francisco, CA 94105-2909

*Travel Agent Magazine*
801 Second Avenue
New York, NY 10003-4404

*Travel & Leisure*
American Express Publishing Corp.
1120 Avenue of the Americas
New York, NY 10036-6770

*Travel Counselor Magazine*
Miller Freeman Inc.
600 Harrison Street
San Francisco, CA 94107

*Travel Industry Personnel Directory*
Fairchild Publications
7 West 34th Street
New York, NY 10001

*Travel Industry World Yearbook—The Big
 Picture*
Child and Waters, Inc.
Box 610
Rye, NY 10580-0811

*Travel Market Report*
U.S. Travel Data Center
1133 21st Street, NW
Washington, DC 20036

*Travel Trade*
15 West 44th Street
New York, NY 10036-6611

*Travel to the USSR*
Victor Kamkin, Inc.
4956 Boiling Brook Parkway
Rockville, MD 20852

*Travelin' Talk Directory*
Travelin' Talk Network
Box 3534
Clarksville, TN 37043-3534

*Traveller Accommodation Statistics*
Statistics Canada, Marketing Division
120 Parkdale Avenue, Room 1710
Ottawa, ON K1A 0T6
Canada

*Travel Weekly*
P.O. Box 7661
Riverton, NJ 08077

*Trends in the Hotel Industry, USA*
PKF Consulting
425 California Street, Suite 1650
San Francisco, CA 94104-2201

*Who's Who in the Lodging Industry*
American Hotel & Motel Association
1201 New York Avenue, NW
Washington, DC 20005

*World Cruise Industry Review*
Sterling Publications
86-88 Edgware Road
London W2 2YW
England

# Index

## A

Abbey, James, 446–447
Accounting
   balance sheet, 135
   cost-of-quality system, 382–383
   division, 239–240
   for restaurants, 135–137
   statement of income, 135–136
ADA. *See* Americans with Disability Act
Adams, Scott, 386
Added-value, 476
ADR, 220–221
Advancement, limited opportunities, 406–407
Advertising, 475–510
   advantages of, 475–478
   agencies, 484
   and added-value, 476
   and featuring low prices, 476
   and quality, 476–477
   and social concerns, 477–478
   audience segmentation (television), 503
   broadcast, 489–492, 503
   budgeting for, 493
   choosing media, 491–510
   claims, ethics of, 593
   closing dates, 498
   competitive advantage, 478–479
   costs of, 503, 506
   creating effective campaigns, 484–491
   database marketing, 504
   definition of, 478
   direct mail, 504–507
   direct marketing, 504
   elements of an effective campaign, 478
   ethics of, 593
   headlines in, 486–488
   hospitality slogans, 481–482
   humorous, 489–491
   in magazines, 496–499
   in newspapers, 494–496
   in trade magazines, 499
   Internet, 508–510
   market segmentation, 482–483
   new media, 508–510
   on radio, 499–502
   on television, 502–503
   positioning, 479–482
   print, 485–489
   telemarketing, 506–508
   word-of-mouth, 478
   working with freelancers, 484
Age discrimination, 591
Agencies, advertising, 484
Aging workers, 404
AIDS, and workplace ethics, 592–593
Airlines
   food service, 96
   ticket sales, 461–462
Alessandra, Tony, 448
All-suite hotels, 181–182
Amadeus reservations system, 461–462
Ambiance, 122–124
American Association of Advertising Agencies, 476
American Express Company, 458, 482–483
American Plan, xxviii, 225
American Society of Travel Agents (ASTA), 466
Americans with Disability Act, 241–242, 324, 407
Apollo reservations system, 461–462
Appearance, and sales, 451
ARAMARK, 101, 103
Areas of dominant influence, 110
Arison, Ted, 308–309
Assessments, in clubs, 275
Assets, 244
Association groups, 158
Association meetings, 284–286
   exhibit space needs, 286
   timing cycle, 285–286
Athletic clubs, 261
Automobiles
   manufacturers, xxii
   travel, xxi–xxiii
Aviation, commercial, xxiii–xxv

## B

Baccarat, 344
Balance sheets, 244–245
Bass PLC, xxx
Baum, Joseph H., 103, 105–106, 516
Behavioral school of management theory, 376–379
Bell, Charles A., 529
Bellagio Casino, 347
Bellstaff. *See* Uniformed service
Benchmarking, 372
Benihana of Tokyo, 124
Bennis, Warren, 388–389
Best Western, 172–173
Beverages
   alcoholic, 148–150
   control, 150
   costs, 148–150
   security and storage, 149
Bicycles, xxi
*Bilu* and *Nili*, 307–308
Blackjack, 341, 344
Blanchard, Ken, 596–597
Bob Evans Restaurants, 130–131
Bohemian Club, 263
Bok, Sissela, 578
Bollenbach, Stephen F., 227
Boorstin, Daniel, xxvii
Boston Consulting Group, 476
Boulanger, xxx–xxxi
Bourges, France, xxv
Breslin, Paul, 417
Brinker, Norman, 91
British and North American Royal Mail Steam Packet Company, xviii
Broadcast media, and advertising, 489–491, 499–503
Brynestad, Atle, 325

Budget hotels, 177–178
Business ethics, 574–582
Business format franchising, 548–551

## C

Caesars Palace, 354
*Canterbury Tales, The*, xv
Capital costs, 243–244
Capture rate, 222
Careers
   as catering manager, 62–63
   as chief engineer, 63
   as controller, 63
   as food and beverage manager, 63
   as general manager, 60–62
   as human resources manager, 63
   as marketing manager, 63
   as resident manager, 63–64
   as systems manager, 64
   food service ladder, 73
   food service management, 81–82
   in casinos, 354–361
   in catering, 66
   in chain restaurants, 65–66
   in clubs, 68
   in food service, 65–68
   in hotel management, 79–80
   in independent restaurants, 65
   in institutions, 67
   in lodging, 59–60
   in meeting planning, 296–298
   in sales, 447–451
   lodging ladder, 72
   path, 71
   with contractors, 66–67
   with cruise lines, 67
Carnival Cruise Lines, 303, 309–312, 315, 320, 323, 334
Carr, Alfred, 577–578
Casino
   games, 344–346
   hotels, operation of, 357–358
Casinos
   careers in, 354–361
   controls and regulation, 353–354
   employees, 349–351

food and beverage department, 358–359
   junkets, 351–353
   marketing, 351–353
   safety and security, 353–354
   solving problems in, 359–361
   terminology, 346–349
Casualization, 120
Catering manager, and meeting planning, 296–297
Catering, 66, 225–226
Catskill Mountains, resorts, xx
Celebrity Cruise Lines, 310
Cendant Corporation, 555–556
Central Pacific Railroad, xix
Certified Meeting Planner, 294
Chain restaurants, 65–66
Chambers, Richard, 439
Champy, James, 385, 388
Chartres, France, xxv
Check-in/check-out procedures, 211–214
Chesapeake & Ohio Railway, xx
Chief housekeeper, on cruise ships, 322
Chili's Grill & Bar, 110
Choice International, 559–560
Circle K, 100
City clubs, 261, 263, 265, 274, 277
City Hotel, New York City, xxvii
Civil Rights Act of 1964, 407
Classical school of management theory, 373–376
CLIA. *See* Cruise Lines International Association
Club management
   as a career, 271–273
   competency areas, 272
Club Managers Association of America (CMAA), 267, 271, 273, 277
Club managers, 269, 271–273
   qualities of, 271
   salaries, 273
Club Med, 247
ClubCorp Company, 269
Clubs

assessments, 275
athletic, 261
careers in, 68
city, 261, 263, 265, 274, 277
corporate, 268–269
country, 264, 266–267, 274–275, 277
dining, 261
equity, 268, 271
expenses, 277
financial control of, 277
food and beverage sales, 276
fraternal, 267
golf, 275–276
history of, 259–260
initiation fees, 275
military, 267–268
operations, 273–277
organization of, 269–273
ownership of, 268–270
professional, 261–262
recreation and sports, 275–276
revenue, 273–277
social, 262–264
sports activities fees, 275
types of, 261–268
university, 264
visitors' fees, 276–277
yacht, 267
CMAA. *See* Club Managers Association of America
Code of ethics, for hotels, 597
Comment cards, 249–250, 328–330
Commerce Club, 263
Commissions, 232
   and travel agencies, 462, 464, 467–468
Communication, from managers to employees, 371
Compass Group, 103
Compensation and benefits, 64
Competency areas, in club management, 272
Competition
   analysis, 442–443
   and pricing, 477
Competitive
   advantage, advertising, 478–479
   benchmarking, 372
   pricing, 438–439

## Index

Computerization, 135, 216–218, 461–462
Computerized cash registers, 135
Concessions, rentals, and commissions, 230, 232
Condominium hotels, 188
Conference centers, 183–184, 289–290
　growth in the U.S., 184
　occupancy and profitability, 184
Contingency school of management theory, 381
Continuing-care retirement communities, 188–189
Contract food companies, 96–98, 102–103
Contract management companies, 104
Contractors, 66–67
Contracts, management, 530–539
Control systems, 242–250
Convention and visitors bureaus, 289
　careers in, 297
Convention groups, 158
Convention Liaison Council, 294–295
Convention services manager, 296
Cook, Thomas, xix, 457–458
Corinth, Greece, xxv
Cornell Club, The, 274
*Cornell Quarterly*, 428–429, 532
Corporate clubs, 268–269
Corporate meetings, types of, 286–287
Correctional institutions, 101
Cost centers
　engineering, 235–239
　marketing, 234–235
Cost-plus pricing, 438
Country clubs, 264, 266–267, 274–275, 277
　financing of, 264
Courtesy, and sales, 451
Craps, 341, 344–346
Crosby, Philip, 383
Cruise director, 322–323
Cruise line food service, 96
Cruise Lines International Association (CLIA), 310, 465–466
Cruise lines, 67
　as fun travel, 310
　birth of modern, 307–309
　history of, 304–312

market segments of, 310
passenger profile, 14
statistics, 303–304
today, 310–312
Cruise sales, 464–465
Cruise ships
　captain, 312–313
　chief housekeeper, 322
　chief officer, 313–314
　cruise director, 322–323
　food and beverage, 316–322
　hotel manager, 314–324
　laws governing, 313, 315
　luxury, 324–334
　medical department, 323–324
　onboard identification cards, 316–317
　organization, 312–324
　purser's office, 316
　service on, 324–334
　shore excursions, 323, 331–333
　"turnaround day," 322
　use of credit onboard, 316–317
Cruise travel, cost of, 325
Cunard Line, xviii, 306, 325
Customer-based pricing, 439
Customers, five types, 482–483
Cyclical menu, 101

## D

Daimler, Gottlieb and William Maybach, xxii–xxiii
Danner, Ray, 428
Database marketing, 504
Days Inn, 408
Decision making, and ethical practices, 596–597
Decotiis, Thomas A., 418
Delmonico's, New York City, xxxi
Delta Airlines, 386, 427–428
Deming, W. Edwards, 382–383
Demographics, 112
　six labor trends, 404–406
Deontology, 581
Developer clubs. *See* Corporate clubs
Dickinson, Robert H., 310–312
Differentiation, 478–479
*Dilbert Principle, The*, 386

Dining clubs, 261
Dining room manager, 225
Direct mail, 504–507
　advantages, 504–506
　costs, 506
　disadvantages, 506
　for recruiting, 415
　sample letter, 507
　sample newsletter, 505
Direct marketing, 504
Disabled persons, 241–242, 324
Discrimination
　as ethical issue, 587–591
　survey regarding, 588–589
Disney, Walt, 389
Diversity of the work force, 406
Divisional expenses, 243
Domino's Pizza, 414–415
　and environmental awareness, 574
Doral Inn, 479–480
Dressing for success, 451–453
Drucker, Peter, 367
DuPont Country Club, 269

## E

Easter Exchange Hotel, Boston, xxviii
Eben/Maurach, Austria, xxv
Economy hotels, 177–179
　top 25 limited service chains, 179
Ecotourism, 45–46
Ed Debevic's Diners, 90–91
Edison, Thomas, xxviii
Elasticity of demand, 439–440
Electricity, controlling costs of use, 238
Embassy Suites, 20–22
Employees
　motivation, 371, 425–428
　nurturing, 372
　recruitment, 414–416
　references, 418–419
　rewarding, 249–250, 333, 425–428
　selection, 248
　training, 330
Employment
　applications, 416–417
　in casinos, 354–361
Empowerment, 248–249, 327–331, 334, 391–392
*Empress of Canada*, 309

Energy costs, 238–239
Engineering division, 235, 237–238
Enkhagen, Linda K., 583–584
Environment, ethical issues, 585–587
Environmental responsibility, 512–513, 532–533, 574–576
  Inter-Continental Hotels and Resorts, 586–587
  Walt Disney Resorts, 587–588
Equal Employment Opportunity Commission (EEOC), 407, 592
Equity clubs, 268, 271
Escoffier, Georgés-Auguste, xxviii
Ethical decision making, 596–597
Ethical issues
  discrimination, 587–591
  environmental, 585–587
  of advertising, 593
  of AIDS in the workplace, 592–593
  others, 585
  sexual harassment, 592
  top 10 in hospitality, 583–584
Ethical relativism, 582
Ethics
  code of, 597
  definition, 573–574
  need for, 595–596
European Plan, xxviii, 225
Exchange programs, 187
Executive chef, 225
Exhibit space, and associations, 286
Exhibitors/exhibit designers, careers as, 297–298
Exit interviews, 428
Expositions. *See* Trade shows and expositions
Eyster, James, 530, 532

# F

Fairmont Hotel, 392
Familiarization trips, 234, 466
Family and Medical Leave Act of 1993, 407
Fast-food. *See* Restaurants, fast-food

Fayol, Henri, 374–375
Feasibility study, for restaurants, 111–112
Fee structure provision, in management contracts, 534–535
Fees, management company, 534–535
Financial controls
  for clubs, 277
  for hotels, 243–244
Financing, loans, 195–198
Firnstahl, Tim, 13, 19
First-in/first-out, 143
Fitness and recreation facilities, as revenue center, 232–233
Fixed
  charges, 243–244
  menu, 129–130
Flagler, Henry, xx
Flags of convenience, 315
Food and beverage
  sales at clubs, 276
  types of hotel outlets, 223
Food and beverage department
  as revenue center, 221–230
  in casinos, 358–359
  on cruise ships, 316–322
  organization of, 224–229
  problems in, 229–230
  support services, 228–229
Food and beverage management, 224–225
*Food Arts* magazine, 516
Food costs, 126
  analysis of, 145–148
  on cruise ships, 319–320
Food courts, 101
Food service industry
  growth in, 54
  top three companies, 54–55
Food service
  and business and industry, 96–97
  and corrections, 101
  and lodging, 95
  and recreational facilities, 96
  and students, 98–99
  and supermarkets, 100–101
  and the health care industry, 99–100
  and the military, 101–102
  and the retail market, 100–101
  and transportation, 95–96

contract companies and self-operation, 99
  on cruise ships, 316–322, 326–330
Ford, Henry, xxiii
Forecasting systems, 242–243
Forrest, Jr., Lewis C., 420–421
Four Seasons Hotel, 367
Foxwoods Resort Casino, Connecticut, 343
*France*, 307
Franchises, top 10 hotel chains, 548
Franchising, 172
  advantages, 554, 556–560
  business format, 548–551
  credit for, 557
  definition of, 545–546
  disadvantages, 560–563
  expectations, 554
  fees, 551–552
  goodwill, 551
  history, 547–551
  how it works, 551–553
  investment, 552–553
  issues, 563
  marketing support, 559–560
  new markets, 563
  opportunities, 564
  owning, 553–563
  product (or trade name), 546–548
  regulations, 553
  restrictions, 561
  site selection, 554, 556
  statistics, 545
  terminology, 545
  training, 557–558
  types, 546
Fraternal clubs, 265
Frazer, Charles F., 478
Frazer, Leslie, 307–308
Friars Club, The, 259
Friedheim, Eric, 462
Front desk agent, duties, 209–215
Front desk, cashiering, 211–214
Fuddrucker's Hamburgers, 593
Full-service hotels, 180

## G

Galileo reservations system, 461–462
Gambling. *See* Gaming
Gaming
 history of, 341–344
 in America, 342–344
 in Nevada and New Jersey, 343
 Indian reservations, 343
 industry size, 344
 odds and profitability, 346
 offshore, 343
 riverboats, 342–343, 360
 slot machines, 346
 specialized terminology, 346–349
 table games, 344–346
Gantt, Henry, 374
Garfield, Charles, 447–448
Gift shops, 230, 232
Gilbreth, Frank and Lillian, 374
Golden Nugget, 347
Golf course expenses, for country clubs, 276
Grand National Hotel, Lucerne, Switzerland, xxviii
Grand Tour, The, xvii
Grand Victoria Casino, 360
Great Depression, 307
Greenbrier Resort, xx
Groen, Lou, 561
Grooming, and sales, 451–453
Grosse Pointe Yacht Club, 267, 275
Guest
 attitudes, 120–121
 comment cards, 249–250, 328–330
 mix, 159–160
 service and satisfaction, 190, 215, 246, 328–330, 384, 422
 service department. *See* Uniformed service
 service, on cruise ships, 319–322, 324–334
Guests
 casino, 349–351
 corporate, 157–158
 types of, 157
*Guide Culinaire, Le*, xxviii
Gutman, Richard, 89–90

## H

Hammer, Michael, 385, 388
Hampton Inn, 392
Handicapped accessibility, 241–242, 324
Hanson, Kristine, 578–579
Harassment, sexual, 592
Hartley-Leonard, Darryl, 392
Harvey, Fred, xxxi
Haussner's Restaurant, Baltimore, 91
Hawthorne studies, 376–378
Henderson, Ernest, xxix
Hewitt, Thomas F., 530, 533
Hilton Hotel & Resorts, 354, 440
Hilton International, 529
Hilton, Conrad, xxix
Hiring process, 414–419
Holiday Inn Worldwide, 486
 franchise training, 558
 history of, xxx, 170
Holland America Line, 305, 307, 312–313
Honesty, 578–579
Hospital food service, 99–100
Hospitality industry careers
 in food service, 65–68
 in lodging, 59–64
 pros and cons, 55–56
 travel-related, 57
*Hospitality Sales and Advertising*, 446–447
*Hotel & Travel Index*, 462
Hotel
 categories, 160–172
 chains, xxx
Hotel Everett, New York City, xxviii
*Hotel garni*, xxvii
Hotel sales, 462–464
 and meetings business, 296
Hotels
 accounting, 239–240
 acquisitions, 191
 airport, 171–172
 all-suite, 181–182
 balance sheet, 245
 categories of ownership, 172
 center city, 160–163
 chains, 173–174
 competition, 193
 construction and occupancy rates, 196
 cost centers, 208, 233–241
 feasibility study, 192–195
 financial controls, 243–244
 financing, 195–198
 full-service, 180
 global trends, 189–190
 highest sales per room by location, 171
 highway, 170–171
 human resources, 240
 independent, 174
 limited service, 177–179
  top 25 chains, 179
 luxury, 180
 mid-price, 178–180
 naming of chains, 175
 number of rooms worldwide, 53
 organization of, 207–209
 pricing of, 174–182, 218
 quality controls, 244–250
 resort, 162, 164–167, 193
 revenue centers, 208
 security, 240–241
 segmenting of, 174–175, 177, 190–191
 setting standards, 247–248
 site selection, 191–192
 statement of income, 244
 suburban, 167–170
 top 25 chains, 173
 U.S. trends, 190–191
Housekeeping department, 218–219
 on cruise ships, 322
Housekeeping
 duties, 219
 guestroom cleaning sequence, 409
Howard Johnson Company, xxxi, 548–549
Human resources department, 240
Human resources programs
 elements of, 407
 evaluating, 428–429
 job breakdowns, 410–411
 job descriptions, 408–411
 mission statements, 408
 productivity standards, 411–414
 recruiting, 414–416
 selection, 416–419
 training, 419–425
Human resources

## 622  Index

changing demographics, 404–406
labor trends, 403–407
legislation, 407
turnover, 406–407
HVAC, controlling costs of use, 238–239
Hyatt Hotels & Resorts, 189, 392, 425, 479

## I

Immigration, 305–306, 404
*In Search of Excellence*, 384, 426
Incentive
    fees, 529
    trips, 287
Incentives and rewards, 426–427
Income, from club membership dues, 274
Independent restaurants, 65
Indian Gaming Regulatory Act, 343
Initiation fees, in clubs, 275
*Innocents Abroad, The*, 304–305
Inns, xxv
Institute of Certified Travel Agents, 466
Institutions, 67
Integrated marketing communications, 441
Interactive Advertising Bureau (IAB), 508
Interactive media, and advertising, 508–510
Inter-Continental Corporation, 529
and environmental responsibility, 586–587
Internal analysis, 444
International Council of Cruise Lines, 303
International Franchise Association, 545
International Hotel and Restaurant Exposition, 283
International Institute for Quality and Ethics in Service and Tourism, 596–597
International Tours, and franchise support, 558–559
Internet
    advertising, 508–510
    travel agencies, 461
Interval
    ownership/timeshare, 184–188
    locations worldwide, 185
Interviews
    conduct during, 74–75
    dressing for, 74
    follow-up, 75
    preparing for, 74
Issuing, 143–144
*It's Good Business*, 578–579
ITT Sheraton. *See* Sheraton

## J

James, Robert M., 531–532
Jefferson, Thomas, xxxi
Job
    hunting, 68–70
    interviews, 74–75
    résumés, 70–74, 83
Johnson, Howard Dearing, 548–549
Johnson, Samuel, xxvii
Jones, Casey, 418
Josephson, Michael, 579–581
Juran, Joseph, 382–383

## K

Kant, Immanuel, 581
Key control, 214
KFC, and training, 557–558
Killington Ski Resorts, 593
Kloster, Knut, 308–309
Kroc, Ray, xxxi, 389–390, 512, 549–551

## L

Labor trends, 403–407
Lansing, Michigan, xxii
Laws of Innkeepers, The, xxv
*LEADERS: The Strategies for Taking Charge*, 388–389
*Leadership Secrets of Attila the Hun*, 426
Leadership, 388–392
    communication, 390
    definition of, 389
    eight key roles, 399–401
    four strategies for, 389
    positioning, 390
    self-development, 391–392
    vision, 389
Leisure travelers, 159
Lettuce Entertain You Enterprises, 371
Lewis, Hunter, 576–577
Lewis, Robert, 439
Liabilities, 244
Lindbergh, Charles, xxiv
Links Club, 263
Liverpool and Manchester Railway, xix
*Lodging* magazine, 505–506
    ethics poll, 583–584
Loss-leaders, 438
Louis XIV, xxx
"Love Boat, The," 309
Loyalty programs, 515–516
Luxury hotels, 180
Lying, 578–579
*Lying: Moral Choice in Public and Private Life*, 578

## M

Magazines
    advertising in, 496–499
    reader demographics, 496–497
Maintenance, 237–239
Malcolm Baldrige National Quality Award, 368
Management companies
    and lenders, 533–534
    and ownership, 530, 533
    and REITs, 530, 532
    history of, 528–530
    incentive fees, 529
    qualities of, 527–537
    top 20, 531
Management contracts, 530–539
    advantages and disadvantages of, 538–539
    and owner input, 537
    approvals, 536–537
    operating expenses, 538
    operator investment, 537–538
    provisions of, 533–538
    reporting requirements, 535
    termination, 537
Management theories
    behavioral school, 376–379
    classical school, 373–376
    contingency school, 381

Japanese influence, 381–382
quality focus school, 381–384
quantitative school, 379–380
systems school, 380–381
Management,
  eight key roles, 399–401
  participative, 248–249
Management-fee structures, 536
Managers
  as leaders, 388–392
  as mentors, 372
  as team builders, 371
  club, qualities of, 271
  eight key leadership roles, 399–401
  five basic tasks of, 368
  goals, 367
  required skills, 369
  responsibilities of, 367–372
  sales, 446–454
  setting objectives, 368
*Mardi Gras*, 309
Market research, 108, 120
Marketing division, 234–235
Marketing mix, 436
Marketing plan, 441–446
  problems and opportunities, 444–445
  situation analysis, 442–445
Marketing
  and franchising, 559–560
  controls, 446
  definition of, 435
  news releases, 236
  objectives, 445
  place, 438
  price, 438–440
  product, 435–438
  promotion, 440–441
  strategies, 445
  tactics, 445–446
  travel and tourism information, 443
Marketplace analysis, 442
Marriott Corporation, 18, 177–178, 189, 372, 482, 517
Marriott, J. W., 103, 176–177
Marriott, Jr., J. W., 372, 428
Maslow, Abraham, 378
Mayo, George Elton, 376–378
McDonald, Maurice and Richard, 549–551
McDonald, Stanley, 308–309

McDonald's Restaurants, 108, 123–124, 128, 389–390, 408
  and franchise encroachment, 562
  and franchise innovations, 561
  and franchise training, 558
  and social responsibility, 574–576
  expansion of, 92
  franchising, 549–551
  history of, xxxi
  marketing of, 92–93
  public relations, 511–513
McGregor, Douglas, 378–379
Meal plans, xxviii, 225
Medical department, on cruise ships, 323–324
Meeting planners
  associations for, 293
  certification for, 294
  duties of, 293–298
Meeting planning, 290
  hotel catering manager, 296–297
*Meetings & Conventions* magazine, and discrimination survey, 588–590
Meetings
  association, 284–286
  choosing a facility, 291–294
  corporate, types of, 286–287
  format of, 290
  location of, 289–291
  objectives, 290
  planning process, 290–291
  role of civic and government organizations in, 289
  room setups, 292
  scheduling, 290–291
  trade shows and expositions, 287–288
Meetings industry
  careers in, 293–298
  impact on hotels, 284
  scope of, 283–289
Melman, Richard, 371
Membership dues, of clubs, 274–275
Menu, 109, 124–134
  categories, 129
  cyclical, 130
  design, 130–132
  fixed, 129–130

  forecasting, 140
  planning, 138–140, 223
  preferences, 127–129
  pricing, 132–134
  specialty, 130
  trends, 129
  variety, 126
Menu-cost spreadsheet, 140
MGM Grand, 356–359
Microsoft *Expedia*, 461, 509–510
Middle Ages, xxv
Mid-price hotels, 178–179
Military
  clubs, 267–268
  food service, 101–102
Mirage Resorts, 347, 352, 354, 356, 358
*Misérables, Les*, xxvii
Mission statement, 12
Model T, xxiii
Monteagudo, Gene, 425
Moonen, Rick, 595
Moore, Robert Lowell, xxix
Moral philosophy, 581–582
Moral values, 576–577
Motel 6, radio advertising, 501
Motivation, four techniques, 425–428
Motor Vehicle Manufacturers Association, xxiii
Mystery shoppers, 249

## N

Nanus, Burt, 388–389
National Arts Club, The, 262
National Coalition of Black Meeting Planners, and discrimination, 588–589
National Restaurant Association (NRA), 85, 406, 415–416
Networking, 416
New York-New York Hotel & Casino, 342, 356
News releases, 236
Newspapers, advertising in, 494–496
Night audit, 214
Nordling, Christopher W., 440
*Norway*, xix, 307
Norwegian Caribbean Lines, 308, 310
Norwegian Cruise Line, xix

## Index

*Notes of a Journey from Cornhill to Grand Cairo*, 304
Nutrition, 122, 126

## O

Occupational Safety and Health Act of 1970, 407
*Official Hotel & Resort Guide*, 462
Ogilvy & Mather Advertising, 487
Ogilvy, David, 487
Olds, Ransom E., xxii
Olive Garden, The, 110, 127
Operating term provision, in management contracts, 534
Operator-reimbursable expenses, 535
Organization charts (examples)
  accounting, 239
  casino hotel, 357
  city club, 265
  corporate or developer club, 270
  country club, 266
  cruise ship, 313
  engineering, 237
  equity club, 270
  food and beverage division, mid-size hotel, 224
  hotel (large), 210–211
  hotel (small), 208
  housekeeping department, 218
  large association's meetings and travel department, 285
  marketing and sales division, 235
  rooms division, 213
Oriental, Bangkok, 420
Overhead expenses, 243
Owen, Robert, 373
Owentsia Club, 267

## P

P&O (cruise line), 304, 312
Pan American Airlines, xxiv
Parker House, Boston, xxviii
Patti, Charles H., 478
PCMA. *See* Professional Convention Management Association
Peale, Norman Vincent, 596–597
Peninsula and Oriental Steam Navigation Company, 304
People's Express, 20
Performance
  measuring, 220–221, 371–372
  reviews, 429
Personal selling, 446–454
Personality types, and sales, 448–451
*Personnel Journal*, 595–596
Peters, Thomas H., 384
Pimentel, Larry, 333
Pineapple, as symbol of hospitality, xvii
Point-of-sale systems, 138, 145–146
Polo, Marco, xv
Positioning, 479–482
Post-opening management fees, 535
*Power of Ethical Management, The*, 596–597
PR. *See* Public relations
Pre-opening management fees, 534–535
Press
  kits, 514
  releases, 236
Pricing
  and advertising, 476
  and yield management, 440
  of hotel rooms, 218
Princess Cruise Lines, 308–309, 315, 318, 324
  and "The Love Boat," 309
Print advertising, 485–489
Private clubs, 259–260
Producing, 144
Product (or trade-name) franchising, 546–548
Product knowledge, and sales, 453
Productivity
  calculating, 412–413
  standards, 411–414
Professional clubs, 259–260
Professional Convention Management Association (PCMA), 286–287
Profitability analysis, 139
Promotion, 440–441
Property management system (PMS), 211–213
Public relations, 510–513
  implementing, 511
  three signs of success, 511
Publicity, 513–514
  definition of, 513
  press kits, 514
  special events, 514
Purchasing department, 228–229
Purser's office, 316

## Q

Quain, William, 440
*Quaker City*, 304–305
Quality focus school of management theory, 381–384
Quality
  consistency, 247
  controls, 10–11, 244–250
  evaluating, 249
  programs, evaluating, 249
  programs, implementing, 383–384
  service, 368, 370, 408
  standards, 247–248
Quantitative school of management theory, 379–380
*Queen Elizabeth*, 307
*Queen Elizabeth 2 (QE2)*, 325
*Queen Mary*, xix, 307
Quick-service restaurants. *See* Restaurants, fast-food

## R

Radio
  advertising, 499–502
  listener demographics, 499–501
Railroads, xix–xx
Rapp, Larry, 334
Receiving, 142–143
Recipes, standard, 125
Recognition programs, 249–250, 425–428

Recreation clubs, 275–276
Recreation facilities 232–233
Recruiting, 414–416
Reengineering, 384–388
 and downsizing, 385–387
 and hotels, 386–388
 definition of, 385
Regemorter, Dedrick Van, 316–317
Reis, Al, 479
REITs, 197, 530, 532
Renaissance, The, xvi
Reorganization, 209
Reporting requirements provision, 535–536
Requisition forms, 144
Reservations, 215–218
 through travel agencies, 461–465
Resort hotels, 193
Resorts
 cost of, 167
 European, 164
 history of, 162–164
 top 25 resort properties, 168–169
 top 5 destinations, 164
Restaurants
 accounting systems, 135–137
 and direct mail advertising, 506
 balance sheet, 135
 beverage costs, 148–150
 budgeting, 137
 casual, 91–92
 controlling costs, 137–138
 controls (financial), 134–137
 controls (operational), 137
 ethnic, 89–91
 family, 92
 fast-food, 92–94
 full-service, 87–92
 guests, 119–122
 health-conscious, 93–94
 history of, xxx–xxxi
 home-meal replacement, 94
 independent, 88–91
 issuing, 143–144
 labor costs, 148
 limited-service, 92–95
 menu, 88–89
 organization, 119–133
 paying, 144–145
 pricing, 87–88
 producing, 144
 profitability analysis, 139
 purchase specifications, 141–142
 reasons for failure, 106–107
 receiving, 142–143
 segments, 86–87
 starting, 103, 107–112
 start-up costs, 107
 statement of income, 135–136
 statistics, 85
 statistics, for start-ups, 106
 storing, 143
 theme 103, 124
 trends, 85–86
Résumés, 70–74, 83
Retirement communities, continuing-care, 188–189
Revenue centers
 food and beverage, 221–230
 front office, 209–215
 housekeeping, 218–219
 measuring performance, 220–221
 reservations, 215–218
 uniformed service, 219–220
Revenue
 for clubs, 273–277
 industry sources, 212
 gaming industry, 344
REVPAR, 220–221
Richfield Hotel Management Inc., 529–530
Riklis, Meshulam, 309
Ritz Hotel, Paris, xxviii
Ritz, César, xxviii, 316
Ritz-Carlton
 and cruise industry, 316
 and employee recognition, 429
 and Malcom Baldrige Award, 368
 and management contracts, 539
 and management philosophy, 383–384
 and quality service, 247–249, 370, 408
Riverboat gambling, 342–343, 360
Roberts, Weiss, 368, 371
Rogers, Isaiah, xxviii
Roman Catholic Church, xxv
Romans, xxv
Room service, 226, 228
Room setups, for meetings, 292
Rooms division, as revenue center, 209–221
Rotterdam, 307
Rouen, France, xxv
Roulette, 341, 346
Royal Caribbean International (Royal Caribbean Cruise Lines), 308, 310, 315, 320, 323
Royal Viking, 325
Rutherford, Denney G., 287–289

# S

S.S. *France*, xix
Sabre reservations system, 461–462
Saint Amand, xxv
Saint Julian the Hospitaller, xxv
Saint Notburger, xxv
Salaries
 of club managers, 273
 of cruise ship food servers, 320
 of unit managers, 69
Sales
 airline tickets, 461–462
 and product knowledge, 453
 and travel agents, 457–468
 and willingness to work, 453
 appearance for, 451–453
 cruises, 464–465
 department, 235, 446–454
 hotel rooms, 462–464
 management, 446–454
 presentations, 456
 tours, 465
 understanding personality types, 448–451
Sales calls
 asking for the sale, 456–457
 following up, 457
 overcoming objections, 456
 preparing for, 454–455
 presentation, 456
 prospecting and qualifying, 454
Sales promotions, 514–518
 loyalty programs, 515–516
 special events, 516
 sweepstakes, 516

Salespeople
  and personality, 454
  basic qualities of, 451–454
  traits of successful, 447–451
Schools of management theory, 373–384
Schulze, Horst, 248, 372
Sea Goddess Cruises, 325
Seabourn Cruise Lines, 310, 324–334
Security
  division, 240–241
  program, elements of, 241
  in casinos, 353–354
Segmentation, 482–483
Selection, 416–419
  checking references, 418–419
  evaluating applicants, 418
  hiring, 419
  interviewing, 417–418
  reviewing applications, 416–417
Sena, Michael D., 505–506
Service
  businesses, 246
  delivery systems, 327–328
  definition of, 5
  delivering, 19–22, 359–361
  importance of, 3–5
  problems in managing, 8–11
  standards, 17–18
Sex discrimination, 591
Sexual harassment, 592
Sheraton Corporation, 596
  and franchise training, 558
  guest satisfaction system, 422
  history of, xxix–xxx
Shoney's Restaurant, 428
Silverman, Henry R., 555–556
*Sirius*, xviii
Site selection
  feasibility study, 111–112
  for restaurants, 110–111
Skills
  inventory, 56–58
  training, 422
Slot machines, 346
Smith, Adam, 581–582
Smith, Thomas, 493–494
Smoking, 121–122
Social clubs, 262–264
Social responsibility, 574–582
Sodexho, 103
Solomon, Robert, 578–579

Sonesta International Hotels, 419–420
Sonneborn, Harry, 550
Specialty menu, 130
Spectradyne, Inc., 230
Sports activities fees, in clubs, 275
Sports clubs, 275–276
St. Michaels Harbour Inn, Maryland, 226
Starting a restaurant, 103, 107–112
  defining the concept, 108–110
  feasibility study, 111–112
  financing, 110, 112
  site selection, 110–112
Statement of income, for hotels, 244
Statler, Ellsworth, xxviii–xxix
Steamship travel, xviii
Stein, Bob, 497
Stephan, Ed, 308
Steward's department, 322
Storing, 143
Stowe, Harriet Beecher, xviii
Strategic
  planning, 12
  service vision, 16–19
Strategic Committee on Respecting the Environment (SCORE), 574
Subway, 556
*Sunward*, 308
Super 8 Motels, 492
Supply and demand, 14–16
SWOT analysis, 12–13, 442
SystemOne reservations system, 461–462
Systems school of management theory, 380–381

T

Table games, 344–346
Tannahill, Reay, xvi
Target
  audience profile, 444
  marketing, 482–483
Taylor, Derek, 448
Taylor, Frederick W., 373–374
Technical assistance fees, 534
Telemarketing, 506–508

Telephone department, as revenue center, 230–232
Telephone deregulation, 231–232
Television advertising, 502–503
Telford, Thomas, xxvii
Thackeray, William Makepeace, 304
Thornblade Club, The, 271
Timeshare, 184–188
  condominiums, 185
  exchange programs, 187
  financial benefits, 187–188
*Titanic*, xviii–xix, 306
Tour
  operators, 460
  sales, 465
Tourism, careers in, 297
Trade magazines, advertising in, 499
Trade shows and expositions, 287–288
Trade-name (or product) franchising, 546–548
*Training for the Hospitality Industry*, 420–421
Training, 243, 330, 419–425
  and turnover, 419
  diversity, 424–425
  hotel employees, 248
  lack of, 407
  with videos, 419–420
Transatlantic travel, 305–307
Trans-Siberian Railroad, xix
Travel
  clubs, 461
  psychographic research, 41–42
  reasons for, 39–41
  three important factors, 38–39
Travel agencies
  accreditation of, 461
  and commissions, 462, 464, 467–468
  commercial, 459
  consolidators, 460–461
  cruise-only, 460
  direct-response, 460
  full-service, 459
  group and incentive, 459
  history of, 457–459
  in-plant, 459
  Internet-based, 461

## Index

reservations systems, 461–464
tour operators, 460
types of, 459–461
work of, 461–465
*Travel Agent* magazine, 462
Travel agents
  associations for, 466
  certification, 466
  training of, 465–466
Travel and tourism industry
  impact of, 33
  interrelation of, 37–38
  nature of, 32–34
  planning and responsibility, 46
  size of, 34
  social impact of, 44–46
*Travel Weekly* magazine, 464
Treasure Island (casino), 347, 356
Tremont House, Boston, xxvii–xxviii
Trends
  affecting travel, 31–32, 42–44
  and political changes, 30
  and population changes, 29
Trippe, Juan, xxiv
Trollope, Anthony, xix–xx
Trout, Jack, 479
Trump Hotels & Casino Resorts, 355
Truth-in-menu laws, 595
Turnover
  and poor training, 419
  reasons for, 406–407
Twain, Mark, 304–305

*Twelve Points of Seabourn Hospitality*, 327–328

## U

U.S. Postal Service, xxiv
U.S. Signal Corps, xxiv
Uniform Franchise Offering Circulars, 553, 569–571
*Uniform System of Accounts for Hotels*, 243
*Uniform System of Accounts for Restaurants*, 135
*Uniform System of Accounts for the Lodging Industry*, 243–244
*Uniform System of Financial Reporting for Clubs*, 277
Uniformed service, 219–220
Union Pacific Railroad, xix
United Airlines, 427
*United States*, xix, 307
University clubs, 264
Utilitarianism, 581–582

## V

Vacation ownership, 184–188
  exchange programs, 187
  financial benefits, 187–188
  hotels' role, 186–187
Value, importance of, 477
Voice mail, 230

## W

Walt Disney Company, 13, 22–24, 35–37, 427–428
and environmental responsibility, 587
Water, controlling costs of use, 238
Waterman, Jr., Robert A., 384
*Webster's New World Dictionary of Media and Communications*, 511
Weiner, Richard, 511, 513–514
Wendy's Restaurants, 502
  marketing, 559
West, Chuck, 308
Westin Hotels & Resorts, 480–481
Westours, 308
Wheeler, Sharon K., 440
White Star Line, 306
Wilson, Kemmons, xxx, 170, 389, 549
Windstar, 310
Women workers, 404–405
Work sampling, 418
World Trade Show, The, 289
World Wide Web, 508–510
Worldspan reservations system, 461–462
Wuster, Thomas D., 476
Wynn, Stephen A., 347

## X-Z

Yacht clubs, 267
Yale Club, 264
*Yankelovich MONITOR*, 121
Yankelovich Partners, 42–44
YEGA, 13, 19
Yield management, 216–218, 440
Zagat, Tim, 516